A TAPESTRY OF JUSTICE, SERVICE, AND UNITY

History Project Director and General Editor: Arleon L. Kelley
History Project Mentor: David Bundy

Contributors
David P. Baak
Judith Bennett
Dorothy G. Berry
David Bos
Peg Chemberlin
Robert Grimm
Roberta Grimm
Sr. Paul Teresa Hennessee
Horace H. Hunt
Kathleen S. Hurty
Arleon L. Kelley
Alton M. Motter
Charles W. Rawlings
Mary R. Sawyer
Charles R. White
Hugh Wire
Lawrence E. Witmer

A TAPESTRY OF JUSTICE, SERVICE, AND UNITY

Local Ecumenism in the United States, 1950–2000

National Association of Ecumenical
and Interreligious Staff Press

Tacoma, Washington
2004

Printed in the United States of America

ISBN 0-9747290-0-0

10 9 8 7 6 5 4 3 2 1

The paper used in this publication meets the minimum requirements of the American National Standard for Permanence of Paper for Printed Library Materials Z39.48-1984.

CONTENTS

PREFACE

Arleon L. Kelley

A National Association of Ecumenical and Interreligious Staff (NAEIS) interest group gathered one afternoon in the summer of 1993 on the porch of the old lodge at the YMCA camp on Lake George, New York, to discuss the possibility of developing a new history of local ecumenism. Interest in the project was piqued in part because a then-recent publication of the World Council of Churches' Dictionary of Ecumenism had only one short entry on local ecumenism and that featured a group in England. There was no mention of the thousands of local ecumenical organizations across America that are the underpinnings of American ecumenical life. After a lively discussion, the group of about twenty people decided that, for the sake of the thousands of people who through the decades had shared a faith vision of serving their community, working for justice, manifesting the unity of the Church, and being the public face of the Church, this work should be chronicled. When I reported this to the whole NAEIS conference, it concurred, and I agreed to take the idea to the Ecumenical Networks Commission of the National Council of Churches of Christ in the USA (NCCC/USA), seeking their partnership.

In behalf of NAEIS, I proposed to the Ecumenical Networks Commission of the NCCC/USA in 1994 that a project be commissioned to research and publish the history of local ecumenism between 1950 and 2000. It was adopted, defining local ecumenism as the World Council of Churches did, as any ecumenical expression below the national life. After several attempts to initiate the idea, I agreed in 1997 to direct the project by developing a collaborative team, beginning upon my retirement in June 1998. In 1999 the Ecumenical Networks Commission was disbanded, and along with it some $25,000 in project funding was lost. I arranged for the project to be placed under the auspices of Christian Theological Seminary, Indianapolis,

Indiana, as a part of its ongoing tribute to longtime NAEIS member and Indiana ecumenist Dr. Grover L. Hartman. (The seminary is an ecumenical seminary sponsored by the Christian Churches, Disciples of Christ, with a long history of teaching and research in ecumenical concerns.)

Seventeen ecumenical colleagues volunteered for the task. New money was raised from several benefactors, and the team first convened in 1998 for five days of work at Bangor Theological Seminary just before the NAEIS meeting at Bar Harbor, Maine. The team was to meet for several days of work in each of the next three successive years. We completed a survey of local ecumenism, over two hundred videotaped oral history interviews with many of the "actors" who had played leading roles in the local ecumenism drama over these years, and collected an extensive archive of material from across the nation, now deposited with the Grover L. Hartman archives on local ecumenism in the Christian Theological Seminary Library. We (the writing team) have also developed narrative stories on about twenty different local arenas, each of which has played a role in the work of local ecumenism over these fifty years. We believe these stories, when seen as a whole, will tell the story of local ecumenism.

There are numerous persons who have made this project possible. Among these are people and organizations that have made generous financial contributions that have enabled both our team's work and the publication of this volume. They include the Gemmer Foundation; Robert and Roberta Grimm of Buffalo, New York; Arthur Sternberg of St. Paul, Minnesota; J. Stanley Hill of White Bear Lake, Minnesota; the United Church Board for Homeland Ministries; and the former Ecumenical Networks Commission of the NCCC/USA.

We also wish to acknowledge the contributions of team members who did not make written contributions but who made significant contributions to the team's work. These include Rev. Leland Collins of the Georgia Christian Council, the Rev. Margrethe B. J. Brown, formerly of the Presbyterian Church ecumenical office, and the Rev. Scott Schiesswohl, pastor in the United Methodist Church and formerly executive secretary of the Indiana and Wyoming state church councils.

Our mentor, Dr. David Bundy, was invaluable to the team's work. He keynoted our first meeting at Bangor Theological Seminary and hosted, as well as guided, our three meetings in Indianapolis. His move from Christian Theological Seminary to Fuller Theological Seminary during the manuscript preparation process deprived us of his planned written contributions. Nonetheless, his stamp is on much of this book.

Annabelle Hartman, ecumenist, educator, mother, lifelong partner of Dr. Grover L. Hartman, and lifetime member of the National Association of Ecumenical and Interreligious Staff was most helpful in assisting in the initiation of the process and responding positively to our overture that our work be deposited in the Grover L. Hartman archives at Christian Theological Seminary.

We must also acknowledge the contributions of Christian Theological Seminary, which has provided the services of mentor Bundy gratis, is providing the archive space, has hosted three of the team meetings, and has provided the educational umbrella for the project's resources at no cost to the project. Our thanks to President Edward Wheeler and Vice Presidents Austin Greene and Dean Ramga, as well as presidential assistant Kate Bell, for making this possible.

We also wish to acknowledge the contribution of Dorothea Anderson, our copy and production editor. Her editing skills and long experience publishing books have made this book a reality.

Finally, we wish to dedicate this project to the memory of two of our team members who died during our team's journey together. The Rev. Kinmoth Jefferson, United Methodist pastor and longtime ecumenist, and one who often invented, influenced, and lived the modern history of Urban Ministry, died before his written contributions were completed. However, his contributions to the team's work in the annual work sessions were invaluable. He was a walking encyclopedia of the church's urban and justice work from the late 1960s to the end of the century. Many of his ideas are reflected throughout the book. Also, our oldest and one of the most active of our team members, the Rev. Dr. Alton Motter, died in the summer of 2003. He was in his mid nineties and was always prodding the editor. In a June 2003 communication he provided a long list of review and marketing suggestions and asked when we could begin our companion second volume of reflections on the history. Alton was the consummate ecumenist and will be greatly missed. Thank you, Kim and Alton!

1

LOCAL ECUMENISM IN HISTORICAL AND CULTURAL CONTEXT

Arleon L. Kelley

The Rev. Nate VanderWerf became the first director of the National Council of Churches of Christ's Commission on Local and Regional Ecumenism in 1969. Early in his tenure he wrote a paper, "The Fabric of Ecumenism." This phrase caught on to describe how the warp of the denominations (vertically arranged) and the woof of the nation, regions, and localities of America (horizontally arranged) are woven together in ecumenism in the United States. Local ecumenism[1] includes all those threads of the woof except the national strand. Yet, local ecumenism is not just a two-dimensional fabric. It is multi-dimensional. It is more like a tapestry. When you look at it, the design has depth that stands out in relief, in a third dimension. Local ecumenism is more than the nation, regions, and localities woven with the denominations. It is the nation, regions, localities, and denominations inextricably woven in and through the culture with all its values, traditions, and institutional richness—an integral part of the tapestry of American life.

Local ecumenism has been evolving in American religious and community life for nearly two centuries and is the public face of the Church in countless settings—the Church in action. Yet this story is rarely told. And when it is told, it is usually in bits and pieces from a denominational perspective or sometimes as a part of community history.

This book seeks to understand and chronicle local ecumenism in the latter part of the twentieth century. We believe local ecumenism is a phenomenon of both cultural and theological importance in America's history and is unique in the world. Some Western European countries have local expressions of ecumenism, but for the most part these are quite different from local ecumenism in the United States. What are the sources of local ecumenism in the United States that makes it a unique phenomena? Arnold Toynbee has suggested that higher religions often emerge in highly developed civilizations that are really "societies of a different species."[2] We believe that American local ecumenism may have such qualities. In the nineteenth century, local ecumenism developed when two strong forces, denominational diversity in the community and volunteerism, joined to make communities better places to live. The motivation was biblical faith that caused a yearning for unity and justice. This motivation, when confronted with the needs created by the emerging industrial and democratic society, required action. The action in turn created a potent force for unity among the people of faith and their churches to care for those who needed a cup of cold water, as well as to deal with the injustices that caused that need.

Local Ecumenism Permeates Much of Life in the United States

We will use the term "ecumenism" to describe what Christians and churches commit to one another and, hence, are and do together. In its broader sense ecumenism describes what people of faith and faith groups commit to one another for their mutual benefit and the common benefit of the larger community.

At the end of the twentieth century there were more than fifteen-hundred staffed ecumenical, community, interfaith, and other forms of multi-congregation organizations in the United States.[3] These include the regional Commission on Religion in Appalachia (CORA), which includes parts of thirteen states; forty-seven state councils/community/conferences or forums of churches; at least sixty metropolitan ecumenical organizations; perhaps five hundred interfaith organizations, approximately one hundred with some staff, twenty-seven of which are metropolitan and two statewide in scope; ninety-two local councils/urban ministries; more than one thousand community/neighborhood ministries (involving congregations of two or more denominations); other specialized ecumenical ministries, such as communication councils; and countless ministerial associations and Church Women United (CWU) units in communities. In addition, there are well over two thousand Ecumenical Shared Ministries (ESM) in the United States[4]—congregational situations where two or more congregations of two or more denominations share worship, a pastoral team, facilities, and mission. Over the fifty years of our study, the most prominent local and regional ecumenical expressions in America have included the following:

Community Ministries. Leaders in community ministries have identified well beyond one thousand of these groups, and they estimate there may be as many as two thousand such groups across the country, making this ecumenical expression the fastest-growing in the United States. These organizations are defined as ministries provided by two or more congregations of different Christian denominations or faiths (e.g., Jewish, Muslim, Hindu) in an identifiable community or neighborhood. They are funded by the participating congregations, by individuals, and through grants from foundations and government agencies. Although most have coordinating staff, they depend heavily upon volunteers. Their concern is almost always totally focused on meeting basic community needs for food, shelter, and care. They may run a food pantry or provide soup kitchens, run youth programs, or provide tutoring, housing, or employment referral. They counsel and protect battered spouses and children, provide remedial education, and ensure good nutrition. They provide health clinics and services for the poor. Some are deeply involved in justice issues and some come together for significant celebrations and worship experiences.

Local Councils. The one hundred or so local councils typically serve cities of less than a million population, counties, or even towns or villages. Membership is most often by local church, as is the funding. Some, like the Long Island Council of Churches, have program budgets with grants in the millions of dollars. Local councils usually enable congregations to be in communication, deal with ethical issues in civic life, pool resources to meet community needs, and develop a significant sense of being a part of the "faith community" among the congregations of an area.

Metropolitan Councils/Conferences of Churches. The sixty or so Metropolitan Councils serve cities of one million or more and are as varied as the cities they serve. Most have membership from denominations, and many also have ways to include local congregations, ministerial associations, and community ministries in their governance. They are Christian, although many include interfaith dialogue as a priority. Their support is from the regional denominational body, congregations, individuals, and special grants from government or foundations. In New York City the Council is composed of denominational representatives as well as representatives from the five borough councils and focuses largely on public policy, advocacy, and institutional chaplaincy, leaving other work of direct services to the borough councils. Other metro councils, like the Indianapolis Federation of Churches, in addition to a variety of services and programs, focus on making neighborhoods viable communities. The Indianapolis Federation endeavors to be inclusive of all churches, i.e., all races and ethnic groups as well as all theological persuasions, and to become an enabling bridge institution for community. Metropolitan councils typically include the following activities in their ministry: broadcast ministries (with local radio and television stations); direct care giving, e.g., AIDS ministry, elder care, preschool day care; community volunteers; programs for housing/homeless; interfaith dialogue; programs to counter racism; services for spirituality and aging; immigration and refugee concerns; environmental education; and church planning for neighborhood congregational clusters, faith discussions, and celebrations around holy days, as well as civic holidays such as Labor Day and Thanksgiving. As an example, the Lehigh County Conference of Churches in Pennsylvania provides chaplaincy in hospitals and jails, migrant ministry, a variety of social service programs, a soup kitchen, and street ministry.

State Councils/Conferences of Churches. Forty-seven of the fifty states plus the District of Columbia have state ecumenical organizations. Many trace their origins to the many nineteenth-century lay social movements. Today most have a membership and governance largely rooted in denominations. Many also have representation from metropolitan and local ecumenism as well as from Church Women United. Financial support is most often from the regional member denominations. All state expressions, except Arkansas, which is interfaith, are Christian, in that they do not include membership from the Jewish, Muslim, or other faiths.

State Councils range all the way from very small programs with nominal budgets to multi-million-dollar direct service organizations. Program focuses often include the following: direct service for the poor, youth, and homeless; faith and ecclesial issues; public policy/advocacy with state legislatures largely focused on issues of justice and welfare; public witness on ethical issues; urban and rural ministry coordination; and ministry in state institutions, e.g., prisons and mental health facilities.

Regional Ecumenism. Regional ecumenism is multistate or within one state. Multistate shares geography, topography, culture, economy, and sometimes religious heritage. Several such regional councils or commissions were formed by denominations in the 1960s and 1970s. Examples were in New England, Appalachia, the Lower Great Lakes, the Upper Great Lakes, and the Great Plains, and membership was usually rooted in national denominational home mission boards and often included state councils. The focus was on collaborative mission. After thirty years, only the Commission on Religion in Appalachia remains—still strong with mission expenditures of about one million dollars per year.

The second regional approach is within a state. These councils usually include a metropolitan center and its surrounding area of smaller cities, towns, villages, and rural communities. One of the strongest and oldest is Christian Associates of Southwest Pennsylvania, which includes Pittsburgh. There are perhaps a dozen or so other examples, including the South Coast Ecumenical Council around Long Beach in California and the Northern and Southern California Ecumenical Councils centered around San Francisco and Los Angeles, respectively.

Interfaith Councils and Organizations. Interfaith Councils are the second-fastest-growing area of cooperative religious life in America after community ministries (many of which are interfaith). These have developed in every sphere of life, from the neighborhood to the city, state, and region. There are perhaps as many as five hundred such organizations in the United States, with perhaps one hundred or so with staff. As indicated above, twenty-seven of the largest cities or counties in America have evolved from a Christian ecumenical council to an Interfaith Council or organization. Some, like the Interreligious Council in Central New York (Syracuse) or Wichita Interfaith (Kansas), still have a Christian ecumenical dimension built into their life, although under the larger interfaith umbrella. Others, like the Interfaith Council of Washington, D.C., or the Berkeley Interfaith Council in California, have uniquely interfaith functions while a parallel council of churches cares for the uniquely Christian concerns and ministries in the same city. The metropolitan or citywide interfaith councils are rooted in a concept of the unity of faiths for the sake of the unity of humankind and earth. These focus on dialogue, brother/sisterhood, human rights, justice, and significant community celebrations. Some also engage in comprehensive community service ministries.

Other Local and Regional Ecumenical Expressions. Other expressions are not quite as common. There are free-standing communication or broadcast councils in large media markets such as Detroit, New York, and Chicago, which have usually developed where the metropolitan councils were confined to the major city instead of the whole media market area. There are urban ministries that focus on resolving the deterioration of neighborhoods and housing as well as ensuring that the ministry of the Church is provided in all parts of the city. Often urban ministries have generated "community ministries" within urban neighborhoods (described above). Others are focused almost entirely on systemic and urban power issues or on community organizing. There is church-based community organizing, a model that uses the resources of the congregations as a base for organizing people in poor and deteriorating neighborhoods to deal with their problems and renew their churches and neighborhoods and to empower them in the political process. Rural ministries are similar to urban ministries, with the emphasis usually on the renewal of the church and the community. The joint strategy and action (JSAC) model has provided a forum for the regional denominational bodies to meet together, evaluate mission opportunities in common, and then pool resources to fund justice and service ministries in a defined metropolitan, state, or regional area. Church Women United (CWU) is a grassroots organization of church and sometimes synagogue women that is dedicated to the study of issues, advocacy, some direct service, and significant community celebrations. In many settings across America CWU uses its understanding and skills to become the big player among ecumenical and interfaith organizations. Ministerial associations are found in most communities and are a way for the ministers of different churches in the same community to pray, study, be in fellowship, and coordinate work.

Local ecumenism, far more than national denominational ecumenism, is built on the voluntary principles that are so important to the fabric of American life. The numbers of people engaged in ecumenical and interfaith activity in any given month is gigantic, and the dollars expended annually dwarfs the mission budgets of most denominations. Local ecumenism is about partnerships—among concerned people, churches, and regional denominational bodies—and sometimes includes the resources of cities, states, and the federal government.

Historical Roots of Local and Regional Ecumenism

Local ecumenism in the United States is rooted in five historical phases over two centuries. The first phase of grassroots ecumenism was the development of camp meetings and mission societies well before the Revolutionary War. Camp meetings were a frontier evangelistic and fellowship development where people from different denominations on a sparsely populated frontier came together to camp, learn more about their faith, bring their neighbors to Christ, and perhaps become a community. Such camp meetings sometimes spawned unity movements that became a denomination—for example, the Christian Church, Disciples of Christ. At the same time these ecumenical camp meetings also strengthened other denominations, like the Methodists, who moved with the wagon trains from frontier to frontier. At this time, Christians on the East Coast were organizing volunteer societies to take the Gospel to the native peoples.

Another building block was the lay Sunday School and social justice movements that began in earnest by 1830. The Sunday School movement developed as a way to teach children who worked on farms or factories how to read and write, using the Bible. By the 1840s, the abolition movement as well as the forerunners of the temperance and other justice movements were being organized among the churches of the north. These, and numerous other largely lay-driven movements, would transform American society.

A third developmental stage began at about the time of the Civil War and encompasses the emergence of social ministries (hospitals, settlement houses, and YMCAs and YWCAs), as well as the initial systematic theological reflection by people such as Walter Rauschenbusch. This initial work focused on the biblical mandate of mission to the needy, and over the next twenty-five years matured to reflect on the nature of the Church in the world. This was also the time when the immigrant churches began earnest faith and order discussions.

The fourth stage began at the end of the nineteenth century and might be identified as the era of Councils/Federations of Churches. The beginning of the second decade of the twentieth century was a time of immigrant (Protestant) church mergers and saw Protestant ecumenism become influential. For example, John Foster Dulles was a founder and Arthur Fleming was a president of the NCCC/USA. Both served in the cabinet under Eisenhower. The ecumenical public church and the power brokers in the society were almost indistinguishable. This influential era of Protestant ecumenism lasted through the late 1960s. Perhaps the Detroit Assembly of the National Council of Churches in 1969 signaled the end of Protestant hegemony in American ecumenical life.

The fifth phase of ecumenical development has its roots in the 1963 first session of Vatican II but began to flower in the late 1960s when we see a post-triumphal ecumenism emerging. It is an ecumenism focused on solidarity with the marginalized, as well as service, justice, and faith and order. Most notably it was a time of reshaping local and regional ecumenical life to be inclusive of Roman Catholics and often of many faith groups; of bilateral discussions; and of multilateral work on mission as well as on Baptism, Eucharist, and Ministry. For Protestants, the Consultation on Church Union process began, which after nearly forty years has now given rise to the Churches of Christ Uniting, as well as the theological work rooted in understandings of power, solidarity with the poor, inclusiveness, diversity, particularity, and universality—each of which has radical implications for both ecumenism and the ecclesiology of the Church.

The Taproots of Local Ecumenism

These five phases are rooted in the spiritual, missionary, justice, and freedom impetus of the eighteenth and nineteenth centuries. There are several historical taproots. One taproot in the original thirteen colonies was religious pluralism. Several colonies were initially homogeneous religious groups that fled persecution to establish a colony as a safe haven for spiritual experiment. Whether establishing a church, as in Virginia, or seeking religious freedom, as in Maryland, Pennsylvania, Rhode Island, and Massachusetts, the ecumenical history of these colonies in dealing with the "others" is different than on the frontiers of our country. When the colonies were forced to deal with one another they also had to deal with their religious pluralism. When forming a common national government they faced the internal tensions brought on by religious assumptions (e.g., Deism, Trinitarian, Unitarian, establishment). The question they were dealing with was, How do we live with religious pluralism?

The intellectual roots of Dr. Benjamin Rush (signer of the Declaration of Independence) were in Republicanism, Scottish enlightenment, philosophy/medical thought, and millennial Christianity. Rush devised a social moral agenda around which he believed all parts of this religious pluralism could rally, transcending the sectarian views of the various denominations and philosophies. He suggested that there was a way to develop an awakening spirit of shared religious activism (ecumenism) outside the realm of theology. Indeed, his work became the basis for an enlightened Christian reform vision for individual, society, and world. His pamphlets on drunkenness, slavery, tolerance, women's participation, and education developed a sense of social piety and an agenda that could cut across sectarian boundaries (it might be argued they also developed the basis of civil religion and America as the new Israel).[5]

In that same tradition, Lyman Beecher, a few years later, called American Christianity to become a "third force" in politics. Voluntary societies, rather than just being institutions of "moral enlightenment," should act as "a sort of disciplined moral militia."[6] These voluntary societies were the forerunners of local ecumenism and were largely composed of laypersons drawn from the ranks of the numerous local churches in the community. Their focus was largely those areas outlined in Rush's tracts: drunkenness, antislavery, tolerance, women's participation, education, mission, and the wellbeing of the community's youth.

But perhaps the greater taproot for local ecumenism lies in the nature of new frontier communities, where people were required to fashion a community from among persons with no common history and to develop common myths and values, i.e., common spiritual stories. These communities were often composed of immigrant peoples. Local ecumenical expressions emerged from this crucible of interaction, as common ground to solve the vexing local problems of the time.

It is true that most ethnic groups brought their church with them as they moved west. But in most early eighteenth- and nineteenth-century frontier communities there was not enough critical mass of persons from one faith tradition for viability, and perhaps even more important, the religious understandings imported from another time and place did not always address the realities of frontier life. So they organized class meetings or lay-led congregations for adults, Sunday Schools for children, and camp meetings to break the isolation.

At the same time, frontier life energized the development of another form of ecumenism. Churches and their laity began to develop numerous eleemosynary organizations—hospitals, schools, and youth and settlement houses—especially in the last two-thirds of the nineteenth century. These organizations, when joined with Benjamin Rush's social piety, gave rise to a variety of movements such as temperance, abolition of slavery (with its underground railways), and suffrage for women.

Although deeply rooted in the spiritual life of the emerging frontier, much of the reflection on the reasons for all this bridge-building, spiritual discovery, movements for justice, service in the community, as well as mission to the rest of the nation and beyond, did not begin to be integrated systematically until late in the nineteenth century. It is in the writings of Walter Rauschenbusch and John R. Mott, a full century and more after Benjamin Rush and four to six decades after Lyman Beecher, that we begin to get something like a systematic exploration of the "life, work, and mission" impulse of the American church. At the same time Horace Mann and others were reflecting on the educational vocation of the churches.

At the end of the nineteenth century and in the first decades of the twentieth century another American ecumenical taproot emerged. Faith and order discussions began among the immigrant churches—largely focused on creedal beliefs and ecclesiology. This discussion in turn began an uneasy discussion between the local conciliar instrumentalities and the denominations. In many ways it was a discussion between the conciliar-rooted propensity for "life and work" and the immigrant churches' propensity for "faith and order." By the end of the nineteenth century these discussions led to the discovery that two areas shared were mission and Christian education. So, although many of the historic mission efforts and nearly all of the Sunday School efforts of the American church were embedded in lay ecumenical movements such as local councils, by the late nineteenth and early twentieth centuries many of these movements were quite successful in rooting themselves also in the life of the denominations.

The great divide in the theological taproots underlying American Protestant Christianity began as the Fundamentalist/Modernism debate at the turn of the twentieth century, and the split was very evident by the 1920s. Some have argued that the fissure in American Protestant Christianity developed as the shift occurred from an agrarian to an industrial society; others have seen it as the result of "classism" defined by education and income; some have seen the cleavage rooted in the struggle between those who were seeking to find ways for persons of faith to participate in modern society as opposed to those who were alienated from modernity and sought to maintain the old ways; others have seen it as a struggle between a particularistic Christo-centric personal "salvation faith" understanding versus a more universal Social Gospel understanding; still others say it is simply a conservative/liberal split; in recent years it is often typified as the fundamentalist versus ecumenist separation. But it remains a significant separation within the faith community defined not only by theological understanding but also by worldview. The phenomena now cuts across denominational boundaries. Every old line denomination, including the Roman Catholics as well as many of those who have traditionally defined themselves as evangelical, seem to embody variations of this separation.[7]

In sum, by the late nineteenth century, local ecumenism, and the larger state and national associations it created, became the principal carrier of values that were to lead the United States into the twentieth century, e.g., unity, global worldview, justice, individualism, hard work, and community, while at the same time it challenged the individual Protestant denominations to deal with their diversity and mission theologically and ecclesiologically (Social Gospel, early mission conferences, and the first Faith and Order conferences).

The Place of Ecumenism in Contemporary American Cultural History

Toynbee talks about the "emergence of the higher religions as societies of a different species"[8] within the broader host society. Diverse denominational Christianity, in general, and ecumenism, in particular, was a distinctive religious development within the context of the larger American civilization. By the last half of the twentieth century new and radical changes had emerged in the United States in both the role and the shape of religious life, coming both from within and from without. The internal changes were formed within ecumenical Christianity by the influence of external cultural changes. The response to these external forces has driven ecumenical theology even further apart from fundamentalist theology; ecumenical Christianity seems to be becoming more akin to the biblical Old Testament's "faithful prophetic remnant," or what Toynbee calls a creative minority, than the all-powerful Christendom of earlier centuries.

Religious Life in Social Context, 1950–2000

After the rather benign 1950s and certainly by the 1970s, it was clear that some sort of fundamental social transformation was under way in American culture. Peter Drucker says, "Work and work force, society and polity are all, in the last decades of this century, qualitatively and quantitatively different not only from what they were in the first years of this century but also from what has existed at any other time in history; in their configurations, in their processes, in their problems, and in their structures."[9]

Many institutions, mores, and values that were held sacrosanct after World War II, in education, religion, government, or community life, have been challenged, overthrown, or radically changed, especially since the 1970s. And subsequently in the 1980s both a conserving backlash against such rapid change and a radical deconstruction of Western cultural myths has set in. By the mid-1990s, America's attitudes were returning to a somewhat transformed middle ground, rooted in a newfound prosperity and founded on the "triumph of unabashed capitalism," technology, societal complexity, and instantaneous communication. By the end of the century there was a diminished middle class—traditionally the backbone of church life.

These trends found parallels in American religion. Following World War II a trickle of immigrants from Asia and the Middle East began. This increased in the latter quarter of the century; with these newcomers came new religions. Americans learned that Hindus, Sikhs, Buddhists, Muslims, as well as persons of other faiths, do not always share Judeo-Christian assumptions. This made for an even more religiously diverse society.

Yet in the 1950s institutional Christianity was expanding. Probably more new congregations were started in this period than in any other period in our history. Denominations were growing. Worship attendance was at a peak, and church membership, as a percent of the population, stood at an all-time high. Two thirds of the population claimed formal religious affiliation. Councils and federations of churches reached peak institutional strength. They were well organized, staffed, and funded. The National Council of Churches of Christ in the USA had just been formed in 1950, two years after the formation of the World Council of Churches, the flag bearers for this new Protestant Christianity. Most communities, counties, cities, metropolitan regions, and states had some form of ecumenical organization by the end of the 1950s. Yet these great strides toward cooperative ecumenism, when mixed with the equally great denominational hubris, were to lead to an unraveling of the fabric of ecumenical life in the late 1960s and beyond.

One example was in the field of Christian education. In the early 1950s, soon after the formation of the NCCC, the denominational members of the Division of Christian Education agreed to two fundamental documents that would change the face of local ecumenism. One was the "Common Philosophy of Christian Education." The other was a "Common Basis for Curriculum." These documents were designed to make it possible for all the participating denominations to develop common curriculum materials—as had been done in many state Sunday School associations a century earlier. But the promise was not to be realized, perhaps because each denomination had its own publishing house, dependent in large measure upon revenues from Christian education materials. Most of the denominations took the two common documents, hired their own curriculum developers and writers, produced their own materials, trained their own field staff to teach their churches how to use the materials, and by the early 1960s had withdrawn their support for the myriad of conciliar-based Christian educators who could have trained people to implement the common curriculum.

The problems were further compounded when many denominations adopted an "intergenerational" approach in the 1960s, effectively putting both ecumenical and denominational youth, men's, and women's ministries out of existence. Thus, successes in the early part of the period initiated by the Christian education movement and adopted by the denominations resulted in the dismantling of a century-old ecumenical Christian education and curriculum development system as well as ecumenical youth, men's, and women's ministries. The prevailing—perhaps subconscious—attitude of the heady late 1950s was that there is nothing worth doing that the denominations could not do better by themselves, resulting in the predicaments that both the denominations and their now largely "wholly owned" ecumenical expressions face today—both institutionally and economically.

There was one attempt to regain the unifying impulse of the post–World War II period. The Blake-Pike proposal of 1960 urged that the mainline churches join in consultation to find a way to be "one," the proposal for a Consultation on Church Union (COCU). But the Consultation was often viewed with suspicion by ecumenical organizations because it was seen as competition or seen as draining resources from conciliar ecumenism—the nine COCU members were often the main supporters of local ecumenism. Another important event occurred in 1961 when Pope John XXIII called for a Second Vatican Council to be convened in 1963. By mid decade there were exhilarating new ecumenical possibilities to displace many traditional Protestant ecumenical expressions—some of which had found their reason for existence in being anti–Roman Catholic.

Nonetheless, by the second half of the 1960s and into the 1970s, the challenge to dominant values, mores, and institutions—manifested in the hippie movement, Woodstock, the civil rights movement, the urban crisis, the antiwar movement, and the liberation movements—became the main forces challenging the dominant cultural institutions. Churches and their various local ecumenical expressions were not immune. At the same time, all the change led many people of faith to search for ways to replenish their spirit or just turn inward. So in the old line denominations the agenda changed from justice to spirituality. The allegations against Presbyterian Angela Davis, Black Power advocate and alleged Communist, became a symbol used by conserving elements in the churches to argue against the justice work of the churches and their ecumenical vehicles. Money was withheld by contributors to home mission activities which diminished the availability for significant justice ministries in many denominations. In the end many activists turned inward in their spiritual journeys, while others simply left the churches and pursued other personal, sometimes materialistic, goals.

In the 1970s, cults emerged—probably in response to this radical cultural change—each with a new and alternative institutional and eschatological vision for religion. Jim Jones and Rev. Moon are illustrative. The culture wars also began in this decade, first in higher education, then in the church, and finally in politics. These value struggles emerged in most Protestant denominations with the organization of conservative "watch dog" groups, e.g., Presbyterian Laymen, the Institute for Religion and Democracy (IRD), and the Good News movement. These groups focused on patriotism, patriarchy, narrow theological understandings (if not fundamentalism), anti-ecumenism, and anti-homosexuality.

Independent churches, mostly outside the old line denominations but heirs to the historic Fundamentalist split of the 1920s, were more concerned with reclaiming past values (but perhaps never the dominant values) than with developing alternative religious institutions. Claiming to be "evangelicals," such persons as Pat Robertson and Jimmy Swaggart used paid radio and television programming (which they had pioneered in the 1930s and 1940s) rather than religious institutions as the means of communication. These televangelists were successful in bypassing the churches that had been the institutions that historically had mediated values. This self-styled radical response to the religious and social upheavals of the 1960s and early 1970s became the first glimmer of religious social/value reactionaries, soon to be known as the political Religious Right. By the 1980s the goal of the Religious Right was to impose its agenda upon society through political power. The leaders claimed they were a principal influence in electing to the presidency Ronald Reagan and both George Bushes. In some states they were successful in taking over the Republican Party; in the 1994 elections and again in 2000, the Religious Right claimed success for electing a Republican Congress.

Three other phenomena were developing in the religious landscape that would also have an impact on ecumenical life. One was the emergence of "New Age" religions. Secondly, new waves of immigrants brought Islam, Hinduism, and many other living faiths into American communities. Finally, Christian Pentecostalism began to emerge as a new force in American religion. By the 1990s Pentecostalism was perhaps the fastest-growing segment of Christianity. There were now as many practicing Muslims as practicing Jews in the nation, and Hindus, Sikhs, and others, when taken as a group, were larger than the Muslims and the Jews together. Religious pluralism, representative of the whole world, had become a reality.[10]

Amid all these changes and new complexities, local ecumenism often found itself marginalized and its resource base shrinking along with the strength of its denominational partners. Local ecumenism often responded by including new partners from other faith traditions, thus transforming itself into interreligious councils in many places across the nation. Indeed, in this process the mission of serving the human community and transcending long-established boundaries often became increasingly clear and defined the nature of faithfulness for many. This also created a greater wedge between ecumenism and the evangelical right. By the end of the century, the dividing issues in both religion and society were racism and views on hierarchy/patriarchy, nationalism/globalism, sexuality, social class, welfare, and wealth, and cut across all faith groups.

At the same time the secularization of our society and other factors have caused many to avoid the divisive forces within the churches by dropping out of religious institutions completely. Indeed, it has been said on many occasions that the largest alumni association in the nation is composed of those raised in the churches. The percentage of the population participating in the life of the churches or who are members of the churches had dropped from about two-thirds in the 1960s to less than half in 2003.

Making Sense of Historical Developments, 1950–2000

The events of this period were played out against the much longer and larger drama of American civilization. In this period we see a largely mature American culture, doing what mature cultures do. Some groups are committed to the past, trying to make "sacred" their memory of what our cultural institutions were, while other groups are trying to canonize our past cultural values and myths and are trying to gain the political power necessary to ensure their views will prevail. At the same time there are many groups that are committed to the future—to renewing and rebuilding our institutions, values, mores, and myths to address contemporary needs. Prophetic Christianity is dedicated to this latter work. Local ecumenism, at its best, has been an avenue through which that hope is focused into action.

By the last half of the twentieth century there were at least four dominant forces shaping local ecumenism. First, the great Fundamentalist debate of the 1920s caused a schism within Protestantism that had detrimental consequences for local ecumenism in the last half of the twentieth century. This schism was a contributing factor in the loss of Christian hegemony and a muting factor in the prophetic voice of ecumenism. Second, Vatican II revived nineteenth-century work toward an integrated pluralistic Christianity, often giving new life to local ecumenism. Third, cultural divisions opened up, including the culture wars, between those who try to conserve the past organizational structures at all costs—conservatives—and those who care little for the organization but are committed to the values of the past—reactionaries. Within each of these roles there are prophetic stances and destructive stances. Local ecumenism is often the carrier of these prophetic voices. Fourth, the arrival of large numbers of immigrants, members of historic world religions, opened new avenues of dialogue and work, beyond the normal Jewish-Christian dialogue and the usual ecumenism. This gave impetus for Christian ecumenism to become interreligious ecumenism.

Some Ideas to Test from the Stories of Local Ecumenism

The period from 1950 to 2000 has been a time of radical cultural and religious change in the United States. We believe that local ecumenism has played a role as an initiator of change, providing a cup of cold water and advocating for justice and, by its very presence, acting as a sign or a sacrament, pointing to the unity intended for all humankind. It has been the public face of religion. If there is validity to these claims, then we wonder, is ecumenism a special species of religion borne out of cooperation, inclusiveness, and equality, and unique to religious life generally?

We are also curious about the developmental history of local ecumenism—the Story—during this fifty-year period. How does what we have been instruct us about what we can become?

It is also our hypothesis that American local ecumenism developed as it did in the nineteenth and twentieth centuries as a hopeful spiritual and religious counterwitness to the excesses of the dominant cultural forces of nation-statism, industrialism, and materialism with their resulting global economic imperialism and domestic consumerism. We believe the modern ecumenical impetus cannot be divorced from these cultural dynamics—indeed, it is our hypothesis that local ecumenism has been forged on this anvil.

At the same time, we will test the idea that the dynamics within and among the American churches have been both the bane and the blessing of local ecumenism. For example, it is unchallenged that Vatican II opened new vistas of possibility for local ecumenism. Yet, especially in this fifty-year period when local ecumenism had increasingly tied its life to that of the denominations, the now problematic institutional struggles within denominations may mean that the future of local ecumenism lies elsewhere.

We will be examining the stories that follow for theological implications. For example, has local ecumenism embraced fundamentally different theological worldviews from those prevalent in more traditional Christian settings? We hypothesize that local ecumenism has developed an underlying organic theological understanding based in the Body of Christ image. Such an image, when tied with creation spirituality, not only sees all as sacred and all as connected, but it also diminishes the separation between sacred and secular. God is not separate from any part of the creation. This theological direction, if it is real, is in striking contrast to underlying denominational theological assumptions that differentiate one from the other and argue denominational sovereignty, which is not unlike machine-era images of discrete parts.

We will also be looking at the ways local ecumenism has enabled people of faith to transcend traditional boundaries of gender, race, patriarchy, superpatriotism, unemployment, income disparity, ecological degradation, misuse of power, and the so-called dysfunctional aspects of the machine era.

We will explore the role of local ecumenism in transcending the boundaries between world faith traditions. What has been its role in moving insular and triumphal Christian positions to become more open to dialogue, interaction, and shared service to the community?

Finally, we will use the experiences of local ecumenism to reflect on the question, How can the ecumenical worldview help us deal with the emerging imperial worldview of economic and other means of dominance? Many across the world believe that as Americans we are in the "belly of the beast" that is dedicated to world domination. If so, what is the creative mediating faith worldview that can be sacramental for the future of humankind, in communities across America, in our nation, and beyond?

To these questions we now set our hand.

Notes

1. "Local ecumenism" is a term used by the World Council of Churches to describe any ecumenical activity that is happening within a global region (several nations in a shared part of the world) or a nation. In the United States we have described it more fully as local and regional ecumenism. By "local" we in the United States usually mean ecumenism in a community, city, or county, and by "regional" we usually mean multistate, state, or multicounty ecumenical organizations. For the purposes of this book we will talk about all these configurations in the United States in World Council terminology. That is, all ecumenical formulations in the United States that are not national will be called local ecumenism.

2. Arnold Toynbee, *A Study of History* (Oxford: Oxford University Press), p. 485.

3. Eileen W. Lindner, ed., *The Yearbook of American and Canadian Churches, 1998* (Nashville: Abingdon Press, 1998), pp. 203–236.

4. *Ecumenical Shared Ministry and the United Methodist Church* (CHARIS Ecumenical Center, Concordia College, Moorhead, MN 56562, 1995).

5. See Robert H. Abzug, *Cosmos Crumbling: American Reform and the Religious Imagination* (Oxford and New York: Oxford University Press, 1994), pp. 18–19. "Rush's own background in Presbyterianism, Quakerism and Anglicanism reflected only part of the religious spectrum that had learned to live together within Pennsylvania. Finding a ritual life that would bring Christians together meant drawing upon a cosmic vision outside the individual sects, yet celebrating the general human virtues associated with each" (p. 19).

6. Ibid., p. 45.

7. See pp.12–98 in Ross Sanderson, *Church Cooperation in the United States: The Nationwide Backgrounds and Ecumenical Significance of State and Local Councils of Churches in Their Historical Perspective* (New York: Association of Council Secretaries, 1960).

8. Toynbee, *A Study of History,* p. 485.

9. Peter F. Drucker, "The Age of Social Transformation," *Atlantic Monthly,* November 1994, pp. 53–80.

10. Diana L. Eck, *Encountering God: A Spiritual Journey from Bozeman to Banaras* (Boston: Beacon Press, 1993).

PART ONE.
A STORY OF GENERATIONS

The vision for the unity of the church—community wholeness, service, and justice in all the earth—is like a patchwork quilt or a tapestry passed from one generation to the next, all the while becoming new for each new generation. This continual renewing of a Christian vision and the passing of that vision to the next generation is lived out locally in America.

Living one's Christian vision where one lives and works is fundamental to being Christian and to the nature of ecumenism. Places themselves change and the context of life in these places changes dramatically with changing technology and social conditions. The twentieth century has seen transportation change from horse and buggy to travel to the moon. It has seen communication change from telegraph to cell phones, Internet, and video conferencing. It has seen our culture change from "home grown participatory entertainment" in the first half of the century to spectator activities ranging from television, to movies, to sports that pay tens of millions to a few for the enjoyment of hundreds of millions in the last half of the century.

So we chronicle the effect of these changes on our communities, even as we chronicle one family's continuing, yet changing, commitment to the ecumenical vision in their community. The commitments of each succeeding generation are testimony to making the vision of God's shalom ever new and compelling, generation after generation. And that story in turn becomes the story of ecumenism in a region of northern California and beyond "to the whole inhabited earth."

2

THE GENERATIONS OF ECUMENISM IN NORTHERN CALIFORNIA

Hugh Wire

In April 1992, a U.S. military air transport landed in Moscow just before Easter with a cargo of family-sized boxes of food from the San Francisco Bay Area. Distribution of the boxes was surprisingly well organized by volunteers in Moscow, remembers Jan Leonard, a volunteer with the Council of Churches of Santa Clara County who had flown with the cargo. "We went with some Russian volunteers and a load of boxes to one of those gray government housing projects. A group of older people was waiting for us. They came up one at a time when their names were read. The Russian volunteers had a list already made up." Each box had the same items: five pounds of sugar, five pounds of flour, rice, canned meat, dried soups, cooking oil, powdered milk, tea, and a full pound of hard chocolate. But donors in packing them often added something extra. "I watched one old woman find toothpaste and a toothbrush when she opened hers. She laughed and laughed, and pointed to her mouth where she had no teeth. But through an interpreter I heard her say it was fine because she knew who she was going to give these to."[1]

How it happened that Jan Leonard would travel in the hold of a cargo plane to Russia with a relief effort offers a window on the last half century of ecumenical life in the San Francisco Bay Area of California. The roots of this event lie in the piety and practices of Anglo-Protestant ecumenism whose changing nature in Northern California this chapter will describe.

A Collaboration

"Near the end of 1991 Suzanne Robinson came to me and asked if we could organize support for a Russian relief effort," says the Rev. Ben Fraticelli, a Puerto Rican Disciples of Christ community organizer who was executive director of the Northern California Ecumenical Council in the first half of the 1990s. After the breakup of the Soviet Union and in the chaos of the new economic system the media were reporting news of great hardships, particularly for the elderly and children. "Charity wasn't what we were doing in the Council," asserts Fraticelli, "but Suzanne was very persistent. She wanted access to the bishops. She already had found that the U.S. government was ready to fly donated relief supplies. One of our strongest board members, Nancy Nielsen, thought we ought to help, and that gave us Lutheran support." Suzanne Robinson, an active Catholic laywoman, well connected to the San Francisco Archdiocese, who lives in Marin County on the north side of the Golden Gate Bridge, was invited to that next meeting of bishops and executives hosted by Fraticelli. He remembers the enthusiastic embrace of the project by Bishop Anthony of the Greek Orthodox Church, which brought the others along. "We became the facilitators of what really became a broad community effort. We could not and did not have to do the work ourselves. Suzanne saw to it that the work got done."[2]

"When I first went to Fr. Gerald O'Rourke, the archdiocesan ecumenical officer, he told me to go get the Orthodox involved first," remembers Robinson. "I then found a wonderful man in San Francisco, an Orthodox layman, who already was gathering things and shipping them in containers. He was collecting money. Doing the whole thing, but it was so slow and hard."[3] Robinson already had found a partner, a woman from Moscow who on a visit to Seattle had been struck by the important civic role of volunteers and had gone home to organize a volunteer service organization, something quite new at that time in Russia. This group could receive and distribute relief supplies.

A team quickly grew around Robinson to raise money, decide on relief goods needed, organize to gather them, and secure a warehouse. Meetings were held in the basement of St. Mary's Roman Catholic Cathedral in San Francisco, with Ben Fraticelli skillfully guiding the process among actors coming from a variety of cultures. There were bishops and denominational executives or their proxies. There were lay leaders from the Greek Orthodox Church and from the Orthodox Church in America, who were not used to working together, and others from activist Catholic and Protestant congregations who had long practice in grassroots organizing. There were a few like Jan Leonard from local councils of churches and a core from the Russian community center.

Under the Northern California Ecumenical Council's auspices a separate bank account was opened and thousands of dollars received. Substantial help moving and storing goods came from volunteers from the Russian community center in San Francisco. Hundreds of boxes with packing lists were distributed to churches and community groups. These were filled and picked up within days of their distribution. "We from the religious community were the conveners, but Suzanne got everybody involved," remembers Fraticelli. "This was a whole community's response to a need."[4]

Bishop Anthony and Rev. Gerald O'Rourke flew to Moscow ahead of the cargo flight with two Protestant religious leaders from the Bay Area and had an audience with Metropolitan Alexi of the Russian Orthodox Church. They attended the first Mass in seventy years in the Cathedral of Dormitian in the Kremlin, where Bishop Anthony joined with other visiting Orthodox bishops in concelebrating the Mass with the Russian Orthodox hierarchy. As they processed after Mass, Metropolitan Alexi invited Rev. O'Rourke to join them for a special lunch and to bring a greeting from San Francisco's Roman Catholic Archbishop. O'Rourke would speak later of how the opening of Russia to the West and to its own past culture was creating vast opportunity for the Russian Orthodox Church but was also a threatening experience of losing familiar space. To have been present that day and to be welcomed as a Roman Catholic by the Russian hierarchy in spite of the threat he represented had been "an historic moment and an extraordinary privilege."[5]

Ecumenical Life: Response to Impulse and Times

This story is the essence of local ecumenism—how people are prompted to cross borders of tribe or culture. This process is the constant in ecumenical religious life as people are drawn into overcoming barriers, finding allies, and doing work that fulfills visions of what is good. The impulse to cross borders has various sources. Of a venture earlier to Nicaragua in 1984 Jan Leonard says, "I wanted to leave a piece of myself there." People are moved by compassion, but also seem to be acting out of a sense of responsibility to their institutional role (Jan Leonard and Suzanne Robinson reflect both), or through their identity in a particular community (members of the Russian community center), through the vision of a good society (Ben Fraticelli), or through the vision of the good church (Nielsen, O'Rourke, and Bishop Anthony). Sometimes these values lead to conflict; but often as in this case the impulse unifies separate individuals into a community. An impulse to include is key to ecumenical life. Whatever its source, the actors from religious communities identify this impulse as coming from their faith, their experience of God, or their commitment to a religious community.

But if the impulses of compassion and its sisters are keys to this collaboration, still another is the shape given it by the times. Glasnost in Russia gave the U.S. administration opportunity to share American values with a former opponent. Both glasnost and the U.S. government gave the media access to heartrending stories that moved Robinson and others to act. The readiness of the first Bush administration to fund private initiatives of both business and nonprofit organizations for Russia permitted the actual birth of Robinson's idea as a viable project. This confluence of external forces illustrates a second critical facet of ecumenical life: It seizes the moment.

Councils of Churches

While not the initiator or even the container of the ecumenical life exhibited by that event, the Northern California Ecumenical Council was the essential convener of the collaborators. "We had the history of organizing collaborative action on social issues among religious communities going back fifty years, and we could talk to the bishops."[6] In the late 1940s the new Northern California Council of Churches had been at the center of community response to postwar needs in China and Korea.[7] Its successor organization, the Northern California Ecumenical Council, could play the role it did because it still served as an outlet for an Anglo-Protestant piety that has fueled Protestant social witness for nearly two centuries.[8]

Until recently such Protestant councils of churches could claim to be the epitome of the public expression of the ecumenical impulse. Even today, this impulse is shaped by forms created at midcentury by the Anglo-Protestants.[9] But we will see how the impulse toward inclusion now found in African-American churches, Roman Catholic churches, Evangelical churches, Jewish synagogues, and immigrant movements increasingly leads these other streams to shape ecumenical and interfaith life in California today.

John Dean Crummey

The story of the ecumenical roots of this Russian airlift can be told, in part, through the work of three generations of the John Dean Crummey family. The family roots are in the agricultural economy of Northern California. Born in the Chicago area in 1878, John Dean Crummey came with his family to Los Gatos in the Santa Clara Valley (later to be known as Silicon Valley) in 1888. His maternal grandfather, John Bean, had come west in the early 1880s, bought an orchard in Los Gatos, and began a business to fill a need of other orchardists, the Bean Spray Pump Company. John's father, David Crummey, then followed to work for Bean. Family tradition has it that John Bean was a great inventor but not much of a businessman.[10] Sales of the company in 1886 were $9,000.

At the turn of the century Bean, in semiretirement, invented a continuous spray pump that enormously improved on existing sprayers by putting out enough chemical to combat a scale that was devastating the valley's fruit trees. Son John, new to the the family business, took a sample of the sprayer on the road. Traveling throughout central California by bicycle he sold more pumps in four months than the company had sold in ten years.[11] This would result in annual sales of $1,750,000 by the time the company was merged with another to become the Food Machinery Corporation, with John Crummey as its first president. John turned over the presidency in 1940 to Paul L. Davies, his son-in-law, who is credited with the diversification that led the corporation as FMC to become a worldwide force in chemicals, food manufacturing equipment, and defense. Crummey would continue to be involved until his death.

Following his first successful sales trip by bicycle, John traveled across the country building the business. His first transcontinental trips were all by coach. Not until after his seventh cross-country trip would he decide to spend an extra two dollars for a place in a sleeping car. If there were children near his seat, he would play with them and volunteer to watch them if the parents wanted to go to the dining car. The story is told that earlier, when the Bean Spray Pump Company needed to expand to meet the demand for the new spray pump, John took his bank book in for a crucial two thousand dollar loan. The banker, seeing the record of saving he had on his small salary, made the loan. "Any young man that can live and save on what you have been making ought to be a good risk."[12]

John Crummey taught Sunday School at the First Methodist Church in San Jose for fifty years. His oldest daughter, Beth, still talks about what a wonderful experience she had growing up in that church. As the company prospered, his family, now including five children, moved to the edge of San Jose. On the edge of an orchard he built a big home with a pool and space for children and guests to play. Jan Leonard says she still meets people who tell of going in their youth to church picnics and parties at her grandfather's home.[13] The church's members included the mayor of the city, the city librarian, and professors from San Jose State. John was an active Rotarian, attending meetings wherever he traveled, and travel he did, around the world. He was president of the Board of Trustees of College of the Pacific (now the University of Pacific), following his father, who had been treasurer of the college when it was still in San Jose.

In retirement John became the founding president of the Council of Churches of Greater San Jose in 1942 and a major supporter of efforts to expand the reach of Protestantism in the Santa Clara Valley and beyond. He and his first wife, Vivan, were active supporters of the program of released time religious education, which the Council of Churches was ready to implement within months of the enabling state legislation in 1943. They provided a mobile school room and equipment and helped fund a program that would reach twenty-six schools. This effort would define the Council for its first ten years. Shortly after the Council's effort at released time education began, the new San Jose Association of Evangelicals organized a separate effort, even though some of their churches had been part of organizing the new Council. Crummey worked to overcome the split in order to expand Protestant influence, helping to call a director of the Council's program who was given the mandate to combine the two programs. This attempt at Protestant unity failed but not for Crummey's lack of trying. In 1953 when the Santa Clara County fairgrounds were considering parimutuel betting on horse racing, John Crummey presented five thousand signatures in opposition. The county's supervisors refused to move ahead on voting on betting, saying that building stables would be too expensive, but not acknowledging the weight of this opposition.[14]

Clifford Crummey says his father was ecumenical as a businessman, and the house was often filled with religious figures from the college and church. But there were limits to who might be included. Cliff's grandfather, David, defiantly wore orange on St. Patrick's Day and his father was anti-Catholic in his sentiments, even though his best friend was Catholic. When the Northern California Council of Churches endorsed the table grape boycott of the farmworkers in 1968, Cliff remembers, "He called me up when that hit the press, and said, 'You know Chavez is a communist.'" Reflecting on other differences in perception he had had with his father, Crummey acknowledged, "I suppose it is part of the times."[15]

Jan Leonard, Clifford Crummey's daughter, remembers her grandfather as a man of principle. "When I was getting ready to go off to college at the University of the Pacific, he took it upon himself to take me aside and give me his best wisdom about how to stay true to myself."[16] An interviewer in the *San Francisco Examiner* asked the 85-year-old Crummey the secret of his success: "Two 10 percents did it. From the time I first started to earn money, I put 10 percent in savings and 10 percent went to Christian work. I never have missed all these years on either one. Nowadays I've raised the church's 10 percent to 30 percent. You'd be surprised what a lot of good can be done."[17]

John Crummey's philanthropy was very purposeful. He made it a policy never to put out more than 25 percent of whatever project was being supported, so that others would be encouraged to stay involved. Family purposefulness about money passed on to succeeding generations. Jack Chinchin, one of John's older grandsons, first went to work as an orchardist, but after a conversion and then seminary went to Liberia and with his family developed a Bible school teaching indigenous leaders. All this had been funded for years through his mother's part of the family's money. Clifford Crummey, John's middle son, intending on not leaving wealth to his own family, distributed the majority of the family funds he had access to before his death to church and social justice causes. Faith Davies, John's second daughter, became a major benefactor for civic causes in San Jose and beyond during her long life.[18]

In the prime of John Crummey's life, Protestantism nearly attained the status of an established religion. A San Francisco religious study made by Protestants in the 1940s found that only one-third of the population was Roman Catholic, leaving great latitude for Protestant mission and a potential majority to be rallied to a Protestant vision.[19] Men like John Dean Crummey were prepared to lead the rally.

THE BIRTH OF THE NORTHERN CALIFORNIA COUNCIL OF CHURCHES

"The spirit and the aim of the ecumenical movement in California is summed up in Charles M. Goethe, prominent Methodist layman and philanthropist of Sacramento," begins the story of the Northern California Council of Churches as told by Paul Shelford, its second executive director.[20] When Clifford Crummey was seeking to reestablish a legal base for a Protestant lobby in Sacramento in the 1960s, the secretary of state said that the name they sought, California Council of Churches, had already been taken. On a document from the 1930s were the names of both Goethe and his own father.[21] Goethe's work to express the impulses for inclusion were entwined with Crummey's but had begun earlier. Charles M. Goethe had been one of the few laity from the West in on the founding of the Federal Council of Churches in 1908.

Goethe's vision was shaped by what he saw taking place in foreign mission. While he and his wife were visiting Korea in 1911 they had seen the mission bodies coming together after years of scattering their mission wherever opportunity had led them, often putting them into competition for converts in the same village. This new coordination had meant one mission body would transfer its congregation to another body where that group already had a stronger cluster of congregations, in order to promote effectiveness in using resources for mission. "This to us was amazing. Since childhood, we were accustomed to nothing but denominational competition." The Goethes brought back to California the vision of the missionary Methodist bishop in Korea, Edwin Harris, for shared planning for mission in order "to revitalize the Protestant Church in the USA and weld it into a powerful weapon for organized unselfishness."[22] The Federal Council's executive, Charles S. McFarland, attempted to slow this enthusiasm for federation in the West: "They might spill the beans to attempt to start too soon in the West."[23]

Goethe persisted, and in December 1912 the decision was made to create both the Sacramento and the state church federations, building on practices of cooperative mission already developed in the Sunday School movement, the temperance societies, and the YMCAs and YWCAs. A major motive for this federation movement, as reflected in a fundraising letter from 1913, was "to make effective through legislation the Social Creed of the Church and to unite the churches of the State in all efforts at human betterment."[24] The Federation was heavily involved between 1917 and 1927 in an ultimately successful effort to sustain support for legislation dealing with prostitution by padlocking these establishments. Goethe and the Federation organized sympathetic legislators and civic leaders to give the campaign highly visible support, and their strategy became a model for similar movements across the country.[25]

In 1935, perhaps in response to the way resources were being mobilized to deal with social need under federal programs, a broad range of California Protestant church leaders came together to create a body under which all forms of Protestant cooperation in the state would be united—Sunday School work, mission education, planning for new churches, as well as legislative advocacy in Sacramento.[26] When this failed for lack of leadership (the committee never got an executive secretary) as well as the lack of funding, Goethe was to guarantee the finances of a northern area committee struggling to continue cooperative Protestant work there. He and his wife underwrote $2,000 of the $5,000 that was committed to bring a Disciple

Christian educator, Abbot Book, from St. Louis to be the first director of the new Northern California Council of Churches.[27]

The Apex of Protestant Inclusion

The accomplishments of Abbott Book in his first years of a long stewardship in the Northern California Council of Churches reflect the capacities and fruitfulness of the ecumenical activities Crummey and Goethe expected to see flourish. Only four denominational staff and three congregations were ready to launch the Northern California Council of Churches when Abbot Book arrived in April 1942. Book began with a desk in a dentist's office in San Francisco. His real office was his car. In his first full year he visited ministerial associations or councils of churches in over sixty cities and towns. His first project was to convince these groups to sponsor a local Sunday Convention in their community, with the new Northern California Council of Churches furnishing leadership. With local arrangements committed, he then got the denominations to send staff to each community to preach and lead workshops with their own congregations in the morning, to be followed by a union evangelistic rally in the evening, with an offering taken for the expense of the convention and for the Northern California Council of Churches. By the end of 1943 these local Sunday Conventions had been held in 41 communities. Protestant congregations and denominations had been touched, from small to large, conservative to liberal, urban and rural.[28]

Other events followed in the next years in local communities, including religious census, visitation evangelism, leadership training, and other institutes and conventions. Karl Irvin Jr., later one of the pillars of the California Farmworker Ministry and regional minister of the Disciples in Northern California, remembers that while he was in a student pastorate in a small Sacramento church, Book turned up there one day to urge his participation in the work of the Council. "I think all he had going was papers in the trunk of his car and a list of names, and he proposed to add me to it. I think I agreed. He was so sure of the importance of it all."[29]

Church at Work began publishing monthly in September 1943 and was supported by Charles Goethe as head of a new communications committee for the Council, providing a vehicle for Book to continue his work to form the network among Protestants. In that very first issue Book could claim that common work had grown in less than a year to a budget of $18,000 and a staff of five, including a weekday education director, a minister in Marin City for united Protestant work with shipyard workers, a half-time fund-raiser, and a prison chaplain to serve men and their families. Funding for the latter two staff came nationally from denominational sources. There was also a new office at the YMCA.[30]

In spite of difficulty in finding leadership and funding for conciliar work in February 1943, the new Council held its first annual meeting at Hotel Whitecotton in Berkeley, at which time 16 vice presidents and 82 members of an administrative board were named. The Rev. Halford Luccock from Yale University was the preacher for that first annual gathering.[31]

Book's connections were not limited to California. He instigated collaboration among four state councils—Washington, Oregon, and Southern and Northern California—to begin in 1945 the "Church Hour of the Air" originating in Hollywood on the Columbia Broadcasting System, with Chet Huntley as host.[32]

In 1951, the annual dinner of the Council was held in the Shrine Auditorium in Oakland, seating 1,200. Two hundred more were turned away. Ralph Sockman was the speaker and Governor and Mrs. Earl Warren came as honored guests. Council membership by that time included 26 different denominations and religious organizations, bridging social class and ideology, though firmly anti-Catholic.[33] *Church at Work* regularly contained broadsides against "the dangerous and growing public influence in the matter of an ambassador to the Vatican," funding for parochial schools, and its support for gambling in the form of bingo.[34]

Why Did Councils of Churches Flourish in the 1950s?

Denominations, seeing their constituencies growing through immigration and the returning of families to church membership after the war years, could come together not out of need as in the 1930s but with a sense of opportunity and capacity. The state was gaining newcomers after the war, often young and with families, and church was a part of creating these new lives. Experiences of shared sacrifice in the war effort created a culture encouraging commitment to public participation by giving Americans a taste of the rewards of civic participation, suggests Paul Shelford, Book's immediate successor as executive of the Council. Undergirding much of the will for conciliar work over the years was the meeting of denominational superintendents that had existed since early in the century. "Comity when I came to the Council nearly ten years ago was to provide a monthly opportunity when the Denominational Executives would meet to protect their interests and see who could strike the best bargain. Comity has changed," Book wrote in 1951. "Twenty-five or more superintendents meet month by month with the concern that the vast areas of our jurisdiction that are unchurched have the Christian witness as proclaimed by our Protestant Faith and adequate houses of worship and buildings for education and social life."[35]

Book had an effective plan that he executed superbly. The change from a poorly funded sole staff position to a fully articulated regional organization in one year is extraordinary. And he enjoyed responsive national church connections. Leaders from the east coast came regularly to counsel and speak and fund.

Most important, mature Protestant leaders in California were ready and able to build on their values in public space. Through 1957 the Council never ended a year in the red, Episcopal Bishop Sumner Walters would write, "because Goethe and his wife met current deficits as the program developed."[36] Five persons were made life members of the Northern California Council of Churches. Four, including Goethe and Crummey, were prominent business and civic leaders. Protestants had access to power in the world—political, economic, and cultural—and that world was ready to follow their leadership.[37]

The Cultural Shift in the 1960s and 1970s

In 1972 the Rev. Clifford Crummey left his position as executive director of the Northern California Ecumenical Council to become pastor of Trinity United Methodist Church in Berkeley. "The commitment to urban ministry from the denominations was gone. We were running out of money."[38] The issues he had faced during five years at the Council he had found to be extremely complex. "I think in a lot of ways my social involvements have come kind of hard for me." In 1999, far into retirement, Crummey became one of the California United Methodist pastors who, against the rules of the denomination, officiated at the holy union of a much beloved, older lesbian couple. "But in this whole [matter] of homosexuality I was one of the slow ones to come along. . . . My whole relation to social problems—to go against the church—is just very difficult. But I just got to the place where I felt the church was wrong."[39]

His memories of the grape boycott were equally painful. Fellow Methodist pastors had condemned him for splitting the church. In hearings in the Central Valley after the Council's board had voted to support the grape boycott, men and women from smaller farms contrasted the vulnerability of their situation with that of the corporate farms who could ride out a challenge and pass its cost on to others. But Crummey had been persuaded, as were many other church leaders in the late 1960s, that resistance in churches to the claims of the farmworkers was wrong. "We had no idea what we were doing," says Crummey, though the United Church of Christ conference minister, Richard Norberg, had taken part in the Easter pilgrimage of Cesar Chavez from Delano to Sacramento in 1966. Strongly supportive also was Karl Irvin Jr., Disciples Regional Minister, who for three years had been the chair of the California Migrant Ministry Committee. Chris Hartmire, the charismatic director of the California Migrant Ministry, was adjunct staff to the Council and a "good friend." "He convinced us that the only way any real good could be accomplished was through these political means, giving power to the farmworker, and the way to do that was to help Cesar Chavez organize," says Crummey. Other Council constituencies like Church Women United and the leaders of the Council of Churches of Santa Clara County were defining themselves by their support of the farmworker movement.[40] But the senior Crummey's dismay was shared by many. By the end of that struggle, the involvement in the Council from communities in the Central Valley that had been so rich under Book was over. Not only was Cliff Crummey on a different path than his father's, but Bay Area Protestant church leaders were shown to be removed from the world of business and agriculture that had responded so strongly to their predecessors.

The Ecumenical Education of Clifford Crummey[41]

Cliff Crummey had graduated from the College of the Pacific and gone on to Boston University School of Theology, where influential professors at his college had been trained. He then began serving as a pastor in Methodist churches, first in Corning in the northern part of California's Central Valley and then in Mill Valley across the Golden Gate Bridge from San Francisco. In both pastorates he would find fellowship and support from other Protestant pastors. Cliff says he became troubled by the quality of pastors joining the chaplaincy during World War II. He left his young family with his parents in San Jose and volunteered for the Navy chaplaincy. Religious commitment brought him to public service as it did his father. He came home to work on a doctorate in Chicago and then became associate pastor in Palo Alto, the most important Methodist congregation in northern California. He moved on to Stockton in the 1950s and served eight fruitful years as pastor of Grace United Methodist Church, a growing congregation near the university where his father had been trustee president and where Cliff had attended and his children would later study. The bishop asked him if he wanted to come to San Francisco to be district superintendent. Cliff had had no love for the city. "I had a father who was well placed in the Methodist Church. The Bishop and everybody knew him. I had a connection." This was 1960. And he learned from the city.

A major source of this learning was Glide Memorial Foundation. The foundation had been created by the family of Charles Goethe's wife, Mary Glide Goethe, in memory of her father and was accumulating income. Though associated with an urban church, the foundation had no program and desperately needed to do something to meet the requirements of being a charitable foundation. Cliff became involved with creating a staff to reach out into a city the church did not understand. Cecil Williams was one of a cluster of gifted leaders hired then, and over the years was to lead Glide Memorial Church to become a model of urban Christian witness. Poverty and racism were two urban realities already acknowledged by the 1960s. Not widely understood at the time was San Francisco's large gay and lesbian population. One of the Glide staff made connections in this community, a council on religion and the homosexual was formed, and when the gay community began to assert itself and felt it needed protection, it was Cliff and other clergy who were called to come to the first of its balls in their collars to face the police: "I was the one who went to the Bishop [after a press report of a North Beach incident]. I had to call the Bishop [about] what had happened."

A national effort was taking place in the early 1960s among Protestant denominations to collaborate in urban ministry. United Methodists were not joining it nationally, but Cliff was asked by the denomination's mission board to attend national meetings of the Joint Strategy and Action Commission (JSAC) as an observer. In San Francisco a strong group of urban denominational staff—UCC, Episcopal, Presbyterian, Baptist, and with Cliff representing the United Methodists—collected around the same idea. The Presbyterian urban ministry leader, Bill Grace, brought Saul Alinsky in for the group to train clergy in community organizing. Alinsky's controversial strategies of organizing around complaints of the community (first tried with residents behind the Chicago stockyards) against the power base gave urban pastors a sense of some traction in dealing with change. Cliff brought Alinsky back again to train United Methodist clergy throughout the city. Coalitions of congregations working in community organizing have grown steadily in the Bay Area in number and reach ever since.

When Crummey's term as District Superintendent was up in 1966 the United Methodist Conference created a position for him as the Methodist Conference's urban minister. But when Paul Shelford resigned as executive director of the Northern California Council of Churches in 1967, his friends among the urban specialists proposed to Cliff that he be hired and they would "take over" the Council.

Staff responsible for urban ministry of their denominations had been meeting regularly, hosted by the new Episcopal bishop, Kilmer Myers, to collaborate in their social ministries. They organized themselves under the Council shortly after Cliff Crummey had become executive director as the Joint Strategy and Action Commission and had hired as director a Presbyterian urban specialist from New York, the Rev. Bob Davidson. It was Davidson who brought to the Council's board in 1968 the request from the California Farmworker Ministry that the board endorse the grape boycott.

Crummey says, "We [JSAC] saw the Council losing relationships with all kinds of these [advocacy] agencies—for peace, all the social issues, the black problems, and so on. So the same team was largely responsible for our beginning to decide to redo the Council and include all of these. So we started to work, and we decided we ought to get a new name, we ought to ask people to all join again, and the Catholics were joining all over the country. Folk in the specialized agencies rushed to join under the Council Table—people who had been on the fringes." Many were to continue in dynamic monthly meetings to share strategies for another decade, and some continued to relate to the Council for the rest of the century. Securing the official participation of the Catholic dioceses was another matter.

Caught by Cultural Change

In the spirit of the 1960s and of Vatican II, the Protestant anti-Catholicism of the previous decades had changed to embrace euphoric mass gatherings of Catholics, Orthodox, and Protestants. Cliff remembers his wife playing the hymns at these gatherings, and once when a reader failed to turn up, of his son reading scripture. All was not smooth in the new relationships. The last of these large gatherings, when the energy for them had run its course, Cliff adds, was in Grace Cathedral. With Archbishop McGucken seated up front, and Cliff sitting in the midst of a group of Catholic nuns, Episcopal Bishop Pike pointedly invited all to the Eucharist, leaving Cliff and the nuns very uncomfortable.

The Archdiocese had created a very active council on race, evolving into a social justice commission that gave Catholics a strong vehicle for engaging with others in dealing with social issues. Led by Catholic and Jewish leaders and involving both black and white Protestant leadership, a San Francisco Conference on Religion and Race in 1963 began a course of demonstrations and lobbying, often with good results, throughout the civil rights struggles of the rest of the 1960s.[42] So there was hope that Roman Catholics and Protestants could meet together in this new ecumenical council. "I went to see the editor of the Catholic paper, a fellow I know. He was later a bishop, very good man. I asked how I should approach this," says Crummey. He told me that "you ought to go see the Archbishop by yourself. If you take a team then he will have to have a team. . . . So I made this appointment. It was a wonderful, wonderful time. McGucken is a very interesting man. I explained it all. He said, 'I am interested, but right now I am having trouble with social issues all around the place, and I am building this new cathedral and we have opposition.' I said, 'When do you expect to dedicate it?' He said, 'I am thinking about sneaking out some morning at 4 A.M. and dedicating it all by myself.'" "You know there were going to be pickets and all," Crummey added in his telling. "It was a wonderful conversation. But the net result was that it was not the right time or the right place and we had to go without the Catholics."

Almost as rapidly as the Northern California Council of Churches had bloomed when Book first arrived in 1942, the Northern California Ecumenical Council seems to have withered in the 1970s. Within the next four years the JSAC-inspired strategy of joint urban work began to unravel. Urban ministers were not replaced by the regional judicatories when they left. Neither the new Presbyterian nor Disciple urban ministers trusted the strategy of JSAC. Looking back on those years Ben Fraticelli, the Disciple urban minister in the early 1970s, was still ready to charge that JSAC strategy functioned as an effort to gain power for the denominations rather than to empower poor and marginalized people.[43] Newer judicatory leaders were not ready to keep the commitments of predecessors, perhaps affected, as American Baptist leaders were later to make very clear, by the alienation of their congregations from the Council for its support of the grape boycott.

Perhaps denominational leaders were all affected by something more pervasive. In the 1970s there was a turning inward among not only Catholics but also by others in mainline churches to consolidate past gains in the face of the divisiveness of social issues. Meanwhile, church fellowship of mass gatherings, as at Book's annual meetings in the 1950s and at the Catholic-Protestant worship in the early 1960s, gave way to the spirited and spiritual demonstrations of marches and vigils of civil rights, boycotts, and peace rallies during the 1960s and early 1970s. These events took place outside ecclesiastical boundaries, even though celebrated and promoted by para-church groups that now gathered at the Council Table—for instance, the Religious Conference on Religion and Race in the 1960s and Clergy and Laity Concerned about the War in Vietnam in the 1970s.

Cliff Crummey's path had taken him beyond where his father and siblings were comfortable. While the family's business evolved from food machinery to building tanks during the war and though he had volunteered to serve as a Navy chaplain in World War II, he had been interested in pacifism. Though remaining loyal to the church of his father, he had followed a path that would land him in that "worst" argument with his father over Cesar Chavez. He had let his soul be captured like many others of California's lay and ordained religious leaders in the late 1960s by Chavez's charisma. Following the lead of the piety of his father, the times had led him to forge an alliance with the son of Catholic fruit pickers in orchards of his father's contemporaries. Cliff had watched congregations transform, seen the engagement of their ministers and laity with social issues, and watched transformation in society. Then he saw the process falter. In 1972 he took an appointment as pastor of the United Methodist congregation serving the University of California campus in Berkeley. In warm testimonies to his long and fruitful ministry given at his memorial service in 2000, there were stories of his personal contributions to pastoral ministry in Palo Alto, to urban ministry in San Francisco, to opportunities for young women clergy in Berkeley, and to education through gifts from his family's funds. All the stories were of his role as a United Methodist with Methodists. Forgotten were his years in the center of the unfolding ecumenical drama in Northern California.

The 1990s, When a Thousand Flowers Bloomed: Janet Crummey Leonard[44]

Jan Leonard's participation in the conciliar movement has been quite different from that of either her father or grandfather, though she followed the same path of a vigorous Wesleyan piety. "What my father was learning about the city in the 60s, I missed," admits Leonard. She was in college in Stockton, taught a year nearby, got married, and then moved to the city of her grandfather, San Jose, because of her husband's job with General Electric. Jim Leonard's family had been active members of the Stockton United Methodist congregation that Cliff Crummey had served as pastor in the 1950s. When the new couple came to San Jose, they immediately looked for a Methodist congregation. Her grandfather's church, First United Methodist, had given way to congregations serving the suburbs that had grown up in former orchards. The couple tried First United Methodist in nearby Campbell. Jan says the perceptive associate pastor visited them and sent them to another Methodist congregation, hidden on a back street but closer to their new home. Roselawn United Methodist Church was a small congregation, organized when the prune orchards were being replaced by homes. It was served by a capable woman pastor and reflected the hospitable Christianity the Leonards were used to. The Leonards stayed. Two daughters came, and Jan Leonard remembers the 1970s as a busy time. A year in the Boston area in 1979 woke her up to responsibility for her own religious life. "We were sending the children to Sunday School at the nearest congregation and finally felt we ought to go ourselves. It was Congregational. They changed pastors, and I became aware that this new one was preaching and teaching a conservative faith that upset everything I assumed was sure. In fact, I left that church for a while and went off to a Methodist congregation in another town just to reassure myself that the world was still as I was used to." Reassured she came back to the Congregational church and she and her husband sang in its choir. She began a period of reading, searching for the voices that spoke to her. She decided she did not have to fight everything, but could approach each worship service expecting to find something she was meant to receive.

When the family returned to San Jose in 1980, Jan joined Roselawn's peacemaking group, Micah 4. Most members were women and most had long practiced to "be taught God's ways, that they might walk in God's ways" (Micah 4:2). Through them Jan was introduced to the Methodist Federation for Social Action, a loose-knit network of people like herself "that before I did not know existed." Perhaps some members of Micah 4 were related to peace-oriented ecumenical agencies that gathered monthly around the Council Table in San Francisco.

In the summer of 1984, Cliff Crummey, now retired, and his wife, Ethel Elizabeth, joined one of those organizations affiliated with the Council, the Nicaragua Interfaith Committee for Action, in a "fact finding" trip to Nicaragua. Jan was encouraged to join them. "I was pulled, but the trip did not feel like me." But in summer 1985, Jan, her daughter Amy, and her mother took a peace ribbon made in Micah 4 meetings and joined the thousands wrapping the Pentagon, with enough left over to begin wrapping the White House. This act mobilized a response to a desire for peace that even far exceeded dreams of those who gathered monthly around the Council Table. But the question of Nicaragua haunted her. She believed that "fact finding wasn't what I wanted to do. But I wondered if it was fear that kept me home. Then in the fall of 1987 I saw somewhere a little announcement about a group going with Habitat for Humanity to build houses. I knew that was for me. This was something that would let me leave a piece of myself there."

Over the next year after her return from that trip she became part of creating a small ecumenical agency, Seeds of Learning, that like Habitat would focus on building and supplying one-room schools in Nicaragua, combining workers from the United States with participants from the local community. Also beginning in 1988, for a ten-year period she became involved with the Social Education and Action Committee of the Council of Churches of Santa Clara County and then joined its board. Like Micah 4, the Social Education and Action Committee had at its core a group of persons schooled in the spirituality of action for peace and justice, some having begun their work in the county in the 1950s in migrant ministry in Santa Clara County. Jan was drawn through them into work with the homeless. She led a long process through which her congregation became persuaded and then enthusiastically committed to invite homeless persons into the church for a month each year to sleep and eat.

In the early 1990s she mediated between the board of that Council and a contentious venture into interfaith work it had begun. Many in the Council felt it had not finished the work of building connections among Christians, harking back to John Crummey's founding concern for building a solid Christian front. Her own search for authentic faith led her to move into interfaith collaboration in the Bay Area. Eight years later she and her husband would welcome a Hindu son-in-law into their family.

None of Jan Leonard's siblings or her two children are active in church. But all have lives that engage them in serving human need—through their work in probation, homeless agencies, and counseling. After five years on the board of the Council of Churches of Santa Clara County, Jan declined to be renominated, though she continued to meet with its Social Education and Action Committee. "That was not my call." And after ten years on the board of Seeds of Learning she also declined renomination. She is actively available to her grandchildren, kept conveniently near by their parents. Her engineer husband who had begun accompanying her to board meetings of Seeds of Learning is now its president. "As I become more settled, he becomes more restless, pushing for change, as if we were changing places." Her inner journey continues, but her activist leadership fades, at least for now.

Jan Leonard, like her grandfather and father, has been a loyal participant in United Methodist congregations. Like them her life reflects a vigorous

Wesleyan piety, sharing the belief with John Wesley that all the world is her parish. Like them she has practiced the volunteerism that characterizes American civic life. But John Crummey could approach the world as a place where he had power, as did the ecumenical organizations of his time. Cliff Crummey could deal with the world through the instrumentalities of the church, in which he had power. Jan Leonard comes to the world in the company of individuals of faith who, as outsiders to the world, have to seek a moral power that is an alternative to it. While a vigorous piety continues to drive their participation, these people have moved from the center of social and political power to the periphery. To the extent that Jan Leonard is representive, people with this kind of calling are not readily building enduring institutions. They are moving bodies who can be captured only for the moment when their journey parallels that of another.

Diminished Fortunes of the Northern California Ecumenical Council

By the time Jan Leonard's path intersected that of the Northern California Ecumenical Council in 1992 that organization had been reduced to two part-time professional staff. Its board was still nominally representative of member denominations but relied chiefly on the willingness of incumbents to remain. The Oakland Council of Churches, whose leaders had been among the small group to create the first state church federation in 1912 and who had been in the forefront of the birth of the Northern California Council in the 1940s, had been transformed into a social service agency during the 1960s, detached from the churches. The San Francisco Council of Churches, a pioneer in many social services in San Francisco and another pillar of the regional conciliar movement, would cease to exist in the 1980s. At the turn of the century, the Northern California Ecumenical Council has struggled to transform itself into an interfaith agency, the Northern California Interreligious Conference, but faces the threat of extinction.[45]

The history of the Ecumenical Council following Clifford Crummey's resignation includes a series of talented executives. Each brought a vision but then left with that vision unfulfilled to pursue it elsewhere.

Lynne E. Hodges, Crummey's immediate successor, was recognized in 2001 by the American Baptists with the national Luke Mowbray Ecumenical Award for his lifetime of ecumenical service. Another nominee in that year was Joan Brown Campbell, who most recently had been General Secretary of the National Council of Churches.[46] Hodges had been active with American Baptists as a pastor and as the denomination's urban minister in

San Francisco in the late 1950s and early 1960s. He responded to a call to a church in Tacoma, Washington, where he helped organize and then lead the city's first human relations commission. When he was installed in 1973 as executive of both the San Francisco Council and the Northern California Ecumenical Council, the speaker was Philip Potter, General Secretary of the World Council. Hodges became involved in responding to issues of intergroup tension and to disasters, including Jonestown.

Hodges led the two Councils to take over a derelict eight-story building on San Francisco's Market Street on the edge of the Tenderloin district and then tried to persuade denominations to establish their offices in a common ecumenical center. Failing in that, nonprofits, many with a religious base and some operating as affiliates of the Ecumenical Council, took up residence in the building. The San Francisco Council of Churches had responded to the challenges and opportunities for service of the 1960s to become a major subcontractor for services funded by government agencies, particularly with children and the elderly. Doneter Lane, a charismatic Baptist lay leader, led the San Francisco Council in adding programs that would provide meals for poor children all across the city during school vacations. As the 1970s progressed into the Nixon administration, the San Francisco Council had financial difficulties through cutbacks in its contracts, as federal money for social programs declined. The lease on the ecumenical center was given up, and the two agencies moved to smaller spaces in the office building next door. This ecumenical space allowed the San Francisco Council to host a meeting in its home with Msgr. John Quinn, the new Archbishop of San Francisco. But this did not, in the end, turn out to be a workable model for conciliar ecumenism in the 1970s. Lynne Hodges left the Council after five years to serve as a local pastor, where he became involved in a close partnership in community affairs with the pastor of St. Leander's Catholic parish.

John Pairman "Jock" Brown, Hodges's successor in 1978, had become chair of the Council Table in 1975 while he was western coordinator for Clergy and Laity Concerned about the War in Vietnam. A scholar of the early Christian period, Brown had been drawn into causes of radical religion when he arrived at Berkeley in the 1960s, became a cause célèbre when his contract at the Episcopal seminary in Berkeley was not renewed, and had his picture taken with Ho Chi Minh in Vietnam while on a peace visit in the early 1970s.

Jock Brown was interested in how the Council might foster radical discipleship. Under the umbrella of the Ecumenical Council were many small faith-based agencies dealing with peace, immigration, human rights, hunger, and farmworker issues. As armed struggles grew in Central America, for example, the Council Table had become a major place where strategies were made among Bay Area activists to alert the churches and through them the public about abuses of human rights the government was supporting.[47] The Council became increasingly defined by the activist agencies it sheltered. "When the Board met, it was chiefly the Council Table in another form," observed Brown. These dedicated laity with a few clergy were the minority who carried the vision and were willing to work for it, Brown notes. The budget at this time was about $200,000, providing for two part-time core staff and budgets for several of the affiliated agencies. Brown was a careful steward of what he saw as Council resources, human relationships, and causes, but "I don't think these sorts of ventures are intended to last that long," he reflected in an interview in 1999. The Council moved from trying to be an ecumenical or interdenominational center to being a center sheltering ecumenical activists. But even this more modest vision was not something that could last.

Brown left the Council in 1983 to continue full-time in research that has resulted in the publication of over fifty scholarly articles in various journals and three volumes published by Oxford University Press. His has been a lifelong work to find in the formative period of Christianity a fresh vision from that period of our obligations for building a just society today.[48]

To replace Brown, Council leadership brought in John C. Moyer, a Californian and a Presbyterian with a demonstrated commitment to ecumenical justice advocacy. He had been the ecumenical campus chaplain in southern California and then at the University of California in Berkeley. Moyer had then worked in Europe in a program funded by the World Council of Churches bringing together people separated by different Christian and national traditions to work on issues of urban life. By the early 1980s he was back in the Bay Area creating a network among religious radicals and union activists around issues of economic justice. At the Ecumenical Council, Moyer, drawing from Europe, sought to make it a vehicle for bold ecclesiastical witness, bringing together sympathetic denominational leaders of Orthodox, Euro-Protestant, African-American, and Roman Catholic churches, with some notable successes. Building on his work in Europe and in the Bay Area on coalition building, Moyer led the Ecumenical Council into a coalition committed to end apartheid in South Africa. The coalition of the ILWU (Longshoreman Union) and a wide variety of church, labor, and civil rights groups closed the Port of San Francisco to all ships carrying South African cargo, a story covered in the *New York Times*. Following on this experience Moyer led the Council into a similar coalition with the ILWU after the government in Korea had imprisoned opposition leader Kim Dae Jung, leaving rights activists fearing for his life. Longshoremen threatened to strike, preventing shipping from the west coast to Korea. Moyer mobilized the public support of bishops and executives. When later in a remarkable reversal of his fortunes, Kim Dae Jung was inaugurated as president of Korea in 1999, he was to invite as his guests Moyer, Rev. Gus Shultz, who had been bishop of the Association of Evangelical Churches at that time, and Herb Mills from the Longshoreman.

To fund itself, and consistent with the vision of making a global witness, the Ecumenical Council in the late 1970s had become the umbrella agency for contracts for refugee services throughout northern California, growing under Moyer's leadership in the 1980s to a one-million-dollar budget. But by 1990 federal funding for refugee services was being drastically curtailed, and the Ecumenical Council itself was facing a serious financial crisis. So in 1990 Moyer left the Council, discouraged after seven years. "The denominations just didn't want a global witness." Moyer returned to Europe, this time to Geneva to direct the program of Frontiers in Mission, supporting global networks of workers for urban justice. Moyer and the board had not found the role of mobilizer for ecclesiastical witness to be sustainable.[49]

Ben Fraticelli was asked by the Disciples Regional Minister in 1991 to help the board work its way out of these contracts that were now costing the Council more than it received from them. Fraticelli defines himself as a Puerto Rican community organizer.[50] As a child he was a convert to the Disciples because of the kindness of members of a Disciples congregation to himself and the other children in his family, which had moved in the 1940s into the church's neighborhood in Hayward, on the east side of the San Francisco Bay. He was trained both in the ministry and in public health, worked as a Disciples pastor and community organizer in Dos Palos, a rural Central California community, in Florida for the National Farmworker Ministry, and beginning in the late 1960s as urban minister for the Disciples in northern California. When the funds ran out for specialized urban ministry in the early 1970s he served the Disciples in Paraguay in a large community service ministry. Returning to Northern California, with no place in the church for his gifts in community ministry, he began consulting in community public health in the Bay Area.

Ben's relation with the Council evolved from consultant to part-time executive as he began resolving the issues around the contracted services. He found himself in harmony with the earnest search that members like Nancy Nielsen of the Council's board were ready to make for an effective voice for faith in public life. He says he was hoping to find again a role for himself in the church linking religious institutions and work for the public good. The Russian airlift was such an effort.

After its work in the Russian airlift, the Ecumenical Council teamed up with the World Council of Churches and the National Council of Churches in 1993 to organize a Bay Area hearing on racism, part of a global emphasis of the World Council. A year of work gathered a wide variety of community organizations that gratefully responded to the opportunity to give testimony to suffering widely ignored by the rest of society. Juliet Twomey, who had provided effective staffing for the Northern California Ecumenical Council on the hearing, was then asked by the World Council to help draft its report of all its hearings. Yet, subsequent efforts by the Ecumenical Council to follow up with local congregational leaders with antiracism training did not prove sustainable. Except for the Oakland Catholic Diocese there was little demand. And offering itself as a convener in places where church and world could meet on common concerns also did not prove to be a service for which there was a constituency. The Council's debt was reduced, but so was income. Fraticelli left the Council after four years to return to public health work. There he would lead community empowerment programs that put resources of public and nonprofit health agencies into the hands of leaders living in marginalized communities.

Following the resignation of Cliff Crummey in 1972, the Northern California Ecumenical Council through the enterprise of its executives continually experimented with its business plans. The Council tried serving as an ecumenical center, as a center for Christian activists, as a mobilizer of ecclesiastical global witness, and finally as a convener of leaders from church and world to focus on pressing issues. In spite of successes in each role, it could not find a sustaining constituency.

Beginning in the mid-1990s, with almost no remaining funds, the board decided to try to create yet another space for itself. Board members could remember how over the years the Council had succeeded in bringing together people to focus on pressing social issues. By 1998 it had refocused itself as the Northern California Interreligious Conference with a bequest to fund staff for a year.

Many Different Ecumenical Forms Emerge

But space for this refocused ecumenical organization to flourish in had diminished. The vacuum created by the diminished council and the continuing ecumenical needs opened the door for *ecumenical change* and perhaps innovation. The diminished council and the changing times brought new experiments and sometimes strong competitors for each of the council's historic roles. For example, on the ecumenical front a new Ecumenical Ministries in Northern California included not only the Protestant bishops and executives that had formed the core of the Council's board in the early 1970s but also several Roman Catholic bishops and nominally, at least, Evangelicals. This organization had grown in the 1990s out of meetings Moyer had been hosting of Protestant and Orthodox denominational executives. They sought a fellowship that was inclusive of Roman Catholics and Evangelicals, which meant to them an organization not encumbered by the public positions taken by the Ecumenical Council over the past twenty years, particularly on women's issues and economic justice. Lacking lay support for their Ecumenical Ministries, however, the bishop's and executives' own interest would wither within the decade. By the same token denominational leaders were seen to be no longer a natural constituency for any conciliar effort, particularly as an inheritor of the traditions of the Northern California Ecumenical Council.

Another unfilled arena was to provide a collaborative *center for activists* to coordinate and stage their work. In the 1980s, in response to the bitter struggle in El Salvador, churches and synagogues were gathered into several covenants in the Bay Area in the sanctuary movement. Whereas the activists around Central America in the 1970s had gathered at the Council Table, those passionate about the sanctuary movement in the 1980s formed their own center for networking and operated their own strategies for engaging support from congregations and from the public. When the sanctuary movement faded in the 1990s, the cause of immigrant rights began to be carried by immigrant organizations, with some congregations, usually containing immigrants, also actively involved. An important center of dealing with public justice issues had moved beyond the Anglo-Protestant world and the conciliar world.

There was also need for *mobilizing religious witness* in time of crisis. At the time of the Loma Prieta earthquake in 1989 in San Francisco, Oakland, San Jose, and Santa Cruz, interfaith organizations were created. In the absence of a council of churches in San Francisco, this interfaith response mechanism grew into the San Francisco Interfaith Council. Its capacity to live beyond its founding purpose came from a Jewish/Catholic/African-American alliance formed in the 1960s as the San Francisco Council on Religion and Race. This had been staffed by Rita Semel as part of her duties with the Jewish Community Relations Council. Semel, at that time retired from the

Community Relations Council, became executive vice president of this new collaborative, which was to pick up many of the functions unserved by the diminished Council. With her extensive connections in both religious and civic communities, she drew active participation from her own synagogue, of which Senator Diane Feinstein is a member, and from other "big steeple" congregations, including St. Mary's Roman Catholic Cathedral, Calvary Presbyterian Church, the largest and one of the oldest Anglo-Protestant congregations, and Third Baptist Church, whose African-American pastor has been a county supervisor.

When the San Francisco Presidio was decommissioned and buildings made available for public use, Semel led an effort to make the base's chapel an interfaith center. Paul Chaffee, formerly a staff member of the San Francisco Council, has made the chapel into a viable gathering point for individuals from many faith traditions in the last part of the 1990s.

It was at this time that the Episcopal Bishop of California, William Swing, conceived a new international interfaith organization, United Religions. Still in its infancy, United Religions affords these and other leaders of interfaith organizations a network that lets them support their impulses for crossing borders of culture and discovering new things about themselves and potential allies for good work.[51]

Still another area of ecumenical need lies in *enabling congregations.* A vision animating the work of councils of churches in both John and Cliff Crummey's years, this is served today in the Bay Area through the parish-based community organizing that the urban ministers introduced to San Francisco in the 1960s. Pacific Institute for Community Organizing (PICO), cofounded by Rev. John Baumann, S.J., has succeeded over twenty-five years in building a constantly growing network of congregations that are given expert staff assistance in their community ministries. PICO has succeeded in getting funding from foundations and businesses to support its work not only in the Bay Area but around the country.[52]

In the Bay Area, the San Francisco Foundation developed its FAITHS Initiative in the early 1990s. Seeing congregations as valid instruments for community change, the staff of the foundation has provided grants, technical assistance, and opportunities for congregations to learn from each other and to collaborate. The focus has ranged from support of work responding to welfare cutbacks, to antiracism work, to support for new ministries with the elderly, all reminiscent of activities that local councils had undertaken in the past. One stated aim of the initiative was to model for other foundations the virtue of supporting these long-lasting community organizations as vehicles for the service and change they sought to promote through their funding.[53]

The California Council of Churches, historically the Sacramento-based statewide arm of the churches for public policy advocacy, has gained substantial foundation funding for its work of empowering local congregations' initiatives to help people move from welfare to work, to provide child care, and to create health ministries. "I think it is probably a narrow window of opportunity we have for getting this kind of support, and the challenge is to build capacity before the faith community moves off their radar screen," suggested its director, Scott Anderson, in May 1999.[54] The FAITHS Initiative and the California Council of Churches have been reaching beyond the mainline, or Euro-based, Protestant congregations, to immigrant, evangelical, storefront, and nonwhite churches, anticipating the inclusion of these varied actors seen now in the Bush initiative.

The ecumenical impulse is quite alive. The successors to the Northern California Council of Churches have increasingly not been among the majority of the people carrying the impulse. Access to the people passionate about causes, access to religious leaders and congregations who are serving their neighbors, and access to the resources that can support causes and ministries are all in other hands. The good news is that the needs are being fulfilled by these newcomers to the ecumenical scene.

Continuity and Difference across the Generations

There is a tradition that continues in the Crummey family and in the ecumenical structures they have been part of. It originates in Anglo-Protestant piety, the social gospel of the turn of the nineteenth century. Today its children are likely not to be members of Anglo-Protestant churches. They well might be working in public and private institutions that serve human need—unions, nonprofits, or governmental. If they are serving in religious organizations those might be animated by other religious traditions, particularly African-American, Roman Catholic, Jewish, or even Buddhist, Hindu, or Muslim.

Clearly, living by principle, as Jan saw her grandfather do, carries through the generations of the Crummey family. Just as clearly, a value structure that demands participation in public life according to these principles carries across the generations. Loyalty is a key, loyalty to family, even in the midst of differences. These three Crummeys have known pain when they have found themselves at odds with particular values of their family or congregations.

But principle will lead them to follow their own paths. So each in his or her own way has that ability to act on this vision.

At the same time the sense of their community has shifted. John's was defined by Protestantism of the middle class, and by his status as an owner. Cliff's by persons that shared social/spiritual values, leading him beyond both Protestant and middle-class boundaries and his status as a professional. Jan's community has been defined in part by the community of women and by what it means to have the status of a volunteer. Her brothers and her children, still drawn by family loyalty and as carriers of its values, are also defined by the values of current culture that atomize society, forcing all to invent their responses.

This seems to have happened because religious institutions have never had deep roots in Northern California. "The only religious center that continually impacts and reflects the life in the city is Grace Cathedral (Episcopal)," says John Pairman Brown, biblical scholar and religious social activist who was the executive of the Northern California Ecumenical Council in the 1970s. "It actually succeeds in containing San Francisco's history within it. The Catholics, though the strongest religious force, are still too focused on establishing themselves to create any institution that can play this role in our society."[55] Religious institutions are not often significant players in the wider public arena. The times do not favor traditional institutions of any kind in California. Religious institutions in particular are overwhelmed by change,[56] and demographic change above all, because of the constant flow of new people into California. Indeed, when one looks more closely at the story of the rise and decline of the Northern California Council of Churches and successor Ecumenical Council one sees clearly how this institution's rise and fall has been closely related to the rise and decline of Protestantism and of significant Protestant leaders in California society.

Weak ecumenical and religious institutions in the Bay Area have resulted in ecumenical entrepreneurism, which is probably a consequence of other widespread changes in the culture. Joan Connell, religion editor of the *San Jose Mercury News* in the 1980s, said that she and Don Lattin, religion editor of the *San Francisco Chronicle*, had agreed that half their coverage should be about the spirituality outside organized religious institutions.[57] Connell was pointing toward the sort of fluid networking that cultural critics find running through love and work as well as spirituality in the twenty-first century.

Jan Leonard's grandfather, John A. Crummey, was one of a handful of persons instrumental in creating the network of councils of churches functioning in midcentury in northern California. Such Protestant councils could often command attention. The Rev. Dr. Clifford Crummey, Jan Leonard's father, was the executive director of the Northern California Council of Churches from 1967 to 1972 when it made its most ambitious effort to change with the times and meet the demands of urban life. Then leaders of both Protestant and Catholic churches felt compelled by the times to organize among themselves to try to evoke and provoke the better nature of the society. At that time it seemed to activists that if they would organize themselves they could carve out separate space in the culture where their values could be carried out. Yet by the 1980s and 1990s the role of the Council changed yet again. Jan Leonard was one of several lay activists, primarily women, who brought the energy to a short-term collaboration for service. The Council was no longer initiator or even convener. It simply provided the legal and facilitating umbrella for the volunteers.

The story of the perspectives and work style of these generations suggests how changing times shaped the different role each would play in the same institution, the Northern California Council of Churches and its successor. The extent that this institution could serve to mobilize the ecumenical impulse in different times is made clear by looking at this changing role of the members of one family. That three generations of the same family continued to be involved in the same institution, even in spite of all the changes of the times, suggests the enduring power of the Anglo-Protestant piety that created the Northern California Council in the first place. But local ecumenism in the Bay Area had evolved into "situation-centered ecumenism." The Russian airlift is the story of the initiative and collaboration of individuals expressing their spirituality in response to a specific situation of need. Jan Leonard's participation in this airlift and generally in ecumenical life was an expression of her spirituality and not necessarily of her commitment to an institution. In fact, the way the airlift was done made it clear institutions no longer captured the essential core of ecumenical life in California, in contrast with a half century earlier, when local ecumenism was largely Protestant and rooted in an institution. A generation earlier, Jan Leonard's father had steered the organization through a major transition. A generation before that, her grandfather had contributed to the creation of the Northern California Council of Churches, partly because he believed that what he stood for had to be given institutional form.

The rapidity of social change over the last half of the twentieth century favors the "entrepreneur" and the "start up" over the "manager" and the "continuing institution." This near truism of church growth is reflected in the fortunes of organizations that seek to empower and connect actors in the religious community. All of the leaders of the Northern California Council of Churches and its successor were persons of notable character, charisma, and achievement. All were markedly entrepreneurial.

That capacity was not sufficient. Newer organizations continually surpassed them in the last thirty years. For example, PICO, born in the 1970s with the single aim of empowering urban congregations, survived to achieve what the Northern California Ecumenical Council with a similar aim but built on an older foundation could not. PICO had a single aim, not many. Sheer population growth guarantees that mainline Protestantism would have a smaller share of the public market. The shift in Presbyterian participation over a wider timespan at the University of California in Berkeley from the turn of the century until today suggests something of the difference. In 1900, 17 percent of the students were Presbyterian. Estimates today are on the order of tenths of one percent. Though San Jose's mayor was a member of First United Methodist in the 1940s, during the 1990s its mayors were the descendants of an early Irish settler and of a Jewish woman and the son of one of the colleagues of Cesar Chavez in organizing resettled migrant workers.

Moreover, there is the change of culture. Karl Irvin Jr., who welcomed Abbott Book to his student pastorate in the 1950s, in the 1960s became a champion of Cesar Chavez, and in the 1970s was an activist denominational executive and mainstay of the Northern California Ecumenical Council, feels now that perhaps the lasting legacy of the 1960s was not the social activism but the cultural change reflected in the human potential movement. "Why, it was a Republican state legislature that put toilets in the fields," he proclaims. "We all were infected by the humanism of that time." It was not a concern about justice that would move Republicans, but their identifying with the indignity of having no toilets. In some way the Crummey legacy has been carried into the present through ways of honoring the potential of being human. It is fine with Irvin that no one needs to coordinate these community improvements. He sees neighborhood groups popping up in Stockton where he lives. Grassroots activity, naturally interfaith because of the diversity of the city, gives him hope for the future.[58]

Perhaps work that links a sense of hospitality toward an undefined community with focused action on achieving particular human good is sustainable only by the initiative of persons. Perhaps the ecumenical impulse cannot survive wedded too closely to institutions. Even Abbott Book, whose work would continue past his retirement in 1957 until the JSAC young turks took it over from his admiring successor in 1967, would experience a hiccup in the latter part of his career. An abortive campaign in 1955 to raise half a million dollars to fund all levels of ecumenical work left the Northern California Council with its first debt since 1942.[59] Perhaps even by 1955 the conditions that made his business plan so effective in 1942 had shifted sufficiently that this failure was a precursor to the need for change that Crummey sought and failed to achieve. Finding the mixture of vision and opportunity is always a matter of something beyond competence. But personal persistence brings companions along the way. Persistence can find opportunities for extraordinary witness, as has occurred in these and other ways in northern California in the last half century.

Notes

1. Jan Leonard, videotaped interview by author, June 30, 1999 (tape has very bad sound).
2. Ben Fraticelli, videotaped interview by author, August 30, 2000.
3. Suzanne Robinson, telephone interview by author, August 30, 2000.
4. Fraticelli, videotaped interview by author.
5. Gerald O'Rourke, telephone interview by author, August 30, 2000.
6. Fraticelli, videotaped interview by author.
7. Paul K. Shelford, *Protestant Cooperation in Northern California* (San Francisco: Northern California–Nevada Council of Churches, 1962), pp. 85–89.
8. Contemporary Protestant impulses toward service to the poor and advocacy for social justice can be traced through the movements of the 1960s back to the social gospel movement of the turn of the century and back yet further to the revivalism of the early 1800s. See Hugh Wire, "Uncovering a Theology of Social Ministry: A Case Study" (D.Min. dissertation, San Francisco Theological Seminary, 1987), pp. 151–186. See also Ronald C. White and C. Howard Hopkins, *The Social Gospel: Religion and Reform in Changing America* (Philadelphia: Temple University Press, 1976).
9. From discussion of the Protestant imprint on ecumenism by Arleon L. Kelley, in 1996 draft of chapter on Protestant-Catholic ecumenism. The Protestant vision of the representation of many in one voting body as a sign of ecumenism made difficult the participation of Roman Catholics or many African-Americans who experience Church differently.
10. Leonard, telephone interview by author.
11. Clyde Arbuckle, *History of San Jose* (San Jose, Calif.: Memorabilia of San Jose, 1986), p. 188.
12. *San Francisco Examiner*, December 1, 1963.
13. Leonard, telephone interview by author.
14. G. Arthur Cassidy, *Heritage and Hope: A Brief History of the Santa Clara County Council of Churches* (San Jose: SCCCC, 1976), pp. 1–7 (archives of the Council of Churches of Santa Clara County, Holy Redeemer Lutheran Church, San Jose).
15. Clifford Crummey, videotaped interview by author, June 22, 1999.
16. Leonard, videotaped interview by author.

17. *San Francisco Examiner*, December 1, 1963.
18. Leonard, telephone interview by author.
19. *Church at Work*, January 1947, in Graduate Theological Union Library. See also H. Paul Douglass et al., *The San Francisco Bay Area Church Study* (Committee for Cooperative Field Research of the Federal Council of Churches et al., 1945), also in Graduate Theological Union Library.
20. Shelford, *Protestant Cooperation in Northern California*, p. 40.
21. Crummey, videotaped interview by author.
22. Charles M. Goethe, quoted in Shelford, *Protestant Cooperation in Northern California*, pp. 41–42.
23. Ibid., p. 42.
24. Ibid., p. 42.
25. Shelford, *Protestant Cooperation in Northern California*, pp. 43–44.
26. Ibid., pp. 68–72.
27. Ibid., pp. 74, 78–79.
28. Ibid., pp. 80–81.
29. Karl Irvin, Jr., videotaped interview by author, May 17, 1999.
30. Shelford, *Protestant Cooperation in Northern California*, pp. 83–84.
31. Ibid., p. 82.
32. Ibid., pp. 94–95.
33. Abbot Book, *Church at Work*, March 1951, in Graduate Theological Union Library.
34. *Church at Work*, September and October 1951, January 1952.
35. Shelford, *Protestant Cooperation in Northern California*, p. 91.
36. Ibid., p. 47.
37. Ibid.
38. Unless otherwise noted, direct and indirect quotes are from Crummey, videotaped interview by author.
39. Conversation with author just after Crummey had participated in the service.
40. Cassidy, *Heritage and Hope*, pp. 23–36.
41. All of the following section, unless otherwise noted, is from Crummey, videotaped interview by author.
42. Rev. Eugene Boyle, videotaped presentation, March 23, 1999.
43. Fraticelli, videotaped interview by author.
44. This section is based on interview with Jan Leonard by the author, June 23, 2000, and from personal knowledge of the author, who has worked with Leonard in the Council of Churches of Santa Clara County and in Seeds of Learning.
45. Catherine Coleman, contract worker, personal communication, May 7, 2001.
46. Lynne E. Hodges, personal communication with author.
47. The other center was the Social Justice Commission of the San Francisco Archdiocese. Networking between the two was very productive, in the author's experience.
48. Material for this section comes from videotaped interview with John Pairman Brown, May 5, 1999.
49. John C. Moyer, email message to author, May 24, 2001.
50. Material in this section comes from Fraticelli, videotaped interview by author.
51. Rita Semel, videotaped interview by author, May 17, 1999.
52. John Baumann, videotaped interview by author, March 6, 2000.
53. Dwayne Marsh, director of the FAITHS Initiative, videotaped interview by author, June 30, 2000.
54. Scott Anderson, videotaped interview by author, May 14, 1999.

55. Brown, videotaped interview by author.

56. A study of membership trends in twenty Lutheran congregations in Santa Clara Valley Conference of the ELCA made in 1994 showed that membership in virtually all had peaked in the 1960s and all had declined since, some precipitously (Sierra Pacific Synod, ELCA, Oakland, Calif.). A study by the Catholic diocese of San Jose in the late 1990s determined that without some unforeseen change there would be one priest for each two parishes twenty years ahead (Diocese of San Jose, Santa Clara, Calif.). A committee of the Presbytery of San Francisco surveying the status of Presbyterian congregations in 2000 determined that up to half were in decline with little prospect for their future growth without substantial intervention (Presbytery of San Francisco, Berkeley, Calif.).

57. From conversations in 1989 in San Jose with the author.

58. Ibid.

59. Shelford, *Protestant Cooperation in Northern California*, p. 96.

PART TWO. LOCAL ECUMENISM CONFRONTS ITS EXCLUSIVENESS

Ecumenism is rooted in a vision of the wholeness of the Church as a sign, if not sacrament, of God's intended wholeness for the whole creation. Wholeness requires the freedom for gifts of all to be mutually shared, boundaries broken down, and the integrity of each cherished. Yet at the same time, the social fabric has historically tended to protect the privileges of the status quo—which has traditionally divided the people of the world by economic and social class as well as by gender, race, sexual orientation, and hierarchies of power, if not patriarchy. The Church has not been immune from boundary building and indeed, from boundary tending—a denial of its very message and nature.

Historically, American ecumenism has been largely the preserve of Euroamerican churches and has reflected largely agrarian values in the midst of an emerging industrial culture. Women were often excluded, as were people of color and different faiths and sexual orientation and people of the lower classes. One of the remarkable transformations of the last half of the twentieth century, and especially of the 1960s through the 1980s, has been the moves of the Church and American culture to ever greater circles of inclusion. We are learning to be open to persons of other faith traditions, within and beyond the Christian tradition. And we have diminished the boundaries among the races and between the genders, and to some degree, among the classes, as well as among the power "haves" and "have nots." Yet, by the last decade of the second millennium we have seen tremendous backlashes trying to rebuild the walls of separation, while at the same time global corporations are pursuing an economic strategy that builds ever higher walls between the rich and the growing numbers of poor in the world.

3

ECUMENISM IN EAST HARLEM: THE PARENT OF ECUMENICAL URBAN MINISTRY

Sr. Paul Teresa Hennessee

Editor's Note: One could argue that the beginnings of the Church's concern for the city came from Walter Rauschenbusch's ministry (and theological reflection on it) in Hell's Kitchen on the central westside of New York City shortly after the Civil War. Among other things, his work created a new awareness among people of faith about the devastating conditions in many urban ghettos. It also created a network of settlement houses in New York and countless other cities in the United States. Rauschenbusch's work developed into a theological body of material that became the basis for the Social Gospel that was an influential rationale for much of the work done by local ecumenism in the United States.

We believe that a rebirth of the Church's concern for the city came out of East Harlem soon after World War II. And even more than in the Hell's Kitchen, this "Hell of Manhattan" was to move the urban church movement far beyond just a social services ministry. The rebirth that came from East Harlem drew upon European theology from the era before World War II, sometimes called neo-orthodoxy, but perhaps better called radical discipleship. It was rooted in the transforming power of worship, nurture, and community, which in turn led to a radical commitment, witness, and advocacy. Because of these influences, the East Harlem Protestant Parish experiment went far beyond the services and tutoring models of the settlement house. It called people to an intense Christian discipleship and, we believe, to a model of urban ministry that was to become the basis for the way churches approached the city across the nation in the last half of the twentieth century. And something radically different was desperately needed in the cities among the Protestant churches. Sociologists of religion such as Professor Sam Kinchloe at the University of Chicago Divinity School and urban mission executives such as Truman Douglass, related to both the Federal Council of Churches Home Mission Division and later to the Congregational Church's Home Mission Board, had for many years been documenting the movement of Protestant churches from the central city to the suburbs. Churches were following the prosperity of their members. And in following their constituencies, they were paying little attention to those groups who then moved into the old neighborhoods. By the conclusion of World War II, Protestant urban congregations of old-line denominations were quickly becoming exclusively middle and upper class, with little concern for, or appeal to, the working people who were now marginalized and left behind. The pattern was similar for Roman Catholic congregations, but with one significant difference. Often as these members moved from the old immigrant neighborhoods, a parish church, though greatly diminished, remained in the old neighborhood as a new strong parish was established in the suburbs. This left Roman Catholics with at least some infrastructure for ministry—although in many cases with little strength left or little real influence in the inner-city community. The East Harlem Protestant Parish was among the first of such attempts to bring ministry and witness back to those left in the old poor neighborhoods, and certainly the most visible nationwide.

The East Harlem Protestant Parish as Modern Urban Ministry Progenitor in America

Harlem is a crowded, creative, and confusing area both east and north of Central Park in New York City. Its population is diverse, made up of many immigrant and ethnic groups. Its apartment buildings, tenements, and high-rises range from slum shabby to good quality. The streets are vibrant with activity and at the same time often marked with tragedy. Harlem is a place of chaos and creativity. It is the whirlwind that has generated great jazz, comedy, drama, and dance. It is also this whirlwind that has often left the debris of human brokenness along the streets in summer's stifling heat or huddled in shabby unheated tenements in winter. Yet, in the words of the Rev. Dr. George "Bill" Webber, "it is a great place to live."[1] And so it has been for him and his family for the last fifty-three years. The vibrancy of Harlem not only produces great creativity, it also attracts it.

Such was the case when Don Benedict and Bill Webber, World War II veterans and just finishing Union Theological Seminary in New York City, were attracted to East Harlem in 1947–1948. They were struck with the contradictions between their theological understandings of "go ye into all the world" and the fact that East Harlem,[2] right on the seminary's own back doorstep and one of the most densely populated places in all of the United States, had been largely abandoned by the Protestant (mainline) churches.

Here was a mission field that was not halfway around the world. The inspiration for the missionary endeavor in East Harlem came from Benedict, in his first year as a Divinity student at the Union Theological Seminary in New York. Benedict began looking for ways he could respond to the Lord's command to "go into all the world and preach the Gospel." The problem of East Harlem and particularly the lack of presence of the Protestant church there was greatly weighing on his mind and heart.

He had seen this teeming neighborhood and thought it to be just as much missionary territory as were the foreign lands to which many of his fellow students were going. In the United States, generally, and in other parts of New York City, religion seemed to be alive and well, but East Harlem was neglected and isolated. In 1947, this incongruity increasingly bothered him. He was concerned that the Protestant churches had abandoned East Harlem along with the successful people who had managed to leave the ghetto.

As with all missionaries who are conscious of the broader picture and connectedness of all people, Don Benedict's personal experiences had led him to this kind of thinking and perception and to his conviction that he was being called by God into the mission field of East Harlem. He was a military veteran whose service experiences had also broadened his vision. Indeed, one chronicler states that Benedict approached the ministry in East Harlem with military precision.

In the lives of each of the founders of the East Harlem Protestant Parish, Don Benedict, Bill Webber, and Archie Hargraves, an African-American minister (the only one ordained of the initial three who began the ministry to East Harlem), there had been a spiritual search that led to an understanding of God's call for their lives and vocations. It was probably most dramatic for Norm Eddy, soon to join the team. He reported that he had experienced, on the actual road to Damascus, in Syria, "a sudden spiritual sense of the oneness of all of God's creation and of his unity with all of creation," while he was serving with the medical corps in Syria during the war. He knew then that he wanted to dedicate his life to helping other broken people experience that sense of oneness of creation and unity with the Creator. Where was the need more evident than in East Harlem?

All four of the founders had served on active duty in the armed services during World War II, which broadened worldviews and understandings of relationship with all people and all of God's creation. Key to understanding mission in the East Harlem Protestant Parish founders was the passage from the prophet Isaiah: "The Spirit of the Lord is upon me, because he has anointed me to preach the Gospel to the poor. He has sent me to heal the brokenhearted, to preach deliverance to the captives, and recovering of sight to the blind, to set at liberty those that are oppressed, to proclaim a year acceptable to the Lord" (Isaiah 61:1–2). Bill Webber, writing about the experiences of East Harlem in his book *God's Colony in Man's World,* states that he does so "only in the hope that they point to our common task and may assist in understanding the nature of mission wherever God has placed his witness."[3]

Author, teacher, and for many years pastor in East Harlem, Letty Russell, in writing on Christian education in her book *Christian Education in Mission,* has said that there can be no education without a witnessing community. "Christian education is participation in Christ's invitation to all people to join in God's mission of restoring men to their true humanity."[4] The goal the Parish set its mind to was "helping to restore the people of East Harlem to their true humanity."

Over time, the founders and staff of the East Harlem Protestant Parish became a crowd of witnesses in their being and doing in this soil that needed much tending. They set about trying to bring the Gospel to the people, but they also attended to those debilitating circumstances that were preventing people from having dignity so that they could respond to the message of Christ. How did this story come about?

The Survey

A 1947 survey of East Harlem[5] that Benedict and Webber completed in order to make their case for mission support in East Harlem found that the needs of the area were huge and the dynamics of the area hard to fathom. It was an area with the highest rates of social dysfunction of any place in the city, i.e., the highest rates of venereal disease, tuberculosis, infant mortality, rat bites, drug use, unmarried mothers, divorces, loan sharking, and malnutrition. Many times an apartment would house several families. In one case they found twenty-seven people, including seventeen children and an eight-day old baby, in a two-bedroom apartment. In another case, a coal bin in the basement of a tenement was home to several families.[6]

Their survey found that the church in East Harlem had three most prevalent forms—storefront Pentecostal, traditional Protestant, and Roman Catholic. The survey noted a large number of storefront Pentecostal churches, many of which were founded by families in the area and were carried on from one generation to the next. Their way was to "spiritualize" life, so people's attention was directed to the future blessings of Heaven, hence not addressing the everyday cares and concerns of the people. Because of this, their influence was minimal in this area of high crime, high violence, high rent, and all the other social ills that daily plagued the people of East Harlem.

While both Roman Catholic and Pentecostal churches had some faithful adherents, neither reached a significant proportion of the population. And most all the old-line Protestant churches had left the area. Only a few were left behind, none with much institutional strength. It seemed that the churches were largely irrelevant to the people who lived there. The survey estimated that only about 1.5 percent of the population had any meaningful relationship with any congregation in the area.[7] For the rest, the church did not exist.

The Experiment

It was in this context that Benedict, Webber, and Hargraves began their experiment in urban ministry. Together over the next decades they "rolled up their sleeves and got their hands dirty." First, they cultivated the leaders of the denominations' home mission boards. In January 1948, Benedict and Webber traveled to Buck Hill Falls, Pennsylvania, to meet with the Division of Home Missions of the Federal Council of Churches. They had ten minutes on the agenda to put their research and plans for an experimental parish in East Harlem before the board. The proposal was for a three-person team to work in East Harlem for three years, working as a team on the whole program, but with each having responsibility to establish a new congregation. The three new churches would each lease a storefront for one hundred dollars per month. The ministers would live near their churches and would begin their work with systematic calling, giving recreational leadership, and working with the various social service agencies. As soon as interest was aroused, they would start a Sunday School in each of the buildings and then eventually a worshiping congregation. The ten minutes turned into an hour, and in the end, the Baptist, Presbyterian, Methodist, and Congregationalists agreed to support the project with a $10,200 grant for the first eighteen months.[8] In time the Reformed Church in America and the Mennonites, as well as others, also participated.

As the work developed, Norman Eddy soon joined what was becoming known as the Group Ministry, followed by other early members such as Letty Russell, George Calvert, George Todd, John Crist, and Hugh

Hostetler. Realizing that if their ministry was to be effective among the people of East Harlem, they, as a team, must manifest wholeness. They began by developing a covenant for the team, i.e., the Group Ministry, to live by. The Group Ministry's covenant was built around four disciplines. First was the discipline of daily prayer and common Bible reading. Second was an economic discipline of not being paid according to their qualifications but according to their need. The third covenant was vocational. "This involved a commitment to their common calling to proclaim the Gospel in the city slums; it included the monthly submission of their work and their plans and their problems to the rest of the Group for criticism; and it called for an undertaking to make no change in their vocation without consulting the Group."[9] "And finally there was a political discipline. The members of the Group were to hammer out a position on all political and legislative issues affecting East Harlem and then work for that position, or else, if conscience would not allow, to hold their peace."[10]

The Group Ministry was one of the geniuses of the experiment. It provided these "outsiders" with a faith and life support group as well as a reference point. History had shown that a pastor, by himself or herself in a difficult inner-city pastorate, would often soon leave because of loneliness and discouragement. The Group Ministry helped all who had covenanted to be sustained and supported both spiritually and emotionally. The Group Ministry's turnover was very low for an inner-city ministry.

With these commitments to each other, the sense of mutual support they shared, and the grant in hand, the initial three went to work on the second phase of their dream, beginning on a hot day in August 1948. A storefront was soon opened on East 102nd Street, followed by others on 100th and then on 104th Streets.

Because of the dramatic and good experience gained from the experiment, the team was certain that they had found a way to be in ministry in the inner cities of the United States. So, three years after the founding of the Parish, Hargraves and Benedict, with the permission of the Group, "went on the road" to sell the good news of their experience to other cities. After presentations in Boston, Cleveland, Chicago, and several other cities, they decided the conditions were right in Chicago (Hargraves) and Cleveland (Benedict) to start similar urban ministries. Students who had interned in East Harlem and participants in these two new ministries in turn spawned hundreds of other urban ministries over the next forty-five years.

These disciples of the East Harlem Protestant Parish reached, at one time or another, almost every large urban center in the United States. By the

1960s this Urban Ministry Movement also produced urban training networks in most of the large cities of America, like that established by Robert Bonthius alongside Benedict's work in Cleveland. The Urban Training Institute in Chicago taught hundreds of middle-class "would be" ministers the reality of urban life, with its famous "plunge" that sent these trainees into the urban ghetto for about a week with no money. This Institute eventually evolved into a seminary consortium for training pastors for urban ministry known as SCUPE.[11] This same impetus led Rev. Joseph (Joe) Matthews to create what was to become the Ecumenical Institute in Chicago. And there was the Fifth City project in the slums of Chicago, rooted largely in the "peace churches." These, in turn, found much in common with Alinsky's Chicago-based Industrial Areas Foundation for community organizing. We can add to these the experiments in Detroit and other places with a ministry or chaplaincy to industry, pioneered in part by Byron "Bud" White, a minister in the Reformed Church of America.

THE EVOLUTION OF THE EAST HARLEM PROTESTANT PARISH AND THE EMERGENCE OF EAST HARLEM INTERFAITH

Our story continues with the East Harlem Protestant Parish and its partner and in some ways its successor, East Harlem Interfaith. Most of the early staff stayed in East Harlem to continue the evolutionary process of being "God's colony" and witnesses to the power of justice, wholeness, service, and community in transforming East Harlem.

The Parish was an ecumenical experiment in urban neighborhood transformation. While the term "ecumenism" was not yet part of the founders' vocabulary or of their formal intent, they did want to get people and church groups involved with each other and, most of all, working for the material, as well as the spiritual, good of the people of East Harlem. And they quickly realized the indivisible nature of the ministry of "presence." The Group Ministry was ecumenical and so was the presence.

Norm Eddy said in a taped interview that from the beginning of the efforts of the East Harlem Protestant Parish "we had a Protestant ecumenical approach." This was because of their intent to reestablish the presence of the missing Protestant witness. Norm goes on to say that in the beginning "there were tentative ties because in those days back in the 40s and early 50s there was really very deep division between many, many branches of Christianity." He says further that it was compassion more than anything else that led various pastors to share their facilities when needs arose.

Yet, from its beginnings and because of the way it evolved in its first two decades, it is evident that the East Harlem Protestant Parish, and later the East Harlem Interfaith, was vitally involved in church-dividing and church-uniting issues at the local level. First they developed the Group Ministry's Covenant, firmly based on theological assumptions. Then early on, the Group agreed to not let their denominational differences interfere with the central vocation they shared, i.e., to bring the message of Christ and Christ's transformation to East Harlem. Under the tutelage of visiting theologians like Hans Hoekendijk and many others, they were able to confront the strengths and weaknesses of this approach and make creative modifications so as not to perpetuate the historical denominational divisions or the historical ecumenical divisions between the streams of Faith and Order and Life and Work. Rather, in response to the Gospel imperative that requires both works of justice and reflection on human beings' relationship to God and to each other, they were largely able to transcend these traditional divisions.

The Parish began to face the exclusiveness of many of their practices. Eventually, out of experiences of accepting the "other," the Parish became a part of the ecumenical theological experience of inclusiveness. This experiment, as much as any other in post–World War II America, developed the reflection-action-reflection model of "doing theology." The East Harlem experiment was a circle, if not an upward spiral—of research, then action for justice and transformation, and then again contemplation and research. It also pushed the ecumenical challenge of inclusiveness, beginning with the professional staff. The African-American presence was evident from the beginning in the person of Archie Hargraves, the ordained member of the founding team. And, inclusiveness became a hallmark of the work in East Harlem.

Inclusiveness made the Parish and later East Harlem Interfaith centers of vibrant urban ecumenism. Vibrant because they were able to involve groups whose lively presence and engagement had been historically largely bypassed by the churches. They were able to build their life around the so-called minorities or normally marginalized people—African Americans, Hispanics, and women members of Roman Catholic congregations. These groups have often been taken for granted or they have been ignored in the more well-known histories of ecumenical involvement.

Among the churches present in East Harlem are three Roman Catholic churches that had served numerous waves of immigrants to what was not yet called "El Barrio." As some observers saw it, the Roman Catholic Church was so overwhelmed with groups from all parts of the world, who needed help in adjusting to America while still holding to their own cultural identities, that the church's response to needs was parochial in the strictest sense of the word. There was no real ecumenical involvement by the parishes of the Roman Catholic Church and there was little in the way of community ministry by these parishes. These parishes largely lived in their own cocoon.

According to Norm Eddy, Hispanic Pentecostal churches were among the first to share some of their church and storefront spaces for day care and other services. Other churches were slower to respond.

The diversity of participation in the ecumenical ministry in East Harlem did not stop there. Women were also key. Many of the Parish success stories revolve around the hard work of women. And there are many stories about women responding to the call of Vatican II for the Roman Catholic Church to become more ecumenically involved—women within a male hierarchical church. They were not directly assigned by the local Bishop but by their religious congregations. They were mostly white, with a few African-American sisters, living and working in the ghetto. These women were there because their congregation's charisms, or special gifts, were to be manifested in mission and ministry to the poorest of God's family.

East Harlem Protestant Parish was inclusive rather than intentionally ecumenical. It was more an experiment that transcended denominations and included all sorts of people. It was a ministry of compassion. True, the Board that oversaw the Parish was composed of members from Home Mission agencies of the funding denominations. This, however, was not so much ecumenical as it was denominational cooperation to experiment with a problem that was bigger than any one congregation or denomination could tackle alone. The Group Ministry that initially ran the day-to-day operations of the Parish intentionally did not allow discussions about denominational differences, thus implying that their ministry of compassion transcended these denominational differences. Other than that one of the congregations in the parish was an old Presbyterian church pastored by George Todd, who was part of the Group Ministry, and that the Presbytery was one of the sponsors of the Parish, the evidence indicates that the Group Ministry made little in the way of direct effort to involve itself with the other churches in the community. At the same time, the first three congregations started were not directly denominationally affiliated. So, in the Parish's first decade or so of existence, it really did reflect "God's Colony," not a denominational colonization.

Another way of seeing this progress in the Parish was in the language of the "Body of Christ." In the Local Ecumenism Working Paper prepared as a contribution to development for the design of this historical study of local ecumenism, Arleon Kelley wrote, "It is no accident that ecumenism has come to understand anew and describe itself as "the Body of Christ," connected, relational, organic, universal and global."[12] Even though the Parish was founded to meet spiritual and physical needs in a broken community, it was something of this understanding of the Body of Christ, and of the relationship to all the members of the Body of Christ in the area, that led to the founding of the East Harlem Protestant Parish.

The vision of the founders was not accidental. They were being guided to East Harlem exactly because of this understanding of the interconnectedness of all things. And while their intent remained to bring the Gospel of Christ to a neglected part of the city, they soon discovered that they had to address all aspects of the lives of these neglected members of the Body of Christ if not only the church but also Christ was to have deep meaning in the lives of the people. A few churches that were present in East Harlem but who were not a part of the East Harlem Protestant Parish offered help to some. But for too long the churches, as a whole, had not given enough attention to the problems of everyday existence that caused people to feel that God—and the church—had indeed abandoned them.

The Parish founders believed in their relationship to the Body of Christ and in giving witness to their belief in this understanding. Witness was very strong. They shared their growing understanding of the unity Christ gives. The outreach that was done, getting to know the people of El Barrio and responding to the problems and queries the people themselves presented, cut to the very heart of the spirituality (although perhaps dormant in many) of African Americans and Hispanics. Their very foundational belief is that God has a part to play in their daily existence even if at times there is resistance to God's activity in their lives.

Through these understandings and relationships that developed within and among the Parish churches, a nucleus with a strong sense of community grew in East Harlem that made the need to reach out to the other congregations in the area an essential next step, so that other congregations might also share in the connectedness of the Body of Christ. This was a task of witness to the disparate parts of the Body. It was a matter of communication. It was a matter of manifesting the church's unity.

In his book, *God's Colony in Man's World,* Bill Webber writes:

> I suspect that the chief impediment to the effective communication of the Gospel today is the simple fact that the pattern of life in the typical Christian congregation does not clearly or visibly embody the nature of

> the Gospel it proclaims. It is this Gospel which points to the ultimate unity of all men in Jesus Christ. Far too many people are gathered into particular congregations because of cultural homogeneity rather than as a result of a radical confrontation with the Gospel. We are united by nature and not by grace. . . . Only when the church comes together at the point of its common unity in Jesus Christ, then the natural human differences can be overcome. (pp. 71–72)[13]

Communication and manifesting unity were tasks not yet fulfilled if the churches of East Harlem were to be the Church. "God's colony" could no longer ignore the others of faith who were in the community and was eventually drawn into relationships with these and their churches. This sense of urgency emerged in the mid-1960s as the Parish was building its church buildings and the early team was branching into other areas of ministry. For example, Norm Eddy was involved full-time in the ministry with people with drug addiction—a ministry begun by the Parish. And at about the same time, Bill Webber was to become the president of New York Biblical Seminary, later known as New York Theological Seminary—a seminary that under his leadership was devoted especially to preparing indigenous city residents/students for Urban Ministry. And East Harlem was still the laboratory for much of this educational endeavor.

East Harlem Interfaith, Inc., founded in 1969, was initially called the East Harlem Cooperating Christian Churches. This earlier organization was trying to bring together not only the people but also the Protestant churches that by then had returned to East Harlem. According to Norm Eddy, it was "an experiential introduction to interfaith, ecumenical, interracial, intercultural life" that was a delight to him as the embodiment of his experience of being united with all people and all creation so many years before. Again, as Norm Eddy says, "it was an attempt at ecumenism although they did not use that word." They were, however, very conscious of attempting some kind of unity in East Harlem.

It is not surprising that Norm Eddy became the first coordinator of East Harlem Interfaith (EHI). In its beginnings, Eddy, through the fledgling EHI, took the initiative to reach out to the other churches in East Harlem in order to see his dream of unity and connectedness fulfilled. It is clear his own personal spiritual experience and his awareness of diversity and pluralism had led him toward this sort of ministry. In a taped interview he stated: "When I got into ministry I was always very sensitive to the working of the Spirit in other people. . . . I've always yearned to see unity among Christians." Like the leaders of Parish had done before him, he began reaching out by doing a survey of the churches in East Harlem. In that early survey he found that the churches in East Harlem dramatized both the pluralism of denomination and of ethnicity. Just as housing ministries, drug ministries, police relationships, regular garbage collection, sanitation, health clinics, and public advocacy were to become systemic justice outcomes of the Parish, the formation of EHI was also a next logical development as a means of weaving together the expressions of the Church in the area as the Body of Christ. It worked to a large degree. The East Harlem Interfaith Annual Report, 1980–81 (p. 49), indicates that the following congregations were associated with EHI:

Black Baptist churches	20
Independent black churches	27
Black Pentecostal churches	18
Black Protestant denominational churches	14
Spanish-speaking American Baptist churches	2
Independent Spanish-speaking churches	4
Spanish-speaking Pentecostal churches	43
Spanish-speaking Protestant denominational churches	9
Numbers of Orders of Religious Sisters	11
Total	148

Yet, this shows that there were few Roman Catholic parishes involved with the Church in East Harlem. It was the Religious Sisters that represented the Roman Catholic Church. They came in droves from many parts of the United States—these women who had made public vows of chastity, poverty, and obedience in the Roman Catholic Church. Each came because the charism (the special gift) of their communities, also found within each individual sister, brought them or sent them or compelled them to come to East Harlem to work with the poor. Some were already in Harlem in other settings, often in schools. Among these were the Sisters of Notre Dame, Sisters of Charity, Sisters of Mercy, Sisters of St. Agnes, and Sisters of St. Ursula, to name a few. The Franciscan Sisters of the Atonement had been in social and parish ministry from their founding and had always worked with the poor, taking census and making home visits for many other parish services. The Little Sisters of the Assumption had deliberately chosen to move their congregation's Home Health Agency from the other boroughs to Manhattan's East Harlem because they saw that this area had the greatest need and that to be effective they needed to work and live among the poor. Each sister was unique, with unique gifts and talents and representing differing aspects of the presence of Christ on the streets and in the tenements of El Barrio.

How much outreach was done by Roman Catholic parishes is difficult to determine. One person told me that he never saw a Roman Catholic priest walking around the streets of East Harlem. On the other hand, many of the Religious Sisters were deeply involved in the fabric of the community. Religious Sisters of the Roman Catholic Church did visit the people of the tenements. These sisters made many a follow-up visit to both Catholics and non-Catholics. They were teachers, they were social workers, they worked to meet recreation needs, they provided health care, they advocated for many causes of justice, and many even involved themselves in political concerns. They were the face of Roman Catholic ecumenism in East Harlem. And they were actively involved in the formation of East Harlem Interfaith.[14]

With the formation of East Harlem Interfaith, the East Harlem Protestant Parish and the Roman Catholic Sisters had found a way to involve the rest of the Body of Christ in the justice and spiritual ministries it had pioneered, because issues related to housing, sanitation, banks, garbage, health, safety, and the police became the agenda of the EHI. It could be argued that the Parish had passed responsibility for the community's well-being to the broader Church, except it did not mean that the Parish, in the forms it took after the late 1960s, was not involved.

The Parish had not created an agenda and then foisted it off on the other churches of East Harlem. If the East Harlem Protestant Parish was "God's colony," it is one role of such a "creative minority" experiment to find what works. The Parish had shown many outreach ministries to be viable in responding to real community needs. And when there was a successful model, the broader Church community and often the political instrumentalities can share in the responsibilities. That had been the role of ecumenical groups throughout the nineteenth century. That was the role of the Parish in Harlem in the last half of the twentieth century. The Parish had been successful with such things as drugs, sanitation, housing, and health issues. It was time to broaden the base. And EHI provided a broader base.

East Harlem Interfaith has existed for thirty-two years and the East Harlem experiment for fifty-six years as of 2003. These have been beacons for justice and unity. They have won some significant battles for the community. East Harlem Interfaith implemented many of the ministries begun by the East Harlem Protestant Parish, but on a broadly ecumenical basis that included all Christians. They have had success in keeping a commercial bank in the area. They have provided programs for single mothers and their babies. They have been advocates for branch hospital clinics in the area. They have held services of commemoration and celebration for all the people of God in the area. And the list goes on. EHI has made a difference in the community, in the lives of people in the community, and in the relationships among the churches. It also has been through some difficult times and has had numerous staff turnovers. At last report it was being kept alive mostly by volunteers, and many fear that waning support will mean its demise.

Financial support has long been an issue. East Harlem is poor. The member churches of EHI are barely self-sufficient. Outside church mission support has all but dried up. Foundation grants are increasingly difficult to get. So EHI has found itself with inadequate monetary and leadership support. The experiment is now two generations old. Leaders of the churches die or move. The population dies or moves. The remaining "creative minority" changes, with maybe half or more leaving as lives become more grounded and organized. New immigrants come who have never heard of the East Harlem dream, let alone share it. The needs of the community and the churches have not changed significantly, but the ability to support "God's colony" in this hard land has. The story will continue—but in what way?

Conclusion

As we have seen, East Harlem Protestant Parish and East Harlem Interfaith have become somewhat known; but in other ways much of what both have accomplished has been overlooked or at least has escaped wide public notice. This may be so in ecumenical circles because of this very involvement on the ground, in the streets, in the very lives of people, rather than involvement at the tables of theological discussion on Christian unity or life and work.

The East Harlem Protestant Parish was founded to go into the unknown territory of East Harlem to spread the Gospel of Jesus Christ, where there was no visible Protestant Church witness, and to restore the dignity of oppressed human beings. East Harlem Interfaith, with its various committees, carried on this vision until its near demise in the 1990s. The East Harlem Protestant Parish and East Harlem Interfaith were certainly voices in the wilderness in those early days of neglect of the residents of East Harlem. People became ecumenically involved because of a deeply personal experience of having seen a wider picture and a broader view of life and of their place in that picture. A missionary spirit soon grew following the initial conviction and commitment.

Characteristics of the ministry in East Harlem are identification, presence, and witness. Creative interaction with people will, in time, develop all three of these characteristics and become an invitation to others. That is how the first Church developed, as told in the Book of Acts. Those who join become a creative welcoming community that attracts others. Together these join in ministry to individuals, to groups, and to the community. As a community they are able to call the even larger community to responsibility. In the end there is transformation. And that transformation reaches out and becomes a model for others—across the United States and, in the case of the East Harlem Protestant Parish, to Europe, India, and beyond. But in the crowded city, it is transformation on a treadmill. It is transformation for the moment. Soon the actors change and the process must begin all over again. Was the Parish a success? Yes, for its time it was. It seeded a variety of permanent institutions that will remain well into the future—ranging from local congregations to health facilities, drug facilities, and family care facilities.

The experiment went on to influence the way churches engaged in ministry in cities across the United States and around the world. The East Harlem Protestant Parish is the womb from which much that became known as the Urban Church Movement was born. Hargraves was a major player in all that happened in Chicago. Webber educated a generation or more of indigenous urban clergy with hands-on experience in New York City in general and Harlem in particular. Benedict shaped urban ministry in Cleveland and in the newly constituted United Church of Christ. Todd took the model to India, held the national urban ministry desk in the Presbyterian Church, and became the director of urban mission for the World Council of Churches in Geneva, Switzerland. Letty Russell educated two generations of seminary students in inclusiveness and urban ministry at Yale. And Norm Eddy devised a successful means and the public policy to support it to help people addicted to drugs. These are witnesses unto the ends of the earth—witnesses that stretch far beyond the original vision of Benedict and Webber.

And at the same time, the witness continued in East Harlem. People there are still experiencing what it means to be a part of the Body of Christ. These witnesses far transcended the confines of ethnicity, color, race, gender, economic status, sect, or denomination. It is ecumenical witness in its truest form.

Notes

1. From phone interviews with George "Bill" Webber and Norman Eddy in January 2003. Rev. Webber was one of four Union Theological seminarians who pioneered the East Harlem Protestant Parish in 1947–1948. Others included Donald Benedict, Norman Eddy, and Archie Hargraves, soon joined by Letty Russell and hundreds of other seminary students, interns, and volunteers over the next two decades.

2. East Harlem stretches from 96th Street to 125th Street in Manhattan and is bounded by the East River on the east and Central Park on the west. The population of the area is about a quarter of a million people. In one case, Benedict and Webber found more than four thousand people crowded into twenty-seven tenement buildings in one block.

3. George W. Webber, *God's Colony in Man's World* (New York: Abingdon, 1960), p. 71.

4. Letty Russell, *Christian Education in Mission* (Philadelphia: Westminster Press, 1967), p. 35.

5. This survey was supported by the New York City Missionary Society, related to the Congregational Church. Kenneth Miller was then the president. See Bruce Kenrick, *Come Out the Wilderness: The Story of the East Harlem Protestant Parish* (New York: Harper and Brothers, 1962), p. 30.

6. Ibid., p. 3–4.

7. Ibid., p. 20.

8. Ibid., p. 30.

9. Ibid., p. 33.

10. Ibid.

11. The involvement of the seminaries has been important to the Urban Church Movement. This involvement ensured that seminary graduates had at least one course in the urban church and often a cross-cultural experience in the inner city. It put the urban church back on the church's radar screen. More importantly, it meant that there was formal theological reflection occurring to undergird the movement.

12. "Toward a Design" was a part of the proposal for this history project. It is deposited in the archives of the Local Ecumenical History Project in the library at Christian Theological Seminary, Indianapolis, Indiana, 46208.

13. Ibid., pp. 71–72.

14. Interfaith, as it is used in East Harlem, refers to Protestant, Pentecostal, and Roman Catholic participation. It does not include other historic living faiths such as the Muslim or Hindu faiths. The EHI has some relationship with the Black Muslims.

References

Cole, Mary. *Summer in the City.* New York: P. J. Kennedy and Sons, 1968.

East Harlem Interfaith Annual Reports.

Kenrick, Bruce. *Come Out the Wilderness: The Story of East Harlem Protestant Parish.* New York: Harper and Brothers, 1962.

Livezey, Lowell W. "Church as Parish: The East Harlem Protestant Parish." *Christian Century* (December 9, 1998): 1176–1177.

Russell, Letty M. *Christian Education in Mission.* Philadelphia: Westminster Press, 1967.

Russell, Letty M., Clyde Allison, and Daniel C. Little. *The City: God's Gift to the Church.* Division of Evangelism, United Presbyterian Church in the U.S.A., 1960.

Webber, George W. *God's Colony in Man's World.* New York: Abingdon, 1960.

4

PRAYER, POWER, AND PROPHETIC ACTION: CHURCH WOMEN UNITED

Roberta Grimm and Kathleen S. Hurty

Church Women United and its predecessors have been an effective and powerful ecumenical force in local communities, at the state level, and in national and international spheres. The work of these groups has enhanced the broader local ecumenical scene and contributed generously to the social culture of the last half of the twentieth century. This is a story of local ecumenism at its best, i.e., a movement that began in local communities and then spread itself statewide and then nationwide. Finally, it has developed alliances worldwide. The stories told here are illustrative of a venerable, if at times vulnerable, ecumenical movement among women.

Women in communities across the United States had been meeting across denominational lines long before the United Council of Church Women (UCCW), the immediate national predecessor of the CWU, was officially formed during the week of Pearl Harbor at Atlantic City in December 1941. This United Council of Church Women became Church Women United in 1966.[1]

Consider the women of Rochester, New York. While not the first to organize, these women came together in 1922 shortly after women's suffrage came into effect following the ratification of the nineteenth amendment by Tennessee (1920). At this time the world's first radio broadcasting station went on the air, the new Ku Klux Klan was gaining political power, and Hitler was reorganizing the Nazi Party. Eighteen Rochester women from seventeen churches and eight denominations met at the request of the Rochester Federation of Churches to form a Women's Council. Among early efforts were sponsoring a daylong public World Day of Prayer meeting, securing volunteers to help foreign-born mothers, opposing the first bathing beauty contests at Atlantic City, and supporting the eight-hour-day labor law.

Early stories focus on conversations local leaders had in the midst of this national call to fight the bigotry and cruelty represented by Nazis and fascists. National organizing began and CWU was born in this chaotic milieu. As Margaret Schiffert describes,[2]

> The foundations of Church Women United were laid in the shadows of world crisis. It was less than a week after Pearl Harbor Sunday when the constituting convention of the United Council of Church Women met in Atlantic City. Many of the participants were still numb from the shocking turn of events as they tackled their goal to integrate the work—of three interdenominational women's groups representing women from seventy Protestant denominations—as a coordinated approach. While some questioned the wisdom of starting anything in the aftermath of the country's plunge into world conflict, most felt themselves driven by a new urgency. The circumstances surrounding this beginning still influence CWU priorities. The mandate accepted in Atlantic City inspired the "People's Platform for a Global Society" thirty years later and remains key to programs in the 1980s [*and to this day*].

The significant Atlantic City event had a long and local history. Margaret Shannon describes this inherited local legacy:[3]

> What the women of 1941 had going for them was the foundation work of others during the previous 40 years. . . . In 1941 there already existed hundreds of united organizations in local communities. They had come into being on their own momentum and had a variety of forms and names such as missionary unions, federations of church women, local councils of church women. Some of them were at least 50 years old at the time the new national organization was being proposed. There is some evidence that some of them went as far back as 1868. The Women's Missionary Union of Springfield, Missouri, for example, dates from a day in 1887 when its constitution was adopted at an all day meeting where 300 women from 11 churches were in attendance. A survey of the Federal Council of Churches around 1926 reported a total of 1900 of these local united groups.

Thus, ecumenical work in local communities and states had an early beginning, not only through women's work but also through the councils and federations of churches.[4] It was the women in local communities who prodded, pushed, and supported much of that ecumenical effort and kept it going when spirits sagged.

This healthy grassroots constituency was a boon for the proposed United Council of Church Women (UCCW), predecessor of CWU. By 1940, thousands of local groups were using material produced by the National Committee of the World Day of Prayer. These groups were a place where women developed a sense of freedom in decision making about their own plans and actions. "It was an intangible sort of freedom," said one CWU leader at the time, "but real enough to women who had not previously experienced it within their own churches."[5] To this day in CWU there is a paradoxical sense of place that contains both commitment to a larger common mission and local autonomy that values creative freedom to pray and act in powerful ways that honor local diversity. Perhaps this factor, more than any other, provides the conceptual basis for an understanding of CWU as "movement."

Spurred by this desire to work together, and by the effectiveness of grounded local ecumenical efforts, women leaders of the churches came together nationally in 1941 and formed the United Council of Church Women. Having experienced the power of women working together ecumenically in local places and challenged by global crisis, the women in Atlantic City organized quickly and purposefully. It was a recognized collaboration between the local and the national that was to be characteristic of the movement long into the future. The strengths of its beginnings are notable. As one researcher notes: "It is arguable that UCCW may be the first and largest autonomous middle class interracial, intercultural and interdenominational lay evangelical venture in gender distinct ecumenism."[6]

Given the crisis of World War II, the concern raised by women in this newly organized national ecumenical setting was to find a collective way to challenge the idea that war was the only solution to major global conflicts or that people had to kill each other in order to accomplish a common good.

Providing a common voice for peace became one major focus of the UCCW in the early years, and this caught the attention of Eleanor Roosevelt as she brought her voice and influence into the formation of the United Nations as a vehicle for global peacemaking.[7] The leaders in the early years of the UCCW, already gifted by a local-global sisterhood through World Day of Prayer linkages, were persuaded by Eleanor Roosevelt's example and arguments, along with burgeoning interest among many women around the country, to dedicate efforts to peacemaking by urging support of the United Nations. Tied closely to the formative work for the United Nations was a commitment to human rights.

A young university student writing at the outbreak of the war, Esther Hymer, reflected on this effort. (Hymer later became the director of the UCCW Christian World Relations and United Nations Office.) "You spent your evenings rolling bandages and you were concerned each day with the news of war," she said. "Becoming emotionally involved, you felt the destruction of everything you had worked on." Invited to a conference in Chicago on the cause and cure of war, she met "women who were just towers of strength." The women focused on studying the causes of war in order to know how to "cure war."[8] She went on to say: "And there were these studies . . . that moved you over to economic problems, to the lack of trade, to hunger, to the lack of human rights . . . all these things that led to the fact that peace was more than the absence of war. That peace was learning to understand each other, that it was the respect of other people. . . . I realized that the United Church Women was satisfying to me because it brought together this drive to utilize fully the tension of public life, that public life could be directed toward building a just society."

The way these United Church Women worked, studied, and prayed raised their awareness. They learned to "think globally by study and prayer and then to act locally." These local initiatives were a central contribution, then, to the coalescing of the movement now called Church Women United—and its early passions were prayer and peacemaking. The movement's base and strength is local—its outlook and impact are global. Compassionate face-to-face work in local places somehow stimulated the capacity these women had to keep the faces of their global sisters in front of them. Local energies were generously and creatively spent, but there seemed always to be time for links with those who lived in other places—"mission fields"—in war-ravaged nations and other places of poverty and suffering around the globe. It is out of this local ferment that a national Christian women's ecumenical movement took root. A decade of organizing and expanding followed.

The organization's stated purpose was "to unify the women of the churches for Christian, civic, and social endeavor, by the exchange of experiences and inspiration, in harmony with the general movement of the Church Federation; and to promote the functioning of organized women's work with social agencies." The central mission and common goals of the movement illustrate the best of collective effort. Church Women United became a racially, culturally, and theologically inclusive movement of Christian women, celebrating unity in diversity for a world of peace and justice. The movement has four stated goals: [9]

- We intend to grow in our faith and to extend our vision of what it means to be Christian women in society today.
- We intend to strengthen visible ecumenical community.
- We intend to work for a just, peaceful, and caring society.
- And we intend to use, responsibly and creatively, the resources God has entrusted to us—our intelligence, our time, our energy, our money—as we carry out the mission of Christ through Church Women United.

At the Halfway Mark of the Century

Ecumenical life took on a new global framework in the organization of the World Council of Churches in 1948. In 1950 the National Council of Churches of Christ in the USA (NCCC/USA) was formed, drawing together a number of precedent bodies. It was a period of expanding institutionalization of ecumenical work. In addition, institutions were becoming increasingly bureaucratized. The churches were no exception to this trend so evident in the wider social arena.

However, in good faith and in the growing spirit of unity among the churches, the United Council of Church Women chose to bring women's voices into the new ecumenical body in 1950 and thus became an initiating partner in the formation of the NCCC/USA. The challenges of the 1950s engaged the Council and the women who worked within it. North Korea invaded South Korea, and Senator Joseph McCarthy conducted hearings before the House Un-American Activities Committee. Rosa Parks and African American women organized a bus boycott in Montgomery. Long-established relationships with the women of Korea through World Day of Prayer were continued; support for the United Nations was not dampened; and church women, who had been working together across color lines, gave impetus to the burgeoning civil rights movement.

Work on human rights continued from early beginnings, with a decidedly local focus, and with a commitment to see the United Nations as an essential vehicle for peacemaking. Local stories told of the involvement of church women in lifting up information about the United Nations. In a memo dated February 20, 1952, Dorothy Lewis, Coordinator, U.S. Station Relations, UN Radio, gave a progress report on the UN Communications Campaign, noting the commitment of the United Church Women of Kansas to reach their statewide membership. She went on to say that "all Kansas City churches and church organizations will combine to reach their membership. As a result of the campaign many stations are reinstating UN programs or asking for new ones." The local stations have expressed surprise, she said, by the increased interest in the United Nations. In this same memo, Topeka, St. Louis, Chicago, Madison, Milwaukee, and Des Moines were mentioned positively as well; and while no mention was made specifically of the work of church women, it is likely that this campaign was seen as a rallying point for local CWU activism throughout this area.[10]

By 1958, Esther Hymer, noting wide interest in the United Nations among local UCCW constituencies, designed a series of UN seminars to further knowledge and understanding of the issues. State councils sent busloads of participants, and for several years approximately 1,500 women came each year to explore the work of UNICEF, the Commission on the Status of Women, and other agencies in the United Nations, giving particular attention to the needs of women and children. These activities were based at the Church Center for the United Nations (CCUN), where CWU was one of the earliest tenants. Local volunteers were essential to the work of the seminars and developed a close-knit and tenacious coterie of women who worked hard to keep interest in the United Nations alive in later years.

Yet, less than two decades after becoming part of the NCCC/USA, the relationship with the National Council of Churches began to fray.[11] Increasingly, the church women's plans and activities were confined and limited by the decision-making processes in the council, the women retained little control of the money they were raising, and the local ecumenical church women's groups involved an increasing number of denominations not present within the National Council. As was typical of most bureaucratic institutions of this time, patriarchy was painfully evident. Men (predominantly white men) controlled the organization, making the decisions and running the programs. One of the factors leading to CWU's decision to break away from the NCC had to do with the fact that the NCCC/USA did not have as broad a membership as the local units of CWU represented. CWU wanted to focus on increasing the participation of Roman Catholic and Orthodox women as well as women from many other Christian denominations. For these reasons, it became clear to the women that separation from the NCCC/USA was the best way to work for economic justice for women, to shape an agenda of peacemaking, and to enlarge opportunities for women's leadership within the life of the churches. The women formally announced their decision to leave the NCCC/USA in 1970 and became an independent organization, Church Women United. The ties were severed as amicably as possible, and a relationship with the council has continued over the years.

Before leaving the council, the women decided to initiate the formation of a women's caucus within the NCC to continue to use this national forum for putting women's issues on the agenda of the churches. The caucus represented women of all colors and modeled shared leadership and cohesion, effectively raising feminist themes during the next several decades. African American women, notes Hartmann, were highly visible in the caucus and as its conveners. A particularly important event in 1974 underscores the influence of CWU on the NCCC: "Even more beneficial to church feminists was the election of Claire Randall as general secretary of the NCC in October 1974, an event the *New York Times* characterized as 'a break with 2000 years of tradition.' Although the council president changed every three years, the general secretary served five year terms; in addition, Randall was reelected in 1979. Moreover, the general secretary, not the president, was in charge of running the organization on a day-to-day basis. . . . Randall's election as the highest staff executive was thus much more than symbolic for NCC feminism."

Contributing to Randall's effectiveness in this arena was the fact that she came to the NCC from CWU, having most recently served as Associate General Director of CWU. Her work in CWU bridged feminism and theology, economic justice, and artful ecumenical worship. It is also interesting to note that following her terms of service at NCC, she was elected president of Church Women United.

As is often the case, as national decisions were being discussed and actions taken, local work continued apace. While not unaware of national maneuvering, the determination to plan and proceed locally was often tempered by more immediate commitments and needs. This did not mean that national initiatives found no place in local agendas, nor did it mean that stimulus to prayer and action from the national unit was unheeded. Local work was continuously informed and shaped by joint efforts within the whole movement. And local experience influenced national thinking and action as well. But the delicate balance of local-national-global linkages and interests depended on broad communication, as well as shared commitments, and the interaction was not always easy in a time of rapid social and ecumenical change.

Ruth Segerhammar, California CWU state president at the time of the 1972 national assembly held at the Los Angeles Convention Center and later a CWU national vice president, reflected on the exhilaration of the national assembly and candidly critiqued its shortcomings from the standpoint of the host group. She closed with a comment descriptive of the way CWU sees itself: "It reminded me again and again that we are not an organization that has arrived, but a movement of Christ's women—unafraid—moving together into the whirlwind of our time."[12]

Church Women United Is Rooted in Inclusive Celebration of Spirituality

CWU emerged from the need of women to celebrate their spirituality and change their communities across America. This spirituality was celebrated across congregational and denominational boundaries long before the twentieth century and almost always resulted in some sort of action or mission. Prayer was from the beginning a significant source for women's activism in local settings, stimulating and shaping action for justice.

In 1887, Baptist Mrs. Helen Barrett Montgomery, Episcopalian Mrs. Henry Peabody, and Presbyterian Mrs. Mary Ellen Jones decided to inaugurate a "day of prayer." From its beginnings in 1887, this day of prayer for confession of individual and national sins, "with offerings that appropriately express contrition,"[13] has become a movement of global proportions. For many years women in local communities prayed and worshiped together in words and stories crafted by women, always with a broad theme that encompassed the world. By 1911, for example, in Buffalo, New York, women were meeting interdenominationally for prayer, study programs, social times, and sometimes projects. Christian women in communities around the United States were finding ways to come together, despite the arbitrary boundaries of denominations, class, and race, to put their faith into action, almost always beginning with prayer, as had been true of the women of Buffalo and Rochester. Throughout its history, CWU's collective prayer and worship days focused attention on the needs of self and others. Fervent prayers often led to energetic collective action.

These times of prayer spread, and by 1927 they became known as the World Day of Prayer. These praying women continued to gather in local communities, involving themselves in matters of mission and ministry. Some participated in the suffrage movement, others in the temperance movement. Some designed local projects of compassion, organized local ecumenical groups, served as teachers and nurses in struggling communities, or answered the call to "foreign" missions. The seeds of a new movement had been planted in rich soil.

Church Women United now serves as the national committee for the international World Day of Prayer movement, observed currently by women in more than 177 countries around the world. Complemented in many communities by two other prayer days—called Celebrations— women also gather under the banner of May Friendship Day (inaugurated in 1938) and World Community Day (instituted in 1943 through the persistent efforts of

Mrs. Albert Palmer). These Celebrations, which are the heart of the present movement, were well under way long before 1941, when Amy Ogden Welcher became the first president of the United Council of Church Women (UCCW). This dynamic relationship of collective global effort—this relationship of faith to life—was formed around a pattern of circularity: "Worship, study, celebration, action. . . . When CWU identifies these as its context of involvement, it envisions them not as stages of a linear journey but in a circular configuration. No starting point, no ending. One grows out of another, leads to another, derives strength from another, gives strength to another, much as the local, state and national units of CWU interact. . . . The style is easy to accept if they see themselves within the larger human sphere and are committed to a circle to which there always is access."[14]

Local World Day of Prayer events are planned and conducted locally, using resources centered on services written each year by women from a different country in the belief that prayer focuses local-global connections. It is, in the words of Mary Zambrano, a CWU leader from Southern California who attended a richly multicultural local WDP service written by the women of Samoa for 2001, a visceral global connection: "The World Day of Prayer worship service was so skillfully put together—we really spent most of the time in prayer, and I felt as if I had been in Samoa by the time it was over."[15]

Church Women United has been in the spiritual vanguard for a long time. It is noteworthy that the celebrations of church women—World Day of Prayer, May Friendship Day, and World Community Day—have included discussions, prayer, and action for many of the crucial social issues of our day long before they became politically correct or were given attention in churches generally. Examples include active work on race relations from the 1950s, formation of Women in Community Service (WICS) to assist low-income women to rise from poverty and the development of global relationships through Causeways in the 1960s, concern for the environment in the 1970s, the call for forgiving the debts of developing countries in the 1980s, and concern for toxic waste dumps near the homes of the poor and people of color and multilingual leadership development for women working in local communities in the 1990s in WomenLinC (Women Leading in Community). The pluralistic aspect of our society is being recognized now, but as early as 1969 Church Women United issued a statement on pluralism that included this phrase: "We resolve to speak up each time there is a violation of the rights of any individual or where there is a belittling of any race by careless generalization."[16] The call to the Christ Way has been the critical call for this movement that has moved so many mountains.

Another way CWU celebrated its spirituality was by helping others worship. The multi-year project of Illinois CWU to build a chapel at the Dwight Correctional Center in Dwight, Illinois, a women's prison, is an example of such efforts and was impressive in vision and scope. The chapel was to provide a place for spiritual nurture for the women inmates. In addition to worship, the building would also provide a place for counseling and for the teaching of parenting skills and a children's visitation and care center, encouraging the women "to become better citizens once they are released again into our communities." Their focus on "trying to help women and children in poverty work themselves out of their situations" was chosen as a part of the national CWU Imperative on Economic Justice for Women. CWU constituents collaborated with other church organizations to raise more than half of the $600,000 required and persuaded the state of Illinois to set aside $100,000. The rest was raised through foundation grants developed by CWU with the assistance of a grant writer from Lutheran Social Services.[17] It is a tribute to the audacity, skill, and persistence of these Illinois church women that such a major project met with such phenomenal success. Spirituality and prayer have taken many forms. These are the foundation of the CWU movement.

CWU—Diminishing National and Church Boundaries, Building Global Partnerships

When Pope John XXIII opened the Vatican doors and old boundaries fell, it was not long before Roman Catholic women, including nuns, could do openly what some had been doing covertly for several years—participate in local units of Church Women United. They soon became staff members, leaders, and officers, enlarging the vision and enriching the programs. These contributions and faithfulness have made a tremendous difference, serving to expand the movement and deepen its spiritual roots. Special mention should be made of Sr. Marjorie Tuite who stood solidly against racism in the United States and for peace in Central America. She traveled the United States combating racism and worked with the Witness for Peace program, spending considerable time in Central America. She was considered a saint by the women of Central America, who sat up all night mourning her death and celebrating her life.

An example of hands across national boarders is the Fellowship of the Least Coin. In 1956 Margaret Shannon met Shanti Solomon, a leader in the church of North India. They were on their way to a meeting in Alaska, something Shanti Solomon said would never be possible for Indian women in the villages she knew. A woman of great faith and devoted to the power of prayer, Shanti Solomon conceived the idea of an offering of prayers and money that would help women all over the world to both give and receive.

That very year she established the Fellowship of the Least Coin, an international movement of prayer, reconciliation, and peace. When women gather in their local prayer services or denominational meetings or when they have a special blessing in their lives they put aside the "least coin" of their country. This has lifted the status of women even as their prayers have been lifted, "all scattered by the seeds of one woman's enthusiasm." Offering the least coin of each country allowed women to make their prayers concrete, but also made all the women's contributions equal, rich and poor alike. Thus each year hundreds of thousands of dollars have been collected to provide grants for women's programs of education and health throughout the world. On October 15, 1998, Shanti Solomon died in Delhi at the age of 78. The Fellowship of the Least Coin continues as a loving tribute to this remarkable woman.

Another example of the international scope of the movement took place immediately after World War II when the United Council of Church Women sent a care package to Greece. The women felt good about this but had no idea of the extent of the starvation in Greece. In 1979 the Church Women United of New York state held the annual assembly at Schenectady. The priest of the Greek Orthodox Church, who had recently been hospitalized, had agreed to hold a dinner in his church for CWU as part of the meeting. The women of the Orthodox church prepared a beautiful Greek meal with all the special touches. Following the meal, after the CWU women had expressed their gratitude, the priest rose to say a few words and tell his story. As a boy in Greece during the war, his family had had a really hard time surviving. A care package from church women in the United States had come to his family. He vowed he would never forget what it meant to him and his family. Later he became a priest and came to this country. The gala dinner was his gift in appreciation for that long-ago package that had meant so much.

The global reach of CWU is told in music and story. "One Woman's Hands" is a favorite song of CWU because it expresses what one woman can achieve. In the early 1960s Ruth Colvin in Syracuse, New York, was astonished to realize the extent of illiteracy among the adults in the United States. A project that began with the collection of reading materials in an old refrigerator expanded to become a worldwide ministry in literacy as Literacy

Volunteers was born. At first this project was supported by the local United Church Women. Later it was endorsed by CWU of the state of New York and by the national office of Church Women United. Ruth Colvin and her husband, Robert, have devoted their lives to traveling the world carrying the gift of reading wherever they go. Literacy Volunteers of America has made a tremendous difference in the world.[18] The power of one woman cannot be denied! Indeed, CWU is a local ecumenical phenomenon with impact ranging from community to nation and encircling the globe.

Church Women United Moves Seamlessly from Prayer to Justice

Impacting the global-local ecumenical scene in the second half of the twentieth century, along with the formation of the World and National councils and the ecumenical impetus coming from Vatican II, were the significant social revolutions of the postwar era, growing anger and anguish over racial injustice, the civil rights movement, the women's movement, the radical nature of a biblically grounded feminist/womanist/mujerista theology, the antiwar movement, the farmworker movement, challenges to the support of the United Nations as a peacemaking body, and the general ferment of the sixties and seventies. The time was ripe for changes and new ways of thinking. For example, because the participation of Roman Catholic women in the movement in local places preceded Vatican II, the women of CWU were strong advocates for a more inclusionary ecumenism among the broader ecumenical circles like state and local ecumenical councils. And inclusive celebrative and prayer activities with their accompanying social action components have moved women far beyond the stereotyped "church lady" image. If women have a need for celebration, women also have a nose for needs—a family in need of support, a hungry child, a lonely homeless person, assistance for victims of abuse, help for an ailing neighbor, a call for civil rights, a way to stop wars. These local experiences of needs, when networked together by state and nation, have challenged the prayer, fellowship, and actions of women in communities across the nation. The stories of advocacy and action rooted in prayer and Bible study are many. Justice is the focus of these stalwart women in local communities—women who put feet to their spirituality and organize for action. Their causes include racial justice, economic justice, environmental justice, and social justice. The local and global are linked. Compassion, bravery, and, at times, panache, are modes of collective effort. Why?

Often the first step was to offer money collected through World Day of Prayer offerings as grants and loans to women from the country that had prepared the World Day of Prayer materials for that year, for some domestic grants and loans, and for support of ongoing ecumenical work through CWU. While possibly a "safe" way to become involved in the world's problems, the gifts often became the starting point for further localized actions and determination to work on root causes. The print resources provided avenues for other collective actions to be taken, frequently supplemented by local needs, and often linked to the global scene through the presence of immigrants and refugees in the community.

One example is from the early 1950s. Fear and suspicion were rampant in this, the McCarthy era. Innocent persons were suspiciously screened. In some instances people were required to sign loyalty oaths. Many careers and some lives were ruined. Members of United Church Women were horrified. Under the leadership of Florence Partridge of the Evangelical United Brethren Church, a committee attempted to develop the UCW Loyalty Oath. It was a bold and powerful statement at a time when "men in responsible positions and self-appointed groups were spreading distrust of churches and citizens with which they disagreed." This is a portion of the antiphonal Loyalty Oath of United Church Women:

> This is God's world.
> **We do believe**.
> Earth might be fair.
> **We will strive to do our part in making it so.**
> Fear comes from the unknown.
> **We will know**.
> We ourselves may, for our beliefs, face disapproval, insinuation, or slander.
> **We will stand**.
> It is our heritage from the Old Testament, from Greek knowledge, from the American founding fathers (and mothers) and from the Christian Gospel of love, to think freely and speak freely our thoughts.
> **We dare to speak out.**[19]

The remaining words of the Loyalty Oath of CWU promise to study, discuss, and understand the issues at hand. An appointment was made with President Eisenhower. Rev. Mossie Wyker, Abbie Clement Jackson, Dorothy Dolbey, Leslie Swain, and Mrs. MacLeod were scheduled for ten minutes with the president. He remained with them for thirty minutes and also agreed to speak at the Atlantic City Assembly in October 1953, a promise he kept.

Work throughout the country went on in different degrees of intensity and complexity. In Tennessee, the Nashville Unit describes its collection of Peace Petition signatures along with the collection of ditty bags as gifts for the homeless, for women in prison, and for the children in the correctional youth center.[20] Work against violence on television is illustrated by the Ohio CWU's efforts and actions through "TV Tune In, USA."

North Dakota CWU's work against nuclear power is a powerful story of women at work for justice and against nuclear contamination of the environment and the nuclear arms buildup.[21] Calling communities to action, they created a vision of the "Peace Garden State," noting that North Dakota was the third largest nuclear power in the world. In partnership with Sr. Marjorie Tuite and twenty-eight others, they designed a Peace-with-Justice bus tour of the state in 1983. In addition to visiting silos and silos (farm feed storage and nuclear storage), they visited the Listen Drop In Center, an adult abuse center, a rape crisis center, Minot Air Force Base, Governor Olson, the United Tribes Technical Training School, and the state penitentiary. They had a significant impact on the state's consciousness.

CWU's strong efforts to curtail violence, both on a global scale as well as in local communities, resulted in a comprehensive social policy statement on violence, adopted in 2000 after two years of discussion and deliberation in local units and insisting that, in addition to the violence of personal and psychological abuse, militarism and economic inequity are forms of violence that particularly affect women and children. CWU uses this policy to speak out in the public and legislative arenas for the Violence against Women Act, for labor justice, for adequate welfare reform that makes a difference in women's lives, and against gun violence. Overall, CWU understands communities of faith and hope to be those places in which violence and fear can be transformed into love. However, it is simultaneously necessary to enact and implement laws that enable people to find ways other than violence to solve their problems.

A CWU Resolution in 1981 on gun control calls for the licensing of gun owners, the registration of handguns, and the reduction in the proliferation of handguns through a moratorium on the manufacturing and importation of handguns. This policy, along with the aforementioned policy against violence adopted in 2000 under the quadrennial theme of "making the world safer for women and children" made it possible for CWU to become a major partner in the ecumenical advocacy around the Million Mom March in 2000. As was stated in the briefing in Washington, D.C., at the time of the event, "when weapons of death, such as guns, are easily available, the opportunity to perpetuate an act of fatal violence increases. . . . Church Women United names access to guns as a significant culprit in continuing the cycle of violence in our society and in our world."[22] As the Violence Policy acknowledges, much of society lives by a model of power by domination—"power over" others, which often leads to destructive violence, rather than "power with," which builds human community.

CWU and Civil Rights: Mothering a Movement

Racism and civil and human rights were a local agenda that became a national concern for CWU women. CWU was a pioneer in the movement toward racial equality. It is in this arena that CWU's power of collaborative change, growing from local compassion and organizing skill, is perhaps best illustrated. Martha Wiggins's Union Theological Seminary doctoral dissertation on Church Women United and the civil rights movement talks about CWU women as "mothers of the movement" against racial bigotry.[23]

In the 1960s there had been a national emphasis entitled "Assignment Race." A 1981 Proclamation on Racism, issued by Dr. Thelma Adair, president of CWU, signaled a second national corporate response by CWU to the resurgence of racism in the United States. It proclaimed, in part, that "Church Women United, rejoicing in God's gift of diversity and celebrating the infinite worth of each person created in God's image and loved by Jesus Christ, deplores the malignant resurgence of racism in our society. . . . Empowered by God's Spirit, we renew our commitment to work for the elimination of the root causes of racism and for full human dignity, liberty, equality and justice for all people."[24] Adair's proclamation resulted in a second national program emphasis, called "Reassignment: Race." This program took on local color and flavor as church women worked on consciousness raising, skill building, and action projects focused toward a broad-based platform of issues: hunger, health, environment, education, crime and criminal justice, family, housing, employment, human rights, peace, and military spending.[25]

Racism was a justice issue for Church Women United very early in its history. Church Women United chapters began to organize against racism even before World War II, and in fact were leaders in this movement long before more established church bodies. For most women in local units, this group was the first racially mixed group in their city and for many the first opportunity to meet face-to-face and on equal grounds with women of a different race. In Syracuse, CWU joined in coalition with other women's groups in the city to work with the Mayor's Commission on Human Rights to foster the spirit of integration and eliminate all forms of discrimination. One early effort concerned the use of black mannequins in the city's department stores. The women decided that there were not enough black mannequins downtown, so they did research, organized, and were successful in persuading several of the department stores to diversify in this way.[26] The Syracuse CWU also made intentional plans to combat racism in the 1960s by organizing a group called Interview, an integrated group with a fifty-fifty ratio of black and white that met regularly, learned to trust one another enough to share their own deep tendencies toward racism, and ultimately shared overnight retreats, becoming good and supportive friends.[27]

In the early days in the South, May luncheons were replaced by May teas, because it was still awkward for black and white women to sit down at table together. Many beautiful stories of racially charged incidents in which women triumphed and equality reigned are told in the history of CWU by its first executive director, Margaret Shannon, in her book *Just Because.* In its own way this showed the intentionality and serious purpose of this movement to eliminate racism among women of faith. Coretta Scott King was a member of the Board of Managers at that time, continuing until well after her husband's assassination in 1968. In 1980 another campaign was begun with the theme "Reassignment Race." Again in the first year of the twenty-first century, the theme chosen for the May Friendship Day Celebration was "For Such a Time As This! A Call to End Racism."

Collaboration and coalition building proved very productive. An example is the 1964–1965 Wednesdays in Mississippi Project of the National Council of Negro Women in collaboration with the YWCA and in partnership with CWU: "As of this writing, the United Church Women is the single integrated national women's group in Jackson. Although its membership is not large, it is unequivocally dedicated to working in a completely integrated fashion. Last February, its annual meeting and luncheon, held in a Jackson hotel, was attended by 75 Negro and white women. With Ann Hewitt as president of the state group and Jane Schutt as president of the Jackson chapter, the United Church Women [UCW was an earlier local name for CWU] have forceful and able leadership, and can be expected to grow in influence."[28]

CWU women also participated in interracial prayer fellowship groups and the Jackson Interfaith organization: "Perhaps the most heartening interfaith experience of the summer was the July meeting of the Jackson Interfaith organization at which a Chicago team member, the National Chairman of Christian Social Relations for the UCW, Elizabeth Hazelden, was the featured speaker. Although Jackson Interfaith has technically been "open" from the beginning, this was the first time local Negroes had attended a meeting. The Negroes were made to feel welcome; several joined the organization before the evening was over. One Chicago visitor was so impressed by this experience that she returned home determined to make sure that Negroes were invited to her own interfaith group—an omission she had apparently not noticed before."[29]

Links between human rights and civil rights gathered steam in the 1960s. Laura Crayton McCray, an active National Baptist Convention member, finds the "approach as made by United Church Women proximating more nearly the pattern as set by our Christ as we are able to interpret our limited experiences in the area of Human Rights; working as Servants in helping to create better mutual understanding among the peoples of this world." She describes the organization of the Tuskegee Council of United Church Women:

> Even from the beginning the UCW story caught my ear. I was impressed with the concerns expressed. I remember how we stopped to ask God's blessings on the women of Alabama as they were considering whether or not the Tuskegee Council could become a part of the work of the State of Alabama—having Negro members. . . . At that time one never knew the results of a meeting where Negroes and white persons met together. Just in case, I took a bar of soap and my toothbrush in case we would necessarily have to remain overnight against our wills. It was at that meeting that our State President, Mrs. Henry Collins, and the women assembled exhibited their best as Christian women and as Servants of God—ready to do His will. Since that day, it has been as if we were one family in Christ.[30]

McCray went on to describe her participation in a Canadian-American Consultation on Human Rights in March of 1966. Describing the discussion of the diverse group around likenesses and differences and "concern for international problems other than our own," she noted that "we lived, ate, and grew in love together over the concerns of ourselves and others." McCray's roommate was Gray Cameron from Tennessee. Noting the importance of the confrontations at the consultation, she describes their tearful parting. Gray (noting her first experience sleeping in a room with a Negro) said: "If I had the opportunity to choose again, Laura, it would be you." "The feeling was mutual," concluded McCray.[31] Commitment to human rights is built through tenacity, passion, and relationships of trust and understanding, with very local, face-to-face contact being essential. It is also noteworthy that human rights and civil rights were seen as cut from the same cloth. One cannot speak of one without taking account of the other.

Social and Economic Justice

Concern for children around the world was another human rights concern. Consequently, UNICEF had high priority in the life of CWU. From the sale of holiday cards, CWU became the third largest contributor to UNICEF among all nonprofit organizations. An article by Betty Stanford, Western Regional Director of UNICEF, entitled "U in UNICEF," focused on encouraging CWU units and members to support Trick-or-Treat for UNICEF, sell UNICEF greeting cards, and use UNICEF's multicultural and international cooperation educational materials. That article quotes CWU leader Lucky Phelps: "'Why do we keep trying to change the world?' asks CWU's WCD Chairperson, Lucky Phelps. She gives her own very important answer, 'It must be because we believe we can do it.' And we can—by giving health and knowledge and hope to the world's children."[32]

CWU was also moved to work in the poverty arena because American women were realizing that women in most parts of the world were and are among the poorest of the poor. They were being denied their humanity. Children are hungry and emaciated and lacking in clean water and appropriate education. Suffering is everywhere. Women and children are abused. In prayer, women probed these dilemmas, laying before God a challenge they themselves could not avoid. In a 1988 address to Church Women United in Alaska, Dr. Sylvia Talbot, then national president, voiced the challenge: "We can no longer tolerate poverty among women and children."[33] According to Talbot, CWU was training women in every state to raise and reflect on the issue of the growing poverty of women and children—to develop skills for working with groups, resolving conflict, increasing involvement and taking action, as well as interpreting action to the wider public. Talbot's words reinforced the principle that from the beginning prayer and action are interwoven into the life of CWU.

But these words were really being drawn from the experiences of local units of CWU that had already begun to approach the very serious poverty of women and children in the United States, as well as in the world. Seeking the root causes of poverty, making the world safe for women and children, and supporting families constituted three of the areas of concern in all the cities and towns and villages where units of Church Women United met. It was not long before local units introduced or supported safe havens for battered women and provided after-school programs for latchkey children.

As a response to the needs of women and children in poverty, women of CWU have originated, staffed, and supplied dining rooms and food pantries for low-income families. But more than that, there have been the many efforts of helping welfare women with their educational and employment needs, as is amply demonstrated by a program in Rochester, New York. The Rochester unit also established a housing program that included settling low-income families in newly restored housing and remaining in contact with them to help them with such things as maintenance and care of their house and good nutrition. These programs later gave way to a metropolitan-wide expansion of the Habitat for Humanity program. But CWU was the instigator in responding to these concerns.

From their celebrations and prayer, Church Women United focused energy not only on issues of women's poverty, but on justice generally. In Rochester, Syracuse, Buffalo, and New York City, women of CWU formed "Court Watchers." This presence in the courtrooms made it much more difficult for judges to discriminate against any group of people, persons of color, or persons with language difficulties. Court Watchers was a silent but powerful presence. In Syracuse, CWU women rode with the policemen on their beats, usually a black and a white woman together. They noted how the police responded to domestic crises and street scenes. They were also influential in changing the tests required of police officers, so that the language of the questions was clearer for all being tested.

Many local units of Church Women United have been involved in prison projects. These have ranged from the giving of personal gifts at Christmas time, to leading workshops and making visits to inmates, to providing picnics and outings so inmates and their families might be together. CWU women have become mentors and teachers to individual prisoners in Asheville, North Carolina, and other places where this is permitted. Local units have created and staffed visiting rooms for families of inmates and supported halfway houses for women prisoners returning to society. Like other efforts to stand for peace and justice, these projects have been carried out in answer to Jesus' words, "I was a prisoner and you visited me."

In Connecticut, the Fairfield CWU unit collaborated with the Council of Churches in Bridgeport on a homeless shelter for "youth-in-trouble-with-families." The church women in Willimantic raised scholarship money for women for job training as licensed practical nurses. In the Greater Hartford unit the work focused on housing and advocacy, and a statewide hearing on Economic Alternatives in Connecticut was sponsored by Church Women United.[34]

Not only economic justice but environmental justice engaged the women of CWU. Louisiana CWU's "Environment Stewardship Report" by Lorena Pospisil praises the accomplishments of local units in stopping the use of styrofoam products in churches and homes, while offering new challenges such as the urgent call to stop the demeaning and debilitating practice of exporting hazardous waste abroad, especially to economically deprived countries. Given that the United States creates more waste per person than any other country and that the content of that waste has become more destructive as the years progress, Pospisil urged CWU to be in the forefront of the campaign to stop waste dumpers from making profit from poisoning the environment, globally as well as locally.[35]

Peacemaking

CWU also collaborated with peacemaking groups such as the Religious Committee on SALT (nuclear nonproliferation treaty). CWU brought "foot power" and "pen power" into the political arena on issues of peace and demilitarization. Organizing support for the Salt II Treaty served as one way of acting on CWU's ongoing concern for peace and disarmament and engaged a number of groups. "We have committed ourselves to work cooperatively, to shape the national debate on SALT II, and to work for ratification of the Salt II Treaty," said Lois Hamer, chair of the Peacebuilding Task Force of the Southern California/Southern Nevada CWU state unit.[36] CWU women from many states traveled to their state capitals, worked with their senators and representatives, and helped shape the national debate.

Millie Moser, then president of the state unit in Southern California/Southern Nevada, wrote a letter to her constituents about a leadership choice she made, related to the unjust treatment of refugees from Central America and consistent with the goals and mission of CWU. This story regarding the power of demonstrating for justice illustrates the dilemma leaders face in presenting a public message through presence and foot power, while at the same time recognizing that not all agree with such action. She writes:

> Dear Sisters in Christ: I want to share a very important process that is happening in my life. For the past six months I have been one of the

> church women participating in demonstrations around the issue of extended voluntary departure status to all El Salvadoran Refugees. We have attempted to raise the issue and keep the public aware of the extreme inhumane atrocities in El Salvador, and point out that there is something that we can do. Title 8, Code of Federal Regulations, 242B, voluntary departure prior to commencement of hearing, clearly states the District Director can grant voluntary departure status for one year. On Monday, March 15, along with 15 other church women, I sat in the District Director Michael Landon's office in the Federal Building to remind him of this code. He would not meet with us. (We had tried to set up an appointment on three different occasions.) At 4:30 the office and building closed, and we were arrested. We were cited with a non-moving violation amounting to a $25 fine. My decision to join in with these women from many denominations: Methodist, Disciples of Christ, Unitarian, Roman Catholic, Episcopalian, came after much prayer. I am painfully aware that many of you reading this would not think of doing such an act. However, I consider this to have been a privilege I did on behalf of all women—in solidarity with our sisters living in El Salvador or as refugees here in California. I ask your prayers.[37]

Moser's decision was made prayerfully. She was acting as an individual, but of course she was also known as the president of CWU in that area. In working for justice, personal power and organizational power go hand in hand. A sign of the power of standing firm, of solidarity and sisterhood, was quickly evidenced when just a month later, in May 1982, the Leaders Council supported her action in a unanimous vote by expressing

> commendation, appreciation and support for the stance of our President Mildred Moser, and other denominational leaders in regard to the safety and voluntary departure status of El Salvadoran refugees. We recognize the possibility of an undesirable alien being permitted to remain in this country, but we believe justice and human rights have prior claim. We thank God for the courage of our leaders in peaceably protesting national policy without regard to their own personal cost. We offer this resolution of confidence and support for our President, Mildred Moser.[38]

The actions of the Coalition of Religious Women in which Moser participated and which CWU supported were given much press and TV coverage.

Moser's leadership also included peacemaking, and she was quick to give credit to others. In one of her columns as president she notes Florence Green's creative leadership in developing a "scroll" of hundreds of CWU women dedicated to peace building. "We picture ourselves as women of the covenant," Moser said, interlinked with women the world over. She challenged her constituents to see 1983 as a time of new urgency because of the specter of nuclear annihilation. "Let us envision ourselves as holding the keys to peace," for we are, she said:

- Unwilling to live in luxury at the cost of another's survival.
- Unwilling to be silent as the nuclear arms race tears on at breakneck speed and glib comments are made about "limited nuclear war."
- Unwilling to be part of injustice wherever it is found.
- I invite, no urge, our units to use the new Wellspring, NO PEACE WITHOUT JUSTICE, for the theological basis for peacemaking.

"We have the power to co-create with God a new call to peacemaking," she concluded. "Happy are those who create a world in which violence is confronted and cast out and in its place preparations are made to live in love for the well-being of all people."

Since 1955 CWU has conducted "Causeways." It is an international and domestic (urban) exchange between American Christian women and women of other nations and ethnic backgrounds. Causeways offers opportunities to meet across geographical divides in order to express mutual support and solidarity in the search for justice, peace, and global community.[39] The Causeways exchange programs have been numerous and varied, for example, the Michigan CWU-sponsored trips to meet Christian women in Cuba. There have also been exchanges with Russia, Serbia, Haiti, and many more. They are successful in the sense that each participant has the opportunity to experience the reality of other women in a different part of the globe.

Local efforts to build a global awareness of peacemaking efforts have also been important in the life of CWU. For example, the Peace Ribbon project and the Idaho Peace Quilt are state efforts designed to use women's handiwork to create community symbols to draw the public's attention to peace issues.

Closely related to these diverse concerns for peace was the "People's Platform for a Global Society." This effort grew out of listening to women describe their lives and hopes for the future. CWU state units collected ideas from local units that were collated and in 1976 presented to President Carter in the White House in the form of a Mandate for Action. Copies of state responses were put into a brightly covered book, currently on display in the Women's Museum in Dallas.

Another example of the justice and peacemaking concern comes from the mid-1980s. The national president of CWU, Thelma Adair, and the staff person in charge of Celebrations, Dorothy Wagner, chose a group of women in Hawaii to write the May Fellowship Day Celebration for 1987. Some of the women were native Hawaiians; all of them deeply regretted the loss of their traditions and their heritage. The service was highly critical of the missionaries who came to Hawaii with their cold northern ways and their strict pious notions, eliminating customs the people held dear and placing the American flag beside the Cross. As so often when colonial powers invade another culture, they took over resources and crushed traditions that gave indigenous people their identity. There was conflict over the service, even on the mainland, but some healing could begin when the United Church of Christ (part of its heritage is the Congregational Church that first sent missionaries to Hawaii) published a formal apology to the Hawaiian people, especially the Native Hawaiians, for any hurt and/or loss they have felt in their traditions with the coming of the well-meaning missionaries. A matter of apology, like forgiveness, has a very Christian ring to it.

More recently, CWU has initiated a series of "Helpshops" as a way to engage women in social and economic justice concerns. A series of Helpshops in the southwest illustrates the intensity of commitment to networking among and nurturing local units as they moved toward action in collaboration with others in the community. Borrowing an idea from the Christian Church (Disciples of Christ), CWU in Southern California/Southern Nevada planned and organized training meetings in each area of this state unit to "give women new hope and confidence as they cooperate in study and action."[40] This mutual nourishment built excitement as well as skills. This issue of the newsletter carried the story of a local unit in Bonita, California, which organized a task force under the leadership of Beatrice P. Russell to deal with anti-Semitism, racism, and the Ku Klux Klan.

In Alabama in 1983, CWU planted roses and azaleas in the yard of John Knight, a county commissioner, after a ten-foot cross was burned in his yard by the Klan. He had been a spokesman for a group of African American leaders protesting civil rights violations. Local papers carried front-page pictures of this creative event.[41]

Very willing to deal with controversy, CWU women in the South ran a series of Workshops on Controversy to help improve human relations in the community by:

1. Increasing the sensitivity of each individual to the feelings causing the reactions of others.
2. Developing more perception in order to recognize situations in which poor human relations cause an impasse.
3. Providing methods and practices to use in working with others in tension situations.
4. Developing new skills in listening to what other people say in order to understand their interests, motives, and purposes.
5. Exploring the real motives for one's own behavior in a controversial situation.
6. Applying this learning to other community situations so that controversial subjects may be freely introduced and discussed and action can begin.[42]

Inclusive Language

Spoken language is perhaps the most sophisticated means of expressing one's deepest thoughts and feelings. Language shapes us even as we shape language. Church Women United has been a leader in promoting inclusive language. One of the Wellsprings studies, "Speaking of God," written by Shannon Clarkson and Letty Russell for CWU, was studied by women all over the United States. Adherence to inclusive language became a policy in editing all the Celebrations. Thus great care has been taken to avoid sexist language wherever possible and to make clear that white and light are not necessarily superior to the blackness of night, which reveals the stars, the dark of the womb from which we are born, and the shadow side of ourselves, which we must confront and love. This shift has lifted the self-respect and hopes of many women and has expanded the vision of God to include "creating woman in her own image."

In no place was this more evident than at an event sponsored by local women in Minnesota. The "Decade of the Churches in Solidarity with Women," declared by the World Council of Churches, 1988–1998, was little known either by the churches or the women. Halfway through the decade, a creative and artistic ecumenical group of women planned the Re-Imagining Conference of 1993 in Minneapolis, Minnesota. Never has there been an affair more maligned and less understood, more publicized without recognizing the very heart, soul, beauty, and promise of such a stellar event, planned solely by the feminine heart of women—perhaps the half-broken heart of woman. It was not only ecumenical but also international in scope, utterly inclusive within the Christian tradition, richly garbed in music, art, drama, dance, poetry, and magnificent prose. Not only were the leaders involved, but every participant was engaged in these wondrous modes of praise and thanksgiving. There was warmth and encouragement, the honoring of loving relationships, enticement to creative theological thinking, challenges, and a real sense of community—an oasis for women in a still patriarchal society. It was, for many, a breakthrough, one many conservative and narrowly fundamentalist groups could not understand, could not abide, could not countenance. But for those who attended it was a soul-satisfying experience never to be forgotten. The Re-Imagining Conference, while not sponsored by CWU alone, symbolized the epitome of CWU's search for women's spirituality. It was also a significant illustration of women asserting their place in the civil discourse.

Women in CWU have been deeply concerned about justice, yet it has not always been natural. Because, at the same time, women in CWU have had struggles with apathy, ingrained patterns of bias, lack of thoughtfulness, and sometimes naiveté. Sometimes even their weaknesses contributed to their effectiveness. In her own words, Francis Pauley, a southern activist and community leader, said that the rationale for giving civil-rights-activist CWU women certain tasks in part is because of the public perception that church women are gentle and nonradical by nature.[43] Yet, in spite of their perceived "church lady" natures, the women who sought change collaboratively through CWU were powerful, committed, and prayerful advocates for a transformed society and were active in working to transform it.

Justice, in all its dimensions is difficult work. There were notations from reports reading as follows: "Apathy is the biggest problem." "It is easier to work *for* rather than *with* someone different from oneself." "Sometimes we fear that we were seen as 'lady bountiful' from another generation."[44]

Women, Feminism, and the Power of Collaborative Change

Moving from prayer, to generosity, to prophetic understanding and action was a natural step for CWU women when the human family was endangered or in any kind of need. Any situation or crisis that diminished justice within the human family was a challenge to be met.

It is clear that CWU women were pioneers in, were affected by, and brought considerable insight to the larger women's movement and the second wave of feminism that came to life with the publication of Betty

Friedan's book in the early sixties. United Methodist Women's Division Executive Director Theresa Hoover, speaking in 1983 to UMC women, put it succinctly: "Out of long commitment to women [we] understood at once what the secular feminists were struggling with and in revolt against. These intelligent, angry younger women articulated our frustrations also. Their analyses deepened our understanding of the systemic oppression of women. Their determination to revise patriarchal culture and politics energized us."[45]

Hoover, an ecumenical activist in the National Council of Churches and in CWU, perhaps more than any other leader in these times, articulated the essential links between racism and sexism, an integration that clearly grew out of the "long commitment to women" evidenced by numerous linked experiences in many local areas. While Hartmann's comments pertain to a national perspective and study—i.e., in addition to CWU, the International Union of Electrical Workers and the American Civil Liberties—it is important to note that Hoover's thinking was shaped by her profound knowledge and understanding of the effectiveness of local action. Hartmann notes: "As an African American woman, Theresa Hoover lent particular authority to the task of incorporating women into a civil rights and social justice agenda, just as Pauli Murray had done in the ACLU. Nor was Hoover alone. Black women provided inspiration and leadership to the feminist cause within the National Council of Churches at a greater level than in any of the other organizations considered here. African American women's considerable presence and leadership among NCC activists ensured that inclusivity and anti-racism formed an integral core of the feminism they constructed."[46]

The power of CWU's local collaborative efforts for justice includes any number of localized and liberating stories, as women's consciousness grew from generalized concerns about women's oppression to a more specific theological and sociopolitical clarity about what it means to be "woman, created in the image of God." For example, special relationships with the women of a divided Korea continued to be important throughout the last half of the twentieth century. These were made possible in part by the courageous efforts of Dorothy Wagner and the World Day of Prayer linkages that she nurtured. As recently as the year 2000, CWU was represented in a delegation to North and South Korea by Kathy Jeffries, CWU activist from Tennessee.[47]

In a 1972 local newsletter from Parsons, Kansas, the question is posed: "Church Women United is interested in Women's Issues!!! Are you?" The article described "a course of special concern on the roles of women in our changing world," a cooperative effort with the Labette Community Junior College and CWU of Parsons. The instructor for the six-week series was Anita Herrick, a student at St. Paul's School of Theology in Kansas City. A nursery was provided during all sessions.[48]

A local unit in San Diego presented a program in 1974, "Women Uniquely Employed," after combing their local unit for stories: "Scheduled to tell of their work experiences are a linewoman who climbs telephone poles, a policewoman assigned to patrol car duty, San Diego Zoo's first woman animal keeper, a TV director-producer and a full-fledged lady auto mechanic. The search for an ordained woman minister continues."[49]

The feminist movement often took on a biblical and theological tone. Grace Moore, in Southern California/Southern Nevada, set the problem in the Mother's Day motif to ask the question, "Are we interested in expanding our understanding of the human-divine relationship by drawing from the experience of women?" She noted biblical texts such as Isaiah 46:3, Psalms 22:9; Psalms 71:6, Isaiah 66:9, and Deuteronomy 32:18 that used the imagery of pregnancy, midwifery, and birthing to enlarge understanding of God, and went on to say: "When God is imaged only in one human sex, idolatry surfaces, and subtle, exclusive linking of primarily the male sex with God tends to make of that sex a god. The totality of God is forgotten. That both women and men are the image of God is negated. We remember the God who rules and forget the same God who births. In that forgetting, women too are diminished/forgotten. If we as Christians would follow Christ, a primary task is to be Mothers in a holy sense, and to call on God our Mother as often as we call on God our Father." When Dr. Sylvia Talbot, then president of Church Women United, was asked in 1988 about the status of women in America, she responded, "I think it's scandalous; we have not made much progress. We have provided for a very small number of women at the top, but the vast majority are hurting out there. The U.S. hasn't even ratified the United Nations Convention for the elimination of discrimination against women, so we are way behind some countries in that area."[50]

The reporter commenting on Talbot's speech noted her assumption that the church may be partly at fault. "'Major obstacles for women, according to a recent UN study, are traditional attitudes and practices, many of which are institutionalized by the church,'" Talbot sighed. The whole life of Church Women United, Talbot claims, is based on the principle of equality among women and men. Women must have their fingers on the pulse of national life, must be involved in politics, must learn to change things. Talbot spoke boldly about the redistribution of wealth across social strata and the necessity of commitment to a deepened understanding of what human dignity is all about—illustrating once again the common CWU notion that feminism with a theological base is undeniably and essentially connected to social and economic justice."[51]

Many church women were actively involved in the women's movement, while others—without articulating the links to "liberation"—put their skills, energies, creative insights, and passion to work in projects of great effectiveness. Whether modest or massive in scope, women designed challenging projects, networked with others to gain support, followed through with persistence, and seldom sought sole credit for their undertakings. The stories are fascinating tales of multitasking, organizational skill and credibility, collaboration and networking, and down-to-earth actions growing out of care and compassion. Many projects were stimulated by the national CWU imperative calling for economic justice for women. The eighties and early nineties were fraught with losses of jobs through unemployment, loss of billions through savings and loans scandals, and billions spent on military efforts such as the Gulf War. In this context, women are hit the hardest and poverty among women is likely to increase.

Women staff members Carol Barton, Frances Kennedy, and Ada Marie Isassi-Diaz supported and nurtured these efforts and collected and shared data about the more than five hundred local units that developed action around economic justice. A booklet, "Making Connections: Economics and Women's Lives," served as stimulus. Exciting new models of collaboration emerged. For example, the role of active learning in CWU has always been associated with faith moving into action. Education is a form of collaborative action and action often leads to deeper learning. Challenges call for prayer, which in turn calls for action. It is part of the circularity that has marked the life of the movement since its beginnings.

In 1994, under the leadership of the General Director, Patricia Rumer, CWU received a grant to initiate a program in collaboration with the Kellogg Foundation, Women Leading in Community (WomenLinC). At the beginning of the twenty-first century, this program has become multilingual, with materials translated into Spanish, Korean, and Malayalam (a language spoken by women from the Mar Thoma Orthodox Church with origins in South India). This major women's leadership training program for social and economic transformation was shared with the global ecumenical community at the World Council of Churches meeting in Zimbabwe in 1998 through an additional grant from Kellogg. Built on the concept that local community involvement is essential for any significant change, it is designed as a process rather than a program, with a methodology that is participatory and collaborative.

The actions growing out of the workshops are focused on locally determined needs rather than nationally directed projects. An example of local efforts is the story from a community where a small CWU unit, participating in the WomenLinC process, built a community-wide coalition including school district people, city officials, community leaders, parents, and students to tackle issues of racism in the schools. The outcome was a series of activities in the public schools culminating in Respect Day, which was broadly appreciated. In each region of the country there are at least twenty trained volunteers who are now prepared to lead WomenLinC workshops, multiplying the effect of the process and effecting social change.

And What of the Future?

As the twentieth century ends and the next begins, CWU, as an ecumenical movement, is facing challenges both external and internal. Many of these are long-standing. Has CWU lost its bearings? Many local CWU units have become discouraged, and some have disbanded. As constituency ages, the questions of local leadership are compounded. The ongoing challenge to recruit new participants remains, and new styles of leadership are not always welcomed. Board development needs to be enhanced, and board and staff roles need clarity, particularly at the national level. Increased attention needs to be paid to the World Day of Prayer Units—local groups that meet once yearly to conduct the WDP celebrations and which outnumber regular units three to one. Fresh models of advocacy and action are found in some local CWUs and need to be studied. A major effort for financial development at all levels of organizational life needs to be implemented. Creative work on Young Church Women United, initiated in the northeast and replicated in several places, needs active support in all areas of the country.

If CWU is to live up to its commitment to peace, justice, and human rights, and honor the foremothers that gave it life and vitality, it will have to change radically—for women's lives have changed immeasurably over this sixty-year time period. It is likely that CWU will live on for a while in local places with local commitment and passion—led by women actively engaged in a committed medley of prayer, Bible study, advocacy, and action. State and national advocacy will continue to be done in some arenas and World Day of Prayer international efforts will continue through dedicated global impetus and planning. But CWU, like many other women's organizations today, will need to adapt to the future, honor its true mission, discard dysfunctional behavior when it crops up, and welcome today's young women generously if it is to remake itself into a healthy organization for the twenty-first century.

Perhaps the finest description of this movement of Christian women, as well as a wonderful tribute, is expressed in this poem by Margaret Shannon.

> A Cathedral
> to the glory of
> Jesus Christ our Lord
> is being built each moment
> as hand touches hand.
>
> We long for . . . listen to . . . lift up
> and love one another, so that
> all in each place
> may offer others gifts God has given us:
> Integrity in relationships,
> Joy and Peace in faithfulness,
> Strength to do more than we ask or imagine through the Church.[52]

NOTES

1. In this chapter, Church Women United (CWU) will be used to refer to the movement that was organized in 1941 as the United Council of Church Women (UCCW), unless speaking specifically of matters related to the earlier name. From 1950 to 1966, while a department of the National Council of Churches, it was referred to as United Church Women (UCW).

2. Margaret M. Schiffert, "Church Women United: On the Dynamic Diagonal," *Ecumenical Trends*, April 1985.

3. Margaret Shannon, *Just Because* (Corte Madera, CA: Omega Books, 1977).

4. See Arleon L. Kelley, Kathleen Hurty, and Margrethe B. J. Brown, "Historical Reflections on Councils of Churches in the U.S.," in *Midstream* 32, 4 (October 1993). See also Ruth Rouse and Charles Neill, *A History of the Ecumenical Movement 15-17-1948* (Philadelphia: Westminster Press, 1954), especially pages 307–349, and Ross W. Sanderson, *Church Cooperation in the United States* (New York: The Association of Council Secretaries, 1960).

5. Calkins, quoted in Shannon, *Just Because.*

6. Martha L. Wiggins, dissertation in progress, Union Theological Seminary, New York, New York, 2001.

7. From Shannon, *Just Because:* "The first biennial assembly of UCCW occurred in Cleveland in December 1942. . . . Having received a report from their seven delegates who had participated in the Study Conference of the Churches, 'A Just and Durable Peace,' held in Dayton in April 1942, the assembly was pleased when Mrs. Albert Palmer (of Chicago) made a motion that a day be set aside in the fall of 1943

for the study of peace by church women. This proposal turned out to be of great significance to the future of the movement." A day of united study was called for on November 11 with the theme, "The Price of an Enduring Peace." (I sigh with regret!) A ballot was signed in the last ten minutes with the questions: "1) Should we urge the United States to join and take its full responsibility in a world organization; and 2) Are you willing to continue rationing of food, gasoline and other wartime restrictions in order that the needs of victims of the war overseas be met? The office sent out 90,000 leaflets. . . . within twenty-four hours *Churchwoman Magazine* published an article indicating that 36 states and the District of Columbia had reported. 83,134 women voted that the United States should join and take its full responsibility in a world organization. 630 voted against. On the second question, 80,395 women voted a willingness to continue for a period after the war such wartime regulations as ration of food, gasoline, restriction of travel, etc." Finally, on page 28 of *Just Because* is the following quote: "By November 24, 1,350 communities in 46 states had reported to the UCCW office. The Press picked it up immediately and Eleanor Roosevelt wrote from the White House a note of congratulations. UCCW was one of the 75 organizations participating in a conference sponsored by Mrs. Roosevelt the next June (1944) at the White House on 'How Women May Share in Post-War Policy Making.'" What a loss we have sustained in the philosophy of such leading women as Eleanor Roosevelt!

8. Oral history interview of Esther Hymer, Director, Christian World Relations and UN Office, 1957–1964, Church Women United Records, United Methodist Church Archives: GCAH, Madison, N.J. (hereafter referred to as Archives) 1225-2-4:06.

9. Approved by the Common Council, September 1985.

10. See Kansas folder in Archives: 1225-3-2:23.

11. One of the best analyses of the relationship of UCCW to the Council and its subsequent departure from the Council is that written by Susan M. Hartmann, *The Other Feminists: Activists in the Liberal Establishment* (New Haven: Yale University Press, 1998).

12. Ruth Segerhammar, *State News, Church Women United of Southern California/Southern Nevada* 30 (Feb. 1, 1972).

13. CWU History Note, in Finding Aid, Archives.

14. Margaret M. Schiffert, "Church Women United: On the Dynamic Diagonal," *Ecumenical Trends,* April 1985.

15. Comment by Mary Zambrano, former president of CWU state unit in Southern California/Southern Nevada. Personal email to Church Women United, March 4, 2001.

16. Archives, Proceedings, Annual Meeting, 1969.

17. Letter from Dorothy Yeoman to Claire Randall, September 19, 1989 (Archives).

18. Since that time Literacy Volunteers of America has joined with Laubach Literacy to become a very strong Pro-Literacy World Wide/New Readers' Press.

19. Schiffert, "Church Women United," p. 66. For complete story, see pp. 65–69.

20. Letter from Margaret Jones, Nashville, Dec. 1990, Archives.

21. Archives: Box 1225-3-2:48; Notes from June 1983 Newsletter.

22. Comments by Kathleen Hurty, CWU Executive Director, and Ann Delorey, Director of CWU's Washington Office, at the Ecumenical Briefing, Million Mom March, May 13–14, 2000.

23. Wiggins, dissertation.

24. Quoted in *State News: Church Women United of Southern California/Southern Nevada* 40: 4 (April 1981).

25. These were the issues defined in the People's Platform for a Global Society, the culmination of a process of collecting issues attended to by local and state units throughout the nation in 1976.

26. Archives: 1224-4-2:16.

27. Roberta Grimm, Some Memories of Church Women United, May 2001.

28. Quoted in *State News: Church Women United of Southern California/Southern Nevada* 40: 4 (April 1981).

29. Interfaith organizations usually include Christians and one or more of the other world's great faith traditions, such as Jewish, Muslim, Hindu, Buddhist, or Sikh. However, sometimes interfaith terminology has been used to describe a Protestant and Roman Catholic organization, or at other times to describe an organization that includes Black Christians and White Christians from different Christian denominations.

30. Oral history interview, Laura Crayton McCray, Archives: 1225-2-4:26.

31. Ibid.

32. Stanford, *State News: Church Women United of Southern California/Southern Nevada* 33 (October 1975).

33. Sylvia Talbot, "Church Women Unite against Poverty," *Together*, the newsletter of the Archdiocese of Anchorage, Alaska, 1988, edited by Virginia L. Peri.

34. Archives: 1225-3-2 CT 108; letter from Frances Kennedy to Bettejane Karnes, Nov. 26, 1993 (Archives).

35. Correspondence between Lorena Pospisil and Carol Barton, 1991 (Archives).

36. Lois Hamer, "The Ecumenical Woman," *State News: Church Women United of Southern California/ Southern Nevada* 38 (Nov. 1979).

37. Millie Moser, *State News: Church Women United of Southern California/ Southern Nevada* 41: 4 (April 1982).

38. Board action, noted in *State News: Church Women United of Southern California/Southern Nevada* 41: 6 (June 1982).

39. CWU History Note, in Finding Aid, Box 64, Archives.

40. *State News: Church Women United of Southern California/Southern Nevada* 40: 6 (April 1981).

41. Archives: 1225-3-2. Alabama, 101.

42. Archives: 1224-4-2:05. Rosa Page Welch account by Laura C. McCray, re CWU and Racism in Tuskegee, Ala., 1957–1959. Workshops on Controversy Folder also includes Interview on June 5, 1974, with Rosa Page Welch, Margaret Shannon, and Elizabeth Haselden, Evanston, Illinois.

43. Kathy Nasstrom, *Everybody's Mother, Nobody's Fool: The Story of Frances Pauley* (Chapel Hill: University of North Carolina Press, 2000).

44. Ibid.

45. Quoted in Hartmann, *The Other Feminists*, p. 92.

46. Ibid., p. 95.

47. See report of Korea trip sponsored by the Partnership with Women Project in which CWU participates fully in *Churchwoman* 4 (2000).

48. See Kansas, Local (Parsons), Archives: 1225-3-2:22.

49. *State News: Church Women United of Southern California/Southern Nevada* 32 (April 1974).

50. Talbot, *Church Women Unite against Poverty.*

51. Ibid.

52. Shannon, *Just Because*, p.169. The poem was written in December 1965.

5

LOCAL ROMAN CATHOLIC AND PROTESTANT ECUMENISM

Arleon L. Kelley

Many Councils of Churches have had a history of Catholic bashing. In my inaugural address as the new executive of the New York State Council of Churches in early 1988, I talked about being inclusive. I spoke of including African American churches, evangelicals, Roman Catholics, Metropolitan Community Churches, and others in the state's ecumenical life. A few days later, one of our officers took me aside and told me in so many words that he made his rather substantial contribution to the Council so we could stand strong against what he saw as a Roman Catholic grab for state money to support their schools, hospitals, and social positions. He would not support a Council that did not support his position. I had a similar thing happen in my experience nearly twenty years earlier. In 1969 I became a part of the initiating staff team for the new Ohio Council of Churches, which included Roman Catholics for the first time. Many Protestants in Ohio were so worried about Roman Catholic efforts to have parochial schoolchildren bused to school and supplied with books that a coalition of those sharing that concern was set up outside the Council. After all, "you can't trust those Roman Catholics." And of course similar feelings prevailed in issues of reproduction and contraception.

Yet, the mid-1960s had ushered in the beginning of a transformation in the American Roman Catholic and Protestant relationship that, in turn, has transformed many ecumenical organizations over the last thirty-five years of the twentieth century. And, in a small way I was privileged to participate in that transformation even before Pope John XXIII convened Vatican II. In the summer of 1961, prior to beginning my doctoral studies at Boston University, I was invited, along with my spouse, to join a twelve-week travel seminar in Europe to study the European rural church movement. While traveling to visit the Waldensians in Northern Italy, Bishop Samuel, a Bishop in the Syrian Mar Toma Church of South India, who was traveling with us, received a communication from his Patriarch telling him that arrangements had been made for him go to Castile del Gondolpho (the Pope's summer residence) to bring the Syrian Mar Toma Church's greetings to the recently elected Pope John XXIII. He was invited to bring five other persons, each from a different denomination, and an interpreter with him. I was one of the five.

The private audience was set for a fifteen-minute period an hour or so before the public audience and mass for the throngs waiting to see the new Pope. We were taken to a room in the undercroft and found him seated with an attending Cardinal at his side. Bishop Samuel proceeded to him with the five of us flanking him. He bowed, read the Patriarch's greeting, and placed a gift from his Church at the Pope's feet. Through our interpreter, Viela Williams (an Italian Waldensian woman married to Welshman Glen Garfield Williams, who later became the Executive of the All European Council of Churches), Pope John expressed his thanks. Then, as Bishop Samuel turned to go, Pope John XXIII called him back and asked each in the group to introduce himself, which we did through our interpreter. As our leader, Dr. Herbert Stotts, expressed our gratitude for being received by the Pope, the attending Cardinal began to usher us out. The Pope spoke sharply to the Cardinal and he replied in kind. (Well, Italian always seems sharp to me!) The Pope then told our interpreter he wanted to ask us some questions. He asked us about our churches (denominations) in the United States and about the religious climate in the United States. Much to the evident consternation of the Cardinal, who kept whispering something to Pope John, we spent nearly forty-five minutes answering his questions. (After we left, we asked our interpreter, Viela, what the Cardinal was saying to the Pope during our conversation. She said the Cardinal was saying, "Get these separated brethren out of here; we have more important things to do." And the Pope was saying to him, "No, these are my friends and I want to talk with them.")

Perhaps it was his curiosity, as well as discussions like this with us and others, that led Pope John XXIII to surprise the Curia and most officialdom of the Roman Catholic Church with a call to convene Vatican II, a council of the Church that was to throw open the windows and let a fresh breeze flow through. One of Vatican II's specific missions was to examine ecumenical relationships. And, of course, the first session of Vatican II began that very process, with many observers and representatives from the Orthodox and Protestant churches invited to be in attendance. Within the first two years after that first session in 1963, the deliberations of Vatican II began to transform the shape of local ecumenical relationships in the United States.

By 1964 conversations were beginning between Roman Catholic leaders and leaders of the Protestant and ecumenical forces in regions such as Appalachia and the Great Plains and in states such as Texas, New Mexico, Oregon, Washington, Montana, and Ohio, and in several cities such as Milwaukee; Worcester, Massachusetts; Houston; and Poughkeepsie, New York. Indeed, New Mexico became the first state in the nation (by two months) to receive Roman Catholics as full members of its Council. Shortly after session one of Vatican II, the Archbishop of the Archdiocese of Santa Fe met with Rev. Harry Summers, then executive secretary of the New Mexico Council of Churches, made formal application for membership, and was received. At that time, the Archdiocese included all of New Mexico. Since that time, two additional dioceses have been created, and they too have become members of the successor organization, the New Mexico Conference of Churches.

Two months after the Santa Fe Archdiocese joined the New Mexico Council of Churches, Texas became the first state with multiple Roman Catholic dioceses to join Protestants in creating a new state ecumenical organization. The new Texas Conference of Churches replaced the former Texas Council of Churches. These may have been among the first local and regional expressions of Protestant and Roman Catholic ecumenism, but they have not been the only ones. A study was completed in 1975 by the Rev. David J. Bowman, S.J., for the National Council of Churches Commission on Regional and Local Ecumenism and the Bishops' Committee on Ecumenical and Interreligious Affairs of the United States Catholic Conference.[1] Of those ecumenical organizations reporting in the study, at least 121 state, metropolitan, county, or city ecumenical instrumentalities had some form of Roman Catholic involvement. In at least 58 ecumenical organizations (45.2 percent) the Roman Catholic Church was a full member.[2] And 109 of the 165 Roman Catholic dioceses in the United States had formed ecumenical commissions.[3] According to the study, some 95 (88 percent) of those 109 dioceses had some sort of continuing relationship with a local or regional ecumenical organization. The first decade after Vatican II revolutionized ecumenical life in the communities of America, and along with it local and regional ecumenical instrumentalities.

One of the reasons for this progress was the spate of "living room dialogues" that were organized in communities across the nation shortly after

Vatican II. Many Roman Catholic and Protestant laypersons were anxious to learn about one another once the official barriers fell. Partly spontaneously, and partly organized by local dioceses, denominational judicatories, and ecumenical organizations, thousands of these meetings took place in homes across America. Study guides were developed, usually for six sessions over six weeks. In many cases these groups continued for some time as prayer and fellowship groups. Some 15 percent of those Roman Catholics and Protestants who came together later in ecumenical organizations indicated that these dialogues were the principal impetus. An equally important reason for coming together was the interest of Roman Catholics and many councils of churches in Faith and Order work (16 percent).[4] Yet, the same study indicated that the most important reason was shared concern about community issues (35.7 percent),[5] and, of course, this impetus of shared concern about community issues tapped into the historic sources of America's local ecumenism from the nineteenth century forward. As has always been true in ecumenical organizations, the respondents and especially the Roman Catholic respondents felt that "there is a tendency to ignore issues where consensus within the ecumenical agency does not exist."[6] The motto of local ecumenism has always seemed to be to "do together what we can and separately what we must." That view makes room for Roman Catholics, just as it had previously for many other diverse Christian groups.

The Bowman study goes on, through a case study method, to detail the historical development from a cross section of sixteen representative places where Roman Catholic and Protestant ecumenism had developed. The sixteen were chosen to be representative of geographic—county, city/metropolitan, and state—spheres of ecumenical experience. The states chosen were Montana and Louisiana; the cities were Kansas City, Louisville, Cincinnati, and Philadelphia; the counties were San Diego, Dutchess (New York), Genesee (New York), and York (Pennsylvania); the metropolitan areas were Charleston, South Carolina, Bridgeport, Connecticut, and South Bend, Indiana. A parish in Southbridge, Massachusetts, and the personal work of one person in Manhattan in New York City were also profiled. In essence each of these places represented a different approach to Roman Catholic and Protestant ecumenical life. No two were initiated the same way, nor did they develop in the same way. Perhaps the only thing they had in common was the vision of one or more people that the churches could work together, even if they could not be one church together.

Indeed, in these sixteen studies, as well as in New Mexico and Texas, the story of how Roman Catholic bishops pursued ecumenical participation and membership or participation in ecumenical agencies was very similar to the story of Bishop James Malone of Youngstown, Ohio.

Pouring New Wine into Old Wineskins

In a videotaped oral history, Bishop James Malone[7] details how he returned from the first session of Vatican II so excited about the new ecumenical possibilities that he began within a few days of his return to search out ways for his diocese to become involved ecumenically. His actions provide insight into how welcoming many of the Roman Catholic leaders, like those in Texas and New Mexico, were to new opportunities for exploration of new relationships with the Protestant churches. After a bit of probing, he felt that the Youngstown Council of Churches probably was not the best place to begin. The Council had a history of being a Protestant bulwark in a predominantly Roman Catholic steelworkers' town. There was too much animosity on both sides. But he then called Dr. John Wilson, executive director of the Ohio Council of Churches, and was told that the Ohio Council had just voted to begin a process of exploring how to reshape its life and that certainly the Roman Catholic dioceses in the state would be welcome to become a part of that conversation. After a year or so of preparation, five dioceses became members of the Ohio Council's Ecumenical Study Commission in 1967 (Steubenville and Cleveland Dioceses refrained).[8]

After another year of formal conversations, the churches in Ohio created a new Ohio Council of Churches on November 12, 1968.[9] By September 1969, Carlton Weber, a United Church of Christ urban church staffer, was elected as the organizing executive. In October 1969, I, as a United Methodist on the staff of the Indiana Council of Churches, joined the organizing staff team, followed in early 1970 by Henry Gerner, a United Methodist serving as the ecumenical campus minister at Bowling Green University. I organized the Council's Division of Church and Community, under the chairmanship of Bishop James Malone, and Dr. Gerner organized the Council's Division of Church and Society. Rev. Robert Greatz, a Lutheran pastor and a leader in the Birmingham bus boycotts, was called as the first director of the Public Policy Commission—later known as Ohio IMPACT. This was the public policy and legislative arm of the Council. Rev. Weber provided overall administrative guidance and staff services for the Faith and Order Commission, which was chaired by Bishop John Burt of the Episcopal Diocese of Ohio (Cleveland).

The organization of the new Ohio Council of Churches, as well as the others where Roman Catholics became a part of ecumenical life, required two conversions. One was the conversion of Protestants to create an openness to accept Roman Catholics and the second was a conversion of Roman Catholics to be open to dealing with Protestants. Br. Jeff Gros observes: "A key element of the decree on ecumenism is conversion, a conversion that implies not only a *metanoia* of all Christian hearts, but also a change of the institutional heart and structure.[10] [Since Vatican II] this conversion theme has become central to an emerging ecumenical literature (and structures), and was a fundamental spiritual motif."[11]

Conversion it was in Ohio, but not generally of the sort experienced by Paul on the Damascus Road, i.e., it was not instantaneous. Rather the conversions occurred through long conversations and careful negotiations. In Ohio the two years of preorganizing negotiations had dealt quite well with such issues as purpose, governance, and representation. They had even dealt with some of the earlier post–World War II dreams of B. F. Lamb, executive director of the old Ohio Council of Churches from 1920 to1951.[12] He had dreamed of the creation of a "Temple of Good Will" in Columbus to house many national denominational headquarters as well as to become the headquarters of the newly proposed National Council of Churches of Christ in the USA. Of course that never materialized because the Rockefeller brothers gave millions of dollars to build an Interchurch Center on Riverside Drive in New York City. But Dr. Lamb had raised millions of dollars through annuities, wills, and gifts for the Temple of Good Will, and these assets were largely invested in downtown Columbus properties—a hotel, several office buildings, a multistory parking garage, parking lots, and others. All parcels related to a master plan for the Temple of Good Will were to be located on the near northwest side of downtown Columbus. The area was to be bordered on the east by High Street with properties on either side of West Spring Street nearly reaching the Olentangy River to the west.[13] How could a new Council be rid of this historic baggage? The solution was for the old Council partners to become stewards of all this through the creation of an Ohio Council of Churches Foundation, with Dr. Wilson as executive—as a retirement job. The Trustees of the Foundation were leaders from the old Council structure. This solution cleared the way to not encumber the new Council while providing for the former leaders to have parts to play.

Another thing that ecumenical agencies, inclusive of Roman Catholics, held in common was early agreement on Christo-centric theological foundations for ecumenical life. For example, the new Ohio Council of Churches envisioned by the Ecumenical Study Commission was based on a

Christo-centric preamble and reaffirmed ecumenical principles that had essentially undergirded that Council for years. Among the items in the purpose statement were the following:

- To enable the Christian Churches of Ohio to realize more fully their essential unity in Christ
- To confront together the needs of the people and churches . . . develop[ing] such cooperative work as will most effectively serve those needs
- To encourage consultation and coordination of effort among the churches of Ohio as they seek to fulfill their common mission
- To assist in the development of ecumenical agencies in the counties, cities, and communities of Ohio
- To maintain a mutually helpful relationship with such ecumenical agencies throughout the state, nation, and world[14]

In most every place where Roman Catholics actually became a part of formal ecumenical life, there were great celebrations designed to dramatize a new day and a new way of being Christian together. Perhaps in no place was it more dramatic than at the spectacular celebration of Roman Catholic official full membership in the Ohio Council of Churches on Pentecost, May 18, 1970. It began in the morning. The congregations of all denominations across the state joined in a common litany of prayer for the new endeavor.[15] This made it a shared experience involving the hundreds of thousands of Christians across the state, with the Pentecost celebration to be held later that day in Columbus. The event was highlighted by a colorful ecumenical procession through the heart of Columbus as officials and delegations from local, state, and national church bodies joined in the Ohio Festival of Ecumenical Witness. The *Ohio Christian News* described it this way:

> Two 7:00 P.M. parades, one Protestant (originating from the Episcopal Cathedral), one Roman Catholic (originating from the Roman Catholic Cathedral), representing two historic streams of the Church, merged into one amid colorful banners and church college marching bands while some 2,000 delegates from churches across the state processed the one mile from St. Joseph's Cathedral past the State Capitol to the Veterans Memorial Auditorium. . . . Participating in the 8:00 P.M. festival were [a whole host of ecclesiastical, state, and community dignitaries are listed].[16]

It was a time of ecumenical euphoria. The occasion dramatized a new day and a new birth!

However, reality has ways of bringing euphoric times back to earth. There may have been a conversion in acceptance, but organizational practice is always another matter entirely. In Ohio, as in other places, the institutional culture and decision-making processes among Protestants have always been very diverse and often unique to a given tradition. For example, Presbyterians work by a very rational committee process, while African American churches work much more under the direction of a significant leader. Councils had learned to deal with those differences to some extent, but the process within the Roman Catholic dioceses was still different again.[17] Roman Catholics were not accustomed to diverse patterns of decision making. Differences in how work gets done and decisions get made became very evident in a hurry. Within the first year of the new Ohio Council's operations, it faced a crisis in dealing with public policy. It soon became clear that even though the Protestants had thought they had negotiated a single public policy and lobbying office for all the Christian faith groups in Ohio, there were forces in the Roman Catholic Church that felt they needed the Ohio Catholic Conference (which was the Roman Catholic lobbying arm) to continue. In the first place, two dioceses were not even members of the Council, and further, they felt the Council could not effectively lobby for the parochial schools, for the busing of parochial pupils, or for support for social service agencies, such as Catholic charities or Catholic hospitals.

And that was true for a number of reasons. In the first place the Council did not see itself as a "trade association lobby." It was an advocate for "good government," for community well-being, and for those who had no voice, for example, for persons living in poverty who had poor or no housing, for migrants, and for a whole host of environmental, health, economic, religious liberty, and other justice issues. Issues of parochial schools, busing of parochial pupils, or support for social service agencies really were lobbying issues. The negotiations that led to the formation of the Council had said that the Council was to advocate only for those issues where there was an agreed-upon public policy. Many of the Protestants felt that meant there would be no legislative advocacy on issues where there was not agreement. Both Protestants and Roman Catholics felt the inadequacy. After a consultation between the Council and the Ohio Catholic Conference, a compromise was reached—to work together where agreement was possible, with the Catholic Conference lobbying for issues where there was not agreement.

Almost immediately this forced two things to happen among the Protestant constituency in Ohio. One good, one less good. In the area of the "education of the public," busing and support of parochial students was opposed by most of the Protestant denominations in Ohio. The United Presbyterian Church in the Cleveland area developed a coalition on public education outside the Council to generally work from the Protestant perspective. Its staff person was Joan Brown Campbell. Although the coalition's work was good, it was not what the Ohio Council of Churches needed at the time to consolidate its Roman Catholic and Protestant mandate. The Council did not oppose the coalition's work and assisted it with mailing lists, etc., but the better solution the Council pursued was to "drive the conversation upward"—that is, a panel of educational specialists and interested persons from both the Roman Catholic and Protestant church constituencies was convened. It developed a comprehensive policy paper on the "public and its education," which decried the lack of positive values in the normal educational process, as well as the lack of quality educational opportunities for all in the public system and particularly in the central cities. In so doing, the Roman Catholic/Protestant team was able to move beyond busing and the rights of parochial students to find common ground and to forge a consensus around concerns for underserved inner-city youth and the lack of values in the educational process. It proposed the development of an experimental curriculum in values education and worked with Wright State University in Dayton to develop the curriculum. Then, through the Council and local Dayton ecumenical efforts, Protestants joined with Roman Catholics to turn a financially failing parochial school in inner-city Dayton into a demonstration school both for how to work with underprivileged children and as a demonstration site for Wright State's work on values education.

This experiment became one of the sources of the values education movement that developed quickly across America in the early 1970s. Thus, because of the inability of Protestants and Roman Catholics to agree on traditional educational public policy issues, a new sphere of educational creativity was developed.[18] And over the longer haul, through careful consultation, the Council learned how to carefully coordinate the Council's public policy work with the social issues work as well as the lobbying work of the Ohio Catholic Conference's public policy work. Consequently, there were few surprises. This coordination probably would not have happened had there not been a new Council of Churches that included Roman Catholics.

This experience in Ohio of pouring new wine into old wineskins was in no way unique. For example, similar difficulties had emerged in New Mexico around how to deal with controversial social issues where there was no agreement, like abortion and busing. Eventually, the New Mexico Conference of Churches formalized the consultation process into a protocol. As now-retired Executive Secretary Rev. Wallace Ford describes the process:

> As the New Mexico Conference of Churches was living into its new program design and re-commitments on the part of the judicatory leaders, after [its second] reorganization in 1982, the Faith and Order Working Group became clear that ethical and moral differences existing between the member churches posed a potential for (1) causing ruptures within the ecumenical covenant or (2) keeping the theological dialogue severely "boundaried." Especially after a three-year study of "Baptism, Eucharist and Ministry" the NMCC became increasingly convinced that all faith symbols, actions, rituals, and sacraments contained an inescapable ethical dimension which required exploration as much as the classical theological agenda of Faith and Order. In addition, public policy advocacy brought the member judicatories into sharp contrast with each other on particular ethical issues. This contrast was vividly demonstrated when the Archbishop of Santa Fe and the Bishop of the Episcopal Diocese of the Rio Grande, good, long-term friends, testified on opposite sides of instituting health clinics in the public schools, clinics which would dispense sex educational materials.
>
> The NMCC Board of Directors requested that the Faith and Order Working Group explore how ethical and moral differences could be examined within the ecumenical covenant. The Working Group (WG) began its study by looking at a variety of models using conflict resolution methodologies. The members affirmed the importance of moving from zero-sum conditions to win-win dialogue. They also identified some key components of conflict resolution that could be useful to the NMCC and to judicatories seeking to mediate their differences.
>
> Yet there was a certain dissatisfaction with the study. The WG perceived it lacked an ecclesial component and returned to an examination of scriptural texts, seeking to discover what might be learned from the early churches' experience with conflict. From a study of the first Council of the Church as recorded in Acts 15, it became apparent that ethical differences were at the heart of the controversy threatening to split the fellowship of the churches. Looking closely at how that Council turned out, key insights began to emerge indicating how it was possible to affirm common ground in the midst of strong controversy.
>
> Based on these discoveries, the WG developed a protocol that could be used for mediating ethical and moral differences. The protocol in-

cluded steps to be taken, beginning with the NMCC identifying an issue in which there are serious differences existing among and/or within the member judicatories, then authorizing a task force to prepare a study that includes presenting the various perspectives, warrants used for the perspectives, common ground shared by the perspectives, and possible resolution or identification of themes for further study. The complete protocol document can be secured from the NMCC.

To date, the protocol has been used with a number of controversial issues: abortion, end-of-life issues, violence, capitol punishment, ordination, human sexuality, and land use. While the protocol does not have the capacity to change the doctrinal positions of the member churches, it does give the regional ecumenical movement an opportunity to conduct serious conversations about difficult moral issues without tearing the covenantal fabric.[19]

The Work of Ecumenism in Every Community

The practice of ecumenism in this new day of Roman Catholic and Protestant ecumenism not only found new ways to deal with fundamental differences by "driving the conversation upward," it also "drove the conversation downward" in many of the states and regions. It did this by focusing on "horizontal" relationships among the churches in each "place." A whole movement emerged across the nation of developing substate ecumenical life, complementing that historically found in counties and cities. For example, in New Mexico and Ohio that work was begun in the early 1970s with the identification of several substate regions called "functional human communities."[20] Even in Massachusetts where the Roman Catholic and Protestant relationships went quite a different route by the formation of a joint Commission on Christian Unity, leaving the integrity of the historic Protestant council intact, the Council itself had full-time staff who related to and often initiated the formation of substate regional ecumenical organizations that included Roman Catholics—as in Springfield and Worcester. The rather common approach was to convene representatives of local churches and judicatory executives responsible in that area for the purpose of evaluating and reflecting on the life and mission of the church in their area. From this reflection they were then invited to discern and finally develop a common plan of action for their functional area. The NMCC later called these Regional Divisions of the Conference of Churches. There, and in Indiana, Massachusetts, Pennsylvania, and Iowa, and to a lesser degree in several other states, this became an important part of how inclusive ecumenism was developed in each place within each state.

A similar pattern had developed in Ohio even preceding the formation of the new inclusive Council. Most ecumenical organizations in Ohio had roots in traditional Councils of Churches or urban ministries, with an often typical anti-Catholic bias. By the mid-1960s several regional entities had been formed. Among them were the Church World Service/CROP program (with both county and hundreds of local units); the Regional Church Planning Office (RCPO) in Cleveland; the Northeast Ohio Regional Church Planning (NEORCP) in the Akron, Canton, and Youngstown area; the Toledo Metropolitan Ministry (TMM) in Toledo; the Cleveland Urban Ministry; and the Southwest Regional Church Planning (SWORCP) for the Cincinnati, Dayton, and Springfield area of Ohio. Ohio CROP was the largest in the nation, under the leadership of Clyde Rogers and Margaret Brugler, while the regional planning offices were nurtured by Rev. Thomas Kalshoven, one-time director of Research and Planning for OCC, prior to its reorganization in 1968. As in some other states, these were historically Protestant, but became the building blocks for a regional/local ecumenical strategy inclusive of Roman Catholics.

At about the same time the new Ohio Council was being formed, Cincinnati, Toledo, and Columbus were each developing ecumenical vehicles inclusive of Roman Catholics and often modeled more along the lines of an Urban Ministry[21] or a Joint Strategy and Action Committee (JSAC)[22] than a traditional council of churches. In Cincinnati, Cleveland, and Toledo, a parallel traditional council continued for a few years. In Dayton a new vehicle was created, designed to be open to Roman Catholics, but initially with no Roman Catholic participation. The Youngstown Council of Churches remained predominantly Protestant.[23] By the mid-1960s Rev. Byron (Bud) White was instrumental in organizing in Cleveland the Westside Ecumenical Ministries, an early community ministry composed of dozens of local parishes, inclusive of Roman Catholics. On the other hand, the Cleveland Council of Churches did not include Roman Catholics. Membership in WSEM was by parish decision. Membership in the Cleveland Council, as in the Ohio Council of Churches, was by action of the Cleveland Roman Catholic Diocese, and that was not forthcoming.

Because of all this substate ecumenical activity it was decided when the new Ohio Council was formed that one of its two organizational divisions would be the Division of Church and Community. Its purpose was to ensure that every functional human community in Ohio had an ecumenical strategy and that that strategy could be linked to statewide strategies. The Division's mandate was to begin with links to each of these above-mentioned metropolitan and local ecumenical instrumentalities in Ohio.[24] In the areas where there was little or no ecumenical activity, such as in many rural areas of Ohio, it was the role of the Division to work with local church and judicatory leaders to initiate such. And it was a priority of the Division's work to assist the movement of local and regional ecumenical structures to be inclusive of not only Roman Catholics but also of women and ethnic persons. Inclusion of Roman Catholic, African American, and Greek Orthodox churches was not seen as an end in itself, but as an essential component in involving all the stakeholders in defining the ecumenical mission in new and creative ways. The member churches of the Council represented 11,000 congregations composed of almost exactly 50 percent of the Ohio population by the 1970s,[25] and it was felt that people of faith could join together in common cause to become a powerful force for good in Ohio.

Theological and Faith Work

As in Ohio, another common area of work in nearly all new conciliar structures inclusive of Roman Catholics was Faith and Order work. The Faith and Order work in Ohio and New Mexico and especially in Texas was very important to the vitality of ecumenical life. As mentioned above, Ohio's Faith and Order Commission was initially chaired by Bishop John Burt of the Episcopal Diocese of Ohio. He was based in Cleveland and was active in the urban issues of that area as well as being a prime mover in the Youngstown effort to retain the steel mills (chronicled elsewhere in this book). So Faith and Order work under his leadership not only dealt with the great theological issues but also with the vexing issues of the day—race, diversity, and poverty. Perhaps New Mexico became among the most effective in linking its Faith and Order work with its public policy work, as well as in effective local community action. The Protocol described earlier is one product linking faith work with societal mission work.

In Texas, Faith and Order activity became its most effective area of work. Indeed it has defined the Texas Conference of Churches. Its annual Faith and Order conference has been a highlight of its work for many years. By the late 1980s significant work was done by Executive Director Rev. Frank Dietz to make the link between Faith and Order work and public social policy and action. During those years the Texas Conference of Churches enjoyed a good degree of success with this integration. Yet, it also created controversy among some members who wished to reserve all witness for the individual member denominations. Eventually, Rev. Dietz resigned, and while the Faith and Order work has continued as a centerpiece of the Conference's work, it has been separated from the social dimension—probably to the detriment of the ecumenical witness in Texas. (I say this because almost the only thing that all state ecumenical instrumentalities have "given" them as a discrete function is public policy, and by the end of the 1990s Texas was pulling away from that unique area of witness.)

New Mexico, along with other places, has also had an effective spiritual formation program. It holds annual retreats for judicatory leaders and has developed regular work with spiritual life directors and others. One of the most exciting formation activities to develop in New Mexico as well as in Washington state ecumenism (also inclusive of Roman Catholics) has been the development of ecumenical schools of theology. Both New Mexico and Washington (Seattle) have been largely isolated from traditional theological institutions. Because of a shortage of ordained clergy, both were experiencing a need for a means of preparing people in lay ministry. In the Roman Catholic Church, the shortage of priests meant that there was a great need to prepare lay deacons to assist in parish ministry. And, of course, many of the Protestant churches had depended on lay pastors for years. In New Mexico, the NMCC formed an ecumenical board to design a way to ecumenically meet these needs in both English and Spanish. In 1997, the initial year, the school met throughout the winter in several of the regional centers across the state. The New Mexico school was able to enroll a hundred or more students in the first year. It used local, trained clergy and professors from nearby colleges as the instructors, and their qualifications were such that the school was initially accredited by Chicago's DePaul University extension education. In Seattle, an ecumenical board, created by the Washington Association of Churches and the Seattle Church Council, decided to locate graduate theological education in one place. It developed and located a graduate theological education department in the Jesuit's Seattle University. By the end of the millennium it had enrolled more than two hundred students, many of them pursuing a fully accredited Master of Divinity degree.

In addition to these general areas of work, all the Roman Catholic and Protestant agencies have undertaken unique forms of public Faith Expression ecumenical work. Rev. Carlton Weber's history of the Ohio Council indicates that over the thirty-two years since the Ohio Council was formed there have been a great number of effective Faith Expression activities. Weber lists the following: Week of Prayer for Christian Unity; Ohio Pastor's

Convocation; Weekday Released Time Religious Education; Church Women United; Church World Service/CROP; Faith and Order Commission; Theologian in Residence; Key 73; Holy Scriptures (in coordination with the issuance of the New Revised Standard Version of the Bible by the NCCC/USA); Fabric of Ecumenism (to dramatize the fabric of ecumenical relationships); Values in Public Education; Ecumenical Youth Ministry at the Ohio State Fair; worship services at the Ohio State Fair; leisure time ministries in twenty-four of the state and county parks; chaplains in state institutions; campus ministries (through the Ohio Board for United Ministries in Higher Education); interseminary conferences; faith responses to natural disasters; and many ecumenical continuing education opportunities for clergy and laypersons across Ohio.[26] Many of these programs were annual events. And the other councils had a similar diversity of programming. Indeed one of the greatest criticisms of these organizations has been that they try to do too much.[27]

In a study done by Dr. Gary Peluso in 1993, 94 of the 177 respondents to a questionnaire indicated that their organization's median basic program and core budget was between $125,000 and $150,000. But more than a quarter of the respondents worked with organizations with budgets over $300,000 per year, and several of those were over $1 million, the largest being $4.5 million.[28] But the question remains, How could all this be done with such limited resources? In Ohio the annual core OCC budget has usually been between $300,000 and $400,000. The answer is twofold. First, many of these activities were funded by outside grants and fees. The second answer is that Weber estimates that from 400 to 800 volunteers were used each year to plan and implement the programs.[29] This Council, like so many, has become an organization owned by a lot of people. Conciliar ecumenism is almost always a resource multiplier.

Other Expressions of Roman Catholic, Orthodox, and Protestant Ecumenical Organization

Conciliar ecumenism was not the only form that Roman Catholic, Protestant, and Orthodox life took. For example, in Pennsylvania, Massachusetts, and Indiana an additional "super" organization was formed rather than Roman Catholics joining an existing reshaped ecumenical structure. In the northeast, the rationale was that the Roman Catholic membership was so large that if it joined a state ecumenical structure, it would overwhelm the Protestant voice. So in Massachusetts, the Massachusetts Commission on

Christian Unity was formed. The Rev. Gordon White, an Episcopal priest, has been its staff person since its inception. The Commission has been an effective forum for Roman Catholics, Protestants, and Orthodox churches to work together, particularly on things that relate to civility among people of faith and a variety of faith-related issues. For example, over the years the Commission has issued guideline papers on marriage as well as on prayer among persons of different Christian faith traditions. It has also undertaken studies of a variety of theological issues related to the World Council of Churches Baptism, Eucharist, and Ministry study, as well as pertinent issues related to race, culture, and the like. In a very real sense this Commission has become a national resource, especially for inter-Christian etiquette.

The Pennsylvania Conference on Interchurch Cooperation was initiated through the efforts of Cardinal Krol (Philadelphia) and the Rev. Albert Myers of the Pennsylvania Council of Churches. It had been staffed since its inception until his retirement in 1997 by Rev. Myers, who also served concurrently as the executive of the Pennsylvania Council of Churches. The attitudes, especially in the eastern part of Pennsylvania, were similar to those in Massachusetts: If the Roman Catholics, Eastern Rite, and other affiliated churches were to join the State Council, it would overwhelm the Protestant voice. (This view did not prevail in the Pittsburgh and Erie area dioceses, for they were founding members of at least two regional ecumenical organizations there.) So the proposed Roman Catholic alternative was for the Pennsylvania Council of Churches to create and host a new super ecumenical organization inclusive of Roman Catholic churches (of several rites), Orthodox churches of several ethnic origins, and the Protestant churches. The Conference has been an effective "brass roots" expression of ecumenism, being composed of the top denominational leaders. Over the years the Conference has been a place for theological consultation, as well as a place to work together on social concerns, interchurch planning, and disaster response. It has also been a source of much educational activity through conferences and seminars. The Conference has no ongoing staff beyond that provided by the executive of the Pennsylvania Council of Churches and voluntary staffing provided by the partner judicatories. Nonetheless, the Conference has become a solid source of interchurch cooperation among partners who have heretofore often been separated, if not alienated, from one another.

Indiana went in still another direction. The leadership of the Indiana Council of Churches was not ready in 1966 to invite Roman Catholic participation, and the Roman Catholics were not ready to participate. But for the national Human Equality and Housing Justice programs there were ready respondents. In 1967 the Indiana Commission on Human Equality (ICHE) was born. It was formed in part under the leadership of Dr. Grover Hartman, Executive Director of the Indiana Council of Churches. From the beginning it was composed of Roman Catholics, Protestants, and parts of the Jewish community. It had a very highly focused initial mandate related to racial equality and just housing for all. The Commission continued for more than two decades under the leadership of such persons as Rev. Thomas Quigley and Mrs. Robert Green. It developed a number of programs related to mentoring people in the workplace and seminars to confront and reconcile racial, religious, and class conflict, as well as a variety of approaches to providing housing for all.

Transition in Protestant and Roman Catholic Ecumenism since Vatican II

There has been a significant transition from an insular Roman Catholic Church in America to a highly involved Church. The number of ecumenical instrumentalities with full Roman Catholic participation has steadily grown over the thirty-five-year period since Vatican II. The Bowman study in 1975 identified 121 organizations with at least some Roman Catholic involvement and at least 58 with full Roman Catholic membership. The study also identified 109 of the 165 Roman Catholic dioceses that had ecumenical commissions. A survey completed in May 1990 by the Bishops' Committee on Ecumenical and Interreligious Affairs, the U.S. Catholic Conference, found that 75 of the now 179 dioceses in the United States were full members of 34 state councils of churches. Another 28 archdioceses indicated that they were members of regional and local councils of churches. And most of the archdioceses indicated that their clergy were members of ministerial associations and that local congregations were members of local councils of churches or community ministries.[30] So the last thirty-five years have seen ever greater involvement and investment of Roman Catholics in local ecumenical life.

But there are other sorts of transitions that have proven organizationally difficult and have become issues in each of the states mentioned above. For example, the transition in professional ecumenical staff has had a profound effect—most likely because the professional leader is often key to ecumenical life. Grover Hartman observed: "Another conclusion rooted in survey findings is the importance of the ecumenical executive. Where the agencies are showing vitality and relevance we generally find a committed, theologically well-grounded and charismatic leader."[31]

In Texas, Harold Kilpatrick left almost immediately after the formation of the Conference of Churches. He was followed briefly by a Roman Catholic priest and then by Rev. James Suggs, a member of the Disciples of Christ, who was able to firmly root the conference in the judicatories. Rev. Frank Dietz, a pastor in the United Church of Christ, became the next director, and he, as noted above, helped the conference begin translating its Faith and Order work into social ministry and witness, to the consternation of some. When Rev. Dietz resigned, the Conference called Rev. Dr. Carol Worthing as the new executive director, a pastor in the Evangelical Lutheran Church of America who came to her new post with extensive experience as the executive of the Illinois Council of Churches. Dr. Worthing has continued the Faith and Order tradition and has also been somewhat successful in helping the conference continue a limited program of social witness. Her gifts are in administration, theology, and resource utilization. After some time, the conference began to reflect those gifts. Throughout the conference's history with the change of leadership there come different gifts. If the gifts of the leader and the organization fit, life is abundant. When it doesn't match, or there is intransigence, the organization suffers.

This point can be more fully developed in the transitions in the Ohio Council of Churches. In 1992 Rev. Weber retired. After a period during which a long-time senior staff person in the Council served as the interim director, the Rev. Debra Moody, a pastor in the African Methodist Church, Zion (AMEZ), was elected as the next executive. Her leadership led to significant transition in the council for a variety of reasons. First, she succeeded a long-term founding executive director who had given very close administrative supervision for more than twenty-two years. Rev. Moody's administrative style was very different. And she often found the staff to be less than supportive—eventually having to deal with at least two lawsuits. At the same time, she, more so than Rev. Weber, was a very public person. Loyalty to the institution needed to be demonstrated by loyalty to her, but this sort of loyalty was not easily transferable. These style changes gave "permission" for all parts of the organization to question traditional commitments and to change.

Secondly, Rev. Moody came to the Council at the time when the member communions were seriously reassessing their financial capabilities—not just in Ohio, but in most middle judicatories throughout the nation. The result was a funding crunch. The monies committed to the core budget began to diminish, not necessarily because the denominational commitment diminished, but because middle judicatory money was drying up. And, of course, a change in leadership is often an opportunity for denominations to reassess their commitments and the council to rethink its life. It became a smaller and perhaps a more focused organization. About this time Rev. Moody resigned to accept the proposal of marriage to the Christian Methodist Episcopal Bishop, Richard O. Bass.

The process the Ohio Council went through under Rev. Moody's leadership is not unusual for an ecumenical organization after the long tenure of one executive. But it is an experience a bit foreign to Roman Catholic ecclesiology, although not to its eleemosynary social agencies. The good thing was that the Roman Catholic leadership in the council stuck with their commitments even as the changes occurred.

Upon Rev. Moody's departure, an interim was called, ELCA Bishop Robert Kelley of the Youngstown area. Bishop Kelley had not been re-elected because of age. He had a long history of participation with the council, both under Rev. Weber's leadership and that of Rev. Moody. He brought ecclesial stature. He spent a great deal of time listening and sharing what he was hearing, and eventually a consultation of the denominations was called where renewed directions for ecumenism in Ohio were agreed upon. These directions built firmly on the previous foundations, but also focused the Council more narrowly so that the smaller available resources could meet the organizational objectives. The Rev. Rebecca Tollefson, a Presbyterian pastor with extensive ecumenical and denominational program experience, was then called as executive director.

One of the difficult issues has been how to recruit Roman Catholics into professional ecumenical leadership positions. There have been several to be sure; but overall Roman Catholic leaders have been in short supply, or have not stayed in their positions very long. For example, Roosevelt Carter was Director of Communications for the Metropolitan Church Board of Columbus for about two years and then left for a significantly better job in television. A Roman Catholic laywoman was associate director of public policy for the Ohio Council of Churches for three years, then left for a good job with a state elected official. A Roman Catholic priest became the director of the Texas Conference of Churches after Mr. Kilpatrick, but soon found that his bishop needed him back in his home diocese. The Rev. Henry A. Atwell became the executive director of the Genesee Ecumenical Ministries in Rochester, New York. He was effective, but found that his bishop had other responsibilities for him after a year or so. Several women have had professional leadership roles, like Sr. Sylvia Schmidt in Tulsa. She was able to nurture the Tulsa Metropolitan Ministry into a very effective and large interfaith organization. And indeed, she is one of a few Roman Catholic priests or sisters who have served a long term of office with a local or regional ecumenical organization since Vatican II. There have been several long-term Roman Catholic laypersons.

These same stories could be told about Louisiana and many other places across the nation. But the same difficulty in continuity of leadership and vision is seen when the founding ecclesiastical leaders retire or are transferred to a new post in another state. When there is a generational or founding leadership shift, an ecumenical organization can find itself with greatly changed patterns of support—sometimes even finding its existence threatened. Kansas City is a case in point—with the story repeated all too often in other places. The Metropolitan Interchurch Agency of Greater Kansas City (MICA) was born out of the Kansas City Council of Churches with dreams of something more inclusive and far grander by Dr. Randolph (Randy) Thornton (former executive of the Kansas City Council of Churches), the first MICA executive, Bishop Charles Helmsing (RC), and Episcopal priest Rev. Elton Smith, among others. They imagined an organization of the highest judicatories of the churches working together for the social and spiritual well-being of the community. It was not long before Dr. Thornton moved on, leaving MICA in the hands of Rev. James Leffingwell, one of the staff associates. Things continued to go well for a time until Rev. Smith moved to become the pastor and dean of a large downtown cathedral parish in Buffalo, New York. That move and the loss of one or two more of the original visionaries caused a crisis in vision, if not in leadership. Rev. Leffingwell found the support of the organization declining and the social witness fragmenting, and eventually an agreement was made that MICA could not issue any statements unless they were unanimous. Newcomers to the cabinet (the administrative mechanism) did not know the original dream or remember the original agreements.[32] And as a consequence of the growing fragmentation, within a decade of its founding MICA was dissolved.

Yet, for every case where Roman Catholic and Protestant ecumenism has failed there are many more cases that have flourished. In a conversation with Br. Jeffrey Gros, associate on the staff of the Bishops' Committee on Ecumenical and Interreligious Affairs, it was pointed out that Roman Catholic involvement with local and regional ecumenical life continues to grow, particularly at the parish level. Gros's surveys of 1997 and 1998 would seem to bear this out.

Roman Catholic and Protestant ecumenism blossomed on the heels of Vatican II. It largely succeeded in finding effective ways of adjustment to new ways of being and living together. It has now found its stride and the relationships are assumed as normal operating procedure. Roman Catholics have taught Protestants "spiritual ecumenism," i.e., the spirit that binds us to one another. Protestants have shared something of their spirit of action. Both have benefited from the other, and so has the witness of the church in this secular society. The inclusion of Roman Catholics in local and regional ecumenism has been one of the success stories of the last fifty years.

Notes

1. Rev. David J. Bowman, S.J., *U.S. Catholic Ecumenism: Ten Years Later* (New York and Washington, DC: jointly published by the National Council of Churches Commission on Regional and Local Ecumenism [CORLE] and the Bishops' Committee for Ecumenical and Interreligious Affairs, 1975).
2. Ibid., p. 10.
3. Ibid., p. 13.
4. Ibid., p. 10.
5. Ibid., pp. 10–11. The galvanizing community issues were identified as religion and the public schools, clergy education, criminal justice matters, the Holy Year, abortion, housing, the aged, welfare, chaplaincy, and prison reform.
6. Ibid., p. 11.
7. Bishop James Malone, retired bishop of the Youngstown Dioceses of the Roman Catholic Church, a former president of the U.S. Roman Catholic Bishops' Conference, former president of the Ohio Council of Churches, and co-chair of the Roman Catholic and United Methodist Bilateral in the 1970s and 1980s. Videotaped interview in Bishop Malone's home by Arleon L. Kelley in fall 1998. The tape is in the Grover Hartman Archives located at the Christian Theological Seminary library in Chicago.
8. Carlton N. Weber, *Searching for the Church's Oneness: Ecumenism in Ohio, 1968–1992* (Columbus: Ohio Council of Churches, 1993), p. 3.
9. Ibid.
10. Br. Jeffery Gros, *Reception and Roman Catholicism for the 1990s* (a paper available from the Christian Unity Office of the National Conference of Catholic Bishops, Washington, DC), p. 1.
11. Ibid. See Ladislaus Orsy, "The Conversion of the Churches: Condition of Unity," *America* 166, 19 (May 30, 1992): 479–487; Groupe des Dombes, *Pour la Conversion des Eglises* (Paris: Centurion, 1991); "Conversion," *Ecumenical Review* 44, 4 (October 1992).
12. Ross W. Sanderson, *B. F. Lamb: Ecumenical Pioneer* (Columbus: Ohio Council of Churches, 1964), pp. 165–173.
13. Ibid. See site pictures between pp. 207 and 209.
14. Weber, *Searching for the Church's Oneness*, pp. 7–8.
15. Ibid., pp. 49–50, for the text of the litany.

16. Ibid., pp. 48–49.

17. Gros, *Reception and Roman Catholicism for the 1990s*, p. 9, observes the following: "Almost all of the participants in the ecumenical movement presume 'ecumenism' to be the most positive when the partner is most like oneself. The rules of behavior and perceptions of ecumenical agencies, even international gatherings, tend to be formed by the dominant culture. Thus, in the Anglo-American world, there is an expectation that parliamentary procedures will best serve these gatherings, when it may be a foreign way of decision making to some churches and therefore inherently marginalizing for them. Presbyterians and Methodists will always be at an advantage over Orthodox or African American churches, procedurally, in councils where Roberts' Rules are used. . . . When procedures and processes are open to Roman Catholic styles of doing things and the Catholics are sensitive to the procedures of the other churches, a certain mutual reception is demonstrated. On the other hand, one understands quite well when a particular church or group of churches, like the United Methodist—which provides close to half the budget of the US National Council of Churches and would be the largest delegation in any ecumenical event, until Catholics began to be present—or the classical Protestant churches, Methodist, Reformed, Episcopal, Disciples, United Church and American Baptist, have to make some rather radical adjustments when the large, diverse and often quite well organized Catholic delegation begins to gain parity with them in ecumenical gatherings. In places like the planning committee of the National Workshop on Christian Unity great care has to be taken to avoid 1) Catholic domination, especially in coalition with Anglo-Catholic and Lutheran elements; and 2) treating all churches, of whatever size and participation (or lack thereof), with equal voice, to maintain a Protestant agenda as primary."

18. Ibid., pp. 144–150. Weber takes the broader view on public education in his text. The above-mentioned incident comes from the author's recollection of an early approach in 1970–1971.

19. This account was prepared for this chapter by Dr. Wallace Ford, former executive secretary of the New Mexico Conference of Churches. Dr. Ford lives in Albuquerque, New Mexico.

20. Arleon L. Kelley, ed., *Foundations for Ecumenical Mission: The Ecumenical Response to Regionalization in the Church* (New York: Regionalization Study Team, Commission on Regional and Local Ecumenism, National Council of Churches of Christ in the USA, January 1974), p. 20.

21. Urban Ministries flourished following the turmoil in cities during the 1960s. Essentially they were designed to mobilize denominational and congregational resources to deal with systemic urban issues—usually through training, advocacy, confrontation, creation of new housing, working with the poor, etc. These were not settlement houses or hand-out centers, although in some locations some of those activities may have been undertaken.

22. Joint Strategy and Action Committees (JSACs) involved a table for denominational mission and social response peers to communicate, plan, and coordinate funding. These tables were developed in many city, metropolitan, and state areas, as well as in the national sphere. These tables usually operated with seconded staff from one or more member denominations. They were a prevalent and effective phenomenon from 1965 through the late 1980s. United Methodist Norman E. (Ned) Dewire pioneered the concept in Detroit and went on to head the national JSAC network located at 475 Riverside Drive in New York City for about a decade.

23. See videotape "L" for interviews with people in Youngstown, Ohio: Bishop James Malone and Ms. Elsie Dursi, executive director of the Mahoning Valley and

pastor. These videotapes are in the Archives at the Christian Theological Seminary Library in Indianapolis.

24. Some of these regional entities in Ohio had been created partly in response to the National Council of Churches' programmatic response to the urban crisis.

25. Kelley, *Foundations for Ecumenical Mission*, p. 8.

26. Ibid., pp. 54–88.

27. Ecumenical organizations provide a big tent. Their constituencies are diverse and have a myriad of interests. One way an ecumenical organization maintains ownership for its varied constituencies is to develop programs that appeal to this diversity of interests. A focused agenda often meets the needs of the few at the expense of the many.

28. Gary Peluso, principal investigator, from page 9 of an unpublished survey presented to the National Association of Ecumenical Staff (NAES), June 5, 1993. The survey is a small part of Dr. Peluso's Lilly Foundation Funded Study of Local and Regional Ecumenical and Interreligious Organizations (Indianapolis: 1993–1994). This study also included site visits to the Illinois Conference of Churches; Northern California Ecumenical Council and Ecumenical Ministries in Northern California; Georgia Christian Council; Christian Council of Metropolitan Atlanta; Associated Ministries of Pierce County (Tacoma); Seattle Church Council; Washington Association of Churches; Southern California Ecumenical Council–Los Angeles; Wisconsin Conference of Churches; and the Indiana Council of Churches. This list is composed from site visit summaries from NAES. It probably included others, because there are no northeastern ecumenical organizations in the above list.

29. Ibid., Dedication, p. i.

30. Unpublished paper, "A Survey of Roman Catholic Archdioceses' Participation in Conferences of Churches" (Bishops' Committee on Ecumenical and Interreligious Affairs, U.S. Catholic Conference, Washington, DC: January 1990), p. 1. It was noted that in ten of the many states with multiple dioceses all dioceses were members: Arizona, Connecticut, Illinois, Kentucky, Michigan, Montana, New Mexico, North Carolina, Texas, and Washington.

31. Unpublished paper, Dr. Grover Hartman, "Lilly Endowment Survey/Evaluation of Regional and Local Ecumenism in the United States" (Indianapolis), p. 5. The research was conducted from November 1983 to March 1984.

32. Bowman, *U.S. Catholic Ecumenism,* p. 23.

6

LOCAL INTERFAITH ECUMENISM: BUFFALO AND SYRACUSE AS CASE STUDIES

Charles R. White

Most anyone reflecting on the history of local ecumenism in the United States during the last fifty years of the twentieth century will inevitably understand what is meant by both ecumenical and ecumenism (from the Greek *oikumene,* the whole inhabited world). Much writing about this period presumes a model more or less reflective of the Edinburgh Conference of 1910, when representatives of many (but not Roman Catholic) missionary societies met, seeking to "explore the nature of mission and the ways to overcome debilitating divisions"[1] within Christendom. Yet, during these years there can also be seen a movement toward "a 'wider ecumenism,' one which would explore the relations between religions."[2] Commonly, this later movement is referred to as the interfaith movement, and it is increasingly multifaith, having present in some form three or more distinct world religions in its components. Whether these are two asymmetrical movements or a single phenomenon being expressed in different ways is a question beyond the scope of this chapter. Nevertheless, the presence of both dimensions has been a source of lively discussion and sometimes continuing contention within religious life, especially wherever the increasingly pluralistic North American society is most evident.

By 1950 there was growing recognition that the United States was Protestant, Catholic, and Jewish in its principal religious populations.[3] Yet, this diversity reflected the exclusionary policy existing in U.S. immigration law that had precluded Asians from moving to this country since the 1880s.[4] The experiences written about here would probably never have occurred in this country had it not been for the 1965 Immigration Act, which began to undo the racism institutionalized in immigration laws such as the first Chinese Exclusion Act (1882) and the Johnson Reed Act (1924), which had effectively stopped immigration from Asia. In barring Asians, these laws also barred their religions. However, because the laws changed, the ecumenical movement in this nation was dramatically changed during the period from 1950 to 2000. These fifty years are a time in which the United States became

> no longer a country of three religions (Protestant, Roman Catholic, Jewish). Today there are more Muslims than Episcopalians. In fact, there are more Muslims than Presbyterians. According to some counts, there are more Muslims than Jews. Buddhism is becoming an American religion that can be associated as much with Americans of European ancestry as Americans of Chinese, Korean, Japanese, or Vietnamese roots. Islam was brought to America by Syrian and Lebanese immigrants as well as many from India, Bangladesh, and Pakistan. Today the children of these immigrants are doing what Catholics and Jews have done for generations: trying to find a way to be American and faithful to their religious values at the same time. Also like Catholics and Jews, Muslims and Buddhists, Hindus and Jains, and others are discovering how the values and insights enshrined in their religious traditions can contribute to the common good of all Americans.[5]

We have come to an important point in the history of religion as it continues to evolve in the ongoing story of humankind. John Bowker, gazing over an expansive horizon of the past, describes this moment in these terms:[6]

> Through these factors the movement has grown for an opening out of Christian theology from "domestic" criteria of its tasks, whether patristic, reformed, liberal, to take in an active cognizance of other faiths. Other faiths have registered the same impulse. For some Christian theologians there is an arguable extension of the ecumenical instinct from "Christian," however diversely read, to "religious." Is not the *ecumene* . . . [t]he *corpus Christianum*? If Catholic/Orthodox/Protestant learn to abate bigotry, repudiate caricature, and "do" things together, may not Hindu/Buddhist/Jew/Muslim/Christian and the rest do likewise? Why not an *ecumene* of religions?

This contribution is a reflection of one person who has participated in "the wider ecumenism" for more than twenty years, beginning in January 1981. The interfaith movement in this country, as written about here, is as seen from two cities in New York, Buffalo and Syracuse. It also reflects my views as one of the founders of the North American Interfaith Network (NAIN) and my experience for the past eight years while continuing to participate in this movement from California, where I was born and where I have lived for the past eleven years.

THE INVISIBLE OTHER

Local ecumenical life is often dependent upon what leaders and others desire to accomplish and what existing organizations and institutions are willing and able to support. The western and central New York state stories over the past thirty years are examples of such symbiotic relationships. One consequence of this process, often resulting in a hegemony of interests, is that others can remain invisible. The history of ecumenical relationships in western and central New York state are good examples of this phenomenon that has also been experienced in many other places across the nation.

TOWARD THE BELOVED COMMUNITY

Buffalo and Western New York as One Case in Point

There had been a Protestant council of churches in this predominantly Roman Catholic area for many years. Yet it was restricted in membership and function because it did not include Roman Catholics, black churches, or the Jewish community, along with others. Through the financial assistance of the local Margaret L. Wendt Foundation, in 1975, a plan was developed to establish a new ecumenical system to serve the city of Buffalo and the eight-county area of western New York.[7]

The plan met with considerable resistance from the Council of Churches. Nevertheless, the Buffalo Area Metropolitan Ministry Inc. (BAMM) was launched in 1977, building upon the two years of planning that had been funded by the local foundation. At the same time, there was always the hope that a new ecumenical system that would include the constituency of the council of churches could be implemented. Thus, the intent in forming BAMM was to provide an expanded, more inclusive, ecumenical system. Consequently, during the years 1977 to 1996, BAMM was a more inclusive ecumenical organization than had been previously known in this part of the nation.

BAMM was formed as an association of religious communities; thus its membership included districts, societies, and diocesan-type structures. The initial membership included Roman Catholic, Protestant, Orthodox Christian, and Jewish organizations that chose to associate together through this forum. The purpose in forming BAMM was to serve its members and the western New York eight-county area by facilitating dialogue and assisting its members to address quality-of-life issues cooperatively. BAMM was accountable to its members through a board of directors, the directors being designated by the member organizations.

The BAMM Board of Directors invited the Rev. Max Glenn to serve as the executive director in the newly formed ecumenical entity, beginning in 1977; he served until 1979. In January 1981, I began my work as the BAMM executive director, continuing in this position until 1992. Following my tenure, the Rev. Cynthia Bronson served for a couple of years. Then, by 1996, BAMM and the Buffalo Area Council of Churches merged into a new organization called the Network of Religious Communities, serving western New York and the Niagara peninsula in the southern portion of the province of Ontario, Canada.

Buffalo, the second largest city in New York state, encompasses an area of approximately 43 square miles. Its population of approximately 300,000 is dispersed in such a manner that the city has retained strong ethnic concentrations in a diversity of neighborhoods, with boundaries that can be readily defined. Buffalo's growth pattern has been similar to that of many other large cities in the northeast. Although the physical boundaries of the city have not changed significantly since the middle of the 1800s, the population continued to expand until 1950. Since that time the city has experienced a steady population decline due in large part to suburban migration. In addition, a significant decline in industry has contributed to the gradual lowering of the school population with a disproportionate decline in the majority-to-minority ratio.

On April 30, 1976, Federal Judge John T. Curtin cited the Buffalo Board of Education, the superintendent of schools, the commissioner of education, and the Board of Regents for de jure segregation. As a consequence, the court directed the Buffalo school district to submit a design for the desegregation of schools that would outline specific actions to be undertaken to comply with the federal court order.

As Judge Curtin was issuing his 1977 decision, Max Glenn arrived in Buffalo to take up his work with BAMM. There was much concern that the implementation of the court order would result in violence as had occurred in other cities, including, in 1974, an explosion of hatred so intense in Boston that for a while the city became known as "the Little Rock of the North." As a deterrent to such violence, BAMM placed priests, ministers, and rabbis in the hallways of schools and on school buses, using clergy that volunteered for this service. BAMM also set about organizing parent councils in an effort to empower the parents and thereby influence the Buffalo public school administrators to develop educational programs more responsive to the educational needs of all children. The parent councils grew into an organization known as Citizens for Quality Education (C4QE).

The newly formed ecumenical system, BAMM, by becoming engaged in the school desegregation struggle, reversed a long-standing injustice wherein African Americans in the city of Buffalo and in western New York state had been ignored by the larger religious community. This regrettable pattern of behavior by the dominant religious community was evident to anyone who had eyes to see and is recorded in history. For example, a few years earlier the National Council of the Churches of Christ in the USA had been identifying local councils of churches that they designated as model councils, entities to be emulated by others. This designation was reported in a nationally distributed religious journal, *Christianity Today*. And the Buffalo Area Council of Churches was thus designated, although it had few, if any, black churches participating. Moreover, there was no Roman Catholic participation, even though the population of Buffalo was predominantly Roman Catholic. Neither was there Jewish or Muslim participation, although persons associated with both of these religious traditions had been living in Buffalo and western New York state since before 1900.

Working with leadership in the African American neighborhoods on school issues soon led BAMM into other issues as well. Two of the significant engagements were opposing redlining policies of financial institutions withholding loans for residents living in minority neighborhoods and advocacy of human rights for tenants in public housing. These engagements were often in concert with the housing department of Catholic charities and similar specialized agencies of other religious communities.

By January 1981, when I became BAMM executive director, the desegregation of Buffalo public schools had progressed without significant incidents of violence, C4QE had become an independent organization, the Housing Task Force had a considerably larger constituency, and the redlining issues had been somewhat mediated for the moment. There was a desire within the BAMM board of directors to grow into something more than the organization had become in the first four years. At the same time there was also a commitment to continue the dialogue with the local Protestant council of churches. Therefore, whenever possible, BAMM consulted with the council of churches and collaborated with them in program activities.

In 1981 the economy of western New York state continued to be weak, resulting in poverty and poor quality of life for many people living in the area. Shortly after my arrival in western New York, a new hotel opened and announced that 150 persons would be hired. In response, 10,000 people lined up to receive an employment application, hoping for an interview and to be hired. In light of this dire economy, BAMM undertook a multifaceted strategy to assist its member religious communities to more adequately respond to the wide range of human needs that were very evident. The association of religious communities began to develop a hunger response program, Food for All. Following a model used before, including in Washington state where I had been on the staff of another ecumenical agency, the goals of this program were to provide education regarding hunger and poverty, direct food relief to persons in need, and advocate to change public policy that often contributed to poverty and hunger in the area.

While BAMM was developing Food for All, it also joined with others to seek systemic economic justice throughout the "rust bowl." There was increasing recognition that the militarism in the nation and the attendant priorities reflected in the budget of the federal government contributed to the economic difficulties experienced in the region. At the same time, consequences of the growing internationalization of the economy were being experienced. Thus, BAMM found itself making alliances with organized labor, peacemaking groups, activists in the colleges and universities, and others, sometimes having to negotiate and attempt to solve conflicts that arose between these diverse institutions and their various constituencies. Moreover, there were continuing efforts to extend these relationships into the BAMM-related religious communities, usually with little success. The member religious bodies did, certainly, continue to support the association, although not at a level adequate to support the service they received from the ecumenical body.

Of the two expressed purposes of BAMM, addressing quality-of-life issues was the first the association tackled. The other purpose, fostering interfaith dialogue in ways other than working together on community issues in a dialogue of life, developed after 1981. This appears to be a natural progression; yet the dialogue of meaning seems to be inevitable if positive, constructive relationships are to continue to grow and prosper. The dialogue of meaning should not be entered into prematurely; each locality needs to find its own proper time to enter into this dialogue.[8] In October 1980, during my interview with the committee that was searching for a person to recommend as the second BAMM executive director, I mentioned that I did not see any evidence that the dialogue of meaning had begun, although the material describing this interfaith organization presented it as a purpose of the association. Members of the committee told me that the association had not yet found ways to begin the dialogue of meaning. This dialogue did begin during the years that I worked with BAMM. The dialogue of meaning occurred alongside of the dialogue of life, each encouraging the other.

Thus my installation as executive director began this dialogue. There had been no formal installation of Max Glenn into the position of leadership in 1977. But this occurred for me because of the position BAMM had achieved in the life of Buffalo and western New York state and because of the religious identity BAMM wanted to express (although it took nine months to reach a consensus regarding the content of the installation celebration among representatives from the Roman Catholic, Orthodox, and Protestant Christian communities, together with Jewish and Islamic representatives). In September 1981 there was an installation service held in Temple Beth Zion, in Buffalo, with music, scripture readings, and prayers, understood as a para-liturgical celebration.

The success of the installation celebration prompted civic leaders who were planning for the Buffalo sesquicentennial observance to request that BAMM conduct a religious celebration in honor of the city's birthday. The BAMM board of directors accepted this invitation and, with the financial assistance of the Margaret L. Wendt Foundation, a successful event was held on a cold, windy March evening in 1982.

During 1983 the BAMM board of directors formed a commission on interfaith dialogue. The work of this group began with Jewish-Christian relations. The commission prepared a model dialogue program and trained representatives from synagogues and churches. Pairs of Jewish and Christian congregations had representatives engage in dialogue using the prepared materials. The program was so well received that several of the paired congregations repeated the experience to provide opportunities for others to participate. Building on this experience, by mid-1985 the Jewish-Christian dialogue program had progressed to the point that an interfaith group traveled together to Israel on a fourteen-day mission.

Following the travel of this group, a group of priests, ministers, and rabbis began to meet together for Bible study. The study began with the Torah; but soon the group was studying the New Testament, much to the surprise and delight of the priests and ministers in the group. This study continues to this day, although many of the members have changed, and has been meeting for more than fifteen years.

Through the interfaith dialogue commission, BAMM began an annual interfaith observance of the Holocaust that included both theological discussion and interfaith celebrations. In addition, BAMM has sponsored a number of successful interfaith peace celebrations. Throughout the years the number of religions represented in these events has continued to grow. Similarly, BAMM has sponsored interfaith AIDS memorial services.

BAMM began with Christian and Jewish membership, but by 1985 its constituency had grown and membership had expanded to include Muslims, Hindus, and Jains. In addition, while not formal members, there was also growing participation by some Native Americans, some Sikhs, and a few of the Baha'i faith.

There is more that could be written, but this has been recalled to illustrate what can be done in one area in the larger ecumenism. I left BAMM and western New York state in summer 1992. By the mid-1990s, both BAMM and the Buffalo Area Council of Churches were dissolved and a new ecumenical system was formed—the Network of Religious Communities in Western New York and the Niagara Peninsula. It may be too soon to see whether the expanded interfaith network will be able to sustain both the dialogue of life and the dialogue of meaning.

In any case, the nineteen years of interfaith dialogue from 1977 to 1996 have, from the perspective of one locality, begun to confirm the truth of this proposition:

> No human life together without a world ethic for the nations.
> No peace among the nations without peace among the religions.
> No peace among the religions without dialogue among the religions.[9]

Syracuse and Central New York as Another Case in Point

Change is never an easy thing; yet it is often a necessity. The story of transition from a Council of Churches to an Interreligious Council in Syracuse, New York, was one of new needs and old allegiances. Robert Grimm had come to be the executive of the Syracuse Council of Churches in March 1965. It was at the beginning of the urban struggles in most cities in the nation and Syracuse was no exception. The Council was an "old line" council.[10] Three things began to happen almost at the same time. Urban ministry had been initiated by the Methodists (soon to become United Methodists), which in turn evolved into Priority One—a program largely devoted to dealing with racism and mental health; an Office of Economic Opportunity antipoverty organization came into being, and after a year or so the regional office of the OEO took over the local organization, accusing its leaders of improper use of the funds (it was reborn three years later as PEACE, Inc.); and Syracuse University initiated a community organizing training institute, with Saul Alinsky as the mentor. Syracuse was the laboratory where their trainees would be trained. These activities left the Council with rather traditional programs—Christian Education, Protestant chaplaincy services, the summer day camp program at Camp Adelphi, and Lenten and Advent community celebrations.

Dr. Hal Garman, Methodist urban worker and pastor, noted that between 1969 and 1971 "the mind set changed. People turned in and were not interested in other people's problems. The spirit of the 1960s dropped through the cracks." And just at the end of that "curve" the Council, under Grimm's leadership, made a transition from traditional conciliar body with congregational membership to a denominational judicatory-based organization known as the Metropolitan Church Board (MCB). The Roman Catholics became a part of this new ecumenical vehicle with a $10,000 annual contribution and a seconded staff person. This new organization shifted governance to the middle judicatories of the denominations, and the goal was to help the churches be more responsive to urban issues. It was "never radical, always moderate." And at the same time, there were parts of the work in the city, like civil rights, housing, and hunger, where the Jewish community joined forces with the MCB.

As the MCB struggled, Rabbi Theodore Levy, Robert Grimm, a Roman Catholic priest, and a priest from the Orthodox Church in America began to meet concerning a failing housing corporation that had been initiated some years before by the Orthodox. They formed an interreligious corporation to take over these housing units (which also later failed). But from this experience they formed a fledgling organization in 1975 known as the Syracuse Area Interreligious Council (SAIC) as a place for discussion and work on shared community concerns. It went one year without professional leadership but announced a position in 1976 of executive director. Dorothy Rose applied, but another woman was hired. Then after a year that women resigned. The job description was changed into a more proactive role. Rose applied and this time got the job. When she reported to work she found that SAIC had one room, one desk, one chair, one telephone, and nothing else. She had a $21,000 budget. The executive committee said she could decide how much of that to pay herself. With the help of Jack Balinsky, director of Catholic Charities, she went to the Onondaga County job training organization and hired a trainee to provide some clerical help at very nominal cost. Essentially, SAIC was just a big dream.

Meantime the MCB was in stressful times. With the Roman Catholic involvement, many Protestants were concerned that Protestant programs like Camp Adelphi, Christian Education activities—Released Time Christian Education and Vacation Bible School training, for example—and the Protestant chaplaincy programs would be lost. At the same time, more and more Roman Catholic energy was being directed to the SAIC. As a result, Protestant Community Ministries (PCM) was founded "to protect the Protestant witness" in Syracuse. A woman was appointed as the director, but after two years she got married and resigned. Robert Grimm also resigned to take a post as executive director of the Buffalo Council of Churches.

In 1976, Chaplain Howard Rose, chair of PCM, called the Commission on Regional and Local Ecumenism office at the National Council of Churches and asked Arleon Kelley if he could come to take representatives of the churches and the Jewish community, as well as representatives of these organizations, through a planning process with the expressed purpose of helping them find a common life. The community could not sustain competing organizations. After several face-to-face meetings with leaders of the various components to get acquainted, a meeting was called of all interested parties and representatives.

The meeting was held in the cafeteria of the New York State Council Church Center in Syracuse with a little over one hundred people in attendance. A shared vision was built in the first phase of the evening's work. It was a big umbrella under which all religious interests could be included. It provided a sphere for all faiths to work together, but also spheres for the Protestants and Roman Catholics to continue their own programs.

The meeting then moved on to working toward a common interfaith life. The purposes for such an interreligious organization were threefold. First, such an interreligious instrumentality should exist as a place to build relationships among the diverse parts of the religious community. This was later done by dialogue, education, and community celebrations (instead of shared worship). Secondly, the organization was to engage in advocacy and social justice. Over the years it worked on many things—the death penalty, racism, and the School of the Americas, for example. And finally, a new interreligious council must provide hands-on direct services. This was to include issues of chaplaincy, housing, hunger, food pantries, refugees, and many others.

Then the evening's attention was turned to "blockages," i.e., things that might impede such a vision from being implemented. Initially, Rev. Nelson Gates, a Lutheran pastor in the central city and an active participant in the Protestant Community Ministries, continued to argue the two Lutheran conditions for participation in any "ecumenical" organization: the "Evangelical Principle" requiring Lutherans to only be involved in distinctly "Christo-centric" organizations and the "Representative Principle" requiring that governance be representative of "evangelical" religious congregations or denominations rather than just interested individuals. Kelley suggested that the goal should not be creating a traditional ecumenical organization, but rather a community of interreligious organizations within which the Protestants would have a sphere for their own activities. Late in the meeting Rev. Gates got to his feet and publicly reversed his former position and "the deal was made." The group voted overwhelmingly to fold all the parts into an interreligious council. The Interreligious Council of Central New York emerged as a two-year experiment, with Rev. Nelson Gates serving as Vice President for Protestant Concerns. Dorothy Rose was asked to continue as the executive, and under her leadership the two-year trial marriage went well indeed. After two years Rev. Gates announced to the evaluation team, "I have not had a Protestant concern in these two years," and his position was discontinued.

The program blossomed. All the Protestant, Roman Catholic, and Jewish chaplains were assigned to the Interreligious Council's Chaplaincy program, which in turn negotiated for chaplain services (paid for by the institution) in all the county and city institutions and hospitals. Camp Adelphi continued for many years, as did the Lenten and Advent events and work on Christian unity. The Jewish community was very insistent that Christians do those things they needed to do to "get themselves together" for the sake of the larger community. At the same time, the IRC pioneered celebrations for the whole community. A highlight among these was the annual dinner to honor a person or a couple who had made a significant contribution to the community and its religious life.

Refugee services were added as a way for Syracuse to respond to the tragic circumstances of the Vietnamese boat people, as well as refugees from dozens of other countries. The Interreligious Council of Central New York found that it had the credibility to be a convener among groups who shared similar interests but no regular communication. It was able to convene a meeting of state, county, and city agencies concerned with children. A standing-room-only crowd came to hear—mostly social workers who had longed for some coordination for years.

Community-wide dialogues for community and congregational leaders on racism were convened with six hundred showing up for the first breakfast. These dialogues lasted for several years. And of course IRC was active in local and statewide advocacy on any number of community well-being issues. At the same time the IRC founded and funded a regional hunger program (now spun out as a freestanding agency) and a network of church, mosque, and temple-related food pantries, which continue. It has also worked for years with the city to meet the needs of the homeless and the housing of vulnerable people. In many ways, the IRC has become an important mediating structure in the Syracuse area, capable of bringing diverse parties together for the common good.

From the $21,000 annual budget, Dorothy Rose parlayed the program budget, over some 22 years, into the $1.2 to $1.5 million annual figure—much of that government grant and program money. At the same time, as other religious groups came to the community they also became members. Membership now includes Muslims, Jews, Sikhs, Hindus, Buddhists, and Baha'i, as well as Christians. One of the big disappointments has been the very nominal participation from the historic African American churches.

When Dr. Garman was asked what his denomination and the community felt about the IRC he noted that in his opinion a full three-fourths of the community was fully open to the interreligious approach. And most United Methodists generally only knew what they read in the newspapers and in the IRC mailings. Since it seemed to be doing a lot for the community, it therefore must be good. Methodists were very supportive, if not always deeply involved. Only the Evangelicals and the Religious Right wanted little to do with it, because, in Dr. Garman's view, it challenges their narrow view of Christianity.

When asked to reflect on the spiritual foundations of the IRC, Dr. Garman said that IRC:

> demonstrates that there is one divine source of all, and in our particular ways and faith traditions we are choosing to relate to that same divine source. [The IRC as a community symbol] suggests that all relate to one God and we are all Children of that God. We need to realize we are one people with one spiritual source. This then drives all the concerns

> about poverty, economic and racial justice. It drives us into concern for our multicultural, multiracial and multifaith diversity work . . . to toleration and then moving beyond that to living together in community . . . to get beyond the barriers that tear down community and all the "isms." IRC sets an ideal, as a standard and a path. It is much preferable to just an ecumenical or just a Protestant organization. We have grown beyond that even though we may not know it. . . . At the same time, one divine source drives all the ethical issues. The ethical challenge is to remove the barriers and to find a way to enable the economic system to serve all the peoples at the margins so they become mainstream. IRC is the basis for this vision in Syracuse and surrounding communities.[11]

The story of the Buffalo Area Metropolitan Ministries and the Interreligious Council of Central New York are shared all too briefly, but there are innumerable similar stories that could be told of how other multifaith, interfaith, or interreligious councils were formed in such other places as Tulsa, Poughkeepsie, Washington, D.C., and Berkeley. Indeed, the next step was to network at least the leadership of these organizations for mutual support.

Reaching Out to Others

We had been communicating with leaders in other interfaith efforts and found the relationships helpful. Soon after taking up my work as the BAMM executive director in January 1981, the bishop in the Roman Catholic Diocese of Buffalo asked me how many other cities had interfaith organizations. I shared with him and others the information that had been gathered through the November 1980 survey conducted by Bettina Gray, then president of the Berkeley Area Interfaith Council, a project sponsored by the Commission on Regional and Local Ecumenism (CORLE) of the National Council of the Churches of Christ in the USA. The survey had documented that in 1960 there were eight interreligious councils in the nation. Then between 1970 and 1980, "during a surge of religious questing and experimentation, the number of interreligious councils tripled in the United States from eight to twenty-four. Most of these councils were local, 'grassroots' developments, generally unaware of the existence or growth of similar groups, and interestingly, not limited to any one geographic area or size of city."[12]

The report of the survey noted that "such growth has been truly quiet, even unnoticed, but is an amazing development in the expressing of positive relations between religions and religious people." The general isolation among the local interfaith councils was borne out in Buffalo. While BAMM had progressed, religious leadership in the western New York state area had little, if any, awareness of interfaith councils in other cities. During my third year in this position, attending the sixth assembly of the World Council of Churches (Vancouver, 1983) as an accredited visitor presented me with confirmation that we were certainly part of something much bigger. Returning to the Buffalo area following this experience, I began to share resources regarding interfaith dialogue that the WCC had developed, especially after the 1961 New Delhi assembly in which Paul Devanandan "challenged the churches to take seriously the experiences of the younger churches in the newly independent countries, where they had to work and struggle together with peoples of different religious traditions in nation-building,"[13] particularly the "Guidelines for Dialogue."[14] I also enrolled in the Doctor of Ministry program at McCormick Theological Seminary, finding there resources for my understanding of organizational dynamics we were working with, although the faculty offered little understanding of the interfaith religious content that was involved in my ministry.[15]

In 1986 we received an invitation from the Temple of Understanding in New York City to attend a meeting of representatives from interfaith councils located around the United States.[16] The purpose of the meeting was to identify issues of common concern and to explore the possibility of forming an interfaith network in North America. I attended the meeting and found much in common with people from organizations similar to BAMM. Those present agreed to meet again. At the second meeting there were representatives from Interfaith Ministries in Wichita, Kansas, who expressed their intention to hold a national conference. Recalling the 1980 NAES meeting in Colorado, they felt there would be interest and that representatives would come from a variety of interfaith councils from various parts of the nation. It was agreed that the vision presented by the Temple of Understanding and the vision presented by Interfaith Ministries of Wichita were compatible, and that therefore there should be one conference, with one goal of the conference to be exploring the viability of forming a continental network of various interfaith entities. With this agreement, a next meeting was scheduled, to be held in Wichita.

Forming the North American Interfaith Network

The time for the meeting in Wichita was early 1987. Meanwhile, Pope John Paul II had met with representatives of other religions in Assisi on a day in which they came together to pray, although not to pray together—the

World Day of Prayer for Peace on October 27, 1986. Meeting after the Assisi event, with all of its attendant media coverage, the conference that was being planned came to be known as "a North American Assisi." It was modeled much like the Assisi day on interfaith prayer. This turned out to be a significant event, receiving considerable media attention, including an article in the *New York Times.* By the end of the conference in Wichita a steering committee for the formation of the North American Interfaith Network had been constituted. I and the president of the American Council for Islamic Affairs, Dr. Mohammed T. Mehidi, became co-chairs.

It was soon agreed that the next conference would be held in 1990, in Seattle, Washington, with the Interfaith Council of Washington as the host. A committee went to work preparing a charter. Another committee prepared the program for the conference, with the host organization doing most of the planning. The attendance at this conference was about one hundred, in comparison to nearly three hundred in Wichita. Those present affirmed the charter and requested that the steering committee proceed to incorporate the network as a not-for-profit organization in an appropriate state. And it was agreed to hold the next conference in Berkeley in 1992, in conjunction with a conference that was being planned by the Berkeley Area Interfaith Council in anticipation of the 1993 Parliament of the World's Religions.

It was decided to incorporate NAIN under the not-for-profit laws of the state of New York. In Buffalo, an attorney and an accountant were found who were willing to do the necessary work as a contribution to the interfaith movement by assisting the emerging network. As the legal and financial work neared completion, the BAMM board of directors, with the support of the Margaret L. Wendt Foundation, organized a regional interfaith conference, the North Atlantic Region Interfaith Forum (NARIF), held in 1991, with an attendance of about one hundred and fifty. During this conference the NAIN steering committee met. The same group was convened as the initial meeting of the NAIN board of directors.

During the 1992 conference in Berkeley, the charter members of NAIN were officially received, numbering approximately twenty-five, and new officers were elected for the NAIN board of directors. The NAIN members are organized entities that are in one of these categories: a regional or local interfaith, or multifaith, organization located in Canada, the United States, or Mexico; a component of an international interfaith organization located in at least one of the three nations in North America; an interfaith office of a single faith tradition; an academic center focused on interfaith relations; or an interfaith media endeavor. Subsequent conferences, or NAINConnects, have been held in Ontario, Canada, in 1994; Dallas, Texas, in 1996; Columbia, Missouri, in 1997; Winnipeg, Alberta, Canada, in 1998; Chautauqua Institution in 1999; and Southern California in 2000. The membership in the network has grown to about sixty entities in various categories. The 2001 conference was hosted by the Dr. Jessie Saulteaux Resource Centre in Beausejour, Manitoba, an indigenously controlled and run theological training center for native spiritual leaders, following both aboriginal traditional spiritual ways and mainline Christian ways.[17] Interfaith Ministries of Wichita, Kansas, hosted the 2002 conference. And the 2003 conference was held in Columbus, Ohio, hosted by the Interfaith Association of central Ohio. The 2004 conference will be held in New York City and has been scheduled to happen concurrently with the annual conference of the National Association of Ecumenical and Interreligious Staff (NAEIS).

Respectful Presence

As a member of the Presbyterian Church (USA) and an ordained minister in this denomination, I have sought to be accountable to this communion, particularly as I have ventured forth into the beloved community—in the localities where I have lived, throughout North America, and around the world. Therefore, I have gratefully participated in several opportunities this church has provided me to work with others in efforts to deepen and broaden our understanding of the potential and actual interfaith relationships we are experiencing as a particular church and as individuals associated with this church. For a number of years I have served in an informal group of advisors to the Division of Worldwide Ministries and to the staff responsible for facilitating our interfaith relations.

In 1996 I was invited to be part of a group called together to offer advice regarding the increasing number of congregations in the Presbyterian Church that are forging ongoing relationships with congregations of other religions, and particularly interfaith prayer and celebration.[18] In 1993 the Research Services staff of the General Assembly included involvement in interfaith activities as part of the Congregational Annual Report form for that year. Responses from the congregations indicated that at least 10 percent of Presbyterian Churches (USA) had ongoing relations with at least one congregation of another religion, most often a synagogue, and often they were sharing in prayer or worship.[19] We offered this perspective regarding interfaith activities:

> If people of different faith communities meet often enough and find common bonds among themselves, they may begin to develop a continuing commitment to each other and to their mutual quest for ultimate Reality. Such commonality cannot be taken for granted. When it does develop people may indeed find ways to engage in acts that Christians can define as full corporate worship. In most cases, however, people assemble for particular agendas in which the conditions do not call forth what we describe as worship. In these cases, people may indeed celebrate together or even find themselves sharing experiences of personal prayer.[20]

We pointed out that, given these circumstances, there are many decisions to make in the varying situations we will encounter because of the pluralistic society in which we live. We can choose to be primarily observers who minimally participate in what is happening around us, or we can be participants, while still maintaining our primary commitments to the faith with which we are associated. This analysis drew on both biblical material and official denominational policies. We also noted there are limits to interfaith prayer, celebration, and worship for Presbyterians that need to be observed in order to remain consistent with our tradition. Thus, we identified "respectful presence" as a method, a concept, to relate to persons of other faiths. We understand that "respectful presence is authentic attentiveness to the symbolic expressions of other religious communities. . . . [and also] means Christian willingness to offer witness in our liturgical expressions of the presence of God." Thus, "respectful presence goes beyond mere tolerance. It engages Christians in receiving as well as giving testimony to deep religious convictions and actions."[21] There are efforts under way to see whether the concept of respectful presence may be expanded to other areas of interfaith activities, beyond that of prayer, celebration, and worship.

Interfaith Relations and the Churches

During the 1996–2000 quadrennial, the Interfaith Relations Commission of the National Council of the Churches of Christ in the USA, of which I am an at-large member, prepared a policy statement that was adopted by the NCCC General Assembly on November 10, 1999.[22] The Interfaith Relations Commission developed the policy statement in consultation with member communions and with NCCC program units, in particular the Faith and Order Commission, the Ecumenical Networks Commission, and the Black Church Liaison Committee. At a number of stages of development of the policy statement, representatives of other religious traditions were consulted, and they shared responses to the document, contributing to its final form and content.

This is the first policy statement of the NCCC regarding interfaith relations of the churches, at least of its member communions. The policy statement begins by acknowledging the presence of Islam, Buddhism, Judaism, Hinduism, Sikhism, Native American traditions, the Baha'i faith, and other faiths in our nation, while confessing that Christians in this nation participated in attempts to eradicate indigenous peoples and their religious traditions, and prevented Africans held in bondage as slaves from practicing their Muslim religion or other African religious traditions from which they were forcibly separated. These practices have been reversed. And the churches are asked to enter into the struggle for "a new and more inclusive civic identity." At the same time, the policy statement recognizes that "ministry in a religiously plural world raises a number of ecumenical questions," including church-dividing issues of theology, or practice, or a mixture of the two, including the relationship between evangelism and dialogue, concerns about intermarriage, and issues regarding interfaith worship or common prayer."

While there are many questions that remain before the NCCC and its member churches regarding interfaith relations, the policy statement commits this Christian ecumenical body to recognizing the ongoing reality of interfaith relations that need to be maintained with respect, integrity, and mutual service to the common good. Accordingly, it commits the NCCC to staying in relationship with national organizations of many faith traditions other than Christian, while maintaining its Christian identity and mission. Through the actions envisioned in this policy statement, the NCCC and its member churches may someday be drawn closer to recognizing the truth inherent in the larger ecumenical vision, perhaps even to the point at which a community of religions may be affirmed.

A Uniting Vision

From among the most well-known international interfaith, or multifaith, organizations—the Fellowship of Reconciliation, the International Association of Christians and Jews, the United Religions Initiative, the International Association of Religious Freedom (IARF), the Temple of Understanding, the World Conference on Religion and Peace (WCRP), the World Congress of Faith, and the Council for a Parliament of the World's Religions (CPWR)—

the Council for a Parliament of the World's Religions is offering a vision that can provide a paradigm for the larger ecumenism that is emerging in our nation and around the world. This uniting vision is not a theology of world religions, nor a philosophical or ideological commitment, as helpful and important as these will continue to be as each of these organizations progresses. Rather, the CPWR is inviting us to recognize some principles regarding relationships: Namely, we should be seeking convergence and not agreement among the religions and we should be identifying and working with critical issues confronting humankind and all existence. In response to the critical issues, each religious community should be making offerings of service. Then, within each of the religions there should be efforts to understand and affirm these relationships in ways consistent with the particular tradition. This model becomes increasingly essential as we acknowledge the asymmetrical nature of the relationships emerging among unique religions.

Summary

This is an account of one participant in the larger ecumenical movement occurring within the United States, across North America, and around the world. I am a Christian minister who has found myself drawn into experiences way beyond those I ever imagined would occur in my life, and am thus convinced that this work is of the Holy Spirit, of the triune God, the God as revealed through history as recorded in the Bible, the God and Father of our Lord Jesus Christ. What God is doing here is more of a mystery than anything else; but, as a disciple of Jesus Christ, I continue to follow and to respond to each prompting of God, as it may appear through the activity of the Holy Spirit in our midst.

When I began as the executive director of BAMM in 1981, we knew of only thirty-five local or regional councils that were interfaith in membership. By 2000 there were perhaps five hundred interfaith organizations in the United States, approximately one hundred with some staff, twenty-seven of which are metropolitan and two statewide in scope. It is anticipated that spiritual and religious life in America will continue to converge, although not seeking or experiencing unity as envisioned in earlier understandings of ecumenism. Moreover, it is expected that this will be primarily a local and regional experience, thus presenting challenges to national and international denominational institutions of various faith traditions, including those of the Christian churches. The larger ecumenism envisioned here will result in many gifts of service to humankind and to the whole world in which we live, guided by a global ethic that is increasingly visible among us.

NOTES

1. John Bowker, editor, *The Oxford Dictionary of World Religions* (Oxford University Press, 1997), p. 303.

2. Ibid., p. 304.

3. Will Herberg, with a new Introduction by Martin E. Marty, *Protestant, Catholic, Jew* (Chicago: University of Chicago Press, 1983), is a helpful starting point in understanding this background. Yet, Robert Wuthnow, *The Restructuring of American Religion: Society and Faith since World War II* (Princeton University Press, 1990), has become an indispensable reference.

4. See Diana L. Eck, *Encountering God: A Spiritual Journey from Bozeman to Banaras* (Beacon Press, 1993), chapter 2, "Frontiers of Encounter: The Meeting of East and West in America since the 1893 World's Parliament of Religions," pp. 22–44, that began as a keynote address to the inaugural meeting of the North American Interfaith Network, Inc. (NAIN), in 1988.

5. James L. Fredericks, *Faith among Faiths: Christian Theology and Non-Christian Religions* (Paulist Press, 1999), p. 2.

6. Bowker, *Oxford Dictionary*, p. 280.

7. See Rev. Alton Motter, D.D., *How to Survive an Ecumenical Transfusion: A Study of Buffalo Ecumenism in Transition*, April 21, 1975. A copy is available in the Local Ecumenical History Project Archives located in the Christian Theological Seminary Library, 1000 W. 42nd Street, Indianapolis, IN 46202.

8. In the World Council of Churches "Guidelines on Dialogue with People of Living Faiths and Ideologies (1979)" it is recognized that "most Christians today live out their lives in actual community with people who may be committed to faiths and ideologies other than their own. They live in families sometimes of mixed faiths and ideologies; they live as neighbors in the same towns and villages; they need to build up their relationships expressing mutual human care and searching for mutual understanding. This sort of dialogue is very practical, concerned with the problems of modern life—the social, political, ecological, and above all, the ordinary and familiar," Part II, On Dialogue; C, Reasons for Dialogue, p. 16.

The WCC, however, goes on to recognize that "Christians engaged in faithful 'dialogue in community' with people of other faiths and ideologies cannot avoid asking themselves penetrating questions about the place of these people in the activity of God in history. They ask these questions not in theory, but in terms of what God may be doing in the lives of hundreds of millions of men and women who live in and seek community with Christians, but along different ways. So dialogue should proceed in terms of people of other faiths and ideologies rather than of theoretical, impersonal systems. This is not to deny the importance of religious traditions and their inter-relationships but it is vital to examine how faiths and ideologies have given direction to the daily living of individuals and groups and actually affect dialogue on both sides" (p. 20).

9. Hans Küng, *Global Responsibility* (Continuum and SCM Press, 1991), p. 138.

10. This material is from an oral history interview with Robert Grimm by Lawrence Witmer done in 1999. Other materials for this section on Syracuse are from interviews completed by Witmer in March 1999 with Dorothy Rose, longtime executive director of the Interreligious Council of Central New York, and with Dr. Hal Garman, a United Methodist pastor who was at one time the Methodist Urban Minister and then the director of a project on racism called Priority One.

11. From an interview with Hal Garman. Dr. Garman holds a Ph.D. completed with Dean Walter Muelder of Boston University. He dedicated his career as a United Methodist pastor to Urban Ministry and as a central city pastor in Syracuse. This

videotape is available in the Local Ecumenism History Project archives in the Library at Christian Theological Seminary, 1000 W. 42nd Street, Indianapolis, IN 46208.

12. The survey resulted from a workshop on interfaith relations that was part of the July 1980 meeting of the National Association of Ecumenical Staff (NAES) in Estes Park, Colorado. The survey form was sent to thirty-five councils identified by CORLE as being interfaith, seveteen of which responded in writing. An additional eight provided information in response to telephone calls. CORLE and the surveyor acknowledged that this might not have been all of the interfaith councils in the United States at that time, but that it did provide an adequate sample to "understand in [some] detail the nature of multifaith councils, when and why they were formed, what their programs are, and their future expectations and needs." Most of the interfaith councils replying to the survey were Christian and Jewish in constituency or membership, with an occasional report of membership of others, most frequently Muslim, Baha'i, or Buddhist. The survey found that some of these were funded and staffed, with staff ranging in number from none to over 125, the average being between 2 and 5 full- or part-time staff, with between 25 percent and 50 percent of the work done by volunteer effort. Of those reporting, 95 percent were primarily receiving financial support from religious sources; individual assistance was the second source of income; and less than 25 percent of funds were coming from government, corporations, or foundations. Eighty percent of the councils surveyed said that an interfaith network would probably be helpful; however, there was no consensus as to which existing groups could most appropriately develop the needed network.

13. From the entry on Interfaith Dialogue (Dialogue, Interfaith) from *Dictionary of the Ecumenical Movement* published jointly by the World Council of Churches and the Wm. Eerdmans Publishing Co. in 1991.

14. *Guidelines on Dialogue with People of Living Faiths and Ideologies* was first published by the WCC in 1979. Also, BAMM encouraged congregations to participate in the study project, "My Neighbor's Faith—and Mine: Theological Discoveries through Interfaith Dialogue," as this became available, beginning in 1998.

15. In 1998 I was awarded the Doctor of Ministry degree, after successfully completing the requisite courses and reporting on a Christologically grounded and biblically and theologically informed thesis project entitled "Toward Unitive Pluralism: A Case Study in Western New York," applying with modifications the model offered by Paul F. Knitter in *No Other Name? A Critical Survey of Christian Attitudes toward the World Religions* (Maryknoll, NY: Orbis Books, 1985).

16. The invitation came from the Rev. Dan Anderson, who was on the staff of the Temple of Understanding and was intended to express in North America the need recognized by four international interfaith organizations (the International Association of Religious Freedom [IARF], the Temple of Understanding, the World Conference on Religion and Peace [WCRP], and the World Congress of Faith), "for regional networks of interfaith organizations," as identified in a meeting in Ammerdown in April 1988. See Marcus Braybrooke, *Pilgrimage of Hope: One Hundred Years of Global Interfaith Dialogue* (New York: Crossroad, 1992), pp. 108, 111, 302. However, as a series of meetings continued, it was soon evident that a variety of initiatives were converging in these gatherings.

17. The NAINetwork, as it is frequently called, is a nonprofit association with a membership of more than sixty interfaith organizations and agencies throughout Canada, the United States, and Mexico. NAIN's purpose is to provide communication and the mutual strengthening of interfaith organizations and agencies, interfaith relations programs, and offices of religious, denominational, and other

appropriate institutions. NAIN affirms humanity's diverse and historic spiritual resources, bringing these to bear on contemporary global, national, regional, and local issues. Without infringing on the efforts of existing interfaith organizations, NAIN facilitates the networking possibilities of these organizations. NAIN encourages cooperative interaction based on serving the needs and promoting the aspirations of all member groups. In keeping with the networking function, the annual NAIN conference is referred to as a "Connect." NAINConnect 2001 was a very special meeting. NAIN invited a number of First Nations Elders to plan and provide direction for the meeting, which reflected on the content and direction of interfaith programming in North America. Through the theme "Sacred Fires, Sacred Circles," the Elders invited participants to receive the teachings and the practice of the Talking Circle as a way of exploring the importance of reciprocity, balance, and inclusion in their programs. The teachings of the Sacred Fire led us toward the importance of care for the earth at the center of all of our struggles. First Nations Elders Myra Laramee, Gladys Cook, Stan McKay, and Melody McKellar, along with staff of the Dr. Jessie Saulteaux Centre, provided an introduction to First Nations concerns and experience. NAIN encouraged member organizations to give special consideration to the balance of people (faith tradition, age, gender) attending NAINConnect 2001.

The Dr. Jessie Saulteaux Resource Centre trains for native ministry within the United Church of Canada, and honors a "two path" journey of respect for both Traditional and Christian ways. The Centre functions extensively in cross-cultural training and teaching of Traditional ways. The Centre is located in a rural area just outside Beausejour, Manitoba.

18. WCC, "Guidelines on Dialogue with People of Living Faiths and Ideologies," had anticipated that "dialogue will raise the question of sharing in celebrations, rituals, worship and meditation," and "this is one of the areas of dialogue which is most controversial and most in need of further exploration."

19. The summary of this data provided by the PCUSA Research Services staff states: "The overwhelming majority of reporting congregations (75 percent) did not participate in ongoing ministry/relations with people of faiths other than Christianity during the past year. Of the 25 percent of congregations that did, the nature of the ministry or relations was most often joint worship/prayer (64 percent) or social service or community development projects (62 percent). Other items mentioned were: "shared study" (20 percent), "theological dialogue" (17 percent), and "shared political advocacy" (13 percent). Those congregations most likely to have ongoing relationships with people other than Christians were large ones. Smaller churches involved in ecumenical or interfaith activities, however, were more likely to use joint worship and prayer in ministering or relating to others than to use the other activities. . . . When asked to pick from a list of faith communities with which their congregation might be interested in relating in the future, Jewish was the top answer (20 percent), followed by Muslim (7 percent), Buddhist (3 percent), and Hindu (2 percent). Four percent mentioned some other group."

20. *Respectful Presence: An Understanding of Interfaith Prayer and Celebration from a Reformed Christian Perspective*, PCUSA, 1996, paragraph 33.0122.

21. Ibid., paragraph 33.0131.

22. The NCCC/USA policy statement and related materials are available at *www.ncccusa.org/interfaith/ifresources.html.*

7

BLACK ECUMENISM: COUNTERPOINT TO WHITE ECUMENISM

Mary R. Sawyer

African American Christians have been a presence in the Protestant ecumenical movement since its beginnings, both in the United States and internationally. Presence, however, has not always meant being either welcome or influential. Indeed, in large measure it has been the inability to be heard or to have a significant impact in predominantly white movements that has given incentive to separate black ecumenical endeavors. An early expression of black ecumenism developed in the 1930s. Black ecumenism flourished, however, in the period from the 1960s to the 1980s. Some of the black ecumenical movements that emerged during these years were national in scope, while others were local; in some instances, a given organization had both national and local components. Influenced by black consciousness, black power, and black liberation theology, most of these ecumenical endeavors were "nationalistic" in character. Only one overtly sought to partner with white ecumenical structures. Since the late 1980s, ecumenism among African Americans has waned, paralleling the diminished activity and influence of white ecumenism.

The primary focus of this chapter is local expressions of black ecumenism, including both those that were autonomous and those connected with a national body. For the sake of history and context, however, the discussion begins with the experience of blacks in white ecumenism.

Blacks in White Ecumenism

Delegates from the National Baptist Convention and the two African Methodist denominations participated in the World Missionary Conference held in Edinburgh, Scotland, in 1910 and in successor ecumenical movements that culminated in the founding of the World Council of Churches (WCC) in 1948. At the organizing assembly of the WCC, when nominations were put forth for members of the Central Committee, one of the American black delegates pointed out that the list of nominees included no representatives of participating black churches and moved that other names be added. The motion was approved, and Dr. Benjamin Mays and Bishop W. J. Walls became the first black members of the Central Committee.[1]

By the time the WCC was formed, African Americans had accumulated nearly a half century of ecumenical experience in movements based in the United States. Nineteen black delegates were among the more than 4,300 individuals who convened at the Interchurch Conference on Federation in New York City in 1905, and at least one African American bishop, Alexander Walters, became a member of the executive committee. Following two additional meetings of this group, the organizing meeting of the Federal Council of the Churches of Christ in America (FCC) was held in 1908, with delegates from thirty-three denominations. Among these were the three black Methodist denominations and the National Baptist Convention, U.S.A. A total of forty-one black delegates were reportedly present from these and other denominations.[2]

The fact that FCC endorsed the "Social Gospel" movement of the time and accordingly was regarded as part of the "liberal" wing of American Christianity was largely irrelevant for black churches, for racial justice was on the agenda of neither. Among the committees created by the FCC in its first decade was one on "Special Interests of Colored Denominations" and another on the "Welfare of Negro Troops," but neither committee had significant standing. In 1919, in response to widespread racial riots, the Council issued a "call for racial justice in America" and two years later established a Commission on Race Relations.[3]

At this time, each of the black Methodist denominations (AME, AME Zion, and CME) had three official representatives in the FCC, while the National Baptists had a total of six representatives. Of the eight-eight members of the new Commission on Race Relations, however, twenty-five were black. In 1922, Dr. George E. Haynes—sociologist, churchman, and social activist—became the executive director of the Commission, the first black person to hold an executive position in the FCC. Haynes, who also was one of the founders of the National Urban League, initially served with a co-director, William Alexander. Haynes himself was required to raise the money to support the Commission's work, which for twenty-five years was largely limited to public education and the promotion of black-white cooperation.[4]

The Commission on Race Relations sponsored the annual observance by member denominations of Race Relations Sunday, addressed problems of black tenant farmers, and pressed the FCC as a whole to take a stand against lynching and mob violence. Member churches with large southern constituencies, however, refused to support anti-lynching legislation. Even some northern churches declined to condemn the Ku Klux Klan. The Commission on Race Relations was instrumental in establishing local race relations committees in many northern communities; it also provided impetus for both northern and southern church women to engage in interracial work throughout the 1920s and 1930s. But the Commission had minimal impact on the Federal Council itself, which in the first decades of its existence was more concerned with prohibition, World War I, and the Great Depression than with racial matters.[5]

The discrepancy within the FCC between black expectations and white intentions prompted one of its members, AME Bishop Reverdy Ransom, to pursue structural merger of the various black denominations. Failing in this, in 1934 he proceeded to organize a separate black ecumenical body that became known as the Fraternal Council of Negro Churches. Bishop Ransom served as president of the Fraternal Council for four years, then was succeeded by the Rev. William H. Jernagin, a prominent member of the National Baptist Convention, U.S.A., Inc., and one of the Convention's representatives in the FCC. Both Ransom and Jernagin continued to participate in the FCC even as they provided leadership to the all-black Fraternal Council.[6]

Not until 1946 did the FCC go on record officially opposing racial segregation. By that time, the FCC was already in conversation with a number of other interdenominational agencies that in 1950 joined to form the National Council of the Churches of Christ in the United States of America (NCCC). Among the signers of the charter establishing the NCCC were representatives of five black denominations and conventions: the African Methodist Episcopal Church (AME), the African Methodist Episcopal Zion Church (AME Zion), the CME Church (at that time, Colored Methodist Episcopal Church, but shortly thereafter, the Christian Methodist Episcopal Church), the National Baptist Convention, U.S.A., Inc., and the National Baptist Convention of America. In 1966, the newly organized Progressive National Baptist Convention became the sixth black member denomination of the NCCC.

The NCCC came into being just as the strands of the civil rights movement were being woven. These strands—the Supreme Court decision in *Brown v. Board of Education of Topeka,* the increased activism of the NAACP, the rise to prominence of Martin Luther King Jr., and the subsequent organizing of the Southern Christian Leadership Conference (SCLC)—all fostered the ideal of racial integration among both blacks and liberal whites, including within mainline white churches. The Fraternal Council itself had gradually shifted from a nationalist posture to a more integrationist program, especially as it worked through its Washington office for equal opportunity legislation. Some members of the Fraternal Council began to feel that a separate black ecumenical body was no longer appropriate. Anticipating that the newly organized NCCC would address their concerns and share decision making, they opted to support the NCCC rather than the Fraternal Council. Some would later question the wisdom of having placed such trust in another predominantly white organization, where reality often failed to correspond to the ideal. Meanwhile, many younger black ministers and church members were drawn to SCLC and the growing movement for racial justice.

The Southern Christian Leadership Conference as a Black Ecumenical Organization

The civil rights movement was preeminently a movement of the black church. Its leaders were black church leaders; the protest marchers, demonstrators, and boycotters were black church members; church women provided hospitality in their homes to activists from outside the local community; churches constituted the communications network and the fundraising arm of the movement; church rallies provided sermon, song, prayer, and spirit to motivate and sustain those who put their lives on the line in pursuit of justice. This is not to deny the political and financial support also provided by white northerners and by African Americans from non-church arenas, but it is to say that the civil rights movement was both a product of, and an expression of, the black religious tradition.

Membership in SCLC consisted of local affiliate organizations rather than individuals. Although the national office ostensibly was to coordinate and provide support to local member groups, the fact is that the affiliates operated with a large degree of autonomy. In part the affiliate structure was built from local church-based protests initiated before SCLC came into being in 1957. According to one study, between 1955 and 1960, the activities of local church-based groups were distributed as follows: court action, 9 percent; electoral political activity, 16 percent; economic boycotts, 25 percent; sit-ins or other forms of direct action, 35 percent; other, 16 percent.[7] It was the major "movement centers"—in Montgomery, Baton Rouge, Mobile, Tallahassee, and Birmingham, for example—that were instrumental in organizing SCLC; these local centers then in turn became official SCLC affiliates. Typically, the focus of these centers was equal access to public transportation, voting rights, and/or school integration.[8]

Many of the ministers who participated in the first meetings of SCLC either affiliated their home church or affiliated direct action groups organized by them in their respective communities. Frequently, local Interdenominational Ministerial Alliances affiliated, as did local Baptist Conferences. As the movement gained momentum, the number of new protest groups grew accordingly. Typically, in the early stages of a local movement, two or three progressive ministers would come forward from each denomination. Then, as the local campaign achieved visibility, other more conservative ministers would be drawn in. In this manner, the movement itself had a conversion function—a process greatly aided by the fact that the sentiments of the people were usually more in accord with the progressive pastors than with their conservative counterparts.

That the people sometimes led the way was indicative of a dimension of ecumenism that transcended interchurch cooperation. In the early years of his civil rights leadership, Dr. King often lamented the passivity both of many black ministers and of the black population as a whole—a passivity expressed in acquiescence to the humiliation and violence of Jim Crow segregation. But as the movement grew in scope and continued year after year, hundreds of thousands of black southerners found a new sense of integrity and self-worth. This change in consciousness and the attendant spirit of pride and purpose was anchored in a positive valuation of ethnicity and so was strongly communal. Thus, the church-led civil rights movement became ecumenical in the most fundamental sense of the word. Paradoxically, it was this "folk" ecumenism that gave birth to a successor and essentially secular movement known as "black power." The black power movement was a critical factor, however, in the formulation of "black liberation theology," which, in dialectical fashion, then gave impetus to a whole generation of black ecumenical movements. Unwittingly, the NCCC played a catalytic role in these developments.

Black Theology and Black Ecumenism

Like many institutions, the agenda of the NCCC over the years has mirrored the changing social climate and issues of the larger society. While initially skeptical of the civil rights movement, by the early 1960s racial matters had become a prominent interest of the NCCC. Representatives of the

Council were involved in the historic 1963 March on Washington, the 1964 Mississippi Summer Project on Voter Registration, and the 1965 Selma voting rights demonstration. The Council also supported more moderate efforts such as Project Equality, the National Urban Coalition, the Delta Ministry, and the United Farm Workers Movement. Ultimately, it played a significant role in lobbying for the passage of the 1964 Civil Rights Act and the 1965 Voting Rights Act.

Internally, numerous offices were created within its elaborate structure to address matters of concern to blacks as well as to other ethnic minority populations. Among these offices were Racial Justice, Economic and Social Justice, Domestic Hunger and Poverty, Multiethnic Christian Education, and the Commission on Justice and Liberation. Blacks were elected or appointed to administrative posts and were represented on various commissions and committees. Nonetheless, most liberal white officials and staff members of the NCCC were unprepared for the radical turn that the black liberation movement took with its demand for black power. It fell to black ministers working within the white ecumenical structures and white denominations, along with progressive ministers in the historic black denominations, to attempt to interpret black power to their white Christian brothers and sisters. These efforts at interpretation marked the beginnings of black liberation theology and led to the creation of a new black ecumenical organization called the National Conference of Black Churchmen (later, the National Conference of Black Christians) (NCBC).

Thus, even as its earlier promises of genuine integration encouraged the dissolution of one black ecumenical group—the Fraternal Council of Negro Churches—the NCCC's inabililty or unwillingness to share leadership authority, decision-making power, and economic resources more fully gave impetus to a new black ecumenical organization.

NCBC began in 1966 when the Rev. Benjamin Payton, executive director of the NCCC's Commission on Religion and Race, convened a meeting of a few individuals to discuss the hostile reaction of liberal white clergy to black power. One participant in this meeting, the Rev. Gayraud Wilmore, later recalled that "the decision was made to form an ad hoc group called the National Committee of Negro Churchmen and to publish a carefully worded statement of black power that would clear the air, clarify the position of northern (black) church leadership, and point to some theological implications of the concept of power."[9] That statement, signed by forty-eight prominent black church leaders, was published as a full-page ad in the *New York Times;* shortly thereafter, a second statement was prepared on "Racism and the Elections." In November 1966, nearly 150 ministers, all clad in clerical robes, processed to the Statue of Liberty, where the statement was read publicly. Then, with the signatures of 172 black church officials attached, it, too, was published in the *New York Times.*

The following March, at a meeting of one hundred black ministers, the decision was made to form a permanent organization. NCBC's most active years were from 1967 until 1974. Officially it existed until 1982, but long before then it had been superceded by another ecumenical organization called the Black Theology Project. At its peak, NCBC claimed 1,200 members, about 80 percent of them ministers and the remainder laity. About 40 percent came from predominantly white denominations and 60 percent from black denominations. While officers and board members came disproportionately from the black denominations, the strategists, theologians, and commission heads were mostly from the white denominations. Initially, the program of NCBC was organized into three commissions: Theological, African Relations, and Urban Mission and Crisis (also referred to as Economic Development). An Education Commission was added later. Of the four commissions, the Theological Commission was by far the most active and productive.

It was the Theological Commission, chaired by Wilmore, that brought black scholars, including professional theologians, into what initially was a conversation of church practitioners and social activists. James Cone, Major Jones, Henry Mitchell, J. Deotis Roberts, Joseph Washington, and Preston Williams were among those involved in the development of statements on black theology, including one written in 1969 that for many became the normative statement:

> Black Theology is a theology of black liberation. It seeks to plumb the black condition in light of God's revelation in Jesus Christ, so that the black community can see that the gospel is commensurate with the achievement of black humanity. Black Theology is a theology of "blackness." It is the affirmation of black humanity that emancipates black people from white racism, thus providing authentic freedom for both white and black people. It affirms the humanity of white people in that it says No to the encroachment of white oppression. . . . The message of liberation is the revelation of God as revealed in the incarnation of Jesus Christ. Freedom IS the Gospel. Jesus is the Liberator![10]

In 1976, NCBC issued a statement that reaffirmed the 1969 formulation of black theology but also sought to clarify the nature of black ecumenism and its relation to white ecumenism:

> Black theology is the theology of the Black Church. It seeks the reunion of all Black Christians, Protestant and Roman Catholic, in one Church encompassing the totality of the Black religious experience and the history and destiny of all Black people. All efforts to reunite and renew the Black Church serve the ultimate purpose of confirming the catholicity, apostolicity and holiness of the whole church of Jesus Christ in which every race and nation joined together, each contributing properly and equally, upbuilds the One Church of Christ in love and justice. Black Theology does not deny the importance of the interdenominational and ecumenical efforts toward church unity with White and other Christians. Rather it asserts the operational unity of all Black Christians as the first step toward a wider unity in which the restructuring of power relations in church and society and the liberation of the poor and oppressed will be recognized as the first priority of mission.[11]

NCBC as an organization was only minimally involved in hands-on "mission" work. However, many of its members became deeply involved in their local communities in efforts to "restructure power relations in church and society" and to "liberate the poor and oppressed." Influenced by the work of the Theological Commission and by the early writings of James Cone, J. Deotis Roberts, and others, local ecumenical organizations were created in the late 1960s and 1970s in major cities around the country. Prominent among these were the Philadelphia Council of Black Clergy, Chicago Black Churchmen, Alamo Black Clergy, and the Black Ecumenical Commission of Massachusetts—the only statewide effort of its kind. Beginning in the late 1970s and continuing through the 1980s, another cluster of local organizations came into being to address ongoing issues of inequity. From the Gathering in Los Angeles to Concerned Black Clergy in Atlanta to the Church Association for Community Services in Washington, D.C., local clergy took upon themselves the ecumenical mantle. Brief profiles of some of the more prominent of these groups give some indication of the nature and scope of their involvements.

Local Black Ecumenical Efforts

In the East Bay of northern California, the organization of some twenty-five local ministers known as **Alamo Black Clergy** functioned as a combination of SCLC and NCBC. In fact, members of Alamo Black Clergy constituted the nucleus of the SCLC arm in the Bay Area. A major focus of this ecumenical group was the raising of funds from churches and businesses to support community projects, provide seed money for starting small businesses, or provide assistance to existing small businesses. Theological education was also a high priority. Concern about the character of the theological education being provided black seminarians by the Graduate Theological Union in Berkeley prompted conversations with GTU's board of directors that led to the creation of a Center for Urban Black Studies. The Center, in turn, for several years offered courses through the various seminaries in Berkeley, including the Pacific School of Religion.

The membership of the **Chicago Committee of Black Churchmen** consisted of the dozen or so local clergy who were members of NCBC. From 1966 until the mid-1970s, along with theological discussions, the group engaged in social action protests and lobbied their respective denominations to support social programs to address the needs of the black community. The most ambitious undertaking of the group was the development of a proposal for a religio-cultural center to train and retrain black clergy in line with black liberation theology.

Theological education was also very much at the core of the program of the **Philadelphia Council of Black Clergy** (CBC). Once again, this was a reflection of the significant role played by the Philadelphia contingent nationally in the theological work of NCBC. CBC's commitment to the development and dissemination of black theology was institutionalized in the "Council of Black Clergy's Institute for Black Ministries," which became affiliated with Temple University. In addition to theology, the course offerings of the Institute included church history, pastoral care, religious education, and community organizing. From 1970 to 1977, the program offered a three-year master of divinity degree and could accommodate up to eighty students. Among the students were pastors interested in continuing education, laypersons exploring the ministry, and laypersons not involved in vocational ministry but active in the liberation movement. The Institute was an authentically ecumenical venture, with six black denominations recognizing it as a "jointly run seminary for the preparation of their clergy."

CBC was more than just the Institute for Black Ministries. It was a politically astute social activist organization that functioned as the watchdog of the community, a clearinghouse for airing problems, an advocate for the people, a thorn in the side of the establishment. From issues of police brutality to educational inequities to economic development and prison reform, the CBC acted where individual churches could not. The thirty-member board of directors, consisting of the pastors of the larger churches, met monthly to hear community concerns and to formulate responses. Among the objectives cited in its statement of purpose were:

To affirm the cultural contributions of black people in America.
To create a community power to eliminate problems within the educational system.
To work for the redistribution of wealth so black people get their fair share.
To organize the black community for the selection, development, and preparation of black political leadership.
To eradicate slums.
To rid the black community of police harassment, intimidation, and brutality.
To rediscover and develop a way of life that is meaningful to oppressed people and true to the teachings of the Gospel.

Like so many other black ecumenical efforts, CBC foundered on the shoals of inadequate economic resources. However, a successor organization, **Black Clergy of Philadelphia and Vicinity** (BCPV) emerged in 1982. From 1983 to 1990, the new organization—with many members from the old—was heavily involved in mayoral campaigns, taking credit for the election of their candidate; helped establish a minority-owned bank; and established relations with area seminaries and schools of theology that led to its playing a major role in student recruitment, curriculum content, and faculty appointments.

In the 1990s, BCPV became the most comprehensive local ecumenical endeavor in the nation. BCPV continued to function as an advocacy group, but created a new component—Black Clergy, Inc.—to function as the service delivery arm. As a nonprofit entity, Black Clergy, Inc., was able to receive grants from foundations and businesses to underwrite new programs in the areas of education, evangelism, economic development, and health and human services. Black Clergy, Inc., assisted several local churches in creating credit unions, became involved in capital fund-raising, provided investment counseling, and initiated a housing program. Involvements in health and human services ranged from the provision of day care to working with the homeless to assisting uninsured individuals obtain coverage. The organization worked with public school districts to provide tutorial programs and address issues of violence and drug abuse.

In a marked departure from other ecumenical movements, Black Clergy, Inc., gave high priority to evangelism. Under their auspices, some sixty ministers were trained to work with congregations in church growth and at the same time to tie the churches into the citywide social services network.

The scope of BCPV's concern extended beyond the boundaries of its own community. Following a briefing on their activities by a Philadelphia minister to a group of clergy in Atlanta, a new ecumenical effort was initiated in that city. In the mid-1990s, interest was being expressed by clergy in Los Angeles, Chicago, and other cities in transplanting the Philadelphia model to their communities. The appeal of this model inhered in large part in its two-pronged emphasis of "empowering" and "equipping." The mission of BCPV was to "resource the community and develop leadership" to "empower and equip the people to become spiritually and economically self-sufficient."

Second to BCPV, the largest local black ecumenical effort was the **Black Ecumenical Commission** (BEC) of Massachusetts. BEC was unique in becoming a statewide organization and notable for getting its start from a state council of churches. In 1966, the Massachusetts Council of Churches (MCC) established a Commission on Church and Race. Two years later, a subgroup of the Commission was formed called the Steering Committee for the Proposed Local Black Churchmen's Organization. The intent was that this group would be modeled after the national group, NCBC. Early in 1969, an organization was created called the Metropolitan Boston Committee of Black Churchmen (MBCBC), which then proposed to the Council of Churches that its Commission on Church and Race be reconstituted as a Black Ecumenical Commission of the Massachusetts Council of Churches. That recommendation was approved, whereupon the MBCBC took the lead in organizing a statewide Black Ecumenical Commission, with funding provided by MCC. BEC was incorporated that same year, and immediately thereafter received the first installment of a one-million-dollar pledge from the Massachusetts Conference of the United Church of Christ—a pledge that was made specifically as an act of reparation for past mistreatment of black Americans.

The agenda developed for BEC at its first statewide consultation included Black Theology; the Black Church in Mission; Economic (Human) Development; Organized Church Ministries; and Church, Seminary, and Community Cooperation. In order to serve its constituents across the commonwealth, BEC proposed the creation of eight regional area groups, each having its own administrative council and coordinator. Four of the area groups became functional, while the established Interdenominational Ministerial Alliance in Boston functioned as the regional group for that area. BEC became fully independent of MCC in 1971, at which time MBCBC became inoperative as a separate entity.

One of BEC's projects, under the leadership of executive director Jefferson Rogers, was the publication of a quarterly journal, *The Black Church*, which survived through six editions. In the 1970s, BEC functioned as a social activist organization, participating in rallies and protests with SCLC and other civil rights organizations through some of the most racially turbulent years of Boston's history. Key issues were school desegregation and busing, but BEC's interest in education extended to the development of the Black Women Seminarians Project, which was conducted through Harvard Divinity School and involved other area schools as well. BEC operated a youth program providing academic tutoring, social services, and family counseling. Under its auspices, local churches were engaged in statewide voter education and registration campaigns. Efforts were made to increase the number of black chaplains employed at state institutions. For a number of years, BEC operated a federally funded foster grandparents program. The organization was also instrumental in obtaining state grants for social service programs in local communities. BEC supported the development of a black church curriculum for children that included holiday observances and rites of passage.

BEC's board of directors, known as the Covenantal Council, consisted of one to two representatives from each of the functioning regional councils—until 1982, when they ceased to function—and one representative from each of the fourteen member organizations, which included the AME Church, AME Zion Church, a state-level black Baptist Convention, the black caucuses of five white denominations, and several Pentecostal groups. For over a decade, BEC was funded by the UCC contribution, supplemented by reparations payments from Methodists, Baptists, Episcopalians, and Unitarians. The Commission gradually declined in the 1980s, as it resorted to using the principal of its endowment for operating costs and as conflicts persisted between members from white denominations and those from black denominations over the proper program focus. Even so, its tenure exceeded most other black ecumenical efforts.

Los Angeles's most significant contribution to the black ecumenical movement was a clergy group called **The Gathering,** formed in 1978 by 130 members of the more conservative Interdenominational Ministerial Alliance. A major focus of The Gathering was police-community relations, but it also investigated housing conditions and worked to resolve conflicts between black residents and Korean immigrants and businesses. After a few brief years of intense activism and real influence, the group merged back into the Ministerial Alliance in 1984.

Police-community relations were a central concern of a New York–based group as well. **The Organization of African American Clergy** (OAAC)—a play on Malcolm X's Organization of Afro-American Unity—came into being in late 1979 and early 1980 and developed a membership of fifty Baptist, Methodist, and Pentecostal clergy. Police brutality was a singular focus during the early years of the 1980s, until attention was turned to a boycott of the *New York Daily News.* The organization became relatively inactive around 1988, but then was revitalized in 1993 as grievances with the *Daily News* again prompted clergy protests.

Impetus for **Concerned Black Clergy of Metropolitan Atlanta, Inc.,** which dates from 1983, came largely from issues of homelessness and hunger. In 1984, the new organization was instrumental in the launching of another organization, Odyssey III, a nonprofit organization devoted to providing meals, transitional housing, and counseling to trainable and employable men. While homelessness remained a central concern, the scope of Concerned Black Clergy's (CBC) involvement expanded into the 1990s. One of its innovations was the holding of a public forum once a week to which anyone in the community could bring issues and concerns and solicit the aid of CBC in redressing circumstances of social injustice. CBC instituted Mission Uplift, a program to empower the community economically through business growth and development, and Keeping in Touch, a mentorship program for young African American men. CBC also served as a clearinghouse on programs for youth being operated by various churches, in turn making the information available to churches interested in initiating such programs.

Through its own Political Action Committee, CBC involved itself not only in educating its constituencies regarding the political process, but served as a critical forum for political candidates, which then became the point of access to individual congregations. Networking with entities involved in job placement, emergency assistance, housing placement, human relations, and civil rights activity was an equally significant aspect of political engagement. CBC actually represented itself as an interfaith, interracial endeavor, though it was emphatically black-directed. At one point, its membership included some 120 churches and mosques, along with another twenty representatives of non-church organizations, each of which was asked to contribute one hundred dollars a month to the work of CBC. Thus, unlike so many other black ecumenical efforts, it benefited from a broad base of membership and support.

The diversity of these local organizations is further demonstrated by the **Church Association for Community Services,** which was created in 1989 in Washington, D.C. CACS, as it was known, began with thirty-five clergy from the District of Columbia and neighboring Maryland who were concerned about the incidence of drug abuse and violence. Building on efforts already under way by several individual churches and borrowing from a model that had been developed by the Congress of National Black Churches (also based in Washington, D.C.), CACS developed a multifaceted program to respond to the needs of families and youth. An evening program for youth from ages twelve to twenty was established to provide mentoring, tutoring, and athletic and martial arts opportunities, as well as workshops on health care and self-esteem. A crisis intervention center worked both with individuals and families. Parenting education classes and support groups were offered as part of the agenda of strengthening the family. Once a month a group of clergy from the member churches would meet with representatives of social service agencies, the school board, the police department, and other community service programs in a collective effort to address community problems. CACS also initiated a program called Reclaim Our Youth, which provided mentoring and supervision as an alternative to incarceration. At its peak, over 120 churches participated in this ecumenical effort, which was supported by member church contributions.

Aside from traditional ministerial alliances, estimates are that in the 1980s nearly 60 percent of all black churches were engaged in some type of interdenominational cooperation. But two-thirds of that activity took the form of fellowship or evangelistic campaigns with other black churches, while some 10 percent involved joint cooperation with white churches. Less than 15 percent of the interdenominational cooperation involved joint efforts to provide community services or to address community problems.[12]

The local ecumenical efforts profiled here can thus make two claims. First, like ecumenical movements at the national level, they constituted a "prophetic remnant" of the whole of the black church. Second, they pointed to a model of local interdenominational cooperation that departs from convention in its emphasis on social change and in the motif—expressed sometimes overtly, sometimes more subtly—of black liberation theology. Within the larger model are any number of submodels, for local ecumenical movements of this era evidenced a striking range in longevity, complexity of structure, and diversity of programs. What they shared was the common goal of improving the quality of life of their constituents.

By and large, since the 1980s activist ecumenical movements have given way to community development efforts on the part of individual congregations and to the megachurch phenomenon. In a sense, black megachurches are themselves ecumenical entities, drawing members, as they do, from the ranks of those who formerly had been affiliated with a range of denominations. While some megachurches focus on achieving the "good life," others have renewed the commitment to eradicating the systemic causes of poverty and alienation that pervade their surrounding neighborhoods. To the extent that these churches are nationalistic in character—emphasizing black heritage and self-determination—they are unlikely candidates for participation in the larger ecumenical movement. Rather, they are part of the legacy of a mission left unfinished in the 1970s when both church and society failed to grasp the opportunity to make good on America's promise of inclusive democracy. The anomaly is that, even as that failure was in process, one group of black Christians persisted in trying to create a different outcome.

Ecumenism in a Conservative Time

The generation of local black ecumenical groups formed in the 1980s was precipitated in part by the "white backlash" of the 1970s. The turn to conservative politics nationally served to extinguish much of the vitality of the social change movements that for a brief moment had threatened to undermine the power and authority of the white establishment. The backlash of "middle America" led to a withdrawal of many white churches from involvement with black churches and communities. Issues of ecology, hunger, and the status of women took precedence over racial justice. To a large degree, black churches were thrust back upon their own resources. If they did not attend to the needs of the black community, who would? As had happened so often before when entry into American society as full partners was frustrated, African Americans resorted to strategies of self-containment and self-sufficiency. It was this climate and mood that in 1978 brought into being the independent Congress of National Black Churches, to which only representatives of historic black churches were admitted.

One of the signs, so far as black members of the NCCC were concerned, that the organization was disinclined to fully incorporate the agenda of black churches into its own agenda was its three-decades-long failure to elect a president from among the historic black denominations. The NCCC had elected its first black president, the Rev. W. Sterling Cary, in 1972, but Cary was a member of the United Church of Christ. A second black president, M. William Howard, was elected in 1978, but he came out of the American Baptist Convention. Not until 1986 was a president elected from a black denomination: AME Bishop Philip R. Cousin.

Notwithstanding the sense of futility generated by these various circumstances, there were individuals within the NCCC, both black and white, who were unwilling to relinquish the vision of ecumenism as inclusive of both blacks and whites, and of both black and white churches. Thus, the 1970s also saw the founding of another ecumenical endeavor committed precisely to a partnership of black and white ecumenists.

Partners in Ecumenism had its origins in an informal conversation that took place in 1972 during the annual meeting of the National Association of Ecumenical Staff (NAES). NAES, whose membership consisted of the staff of the several hundred councils of churches at state and local levels, received support from one of the NCCC commissions, the Commission on Regional and Local Ecumenism, or CORLE. Participants in the aforementioned conversation included Sterling Cary; Donald Jacobs, a member of NAES; two staff members of CORLE, Arleon Kelley and Nathan VanderWerf; and Ray Kearns, the chair of CORLE. An observation made in the course of conversation about the small pool of black candidates for CORLE staff positions prompted the comment that black churches did not have their own ecumenism—and that white ecumenism was always played by the rules of white culture. Kelley suggested that what was needed was the development of a black ecumenism that could negotiate as an equal partner with white ecumenical organizations, and that this development needed to occur in all spheres of church life and especially in local communities.

Sterling Cary readily endorsed the concept, and the conversation was subsequently expanded to include additional members of NAES, among whom were Maynard Catchings and Lucius Walker. In 1973, the black caucus within NAES called for a program to increase the involvement of both black and white churches in local ecumenical bodies and to direct their attention to the problems of the cities. A keynote speech by Sterling Cary at the 1974 conference of NAES gave further impetus to the idea of a Partners in Ecumenism (PIE) project. After further discussions, which included the Rev. Joan Campbell, a proposal was submitted to the board of CORLE, which in turn recommended the proposal to the General Board of NCCC. The outcome was the establishment of a PIE Program Committee within the CORLE office, with Rev. Catchings—who had become a staff assistant to Clair Randall, NCCC's general secretary at the time—assigned to work with the Partners Project. An advisory group consisting of members of NAES was constituted to work with the project.

The initial charge was as follows:

1. To explore with local ecumenical bodies ways by which Black churches and denominations in their area may become more fully involved in ecumenical life and work.

2. To work with Black churches to stimulate greater understanding and involvement in the ecumenical movement.
3. To find ways that Black churches working ecumenically can link with community programs in their area toward greater service to the needs of people around them.
4. To find ways by which Black ecumenical life can be fully related to the total ecumenical efforts in a given community.

For two years, Catchings and members of the advisory committee visited local communities, met with state and local councils and churches, and at national meetings of NAES encouraged members to hire more African American staff in their local agencies. In 1978, PIE began to develop a more formal organizational structure and convened its first public conference, marking the official founding date. The Rev. Joan Campbell was named national coordinator of PIE, while the Rev. Don Jacobs was named the national director. The first meeting of the national board was held in 1979, at which time the Rev. George Lucas—who for many years had served as the executive director of the Fraternal Council of Churches—was elected as president of PIE. He was succeeded in 1981 by AME Bishop Frank Madison Reid Jr., and then by the Rev. Marshall Lorenzo Shepard (PNBC) in 1984. Serving from 1987 to 1990 was the Rev. Jewett Walker (AME Zion). In contrast to most other black ecumenical groups, the national board of PIE had significant representation of women. Elected representatives came from both historic black denominations and predominantly white denominations.

While unique among black ecumenical endeavors in being located in the "belly of the beast," members nonetheless claimed the same hopes and aspirations that had been held by so many of their predecessors: that the white ecumenical movement would respond to black concerns and that the black church would be accorded a place in the universal Church as a full and equal partner. A 1979 fact sheet described PIE as "an attempt to strengthen the role of the Black Church in addressing *today's crisis facing Black America.* PIE strives to unite black congregations at a local level with one another and, through local ecumenical bodies, with white churches."

The word "partnership" clearly assumed multiple meanings as PIE adopted an agenda of 1) interdenominational action among black churches at the local level, as well as 2) increasing the involvement of blacks both individually and as a body in white ecumenical agencies at the local and national levels, in order that 3) the programs and resources of those agencies could be effectively brought to bear on the living conditions of urban blacks. The initial step in pursuing these goals was the convening of six regional conferences around the country as a way of building a network of key black church persons who, through legislative lobbying efforts, would influence national policymaking. The hope of PIE was to develop permanent regional structures and local chapters; while four such chapters ultimately were established, achievement of this design was frustrated for the most part by the lack of staff and resources. By 1985, PIE's network, which at one time had reached a peak of 6,000 individuals, had declined to some 2,000, about 25 percent of whom were laypersons.

From 1980 through 1986, with the exception of one year, annual meetings of PIE were convened in Washington, D.C. At each conference, one day was designated as a time for delegates to lobby on Capitol Hill for legislation critical to the black community. Aside from this activity, however, PIE conferences were noteworthy primarily for the fact that they constituted the sole forum in which African Americans from both black and white denominations who were committed to ecumenical action and who were still willing to explore cooperative interracial efforts could come together with like-minded individuals. Overwhelmingly, those in attendance were not the bishops, denominational officers, or pastors of the more prestigious churches, but rather were representatives from grassroots churches, ministerial alliances, and local councils of churches who had an interest in social ministry.

In an effort to increase black involvement and leadership in the ecumenical movement, PIE instituted an internship program in cooperation with the Interdenominational Theological Center (ITC) in Atlanta; the program was later expanded to include other schools as well. Ultimately this program was taken over by the NCCC, where it was administered through the office of Ecumenical Networks. In 1984, PIE developed a plan for the delivery of human services in urban neighborhoods by clusters of black churches that were partnered with local ecumenical bodies. But PIE was never able to muster sufficient resources from the NCCC or other sources to implement the plan.

Particularly through meetings of NAES, PIE continued its "consciousness raising" regarding the desirability of ecumenical partnership, relentlessly pressing the need for increased black representation in local agencies. By 1983, twenty-seven local and regional councils of churches were reported to have black presidents—a significant increase, but still less than 4 percent of all councils. Only seven councils had chief executive staff who were black. Throughout the 1980s, PIE staff provided technical assistance to more than a dozen state councils interested in increasing the involvement of black churches. PIE officials also noted increased participation of black denominations—particularly the NBC, USA, Inc.—in the NCCC and by African Americans in the WCC after PIE was founded. An ongoing activity of PIE was advocacy for increased representation of blacks on both NCCC and WCC committees and commissions.

Ultimately, however, through a series of reorganizations within the NCCC itself, the role of PIE was diminished, and by 1990 the "partners project" was nowhere to be found on the organizational chart.

Partners in Ecumenism was the last in a series of black ecumenical efforts that challenged the white ecumenical movement to rectify persistent racial inequities in church and society alike. Other black ecumenical movements despaired of working with the white church, as time and again issues of race were subordinated to more "comfortable" matters. These independent movements, which arose from local black communities, were singularly focused on addressing the needs and rights of the people. PIE was unique in simultaneously seeking black self-determination *and* cooperation with the white particularity. In the final analysis—in spite of civil rights, black power, and black liberation theology and in spite of Jesus' unequivocal prescriptions for equality, justice, and inclusive community—the white particularity was unable to grasp the concept of a pluralism in which real power was shared and all were authentically partners.

Notes

1. For slightly different accounts of these developments, see William J. Walls, *The African Methodist Episcopal Zion Church* (Charlotte, NC: AME Zion Publishing House, 1974), p. 493, and Benjamin E. Mays, *Born to Rebel* (New York: Charles Scribner's Sons, 1971), p. 256.
2. Walls, *African Methodist Episcopal Zion Church,* p. 485.
3. David M. Reimers, *White Protestantism and the Negro* (New York: Oxford University Press, 1965), p. 92. This Commission is variously referred to as the Commission on the Church and Race Relations and the Commission on Interracial Cooperation.
4. Ibid., pp. 92–93.
5. Ibid., pp. 93–100.
6. For an extended discussion of the Fraternal Council of Negro Churches, see Mary R. Sawyer, *Black Ecumenism: Implementing the Demands of Justice* (Valley Forge, PA: Trinity Press International, 1994), chapter 1.
7. Doug McAdam, *Political Process and the Development of Black Insurgency, 1930–1970* (Chicago: University of Chicago Press, 1982), p. 134, Table 6.4.
8. Aldon Morris, *The Origins of the Civil Rights Movement* (New York: Free Press, 1984), pp. 90–91.

9. Gayraud S. Wilmore, *Black Religion and Black Radicalism* (Maryknoll, NY: Orbis Books, 1983), p. 196.

10. "Black Theology," statement by the National Committee of Black Churchmen, June 13, 1969, in Gayraud S. Wilmore and James H. Cone, eds., *Black Theology: A Documentary History, 1966–1979* (Maryknoll, NY: Orbis Books, 1979), p. 101. Also, see the discussion of this statement in Wilmore, *Black Religion and Black Radicalism,* pp. 214–215.

11. "Black Theology in 1976," statement by the Theological Commission of the National Conference of Black Churchmen, in Wilmore and Cone, eds., *Black Theology: A Documentary History,* pp. 341–342.

12. C. Eric Lincoln and Lawrence H. Mamiya, *The Black Church in the African American Experience* (Durham, NC: Duke University Press, 1990), pp. 155–156.

8

NATIVE AMERICAN ECUMENISM: MINNESOTA AS A CASE STUDY

Alton M. Motter

Editor's Introduction

Among the most dramatic examples of local ecumenism confronting its exclusiveness in the last half century are the ecumenical ministries of Native Americans. These fifty years are marked by a profound revolution in the way the dominant population has related to First Peoples in the United States and the way that First Peoples once again understand themselves. The eighteenth and nineteenth centuries and the first two-thirds of the twentieth century saw the dominant population of the United States effectively taking Native lands and driving First Peoples into less productive lands and finally onto reservations. By the turn of the twentieth century, the strategy of the government, although perhaps well intended, was nevertheless destructive to the integrity of the First Peoples. It seemed to be twofold. First, to take the children from the reservation and educate them in the "American language" and culture and in the process try to integrate the younger generations of First Peoples into the dominant culture. Second, to make people on the reservations dependent on government largesse, destroying the self-esteem of many of the people in the process. Of course, there was also the issue that many of the so-called marginal lands, set aside as reservations, were later discovered to be very rich in natural resources, e.g., oil, uranium, timber, and fish. The dominant population began to find ways to "get it back," as though these resources belonged to white people in the first place.

The Church in America in large measure also followed this strategy, and to some extent, invented it. Beginning in the eighteenth century, mission associations were formed in the "Boston States," i.e., New England. The Congregationalists were among the first to form such missionary associations. Serge F. Hummon, longtime United Church of Christ Board of Homeland Ministries staffer, describes it this way:

> *During the waning years of the eighteenth century and the first three decades of the nineteenth century (1783–1830) Indian missionary activity was furthered by associations formed to provide personnel, literature, and Bibles for the expanding frontier. A fear existed that people on the frontier would be paganized. In 1787 the Society for the Propagation of the Gospel among the Indians and Others in North America was organized and incorporated (in Boston) in order to give inspiration and leadership to regional societies. One such group was the New York Missionary Society, which sent a mission to the Chickasaw in the South, in 1799. At this time overseas missions were an emerging concern, but frontier settlements and Indian work were priorities.*[1]

At this same time, before the Louisiana Purchase, priests from French Roman Catholic orders were moving among the First Peoples in what is now Michigan, Wisconsin, Illinois, and Minnesota. For example, Fr. Pierre Marquette was active in converting and baptizing Indians as his exploration party moved across the upper Mississippi River and Upper Great Lakes regions. Thus, the church's mission to the First Peoples was not only to provide Bibles, but also included building schools, winning converts, and developing churches for them. These, in effect, socialized many into Christian, if not American, ways.

Christianity has a self-corrective and transforming possibility built in. The churches provided theological training for a number of young gifted Native persons who felt called to ministry. These Native persons, having studied such scholarly theological works as H. Richard Niebuhr's work on Christ and Culture began to realize that what the churches had been doing in their mission work was destroying the "Indian culture," although they proposed to do it in a most beneficial manner and under the guise of doing good for the Native People. Christ may be for the people, but what the churches were doing was against the Native culture.[2] *By the late 1950s and early 1960s this led, in turn, first to the First Peoples' self-determination movement and by the late 1960s to the First Peoples' liberation movement. Hence, many Christian Indians were able to incorporate and integrate their Christianity and traditional Native values and religion into their lives. It was a transition in the Church from white mission society paternalism to a more equal participation in the Church.*

This pattern was often fostered by local ecumenical initiative. The National Council of Churches, Division of National Missions, had full-time field personnel, most notably William Scholes, who addressed Indian concerns, often working in partnership with local ecumenical expressions. One such case was at Wounded Knee in South Dakota. The First Peoples of southwestern South

Dakota wanted that site for commemoration of the battle fought there and as a place for a "back to basics" Indian settlement. It resulted in a stand off with state and federal authorities. James Armstrong, United Methodist bishop of the Dakotas at the time, with support from other church leaders and the NCCC, became instrumental in a reconciling process that eventually made possible much of what the Native leadership was seeking–although as of this writing some Native leaders from that struggle are in prison on what many believe to be trumped-up charges.

Many other state and city councils also took the initiative. The New Mexico Council of Churches, under the leadership of Harry Summers, worked with some of the leaders of the Navajo Liberation movement at Ship Rock, New Mexico, in the Four Corners area. The work there was generally under the leadership of a historic Episcopal Church mission, but in some of the conflict situations that developed the Council involved itself and the NCCC resources in a mediating role. The Seattle Church Council and the Washington State Conference of Churches have worked together with First Peoples to help them fulfill some of their aspirations during the last four decades of the twentieth century. One of the results is a very beautiful and functional cultural center in the northern part of Seattle, built on grounds given up by the military. But they have also been involved as advocates for the First Peoples in fishing and land disputes. William Cate of the Seattle Church Council and Loren Arnett and John Boonstra of the Washington State Conference of Churches were very much involved in reconciling activities and on occasion as advocates for First Peoples' concerns.

Other examples of local ecumenical involvements include the New York State Community of Churches and its predecessor, the New York State Council of Churches. It has been involved on several occasions with the disputes both within and between the Mohawks over gambling issues and cross-border trafficking in cigarettes. At one time it brokered state land for a dedicated reservation to be used by a back-to-basics indigenous school and communal farm and village. The Council has also been involved in reconciliation processes related to Mohawk land claims. The historic treaties that conferred all the land north of the Mohawk River to New York (all of the Adirondack Mountain areas, which make up perhaps as much as 30 percent of the state) have long been thought to be illegal, as have some of the treaties that involve three counties just east of Syracuse but south of the Mohawk River. Some courts have ruled them so. The court process has been very difficult for both the Mohawks and the New York families that have lived on these lands for up to 250 years. At the same time the Long Island Council of Churches has been involved with some of the Indian land disputes on the east end of Long Island. First Peoples' concerns have been on the local ecumenical agenda in many parts of the nation. However, the case that will be explored in a bit more depth is in Minnesota.

Local Ecumenism and First Peoples in Minnesota

American Indian Ministries have been carried out through these three Minnesota Councils of Churches: the Minnesota Council of Churches, currently headed by the Rev. Peg Chemberlin; the Greater Minneapolis Council of Churches, whose current president and CEO is the Rev. Dr. Gary B. Reierson; and the St. Paul Area Council of Churches, whose executive director is currently the Rev. Dr. Thomas A. Duke. Together, this trio of ecumenical councils has developed one of the largest and most effective expressions of Indian ecumenism in the nation. Marked by a deep sensitivity to social needs, these council leaders developed an almost unbelievable ministry with Minnesota's large American Indian population of nearly 60,000. Native Americans live on eleven reservations within the state, with a total population of 35,282 in 2000. The year 2000 U.S. census report indicates that 24,407 Indians also live in five Minnesota cities: Minneapolis, 12,683; St. Paul, 5,991; Duluth, 2,984; Bemidji, 1,549; and Cloquet, 1,200.

Most Americans are quite unaware of the struggles still facing vast numbers of Indian people. In 1969, I wrote the following editorial, titled "The Red Revolution," for the quarterly news publication of the Minnesota Council of Churches:

> When we speak of today's racial revolution we usually think of the *black* revolution. There is also a *red* revolution. It is long overdue! In some respects the two revolutions are alike; yet, they are vastly different. The Indian, like the Negro, has suffered grave injustices at the hands of the white man. This first American has, however, become the *forgotten* American. Forced to retreat before advancing white settlers; cheated by treaties; defeated in battle; he was then relegated to the white man's "reservations." His way of life was threatened; his sense of values was thwarted, his means of sustaining a livelihood were destroyed.
>
> Rather than see him starve, the white man's government put him on "relief." Gradually, the Indian's initiative was destroyed. Caught between two cultures, he faced hopeless frustrations—frustrations that he

frequently tried to drown with alcohol or remove by suicide. The facts about the Indian today tell their own story:

- His average life expectancy is 45; the white man's is 70.
- Three times as many Indian children die as white children before they are four.
- Some form of mental disorder will strike five Indians for every two other Americans.
- For every one young non-Indian suicide, four young Indians will die by their own hand.
- The unemployment rate among Indians is nearly 40 percent—more than 10 times the national average.
- The dropout rate for Indian pupils before completing high school is nearly 60 percent.
- Seventy-five percent of Indian families have annual incomes of less than $3,000.
- On the totem pole of American life, the Indian is the low man—in job skills, health, housing, education.

When these words were read recently, to one of the Native American council leaders in Minnesota, she said, "With some minor changes, these same words could have been written today—32 years later. Our greatest challenge is to interpret the realities of today's Indian life to non-Indian people."

Minnesota

The far-reaching Indian ministry we see in 2000 began in 1952 within the Minnesota Council of Churches. This ministry was decentralized in 1974, and the two city councils began their respective programs.

Under the leadership of Native American Mary Ann Walt, the way was paved for the Minnesota Council's Ministry. The geographically dispersed Indian communities in northern Minnesota made it advisable for her to work from an office in the city of Duluth. Walt sought to develop a six-point program: To bear witness to the Gospel (Word and Witness); to identify issues affecting Indian people (Advocacy); to create new levels of understanding and cooperation (Bridge-building); to address urgent human needs (Direct Service); to hold grassroots conferences (Education); and to assist in developing Native American leaders (Indigenous Leadership).

Through the years, the records show how some of these aims have developed:

The series of Indian Elders Conferences at the White Earth Reservation Rediscovery Center
Prayer/Talking Circle Meetings for Native and non-Native community leaders
Programs for a "Violence Free Duluth"
The Crazy Horse Malt Liquor boycott
The building of a $300,000 remodeled transitional housing project in Duluth
Dealing with tribal sovereignty related to fishing, hunting, and wild rice gathering rights, based on the 1837 U.S. Treaty with the Chippewa, for the Mille Lacs Indian Band of the Chippewa people
Civil rights legislation
Racism issues
Efforts to recruit college and theological seminary students and faculty volunteers
Negotiations regarding the use of the sweat lodge, the pipe, and the drum for Native American religious observances in Sandstone Prison
Production of two films, "Eagle Can You See Me" and "The Bridge"

Walt's effectiveness was recognized in 1992 when, while much of the nation was observing the five-hundredth anniversary of the arrival of Christopher Columbus, she and her counterparts in the other two councils were leading Minnesota to celebrate the fortieth anniversary of its ecumenical Indian ministry. Later in 1998, she was highly honored for her "26 years of creative Indian ministry" by the Minnesota Council of Churches and several Lutheran synods, which all shared in recognizing her leadership at a banquet held in the Black Bear Hotel near Cloquet, Minnesota.

The Minnesota Council's budget for 2001 provided $56,795 for Indian work, or 10.3 percent of its total budget of $552,063.

MINNEAPOLIS

The unusual significance of the Indian ministry of the Greater Minneapolis Council of Churches was dramatized in 1995 when the $2.2 million, four-story headquarters office building for its Division of Indian work was dedicated. The Council itself moved into this new building. Designed by Indian architect Sun Rhodes and his partner in AmerINDIAN architecture, Daniel Feidt, the structure reflects the rich symbolism of Indian culture. Many symbols are related to the moon, a powerful symbol for the Plains Indians.

Mary Ellen Dumas, director of the division's staff of 23 Indian persons, said that there is now adequate space in this 26,000 square-foot structure to serve some additional 1,600 people.

Recently retired, after serving for fifteen years, she said her division's four basic programs were: *Teen Parenting*, to assist young Indian parents receive prenatal care, finish school, and learn effective parenting skills; *Youth Leadership*, to guide and encourage Indian youth in their educational growth and cultural identity; *Family Violence*, to provide protection, emotional support, information, and legal referrals for Indian victims of domestic abuse; and *Emergency Assistance*, to help Indian people who face unemployment, underemployment, low education or job skills, poor self-image, or poverty. Over 10,000 people annually receive food, clothing, and utility bills assistance. "We're here to help Native Americans of all ages when they come from the reservations. And, after they arrive, they may be having a hard time. Our business is to help and guide them to a better life. We're equipped to do that," she said.

In 1996, she was the ninth person and the first Native American to receive the Preus Leadership Award named after the bishop emeritus of the former American Lutheran Church. Her former young assistant director, Noya Woodrich, now heads the division. She calls Mary Ellen "my second mother," who "showed me how to work with other Native Americans, and what to expect of myself."

The Minneapolis council's major commitment to its Native American Ministry is illustrated by the fact that out of its total annual 1999 operating budget of some $4 million, more than $1.25 million, or 25 percent, goes for Indian work.

St. Paul

The Indian Ministry of the St. Paul Council is carried on through its Department of Indian Work, directed by Sheila WhiteEagle who has served in this capacity for some twenty-five years. The department's ministry is fivefold: *Indian Parenting* assists Indian family members in learning effective parenting skills. It is operated in collaboration with the St. Paul public schools' Early Childhood Family Education Program. *Youth Enrichment*, with after-school and summer sessions, assists Indian children with their own cultural identity and self-esteem. *American Indian Family Center* offers Indian families a "one-stop shop operation" where seven American Indian agencies are housed. These offer immunizations to children, record keeping for families, school readiness, welcoming services for new babies, and assistance in tribal enrollment. *Emergency Assistance* provides emergency supplies of food and clothing and assistance with transportation, education, and utility or housing bills for about 500 families annually. The *Collaborative Planning and Education Program* works with other organizations to evaluate current programs, meet new needs, and assure continuance and stability.

Director WhiteEagle is assisted by nine part-time paid Native American staff persons and some fifty volunteers—divided equally between Indian and non-Indian persons—without whom, Sheila said, "We would not be in business." Serving some seventy families per month, Sheila operates within an annual budget of about $218,900—18 percent of the Council's total fiscal 2000 budget of $1,213,000. Sheila also serves on many community boards related to Indian issues and matters. In 1993, she was the recipient of St. Paul's McKnight Award in Human Service.

In 1995, the Council shared in plans to provide a $1.5 million St. Paul Elder's Lodge, a senior high-rise for 41 Indian elders, the first such Indian-owned facility not located on an Indian reservation. Currently, a new program is the St. Paul Indian Trading Post, where unique Indian foods such as wild rice and Indian crafts can be purchased.

To better accommodate the department's staff needs, as well as those whom they serve, a major building renovation was completed in 2000. Graced by appropriate Indian symbols, this included an enlarged and revamped community room, used for traditional American Indian ceremonies for meetings, birthdays, baptismal and naming ceremonies and for funerals. It also includes a new kitchen, which is widely used. Built at a cost of $80,000, this became a major addition to the Council's present office headquarters on St. Paul's beautiful Summit Avenue. In addition, an adjoining Peace Garden and an International Peace Pole in the garden's center were also dedicated in 2000. Inscriptions on the pole state in many languages, "May Peace Prevail in Our Community." During the dedication and open house ceremony, distinguished religious leaders from many traditions asked for forgiveness for the mistreatment of American Indians, other people of color, and people of different faiths. Many voices were lifted up for peace, justice, and reconciliation.

Conclusion

Native American Ministry in Minnesota is probably unique in the nation in the amount of money invested annually by local ecumenical organizations. It continues to blaze new pathways of service and opportunity among these often forgotten First Peoples. It has traveled far. Supporting these labors have been at least two of Minnesota's theological seminaries. Faculty members and students of St. Paul's Luther Seminary have participated in certain phases of these Council-related ministries. This has been done in order to raise the awareness of the students who are the future spiritual leaders and also to develop the First People's theological experience as a gift to the theological understanding of the larger Church. As native peoples are liberated, we are all liberated.

Even going beyond this has been the United Theological Seminary in the Twin Cities. Located in New Brighton, this ecumenically minded seminary, related to the United Church of Christ, has offered a two-year Diploma in Indian Ministries primarily for American Indian students, but also for non-Indian students seeking to serve in native committees.

And, as we look to the future, let us also rejoice in the encouragement provided by the national American Indian College Fund (based in Denver, Colorado), which in 2001, for example, provided support for more than 2,000 Native Americans who will graduate from thirty-two tribal colleges located in twelve states in the west and midwest. These students have learned first to appreciate and affirm their Native culture and then to negotiate it within the dominant culture. As skilled and highly motivated workers and leaders, these young men and women will undoubtedly help to bring new life and hope to their communities and the whole community.

In spite of these encouraging developments, there could still be some critics. To such possible negative voices, let us recall the Indian saying, "Never judge a man until you have spent a moon in his moccasins." Minnesota's ecumenical leaders have learned not only how to walk in Indian moccasins, but in doing so, are leading the way toward a richer and fuller life for those who were here long before the arrival of most of us on these lands.

Notes

1. Serge Hummon, United Church of Christ Archives.
2. This idea is developed by Wesley Hotchkiss in a paper, "Some Presuppositions in the Work of the Church among American Indians" (Minneapolis: United Church Indian Work Consultation, 1958).

PART THREE.
LOCAL ECUMENISM RESPONDS TO THE CHANGING FACE OF URBAN AMERICA

By the early part of the twentieth century slightly more than half the people were concentrated in the cities. By the last half of the twentieth century nearly four out of five Americans lived in metropolitan areas. Concentrations of people living in limited geographic space often have problems. Those problems are often rooted in the poverty born of economic disparity, community and ethical breakdown, racism, and spiritual emptiness.

It has been the calling of local ecumenism in the city to offer the cup of cold water, to feed the hungry, to care for the sick and brokenhearted, while at the same time to speak the prophetic words of justice to the powers and principalities that are invested in maintaining the status quo.

These stories show how dedicated people are endeavoring to transform the city. Oftentimes the faithful are equal to the task, but in the end the war is sometimes lost. At other times there is transformation.

9

THE STEEL SHUTDOWN IN YOUNGSTOWN AS A CASE STUDY OF ECUMENICAL ACTION

Charles W. Rawlings

During World War II, travelers driving at night near Youngstown, Ohio, would see the horizon lit in great flashes of white light as molten steel was poured out of huge blast furnaces. Even during peacetime, the Youngstown mills, like Pittsburgh's sixty miles away, were wonders of the industrial age, lining the Mahoning River for many miles. The intricacies of the production process brought bituminous coal and limestone to the mills from Appalachian mines by river barge and train. Iron ore came by ship from the Mesabi Range in northern Minnesota down through the Great Lakes and on to the mills by train. The coal was "cooked" in huge ovens that converted it to coke. Ten-story-high blast furnaces turned a mixture of the ore and limestone into iron and mixed it with coke in older open hearth or newer basic oxygen furnaces, turning it into steel.

Poured at 2,500 degrees Fahrenheit, the steel would first be cooled into ingots and rounds until needed, then placed in reheat furnaces and poured semisolid into tube or rolling mills a quarter-mile long that flattened and shaped it into widths suitable for pipe, cars, refrigerators, or battleships.

During the war, the Youngstown steel mills employed as many as 30,000 workers. When the news hit the papers on September 19, 1977, that the Campbell Works of the Youngstown Sheet and Tube Mills would be closed by Christmas, there were 5,000 men and women at work there and another 10,000 in the nearby mills of U.S. Steel and Republic Steel. Another 20,000 people worked in steel fabrication industries or at jobs in the infrastructure of community life.

Although originally written for this volume, a version of this article appeared in *Church and Society*, a journal published by the Presbyterian Church (USA), January–February 2003: "Steel Shutdown in Youngstown: Ecumenical Response to the Opening Hand of Globalization," pp. 71–91.

Over the next three years, the Campbell Works and the Ohio Works of U.S. Steel would be closed, the blast furnaces demolished, and the land totally cleared. Within two more years, most of the even more extensive mills at nearby Pittsburgh, dramatically lining the shores of the Monongahela, Allegheny, and Ohio rivers, would also be obliterated. Sixty-three thousand jobs in basic steel and more than 65,000 other jobs vanished in a hurricane of corporate investment and banking decisions.[1] Together with the OPEC oil price war a few years earlier, this was the opening hand of the new global economy.

Over a concurrent five-year period, local and national coalitions of religious and community leaders from coast to coast organized to challenge actions by steel corporations that destroyed the livelihood of people. The first and most highly organized was the Ecumenical Coalition of the Mahoning Valley where Youngstown is located. The Coalition defined the steel crisis primarily as a moral question, not an economic one, although it became deeply involved in the effort to create a concrete answer. That answer was a worker- and community-owned steel mill that would be modernized with the help of the federal government. How the crisis in Youngstown was precipitated, its underlying causes slowly identified, and ecumenical resistance mobilized for the sake of the community is a morality play of historic proportions. In it can be seen not only the reach of corporate and financial power but also how the argument advanced by the world of business seeks to elevate business decision making beyond moral criticism.

The Justice Department Sets the Stage for a Fall

The story begins in 1969 when Attorney General John Mitchell, appointed by President Nixon, received a report from one of his antitrust division attorneys recommending against approval of a proposed acquisition by a shipping company, the Lykes Corporation of New Orleans. The target was the Youngstown Sheet and Tube Company. Lykes's assets were one-sixth the size of the assets of the steel company: $137 million compared to $806 million.[2] Although the shipping company was then making money carrying materials across the Pacific to the Vietnam War, the antitrust lawyer reasoned that Lykes wanted the huge cash flow from the steel mills for other investment purposes. His analysis was that Lykes would divert cash away from the capital reinvestment and modernization program planned for the huge Campbell Works of Youngstown Sheet and Tube. The result could mean the loss of the nation's sixth-largest steel producer, thus increasing concentration and monopoly in the steel industry and violating federal antitrust law.

Attorney General Mitchell ignored the prediction of his antitrust specialist and approved the purchase by Lykes. Six years later, in 1977, the prediction came true. Having taken out dividends in excess of income and having invested in other acquisitions and properties, Lykes announced the shutdown of the Campbell Works in Youngstown. The mill had not been modernized to meet competition and was losing money.[3]

Background of Growing Awareness among Church Leaders

The Youngstown crisis came at a historical moment when leaders in the church and secular social justice advocacy communities had come to a growing awareness of the corruption of democratic life by the power of giant corporations. A revelatory book had appeared in 1974, *Global Reach: The Power of the Multinational Corporations* by Richard Barnet and Ronald Mueller (Simon and Schuster). Local and national church leaders were reading about transnational corporations that had little accountability to national governments—companies so large they were virtual private governments, sometimes equaling the assets of a half dozen smaller nations.

The Vietnam War, as well as the Cold War, had demonstrated that Pentagon contracts were an indispensable part of the business plan of many companies. Some church leaders had begun sponsoring and participating in conferences on national priorities in an effort to shift government resources to meet human needs. A conference in Cleveland in 1977 had attracted 500 participants. The luster had gone from the image of corporations as good citizens.

The view expressed in *Global Reach* led Bishop John Burt in the Diocese of Ohio (Episcopal) to ask me (who was on his staff) to design a seminar for the Urban Bishops Coalition of the Episcopal Church featuring Richard Barnet in dialogue with the distinguished Christian ethicist John C. Bennett, president-emeritus of Union Theological Seminary. The question was what to do about the ability of the private sector to move globally "beyond accountability to any nation" with potentially damaging effects on the economic stability of families and communities in both the nation where the company was based and in the underdeveloped countries where it could find cheap labor unencumbered by laws that protected workers.

The bishops subsequently decided to work with Barnet's Institute for Policy Studies in Washington to design a series of three week-long "North-South Institutes" for clergy and laypersons emphasizing a new international paradigm, based not on Cold War politics but on North/South, rich nation/poor nation relationships.

Over the next twenty years, as deindustrialization spread and the gap between the rich and the poor grew wider, some of us would turn back more than once to a chapter in *Global Reach* entitled "The Latin-Americanization of the United States"—relevant today, in the new millennium, as the *New York Times* reports that it takes one hundred million Americans to equal the wealth of the top 1 percent of the U.S. population.[4]

Responding to the Crisis

In Youngstown, the aging steel mills were facing difficult competitive conditions that threatened their futures. Eugene Bay and Robert Campbell, the pastors at Youngstown's First Presbyterian Church, were trying to give their management class church members the theological tools to link biblical faith to economic questions. At one of a series of public forums, they had invited the Roman Catholic diocese's social justice priest, Father Edward Stanton, to present the Catholic theory of profit and the common good. On the night before the shutdown announcement, their program had featured Staughton Lynd, who had been writing and speaking on economic life as it affected working-class people and their communities. Lynd had been a professional historian on the faculty at Yale but was denied tenure after a visit to Hanoi during the war. He had become a legal aid lawyer, working now in Youngstown. (Lynd's parents were authors of a famous midcentury landmark study, *Middletown*, that documented the common captivity of local churches to dominant economic forces in their community.)[5] His remarks were quoted right underneath the shutdown story in the next day's *Youngstown Vindicator:* "It is wrong for a company to come to town, allow families to depend on it for a livelihood and leave simply because it thinks it can make a profit elsewhere. . . . It must acquire a greater sense of social responsibility. It must invest its profits where it earned them."[6] When the early edition of the *Cleveland Press* appeared that fateful day, September 19, 1977, with the headline "Youngstown Sheet and Tube to Close—5,000 to be Laid Off," it was dramatic news but not entirely unexpected by religious leaders. After reading the newspaper story, Bishop Burt immediately placed a call to his friend, James Malone, the Roman Catholic bishop of Youngstown.

Personal experience had been a great teacher for both men, who had known each other when they were young priests in Youngstown churches. Malone could remember the 1937 "Little Steel" strike and the day his dad, who was a steelworker, came home with his head deeply cut and bleeding from an attack on the picket line by Republic Steel's company police. Burt as a child had seen Ku Klux Klan crosses burn in the front yard of his own home because his father, an Episcopal priest, had spoken out against racism.

The two bishops authorized an urgent call to Richard Barnet to assist them in evaluating the situation. A week later, Barnet arrived in Youngstown for a consultation, convened by Malone, with other Youngstown religious and community leaders that also included Staughton Lynd and me.

A New Coalition Forms

Over the next several days, calls went out to other denominational leaders and to denominational national offices. Within weeks a hundred national denominational staff and Youngstown church leaders, including the local rabbi, gathered for a Steel Crisis Conference to design a response to what at that time was an unprecedented plant closing.

Key religious leadership locally and nationally wanted to come to grips with a crisis they realized might be only the tip of the iceberg in the new global economic era. For a hundred years, church leaders in America had sometimes embraced socialist ideas as a way of making industrial life serve the community through a democratic process. Because socialism had demonstrably failed in places like the Soviet Union, many clergy and intellectuals had begun to search for some form of community capitalism that could counter corporate giantism. The crisis in Youngstown attracted intellectuals and church leaders seeking to devise new responses to what was happening nationally and globally. One of them was Gar Alperovitz, an economist well known in peace circles for his writing on the decision to drop the atomic bomb on Hiroshima. He had been contacted by Staughton Lynd and was invited to the conference because of his new National Center for Economic Alternatives.[7]

Speaking at the conference, Alperovitz urged an exploration of a community or worker ownership model that could buy the Campbell Works and, with the combined political clout of religious, labor, and civic leaders, obtain federal support for the cost of modernization. It was lost on no one that an unusual configuration of both Protestant and Roman Catholic leaders had begun working together. Alperovitz's argument that the chief obstacles were moral and political, not economic, had a high resonance with the national and local religious leaders at the conference.

The next few weeks saw a flurry of hectic consultations and emergency meetings with Washington, D.C., and with local political leaders, workers, and steelworker union locals. The result was the formation of the Ecumenical Coalition of the Mahoning Valley and its decision to try to reopen the Campbell Works as a community-worker-owned steel mill.

In the early going there was an abundance of outrage throughout the community and in national circles over this closing decision made by absentee owners who had looked to their own interests, caring nothing for the welfare of the Youngstown community. The new Ecumenical Coalition was quickly joined by Methodist Bishop James Thomas of the East Ohio Conference, Rev. John Sharick, executive of the local Presbytery, Rabbi Sydney Berkowitz of the local Rodef Shalom Temple, and the United Church of Christ Ohio Conference Minister Dr. William K. Laurie. Other key local pastors included Rev. Edward Weisheimer of Central Christian Church, Rev. Donald Walton, the Methodist district superintendent, Rev. Diane Kenney, the Protestant chaplain at Youngstown State University, Rev. David Stone, director of a Baptist mission, and Rev. Robert Taylor from Howland Community Church in nearby Trumbull County.

The denominations locally and nationally quickly contributed nearly $350,000 to support a staff to mount a "Save Our Valley" campaign. Rev. Richard Fernandez of Philadelphia, another veteran of the developing consciousness about unaccountable corporate power and the former director of Clergy and Laymen Concerned about Vietnam,[8] was hired as the Save Our Valley campaign organizer. I was seconded by the Episcopal Diocese, as was Father James Stanton from the Catholic Diocese, to work virtually full time in the campaign. Rev. Robert Campbell was seconded a day a week by First Presbyterian Church.

The Campaign to Save Our Valley

The new Ecumenical Coalition first composed a lengthy pastoral statement for which John Carr, on the staff of the U.S. Catholic Conference, served as the principal writer. The statement appeared as a full-page ad in the *Washington Post* and *New York Times.* It said in part:

> We believe that this action by the Lykes Corporation . . . raises profound issues of corporate responsibility and justice. . . . We enter this complex and controversial situation out of a concern for the victims of the shutdown, out of love for our Valley at a time of crisis and out of a conviction that religious faith provides essential insights on our problems and possible remedies . . . Our Judeo-Christian tradition has articulated a highly developed social teaching. . . . The purpose of economic

> life is to serve the common good and the needs of people [and] "the dignity of persons." We believe that industrial investment decisions ought to take into account the needs and desires of the employees and the community at large. . . . economic decisions ought not to be left to the judgment of a few persons with economic power, but should be shared by the larger community which is affected by the decisions.[9]

The statement ended with ringing passages from Isaiah 58: "You oppress all your workmen and strike the poor man with your fist, let the oppressed go free, and break every yoke."

In November, a delegation from the Coalition met with Undersecretary of the Treasury Anthony Solomon, who headed a federal task force to draw up a comprehensive program to counter the growing threat of steel mill shutdowns. Youngstown had underlined the crisis of old steel mills without competitive technology, and Solomon's task force led to a $500 million program of federal loan guarantees (the report had recommended $1 billion).

A study by an outside steel expert commissioned by the local Western Reserve Development Agency estimated that it would be possible to reopen the Campbell Works of Sheet and Tube if the open hearth furnaces were replaced with new technology, such as electric furnaces, and the rolling mills were updated. The cost would be in the vicinity of $300 million.

Separately, the Department of Housing and Urban Development arranged for a $300,000 grant to be given to Gar Alperovitz's National Center for Economic Alternatives to turn such an estimate into a detailed feasibility study.[10]

Central to the effort of the Coalition was the expectation of loan guarantees for modernization costs from the Federal Steel Loan Guarantee Program. In a meeting with Jack Watson, the White House's representative in discussions with the Coalition, Watson had said that even though there was a $100 million limit to loans to any single company, the Coalition's higher need would pose no obstacle to the government.[11]

Bishop Malone presided at most Coalition meetings throughout the campaign.[12] His presence was a metaphor of grace: accepting all the varied religious and nonreligious participants, giving to all the dignity he understood was from God, and turning a bit firm and stern on rare occasions. There were some tensions within the Coalition at the level of the Steering Committee composed of staff and local pastors that guided the coalition work on a daily or weekly basis. Some had always operated within systems using an educational and conciliatory model, others (including me) were practiced in their disillusionment about how large-scale systems worked and the way they showered rewards on those who did not fundamentally challenge them.

Historic distance had also grown for much of the twentieth century between the secular Left, which kept calling for drastic measures to correct or diminish the injustices inflicted by the marketplace, and the churches, which tended to support the idea that American technological and economic progress was a manifestation of God's purpose. The Ecumenical Coalition, however, bridged this distance very comfortably. Few, if any, of its members subscribed to the notion of American exceptionalism or the ideology of progress solely through technology and wealth. The problem in 1977 was what to do about corporate power when it laid waste to entire cities by transferring its capital somewhere else in the world. The problem was called "capital flight." A great variety of socially conscientious people—believers and nonbelievers—found the Ecumenical Coalition's struggle to do something about such corporate decisions worth helping. The most prominent of these were of course Barnet, Alperovitz and his colleague Jeff Faux,[13] and leaders of the new public interest campaign movement that later became Citizen Action, including its able founder, Ira Arlook.

Save Our Valley Savings Accounts

The effort in Youngstown was both energetic and prolific over the next eighteen months. Locally, there were solemn ecumenical services, public rallies, education, and interpretation of community ownership. Nationally, other plant closings began to be announced, and church and community leaders pointed to the Youngstown effort as they developed their own local responses.

The Save Our Valley campaign focused on a unique process in which everyone could participate in supporting the reopening of the mill. All local banks agreed to open Save Our Valley savings accounts where people and organizations could place deposits as a symbol of their support for reopening the mill. The savings accounts meant that both working-class people and large organizations could show their support by making these deposits.

The United Steelworkers Union Fails to Help

Early in the campaign the Coalition struck a major roadblock. The United Steelworkers of America, with its locals in all the Youngstown mills, refused to participate or endorse the proposal for a community-worker buyout of the Campbell Works. Comfortable with long-term escalator contracts (wages went up automatically as the cost of living rose), the international union was no longer accustomed to conflict with management. They were, in fact, parroting the company line that old steel mills had to die and fade away. The International Union was hapless in the face of the new problem of capital flight. It had defined itself as a partner with the big steel companies.

Locally, this led in two divergent directions. There were still a few militant union locals who viewed the international union as an enemy (and were viewed similarly by the international), especially at the Brier Hill plant of Sheet and Tube. Only a handful of Campbell Works workers protested loudly against the shutdown, but they played a major role in explaining worker ownership to other workers.

Most union locals were influenced by many years of comfortable relations with management and had a large number of older workers in their ranks. These older workers began to say, Why should we make trouble, we'll have a good pension. In short, many labor unions had lost the tradition of struggle that had given them birth.[14] The result was a settling-in of the learned pattern of an individualist ethic where each man looked after himself. Many unions were viewed by their worker members as benefits clubs, not communities of solidarity. At no time during the Youngstown struggle did the 5,000 affected workers march down the street to protest what was happening. The largest rally in fact drew only a little more than five hundred steelworkers. Given the historic distance between unions and the churches,[15] and the comfortable union-management relationships that had developed in good economic times, the effect was that the religious community could not rally labor. *More important, it meant the Coalition could be politically isolated.*

Even so, the momentum of the Save Our Valley campaign developed a full head of steam. Non-steel unions in the region, such as the United Auto Workers, made deposits in Save Our Valley accounts. Ecumenical agencies in every Ohio city mounted parallel campaigns for signatures and funds to be placed in the Save Our Valley accounts in Youngstown. Small grants were sent from the Ecumenical Coalition to help these agencies educate and mobilize support.

Over four million dollars was placed in these Save Our Valley accounts, including major deposits from national denominations. All of this was designed to show Washington that there was broad political support for a federal role in helping Youngstown's mill reopen. In the final months of the campaign more than three thousand Ohio clergy and national religious leaders signed a full-page ad in the *Washington Post*—"Mr. President, Youngstown's Job Crisis Is a Moral Issue"—asking Jimmy Carter to support the Coalition's application for the resources needed to buy and reopen the mill.

Business Necessity versus Moral Choice

In the intricate dynamics of advocacy and negotiation that accompanied the campaign for local support, there was a constant fugue and counterpoint around crucial questions: the feasibility of reopening the Campbell Works; those with the political power to shape the answers; and the White House view of the crisis. At stake in the debate was the fundamental contention of business and corporate leaders that economic necessity lifted their decisions beyond the realm of moral choice and moral evaluation. They had to do what they had to do!

In the beginning, the steel industry had interpreted the crisis descending on Youngstown as the result of unfriendly tax laws, the high cost of environmental compliance, and, especially, steel dumping by overseas companies. Dumping referred to steel imports alleged to be coming into the country that represented excess production by foreign steel makers that they could not sell and instead sought to "dump" below the cost of production. This was a difficult cost figure to evaluate from the outside and dubious as an explanation for the failure of U.S. companies to be competitive in price. While it was possible that domestic steel had been injured by the failure of the U.S. government to enforce an anti-dumping act dating back to 1921, the argument conveniently concealed the possibility that steel from Japan was cheaper because it was coming from efficient new technology. Through political influence, steel companies in the United States had supported enactment of a protectionist trigger price mechanism that forced foreign steel to raise prices. But there was little evidence that this enabled domestic steel companies in the United States to gain greater market share.[16] American companies had operated in a dominant comfortable position for decades and were laden with comfortable, entrenched, management bureaucracies.[17] When U.S. Steel and Bethlehem Steel built huge new steel works outside Philadelphia and Baltimore in the late 1950s, they had inexplicably installed the old technology of open hearth furnaces instead of investing in the new more efficient basic oxygen furnaces.[18]

How to Modernize: Brownfield or Greenfield?

It was obvious that domestic competitive viability and success against modern foreign steel companies would require the use of such modern technologies. That was why a "continuous caster" was recommended for a reopened Campbell Works. It would eliminate the whole cooling and reheating step in steel production—delivering steel directly from the blast furnace into the casting and rolling mills. That is also why consultants working for the Ecumenical Coalition recommended a move to electric furnaces that would melt steel scrap, eliminating the costly transportation and conversion of raw materials into iron and then into steel.

For the eighteen-month life of the Ecumenical Coalition (and during subsequent efforts to save U.S. Steel's Ohio Works in Youngstown), the Coalition proceeded on the assumption that a major element in the strategy was to get both government and the steel industry as a whole to pursue the modernization of existing "brownfield" mills in communities like Youngstown—where an infrastructure of rail transportation, streets, utilities, homes, schools, churches, and synagogues had been built and the fabric of community life woven together.

Steel companies had begun to argue for ultramodern "greenfield" mills at a cost that would run into the billions of dollars. It was not an empty threat. U.S. Steel had purchased a large tract of land on the shores of Lake Erie near Conneaut for just such a greenfield mill. If that mill was built it could threaten the viability of a reopened Campbell Works and put the Ohio Works in Youngstown and steel mills in Pittsburgh out of business. The political debate and maneuvering in Washington about how expensive it would be to help the Campbell Works modernize and reopen was aided and abetted by the steel industry, which used greenfield advocacy to argue against modernizing an old mill like the Campbell Works. For the Ecumenical Coalition, the argument was that modernizing the Campbell Works would cost a few hundred million. A greenfield plant would cost a few billion dollars.

The first signal that something quite different was happening came in a dramatic report prepared by Edward Kelley and Mark Schutes for the Ohio Public Interest Campaign. Lykes had claimed that its bankers would not loan them any more money for use at the Campbell Works. But the report disclosed that the same banks that had financed Lykes's takeover at Youngstown were now lending money to Japanese steel companies *for their modernization*. Citibank's loans to Japanese steel jumped from $58.9 million in 1975 to $230 million in 1977, a 391 percent increase. Chase Manhattan loans jumped from $59 to $204 million in the same period, and Chemical Bank from $15 to $82 million. Worst of all, steelworker pension funds were deposited in the same banks, meaning that their own assets were part of a financial pool being used to finance the modernization of foreign mills that would take their jobs away from them.[19]

The second signal came after the fact, but played a role in the story as it was happening. The steel crisis at Youngstown had became a vortex that focused the work of many progressive economists and policy analysts. To understand the impact of subsequent knowledge and developments, it is necessary to move briefly ahead of the story. I vividly remember the afternoon strategy meeting and the stunned silence in May 1980 when the second signal about modernization came. Recent research gathered by a varied group of technical specialists was being presented to us by two of those specialists when we suddenly, collectively, realized that U.S. Steel was neither going to modernize its brownfield sites *nor* build a new greenfield plant at Conneaut. *They were going to begin to get out of the steel business.*

It was a surprise beyond the imagination of any of us. Unknown to the Coalition, the company had been reinventing itself in the context of global economic opportunities. It had abandoned its greenfield plan long before it became public. Covertly, it too was looking to its own interests, not the community's. It would soon change its name to USX—a suitable nom de plume for a company that had concluded that the whole world had now become its oyster to harvest.

Attitudes of Business

Ideas that modify hierarchical ownership have often come under attack in the United States as being socialist. Predictably, this happened to the Ecumenical Coalition. Edgar Speer, chairman of U.S. Steel at the time of the Sheet and Tube shutdown, denounced the Ecumenical Coalition proposal for a community-worker-owned mill in a Chamber of Commerce speech calling it "nothing short of a Communist takeover."[20]

The local business community had at first reacted with others against the closing. As months passed while the feasibility studies were made and negotiations with the government unfolded, they too began to talk about the inevitability of closing the mill. This may have been aided by literature in circulation in business circles alleging that Alperovitz's National Center for Economic Alternatives was trying to orchestrate a takeover of the Democratic Party and Wall Street. When the Coalition's campaign director Richard Fernandez and I went before Youngstown business leaders to give them a progress report on the Save Our Valley campaign, we had expected a warm welcome. Their early reactions to the shutdown had been anger about the neglect of the Campbell Works by Lykes. This time the reception was frosty, and during the question period it became apparent that they now were defending the Lykes decision as just "good business sense."

However eloquently stated, the moral argument from the religious communities where most of these businessmen (yes, men) attended church services on Sunday had little resonance. Theirs was a culture in which business decisions were understood to reflect a natural, one may say, Darwinian, process, where men and women courageously acted according to the necessities of a natural order that God had created. It was thought by them to be a realm that made moral assessment irrelevant and a waste of time.

The Government's Shifting Position

All of these currents had the effect of diminishing the political influence of the religious coalition. Meanwhile, the Carter administration also made a significant bureaucratic and ideological shift, moving away from their early sympathetic stance toward Youngstown and the Ecumenical Coalition. Economic development was taken out of the Department of Housing and Urban Development (HUD), which had given the grant for the feasibility study of the Coalition's idea, and put into the hands of the pro-business Department of Commerce and its Economic Development Administration (EDA).

Support in the Carter administration had come initially from the Treasury Department and its steel loan guarantee program and from HUD, which enthusiastically funded the feasibility studies made by the Ecumenical Coalition's consultants.

This bureaucratic coup d'etat within the Carter administration not only demonstrated its underlying ideological hostility toward the community ownership idea, but it also was drawn from an argument made by the steel industry that the federal loan guarantees proposed for Youngstown constituted a subsidy that compromised unsubsidized private enterprise.[21] This argument was made not only while big steel's banks were investing in Japanese modernization, but while private steel companies themselves actually were beginning to receive loan guarantees.

The great tragedy was that the relationship to the federal government by both the stricken Youngstown blue-collar worker community and the religious community was essentially adversarial. The Carter administration seemed to say, Prove to us that we, the federal government, have a responsibility for the economy and welfare of communities. In fact, the long-standing partnership between government and powerful business interests was the more familiar and reliable relationship. (This, in turn, should throw a cautionary light on the current popularity in 2003 of the idea that the real partnership between government and religion should be for purposes of charity, "charitable choice," leaving justice to the invisible hand of the market economy.)

A Second Adverse Justice Department Decision

A fateful development at the Justice Department in 1979—now in the hands of a Democratic administration—helped cast the final die and replicated the decision of a Republican administration that had started Youngstown downhill in 1969. The Lykes Corporation was petitioning the Justice Department, under "a failing company" provision of antitrust law, for permission to merge with LTV Corporation, a Dallas-based conglomerate that had bought Jones and Laughlin Steel. Once again, the Justice Department's antitrust lawyers concluded that the merger would result in significant increased concentration of ownership in the steel industry "above that allowed by the department's merger guidelines."[22] Faced with this proposed merger, the Coalition had petitioned the Anti-Trust Division to attach conditions to any approved merger that would require Lykes-LTV to continue to buy the products of a reopened Campbell Works. They also concluded that Lykes was in fact not a failing company. The attorney general, Griffin Bell, ruled against his own antitrust staff and waived aside any notion of attaching conditions that would protect a reopened Campbell Works.

Calling what happened a case study in the politics of influence, Staughton Lynd would later describe the interlocking relationships of the White House with Lykes and LTV when faced with a hostile Anti-Trust Division recommendation:

> The Wall Street attorneys for the two conglomerates [Lykes and LTV] then went over the head of the Anti-Trust division to Attorney General Griffin Bell. In doing so they could make use of a southern old boys network. . . . Jack Watson, the White House Assistant who was in charge of a decision about the Ecumenical Coalition's quest for Federal help [had been] in private practice with the Atlanta law firm of King and Spaulding. Griffin Bell was a prominent member of King and Spaulding before becoming a Federal judge. Stanley Rosenkrantz, a partner of the Tampa law firm headed by Chester Ferguson, Vice Chairman of the Board of Lykes, was also a former partner of King and Spaulding. Both were born in Sumter County, as was then President Jimmy Carter.[23]

Lynd then reports the story told to reporter John Greenman by members of the Anti-Trust Division who were lectured on the matter by the attorney general: "He [Griffin Bell] told us we should not treat what the companies tell us with suspicion as in an adversary posture," Erik Kaplan said. "We should put more faith in what they say to us." And John Shenefield quoted Bell to the effect that "here you have businessmen who are in trouble. They are trying to do something. We should try to think of ourselves as their allies."[24]

The merger would be a nearly fatal event for the Coalition proposal. A merged Lykes and LTV (with Lykes still holding other Youngstown Sheet and Tube Properties, including the busy tube mill that was expected to buy 200,000 tons of the reopened plant's product annually and the Indiana Harbor mill that normally would buy some Sheet and Tube products) would mean loss of the captive market at the tube mill and some of the market with other nearby mills. Instead, an LTV merged with Lykes would sell those customers products from its nearby Jones and Laughlin works.

In the early days of the Ecumenical Coalition's effort, Jack Watson, speaking for the White House, had waived the supposed $100 million limit on loan guarantees, saying that the $300 million required for the Campbell Works modernization posed "no obstacle." As big steel asserted its ideologically based objections ("subsidies smack of government interference in the market, the proposal is socialist"), as the Coalition suffered from lack of a partnership with labor (whose partnership was with big steel), and as the original marketing plan was shattered by the Justice Department's refusal to follow its antitrust staff recommendations or attach conditions to the Lykes-LTV merger, the White House now began backing away from its pledge that the official loan guarantee limit was not $100 million. Subsequent documents and interviews years later demonstrated that it kept the Ecumenical Coalition in an application process it had already decided to refuse.[25]

The Ecumenical Coalition kept trying to adapt to the changing conditions. In the final four months of the Coalition's effort, two former steel managers volunteered to help with the strategy for reopening. John Stone, former vice president of Sheet and Tube operations, urged the coalition to work at the other end of the mill process and led them to design a plan for reopening only the finishing mills in the first stage. Frank McGough, former assistant to the manager of the Sheet and Tube's Indiana Harbor plant, helped evaluate the equipment and plan for the phased plant restart. Two major law firms in Cleveland, Thompson, Hine, and Flory and Benesch Friedlander, assisted with financial and organizational planning. The investment banking firms of Warburg Paribas Becker and Lazard Fràres designed placement of the modernization loans with private lenders.

A final package was submitted to EDA and the White House that included a $10 million grant from the state of Ohio, called for a $17 million

UDAG grant—the combined $27 million needed to meet the price established by LTV for the Campbell Works and to create the new company—a $10 million EDA-funded Employee Stock Ownership Plan (ESOP), and $245 million from the loan guarantee program.

The Global Context

The White House rejection as well as the decisions made by the various steel corporations—Lykes, LTV, and U.S. Steel—must be placed in the context of the global firestorm that was to turn great industrial centers from coast to coast into rust belts. In one twelve-month period of that storm, the American machine tool industry lost 60 percent of its business to overseas competition. The steel companies themselves were reeling under the impact of the global economy they had not anticipated.

Still, this same corporate America and its investors simply moved to other green pastures. The workers of the rust belt for the most part were forced to move down the economic food chain. Marriages dissolved, homes were lost, millions of lives were disrupted. When the dust settled, it would be said that this was simply the transition from a manufacturing to an information economy. But the cost was that the average worker 20 years later was making less than he was when Lykes shut down Youngstown in 1977.

Subsequent Events

The other shoe soon dropped in Youngstown. U.S. Steel announced it would close its giant Ohio Works in Youngstown. In this instance, the leader of the union local, Bob Vasquez—unlike the passive union heads at the Campbell Works—was ready to fight. The remnants of the Youngstown coalition conferred with him and his officers and, together with Staughton Lynd, began a new effort to buy this mill, or at least some of its finishing mills, and create a worker-owned facility. The union marched, occupied company buildings, and held mass rallies. And the international union backed them up this time.

The problem this time was that U.S. Steel refused to sell the mill to them. It was during this period that we learned that U.S. Steel was actually getting out of much of its steel business. The union went to federal court and won an injunction forbidding the company to dismantle the facilities. During the injunction hearing Federal Judge Thomas Lambros began with a powerful opening statement:

> Everything that has happened in the Mahoning Valley has been happening for many years because of steel. Schools have been built, roads have been built. Expansion has taken place because of steel. And to accommodate that industry lives and destinies of the inhabitants of that community were based and planned on the basis of that institution: Steel. . . . [I]t seems to me that a property right has arisen from this lengthy, long-established relationship between United States Steel, the steel industry as an institution, the community of Youngstown, the people in the Mahoning County and the Mahoning Valley in having given and devoted their lives to this industry. I think the law can recognize the property right to the extent that U.S. Steel cannot leave that Mahoning Valley and the Youngstown area in a state of waste, that it cannot completely abandon its obligation to that community, because certain vested rights have arisen out of this long relationship and institution.[26]

A new feasibility for purchase study was commissioned and the union local went to trial in federal court to try to force U.S. Steel to sell. It was a poignant scene: three courageous Legal Aid lawyers against one of the nation's largest corporate law firms—Squire, Sanders, and Dempsey—carrying files by the "boat load." To provide some balance to this, former attorney general Ramsey Clark came into the case as a lawyer on the side of the plaintiffs, making the opening speech before Judge Lambros.

In the end the judge moved to safe ground. He gave permission to U.S. Steel to sell one of the rolling mills, not to the workers but to a small firm brought into being behind the scenes, Toro, Inc. The judge was permitted to believe, as his closing remarks from the bench revealed, that he thought he was dealing with the large Toro Corporation that manufactured mowers and snowblowers.

The Dominoes Begin to Fall

A year later, U.S. Steel blew up its blast furnaces and leveled the Ohio Works in Youngstown. Two years later 85 percent of all basic steel jobs in Youngstown were gone and with them 15,000 related steel-fabricating jobs for a net loss of 25,000 jobs. Over the next three years, 75 percent of Pittsburgh's steel industry would be demolished—even the great Edgar Thompson works and the historic Homestead mill were completely leveled—and 175,000 jobs eliminated.[27] Lost in this drama are hundreds of thousands of stories about people who had their hearts broken, who lost their homes, whose spouse died prematurely, or sank into alcoholism, or committed suicide. In the end, the incapacity of our society to care about what was happening to the people is what defeated the many ecumenical coalitions that formed around the country to help them resist a fate that was not inevitable. There were alternatives and there were better choices.

The Preferential Option for Pietism Marginalizes the Ecumenical Community

The fact that the Ecumenical Coalition made its effort with Jimmy Carter in the presidency has special significance. At no time during this combined effort of the national Protestant and Roman Catholic communities did President Carter give the slightest hint of interest. For his administration the issue was always political and economic, not moral. This was of course not unique, as the Coalition's experience demonstrated. Both a Republican and a Democrat attorney general made essentially the same kind of decisions with the same effect: to waive aside antitrust arguments and community interests in support of the wishes of large corporations.

But Carter's embrace of pietism *was* unique, and it had far-reaching effects: helping to establish in the media and in the public mind a religiosity that was quietist with reference to both public governments and the exercise of private power. It is not an accident that ecumenism suffered a dramatic loss of public support and private funding after the time of the Ecumenical Coalition (a trend that began with the backlash against ecumenical and church activism for civil rights and against the Vietnam War). The regression away from ecumenism that came in the last quarter of the twentieth century is directly proportional to the triumph of an individualist piety that can embrace acts of mercy but not acts of justice.

The generation of leaders who unreservedly plunged into the struggle to make Youngstown and similar situations a moral issue viewed from the perspective of biblical faith has now gone into retirement. It remains for a new generation in the churches to overcome this disastrous separation of faith from the world where people live, act, and make choices about moral issues every day (whether consciously or not). For the hour of trial surely will come again, whether because times turn bad and demagogues have new opportunities or because U.S. foreign relations has been defined as a business. In a world of growing inequality, the capacity to act mercifully may exist only if we have first acted justly.

Six Reflections on Labor, the Left, and the Religious Communities

One. When Staughton Lynd wrote *The Fight against Shutdowns,* he made a point of "putting the workers in the center of the story because I think that's where they belong." But the workers seldom saw themselves in the center, except briefly when they stormed the U.S. Steel headquarters building in Pittsburgh (and then went home for dinner) and when Bob Vasquez, the heroic leader of the U.S. Steel union, led a takeover of the local company building (for only a few hours). The workers do belong in the center of their own self-determination process, but little in the experience of these union workers—a post–World War II generation—gave them any sense of having power or influence in either their corporation or their union. For them, the deal was that at the mill you served someone else's purposes and got paid for doing that, and you belonged to the union because it was a benefits club. The memory of struggle by their fathers and mothers was long lost, together with the solidarity and will to mobilize with a collective and community consciousness to resist what was being done to them.

Two. The Ecumenical Coalition had parallel liabilities. Among the participating Protestant denominations their roots lay primarily in the early English, German, and Scoth-Irish settlers who became the ownership and management class of the nineteenth and twentieth centuries. Catholic roots were in the immigrant populations who arrived later to work the mines and mills of the Industrial Revolution. With the exception of Bishop Malone, the Coalitions's largely Protestant leadership was not at all close to working people culturally or sociologically. It was not part of their tradition to teach agency and the dignity of participation to working people, let alone support worker militancy. The Coalition members wanted to do exactly that, but they and their churches had too long walked the road that saluted the moral legitimacy of the wealth and power that built their churches and paid for their costly organs and stained glass windows. The church was no better prepared to change course than was labor.

Three. Not surprisingly, the 200-year-old debate in the United States over capitalism versus various proposals to modify its power and political influence for the public good (ranging from regulatory legislation to socialism) shaped both community consciousness and religious sensibilities in the Youngstown effort. There was a more radical Protestant and Roman

Catholic perspective in Youngstown—certain in its conviction that no invisible moral hand was at work in capital markets—but it coexisted alongside the view that capitalism is an order of nature, a view that invokes an extremely convenient god. Bishop Malone intuitively leaned toward this more radical and activist camp, but his clergy and staff tended to a more traditional recognition of the political reality of power and money. Exacting concessions from market powers, not their transformation through some form of community capitalism, was their practiced inclination.[28]

Four. The relationship between church leaders and intellectuals on the Left also deserves careful scrutiny in the Youngstown story. It was much more the Richard Barnets, Mark Raskins, Gar Alperovitzes, and Ira Arlooks, who had done the hard study and intellectual digging, that helped illuminate the structural nature of the local community predicament in the new transnational economy. They have received little praise and recognition for imagining new solutions within a democratic framework—whether called democratic socialism or community capitalism—and it was and is an evil deed when this rich imagination is trashed in the name of corporate America.

Five. A theology of engagement and advocacy for the oppressed fired the local and national ecumenical community's participation; but there was a missing link and that was the absence of a shared language with the Left about what was sacred in this struggle. Ostensibly and easily, it was the common good, the threat to the human community posed by the private and public forces in play. But at a deeper level there was a mismatch between the institutional traditions and theological roots of the religious participants and the doubts by those on the Left that the religious community's sacred language was any longer efficacious in a desacralized world, or that it afforded anything more than a historic community infrastructure upon which to organize. My view, grown clearer over the subsequent twenty years, is that the Youngstown partners from the secular Left yearned to hear the sacred word of the religious tradition but mostly could not—and this was because economic categories had become more universal and living forms of discourse than religious language. It is equally true that government and corporate officials also heard no moral imperative in the language of the Ecumenical Coalition (a language they considered a form of discourse irrelevant to business and political realities). But when they heard the voice of the Left in the coalition they had a long-prepared and ready category at hand, which was to declare it communistic. The challenge for the future is the recovery of sacred vision and language that aims at concrete economic and political problems in ways that subordinate all that is self-interested, private, or humanly destructive. That must be a sacred language everyone will be able to recognize. The biblical mandate *is* to hold all things in common! "Awe came to everyone, because many wonders and signs were being done by the Apostles. All who believed were together and had all things in common; they would sell their possessions and goods and distribute the proceeds to all, as any had need." (Acts 2: 43–45, NRSV translation)

Six. The Ecumenical Coalition's principal liability needs to be seen clearly. It was led by clergy who, however well intended, were not close to working people culturally or sociologically. The real role of the Coalition, its missionary role, was to try to wed its resistance to injustice to the passive comfort of middle-class church members who had been taught, and had believed all their lives, that there was an inherent legitimacy to economic life even when it wounded them. Retrospectively, it is clear that we all belonged to churches with two religions: one biblical, the other governed by the god of the work ethic—which holds that the successful have done the right thing and the unsuccessful are morally flawed. I remember leaving desperate meetings of steelworkers and local activists to drive to mandatory denominational functions at wooded retreat centers, arriving to the warm sounds of lay and clerical church leaders enjoying their sherry hour. They were concerned, as they thought Jesus had taught them to be, for the victims in society, but they never thought these victims had any moral claim on their own comfortable lives. That's one difference between ethics and piety.

Notes

1. John P. Hoerr, *And the Wolf Finally Came: The Decline of the American Steel Industry* (Pittsburgh: University of Pittsburgh Press, 1988), pp. 589–590. Figures were provided to Hoerr by the Pennsylvania Department of Labor and Industry. Very important in measuring the disaster of job changes for workers is that between 1979 and 1986 manufacturing jobs in the Pittsburgh region declined from 27.9 percent to 15 percent of total jobs in the SMSA, while lower paying service jobs grew from 19.3 to 29.6 percent.

2. For a full description of all Youngstown Sheet and Tube facilities and the history of Lykes and other competing company acquisition attempts, see William T. Hogan, S.J., *Economic History of the Iron and Steel Industry in the United States,* vol. 4, pt. 6. Lykes was "a holding corporation which derived 85% of its sales from steamship interests. This dependence on a business *which requires government subsidies for its existence* and is subject to the tides of political pressure was one of the principal reasons for its drive to expand into non-steamship areas" (p. 1839) (emphasis added).

3. Barry Bluestone and Bennett Harrison, *The Deindustrialization of America* (New York: Basic Books, 1982), pp. 152–153, includes a chart of capital investment

in Youngstown from 1961 to 1977 showing the sharp decline after the Lykes merger. See also the detailed discussion in Thomas G. Fuechtmann, *Steeples and Stacks, Religion and Steel Crisis in Youngstown* (New York: Cambridge University Press, 1989), pp. 41–53.

4. *New York Times*, September 14, 2000.

5. Robert S. Lynd and Helen Merrell Lynd, *Middletown: A Study in Contemporary American Culture* (New York: Harcourt, Brace and Company, 1929).

6. *Youngstown Vindicator*, September 19, 1977.

7. Lynd and Alperovitz in 1973 had co-authored a thin volume entitled *Strategy and Program: Two Essays toward a New American Socialism.* Although not known by Ecumenical Coalition leadership at the time, there is no reason to believe that this fact, if known, would have deterred the Coalition from relationship with them. However, a discussion by phone between Lynd and Alperovitz reported in the Fuechtmann book may explain the sudden move by Richard Barnet at the Institute for Policy Studies to hand his interest in the Youngstown crisis over to Alperovitz. This was a development that, in my opinion, did not bode well for the project. Barnet was highly analytical and objective. Alperovitz was brilliant but more possessed by an outsized drive for self-realization. The Lynd-Alperovitz essay was subsequently used by the business community and conservative government officials to deprecate the Ecumenical Coalition proposals.

8. Started initially by John Bennett and William Sloan Coffin, the organization went through several name changes reflecting changing paradigms and perspectives. It became Clergy and Laity Concerned about Vietnam and then just Clergy and Laity Concerned.

9. Published simultaneously in the *Washington Post* and the *New York Times*, November 29, 1977.

10. Fuechtmann, *Steeples and Stacks,* p. 97.

11. Federal or state loan guarantees are actually privately placed loans in which the federal or state government "guarantees" the loan, thus protecting the private bank from loss while offering them the risk-free opportunity to earn the interest derived from the loan.

12. Episcopal Bishop John Burt was co-chair of the Coalition, but he was based in Cleveland and therefore not able to be present on a constant basis.

13. Jeff Faux became executive director of the major progressive Washington think tank, the Economic Policy Institute.

14. Two years later over dinner, a regional AFL-CIO organizer in Oregon described the problem to me faced by labor as a function of the low social status of blue-collar workers. "The problem is," he said, speaking of his own generation, "we told our children not to be like us."

15. Space does not permit elaboration of this distance but it is very important historically and formed a backdrop to the drama led by the Ecumenical Coalition. Protestant churches had few blue-collar workers. They were inherently pro-management. The Catholic Church, with congregations that did have many blue-collar workers, nevertheless historically pursued a very conservative tack on labor militancy, and few workers looked to the Catholic Church, even if they belonged to it, for help with their labor-management struggles.

16. See the United States International Trade Commission's "Condition of Competition in the Western U.S. Steel Market between Certain Domestic and Foreign Steel Products," USITC Publication 1004, September 1979. "The demand for domestic steel is somewhat unresponsive to changes in import prices," the report noted, pointing to a lack of balance between domestic capacity in the Western mar-

ket and the particular products in demand. See also Hoerr, *And the Wolf Finally Came,* pp. 94ff.

17. Agis Salpulkas, business writer for the *New York Times,* wrote on February 1, 1980: "The litany is familiar. The blame for the industry's troubles fall on outside forces such as imports and interference by the Environmental Protection Agency. No fault is found with the top steel management responsible for the industry's relatively low profitability. . . . 'the trigger price system' helped the steel companies to raise steel prices even when demand was failing."

18. Hoerr, *And the Wolf Finally Came,* pp. 97ff, 423ff.

19. Edward Kelley and Mark Schutes, "Lykes Responsibility for Closing the Campbell Works" (Cleveland: Ohio Public Interest Campaign, 1978); see also "Lykes and Its Banks," 1978, by the same authors.

20. Cited in Fuechtmann, *Steeples and Stacks,* p. 177.

21. Fuechtmann in *Steeples and Stacks* gives a view different from mine, the Coalition's, and Staughton Lynd's in *The Fight against Shutdowns.* Fuechtmann believes the EDA acted honorably and that the Coalition failed to create a solid business plan for a reopened Campbell Works. But the evidence is overwhelming that the EDA from the beginning was never interested and offered no real assistance, remaining an adversary of both the community and the Coalition. Fuechtmann's book, published ten years later, lapses into unspecified and undated references to interviews in which the author's own voice is the sole authority without documentation. On the other hand, Fuechtmann correctly notes the ideological vision of Gar Alperovotz, who actually knew very little about the steel business itself. Fuechtmann's claim is probably correct that John Greenman (later the reporter for the *Warren Tribune*), while still working for the Coalition, interviewed Alperovitz's consultant, Paul Marshall, discovering that he was privately doubting his own projections as to independent feasibility. Alperovitz's response to Greenman, according to Fuechtmann, was that the plan all along had been to get the government to provide jobs by maintaining the Sheet and Tube Company, not to create a successful, independent company. See pp. 220ff.

22. Fuechtmann, *Steeples and Stacks,* p. 219.

23. Staughton Lynd, *The Fight against Shutdowns: Youngstown's Steel Mill Closing* (Singlejack Books, 1982), p. 100. Lynd here draws from the dramatic investigative reporting of John Greenman for the *Warren Tribune,* December 9–14, 1979. As a matter of full disclosure, Greenman had worked for the Ecumenical Coalition before going to the *Warren Tribune.*

24. Ibid.

25. Ibid., see pp. 63ff; Fuechtmann, *Steeples and Stacks,* see pp. 252ff.

26. *Williams v. U.S. Steel,* U.S. District Court, Cleveland, Ohio, Transcript of Proceedings, February 28, 1980.

27. The Pittsburgh story is told in *The Business of America,* a film made in 1982 by California Newsreel and shown on PBS stations nationwide. It opens with footage of the dynamiting by U.S. Steel of its own giant blast furnaces in Youngstown. See also William Serrin, *Homestead: The Glory and Tragedy of an American Steel Town* (New York: Times Books, 1992).

28. Father Edward Stanton, the priest assigned by Bishop Malone to the Steering Committee of the Ecumenical Coalition is effectively supported by Fuechtmann's *Steeples and Stacks* as a man with a more practical view than the outside consultant, Gar Alperovitz, or this writer. Stanton spoke often with Bill Hogan at Fordham, a Jesuit priest and nationally recognized expert on the steel industry. But the human and community tragedy caused by the steel industry is missing from Hogan's voluminous writings on the steel business.

10

GROWING TOWARD COMMUNITY IN ROCHESTER, NEW YORK

Lawrence E. Witmer

An anniversary is an occasion for celebration, remembering, and looking forward. To celebrate the seventy-fifth anniversary in 1994 of ecumenical ministries in Monroe County, New York, I prepared a history of local ecumenical life. For the 1999 National Workshop on Christian Unity held in Rochester, I enlarged and updated it.[1]

Our remembering of ecumenical experiences is often personal. Each of us recalls the people, events, and projects that touched our lives in a special way. Each has a way of describing how God's presence was known through these experiences, usually in helping us break out of our narrowly defined parameters of church life to recognize and appreciate the more holistic Body of Christ. However, this historical overview seeks to broaden personal perspectives. It offers in a few pages a story about the development of relationships among churches and their service to the greater Rochester community over a period of eighty years. It describes how changing social environments and evolving commitments to ecumenical life have found expression, primarily through the succession of conciliar structures created by the churches.

Apart from certain pleasures associated with reminiscence, telling stories about ecumenical life in the past can help us understand the present. Further, an informed historical perspective, joined with a sensitive assessment of present realities, can enable effective planning for the future. Undergirding this effort is a prayer that God's Spirit will guide our review of past decades so current leaders can be empowered to encourage faithful life among the churches in years to come.

In the Beginning: Serving Together through Movements

From the time of the earliest settlement in what was to become Rochester, the church was there. As pioneers moved to the frontier in western New York, they brought their faith and their churches with them. In 1830, just a few years before the city was incorporated, the great evangelist Charles G. Finney first came to Rochester. Revivalism was sweeping the country. Viewed from the churches, the challenge was to build moral character in the pioneers as they were building a new society. Finney's forceful and convincing message brought together people from all the churches, which at the time numbered fifteen. Approximately 400 families were brought to Christian faith and drawn into the participating churches, including some of the city's most prominent citizens. The churches, together, had made a dramatic and significant impact on the young community and its leadership. By the time of the Civil War, Rochester had a population of 51,000 served by 35 churches.

Throughout the nineteenth century, lay movements were a dynamic force for cooperation across religious lines by Rochester citizens. By 1818 the Sabbath School movement was established to help make the Bible accessible by teaching young people to read. In 1822 the Monroe County Bible Society brought together people from many churches around the goal of placing a Bible in every home in the community. Soon thereafter a Tract Society was formed to supply religious reading to canal boat passengers passing through the city on the new Erie Canal. In heeding God's call to send missionaries to Native Americans, China, Burma, and Africa, Rochester lay leaders found common cause and by 1826 organized the Monroe County Missionary Society. Later in the century, local church members were caught up in national movements for women's suffrage, abolition, and temperance. National influences also led Christians to found the local YMCA and YWCA.

However, while many individual clergy and laity were involved in these activities, relationships among churches through the early decades were not always harmonious. The religious heterogeneity in this expanding frontier was a new experience for all. Separate language churches and schools were common for new immigrants coming from various European countries. Doctrinal differences were held rigidly as the basis of identity and distinction for each denomination. Zeal for moral causes such as temperance and abolition brought tension within and among the churches.

By the last decade of the century, frays in the social fabric became obvious, and the churches began to respond in new ways. A serious recession led to widespread unemployment. Labor strikes, child labor, growing slums, corrupted politicians, and many other social ills led many to despair over prospects for Rochester. Facing growing appeals from many local agencies serving the poor and marginalized, church leaders began looking for ways to integrate charitable and religious efforts to meet pressing human needs. In 1901 leaders sought to organize a Federation of Churches to encourage greater collaboration. However, the effort failed due to disagreement on whether Unitarians and Jews should be admitted. Two years later a Ministerial Association was formed among Christian pastors. It served for nearly two decades as a focal point for church leaders, dealing with a wide variety of community and religious issues (e.g., Sunday closings, labor disputes, temperance, and wholesome entertainment for young people).

During the decades spanning the turn of the century, a new social conscience slowly awakened in the churches. Walter Rauschenbusch, a professor at the Rochester Theological Seminary, gave powerful expression to this new sense of moral responsibility. He saw materialism strangling the human spirit and spoke of the need for social salvation. Christians began to see that beyond individual morality there were implications for building social justice through the institutions of modern society.

Swept up in a wave of patriotism during World War I, local churches supported the "war to end all wars." There was widespread sentiment that when the war was over, the world would be a better place and that the churches would have a leading role in building a world in which peace and justice would prevail.

Fostering Cooperation: The Years of Church Federation, 1919–1961

In the aftermath of the war, American hopes for a peaceful and prosperous world were on the rise. The strenuous war mobilization had brought church leaders into many cooperative efforts, and their experiences built new levels of understanding and trust. Further, the Federal Council of Churches had been established in 1908 and had proven a valuable model for coordinating chaplain and relief services during the war years. This movement had already taken root in many other cities. The time was right for building new relationships among churches in Rochester.

From the Ministerial Association came a proposal to establish the Federation of Churches of Rochester and Monroe County. On December 2, 1918, just three weeks after the Armistice, 168 representatives of 53 churches from 9 denominations met in the First Methodist Episcopal Church. A committee of laymen agreed to underwrite for two years an annual budget of $7,500. The Federation was born; it was the first community-wide, interchurch organization in Rochester.

One of the first undertakings of the Federation was a community-wide survey of religious needs and affiliations. A total of 175,000 members were counted in 158 churches. Christian education became an immediate priority. Within a year 300 Sunday School teachers had graduated from the Federation's School of Religious Education. Vacation Bible Schools were greatly expanded. In 1920 the Rochester Board of Education agreed to release pupils from school for one hour each week to attend a religious education program. At first the Federation provided teacher training and curriculum development, but by 1928 it assumed full administrative responsibility for the program. It grew over the years until peaking in 1959, serving over 4,000 students from 59 schools.

Major attention also was given to providing chaplain services in hospitals. Comity agreements guided new church development by the denominations as coordinated through the Federation's Church Extension Department. Community-wide worship services were held at Lent and Thanksgiving. In 1921 the Federation brought together women leaders to form a Council of Church Women (which later became Church Women United). In 1926 a gathering was held to promote goodwill between liberal Jews and Protestants. By 1933 Federation leaders helped initiate the Interfaith Goodwill Committee. With leadership provided by Jewish, Roman Catholic, and Protestant faith communities, it served for more than two decades to enlarge interreligious understanding. Throughout the life of the Federation, ongoing attention also was given to such concerns as evangelism, mission education, social welfare, public health, industry-labor relations, child labor, Race Relations Sunday, prohibition, gambling, prostitution, and Sabbath observance.

During the Federation's forty years, at least thirty-seven churches were founded or moved as the result of guidance by the Comity Committee. Both radio and television were invented, and the participation of churches in using these mass media was channeled almost entirely through the Federation. In 1940 the Federation's name was changed to the Federation of

Churches of Rochester and Vicinity to include the seven-county "trading area" around Rochester. By the late 1950s membership had reached 247 churches of 28 denominations—Protestant, Anglican, and Orthodox.

Patterns of financial support also changed. Four years after its founding, church contributions totaled some $9,000 annually, with 153 individual gifts providing $2,800. By 1959 church gifts increased to $29,135, and 11,339 individual gifts amounted to $65,358. According to Federation records, no other city in the country had a greater proportion of donors to population.

Initially there was suspicion among some church leaders that the Federation was part of a covert strategy towards organic unity. Such was not the case. However, while walls between denominations did not come down, churches grew more conscious of the existence of each other. While many enjoyed the interchurch fellowship, many also yearned for a more substantive unity than federation could bring.

In reflecting on the Federation years at the time of his retirement as executive secretary in 1959, the Rev. Hugh Chamberlin Burr shared these observations:

> It is the genius of the Federation that it is not something superimposed upon the churches but an agency developed by the churches through which their resources are pooled and their potential developed. . . . Through the Federation the churches at first sought to do the things which could be done better together than separately. Through the Federation they continue to do not only these things, but increasingly have developed programs which, were they not being done by the churches together, would not be done at all.

Recognizing a Common Calling: The Council of Churches, 1961–1970

During the 1960s, new community dynamics pressed for change, most significant among them the growing presence of racial minorities in the city. Through the1950s, the nonwhite population of the city had more than tripled, growing from 7,845 to 24,214. Most immigrants came from the rural South and Puerto Rico, people eagerly seeking employment within Rochester's booming economy. However, there was a dearth of unskilled jobs available. According to the 1960 census, only one in five African American adults had a high school education, and less than 4 percent had college degrees. What housing newcomers could find was limited to two areas of the inner city where buildings were severely blighted. Complaints of police harassment and excessive use of force had begun to surface, and there were other indications of growing social unrest. The Federation of Churches paused to assess its mission priorities.

In the wider ecumenical world the "church council movement" had spread rapidly. Following the establishment of the World Council of Churches (1948) and the National Council of Churches of Christ (1950), Church Federations became Councils of Churches in many states and cities across the United States.

With the adoption of the "council" concept, the national denominations signaled a growing awareness of common calling in mission. Their intention was to bring churches together for planning and service in a more comprehensive and coordinated manner than earlier Federations had envisioned. To illustrate, the purposes of the NCCC included "to do for the churches such cooperative work as they authorize the council to carry out on their behalf, and to foster and encourage cooperation among the churches." The Council, as an ecumenical agency, was expected to speak to and call forth the churches, as well as to speak and act on their behalf. As local leaders embraced the council model, they agreed that the structure of the Federation, as well as its mission priorities, needed modification to facilitate their growing commitment to cooperation in meeting the changing needs of the community. By 1961 a new constitution was adopted and the name was changed to Rochester Area Council of Churches (RACC).

At the end of a year-long planning process, the commitment was reaffirmed to continue a strong Christian Education Department. Training for church school teachers and other children's workers would be a major activity. However, the report called for a study of the massive Weekday Religious Education program and the audiovisual library to assess their relative costs and benefits to the churches. Within a year the WRE program was terminated due largely to the difficulty of sustaining funding and the cadre of teachers.

A second major commitment made through the new Council was to establish "program boards" to bring special attention to three emerging priority concerns of the churches, namely, campus ministries, social services, and the inner city. Unlike the departments of the former Federation, which were composed of delegates from a variety of congregations, the new boards would be constituted by denominational representatives. The purpose was to bring these denominations more directly into planning and funding of mission projects, a pattern shown to be effective in a growing number of cities across America. For the new Council, the change reflected the growing importance of denominational structures and leaders in the life of the local ecumenical community.

The Board for Campus Ministry (BCM) was the first organized and soon employed a chaplain-director. Over several years a coordinated chaplaincy program was developed at several local colleges. Its chaplains, funded mostly by several of the larger denominations, offered services to all Protestant students. They also worked closely with chaplains representing denominations not participating in BCM. Its legacy today is the Genesee Area Campus Ministry.

The Board for Social Services developed a plan for support of church-based social services across the community. Funding for the program was to include a large subsidy from the Community Chest; however, that support was not forthcoming. Consequently, the focus was narrowed to pastoral counseling. Training was offered to pastors, and counseling services were provided to individuals and families who sought assistance with problems within a context of respect for their religious beliefs and practices. Its legacy today is the Samaritan Pastoral Counseling Center, an independent self-supporting agency.

By the time the Inner City Board (ICB) took up its work in 1961, some community leaders were expressing grave concerns about the extent and impact of discrimination against racial minority residents in Rochester's inner core. A Federation newsletter included this excerpt from a Council of Social Agencies report: "Activities of the State Committee Against Discrimination that turned up employment discrimination to a greater degree than had been suspected also turned up more resentment on the part of the victims than anyone had known in official circles. . . . The situation, especially with respect to housing, demands justice. The Negro "ghetto" will no longer contain families who can afford and want something better." This concern over race relations came to dominate the life of the Council in the 1960s, and some would contend it shaped local ecumenical life for the balance of the century.

The Inner City Board's first efforts focused on a variety of partnerships with black churches in providing religious and social services for children and youth in the inner city. One notable program brought thirty students from area colleges into several inner-city churches to offer tutoring for high school students.

Greater prominence was given the growing urgency of the race issue in June 1963 when RACC appointed a local Commission on Religion and

Race (CRR) patterned after a national effort. A socially prominent laywoman gave spirited and capable leadership. The issue was not new to her. Twenty years earlier she had led a task force on improving interfaith and interracial goodwill as part of a community-wide Council on Post War Problems. Roman Catholic and Jewish representation were brought into CRR. Meetings were held weekly for several months to help initiate the work. The Commissions chair expressed her perspective on the racial situation in this excerpt from a RACC Newsletter: "At the present moment the greatest need is for a change in the climate of thought in our communities, a new commitment to the fundamental principles of Christ's teachings that our love of God must be expressed in love and concern for our fellow men, that each individual is of such value in the sight of God that it were better for a man that a millstone were hanged about his neck and that he were cast into the sea, than that he offendeth one of God's children."

When a parent group took the city school district to court to stop its open enrollment desegregation plan, CRR, in one of its first actions, filed a brief in support of the program. Other early CCR initiatives concerned open housing, nondiscrimination in employment, and job training for racial minorities.

In the fall of 1963 public awareness of a frustrated and angry black community came at the same time that an aroused and determined clergy and Council of Churches became known. Several incidents of alleged police brutality against black citizens brought black ministers to the fore as spokespersons against oppression of their people. Lack of response by city authorities fed fears of violent retribution against police. Working closely with these clergy, RACC helped organize a protest sit-in at police headquarters. The interracial and interfaith group demanded establishment of a Police Advisory Board through which citizens could help curb police violence. Over 500 persons were involved in maintaining an around-the-clock vigil that lasted ten days. The city council finally capitulated and passed legislation establishing the monitoring agency. RACC used the occasion to call Rochester business and political leaders to help deal with broader issues underlying the unrest in the black community. However, public opinion–as informed by the media–saw the RACC's concern as "alarmist" and exaggerating "the Negro problem."

After several years, the Council's Inner City Board became its Board for Urban Ministry (BUM), through which the denominations undertook their largest cooperative effort ever. Representatives from eight Protestant denominations, the Roman Catholic Diocese, the Jewish Community Council, and the Negro pastors' ministerium made up the board membership. A full-time director was employed, and probably for the first time in the United States, the Roman Catholic bishop appointed a priest as "vicar for the poor" and assigned him to work alongside BUM staff in a Joint Office for Urban Ministry.

In the summer of 1964 a police confrontation with black youth escalated into a widespread riot that lasted through two nights. Resentments noted by earlier surveys fueled the anger. Four people died, over eight hundred were arrested, and more than $1 million damage was inflicted upon inner-city commercial areas. Nonetheless, shortly thereafter a local newspaper editorial complained that the riots and the attention given the city did a "great libel" and went on to insist that "Rochester is perhaps the most unlikely city in America for this to happen!"

In the aftermath of Rochester's race riots and the widespread public denial of its significance, BUM, CRR, and RACC leaders consulted intensively with black pastors and other community leaders. From the pastors' perspective, something was needed to help prevent the futile swing between apathy and violence. Some new dynamic was required to overcome the powerlessness and invisibility felt by so many blacks. Sympathetic leaders in the wider community were convinced that only the Protestant church structures were free enough to do something dramatic to empower the black community. Consequently, after careful research the church leaders turned to Saul Alinsky and his Industrial Areas Foundation (IAF). Alinsky's proven expertise, they believed, could bring together black churches, businesses, and neighborhood groups to establish an effective, mass-based, community organization. The aim was to develop an independent agency that was of, by, and for black residents and was capable of articulating and acting effectively on problems they deemed most critical.

The contract with IAF required the churches to raise $100,000 for two years of support. BUM took the lead, encouraging each member to help in its own way. Funding was sought from local, regional, and national denominational bodies, as well as local congregations and individuals. According to one informed estimate, more than one thousand church members were involved in decision making regarding IAF funding. Their discussions and actions evoked a firestorm of protest. Alinsky was portrayed in the press as an outside agitator who could do no good for Rochester. Many Christians, even those sympathetic to the aspirations of black people, opposed IAF intervention out of fear of the inevitable community conflict that would ensue. Nonetheless, in vote after vote across the churches, support was promised and the funding goal was met. With the assurance of resources from the churches, in March 1965 a broad cross section of black leaders gathered and voted to invite the IAF to organize their community. Six weeks later fifteen hundred delegates in convention launched what became known as FIGHT, a black led and fully controlled effort to turn numerical strength into political power.

FIGHT's early agenda expressed concerns over police brutality, housing conditions, education, and urban renewal. However, increasing the quantity and quality of job opportunities for blacks was soon recognized as the top priority. Attention focused on the Eastman Kodak Company, Rochester's largest employer; soon FIGHT and Kodak became embroiled in an intense public conflict over employment opportunities for unemployed blacks. The community, and the churches, became polarized. Many Christians found it difficult to accept FIGHT's confrontational tactics. Many individuals and churches expressed their opposition by terminating their financial support for the Council. Eventually an agreement was reached which established an employment target, and FIGHT was given a role in recruiting prospective employees. Several years after the conflict was resolved, many would credit FIGHT for helping reduce barriers to minority employment with Kodak as well as with other major companies in Rochester. FIGHT went on to develop significant programs relating to housing, job training, and parent involvement in schools.

BUM's commitment to community organization as an instrument for social justice eventually was enlarged to encompass most of the city. In the view of the religious leaders, all residents needed empowerment through organizations that would enable them to promote their own interests and engage constructively with the new advocacies from the black community. Churches gave key leadership in organizing most of the major neighborhood associations which still serve sectors of the city. Each has worked closely with city officials in physical planning, building code enforcement, public safety, setting social service priorities, and monitoring other services affecting their own residents.

The Council's concern for race relations also found expression in its support of open housing and low-income housing. Using federal programs, a foundation was established to build and operate an apartment complex. Further, as a model and encouragement to church groups, the Council purchased a house in the third ward and rented it to a family. In the aftermath of Dr. Martin Luther King's assassination in 1968, it helped establish the Joint Interfaith Commission, bringing together Protestant, Roman

Catholic, and Jewish leaders to generate support for community development efforts in the inner city. One major grant from the Commission enabled FIGHT to launch its first low-income housing construction project.

Through the decade of turmoil in the Council over racial justice, many noncontroversial activities continued with much support among constituents. These included church school and vacation Bible school teacher training, School of Religion, hospital chaplaincies, and migrant ministries. The Council also sponsored the largest used clothing drive for a city its size anywhere in the United States, and its audiovisual library for local churches was unmatched anywhere. RACC sponsored religious programs almost every day on radio and television. With the mounting involvement of the United States in the war in Vietnam, the Council launched an education and action program focused on moral dimensions of the conflict.

Through the 1960s, the Council found itself on a new frontier where the pressing issue of racial justice demanded change in the traditional ecumenical ministries to meet the challenges of life in the city. In 1966 the embattled Council president, the Rev. George Hill, expressed well the dominant sentiment:

> Perhaps the most important thing that should be said is that the Protestant clergy and laity have emerged as a responsible initiating force in our community. This is something new, and finds its major focus in the work related to the support of the Industrial Areas Foundation. The fact that individual churches, clergymen, and the Council itself were mentioned frequently in the public media, though not always with warmest approbation, seems to indicate that the Christian community is becoming increasingly relevant to the real issues of human life, and can no longer be taken for granted as a bulwark of the status quo. Let us resolve to continue to work on the cutting edge of the human situation, where the risks are great, but the opportunities are greater.

As the decade drew to a close, once again the agency felt great pressure to restructure its life. Given its financial plight, given the growing role of denominations in ecumenical life, and given the prospect of the post–Vatican II interest of the Rochester Roman Catholic Diocese in becoming a full participant in local ecumenical life, once again a redesign process was launched. What emerged in 1971 came to be known as Genesee Ecumenical Ministries (GEM).

TOWARD ENGAGEMENT IN COMMON MISSION: GENESEE ECUMENICAL MINISTRIES, 1970–1991

In establishing GEM, the congregations that had been the members in RACC entrusted leadership of local ecumenical life to their denominational leaders. Eight Protestant denominational bodies, the Roman Catholic Diocese, and the United Church Ministry (the black pastors' ministerium) covenanted to "develop and implement their common mission." Such mission was understood as "the involvement of the church community beyond the local congregation's pastoral care and ministry of word, sacrament, and nurture." Thus, "partnership in mission" became the vision undergirding GEM.

Building on the collaborative experience of the denominations in the Board for Urban Ministry, the intention of the majority was to extend such joint planning to a broader range of social justice concerns. However, some leaders continued to advocate for service activities. The first report of the GEM Program Priorities Committee acknowledged the apparent polarity between mission and service: "Our committee believes GEM must engage in ministries both to the community and to persons, individually and corporately. We ought to do together what cannot be done effectively by small units. Social justice must be the center of our concern."

Integrated planning among denominations was projected in setting program priorities, in developing and implementing activities, in funding, and in staffing mission projects. Throughout the GEM years member churches struggled to establish the communication lines and accountabilities to make this commitment a practical reality. At many points effective collaboration was achieved and with positive results. However, the forces of denominational autonomy often would frustrate the hope for more integrated, shared mission development.

The new GEM Board set in motion an elaborate process to evaluate programs inherited from RACC, to assess current needs for ministry, and to establish program priorities. However, two community crises—both reflecting our society's difficulty with race relations—demanded their urgent attention.

In summer 1971 with city schools heading toward a major reorganization for desegregation, opponents grew more determined and militant. Demonstrations and rock throwing greeted school buses bringing black children from inner-city to outer-city schools. Increased police presence only added to the frustration and anger of antibusing demonstrators. The community crisis led GEM to short-circuit its priority-setting process. The Urban Education Team (UET) was established to deal with the immediate human relations challenge, as well as to address broader issues of quality and equality of educational opportunities.

GEM's UET chose to enter the situation as a mediator, helping the conflicting parties find common ground. Foremost in their planning was to ensure the safety of children and ensure that adults would behave with civility toward one another even when they disagreed deeply. At first UET had difficulty gaining acceptance in this new role because the churches (through RACC and BUM) had been vocal advocates for school desegregation. Its credibility was greatly enhanced when funds were secured from church sources to bring in professional mediators from the American Arbitration Service. UET staff and volunteers, working under the direction of the mediator consultants, succeeded in bringing together for extensive negotiations over several months representatives from all interested parties in the conflict. Student, parent, teacher, administrator, and school board representatives eventually built enough trust to fashion a school safety proposal that subsequently was adopted by the Rochester Board of Education.

This positive experience in working through a community conflict eventually led GEM to collaborate with the American Arbitration Service and other local organizations in founding the Rochester Center for Dispute Settlement. The UET's successful work with parent groups led to eight annual contracts with the federal Department of Education to operate the Education Resource Network (LERN), a program to enhance parent empowerment for participation in schools. ERN's legacy is evident today in city school district programs dealing with parent involvement, magnet schools, school-community relations, and the teaching of civic values.

The inmate rebellion at Attica Correction Facility and the state police's brutal handling of the situation brought to the young GEM a second community crisis. GEM's associate director, a young African American minister, became involved as part of an observer team sent to the prison, located about sixty miles southwest of Rochester. The Episcopal and Roman Catholic bishops issued a joint pastoral letter calling the churches to address the inhumane conditions in prisons. Concerns about police abuse and discrimination in courts had already become the focus of attention for Church Women United and many local clergy. As a clear priority for criminal justice emerged, GEM's Judicial Process Commission (JPC) was born and quickly became a major program.

Over the years JPC provided GEM with significant research, organizing, and advocacy services on a wide range of criminal justice issues. These included reforming the Public Defenders Office; opposing jail expansion and fostering alternatives to incarceration; training for police in community relations; promoting criminal justice reform legislation, including opposition to the death penalty; advocating citizen review of police misconduct; promoting mediation and conflict resolution training in schools and neighborhoods; and developing educational materials and training opportunities for churches and community groups. In appealing for church support, JPC often presented its work from a biblical and theological perspective. JPC personnel also made significant leadership contributions to criminal justice ministries at state and national levels.

The continuing concern over racial justice led GEM into a variety of other activities. The covenant underlying GEM entailed a commitment to support development of United Church Ministry (UCM) to serve a broad cross section of black churches as a denomination-like body. In keeping with its commitment to empower communities for self-determination, GEM worked with denominations to provide funding to staff UCM during a five-year developmental period. UCM gave special attention to strengthening black families, evangelism, training lay leaders, social ministries, and political action. With funding support from denominations, UCM sponsored a full-time ministry to residents in Hanover Houses, a high-rise public housing project that was beset with drug activity and other social problems.

Incidents of police violence against racial minorities continued into the 1970s. Each time a citizen was killed or seriously injured by police, UCM hastily organized protests to provide voice and action options for frustrated and often angry blacks. GEM's Judicial Process Commission provided staff and volunteer support for these actions, and GEM member churches often responded as well. Inasmuch as the Police Advisory Board created in the early 1960s soon faltered for lack of support by the city council, there was no avenue remaining for community monitoring of internal investigations of police misconduct. GEM repeatedly worked in coalition with various groups seeking to enlarge police accountability. Eventually the city council enacted a monitoring mechanism that included an enlarged role for citizen participation.

Building on its 1973 survey of religious needs of inmates in the county jail, GEM secured a commitment from the sheriff to employ a chaplain. An interfaith advisory council was established to select the chaplain and to serve as liaison between this chaplain and the religious community. Council members included representatives from Jewish, Muslim, and evangelical Christian communities, as well as the GEM members.

At the instigation of several prominent black churchmen, GEM established the Rochester Committee for Justice in Southern Africa. Its purpose was to foster solidarity between Rochester residents—and especially their major corporations—and blacks in South Africa working to overturn the apartheid system. Vigils brought attention to local banks doing business in South Africa. Meetings with Eastman Kodak officials encouraged them to use their influence for social change through their business interests in South Africa. To interpret the struggle to churches, schools, and other groups, a speakers' bureau was established. A plan was developed in partnership with the South Africa Council of Churches for a visitation by a delegation of Rochester church and business leaders. The effort was finally abandoned when the South African government refused to issue visas. As a gesture of hope for the future, funds gathered for the visit were reallocated to provide scholarships for South African students to come to Rochester area universities to prepare for leadership in their post-apartheid nation. Education and advocacy efforts continued over the years until apartheid was finally overcome.

During GEM's first five years, interdenominational cooperation in promoting common mission was at times very encouraging and at times very frustrating. In 1976, in an effort meant to encourage even closer collaboration, a significant restructuring was undertaken. Added to the constitution was a preamble that expressed a theological undergirding for the agency not evident initially. Members covenanted "to work together to seek truth, establish justice, and to hasten the coming of God's Kingdom of peace." It also included the well-known Lund Principle (adopted at the World Conference on Faith and Order in 1952), namely, that members would "strive to do all things together except those which doctrine and conscience require be done separately."

GEM's original covenant was expanded to list seven commitments denominations would make to guide their relationships with each other. Furthermore, in changing from a board of directors to an ecumenical strategy board, denominations agreed to send delegates who were leaders in their own mission units and who were empowered to speak on their behalf in GEM deliberations. The new constitution also called for denomination executives to convene regularly and for their mission staff to support the ecumenical agenda. While some benefits from these changes were achieved in the following years, the general propensity for denominational autonomy persisted.

Another reassessment in 1980 led to changes that brought denominational executives directly into ecumenical planning and a broadening of the base of participation in GEM. A tricameral body was created to bring together denomination heads in the Executives Cabinet, denomination mission leaders in the Council of Communions, and delegates from city and town church clusters in the Assembly of Ecumenical Clusters. This latter addition expressed GEM's growing concern to address social and economic inequities across the urban-suburban divide through nurturing "geographic ecumenism." The plan established a Coordinating Committee to keep the three parallel bodies working in tandem and stipulated that one of the executives would serve as GEM president.

While the personal involvement of the executives added a significant element of sanction for ecumenical action in GEM, the three-part structure proved unwieldy. Each body tended to focus on its own priorities. A revised format adopted in 1984 reestablished a unified Board of Directors; however, its members included denomination executives and delegates from clusters of churches as well as the denominations' mission leaders. This design also entailed establishment of three departments—Social Witness, Ecumenical Relations, and Operations—through which the board would exercise its responsibilities. For the first time the concern for Christian unity found organizational expression in GEM.

To seek improvement in financial support, the 1984 constitution required the budget to be separated into two parts, core operations and program. A fair-share formula was ordered to guide denominational giving to underwrite core expenses. Supplemental contributions for specific programs also would be encouraged. Also prescribed was a "metropolitan conference," i.e., a delegated body to represent various congregations, denominational program units, and special ministries that would convene periodically for worship, consultation, and resource sharing. Recognizing the need every few years to redesign the agency to ensure relevance and sustain ownership by denominational leaders, a three-year expiration date was added to the constitution.

As GEM sought to shape its agenda in response to crises in the wider world, major attention was given to the plight of refugees in Asia, Africa, and Europe. In 1979, working in partnership with Church World Service and several denominations, full-time staff was employed to promote refugee resettlement in the community. Many congregations were recruited to serve as sponsors and provide hospitality. Cooperation was cultivated with Roman Catholic, Lutheran, and other refugee resettlement organizations through the GEM-sponsored Rochester Interfaith Council on Immigrants and

Refugees. Over the succeeding twenty years, the GEM project brought to Rochester and the surrounding counties more than 5,000 refugees from famine, natural disaster, war, and oppression.

Another local crisis that claimed GEM's attention was the fiscal situation confronting the city of Rochester in 1980. Due to its shrinking tax base and limitations on its taxing powers imposed by the state constitution, the city's ability to provide basic services for its residents—including public education—was increasingly in jeopardy. One appealing solution was to shift the cost of city police services to Monroe County, which already had a major responsibility for law enforcement in suburban areas. Seeing this proposal as a way to address city-suburban inequities, GEM joined other community groups in an intensive campaign for metropolitan police services. While the campaign failed in a public referendum, it contributed to a later agreement by the county legislature to redistribute sales tax revenue to greater benefit the city.

Taking advantage of opportunities offered by the federal government to enhance the well-being of low-income neighborhoods, GEM continued and enlarged the Volunteers in Service to America (VISTA) Project begun under the Council of Churches. It became the largest single project in the United States, sponsoring in one year as many as forty participants who served in seventeen community agencies. The work entailed community organizing, health care, job training, legal services, and education for migrant farm workers. Similarly, when the Comprehensive Employment and Training Act (CETA) offered federal funds to help unemployed workers acquire job skills through community service, GEM sponsored as many as eight trainees, most of whom served in its sponsored programs.

GEM also continued the function of "social pioneer," helping create new responses to human needs in the community. GEM sponsored a local chapter of Habitat for Humanity to marshal volunteers and donated materials to build houses for low-income families. During these last fifteen years, over eighty houses have been built in Rochester's inner city. Working with Monroe Developmental Center, GEM helped create Respite Cares to recruit and train volunteers to provide in-home care for children and adults with disabilities. Sensitive to the special needs of people with hearing loss, GEM helped organize Hard of Hearing Services to serve as an advocate and resource to churches and other agencies regarding accessibility issues. Another creative partnership was nurtured to bring GEM, local church clusters, and Church World Service together to greatly expand local participation in the annual CROP Walk for the Hungry. Today the annual event yields nearly

$100,000 for the relief of hunger close to home and around the world. Also started by GEM was One World Goods, a project to provide a local market for Third World artisans to enable them to become self-sufficient.

GEM eventually gave renewed attention to serving the needs of congregations. Through nurturing collaboration among Christian Education leaders, the Lay School of Theology was reinstituted and attracted several hundred enrollees each year. Further, a center was created to facilitate resource sharing. Wellspring: Church Resource Services provided educational materials and training opportunities for church educators across denominational lines. GEM also convened denominational leaders to ensure development of new chaplain positions at several area hospitals and to provide support for chaplains serving in all local institutions. Clergy were convened periodically for orientation and discussion of key public issues. To promote interest in the wider ecumenical movement and to pursue its dedication to church unity, leaders from the world, national, and state levels were brought to Rochester by GEM. Conferences were sponsored on key issues, including the "Baptism, Eucharist, and Ministry" document of the World Council of Churches and the plan for "Covenant Communion" put forward by the Consultation on Church Union (COCU). GEM continued sponsorship of the Rochester Friends of the World Council of Churches, which occasionally brought a WCC speaker to town, provided a public forum for local delegates to WCC assemblies, and helped raise funds for the WCC. Additionally, observance of the Week of Prayer for Christian Unity became an annual occasion for gathering in worship.

Recognizing the growing number of people of other faiths in Rochester, GEM cultivated interfaith dialogue and cooperation and helped establish new institutions to ensure that these relationships would grow. Beginning in 1979, the Commission on Christian/Jewish Relations pursued issues of interest to the two faith communities. Concerns included local expressions of anti-Semitism, church-state issues, stewardship of energy resources, teaching values in public schools, observance of religious holidays, Holocaust remembrance, opposition to the death penalty, civil rights, and race relations. Organizing support also was provided in establishing a local chapter of the New York State Labor and Religion Coalition, an interfaith effort to bring attention to justice issues in the workplace. Through other ad hoc projects over the years, GEM recognized in its interfaith partners shared religious values and common concerns for the welfare of the community. These relationships helped lay the foundation for the much enlarged interfaith activity in succeeding years.

The GEM Board eventually became convinced that viable ecumenical ministry in metropolitan Rochester had to be based on a structure more inclusive than what its "coalition of denominations" permitted. Leaders increasingly recognized barriers to communication and collaboration with local church partners. The communication protocol requiring GEM to work through denominations to reach parishes for volunteers and financial support often proved ineffective and frustrating. Leadership and financial resources needed to realize the visions and commitments expressed by the denominations were not forthcoming. In addition, the fact that many congregations, including African American and other ethnic churches, had no local denominational body through which to participate in GEM became unacceptable. Amicable contacts with some evangelical pastors made through preparing for a Billy Graham crusade in 1988 led to new hopes for their participation in a new organization. Further, partner organizations in many activities often were church-supported mission agencies but were not represented at the GEM table.

These and other signs pointed once again to the need for a fundamental redesign of the agency. So, relying on the Apostle Paul's image of the church as the Body of Christ, GEM set in motion a process to find a new way of connecting all the many parts of the body, of bringing them all into intentional community. The result was the emergence of the Greater Rochester Community of Churches in 1991 to carry on the legacy and work of the local conciliar movement.

Growing toward Community: Greater Rochester Community of Churches, 1991–2000

In fall 1988, anticipating the need to once again review the GEM constitution, denominational executives urged that a more thorough reconsideration of ecumenical relations was needed. Building on this interest, the GEM board recruited a broadly representative Redesign Task Force, including members from several denominations not involved with GEM. A year-long process involving surveys, focus groups, and town meetings was set in motion. Results from all these consultations led to a proposal for a new organizational structure for ecumenical ministry.

Three primary commitments previously expressed by GEM members were carried over: to manifest the unity of the church, to nurture one another, and to engage in mission together. However, the basic structure would be changed significantly. Members would include parishes and church-related organizations as well as local ecumenical clusters of churches and denominational bodies. The structure would encourage leadership to arise from a variety of constituencies. Communication and ownership of the ecumenical agenda would be cultivated through an assembly of delegates from all member groups that would gather two or three times yearly. The organization would be led by a board of directors with some members appointed by denominations and others elected by assembly delegates. Broader financial support would be encouraged directly from congregations.

The new name, Greater Rochester Community of Churches (GRCC), signaled an interest in growing beyond cooperation and joint action among denominations. New theological convergences relating to Christian unity (developed through dialogue between national denominations), coupled with the pragmatic experience of local church groups working together, led to a yearning for deeper levels of sharing and collaboration at all levels of church life. Further, the name gave expression to the concern to create a more inclusive fellowship across the theological divide between so-called evangelical and mainline churches. Thus, the commitment expressed in the GRCC covenant is to promote "community" among the churches, a term steeped in the biblical vision of "koinonia."

As GRCC got under way in the summer of 1991, it agreed to continue sponsorship of ministries inherited from GEM, namely, Refugee Resettlement and Services Project, Judicial Process Commission, One World Goods, Commission on Chaplain Services, Commission on Christian-Jewish Relations, and the Rochester Committee for the World Council of Churches. By year end, membership included seven denominations (all those previously in GEM), seventy-one congregations (affiliated with twenty-one denominations), five local clusters of churches, and thirteen church-related organizations.

Growing concern in Rochester over violence was identified by GRCC as its first priority. Recognizing economic deprivation as a major factor underlying violence in families and neighborhoods, GRCC recruited a Task Force on Economic Development, devised a "theology of economic engagement," and became a catalyst for inner-city economic development. Over the following several years major support was given to: creation of a federal credit union to serve residents and workers in areas of highest poverty concentration in the city; advocacy for a supermarket in an area of the city long deprived of such services; and establishment of a micro-enterprise center to support self-sufficiency among people living in poverty through development of small business opportunities.

An early initiative promoted to build community among churches across city-suburban, racial, and economic class lines was the Crossroads Project. Several pairs of congregations were assisted in developing relationships and shared activities among their members. Forums were held to provide information on critical issues, and in some cases, people from paired churches came together to develop a common ministry.

Interfaith relations were enlarged through formation of the Commission on Christian-Muslim relations. Three Islamic mosques, represented in the Greater Rochester Council of Masajid, share sponsorship of the Commission to promote increased understanding and cooperation. An early concern centered on prejudice and negative cultural stereotypes of Muslims. Growing interest in Islam led to many invitations to Muslim leaders to speak with church groups about their faith.

While GRCC began cultivating financial support among its new congregational members, significant reductions in contributions from denominations led to serious financial problems for the new organization. Revenues from denominations declined from $70,000 in 1988 to $42,000 in 1992. After struggling unsuccessfully to develop other sources of revenue, GRCC reluctantly concluded there were serious "disconnects" between the vision and commitments expressed in the new constitution, the financial resources made available by members, and the actual energies and interests of individuals who made up the Board of Directors. Change became a necessity. By the end of 1994 staff was reduced from three full-time employees to one, the organization was simplified by eliminating the three program departments, and volunteer leadership positions were redefined.

As efforts were made by GRCC to strengthen ties with African American churches, commitments were made to give greater prominence to racial justice on the ecumenical agenda. Liaison was reestablished with United Church Ministries (UCM), a key point of connection with African American ministers. This agenda was pursued first through collaboration with the Divinity School in a two-year lecture series, "Dismantling the Legacy of Racism." A second project evolved through the joint efforts of GRCC, UCM, and WOKR-TV in an interracial dialogue program, "Beyond Racism." In addition, GRCC representatives joined community coalitions dealing with fair housing and welfare reform, both having racial justice dimensions, and they initiated conversations with local foundations to encourage collaboration in funding projects in areas of greatest need.

GRCC sustained and/or developed commitments to these other special ministries:

The Refugee Resettlement and Services Project, funded largely by Church World Service and Episcopal Migration Ministries, employs a multi-ethnic staff to assist as many as three hundred refugees each year to resettle in communities throughout western New York.

The Commission on Chaplain Services provides communication among chaplains in various local institutions, serves as a link between chaplains and local churches, and develops advocacy for chaplaincy programs as needed.

The Commissions on Christian/Jewish and Christian/Muslim Relations regularly bring together key leaders from these faith traditions for study, dialogue, and action on common concerns.

An annual Faith-in-Action Banquet recognizes and celebrates with parishes and other religious groups those individual members who put their faith into action to serve people in the community.

The Rochester Friends of the World Council of Churches sponsors occasional speakers and special events to help interpret the work of the WCC.

The Ecumenical and Interfaith Archives acts as a resource for GRCC, its predecessor organizations, and other local ecumenical and interfaith organizations.

In the eight years since GRCCs inception, growing religious pluralism in the community has been a significant influence. Associations of ecumenical leaders with people of other faith traditions are claiming an increasing amount of time and attention. The Interfaith Forum and the Religious Alliance (focusing on dialogue), the Interfaith Alliance (focusing on public policy issues), the Commissions on Christian/Jewish and Christian/Muslim Relations (focusing on issues of common concern), the Interfaith Housing Coalition (focusing on housing and development polices), and the Interfaith Action Coalition (focusing on neighborhood issues) exemplify this rich environment for interreligious relations.

A newly emerging focus for ecumenical engagement pertains to issues in the secular world that pose questions about the kind of community residents want to share in Monroe County. Problems associated with the extreme concentration of poverty within the city, coupled with environmental problems related to uncoordinated suburban sprawl, are opening conversations in which voices from the religious community are invited to help explore "smart growth" and a new "ethic of community."

The Community of Churches struggles to discover and express God's calling to ecumenical life in a religious and social environment that is in great flux across the metropolitan community. While formally the vision of church unity and commitments to close collaboration among the churches remains intact, the traditional ways of expressing ecumenical relationships appear to be of diminished interest. New ways of relating are being explored and tested to encourage Christian unity, to promote common mission among the churches, and to encourage shared life among the churches in the community. This is a time of uncertainty, innovation, and hopefulness.

Note

1. All of the quotes come either from the official documents of the GRCC or from videotaped or audiotaped interviews done by the author with the person identified. These may be found in the Project Archives at the library of Christian Theological Seminary, 1000 W. 42nd Street, Indianapolis, IN 46208.

11

ECUMENISM IN A CHANGING CITY: NEWARK, NEW JERSEY

Horace H. Hunt

When I first came to Newark in October 1963, the city was already undergoing significant changes, some long in the making. Although African Americans had for decades been part of the racial and ethnic mix, they were rapidly on their way to becoming the majority of the population. Already their children were the largest single group in the public school system.

By and large, however, the city leaders who determined the patterns of living, services, jobs, transportation, government, and virtually everything else were doing nothing to respond to these changes, except to resist them or pretend that they had no effect. The school system, which had been the pride of its citizenry and the surrounding area, was deteriorating. Long-established teachers, many of them excellent, were beginning to retire early or move to the suburbs to work in the classroom. Central administrators were responding as if the system needed no adjusting while sitting atop a large patronage operation. Others were either doing what was necessary to hang onto their jobs or planning a safe and secure escape. Even back then classroom results were a major concern although little was done to address the situation. There were a few creative efforts within the African American community to tailor the curriculum and teaching methods to the black community's experience and language. Yet, it seemed a feeble effort.

Newark boasted one of the largest and best public housing programs for a city of its size in the nation. But like so many such projects across the nation, the newer ten- and twelve-story high-rises were already showing the traits of the warehousing of people and families. It was those characteristics that would later lead to the demolition of such structures throughout most of the country. The Central Ward ghetto and its neighboring fringes were dominated by deteriorating and substandard homes. Most of the residents of old multifamily dwellings lived almost continuously in fear of fire, which seemed at times to be an almost daily occurrence among such structures, not infrequently resulting in the loss of life.

The largest city in New Jersey and located across the Hudson River and a few miles inland from Manhattan's Wall Street, Newark was the center of the state's economic activity. Although some manufacturing and processing plants had begun to close or relocate, banking, insurance, transportation, and retail were still thriving. Every weekday the population of the downtown area would double as suburbanites traveled to their places of employment in the central city. However, there was little opportunity for job development or advancement among Newark's poor, largely African American population. The unemployment rate among young black men was two to three times the rate of other population groups in the area. In addition, as new job opportunities began to develop in the suburbs at malls and industrial parks, most central city blacks had no means of travel to such jobs. The convenience of transportation routes and facilities was centered in getting the suburbanites into the city and not city dwellers to new jobs in the suburbs.

When I arrived in 1963, the city government was headed by a former liberal congressman (who in a few years would be convicted of fraud and conspiracy along with some members of the City Council). There was one African American on the Council from the Central Ward, whose job it was to work with the mayor to keep the black community "in its place." In other words, the mayor provided him with enough patronage and token services to make sure that any unhappiness among African Americans in Newark would not express itself disruptively. The mayor was Italian American, as was the city council president and variously two or three of the other six members of the council. Despite their numbers, blacks had no political power, though they did hold a number of middle- and lower-level patronage jobs with the city, especially in the board of education and the housing authority.

The police department was dominated by Irish Americans and Italian Americans. Conflict with members of the African American community was on the rise. The incidence of crime was highest in places like the Central Ward, but the harsh and racist treatment of blacks by white police officers was an increasingly common occurrence. Incidents in the black community between the police and residents were the focus of most complaints to city hall and each had the potential to create a protest that could become large. Most African Americans who were arrested had no legal assistance except overworked public defenders. Many were kept in holding cells or the county jail for months before they were indicted, and even then trial dates were often several months later. Thus, they were incarcerated for sometimes a year or two before they even came to trial. Bail was available for poor people, if at all, only from bail bondsmen who charged exorbitant rates. The mistreatment of incarcerated black people was common.

The city was divided into five wards. The Central Ward was the poorest and overwhelmingly African American. The North Ward was largely Italian American. The South Ward was where most of the city's Jewish population lived. The East Ward was an ethnic mix of Poles, Germans, Italians, Portuguese, and others. The West Ward was partly an extension of the Central Ward and increasingly similar to it in makeup; but another part—a westward peninsula jutting into the nearby suburbs—reflected its suburban surroundings. Increasingly the Jewish population was moving to the suburbs, along with their synagogues, as the South Ward became more and more black. Unscrupulous real estate companies and agents were focusing "block busting" tactics on the west fringes of the South and West Wards in the direction of Irvington, a traditional white ethnic and blue-collar town. However, except for the ethnically diverse "Ironbound" (East Ward), which was cut off from the rest of the city by the main north-south rail corridor, every area of the city was beginning to experience the growing "encroachment" of the Central Ward's African American community.

Newark's churches were in the midst of transition, a transition that was mostly unwelcome in the white community, although some congregations and judicatories were attempting to develop transition and community-oriented ministries. The Archdiocese of Newark was the largest Roman Catholic diocese in a state that was already largely Catholic. Tall spires with crosses on them dotted the landscape throughout the city, but the parishes themselves were increasingly in decline—in membership and in enrollments in the parish schools. The exception was the Cathedral parish and a few parishes in the northern and western edges of the city. A few parish priests attempted to reach out to the newer African American residents of their communities but with only limited success. The exception was one church in the heart of the Central Ward, where its four or five parish priests very intentionally developed an extensive outreach and involvement in the community. Most parishes hung on to their old ways, especially the traditional ethnic parishes, which resisted change and resented the presumed threat to the neighborhood culture by the African Americans who were moving into their neighborhoods or at least to the fringes—"too close for comfort."

White Protestant churches were increasingly struggling to hang on. A few tried to integrate their Sunday Schools if not their memberships. A couple of congregations merged. Fewer still tried creative outreach ministries, which stirred interest and offered promise that for the most part never materialized. The downtown churches, no longer prestigious nor with lines waiting for worship on Sunday mornings as in the distant past, continued as before with some tangential efforts to engage the minority population while attempting to reach suburban commuters with events like weekday luncheon programs. The United Church of Christ and later the Presbyterians hired urban enablers and coordinators who focused on justice issues and community development while also attempting to help local congregations meaningfully deal with their changing situations. The United Methodists had hired a seminarian, Kim Jefferson, as part-time minister of community relations at the end of the 1950s and had sent him to their local church in the Clinton Hill area of Newark. In 1963 he assumed in addition the position of director of the newly reorganized Greater Newark Council of Churches (GNCC).

The African American churches were a typical mix, from large established congregations to small, and even storefront, operations. There were the three Black Methodist groups, the two major National Baptist denominations that met together on the state level, and a multiplicity of others from Pentecostal to a few affiliated with mainline Protestant denominations. There was also a prominent Baptist Ministers Conference of the greater Newark area, which met weekly for preaching, inspiration, and fellowship for the most part; but in time, it also provided some input into the race agenda in the city. Some churches ministered primarily to the black middle and professional classes, a large portion of which lived in the nearby suburbs. Others drew their congregation from the inner city.

Significantly, though responsive to their constituency, Newark's African American pastors, with only a few exceptions, were not involved in the civil rights movement of the time, although some were involved with Martin Luther King's Southern Christian Leadership Conference on the regional and national levels. Unlike other cities where black ministers were in the forefront of civil rights protests and demonstrations, there were only one or two who participated in such efforts, neither of which was Baptist or one of the city's black church leaders. The most prominent of these was soon transferred by his bishop out of Newark. There were some well-known established pastors who became spokespersons when called upon and who also participated in some meetings, especially when the presence of African American clergy was sought, but they were not major players to any degree in the civil rights struggles, either organized or spontaneous, as played out locally in the 1960s.

In addition to all these factors, Newark's social services were being strained by the increasing needs of the people. And a disproportionate measure of those needs were among the African American population. Whenever any analysis of Newark was provided during the 1960s, a litany of indices was routinely offered, such as those mentioned by Tom Hayden in *Reunion: A Memoir* (1988). Hayden was part of an intense community organization effort in Newark by a core of committed SDS students from 1964 until the so-called "disorders": "Newark ranked highest in the country in crime, maternal and infant mortality, tuberculosis, and venereal disease. Unemployment citywide was 15 percent, and much higher in the black community. One third of the city's children dropped out of school, and less than 10 percent achieved normal reading levels. In 1960, 32.5 percent (41,430) of its housing units were officially substandard. Nearly 30,000 of those dwellings lacked internal heating systems, and 7,000 had no flush toilets. There were 5,000 totally abandoned units and 13,000 public housing units—more per capita than any other American city."

Upon arriving in the city, I quickly became involved with the Greater Newark Council of Churches. One could see that it was increasingly becoming politely polarized between traditional interchurch activities on the one hand and the emerging justice needs of Newark's African American community on the other hand. While the director, Kim Jefferson, deftly coaxed the Council's board to take stands on important issues from time to time, a small core of concerned clergy who were active in the GNCC found themselves increasingly active out in the community. In addition to a few civil rights rallies, the most significant one was held just after Medgar Evers was slain in Mississippi. That meeting produced a local issue. It centered on the construction of the new Rutgers Law School building, where blacks were being frozen out of the jobs because of the restrictive practices of the building trades unions. Picketing at the site, organized by groups like the local chapter of Congress on Racial Equality (CORE), occurred on a regular basis. The main significance of this effort was that it said to the city and its institutions that the black community was not going to sit by quietly while living and working conditions for them continued to deteriorate. Even though the picketing was something of a wake-up call for Newark, increased employment opportunities for central city African Americans, even to a limited extent, came only with time and not as a direct result of the picketing.

From 1963 to the summer of 1967 a number of issues directly affecting the black community were coming to the fore. Among these was unhappiness with the city's educational system: deteriorating buildings with some dating back to the last century; lack of adequate textbooks and classroom supplies; progressively poorer learning and test results within the classroom; disruptive pupils in already overcrowded classrooms, most of whom needed supplemental or independent special education programs that were not being provided sufficiently; and the feeling that fundamentally the system was not at all responsive to the students from the African American community. In a few years these concerns plus some money issues led to a prolonged teacher's strike that worsened racial feelings. Black parents resented striking teachers for causing their children to miss weeks of class time, and the teachers' union, although it had an African American woman as president and many black members, was viewed more or less as a group of suburban teachers who cared little about their students. The union was addressing valid educational and economic issues, but as the strike went on for weeks on end, feelings became bitter.

Strife between the police and the black community erupted from time to time, mostly over the actual and perceived mistreatment of central city residents. High-rise public housing buildings were increasingly plagued by maintenance problems, such as elevator breakdowns. As a result, residents would have to carry groceries up many stories and young children could not readily move from the courtyards to their upper-story apartments to go to the bathroom—no public facilities existed on the ground level. Fires in the garbage chutes were regular happenings. In short, normal family life in the projects was becoming virtually impossible. Few if any social service programs were available within the projects themselves, despite the presence of a multiplicity of individual and family needs. These high-rises were little more than warehouses full of poor people with countless problems that compounded the difficulties they confronted in daily living, or in merely trying to survive.

At about this same time a small effort was being made to organize mothers on welfare around these complaints: inadequate income, overworked and unavailable case workers, restrictive and discriminatory practices within the system itself and also in the way some employees treated their clients, and a bureaucracy controlled by the white establishment that was trying to relate, often condescendingly, to an overwhelmingly African American client population. Some of these welfare mothers began to find their voices and increasingly gained confidence in speaking out against injustices in the welfare system as they experienced it locally.

In this period two major issues began to emerge. The first involved the efforts of the state's College of Medicine and Dentistry to move from Jersey

City to Newark where it planned to build a fifty-acre campus in the middle of the Central Ward, thus displacing thousands of inner-city residents. The other centered on the attempt to build a major highway connector right through the middle of the Central Ward. Both attempts were bitterly resented by the local residents who would be most affected and who, typically, were not being consulted. Although the medical/dental school campus was eventually built, it was drastically reduced in size compared to what had been originally projected. The highway was never constructed. Meetings were held with the mayor and city officials in an attempt to get some redress for the people's complaints, but nothing ever happened, except that the mayor tried to make it appear that community representatives were always welcome to come and discuss such concerns with him in his office. As a result not only was the black community increasingly restive, but organizing and protest efforts began to build around these issues.

The GNCC continued to try to be responsive to such developments. Even where the Council was not directly involved, its director, Kim Jefferson, and a small group of urban-oriented and concerned clergy found themselves at community meetings around these issues. They also began to consult with and support one another in these efforts. In addition, some traveled to Selma, Alabama, to join local protests and organizing efforts after the beatings of civil rights marchers there. They joined civil rights and community leaders in regular meetings, which began to be hosted by the Jewish Community Council in its downtown office building. One result of these efforts was Newark's anti-poverty program, the United Community Corporation, with grassroots and local neighborhood participation built into the process. As elsewhere, this local War on Poverty never realized its idealized goal, but it began in Newark as an initiative of local community and civil rights leaders rather than the city administration. This small group of concerned clergy, almost exclusively from mainline Protestant denominations plus a few Catholic priests and the director of the Jewish Community Council, played a prominent role in the process by working with community activists and by insisting that the voices of the inner-city poor be heard and respected.

During this period, tensions within the black community and especially between that community and the white political power in city hall were on the rise. Despite constant denials that Newark could erupt as Watts had, the establishment was increasingly suspicious of any organizing efforts within the community and always on the watch for supposed "outside agitators." On a sweltering July evening in 1967 in the shadow of one of the most congested and trouble-plagued high-rises, a black cab driver was arrested by police for a minor traffic infraction and brought to the nearby precinct house. Word began to spread that the cabbie had been beaten. A crowd gathered outside the precinct and began to throw things at the building. The police responded with a siege mentality. In just a few hours things exploded, and the so-called Newark riots were under way, lasting for several days. (Community people always referred to this eruption as "the rebellion," a rebellion against mistreatment and injustice.)

The GNCC and especially the corps of committed clergy kept in touch with developments though a black American Baptist clergyman who had recently begun a public housing ministry in the Central Ward's Scudder Homes, where he also resided. The group also met with the United Community Corporation and community leaders in the UCC building at the edge of where the rebellion was occurring, trying to calm the situation.

Property damage and looting released the community's anger. African American–owned stores were bypassed while resentment focused on properties and establishments owned by whites. No one was injured until the police began to react, or really overreact, with undue force. As the violence escalated, looters were shot and mothers and grandmothers watching too closely from apartment windows were felled by bullets from the forces brought in to restore "law and order." The governor added national guardsmen and state troopers, which only added to the size of the attacking battalions, many of whose guns were being fired indiscriminately into crowds of looters. While in response there may have been some shooting toward and the killing of one or two police and firemen, it is just as likely, if not more probable, that the policemen's own bullets may have killed some of their colleagues in cross fire. Over two dozen black people, including women and children, were killed, some with dozens of bullets fired into their bodies, in a classic example of the priority of white property rights over black human rights. Representatives of this group of clergy joined others in meetings, initially with the mayor, but then shifting quickly to sessions with the governor, in attempts to get him to pull back the police and the national guardsmen. The onslaught continued for two or three more days with additional killings until the governor finally ordered a pullback. As soon as this occurred, things quieted down almost immediately.

In the aftermath of the rebellion, the provost of Rutgers University in Newark together with the dean of the law school, both committed and concerned churchmen, hosted meetings of community leaders. Prominent among them were civil rights spokespersons and organizers and community representatives from the Central Ward. In time, task forces were organized around the issues of housing, education, health, employment and economic opportunity, welfare rights, and police-community relations.

The clergy group played a vital role in these efforts, and one or more of them, partly by design and partly by interest, became involved in each of these task forces. Although the task forces produced only limited results (for example, clergy began to ride overnight in a few police patrol cars through the Central Ward, and a welfare rights organization came into being), each of the clergy found themselves becoming more of a "specialist" in one of the concerns. Imperceptibly at first but more and more intentionally, the formation of an urban crisis ministry team was taking shape. The following summer a proposed outline of a new metro ministry organization was drafted. An all-day retreat helped to finalize the document, which was then shared with judicatory executives, who like most mainline Protestant church executives at the time were searching for ways to respond to the nationwide urban crisis. Area bishops and executive ministers, along with the directors of national church agencies responsible for inner-city work, were petitioned to come aboard with programmatic, financial, and moral support of the proposed organization. A few months prior, Kim Jefferson had left the Greater Newark Council of Churches to join the staff of the United Methodist Board of Global Ministries. The office of the Council moved to the downtown church I was serving while I acted as interim director. When Metropolitan Ecumenical Ministry (MEM) succeeded the GNCC in July 1969, I was asked to become its first executive director, which I accepted after resigning from my pastorate.

At the vital everyday center of MEM was the staff team, as it was named, which consisted of me, as executive director; a Presbyterian urban coordinator plus the executive presbyter of the Newark area, both of which were housed in the same building as MEM; a United Church of Christ urban organizer; an American Baptist director of a local neighborhood house; the dean of the Episcopal Cathedral; a former Newark United Methodist pastor who had just been named as the first director of a UMC metro ministry with offices across the hall from MEM; an outreach person from the downtown YMCA; a housing and urban specialist from the national Presbyterian office who lived in the area and had worked with us closely before assuming his national position; a young associate from a suburban UMC church; at least one Roman Catholic priest; the director of community relations for the Jewish Community Council; a UMC retired schoolteacher who contributed her time; a local Lutheran pastor; the director of urban work for American

Baptists in the state who had previously pastored a black congregation in the city; and the campus minister serving the campuses of Rutgers Newark, the rapidly expanding Newark Community College, the Newark College of Engineering, and the College of Medicine and Dentistry. We shortly added to our paid staff a United Church of Christ minister, who had recently directed an urban ecumenical agency in his native Puerto Rico, as our specialist in work with the ever-growing Latino community of Newark. A part-time member of our paid staff was a social worker who also did community organizing for an Afro-centric group in the Central Ward. Four of our team members were African American and one was Puerto Rican. Two and one half of our positions were funded directly by MEM. Others who were employed by their church organizations or community groups were co-opted or seconded members of the staff team.

In time, others joined us, while some moved to other positions elsewhere, as did Kim Jefferson. Various urban-minded pastors met with us occasionally as did representatives of various community groups and agencies. We met at least weekly: to hear reports about emerging and continuing issues in the community; to strategize and make assignments; to establish linkages with area churches and denominations who increasingly looked to us for interpretation and guidance regarding their response to the urban crisis; to cultivate relations with black churches; to support community organization initiatives citywide or in neighborhoods around black concerns or for special projects such as housing; and to respond to new and continuing crises, such as a strike by Newark's public school teachers, which had racial overtones.

The staff team continued to specialize, with various members devoting their MEM time to particular issues such as housing and education. Issues arose about the building and expansion of the new medical school campus: issues around size and location, employment of minorities, and health services for the community. The Newark Preschool Council, which was greatly assisted in getting off the ground by the GNCC and whose director, Kim Jefferson, became the first president of that board, was rapidly expanding primarily in local and mostly African American churches throughout the city where most of the classes were held. Rutgers–Newark had a pitifully small black student population, and protests were mounted against the failure of the university to address that issue.

A white vigilante group arose in the North Ward and stirred up anti-black feeling in the white ethnic community. At the same time MEM began to see the importance of also addressing white ethnic needs, as well as those of African Americans and Latinos. For example, a new county jail was built in the heart of Newark, which quickly became overcrowded, limiting inmate services and access to quality family visits.

Police-community strains continued. Much of the area where the rebellion occurred was block after block of virtual wasteland. Scores of deteriorated houses had already been bulldozed, leaving rubble-strewn lots, while others continued to stand as monuments not only to what happened during the rebellion but also to the substandard condition of most of the housing in that neighborhood. The housing authority sought improvements, most of which never materialized or were mostly cosmetic, but in time new town houses began to be built on debris-cleared land. A local priest moved into the high-rise closest to the initial outbreak of the rebellion and encouraged the tenants in their efforts to organize and become self-managing. A number of the junior and senior high schools were becoming flash points of racial tension, or in the case of primarily black school populations, neighborhood grievances about school overcrowding and poor schooling were increasingly voiced.

The staff team continued to keep abreast of these and other concerns, often meeting with community leaders who were involved and/or attending some of the planning meetings that were organized around these concerns. One member of the team, for example, devoted many hours to following what became a prolonged teachers' strike while meeting continuously with community, teacher union, and board of education people. Also during this period MEM became involved in an indigenous voter education and registration effort that helped to elect Newark's first African American as mayor along with a couple of Central Ward activists who became members of the city council. MEM also provided links between this organized effort and those suburban congregations that wanted to encourage the election of a black mayor.

Our style of operation was "to be there for others," for the community and for the churches. We tried to be the eyes and ears of caring and committed servants, serving in the midst of a vortex of urban crisis and change. While our initial and continuing focus was on the needs of the African American community, we attempted to be sensitive to all human needs and the various ethnic groups within the city. We were available to community groups and leaders in ways that allowed us to be used by them even if in retrospect we were on a few occasions manipulated by them. Essential to our ministry was our desire to give voice to the powerless in the community, to let *their* concerns be heard, and to encourage every program design and community development to be self-initiated and self-governed rather than having things done *for* those most affected. MEM also sought to enable collaboration among groups within the community and the city at large. We encouraged church and other resources to become available for new start-ups of community organization and development by interpreting the needs to potential funding sources and helping them to evaluate each situation. While our response was primarily to the human needs of impoverished and powerless persons and groups in the city, we always knew that we were servant ministers, even though not all were ordained, and representatives of the church as well as our denominations who supported us. We were *their* presence in the city.

In addition to our focus on and our involvement in the city itself, MEM worked to involve suburban churches in various aspects of the city's rebuilding and renewal efforts, or to help launch such efforts. The results were inspiring in some cases, but limited. A few congregations in the suburbs formed linkages with local churches in Newark of the same denomination. Some provided student interns who worked in neighborhood programs during the summers. Some key laypeople of these outlying churches helped to spearhead ecumenical efforts to focus on the urban crisis and to work with groups like MEM in their response to it. We also worked with others and especially with the newly formed Urban Coalition of Newark to encourage greater business involvement in addressing the city's needs.

Our emerging design to truly develop a *metropolitan* ministry with city-suburb mutual involvement and interdependence was never realized to any degree of depth or breadth. About this time the national denominations began to feel the financial pinch resulting in staff cutbacks. Funds for groups like MEM became harder to secure; increasingly they were maintenance budgets rather than the kind of financial resources that could enable creative responses and support to either community development efforts or city-suburb church programs.

I left MEM at the end of 1974, convinced that its new director should be African American. However, that did not occur until there were two more white directors and not for several years. Sometime in the late 1990s, in response to a request from Kim Jefferson, whose premature and untimely death prevented him from being able to write this chapter on Newark as he had agreed to do, I wrote the following:

> One of the biggest challenges facing the church in metropolitan areas is still the race issue. Despite noble efforts to encourage racial mixing in churches, including biracial pastorates, there has been little success to

my knowledge. We seem to be in a period where church fellowship across racial lines in exchanges between city and suburb, and within regional and national gatherings, are our most meaningful interactions. However, back in the metropolitan areas, not only is there the factor of racism to contend with, but Blacks and Whites still seem most comfortable in their own church culture. This may be a given that we must learn to live with creatively rather than to try and change it.

Certainly the need for greater racial and ethnic interaction leading to greater understanding still exists and the church can play a big role in this effort as it did historically in the civil rights movement. However, church institutional patterns and differing ministerial styles still can get in the way of progress here.

Central cities are still largely unmanageable, both in the city halls and in the larger institutions such as the public schools. In our current economy there are more job opportunities for central city residents, but hard pockets of unemployment or underemployment still exist. So-called welfare reform has assisted some to become more independent, but in many ways the "reform" is more punitive than curative, and despite the success stories, many previous recipients are worse off than ever. Strides are being made in housing and transportation in some cities, but by and large police-community relations are as strained as ever, especially in black and Latino areas.

Churches still tend to approach these problems, if at all, with the band aid approach rather than by working for institutional change. The problems are mammoth and complex and also compounded by years of institutional entrenchment. (For example, local school boards even in suburban and small communities are notoriously resistant to change.) My guess is that there is less desire by well-meaning suburban church people, in this time of economic contentment and conservative drift, to become involved in urban concerns than during the civil rights era. The major Protestant denominations, which cannot come to terms with their own homophobia, will find it hard to deal with apparently intransigent inner-city and metropolitan concerns.

At the local church level, a strategy of sound Bible study that examines the implications for social justice is still vital. Implicit in this is the need to explore the political implications of social justice concerns. The lessons of the 1960s and 1970s that hoped-for changes in city halls would bring about needed change has only led reformers and change agents to become disillusioned with both political parties, but change is still possible. Grassroots initiatives for gay rights, an end to the death penalty, and political campaign reform show signs of genuine hope. Thus, there are things that local church people as well as congregations or groups of congregations can do to effect political change.

I think that it is important to give support and assistance to those professionals (public school teachers, social workers, health care workers, etc.) who work in the city. I am not sure that churches as such have done this, except where individual pastors are encouraging.

We live in an age where top down (federal government, for example) approaches to social change are largely ineffective or even harmful. Witness the attempt at national educational standards via testing, which does nothing to improve the quality of education in our communities. While programs such as charter schools hold promise as "laboratories" perhaps, their real contribution, and those of other new programs, is in suggesting that school systems need a major overhaul. Church people and other community activists can assist in pushing for such major reform without getting caught up in the latest gimmick. Tutoring, mentoring, and school board involvement are still ways in which church people can make a difference in education.

I am afraid that the hoped-for institutional change efforts of the 1960s and 1970s that churches and judicatories encouraged are no longer as important as agenda items as they were previously. Hard realism has also taught us, and the churches, that such change, if it is to be more than cosmetic or transitory, is hard to come by in this current period. That leaves those of us in the church who are committed to change with less room and ability to influence church agency decision making than perhaps existed previously. It also means that there are fewer resources with which to develop urban strategy programs.

Does this mean despair or the abandonment of metropolitan strategy efforts? I think not. But along with new realism, we need to become more sophisticated, creative, and adaptive. New channels of collaboration must be explored. Strategies of either cities-suburbs or church metropolitan agencies may need to explore new issues emerging rather than continuing old efforts, for example the effort to end the death penalty, which carries strong racial overtones. Increasing economic opportunities of significance rather than tokenism may offer more hope than trying to change basic institutions, which are so resistant to change. Legal efforts still offer some hope, although the present conservative climate is not as encouraging as previously. Through it all, the church needs to stand as a bulwark of racial equality and inclusive social justice. Minimally, this means church strategy must encourage churches to become active and involved in justice issues. Meaningful and relevant church metropolitan agency programs cannot exist in a church that seeks to retreat to worship, evangelism, and moral pronouncements without seeing the fuller implications of Jesus' message for the church and the world in which it exists.

Note: This history and analysis covers MEM and Newark only from 1963 to 1974.

12

FROM COOPERATION, TO COUNCIL, TO AGENT: GRAND RAPIDS AREA CENTER FOR ECUMENISM

David P. Baak

On March 23, 2001, the Third Annual Summit on Racism was held in Grand Rapids, Michigan. Organized by the Racial Justice Institute of the Grand Rapids Area Center for Ecumenism (GRACE) and cosponsored by some seventy-five businesses and community organizations, the summit brought together more than seven hundred persons from all sectors of the community. Nineteen action groups in business, religion, media, education, community, and government met throughout the day—continuing their work on projects begun during the year before. The day was opened by a gripping Diversity Theatre presentation and capped by a presentation by "Talk of the Nation" radio host and author Juan Williams, who commended the audience for taking "the first step in racial healing [which] is the hardest . . . when a person can admit there's a problem and start talking about it" (*Grand Rapids Press*, March 24, 2001).

On May 2, 2001, the *Grand Rapids Press* reported that the Grand Rapids City Commission had voted 4 to 3 to name a new downtown park "Rosa Parks Circle." By May 4, the paper reported that "reaction to Tuesday's decision to name Grand Rapids' newest gathering place in honor of civil rights pioneer Rosa Parks continued to heat up Wednesday, with some officials indicating the matter is not over. . . . Opposition generally has centered on the tenuous Grand Rapids connection to Parks." More than a thousand calls had been received in the city offices, running some 9 to 1 against the decision. On May 6, the *Press* report included an account of the racist and threatening calls made to two of the commissioners and the announcement for a prayer vigil: "A prayer vigil 'designed to bring a spiritual response to the controversy' is being planned by a diverse group of clergy. The vigil, sponsored by the InterDenominational Ministerial Alliance and the Grand Rapids Area Center for Ecumenism will be at the Macedonia Baptist Church."

The Summit on Racism had been established in 1999 to work toward "a racism free community," and one of the hopes of the Racial Justice Institute was to create a "critical mass" of people focused on racial justice. The intensity of the reaction to the naming of Rosa Parks Circle was an expression of the racism that infects many and affects all in the community—all the arguments about process and alternative names related to the park did not explain the disproportionate reaction to a political decision. It would be a mistake to get caught in the euphoria of the success of the Summit and the feeling of a "critical mass" of a crowd of enthusiastic allies and proponents of racial healing. It would be equally shortsighted to dwell only on the racial separation of the community demonstrated by the intense reaction to the commission's action.

For many years racial tension has existed alongside thoughtful and creative responses to racism. The continuing opportunity is ours, suggested this author: "Allow me to remind us of the powerful call to all of us who believe, from II Corinthians 5.16–21, about God's reconciliation and how we fit in it. We become ambassadors of reconciliation and we, together, become the righteousness of God out of which there is a 'new creation'—we are brought to a place we've never been before. God, in us, reconciling the world. . . . If we are not called, here, and now, into the middle of the racial separations of this community, then where, and when—and who?" (GRACE Notes In-site, May 2001).

Many medium-sized communities exhibit a strange combination of arrogance, isolation, and self-sufficiency countered by a hunger for being considered mainstream. Grand Rapids has been like that—both with problems and with solutions. It has certainly not been willingly out of touch with the rest of the world; but often it has not really desired to be connected either. The community's experience has often been one of replicating the problems of other places and also one of reinventing the wheel when it came to responses. That has been true with respect both to the community's experience with racial justice issues and the development of its ecumenical organization, just as both are also reflected in the ecumenical stories of many other communities, as well.

This chapter focuses on racial justice as a primary social and ministry issue to which GRACE responded many times during the second half of the twentieth century. But the discussion is presented in terms of the changing characteristics of GRACE as an ecumenical organization. Each was repeated in dozens of other communities during this period.

There have been several phases in the life of GRACE since its founding in the mid-1940s—from *council* to *association* to *agency*. In the last years of the century, an *integrative* style emerged, and with it the possibility of yet another organizational transformation. GRACE had begun to gather people of faith from throughout the community in order to discern an agenda, along *with* the community, that provided an active, visible witness to the reconciling mission and ministry of the Church.

The Rev. Dr. Russell McConnell was perhaps the pivotal personality in the history of GRACE. He served as the executive director of the organization for seven years (1966–1973) and was the key visionary that led the effort in 1972 to radically change the organization. Many other ecumenical organizations have made similar transitions, though very few so early and so well, as structure and form gave way to informality and locally driven agendas.

The organization also enjoyed stability in its leadership. During this half-century there were only five executives, with two of them spending a combined total of more than thirty-five years in the position. But the genius of GRACE, like many similar organizations, was that there were many other leaders, whose time and energy and commitment both *created* the ecumenical arena and *gave permission* to the whole community to act together. In fact, GRACE was one of the critical factors that made the Grand Rapids community distinct, as newcomers often said, and perhaps even unique. Significantly, the degree to which this dynamic remained in the background of the community's consciousness is the degree to which those who tried to live out the ecumenical vision actually succeeded—living ecumenism, in the best sense, together, every day, in the routine.

Grand Rapids is a western Michigan city of 200,000, in a metropolitan area of nearly three times that number. It shares the economic history of many other upper Midwestern communities, evolving from native (Odawa) river bank village to fur trading to lumbering to manufacturing and service over the past two hundred years. While its ethnic heritage is typically northern European, it is distinctive in that it was settled by French and Irish Catholics as well as by the usual New England–New York Protestants. Its mid-nineteenth-century immigrants came especially from the Netherlands, Germany, and Poland.

The religious population of the community has several distinctive characteristics, in addition to being overwhelmingly Christian. At mid-twentieth century (and into the 1970s), a third of the religious membership was Roman Catholic; nearly as many were members of Christian Reformed and Reformed Church in America (RCA) congregations; about 15 percent were members of mainline denominations other than the RCA; other religious traditions made up the final 20 percent. Active religious affiliation was close to national averages—about half of the population identified itself as involved in the life of a congregation.

The "non-religious" community ethos reflects its religious heritage—both faith and agnosticism are lived out in strongly conservative, categorical, and self-sufficient ways. There have long been rigorous, serious, and high community standards and expectations for personal achievement (money, advancement, invention, etc.), and corresponding behavior has often been separatist, individualistic, and even libertarian. Yet, community members have been intensely involved in religious activity and have long provided strong volunteer efforts throughout the community. This has produced a high proportion of faith-based groups among an overwhelming number of nonprofit organizations. The region has become a leading area for research and production. It has a diverse manufacturing base and provides a high quality of life—for most of its population.

These values and corresponding organizations endure, even though by twentieth century's end the religious community's proportions had shifted dramatically. Roman Catholic membership, while continuing to grow, made up about 25 percent of the religious population, and the proportion of Reformed, mainline Protestant, and Orthodox congregations had declined to no more than a total of another 30 percent (a drop of nearly 20 percent in twenty years). Significant growth took place in independent evangelical-fundamentalist congregations, to nearly 25 percent. Even with dramatic growth in the Muslim and Buddhist communities, faith traditions other than Christian represented less than 5 percent of the religious community at the end of the century.

Comparatively modest in size, Grand Rapids is the core of a fast-growing region of more than a million and a third people. Most of the area's counties grew 15 to 25 percent between 1990 and 2000, with a significant proportion of that growth coming from a diverse immigration of people from eastern Europe, southeast Asia, eastern Africa, and central America. Census data indicates that the white population of Grand Rapids declined from 80 percent in 1980 to 67 percent in 2000. In the last ten years the Hispanic population tripled and all other minority groups grew as well, both in real numbers and in percentage of total population. At the same time, several outlying communities that also grew dramatically remained above 90 percent white. This shift is reflected in the Grand Rapids public schools, where 71 percent of the students in 1972 were white but only 35 percent in 2000. Additionally, 60 percent of the students in the district in 2000 were within federal poverty guidelines (census data reported in the *Grand Rapids Press*, various dates, spring 2001).

These disparities indicate the constant tension and separation along racial/ethnic (and economic) lines experienced in the Grand Rapids area. Inclusion in the high quality of life of the region is often—and visibly—restricted to whites. Again, while not dissimilar from many other communities, racism and response—both positive and negative—have long been part of the character of the Grand Rapids metropolitan area. So, also, is an inextricable connection of racial issues with the religious community and its ecumenical witness. Racially separated as much as ever, according to many in the community, there also have been energetic responses that periodically attempt to provide cooperation and reconciliation. These attempts are also a part of a long-standing community tradition of trying to find ways to work together toward solutions.

Conciliar Style (1947–1972): Grand Rapids Area Council of Churches

The Conciliar style of ecumenism was characterized by an attempt to unite local churches in a single structure and a common agenda of Christian unity that was derived from denominational life and a national ecumenical context.

Beginnings

The Grand Rapids–Kent Council of Churches emerged in the mid-1940s through ties with the Grand Rapids Council of Church Women and the Grand Rapids Ministerial Association. Even though it had no staff, the group conducted a great many activities as a volunteer organization over the next decade. Those activities, which were well-reported in newspaper accounts, included an extensive survey of the community's poverty housing. The council took the lead in the resettlement of displaced persons, primarily from Eastern Europe, established a successful Christian education program, and responded to racial justice issues.

The InterDenominational Ministerial Alliance of Greater Grand Rapids, made up of African American pastors, was also formed in the 1940s. It met regularly, usually twice a month, for fellowship and education and continues into this new century. It is both a forum and a community access point for black pastors. But the need for the organization and its very existence also demonstrate the continued racial separation of the community.

The Council's organization—and early success and stability—had much to do with the charismatic Rev. W. Raymond Prescott, who began a twelve-year pastorate at Burton Heights Methodist Church in 1944 and who, in mid-1947, began a nearly seven-year tenure as Council president. When the Council formally incorporated in 1957 and opened its first office in the Federal Square Building, the Board hired Ray Prescott as its first director. He served in that post until December 1965, when he died suddenly, two months before his retirement and after his successor, Russell McConnell, had already been named.

Setting the Agenda and Speaking for the Church

In those early days, the leaders of the Grand Rapids Council of Churches held a vision of visible church unity and acknowledged the lead of the National Council of Churches in formulating the agenda *for* the churches and *of* the local council. Ray Prescott was one of those attending the founding of the National Council of Churches of Christ USA in Cleveland in late 1950, and he reported that "your Council is a part of that great movement." That point of view was clear in the stated purpose of the Council in its incorporating constitution, in 1957:

> We, the churches of the Grand Rapids area, desiring to make a more convincing witness to our essential oneness in Jesus Christ as divine Lord and Savior as revealed in the authoritative scripture, in order that we may bring an adequate, effective and relevant ministry to the people of this area, reach the unreached with the gospel of Christ, bring the truths of the gospel to bear upon the actions of men, do hereby constitute the Grand Rapids Area Council of Churches.

The statement is clearly optimistic, and there is a bit of bravado in the declaration that "we, the churches . . . constitute," when actually only thirty-three congregations were contributing members of the council that year. The few assumed they could speak for the many, believing the others would come along.

One of the first projects of the newly formalized council was to conduct a religious community survey "so we can speak with authority of religious conditions we are facing," according to Prescott. "We aim to find how many members are in the various denominations or not in any denomination, and what areas are over or under churched. This will aid greatly in the work of the council's Comity committee which helps member denominations plan the geographical layout of new churches, so no area will have too many or too few churches" (*Grand Rapids Press,* June 15, 1957).

The principle of united witness and focusing ministry efficiently is hardly debatable; but when such a principle is externally imposed the results should not be surprising. By 1968, the effort had changed—deteriorated, in a sense—to "a method of mutual reporting on plans to let us evaluate the need with full knowledge of what is contemplated in the area by other churches." In other words, the Council's original vision, as an expression of "United Protestantism," expected that its member churches would defer to the committee's assessment as to which congregation of the several member denominations would provide a Protestant presence for a given neighborhood. At the end of the Council period, there was a general recognition that such a vision had always been unrealistic and that, at most, the committee could make information available to a denomination regarding the neighborhood where it or one of its congregations had decided to begin or extend its ministry.

Racial Justice in a Faith and Order Context

During the early years, councils attempted to move their constituencies—and their communities—by means of a strong Faith and Order perspective that viewed the Church as a relatively (ideal) static and objective entity, a fellowship *(koinonia),* first of all, out of which witness or service flows. The effort toward comity may be the most obvious example for the Grand Rapids Council but it was hardly the only, or the most important, expression. Unified Christian education was also a very effective Council function for some twenty years, into the mid-1960s. Social action efforts over the years were attempts to respond to human need by way of attempts that drew people into an understanding of the Church as *consolidated* or *centralized* and the Council as representative. The Council actively organized an effort to resettle displaced persons in 1947 and 1948. It spoke to the community on the issue of housing in 1947 and again in 1967, as it did, similarly, regarding racial relationships.

In July 1964, Catholics and Protestants rallied in thanksgiving for the passage of the Civil Rights bill in a service sponsored by the Council. Participants included Msgr. Charles W. Popell (St. Andrew's Cathedral), Rev. Jacob Eppinga (LaGrave Avenue Christan Reformed), Rev. James Cochran (St. Paul's Methodist), Rev. R. A. Schley (First Community AME), and Rev. Charles Scheid (South Congregational).

In August 1966, the city school board picked a committee of clergy to spearhead the area's effort toward open housing. A fifty-one-member study committee, chaired by Chester Hall, community leader and a Council of

Churches officer, had proposed that the number one recommendation toward eliminating segregated schools was that the school board "exercise vigorous leadership in enlisting promotion of open housing. The School Board decided to appoint the religious leaders as the nucleus for the committee because they could best 'arouse the moral conscience of the community in meeting this moral responsibility.'"

In June 1967, the Kent County Committee for Open Housing, chaired by Council director Rev. Russell McConnell (who also chaired the city's Community Relations Commission and sat on the Community Mental Health Board), organized a board of directors for a development corporation to initiate nonprofit low-rent housing. Six board members were chosen by the Catholic Diocese, six by the Council, and five by the executive committee of the Open Housing Committee.

In the spring of 1967, many felt optimistic about prospects for racial harmony in Grand Rapids, believing that violence such as that seen in several other cities in the years 1964 to 1966 could be avoided. Others cautioned that an undercurrent of anger and frustration remained. And indeed, in July, in the middle of the open housing discussions, a week of violent riots in Detroit set off a less violent, but no less disturbing, outbreak in Grand Rapids. Most observers agreed the results could have been worse. According to a report prepared by the United Community Services, "the tensions were eased by the work of African American ministers and other community leaders, and by a task force of 12 African Americans and three whites who, before the outbreak, had been working with young people through programs at the recently opened Sheldon and Franklin Hall complexes (Gordon L. Olson, *Grand Rapids, a City Renewed*, 1996, pp. 51–52).

Other attempts by the Chamber of Commerce (Project 1,003, an employment initiative), the Grand Rapids Foundation (police-community meetings), and others coincided with the work of the open-housing effort, the InterDenominational Ministerial Alliance, and the Council of Churches.

In September 1967, day-long talk sessions were held regarding prejudice in Grand Rapids and resulted in three unanimous resolutions for better racial understanding. Forty participants, leaders in local church, academic, governmental, and civil rights circles recommended that

> Open housing legislation on both the city and state levels be enacted with coverage "as extensive as legally permissible."
>
> Conference participants and the community at large support the November 21 school tax millage vote, "since the current situation is prejudicial to the best interests of our children."

The participants hold a similar conference later for older teenagers and for young adults.

The school tax millage passed and eventually so did the open-housing legislation. There is no record of a follow-up conference for young people. There was also no such community-wide response to racial issues again until the 1990s when the community became involved in Institutes for Healing Racism, the various projects of the GRACE/Racial Justice Institute, and similar programs.

While many efforts were attempted by the ecumenical community through the Grand Rapids Area Council of Churches, the authority for the Council to do so rested in the leaders' assumption that the denominations had delegated their authority to a local Council to speak to, and on behalf of, their congregations. A few Roman Catholic congregations joined the Council after the stimulus of Vatican II, including St. Andrew's Cathedral. (This was apparently the second Catholic congregation in the nation to join a council of Protestant hegemony. Such hegemony was a national "issue" for Roman Catholics well into the 1970s. It is now long gone from almost all local ecumenical discussion and effort.) Only LaGrave Avenue Christian Reformed Church, of the evangelical, not mainline, churches, participated in the Council, at an associate level, for a number of years. But most congregations in the area were not involved. By the end of the 1960s, less than 25 percent of the religious community was of mainline Protestant traditions, and only some of these mainline congregations were actually members of the Council. This support was increasingly inadequate to carry out the unity vision.

The Council style was an important model for ecumenical ministry. It led the effort toward Christian unity for many decades and accomplished much. But it was built on the priority of denominationalism of the early century and it was encouraged by post–World War II enthusiasm and the hope for a new world order. And it was external to the life of many local congregations, particularly in an area like Grand Rapids, which was dominated by traditions that had never shared the goal of a "United Protestantism."

ASSOCIATION STYLE (1972–1988): GRAND RAPIDS AREA CENTER FOR ECUMENISM

The Association style of ecumenical activity was strongly inclusive, inviting active involvement of the congregations and relying on them to set its agenda so that Christian unity would be discovered and demonstrated.

Task Force on Ecumenical Development

A Task Force on Ecumenical Development was appointed in 1969 and worked for more than a year to design what was recommended to be a fellowship, an intimate relationship of people." In reaction to the strong council design of the past, as well as in response to current funding and participation realities, hierarchy gave way to grass roots. Rather than setting an agenda for the congregations, the new entity—the Grand Rapids Area Center for Ecumenism (GRACE)—would be an association where program came from its members. The recommendations were approved at the Council's annual meeting in February 1972.

Much of the structure and even the language was familiar. But a major change in style and focus in the life of the ecumenical organization produced an entity that would be radically different from the Council. Neighborhood clusters of congregations, already forming on their own, would effectively put ecumenical action and decisions at a very local level and would become the place of activity for the new organization (fellowship). The Central Unit would provide administration and advocacy (unless that too might be taken on by a neighborhood cluster). Affiliate memberships would be formed to allow congregations to be related to a task force or a cluster only—for a limited time, or permanently. Associate memberships would be established for ministries and individuals.

This configuration was adopted, building on present strength, in order "to reach out and embrace the churches not now involved." The task force minutes indicate that mutual need was expected to bring the congregations together in the clusters and that their presence would demonstrate that ecumenical activity in the community was larger than (but still part of) the formal membership. It was a position taken after long discussions with persons from many traditions, especially with Roman Catholic, Christian Reformed, and Missouri Synod Lutheran representatives. Accordingly, the organization changed itself to attempt to include all congregations and to enable their agenda. GRACE's agenda would be an agenda determined by its constituency.

Letting the Church(es) Set the Agenda

The purpose of GRACE shall be to promote programs and activities that will reflect the concerns of the faith community represented in the greater Grand Rapids area. Recognizing the diversity of congregations, GRACE will not seek to effect doctrinal unity, but shall endeavor to bring together people of concern through joint ministry, based on the strengths and resources of our Judeo-Christian heritage, demonstrating the power of ecumenism.

This GRACE 1974 purpose statement completed the organizational transition and made it clear that now it was up to the congregations to establish programs and, by extension, to (re)establish that visibility for the Church in Grand Rapids. In 1973 the constitutional and philosophical changes began to assert themselves. Rev. Russell McConnell retired, after serving as executive director for seven years. Rev. Gerald O'Conner, former pastor of St. Johns Church of Christ, who succeeded him, had served as the local United Fund Community Services planning director. As with many leadership transitions, the loss of McConnell's personal ties and presence on community boards reduced the organization's visibility.

The new programming style, however, got off to a very slow start because it depended on an active constituency. At its best, the approach could engage ever-larger numbers of congregations, finding room for everyone and responding to an ever-greater variety of issues and reflecting the variety of interests in the faith community. At its worst, however, the approach deteriorated into a passive vigil for someone to take it seriously. With such a small constituency base to begin with, however visible the leadership of the old Council had been, GRACE lost members (to a total of fifty-three congregations in 1975) and programs (the January 1975 issue of *GRACE Notes* indicates three cosponsored events and no ongoing initiatives, which had been the hallmarks of the past decade). By 1976, the position of executive director was reduced to part time, and in May, Rev. O'Conner resigned.

When the Rev. Vernon Hoffman took on the part-time executive director's role in fall 1976, it was clear that implementing the GRACE design, and, indeed, saving the organization, would require something more than a passive response to those who might be interested. Accordingly, the organization followed a style of initiating discussions regarding issues of concern to the congregations and attempting to draw out those persons who would choose to get actively involved if there were a forum. It was an activist orientation—within the limits, however, of its constituency's interests—harking back to a decade earlier, and was often referred to locally as "pragmatic ecumenism."

There was clearly a stronger emphasis on Life and Work programming, long seen as a perspective of the laity and an expression of service (*diakonia*). So, while the organization continued attempts to expand the support for the ecumenical vision and for living into its inclusive charter, it also continued to focus its energy on areas of public witness, which carried its own momentum.

Within two years, the annual report listed thirteen new task forces or initiatives. The Greater Grand Rapids Hunger Task Force had conducted its first Hunger Walk. The first Ecumenical Choir Festival had been held. Groups had been formed that focused on criminal justice, fine arts, South Africa, fair housing, and disaster response, and a new program had been started, Widowed Persons' Service, which would develop into a GRACE affiliate organization and later become a free-standing social service agency. The executive director's position had been full-time since 1978, and the 1979 budget provided for additional staff.

By the mid-1980s, many efforts, programs, task forces, and other initiatives were being sponsored by GRACE. This growth survived another leadership transition when Vern Hoffman accepted a call to a local congregation and I became the executive director in early 1983. Having spent a number of years in criminal justice pretrial alternatives, my social justice orientation was compatible with GRACE's emphasis. Along with its hunger program, GRACE had convened a number of community and congregational leaders in 1981 to respond to governmental funding cuts and the effects of recession. The All County Churches Emergency Support System (ACCESS) was created, providing the leadership and coordination of a community-wide network of emergency food pantries, many of which were housed in congregations.

Other efforts focused on ministry to the aging, media ministries, sexuality, Christian education, chaplaincy, and racial issues. Major events included the dedication worship service for the Grand Center, hosting the national Workshop on Christian Unity, and the development of the Project Plant Hope hunger effort, including sponsoring travel seminars to Central America. The Interim Ecumenical Eucharist evolved into an annual ecumenical communion service. Pentecost services, National Day of Prayer observances, and shelter issues events complemented ongoing efforts such as the Clergy Interracial Forum and the Aging Ministry Council. In 1987, GRACE and its four affiliates (ACCESS, FISH, Habitat for Humanity/Grand Rapids, and Widowed Persons' Service) moved to larger offices with some twenty staff persons and combined budgets in excess of $500,000, with nearly that much more annually flowing through the Hunger Fund.

GRACE actively reached into the congregations to define its programming and attempted, as an association, to actively respond to the concerns of all of its members. While much was accomplished, the organization's energy was dispersed in many directions. GRACE was involved in so many different things that, while it rebuilt its membership, it also lacked focus.

AGENCY STYLE (1989–1999): GRAND RAPIDS AREA CENTER FOR ECUMENISM

The Agency style assertively recruited persons from the religious community to become cooperatively involved in programs that would respond to needs, that would help to shape the agenda of the congregations, and that would also demonstrate the unity of faith of its constituency.

Practice to Principle: Life and Work Focus

The Grand Rapids–Kent Council of Churches/GRACE has always provided programs of importance, but it has always done so with a minority of the community's congregations participating. Additionally, the growth of GRACE programming was often led by laypersons—individuals rather than congregations.

By the early 1980s, GRACE was becoming a social justice agency, with the congregations encouraging their members' participation. At a programmatic level, GRACE efforts such as the Aging Ministry Council and the Clergy Interracial Forum in the mid-1980s actively mobilized the strength of laypersons in the GRACE constituency, not waiting for the congregations to set the agenda. In 1988, a different funding strategy was begun—away from total dependence on contributions: the AIDS Pastoral Care Network (APCN) program received its first operational grant from the AIDS Foundation and then has annually received federal funds; in 1995, the Racial Justice Institute was funded by grants from foundations, businesses, congregations, and individuals; similarly, the Project Zero Mentoring pilot program was initially funded by federal welfare reform monies.

Acknowledging this practice, the Board formally revised the bylaws in 1988 for GRACE to become a directorship corporation, eliminating formal congregational membership. This provided the framework for individuals, congregations, and groups to participate in GRACE programming according to "conscience, interest, or tradition." This activist approach was reflected in the changes to the GRACE mission, although it still included the unity approach of earlier decades. As the 1990s began, the mission stated that GRACE is "a visible expression of the Unity of the Church—cooperating in ministry, seeking justice, and celebrating God's love."

Shaping the Agenda of the Church(es)

Functioning as an agency, GRACE was intentionally leading the religious community into a new way of thinking and acting. It was no longer satisfied with providing an opportunity for ministry with which the congregational constituency could get involved simply if they chose. Now GRACE would continue to respond to the issues of its supporters, but, additionally, taking a lesson from the old Council, the Board was willing to risk speaking prophetically where congregations were unwilling to do so. In the late 1980s, AIDS was one of those issues, as increasingly (still, and again) were the issues related to racial justice.

It is interesting to note that a small committee had followed the same principle in 1986, as it planned the successor event to the educational interim ecumenical Eucharist series of the early 1980s. In January 1987, during the Week of Prayer for Christian Unity, the Lima Liturgy of the World Council of Churches/Faith and Order formed the basis for an ecumenical communion service, with Protestant, Catholic, and Orthodox participants, and with the risks associated with such an effort. It was an invitation to congregations and individuals to participate, but GRACE would lead the community into such an experience whether or not anyone else agreed. No one was asked for authorization for this service, or its supervision. GRACE, as Church, drawing on the authority of its constituency—congregations and individuals, clergy, bishops, and laypersons alike—authorized the gathering itself to celebrate the Eucharist as a way of expressing fundamental Christian unity and, in so doing, to encourage practical efforts toward more structural and institutional cooperation. This was exactly the opposite process than had been followed at a denominational level, where the Eucharist was usually seen as the culminating expression of a unity expressed in visible, documentary agreement.

GRACE, its board, staff, and participants now identified program issues from its ecumenical vantage point—not unlike the earlier council—but did so with a very local focus. Rather than attempting to speak to or for the Church, GRACE encouraged the participation of those interested in a faith response to an issue. An article in the *Grand Rapids Press* in April 1997 indicates the community's positive reception: "'If GRACE wasn't doing this, I don't know where it would come from,' said Bill, an AIDS Pastoral Care Network client. Perhaps nowhere. For 25 years, GRACE has played a unique role in the greater Grand Rapids faith community. It has reached across denominational and social walls to comfort the afflicted, feed the hungry, champion justice and offer the Eucharist to all believers."

Clergy Interracial Forum

The Clergy Interracial Forum (CIF) was a similar program effort, attempting to draw together clergy in response to the racial separation in the community. The CIF had its origin in a response/planning effort begun in April 1983, when more than fifty black and white clergy met at Park Congregational Church. The meeting was precipitated by a crisis over the Grand Rapids public school's superintendency—which degenerated into white and black religious and community leaders pitted against each other, mostly through the media. The group was called together by the Church Community Committee of the InterDenominational Ministerial Alliance.

Continuing as a way for "black and white clergy [to] end our separateness first," Forum meetings were held periodically in 1983 and 1984. Convened by GRACE, these meetings were planned by representatives of the InterDenominational Ministerial Alliance, the Grand Rapids Ministerial Association, and the Grand Rapids Urban Fellowship.

In fall 1984, an extensive congregational pairing, promoting pulpit exchanges and other activities, was implemented. Nearly forty congregations were involved at some level. An unsuccessful attempt to organize an interracial clergy retreat took place in spring 1985. In 1985 and 1986, sessions of the CIF were regularly held and a number of positive interracial activities were conducted because of the linkages and friendships formed through the CIF. These included multiracial participation in GRACE ecumenical services; black and white clergy acting together to help ameliorate interracial tension, mostly among young people, at a local theater complex and a large shopping center; continued pulpit and choir exchanges; and participation in the InterDenominational Ministerial Alliances Annual King Day Services.

The CIF continued to meet into the early 1990s, although with fewer participants and a much lower profile. The meetings often dealt with the tension between the need for "fellowship" (devotions, lunch) versus "action." In all, about seventy-five individuals, mostly clergypersons, participated at some level—the most tangible result was that of getting to know each other. GRACE continued to convene the Forum and provide staff support. The CIF was one of the organizations that then gave rise to the Racial Justice Institute, planning for which began in 1994.

Integrative Style

The Integrative style of ecumenical programming appears to be a blending of the unity and social justice perspectives; it is collaborative and seeks to discern the agenda of the Church and act on it; and, it becomes a reconciling synergy—something brand new—much more than the simple combining of its parts.

Discerning the Agenda of the Church

Much of Council/GRACE history is a mix of Faith and Order (the Unity agenda) and Life and Work (social justice). Perhaps most of the strength of GRACE has been the ability of board and participants to use both approaches, as local conditions have required. But, neither method nor a simple combination of the two seems adequate for the near future. What appears to be emerging—again the practice is driving us toward a principle—is an integrative approach that combines the two earlier emphases and that which is conditioned by insight and contextual constraints. Perhaps it is simply a Mission and Witness approach, where evangelism is carried out within an ecumenical expression of the Church. This is a distinct, if not new, understanding of the Church, one which includes an ecclesial, reconciling role for the ecumenical agency and one which transcends the boundaries that many such local organizations have used for so long. This approach seeks to discern the agenda of the Church and to act on it.

The approach is much more active than was GRACE's style of leading in the early 1990s. The agenda was still shaped, in a sense, *for* the community. Only since 1995 has the emphasis shifted to an agenda arrived at—discerned—in *collaboration with* the community. The earlier style depended on cooperation with a particular program; the current approach, by definition, demands broad community involvement from a program's inception.

Racial Justice Institute

The single best example of this approach is the Racial Justice Institute (RJI) program, the latest expression of the long-standing agenda of GRACE (and of the earlier Council) for working toward racial justice. Planning for the RJI began in 1994 with the Clergy Interracial Forum and the Urban League's Race and Religion Committee. It was increasingly clear how deep the racial separation in the community was. One person's response to an areawide survey indicates a widespread feeling of preference for that separation. "My town is all white. It's been white as long as I can remember. It doesn't bother me that its not diverse. I like it this way, I just feel comfortable hanging with people of my own race honestly." A young African American professional said, "Grand Rapids is open-minded. It's definitely not overtly racist and hostile—just the opposite. But there's a gap between accepting and celebrating diversity. I definitely feel this is a great economic opportunity, but at what expense?" He and his physician wife moved back to the West Coast after a little more than a year (*Grand Rapids Press,* August 22, September 12, 1999).

At the same time, there were many efforts, especially within business and religious congregations and organizations to make things better, but the efforts were not coordinated. The RJI aimed to help put the efforts in touch with each other and, together, to focus on the problems within the community. In 1995 the RJI was funded for three years by three foundations and two businesses; programming began in 1996. The Rev. David G. May, pastor of Mt. Moriah Baptist Worship Center and past president of the Inter-Denominational Ministerial Alliance, became the RJI Coordinator in 1997. His vision and joint leadership with me, as executive director of GRACE, of the ecumenical faith effort for racial justice became key to the success of the larger Grand Rapids community focus on racial issues during the 1990s.

In 1992, a personal contact between Catholic layperson Bob Woodrick, chairman of a local grocery chain, and Nathan Rutstein, author of *Healing Racism,* resulted in further local and national contacts that encouraged the use of the "Institutes for Healing Racism" (and its circle dialogue process) in the community. Also in 1992, committees of the Roman Catholic and Episcopal Diocesan sponsored a joint "study circle" model of discussion aimed at racial reconciliation. Several of the more than forty participants became the core of continuing efforts at racial education and awareness among congregations, an effort that became the Faith Based Institutes for Healing Racism, now coordinated by the GRACE/RJI. At the same time, the Chamber of Commerce Diversity Committee was trying to promote attention to racial justice issues in the workplace, an effort that eventually became the Employers Coalition for Healing Racism. In 1993 Woodrick gave a speech to a gathering of some three hundred business and community leaders that is remembered as a galvanizing moment, becoming the symbolic beginning of what has become a joint community effort, particularly around sponsoring Institutes, in which, at the end of that decade, some 1,500 persons had participated. In 1995, Woodrick also became one of the first major funders of the GRACE/RJI.

Within the mission of GRACE ("to invite individuals, congregations and the community into greater reconciliation"), the purpose of the Racial Justice Institute was "to mobilize persons within the religious community to respond to issues of racial justice." The RJI hoped to create an active constituency, a community awareness, and general support for the program (a "critical mass" that would change community expectations about racial justice). It would provide integrative programming, combining education and action so that any single item would have an obvious relationship to another, as well as to the theological, moral, and philosophical reasons for such a program.

The Youth March for Justice (held each September) was highly successful in drawing attention to the fact that young people suffer from racism in the community. But the march has also given them an opportunity to have a voice, to be heard, and to effect a change. A youth initiative, *Racial Expressions—Youth in Action,* was an outcome of both the Summit on Racism and the March. Congregational partnerships facilitated mutual fellowship and development; congregational partnering options and guidelines were developed to assist in the process. A series of information-gathering sessions, including pastors' groups and a town meeting, were held. Three-session workshops, "The Disease of Racism, Hope for Healing," were provided in a number of congregations. Eight-week and two-day sessions of the faith-based "Institutes for Healing Racism" were facilitated.

In the fall of 1998 the GRACE/RJI brought 150 area business, civic, educational, and religious leaders together for a half-day leadership conference. The conference focused on how racism could undermine the social, cultural, and economic base of a community. Its purpose was to begin a dialogue that would pave the way for a proactive five-year effort to promote cultural diversity and racial healing in the Grand Rapids area. The summit's two-part agenda was to create a vision for the future of racial justice in the metropolitan community and to develop strategies that would provide a platform and action plan for achieving that vision.

On April 16, 1999, the Institute, along with other area organizations, sponsored the community's first Summit on Racism. The response was overwhelming. The Summit attracted a diverse mix of 435 people who came together for the common purpose of learning and sharing ideas. Participants were given the opportunity to make a personal commitment in one of six strategic areas and to attend workshops aimed at establishing actions steps for the coming year. In 2000, more than 550 attended, and in 2001 over 700 persons spent their day sharing progress reports for each action team. Recommitted, the participants left energized and ready to take part in the new plans they had formed.

The summit was itself an action step of reinforcement and commitment, gathering new participants in the process and on the way in a multiyear plan toward a "racism free community." More than a dozen community organizations and more than seventy-five business, education, governmental, and community groups joined GRACE's core constituency in planning, supporting, and participating in the effort. The Summit became an "annual focus on racism in this community" and created a collaboration that became, "by 2001, a 'community project,' involving participant cosponsors and underwriters from every sector." It was both the most visible community collaboration of its type and also a model for a similar Summit on Racism in a neighboring county. It also provided the model for other community efforts in response to poverty and community planning.

The GRACE/RJI called the community of faith to gather around this issue in order to discern a religious community response of racial justice. Many people of faith came to the variety of gatherings. A large number of them were not part of institutional, congregational faith groups, but they, and their organizations, chose to collaborate with each other in the formal programming of GRACE and the RJI—and in the process have participated—even becoming the means of—"the greater reconciliation" of the community.

Through these efforts, and primarily through the Summit, the mailing list of actively interested/involved persons grew to more than a thousand people—part of a growing community constituency that approached a critical mass that would have the energy to create a community expectation for racial justice. The work of the Racial Justice Institute had a significant impact in building such a community consciousness.

The RJI program also had a strongly ecclesial function for many of its constituency: Their witness/mission, their service, their understanding of unity, all were articulated in terms of their experience in and with this program. This was true also for many in the GRACE AIDS Care Network and in the collaborative Mentoring Partners (response to welfare reform). These were all examples—and measures—of an integrative style of ecumenical programming.

Conclusion

In 1996, after two years of study, reflection, and planning, the GRACE Board adopted a Vision that clarified its programmatic maturation. The Vision states: "GRACE is called by God and by the church to visibly enable a collective expression of the kingdom and the reconciling love of God. . . . The mission of GRACE, which arises from that vision, . . . invites individuals, congregations and the community into greater reconciliation as together we provide cooperative ministry, promote justice and celebrate God's love."

Reconciliation expresses well the dynamics of the integrative style and the approach to the future. More than simply fixing two broken parts, reconciliation brings people together in a completely new relationship, into something that we have never experienced before. GRACE is exploring the meaning of the reconciliation inherent in our theology of Christian unity and in the synergism of a reconciling process for all persons working together on an issue, so that, together, we become witnesses to the reality of God.

At the turn of the century, the questions for GRACE that arise out of this style, in addition to the need to understand the implications of the style itself, include an exploration of the nature of its constituency. Congregations, and their members, almost as a matter of course, assume that Christian Unity is part of their self-definition. It seems that they do not participate in GRACE programs to pursue, or even to express, Christian unity. They seem to ask for an action step, as if there has been enough discussion. Then, looking at GRACE, or at any of a number of other agencies in the community, they choose which organization provides the activity to best express their faith. People of faith seem to be involved in programs for personal mission and fulfillment reasons, and there is no inherent reason to act, for example, through the Racial Justice Institute of GRACE rather than the home building of Habitat for Humanity. Neither is seen as more or less an expression of unity. Faith, today, appears to assume unity.

If that is so, why is fragmentation so prevalent and the need for reconciliation so great? And to what is an ecumenical agency called, in every day local terms, especially when that agency has a vision for demonstrating the kingdom and inviting all into greater reconciliation? What is the relationship between GRACE, the Church, and the churches? And what can we learn from the past to help us as we move into the future?

References

Bratt, James D., and Christopher H. Meehan. *Gathered at the River: Grand Rapids, Michigan, and Its People of Faith*. Grand Rapids: Grand Rapids Area Council for the Humanities and William B. Eerdmans Publishing Company, 1993.

GRACE Annual Reports (complete set), *GRACE Notes, GRACE Notes In-Site*, newsletters of the Grand Rapids Area Center for Ecumenism, and unfiled notes and papers, all held at the Grand Rapids Area Center for Ecumenism offices in Grand Rapids.

Grand Rapids Press. Archives and files, held in the Grand Rapids Public Library.

Olson, Gordon L. *Grand Rapids, a City Renewed: A History since World War II*. Grand Rapids: Greater Grand Rapids Chamber Foundation by the Grand Rapids Historical Commission, 1996.

13

THE FOUNDING OF SMITH HAVEN MINISTRIES

David Bos

The 1960s were a time of the shaking of the foundations, in national culture, in institutions and in personal lives. In June 1960, I had just graduated from seminary and had just been ordained to the Presbyterian ministry. I had been married for three years and had two children. We arrived in a small city in upstate New York to take the post of assistant minister in a prosperous, liberal, and relatively large congregation situated in the middle of town. In so doing, I was following a well-established pattern in well-established institutional contexts. Then, in a manner of speaking, all hell broke loose—in my personal life, in my denomination, in society, even in the small city. Seven years later, after the assassination of President John F. Kennedy, and after the eruption of racial riots in several northern cities, I found myself in the employ of the Presbytery of Long Island—but not as a pastor. I was divorced and estranged from my former wife and children, remarried to a citizen of the Netherlands, and conducting a one-year exploration, which was to lead to an as yet undefined experimental ministry.

The shake-up in my life was both an echo and a precursor of widespread changes in the whole social fabric. Who would have thought that within another four years the small city would lose its main industry and the congregation there would begin a downward spiral in membership, which would reduce its size by two thirds. Martin Luther King would be assassinated. The antiwar movement would reach its zenith. Universities would be under siege by radical students and faculty. Feminist, environmentalist, and consumer rights movements all would experience the first stirrings of political and social power. The civil rights movement would evolve into its most militant expressions in the Panthers, the Black Muslims, and black power. And

President Lyndon Johnson would announce his War on Poverty in the wake of perceived vast economic inequalities.

In the churches, "experimental ministries" would spring up in a variety of settings—factories, recreational areas, Wall Street, shopping malls, youth hangouts, and the city streets. Vatican II would bring Catholics and Protestants together in several arenas of cooperation.

These changes affected denominational offices and ecclesiastical institutions. In the sixties, a divorce usually was devastating to one's professional plans—especially if the profession was the ministry. Our divorce was emblematic of a huge wave that was to grow exponentially and generally throughout the 1970s. Church officers and members were not immune. However, as had been true in earlier generations, when the divorce was inevitable I did not feel compelled to leave either my post or the profession itself. Yet, at the same time it caused me to seriously reevaluate my relationship to the profession and reflect on my role as a minister. I was fortunate enough to be able to take a leave of absence from my post to study church history at a Dutch university as a Fulbright scholar. Upon returning, in the midst of this period of self-examination, an opportunity presented itself in the form of an open-ended call from the Presbytery of Long Island. That call was to result eventually in the Nesconset Experimental Ministry, as it was called—a ministry that would develop into Smith Haven Ministries, one of the first "community ministries" in the nation—located in the then-largest regional shopping mall in the United States.

The Presbytery was searching for a way to respond to the many changes that were taking place within its bounds. It was an area that was very much exposed to all the upheavals of the 1960s—at once urban, suburban, and rural, with a Native American reservation in the mix. To its credit, the reaction of the Presbytery was not to "circle the wagons" for fending off the effects of change, as sometimes happens in the Church. The leaders of this effort included General Presbyter, the Rev. William Rambo, native of New York City and former pastor in the Presbytery; Moderator Tom Stewart, pastor of the Roslyn congregation and scion of a distinguished New York state Presbyterian family of many generations; and the Rev. Doug Bartlett, chair of the committee to oversee the Nesconset project. Bartlett was pastor of an experimental "house church" congregation in Commack. These were joined by the pastors of two nearby large congregations, the Rev. William Brown at Smithtown and the Rev. Don Broad at Setauket. To the last one, these leaders regarded the many changes and upheavals not as threats but as opportunities for transformation and discovery of new ways to do ministry.

The great suburban expansion of mainline Protestantism in roughly the years 1945 to 1965 was over. The first numbers reflecting what would be a precipitous decline in membership of urban congregations and younger people were in. Even the suburban base began to reveal weaknesses. The "triple ghetto" (a phrase from Will Herberg's book, *Protestant, Catholic, Jew*) now had to be expanded in concept to include a fourth category—those who declined to identify with any of the above and who felt little social pressure to do so.

The Presbytery of Long Island had been an active partner in forming comity agreements with other Protestant bodies relative to the development of new congregations. These were designed to prevent the circumstances that had arisen in many suburbs where "first units" representing various denominations had appeared within blocks of each other. As the postwar boom in membership began to level off, these first units found themselves struggling to survive and in competition with each other for the diminishing pool of prospective members. Denominational leaders began to confer and consult with each other to substitute cooperation for competition in the field of church extension. On Long Island, William Rambo initiated such discussions among the denominations.

The Presbyterians had taken responsibility for an unincorporated area called Nesconset. Nesconset was located on the eastern edge of the town of Smithtown on its border with the town of Brookhaven. It was on the growing fringe of the metropolitan area and in the midst of residential construction ranging from lower-middle-class to upper-middle-class homes in numerous subdivisions. If the Presbytery had followed the pattern of the 1950s and early 1960s, it would have purchased land and called an "organizing pastor," whose task it would have been to plant a Presbyterian congregation—the Nesconset Presbyterian Church, perhaps.

Several factors, however, gave the Presbytery pause. It was determined that of the many people moving into the area, Protestants were in the minority (about 20 to 25 percent) and that Presbyterians were only a small fraction of those. The great majority were Roman Catholic (50 to 60 percent), people who were joining the exodus to the outer suburbs begun much earlier by their Protestant neighbors. A Presbyterian new church development of the 1950s located not far from Nesconset had not prospered and was struggling to survive in the rapidly changing suburban scene. Nor should one overlook the skepticism that was abroad in mainline Protestantism at the time, about the efficacy of the traditional residential congregation in responding to the challenges of the changing times. The very authenticity of this rock of local institutional life was called into question by certain strains of thought that were then in the ascendancy—strains of thought that might be grouped under the broad rubric of "kenotic theology" (from the Greek *kenosis,* meaning "emptying," as in "Christ emptied himself, taking the form of a servant"). Space does not allow a full description of this theology. However, it emphasized the servanthood of the church and did not place a high priority on the survival of traditional institutional forms.

Thus, for a variety of reasons, pragmatic and theological, the Presbytery eschewed the prevalent pattern of new church development. It was among the first to do so, but by no means was it alone. Protestant bodies throughout the country at this time sought ways to extend their influence and ministry in ways other than through building new residential congregations. Thus, the Presbytery decided to create a position: "Minister to the Nesconset Area." The person who would fill this position would conduct an "exploration" on behalf of the Presbytery. He (and at that time it would almost certainly be a "he"), after as long as a year's process, would recommend a course of action to the Presbytery. In the spirit of the times, there were really no stated parameters on what shape those recommendations might take. A typical Presbyterian new church development was not to be ruled out. Clearly, there was an expectation that God might reveal other options in the course of the year's exploration.

It was an opportunity! I was ready to take on this challenge. Probably, one reason I had received this call was because of an already demonstrated penchant for innovation, having started a student discussion group between students of Union Theological Seminary and Jewish Theological Seminary a few years before and having been one of the founding members of the NAACP chapter in Olean, New York. And especially after the experiences in that first ministry after seminary I shared some of the common misgivings about the relevance of the traditionally structured congregation. So I was eager to strike out in new directions and to start a new life in a new context where my spouse could continue her theological education. In the middle of this tumultuous decade, I shared the basic optimism with the leaders of the Presbytery of Long Island that "God was doing a new thing." Here was an opportunity to be a part of that new thing.

We arrived on Long Island on April 2, 1967, to life in a rental house in a lower-middle-class subdivision surrounded with homes well stocked with watchdogs and guns. In the spirit of "exploration," I began almost immediately to meet with people in the area: ministers and priests and rabbis; social activists; governmental and business leaders; lay leaders of the congregations and parishes of the area; local, regional, and national denominational leaders who carried portfolios related to the area; representatives of institutions of secondary and higher education; and various committees of the Presbytery of Long Island. The leaders of the Presbytery brokered many of these meetings and alleviated, to no little extent, the feeling of isolation for a minister who had just left the shelter of a warm and protective congregation for a venture into the unknown. There was a strong consensus in the Presbytery that the times demanded this kind of an exploration. I noted in one of the first entries in my journal that right from the beginning there was a willingness and even a bias in the Presbytery to try something other than a typical new church development. Other denominations expressed interest and eventually became full partners in the experiment (including United Methodist, Episcopalian, Lutheran, United Church of Christ, and Roman Catholic). But I experienced both the anxieties of a situation that was in many respects lonely and insecure and the exhilaration of an explorer in uncharted territory.

There were four meetings in the first several weeks that were to have a determinative effect on the development of this experimental ministry. The first was with Kenneth Anderson, an African-American elder in the Presbyterian Church in Port Jefferson. He was an anesthesiologist by profession, a member of the Suffolk County Human Rights Commission, and a civil rights activist. Anderson had the temerity to initiate contact with me only days after his arrival on the scene and to invite me to join him that very night in entering and observing a meeting of the MacArthur Club—a local branch of the right-wing John Birch Society. I accepted the invitation with both alacrity and misgivings. That was the beginning not only of a friendship but also of a significant ongoing linkage between the African-American community of Suffolk County and the experimental ministry. Henceforth, this ministry would be an expression of a desire for racial harmony and cooperation. When, four months later, we started to recruit a proposal committee to formulate a proposal to the Presbytery of Long Island, Kenneth Anderson was one of the first to agree to participate and to help shape the proposal. Later, Anderson and I were to serve together on a Presbytery committee to educate ourselves and others about the militant organization known as the Black Panthers.

Because of the meeting with Anderson and others with ties to the Suffolk County Human Rights Commission, we were referred to another member of the Commission, a priest of the Roman Catholic Diocese of Rockville Center and associate pastor of St. Peter the Apostle's parish in Islip Terrace, the Rev. T. Peter Ryan. Ryan and I were the same age, had both established a reputation as advocates of civil rights for African Americans, and were both exponents of post–Vatican II Catholic-Protestant and interfaith cooperation. We also shared a view that there was a need for para-congregational structures that would augment but not supplant the traditional, residentially based parish. In other respects, we were of quite dissimilar backgrounds: the one, of Calvinist and Dutch ancestry, a product of midwestern public schools and eastern establishment institutions of higher education, of essentially itinerant status, and accustomed to situations where Protestants enjoyed majority if not hegemonic control; the other, of rather traditionalist Catholic and Irish ancestry, a product of Catholic schools and Catholic higher education, a Long Island native, and accustomed to majority Catholic communities where deference was paid to the parish priest. Yet, almost from the very first moments of our meeting, we could imagine ourselves as a team—finding a bond in our similarities and a pragmatic complementarity in our dissimilarities. From the beginning, we could envision how each might enhance the reconciling ministry of the other and how our relationship might exemplify the ecumenical intentions of our respective faith communities.

Peter Ryan's involvement, first as a member of the Proposal Committee and eventually as cofounder of the experimental ministry and codirector of Smith Haven Ministries, meant that this project would always be a significant ecumenical and interfaith effort and witness in central Suffolk County. Ryan brought significant Catholic resources to the project—including volunteers and financial assistance from religious orders, priestly and pastoral support from surrounding parishes, and advocacy of the project by the area's Catholic leadership with developers and politicians.

The "Minister to the Nesconset Area" and Father Ryan began to talk about a centrally located ecumenical center. Everyone in the area was aware that a regional shopping mall was being planned. Would the Smith Haven Mall be a suitable location for such a center? Ryan began to inquire about other shopping mall ministries, while I began to talk with those "in the know" about local real estate transactions. Through the Centerreach Rotary Club, I met Gary Katica, a young businessman who headed a real estate agency and was an active layperson in his Greek Orthodox parish. Because of that contact, Katica informed the Proposal Committee that the coming shopping mall would be of proportions hitherto unheard of. Instead of the customary two anchoring department stores, it would have four! Its one-and-a-half million square feet would make it the largest in the country. Its trade area would double in population within the next fifteen years to some 400,000 residents. Noting that some developers of shopping malls had encouraged occupancy by nonprofit service-oriented organizations, Katica encouraged the Committee to explore such possibilities. His company owned a former model home on property adjacent to the mall construction site, and he indicated his willingness to make the building available at a reasonable rent. On the Proposal Committee's recommendation, the Presbytery of Long Island rented the former model home, I moved the office from my home into the building, and after a year, the first programming of the Nesconset Experimental Ministry (NEM) began in the basement there—a coffee house for high school youth called "the Grounds."

Katica also introduced us to his Greek Orthodox priest. The priest proved very interested in the prospect of an ecumenical experimental ministry. He invited me to preach in his church, and eventually the parish became a participant in the ministry. Katica advised our team on how to approach the mall developers (e.g., not through their local representatives but directly to the partners in New York City). There were, therefore, several significant aspects to the Katica connection: It demonstrated that the experimental ministry could cast a wide net in ecumenical participation—not only in terms of Protestants, Catholics, and Jews, but also in the Orthodox Christian community as well. It demonstrated that with wide ecumenical and interfaith participation, doors would open for interfacing with the world of business and commerce (the rental of the strategically located former model home was a very key step leading to the establishment of the Smith Haven Ministries). Finally, it encouraged NEM to pursue a negotiated entrance into the shopping mall as a potential scene for effective and responsive ministry.

About three months into our assignment, shortly after our initial conversations with Gary Katica, we were introduced to Dorothy (Mrs. Alfred) Ryder through William Brown, the pastor of the Smithtown Presbyterian Church where Ryder was a member. She had recently moved to Suffolk County from Brooklyn where she had been vice president of the School Settlement House and named Outstanding Protestant Woman of the Year. She quickly became active on committees of the Presbytery of Long Island. Because of a strong and pleasant personality, good organizational skills, and many contacts reaching back to her childhood congregation in Brooklyn—one of the oldest congregations of the Reformed Church in America—she was a powerful laywoman. I use the term "laywoman" because Dorothy Ryder's engagement with NEM and later with SHM assured that it would be an important site for ministry of the laity and that it would always have strong lay oversight. Furthermore she viewed herself as bringing an essential element of lay leadership into the picture. It is not that she was antagonistic to clergy or to me or my newfound collaborator, Father Ryan. Far from it; but she knew and was convinced of the fact from long years of experience in civic and church matters that there could be no substitute for strong and dedicated lay leadership if this experiment was to succeed. We recognized the gifts that Ryder would bring and, when the Presbytery of Long Island rented the former model home, we asked her if she would chair the House Committee—the committee that would oversee operations in the newly rented facility. She accepted that responsibility and would eventually become the first chairperson of the Steering Committee of Smith Haven Ministries as it began operations in the Smith Haven Mall.

Ryder remained a powerful force in the life of the ministries for the rest of the century as a genuine supporter of the ministry and its executive directors in a number of capacities. But these formal roles were not nearly as significant as the informal role that she played (along with her husband, an architect for the State University of New York at Stony Brook—itself a new and rapidly growing institution) as a counselor and constructive critic for these two young clerics, who were trying to develop an expression of "God's new thing." She would assess the many people and ideas that came forward with an unerring, yet gentle, eye. She maintained a certain detachment that made her a valuable source of objective advice, while never wavering in her support of the project and of the idea of an experimental ministry in response to the changing times.

These introductions to four people who would become pillars in the new ministry tell the story, in its essentials, of the founding of Smith Haven Ministries. These four are the parents of Smith Haven Ministries and the grandparents of the modern community ministry movement. They illustrate the crucial and related dimensions of lay leadership—vital interface with a particular locality, ecumenical and interfaith cooperation, and social mission.

Yet, this does not tell the whole story. The full story would have to include the account of the visionary leadership of the General Presbyter, William T. Rambo, his mentoring of the young team of codirectors, and his brokering of ecumenical support from regional and national ecumenical offices. The full story would have to relate the drama of a *Newsday* journalist friend of Father Ryan persuading a former mayor of New York City (Robert Wagner) to intervene with the developers of the regional shopping center on behalf of the experimental ministry. It would also go into some detail about the inherent tensions that arise when a social ministry establishes itself in a regional shopping mall during a time of social upheaval—the effect, for example, of a student theatrical group in whiteface portraying the horrors of the Vietnam War in the corridors of the mall; or of a young man, excluded from the youth program because of drug use, trying to destroy the mall by setting fire to a pile of cardboard at the rear entrance of Smith Haven Ministries. Nor have we elaborated on the varied programs that went into operation when the Nesconset Experimental Ministry became the Smith Haven Ministries and began operations in the Smith Haven Mall in February of 1970—from a fair housing center to shoppers' child care, from a program for runaway youth to consumers' advocacy, from pastoral counseling to a community information and referral service, from an emergency food pantry to book and art sales.

I resigned from Smith Haven Ministries in spring 1975 for another pastoral position with a community ministry emphasis in upstate New York—handing over the main responsibility for the direction of the project to Father Ryan. The effect of the founding of Smith Haven Ministries on me was to restore some wholeness to a life that had seemed shattered in both its personal and collective dimensions. My hope was that the new community ministry would have a similar impact on the people of central Suffolk County. I attempted to capture this hope in a Preamble to the formal proposal for an SHM to the Presbytery of Long Island, dated October 11, 1967. It might stand as an expression of the hope represented by community ministries that were beginning to spring up across the United States at that time:

> We note that there are many signs of alienation or brokenness in the society in which we live. We are separated on the basis of age, color, place of residence, job or income classification. All of us suffer from these various forms of separation insofar as they contribute to our inner loneliness and lack of harmony.
>
> We affirm, nevertheless, that a spirit of renewal is present and at work in our society. We declare that it is this spirit of renewal that has brought us together from many varied backgrounds and traditions to

consider the unique opportunities for constructive action that a regional shopping center affords.

It is our purpose to illustrate the spirit of renewal by our own unity and cooperation in formulating a shopping center ministry. It is our purpose also, in this spirit, to discover ways of working for the renewal of our society through the instrumentality of a shopping center ministry.

We seek to use the singular and historic possibilities for reconciliation that the market place presents. We understand the word, "love," to indicate a force for renewal insofar as it means not glossing over conflict but using it for the advancement of human values. Thus, among other things, love means to aid the cause of the oppressed and to support and comfort those who despair.

In general, our common confidence in the spirit of renewal causes us to hope for a new day and a new life for our society and leads us to find ways of celebrating the signs of its coming. We invite all peoples from all segments of society to join in this celebration and in this ministry of renewal; and therefore, we find the regional shopping center to be an appropriate focal point of service.

The ministry continues into the beginning of the new century.

PART FOUR.
LOCAL ECUMENISM BEYOND THE CITIES

The United States became an urban nation in the twentieth century, although because of population growth there are still more Americans living in rural America at the close of the twentieth century than lived there a century earlier. These rural Americans provide most of the food and much of the natural resources required to keep urban America and the American economy alive. Yet, like the central cities, rural America has been denied its share of the benefits from its contribution to the whole society. As a result, in the last half of the twentieth century:

- *A higher percentage of the population of rural America lives in poverty than in urban America.*
- *Extractive industries, like coal mining, utilize the resources of rural America, but the profits flow to the city. These industries, at best, provide jobs for a time for rural Americans, until the "vein runs out." They traditionally have left behind poverty and ecological degradation.*
- *Vertically integrated corporate farms have come into being, which profit not from production but from processing and distribution of farm products.*
- *Modern agricultural technology has enabled efficiencies and resulted in soaring farm production.*
- *This in turn has led to the disappearance of the small family farm—an independent way of life that is becoming less and less possible, because it is dependent largely on only the production of food stuffs. In a hungry world, farm commodities are regularly priced below production costs, leaving the farmer the loser.*
- *The independent farmer's income has plummeted, as has the value of his or her land, causing one of the greatest farm crises ever in rural America.*

- *Countless people have seen their hamlets, villages, and towns, as well as their churches and other basic community institutions, devastated in the process.*
- *At the same time, many economically sufficient urbanites have moved to rural America, for recreation and to find a simpler way of life.*

Amid these dynamics have been churches united in regional, state, and county ecumenical bodies that have given a helping hand and spoken a prophetic hopeful word.

14

RURAL ECUMENISM: THE COMMISSION ON RELIGION IN APPALACHIA AS A CASE STUDY

Arleon L. Kelley

Ecumenism over the past half century has had some of its most exciting and effective moments in rural America. As if in a mirror, we see the reflection of the twentieth century's many effective rural ministries in this story of the Commission on Religion in Appalachia (CORA). Just as national denominational home missions boards worked together to create the East Harlem Protestant Parish as an experiment in urban mission, CORA is the product of creative responses to rural needs by many of the same mission boards.

CORA's Roots Are in the Rural Ministry Movement

Home missionary societies, voluntary societies of Protestant Christians, most often Congregationalists, Episcopalians, Presbyterians, or Baptists, and independent of the churches, were formed in many eastern seaboard cities, like Boston and New York, in the 1700s. They carried the Gospel to the Native peoples in the West and formed congregations on the American frontiers. By the beginning of the twentieth century, many of the denominations had home mission boards with departments that included hospitals, homes and schools, rural concerns, and urban concerns. The rural concerns of the churches had come into focus from rural church surveys and two government-initiated programs as well as the trend of people moving from the East to the western frontiers and then eventually from the frontier farms to the city.

In 1862 Congress had passed the Homestead Act, making 160 frontier acres available to all homesteaders who lived on the land for a period of time. That same year the Morrill Act had created the land-grant college system (a college in each state endowed by extensive land holdings given by the government) to provide technical assistance to farmers. In 1914 the Smith-Lever Act created the county extension agent system, 4-H Clubs, and

Future Homemakers and Future Farmers of America in high schools. The land-grant colleges' focus was on the improvement of the family farm as well as rural community life, and the churches often worked hand-in-hand with these land-grant college and agricultural extension programs.

Historically and theologically, American life had been tied to the land and the village. A subtext of the concern was that people leaving the land and the villages to move to the cities and work in the factories might lose their faith and the denominations their rural congregations. In 1889–1890, a decade before the dawning of the twentieth century, the Evangelical Alliance for the United States investigated five rural counties in upstate New York, and over the next seventy-five years, Cornell University and the New York State Council of Churches undertook many innovative projects to strengthen the rural church, its leadership, and its communities.

In 1909 President Theodore Roosevelt created the Commission on Country Life as a response to the movement from local rural economy to a national industrial economy, movement that was disrupting traditional cultural assumptions, in no place more evident than in the rural church. The Report of the Commission on Country Life had this to say about the rural churches: "The fields were small, the people conservative, often there were too many churches in a given community and sectarian ideas were too divisive. As a whole, the churches lacked direction and did not assume social responsibilities."[1] They were dying or barely surviving.

These findings largely concurred with what had been documented by the Evangelical Alliance two decades earlier and led to the founding of the Rural Church Movement in 1910[2] by Washington Gladden, Josiah Strong, William DeWitt Hyde, Graham Taylor, and Ozora Davis. These leaders all had strong roots both in rural America and in the Social Gospel Movement. The Rural Church Movement's formation was preceded by the formation of the Home Missions Council of North America in 1908 and was followed in 1913 by the Federal Council of Churches initiation of its first Committee on Church and Country Life with nationally known conservationist Gifford Pinchot as chair.[3]

Because much of Christian religious myth of the eighteenth and nineteenth centuries had developed around the family farm, specifically, and the rural way of life in general, these changes toward urbanization and industrialization were shocking to many, and the resulting Rural Church Movement was born from the crucible of this transition in the United States. The movement was both denominational and ecumenical. In many of the frontier-born denominations—Methodist, Christian Church, Baptist, for example—the nineteenth-century mode of evangelization had been to form lay-led neighborhood ministries, which had often resulted in churches being formed. Rural neighborhoods were defined by the distance a horse and buggy could drive in a half hour or so to the one-room school or the general store. Such neighborhoods typically had congregations of two or more denominations, often one an ethnic congregation of the dominant ethnic group and the others "gathered" congregations that emerged from the lay ministries described above. As the Evangelical Alliance discovered in New York state, by the late nineteenth century the rural neighborhoods had begun to diminish in importance. Later, with the advent of the automobile and closing of one-room schools, depletion of rural neighborhood populations and resources became epidemic. All neighborhood institutions began to founder—including the churches. In New York, the State Council of Churches joined with Cornell Universitys Land Grant Agricultural College to form a Rural Church Institute whose purpose was to save the rural churches of New York through leadership development, curriculum development, and agricultural extension agent models, as well as the systematic and planned joining of congregations into larger parishes that shared a pastor, or if need be, merged into federated congregations.[4] The goal was to save rural communities and to ensure at least one viable Protestant rural church in each rural community in New York. Similar programs developed in the state councils of perhaps thirty or more of the primarily agricultural and rural states in the United States.

Also instrumental in the formation of CORA were the home missions enterprises of the denominations, which often picked up the rural agenda in states with no state ecumenical agency, like the Appalachian region and western mountain states. There the home missions boards often developed hospitals, schools, and service centers to meet human needs in these underdeveloped and underserved rural areas. Through ecumenical agreements the denominations also developed a mission comity plan that assigned responsibility for evangelism and the developing of new congregations in certain geographic areas, so all could be served and mission resources would not overlap. This work was all coordinated through the Home Missions Council, which became the Home Missions Department of the Federal Council of Churches and later the national missions unit of the National Council of Churches of Christ in the USA (NCCC/USA).

The Rural Church Movement also encouraged the development of the Rural Church Inter-Seminary Movement. The Inter-Seminary Conference for Training the Rural Ministry was first initiated by Dr. Malcolm Dana of Hartford Seminary especially for New England seminaries, but eventually spread to other regions of the nation through the Inter-Seminary Movement. In New England this rural component of the Inter-Seminary Movement even had its own endowment to pay for the gatherings and institutes the organization sponsored. When the Inter-Seminary Movement was in full flower from the 1920s to the late 1960s, it provided opportunities for seminary students to meet with students of other seminaries for fellowship, to read papers, and to discuss major theological issues related to rural America, with the result that several generations of pastors were well trained for rural ministry. It also meant that church leaders often held a rural bias.

CORA itself was formed by the denominational home missions partners in the National Council of the Churches of Christ in the USA, Town and Country Department. In a 1963 meeting in Chattanooga, Tennessee, to set up bylaws, the decision was made that CORA should become a separate entity, which the NCCC/USA governing board subsequently agreed to. CORA was separately incorporated in 1965. Its focus was parts of thirteen states in the Appalachian region of the United States—initially the rural areas of those states. By the early 1960s, the churches that participated in the NCCC had begun to realize that Appalachia was being modernized, traditional rural isolation was breaking down, and many of the health and educational and other mission institutions they had supported in the region were less needed because of the development of public schools and health and other institutions. The churches wanted to move from the paternalism of helping to empowering people and neighborhoods to resolve their own problems.

At the same time, rural leaders were beginning to see the symbiotic relationship between the urban center and the rural hinterland. Before the turmoil of the latter third of the 1960s, the national rural and home missions people initiated two processes, almost simultaneous with CORA's initiation, which had significant impact on CORA, largely because the same people were involved in all three activities. One was an experiment in better understanding the interdependence of the rural community and its churches. It began in 1963 with the formation of the Ecumenical Center for Renewal and Planning (ECRP) located in Merom, Indiana. The national denominational Home Missions/Rural Departments initiated it as the rural counterpart to the Urban Training Center in Chicago. ECRP, with director Rev. Keene Lebold and co-director Dr. Donald Zimmerman, undertook many creative community interventions, as well as the training of many pastors in community and church renewal. I collaborated in many of the ECRP projects in my capacity as executive director of the Department of Research and Planning, Indiana Council of Churches. The collaboration undertook several studies and action planning processes in rural Indiana as a way to better understand what was happening in rural churches in rural America. One of those study processes was in Spencer County, Indiana, a county that borders the Ohio River in southwest Indiana. The intervention was to test the hypotheses that the community and the churches were interdependent and that the church culture could impede the progress of the community, and vice versa. Spencer County was a good study ground because it was intensely rural and had, along with its churches, all the economic and social hallmarks of a dying community. Indeed we found that perhaps much of the county's underlying problem was rooted in the religious culture of the county. There were three ethnic groups in the county of roughly equal size—German Roman Catholics, German Lutherans, and a mixture of other Anglo minorities who were largely affiliated with Methodist, Presbyterian, and United Church of Christ congregations. Historic differences meant that members of one group never spoke with or dealt with members of other groups—either economically or socially, and certainly not religiously. Politicians used those dynamics to control the county, playing one group off the others.

Over a several-year period of intervention by ECRP and the Indiana Council of Churches this changed. The turnaround began when more than a hundred largely lay Protestants (including the German Lutherans) joined with about seventy-five Roman Catholics, first at a meeting at the Methodist's campground near Santa Claus, Indiana, which went so well that a second meeting was set for St. Meinrad's Archabby Church, a community that had just been engaged in a time of liturgical renewal, following the first session of Vatican II. The Protestants, who had heard all manner of rumors about the evils of the Archabby, had to brave stepping onto the grounds and were flabbergasted when they entered the church to find that it was stark white, and that all the pews and statues had been removed from sanctuary and nave. We all sat around on movable chairs in a circle in the center of the nave where pews had previously been. Walls of separation began to crumble with that meeting. The very next morning a Protestant mailman arrived at a parish priest's doorstep before breakfast and asked him to go to Indianapolis to get food stamps for the county. There they found that it was not the state but their own county politicians who would not allow food stamps. This certainly changed the politics in the next election. Indeed, within two years the systems of political, economic, religious, social, and community life were transformed. Most certainly the first session of Vatican II had played an important role in the improved church and community relationships in Spencer County.

A second process being undertaken by the denominational members of the Rural Ministry Department of NCCC/USA was the National Consultation on Church and Community Life. Emerging understandings of rural and urban interdependence, as well as the opportunity created by Vatican II, among other things, led to a proposal to the NCCC Rural Ministry Department that its regular National Rural Church Conference be postponed and instead a national "Consultation on Church in Community Life" be called for 1965. All the denominations, in and beyond the NCCC/USA membership and including the Roman Catholic Church, were invited to participate. More than two-dozen denominations, including Roman Catholic Monsignor O'Rourke of the Roman Catholic Apostlate to Rural America and Rev. Dr. (Father) Bernard Quinn of the Glenmary group, accepted the invitation.

The consultation took two years of preparation. The Consultation Studies Team, that I, a Methodist, co-chaired with Leonard McIntire, a Presbyterian, proposed rather revolutionary views: about the inadequacy of the approach of the historic Rural Church Movement (including its attempts to develop a unique rural theology), the interdependence of rural and urban communities, and the ineffectiveness of unilateral denominational approaches to saving their rural churches, and formulated a new analysis of the socioeconomic forces affecting nonmetropolitan communities. The proposals called for the churches to open themselves to renewal as Church in their neighborhoods and to use their newfound faith relationships to be a transformative force in their communities.[5]

Almost immediately following the Consultation, the Urban Crisis (called Crisis in the Nation by the NCCC) hit the churches with full force, and most denominational resources were needed to respond to this largely urban need. One by one, the denominations radically downsized and merged or phased out their national departments of rural work, as did the middle judicatories, the seminaries, and most state councils of churches. These factors, as well as the values and culture shock waves rebounding across the nation, turned the attention of the churches away from any great concern for a rural and urban interdependency to focus almost entirely on urban needs. The agreements the Consultation reached about ways to mobilize their resources for creative new forms of ministry in nonmetropolitan areas fell largely by the wayside, with some notable exceptions. The United Methodist Church's rural concerns department, under the leadership of Dr. Harold Huff, added staff, including the UCC's competent rural justice activist theologian Dr. Shirley Greene. But the several-person national office for rural concerns in the Presbyterian Church was folded into a larger mission entity under the leadership of Rev. Eugene Huff. By 1968 he hired the Rev. Arthur Tennies (also Director of Research and Planning for the New York State Council of Churches) on a 20 to 25 percent basis to deal with the national rural agenda for the Presbyterians. And by the early 1970s, the National Council of Churches Town and Country Department, under the leadership of Dr. Henry McKenna, was disbanded.

At the same time that denominations were downsizing their rural work, a new group emerged from the Consultation and its old planning committee. This was a much broader and more informal national group of persons from denominations, councils, and public institutions, such as the land-grant schools, called the Non-Metropolitan Issues Group (NMIG). This group or coalition was largely person- and interest-based, rather than being composed of representatives of institutions—as had been the NCCC Town and Country Department. I initially convened this group of perhaps seventy-five to one hundred members. Fr. Bernard Quinn kept the mailing lists and did the communication. It was designed to be a forum for communication on rural issues and a place where people and resources could be gathered to work on nonmetropolitan church and community concerns across America. This group initiated many projects and processes around rural issues over the years and proved its mettle in a number of situations. But perhaps at no other time was it more effective than when the Farm Crisis emerged a decade after NMIG was first convened. The Rural Network, which emerged from the NMIG, continues into the twenty-first century.

The Farm Crisis began in the 1970s and was at least partly a product of our economic system's propensity to expand by going into debt, a system that did not work for farmers as perhaps it did for other businesses—when a crop failed or when inflation carried interest rates to 20 percent or when the value of the mortgaged farm land diminished rapidly. But the Farm Crisis of the 1970s and 1980s also resulted because our institutions—government, education, political parties, the church, and the economy—had all but forgotten rural America for more than a decade. (Chapter 15 will cover the state and local ecumenical response to the Farm Crisis in more detail.)

A final dynamic in the formation of CORA was the political and economic concept of "regionalization," first made popular in the Kennedy administration and made even more important for a time by the Nixon administration's attempts at regional planning and allocation of federal monies through regional block grants. Eventually the churches began to mirror this approach with a series of regional organizations. At one time there were fledgling ecumenical regional organizations in Upper New England, the Upper Great Lakes, the Great Plains, the Lower Great Lakes, Appalachia, and the Mountain States. With the exception of the Lower Great Lakes group, these regional entities were essentially "crisis corridors," well away from the direct influence of the great urban centers. With the exception of Appalachia, these ecumenical regional groups were short-lived. They were formed about 1970 and had largely disappeared by 1990 because they demanded missional resources the church did not have or had allocated elsewhere, while at the same time they seemed to add another layer of meetings, stretching scarce leadership even further. These missions were largely dictated by the needs of the region. For example, the Upper Great Lakes group focused on native peoples' concerns and the problems presented to communities and people by mining in the areas west of Lake Superior, while the Lower Great Lakes group focused on the aging industrial infrastructure from western New York to Chicago. After more than a decade of work, almost exclusively by regional church people and with little national assistance, the groups disappeared.

But the exception was Appalachia and CORA. Because the national church had extensive mission activity in the region, the national churches remained connected with the region through CORA. Indeed, it seemed that what little energy the national churches had left for rural concerns in the midst of the Crisis in the Nation was focused in Appalachia. But there were also other forces beyond the churches that made Appalachia important on the churches agenda.

THE CREATION OF CORA

We have seen that complex churchly and external societal dynamics eventually focused church energy on Appalachia. There were, however many forces in Appalachia itself that were also directly involved in both CORA's formation as well as its staying power into the third millennium. In 1960 John F. Kennedy came to West Virginia to campaign for the presidency. After seeing the conditions of poverty, inadequate housing, and lack of health facilities and schools, Kennedy promised that if elected he would fight the poverty of Appalachia. Shortly after his election, the federal government, in partnership with the region's states, formed the Appalachian Regional Commission (ARC), whose task was to develop a common plan for the parts of thirteen states that made up the region and then to be the avenue for federal resources to "open up" the region with roads and communication, as well as to develop the region's community institutions and economy. National church leadership soon realized that a way to participate in this process was needed—CORA became that vehicle.

In 1956 a meeting of religious leaders in Berea, Kentucky, had called for an Appalachian study. And before President Kennedy's initiative, the Ford Foundation had commissioned a regionwide study of Appalachia. The general study, by Thomas R. Ford, entitled *The Southern Appalachian Region: A Survey,* was completed in 1962, with one of the major dimensions focusing on religion in the region. Dr. Earl D. C. Brewer, professor at the Candler School of Theology at Emory University in Atlanta, served as director of that part of the study. It was a comprehensive study, and upon its conclusion, a consultation of religious and community leaders, "The Church in the Appalachian South," was called in 1963 to study the findings. Fourteen denominations and four state councils of churches participated. The study produced many revelations, but one was that there was the "religion of the executives" and the "religion of the folk." The former had been imported to manage the mining and other industrial concerns, as well as the "mission" institutions, largely from mainline churches, with some being Roman Catholic. But it was the religion of the folk—the indigenous religion—that few bothered to know about or knew how to relate to. But in many ways, the religion of the folk set the tenor of the community, and it became evident that this religious dynamic was deeply involved in the problems and opportunities of the region—much the same as ECRP and the Indiana Council of Churches were finding in Spencer County.

CORA formed indirectly from the Brewer Consultation and came out of the NCCC/USA's working group of national Town and Country and Home Mission executives, along with leaders from the region, including people from West Virginia University and two or three regionwide historic organizations, like the Council for the Southern Mountains. By 1964 this working group had developed some very motivating dreams of what faith communities might do to transform themselves and their work in the rural areas of Appalachia. The initiating meeting of CORA was held in Morgantown, West Virginia, in 1965. A board was organized and the work of developing a constitution and incorporation was begun. At the first board meeting, held at Coraopolis, Pennsylvania, it was decided that rather than having paid staff the group would work, at least initially, on a collegial basis, with Dr. Ernie Nesius, vice president at West Virginia University, becoming the first chair of the exploratory group. Rev. Max Glenn, director of Town and Country work for the Christian Churches, Disciples of Christ, was named the executive secretary, doing all the correspondence, communication, and between-meetings work. Nesius took a sabbatical year from his administrative and teaching responsibilities to become the first coordinator.

Nesius returned to academia after the first year, and the seventeen participating denominations agreed that his logical successor was Glenn, first seconded by the Disciples and by 1968 hired by CORA to be the full-time executive director. He shared the dream from the beginning and had done most of the work necessary to incorporate the organization. He was a young, well-equipped church leader and an enthusiastic visionary. Sr. Lenore A. Mullarney, a Roman Catholic sister with extensive business experience, became the office administrator, and within a couple of years, Rev. Dr. John McBride, a Commission member and Southern Baptist Home Mission Board staffer, became the associate executive coordinator.

The office was officially located in Knoxville. Some say it was located there because the Glenns' children had severe allergies and Charleston was not a good place for children with allergies. But also there were better airline connections to Knoxville than to Charleston—CORA depended heavily upon national rural church leader involvement in the beginning.

In 1966 the Commission stated its organizing purpose in these words: "In the name of Jesus Christ, to engage the resources of the communions and other agencies in activities designed to meet the pressing human needs of the people of Appalachia." By 1967 it was clear that this meant that CORA's intention was to address issues of poverty and building community in Appalachia. The guiding values, called "Basic Guidelines (policies) for CORA's activities" were as follows:

- Give priority to the mobilization of church resources for cooperative action
- Be the instrument . . . for collection, analysis, and dissemination of information and for action
- Recognize that the Church's endeavors in the economic, social, political, and cultural environment must be characterized by a real concern for building human community
- Work for the self-determination and the values of self-development among people

- Mobilize and use church resources in ways that will stimulate and supplement, not substitute for, the resources of public or private agencies . . .
- Respond to human needs in Appalachia as a necessary and valid demonstration of the love of Jesus Christ

The following two are perhaps among the most important of the initial five organizational goals developed:

- Identify pressing human needs . . . [and] their underlying causes and facilitate action to deal with the situation
- Provide a vehicle for the communion's reassessment of existing mission activities in the light of the needs of the people in the region and the potentials for joint action in mission[6]

Several "energy centers" were convened and developed over the first five years to implement these goals. The Appalachian Regional School for Church Leaders (ARSCL) was initiated in 1968 and the Self Help Task Force was developed in 1969. The Appalachia Mission Renewal Project (AMRP) was also among the first task groups developed to "provide a vehicle for the communion's reassessment of existing mission." Another energy center was a Research Task Force—a means of drawing the ecumenical and denominational researchers together to "identify pressing human needs" in the region and to provide the information AMRP required by assessing the Church's resources, redundant mission institutions, and the relative strength of given denominations in various parts of Appalachia. I was the first chair and collegiate staff for this function. Fr. Bernard Quinn of the Glenmary Research Center (later CARA—the Center for Applied Research in the Apostlate) gave primary leadership to the research tasks, producing the first CORA Appalachian Atlas in 1971. Soon the Social, Economic, and Political Issues (SEPI) task force was organized under the leadership of Dr. Shirley Greene, task force chair and seconded by the United Methodist Church to CORA as collegiate staff. In 1973 the Appalachian Development Projects Committee (ADPC) was initiated as a means of supporting and putting many of the funding decisions in the hands of the grassroots community groups. As such it soon replaced the AMRP, which essentially made the mission planning a collaborative process with the grass roots, rather than an activity just for the denominations.

From the beginning Dr. Nesius felt strongly that somehow the Church needed to get beyond the churches, that is, the Church needed some new experiences in eliminating poverty and developing community—new vision, new experience, and new models. So one of the early actions of the Commission was to approve this focus in three experimental locations: one near Clearfield, Tennessee, another in Scott County, Tennessee, and the third in Jackson County, Ohio. CORA's relationship with these locations continued for a number of years.

The five executive coordinators that span the first thirty-five years of CORA (until 2000) each represent leadership and gifts that were timely for CORA and the region. Nesius was a rural expert who could relate to the emerging power of the federal government's Appalachian Regional Commission (ARC) in the new Appalachia that was developing. Max Glenn brought the expertise to root CORA deeply in the life of the churches as well as the ability to develop a sound forward-looking organization through the research, management by objectives, and evaluation process. He was deeply concerned for the mission of the church and the people that mission served. When he moved on a decade later, one of the parents in the formation of CORA and Glenn's long-time associate, John McBride, a former Southern Baptist Home Missions missionary and executive, took the helm, with a missionary's zeal and sophisticated mission know-how. Not only did he further the directions that Glenn had initiated with the Commission but he also led the organization through the first serious assessment of its life and helped it streamline and focus on working with grassroots groups, concerns for justice, and parish development, along with resource mobilization.

Jim Sessions, a United Methodist minister with long experience in the civil rights and labor movements, became executive coordinator during the first years of the Reagan administration. He brought a passion for economic and social justice and updated organizing skills to CORA. There was a certain "goodness of fit" that made those years very creative for CORA and the region. It is true that God prepares people for the *kairos*—life-changing moments when need, resources, and leadership come together to make a transformative difference.

Tena Willemsma, the executive coordinator (later executive director) who followed Jim Sessions, came to Appalachia as a VISTA volunteer in West Virginia and never left the region. The abiding passion for justice she brought to the chief leadership position in CORA was honed by grassroots organizing in West Virginia and work on mining justice issues for CORA, as a seconded staff of the Roman Catholic Diocese of Richmond. She then worked nearly a decade and a half as CORA's staff coordinator for the Social, Economic, and Political Issues (SEPI) task force (following Dr. Shirley Greene), and served as the interim executive coordinator while Jim Sessions was on sabbatical. She nurtured the soon-to-be-pivotal Economic Justice Theological paper from its beginning—pivotal because it became the blueprint for more than a decade of CORA's work in the last decade of the century. This, along with her work for women's inclusion and the inclusion of all marginalized persons, were her greatest passions. It was CORA's good fortune that soon after the Commission finally adopted economic transformation as its focal mission in the early 1990s she was elected to take the CORA helm.

Throughout its history CORA pioneered new ecumenical organizational ground, always attempting to be something other than another ecumenical bureaucracy. It saw its small core staff as facilitators or coordinators of the work the denominations decided to do together. It understood itself as an information exchange or a system of communication, sometimes generating information, sometimes processing it and making it more usable, and sometimes serving as a conduit for information.

In CORA's first few years it was quite successful in defining the organizational question—what is CORA?—by clearly defining and dramatizing its mission and goals. Within the first five years it was also very successful in defining, for that time, how it would organize its life and resources for greatest effectiveness. However, before the end of the first five years, CORA, through the work of Appalachian Development Projects Committee (ADPC) and because of the weariness of national denominational executives always being called to Appalachia for another round of decision making or governance issues, began to understand that seventeen national denominations and thirteen state councils were not a real grass roots.

CORA and Inclusiveness

After more than five years, the "who" question was still largely unanswered in CORA, as it was in so many ecumenical organizations across the nation at that time. Patriarchy and hierarchy were increasingly being questioned. As a people, we were becoming aware that life in general and ecumenical life in particular should not be controlled by mainly white males and often by distant clergy, who had been accustomed to "being the leaders" (often dubbed the "brass roots"), with women, local folk, and people of color serving largely in supporting roles. The principles of self-determination and egalitarianism were being explored. We were learning that one did not do things "for" people, but rather should be working in enabling ways so that "folk" are empowered to do that which they need to do. So, early on, really within the first two years of its life, CORA began the journey toward becoming participatory and egalitarian and more rooted with the people, churches, and organizations in the region.

The pressure that energized CORA took several forms, with many intense debates, but over the years CORA eventually, and sometimes haltingly, dealt with five different dimensions of inclusiveness. One related to the denominational relationship with the funding of projects. CORA had developed a Joint Strategy and Action (JSAC)[7] style funding table in the ADPC so that the denominations could work together and coordinate their responses on funding requests. The mid to late 1960s was a time when self-determination was becoming very important, so it was not long before the funded groups were asking for a voice in the process. In 1970 the Commission voted to give grassroots-funded projects 51 percent of the vote on funding decisions in ADPC. The next year, however, with denominational money threatening to dry up, a compromise was worked out that gave the projects significant, but not majority, involvement in the evaluation and funding process.

Another participation issue came as the national denominations sought to "devolve" their role in favor of more middle judicatory participation. By the late 1960s the denominational caucus idea was agreed upon, and by the mid-1970s John McBride reported in the 1974 Annual Report that there were thirteen active denominational caucuses among the seventeen member denominations, as well as a conciliar caucus among the thirteen state councils, one regional council (Christian Associates of Southwest Pennsylvania), and the national member council. The denominational caucuses were composed of people from each denomination throughout the region and eventually became very influential in the selection of commissioners from their denomination, as well as in the cyclical long-range planning processes that has guided CORA's life.

A third inclusiveness issue—the participation of women—was somewhat later in surfacing in the Commission's awareness. In 1973, as in earlier years, there were only two women Commission members and a third who was an alternate member.[8] One of the two members, Rev. Elizabeth Hartzfield of the Disciples of Christ, was also on the board as vice chair. By 1974 the Women's Caucus was organized, with leadership assumed by Tena Willemsma and Joyce Dukes. The Caucus was initially composed of staff, collegial and associate collegial staff, those few women on the Commission, and others who were participants in the caucuses and projects. As time passed, the Caucus was successful in getting more women into key spots, advocating successfully for the Commission to use inclusive language, raising the gender issue in employment opportunities across the region, developing theological reflection on the family, and promoting economic justice in the region, to name just a few of their concerns.

A fourth foci of concern about who should be a part of CORA had to do with race. This concern became a commission-wide concern about five years after the Women's Caucus was formed, even though the 1972 SEPI priorities had included concern about the participation of both women and minorities. The minority concern took two forms. First, there was little, if any, participation of African American churches in the initial organization of CORA, and where there was some relationship, as in the National Baptists through the Southern Baptist Home Mission Board or the Christian Methodist Episcopal Church (CME), there was very little participation. (With the arrival of Bishop Lindsay in the region in the last decade or so, the CME has become very active.) So what little black participation there was in the first two and a half decades of CORA's life came largely from either the funded projects or from the African Americans in predominantly white denominations—especially the United Methodist and the Presbyterian churches. By 1973 Pearl Jones had joined the staff as the receptionist and bookkeeper. By 1976 Almetor King of the Poor Peoples Self-Help Commission in Knoxville, but representing the Council of the Southern Mountains, was emerging as a leader and eventually became a board member also. But it was well into the later 1980s before CORA began to even think beyond the token stage, not coincidentally perhaps, with the development of a CORA concern for urban Appalachia. The assumption had always been that rural Appalachia was white—although there had always been persons of color—black, native, and now Hispanic—in rural Appalachia, some as miners and others as workers or subsistence farmers. But it was not until the early 1990s that the issue came back on the CORA agenda, after a presentation to the Commission on Institutional Racism by Joe Barnett of Crossroads Ministries in Chicago, the development of a People of Color Caucus, and contracting with Ron Davis (he spells his name ron davis) to help CORA address the issue. By 1999 the Commission had adopted a full plan to face its racism over the next several years. In recent years, several African Americans have been commissioners, board members, or officers.[9]

The final question about who should be included was whether CORA should be an interfaith or a Christian organization. Over the years Unitarian, Jewish, Muslim, and Baha'i organizations had joined with CORA on justice issues or had on occasion used the humanitarian capabilities of CORA to access the region. This raised the question, mostly within CORA itself, of whether CORA should become more faith-inclusive. From 1994 to 1997, simply discussing the question internally was divisive. One communion, the Reformed Church in America, either assumed the discussion was inappropriate or prejudged the outcome and subsequently withdrew its membership in 1997 because it would not be a part of an interfaith organization. In the end, it was decided that CORA should remain a Christian ecumenical organization but should regularly convene meetings around regionwide concerns that included all faith groups that were interested in participating. An Appalachian Summit on the emerging needs was convened in March 1999, and Baha'is, Unitarians, and several humanists participated, in addition to the CORA membership. At least for the present, most are comfortable with this arrangement.

There are other major but unheralded stories that are part of the thirty-five years of the CORA experience. One has to do with CORA involvement in community development. Another is the extensive energy invested in justice issues. Still another has to do with the renewal of the parish. Finally, there is a story to tell about CORA's involvement in developing and advocating for inflow of resources into the region.

Constituent bodies often have different ideas about how to pursue societal and religious change. Some are committed to development, community-by-community and church-by-church. Others are committed to activist participation in systemic justice issues and grassroots empowerment. Still others are focused primarily on the renewal of the religious system itself. All these interests, along with a plethora of less evident undercurrents, have been present in CORA from the beginning. And perhaps the miracle of CORA is that these have been woven together into a whole, with only occasional friction and breaks in the fabric.

Within the first ten years of CORA, each of these views was orchestrated by strong advocates. The community development banner was held high by Ben and Nina Poage, Dwayne Jost, Glenn Biddle, Marie Cirello, and many others. Social and economic justice concerns were advocated by Shirley Greene, Don Prang, Tena Willemsma, B. Lloyd, Joyce Dukes, Jim Sessions, and Bill Troy, to name only a few. And the concern for parish renewal and development had its advocates in people like Karl Jones, Gladys Campbell, Sandy Elledge, and Harold McSwain.

Development or Justice?

The grassroots self-help community development perspective had its focus in teaching and developing ways for people in the small communities across the region to do things that would make their lives economically sustainable while offering an acceptable quality of life. Through the Human, Economic, Appalachian Development (HEAD) unit of CORA (it has had various names), first initiated by the Rev. Ben Poage, much was accomplished in the first fifteen years of CORA's life. The Rev. Glenn Biddle, a United Methodist pastor and director of the Jackson Area Ministries in Jackson County, Ohio, was the visionary chairperson of the first HEAD task force. Because of his leadership, and the work of the husband-wife team of Ben Poage (Christian Church, Disciples of Christ, minister with an undergraduate degree in agriculture) and Nina Poage (a Ford Foundation Fellow in Community Planning), who invested a major portion of their professional lives in community development, much was accomplished: improvement of the native crafts, including creation of a federation of Appalachian craft groups and Appalshop (to nationally market crafts from the region); feeder pig and rabbit breeding cooperatives; sustainable grassroots agriculture; a wood pallet cooperative; a furniture factory; a food service cooperative; a feed mill; and credit unions—to name just a few. Part of the time the Poages were CORA staff and part of the time they were not, but their interest and work in grassroots development inside or outside CORA never faded over the years. Nina became a city manager for a time, but she came back to a CORA-based ecumenical community development project. Ben went on to become an executive for the Disciples of Christ in Kentucky, but all the time both he and Nina were leaders in CORA.

There were many times when the concern for grassroots, self-help economic development fell on hard soil in CORA. It seemed that many of the leaders in CORA could not understand it enough to give it equal importance with grassroots organizing (which, in fact, it was, plus technical assistance) or with the SEPI justice concerns. Yet many of the projects undertaken by HEAD were very successful, and the added economic value developed in the region by HEAD was once determined, in an evaluation of the HEAD program, to be in the millions of dollars.[10] These enterprises had not only created more than 300 jobs in the first seven years, but HEAD was also able to raise $1,200,000 from outside sources to continue developing the self-help community development model. Although some $232,000 came from the churches, nearly one million dollars came from outside the religious systems. At the same time, HEAD was successful in creating a "free standing" Appalachian Development fund "in order to provide a localized and specific source of grant funds for Community Economic Development (CED) in the region."[11]

But HEAD always seemed to have political problems within CORA. It was probably too "hands on," too rural, and too successful to fit the psyche of many church leaders of the day. It was also too efficient in raising money, which some of the leadership would rather have spent on social issues or grassroots-issue organizing. The social crises of the 1960s and the Church's response, as well as laypeople's reactions to that response, had put the Church under great stress—not only financially, but also in "hanging together for common mission." On the one hand, leaders were embattled, but on the other, by the 1970s what national resources the Church did have had been committed to advocacy and activist justice, with the social systems being the target. In contrast, for many, community economic development was local, incremental, non-systemic, and safe. Further, it was also a model not unique to the churches, i.e., it was perceived as a secular model (of course grassroots community organization was also a secular model). So many of CORAs leaders did not see how HEAD fit their vision of the justice agenda. By the end of the 1970s, HEAD was phased out in its "hands-on" form. Yet the interest did not die. HEAD continued as a separate but related organization. And the concern for community and parish emerged in the next phase of CORA's life under the rubric of community and parish development, which coupled the religious parochial concerns with cooperative parish renewal/development and community renewal/development.

The Parish and the Community

Concern for the parish in its community setting had been a concern of CORA from its earliest day—not surprising, given CORA's origins in Town and Country work. Yet from the beginning it was a subsidiary concern of the Commission. However, in 1978 the Parish Development Task Force became one of the standing units of CORA, organized under the leadership of Peter C. Fulghum, the first chair. The task force defined parish development as "the intentional process of maximizing the resources available to a local congregation to the end that the local congregation may most effectively be the church in mission."[12] Although parish development had been advocated as an appropriate role for CORA from its inception, it, like community development, was a contentious issue, but for different reasons—in this case, contentious because about half of the partner denominational members, out of the assumption that they were "sovereign," believed it was the sovereign responsibility of the denominational judicatory to oversee and care for the needs of "their" congregations. But an almost equal number of CORA leaders believed that for the sake of the community (and the nature of the Church) parish development needed to be done on an ecumenical basis. This view argued, as had the 1965 National Consultation on Church and Community Life, that one needed to view all the congregations in the community as making up the Church, and therefore their development had to take into consideration each of the congregations in the context of all the congregations, so that the whole Church would become a positive force for the community's renewal. As the definition indicates, the initial CORA compromise was to talk about a local congregation in mission. This approach allowed the ambiguity of whether the mission was to the community or only to "souls" disembodied from their communities.

There were other forces that brought parish development to the fore. One occurred when the Christian Reformed Church joined CORA. Congregational renewal and parish development was one of that denomination's passions and it was able to make one of its missioners available to lead parish development for a time. Another impetus for CORA's involvement in parish development was the several years of experiments undertaken by the Hinton Rural Life Center, outside of Hinton, North Carolina, almost on the border with northern Georgia. Dr. Harold McSwain, initially under the tutelage of Dr. Earl D. C. Brewer, along with Gladys Campbell, had been experimenting with renewal of small rural congregations by linking them and their pastors together and then training them to become "cooperative parishes." The model worked well for them, as it had for United Methodists in other parts of the nation. Both McSwain and Campbell were delegated to CORA to represent the UMC, and as such pushed for experiments in ecumenical cooperative parishes. For them, cooperative parishes had never been only about saving the rural church but also about ensuring that the rural church had enough strength to be a force in community ministry or community renewal. However, often it seemed that only a few in CORA could really hear the last half of the argument, so this advocacy had many of the same political problems in the CORA decision-making process that had plagued HEAD in community development.

By the late 1990s this area of concern also included CORA's demonstration project of "Church and Community Renewal," which was a new iteration on the themes of parish and community renewal and development rooted in CORA's 1970s history. Three experimental projects were undertaken. One in Cleveland, Tennessee, with Brenda Hughes as local "animator," resulted in the formation of the Bradley (county) Initiative for Church and Community (BICC). Another was in northeast Pennsylvania, with Karl Jones giving oversight. A third was the Kentucky Ecumenical Economic Project (KEEP) with Nina Poage as enabler. These projects used various methods, including a scripture study method developed in Iowa during the Farm Crisis by Rev. Dave Ostendorf.

Leadership Development

Another force that created a climate for parish development was a concern for development of lay church leadership in the region. One of the expressions of this concern was the Joint Educational Development (JED) project, undertaken in cooperation with CORA, beginning in about 1971. JED was a national Christian education consortium of approximately the same denominations that made up CORA. A February 1972 Consultation in Maryville, Tennessee, set the task of developing local church curricula uniquely appropriate to lay people of the Appalachian culture. Although this work was never completed, it did put leadership development on the CORA agenda.

An earlier energy center in CORA concerned with professional leadership development was the Appalachia School for Church Leadership (ARSCL), which CORA developed in partnership with West Virginia University. (These partnerships between land-grant universities and rural church interests had been happening across the nation for more than a half century.) A CORA and WVU joint committee developed a thorough summer program to provide training to Appalachian, and occasionally other, rural pastors to enable them to better understand and serve their contexts. West Virginia University appointed Lutheran pastor and scholar Dr. B. B. Mauer to its faculty to initiate this program. A bit later Dr. Jack Rogers joined him, to implement ARSCL as well as to develop other continuing education programs for clergy, in cooperation with CORA. The program ran for about twenty years. In the early years it had as many as 150 participants, then averaging around 100 participants for several years before tapering off somewhat. With Dr. Mauer retired, and when Dr. Rogers also retired, the university chose not to continue the program.

Still a third professional church leadership development effort began in 1983 when Dr. Mary Lee Daugherty started the Seminary Project, designed to make possible an Appalachian exposure for seminarians. By 1985 the project had evolved into the Appalachian Ministry Educational Resource Center (AMERC) in collaboration with CORA. AMERC is a consortium of from 26 to 30 seminaries, mostly outside the region, that join together to provide opportunities for their faculties and students to become familiar with the Appalachian context and to prepare ministers for ministry in Appalachia. In June 1985, the first six-to-nine-week-long courses were held. These were followed each year with a one-month January term. AMERC developed a great deal of resources and influence, especially within the seminaries. In 1998, the semi-retirement of Dr. Daugherty and changing needs of the seminaries, if not the nature of ministry, led to a major reassessment and new direction. Ben Poage, recently retired from responsibilities with the Regional Disciples of Christ staff, became the interim director and then the executive director. The new model was for AMERC to enable the member seminaries to develop the training programs and for these programs to be open for student participation from any of the AMERC member seminaries. Over the decade and a half that it has been in existence, it has trained several hundred seminary students and honed the skills of dozens of professors.

Social and Political Issues

Unlike grassroots community development and parish development, Social, Economic, and Political Issues (SEPI) commanded the attention of the Commission almost from the time of its organization. SEPI was exciting. It did theological reflection work. And it was always where the action was in the region, whether in a hospital, or at a miners' strike, or focused on land ownership or mountaintop removal. Indeed, SEPI had great collegiate staff leadership as well as denominational leaders. Its focus was always broadly defined as justice, up until 1986, at which time the Commission began a six-year dialogue that ultimately defined its purpose more narrowly. It then agreed to focus all its energy on Appalachia's economic transformation (economic justice).[13] But that gets ahead of the story. Let's go back to the beginning. As noted above, soon after CORA was organized, Dr. Shirley Greene, a UCC pastor theologian and a rural specialist with an abiding interest in justice and particularly rural justice, was hired as a staff associate by the United Methodist National Mission's Rural Ministries unit and then seconded half-time to CORA to lead the justice work. The energy center he was to nurture became the SEPI Task Force. Greene had been a conscientious objector during World War II and had been assigned to the Merom

Rural Life Center in Merom, Indiana. The center had received a large number of German prisoners of war. Greene developed relationships with the local farmers and developed a program so that the farmers and the prisoners became partners and a community of effort in the production of food—a very reconciling action. After the war he stayed on and continued the Center as a place to enrich and renew rural life in that area of Indiana as well as in nearby Illinois rural communities. When the UCC was formed in 1959 he had became one of its national rural specialists. (After his time with CORA, married to a rural pastor, he followed her to a Wyoming parish, where he started, and staffed, the Wyoming Coalition of Churches, and then moved once again with his spouse to retire in New Mexico.)

The SEPI Task Force was central to CORA's life because it helped the church people of Appalachia reflect on their situation and then to reflect on the Gospel mandates. This situational and theological reflection model was used very effectively to help both the member denominations and the people locally to come together in prophetic action. At the same time this method was augmented by some very solid organization that blanketed both the member denominations and the region. SEPI, of all the energy centers of CORA, was perhaps the most effective in using collegiate staff.[14] These staff joined in the common task of using the reflection and action model among their own constituencies, as well as with grassroots groups on social issues and problems. Usually, a collegiate staff person also served as point person for each issue identified for CORA attention. This model multiplied by many times the work that could be done on an issue and especially the numbers of people who could be involved. A second dimension was the collaboration with local, regional, and state councils in the region. State councils usually had a legislative arm, concerned with legislation in each state. CORA and these councils worked together to form state SEPIs, that is, clusters of people from churches in each state who also reflected and worked on social and public policy issues of common concern.

Thus, with this method and this organization, CORA was able to be an effective witness and advocate in the region for social justice. The issues addressed and worked through to resolution have been many. From the very beginning, because the largest industry in central Appalachia was coal, coal miners were a concern, and CORA stood with them on many picket lines. The health of miners was another concern. CORA worked with the unions and public health groups to ensure cleaner, safer working conditions, as well as social and health services for those who had black lung disease. Another mining concern had to do with contracts that required all the mined coal to leave the region, leaving none to heat the homes of those who mined it or who lived in houses over the mines. Early on, Project Operation Coal addressed this issue, with modest success in diverting some coal for local use. Still another related issue had to do with land use and land ownership. A study co-sponsored by CORA showed that well over half the land in central Appalachia was owned by outside interests—usually mineral interests. In some counties, outside ownership exceeded 80 percent. The study also determined that these companies had worked with local officials to keep the taxes on these lands extremely low, so that that the tax base for local schools and services was almost nil. Further, it was found that even lands apparently owned by local people often had had the mineral rights sold, meaning that a mineral company could come on this land at any time to dig for coal or other minerals, with no consideration of surface rights, and leaving no recourse or royalties to those whose house and livelihood came from the land. Finally, CORA worked with other progressive forces in opposing mountaintop removal by big strip-mining companies. Such actions left people in rural areas feeling powerless, because so many of the decisions that affected their communities and land were actually being made by people who lived outside the region.

Perhaps one of the most controversial witnesses of CORA, through its SEPI component, came during the Pikeville, Tennessee, Methodist Hospital strike. The Pikeville hospital was originally a mission hospital, established and still accredited by the United Methodist Church. The conflict was over wages for the workers and the right to organize a union. The hospital played hardball, typical of many corporate attitudes in the region. Workers found themselves locked out from their jobs and scabs taking their places. It was a tragedy for the workers and an embarrassment for the Church, which had long affirmed the right of workers to organize and the necessity for every worker to be paid a living wage. At the request of some United Methodists, CORA became involved, sending people to stand on the picket lines in solidarity with the workers and sending representatives to reason with the local hospital board and the local ecclesial leaders—but for a long time, to no avail. Eventually a compromise was reached, but most felt that justice did not prevail for most workers.

It was SEPI that also led the way in including women and minorities in the life of CORA and other public institutions of the region. After Shirley Greene left his post with the United Methodist Church and moved to Wyoming, Tena Willemsma became the staff person for SEPI. In her very thorough and effective manner, she and Joyce Dukes, along with other women on the board, commission, staff, and funded projects, began a consultative process of confidence-building through biblical reflection, context analysis, and sharing that empowered them to demand and subsequently take their place of leadership in CORA and throughout the region. This several-year process of empowerment produced great rewards in CORA's life and throughout the region because it liberated tremendous leadership energy. At present, the board is about half male and half female, the executive committee has two males and two females (two are black and two are white), and several of the committees are chaired by women.

By the 1980s under the leadership of Jim Sessions as executive coordinator and Tena Willemsma as SEPI staff, the attention of SEPI turned more directly to economic justice. The Reagan administration years diverted much of the "grassroots helping money" from the local communities and region to the national defense budget. Welfare benefits for the poor, like food stamps, became more difficult to obtain and grants for grassroots development more and more scarce. All of this heightened CORA's concern for better employment opportunities and fair wages. Bill Troy joined the staff of CORA as a United Methodist missioner with a specific focus on employment justice, including developing the industrial base to provide jobs, as well as assisting in the organizing that empowers workers.

When all these things SEPI had initiated were added together, along with the earlier experiences of HEAD, it became very evident to many that Appalachia's overarching problem was economic justice. In the early 1980s, CORA, at SEPI's request, commissioned a Working Group on the Appalachian Economic Crisis (ECWG), composed of a diverse group of people from a variety of backgrounds, to "investigate the root causes of the Appalachian economic crisis" and to "develop a set of recommended strategies and actions for CORA, grounded in a comprehensive analysis of the Appalachian situation."[15] After two years of work, which included theological reflection, analysis of mounds of information, and hours of discussion, the working group was able to document "an unprecedented lack of opportunity for personal, family, and community well-being in the present economic climate of the Appalachia."[16] It became clear to the working group that Appalachia's lack of opportunity could not be reversed without significant changes in the economic values and practices that affect the people and institutions in the region. In short the report called on CORA to use all its energies to bring about economic transformation in the region. Such a call was not particularly new to CORA. One of CORA's early leaders, Presbyterian pastor Dr. Jack Weller, had made such a call in his book entitled *Yesterday's*

People. Many had taken offense with the title, but in it he had argued quite persuasively that since Appalachian people had not really yet entered the industrial phase of societal development, they could jump straight to the post-industrial era. In any case, the ECWG report was cautiously received, and the recommendations were not adopted. A process for grassroots groups, denominations, and regional ecumenical bodies to study and discuss the report was set in motion, and eventually, in 1993, some seven years later, CORA adopted economic transformation as its principal organizational purpose. That shift meant that everything that CORA did had to answer the question, How does this activity contribute to the economic transformation of the region? Or does this activity contribute to continuation of the status quo? If it did, then that CORA activity had to be jettisoned. This step turned all of CORA to an economic justice agenda, which, after all the years of paternalism and economic patchwork, seemed an entirely reasonable way to go.

At this writing, the effort seems to be working—although ever so slowly. What CORA is intentionally about is creating the conditions from which economic transformation may one day occur, perhaps in the twinkling of an eye, not unlike the way the Berlin Wall toppled, which after decades of working to create the right conditions finally fell almost of its own weight. However, this organizational purpose does not mean that CORA has abandoned grassroots organization or community or parish development, grassroots economic consciousness-raising, or even its volunteer program. Rather it means that each of these activities has strengths to contribute to economic justice. For example, when volunteers from the north come to work in Appalachia it becomes an opportunity to develop their awareness of the economic injustices found in the region. So with singleness of purpose and broad support for that purpose among the constituent denominations and the various grassroots constituencies, many would say that CORA is even more effective today than it was at its inception. The issue now is, Can CORA continue to generate financial support for this rather radical Gospel imperative? Money is easier to come by to "help" the poor. It is more difficult to come by when you are empowering those with little power to gain greater power.

The economic transformation agenda has created many partnership arrangements for CORA with economic and environmental justice working groups in the National Council of Churches and the World Council of Churches. Both have agreed that Appalachia is America's Third World Country.

Conclusion

Surely CORA is a sort of crown jewel in the largely vanished Rural Church Movement. Yet there are other even newer effective experiments too. The Town and Country church enthusiasts in the United States and parts of Europe have developed a new tactic in the creation of professional rural chaplains. Rural chaplains emerged, in part, as a way for specially trained pastors to give support to struggling farmers, but also as a way for the Church to place professional assistance in key rural communities, helping both church and community define and address issues negatively affecting the quality of rural life. Rural chaplains continue the Town and Country movement concern for spiritual support even as CORA has continued the concern for rural justice and community development. All this work is in the tradition of Washington Gladden, Gifford Pinchot, and countless others who have worked together ecumenically to increase the quality of rural life. Probably both CORA and the rural chaplains differ from some of their forebears, however, in that they are less concerned about the institutional church's survival in the community than they are the flourishing of the people and their communities. When that happens the churches will flourish, too, because when the people and their communities flourish, so will their institutions, including the Church. In the end, rural ecumenism, at its best, whether in Appalachia, upstate New York, Iowa, Kansas, Illinois, Pennsylvania, the Dakotas, Ohio, Indiana, Illinois, or Nebraska, is focused on one thing: improving the quality of the people's spiritual life so that they are empowered to create the communities they require and so they are able to participate responsibly in the whole inhabited earth. Rural ecumenism, at its best, has enabled the church to be the Church in each place across nonmetropolitan America. And so it will continue as an enabler of Church.

Notes

1. Report of the Commission on Country Life, Executive Branch, U.S. Government, Washington DC, 1909, pp. 139–141.

2. Mark Rich, *The Rural Church Movement* (Columbia, MO: Juniper Press, 1957), p. 46.

3. Ibid.

4. Federated congregations retained affiliation with more than one denomination. Sometimes individual members retained their membership in one of the federating denominations. However, all local church functions were conducted as if it were one church, with one pastor or pastoral team.

5. Arleon Kelley and Leonard McIntire, eds., *Ecumenical Designs* (New York: Steering Committee of the Church and Community Life Consultation, Rev. Harold Huff [National Methodist Staff], chair), 1965.

6. Commission on Religion in Appalachia Organizational Documents, 1965.

7. Joint Strategy and Action (JSAC) was an interdenominational, if not ecumenical, effort in which middle and national judicatories came together to jointly evaluate projects and their proposals for funding and then make collegial funding decisions. JSAC had a national board and office located at 475 Riverside Drive, in New York City. Dr. Norman E. Dewire was its first executive. Although it existed for about fifteen years from the 1960s until about 1980, it was most influential in the late 1960s and early 1970s.

8. CORA 1973 Annual Report (Knoxville, TN: CORA, 1973).

9. African American commissioners who were leaders in CORA included Almetor King, board; Rev. Homer Davis (UMC), chair of ADPC, vice chair, etc.; Judith Hill (UMC), vice chair; Rev. Sylvester (CME), secretary; and Karna Burkeen (UCC), personnel and nominations chair.

10. Arleon Kelley, organizational evaluation documents for the first ten-year review, 1975.

11. CORA Report of Accomplishments (Knoxville, TN: CORA, 1978), p. 20.

12. Parish Development Report, published in the 1978 CORA Annual Report, p. 2.

13. Report of the Working Group on the Appalachian Economic Crisis, *Economic Transformation: The Appalachian Challenge* (Knoxville, TN: CORA, 1986).

14. Collegiate staff were denominationally employed staff who were contractually seconded to CORA for a portion of their time each month to undertake a specific task for CORA in behalf of all the member denominations.

15. Report of the Working Group on the Appalachian Economic Crisis, *Economic Transformation: The Appalachian Challenge* (Knoxville, TN: CORA, 1986), p. iii.

16. Ibid.

15

THE STORY OF THE FARM CRISIS: KANSAS AS A CASE STUDY

Dorothy G. Berry

The second half of the twentieth century began with an increasing optimism on the part of the American people—reflected in church life as well. The war was over, nations were coming together in an organization that held the promise of assuring that such a global conflagration would not occur again, and the churches were experiencing an influx of people serious about giving thanks and providing their children with the experience of the Christian faith. It was a time of almost unbridled optimism about the future, and the economic prosperity stood in sharp contrast to the dark days of the Depression. In the middle of the country, in the Great Plains, the optimism was palpable. Electricity had come, and government agricultural policy was being built on the lessons learned about care of the land during the past quarter century.

Councils of churches, both city and state, were maturing, the increase in membership in all mainline denominations translated into serious programs to be sure all of society benefited from the prosperity, and there was a healthy supply of persons, both clergy and laity, willing to devote time and financial support to ensure the success of the ambitious programs.

The national Office for Councils of Churches, a department of the National Council of Churches, was looked to for guidance, and a remarkable degree of voluntary uniformity prevailed. Suggested organization of council structures, even to the wording of the by-laws, was provided by the national office and gratefully accepted. It was a time of dreaming big dreams for the future and working together.

The turmoil of the 1960s was far more evident on the two coasts than in the Great Plains. Agriculture was still king in most of the Plains States, and, while the big cities began to experience the symptoms prominent on the coasts, the rural cities and towns watched with distant amazement, confident that their life would not be disrupted.

Vatican II

The Vatican Council and the election of the first Catholic president affected the life of the city councils as the excitement and curiosity of clergy and laity in both Protestant and Catholic circles caused a reaching out after a long period of uneasy and almost total separation. Serious theological conversations began at professional levels; inquisitive questioning characterized the local scene. (I remember one priest, in a moment of honest sharing, asking, "Do we Catholics look different to you? You Protestants look and act so different from us!") Creative relationships were building, both within the councils and individually, and enthusiasm about the coming together of the Christian Church ran high.

The first Catholic parish to join a council of churches occurred in Tulsa, Oklahoma. The Church of the Madelene, led by a highly committed ecumenical and social action priest, Fr. James McNamee, with the full support of Bishop Victor Reed, broke the Protestant domination of the council of churches and in 1965 became the first Catholic parish member of a council of churches. By the late 1960s, by concentrating on the social action agenda, Catholic parishes and Protestant local congregations were working closely together as if it had always been that way.

New Mexico was the first state to include a Catholic diocese in its ecumenical agency membership. In 1964 the Santa Fe Diocese became a full member of the New Mexico Inter-Church Agency, predecessor to the New Mexico Conference of Churches. In February 1969 the Texas Council of Churches accepted into full membership ten Catholic dioceses, the first state Council to include almost the entire Catholic population in its membership (the Lubbock Diocese joined in 1983). To mark the momentous promise of these events, and in recognition of the particular definition of "council" in Catholicism, the term "council" was changed in each case to Conference of Churches. By 1984, seventy-one dioceses in thirty states had become full members of the state ecumenical agency.[1]

In rural towns, the neighborly relationships among Catholics and Protestants were reinforced by the new openness to asking each other questions about their faith and church life, heretofore politely avoided. A new sense of community was being engendered. Protestants and Catholics alike mourned deeply the death of Pope John XXIII, and the subsequent assassinations of President Kennedy and. Martin Luther King Jr. united Catholic and Protestant Christians even more deeply into one community.

Troubling, however, was the Vietnam War. In every town and city, young men were being called into the armed forces, and sentiments of patriotism clashed with honest feelings about the immorality of that war. Towns and cities alike found themselves conflicted, and the churches were no exception. Numerous pastors, particularly in free churches, found themselves suddenly dismissed because of the decision of a son who either went to prison for resisting the draft or who went underground. Those in rural communities found their lives similarly disrupted.

Conciliar Program Expansion and Change

Young people were particularly affected by these events. Nationally, one of the casualties of the turbulent 1960s was ministry with young people. Formerly an area of vibrant intervention in the lives of high school and college students that resulted in many entering various areas of service both as clergy and laity, youth work was completely shut down by most of the mainline denominations between 1965 and 1967, which also caused the end of the creative national program, the United Christian Youth Movement. The denominations were not indifferent to young people and their concerns but found the pressures of addressing severe national questions overwhelming and the need to shift resources unavoidable. In many areas, including the Plains States, the resulting gap of concern and programming for young people was filled by the city Councils of Churches. Local congregations still continued their efforts with local youth, but the opportunities for larger gatherings that had spurred the imagination and creativity of so many youth were lost.

The restless period for young people nationally, characterized by the press as the "flower children" era, presented enormous challenges for city Councils, which by and large were met with determination and creativity. Coffee houses as gathering places for rootless young people, drug prevention and care programs for young people who had succumbed to experimentation, challenges to laws that criminalized adults who attempted to provide safe space for runaway young people, and community services organized to divert young people from municipal court systems are all examples of the way city Councils strove to meet the needs of a new emerging generation. In rural communities, the attraction of life in the city and the opportunities it held increased, and fewer and fewer young people opted to "follow in dad's footsteps" by remaining on the farm.

Councils of Churches throughout the country found themselves immersed in creative programs to address racism, at the same time providing counseling for young men facing the draft and discussion opportunities for those trying to make sense of U.S. participation in Vietnam. Events were happening too quickly for decisions at carefully planned meetings of boards of directors, and Council executives often found themselves on the front lines attempting to provide nonviolent leadership in provocative situations. Storm clouds were gathering in Washington, unnoticed at the time, which would further complicate the picture and temporarily cloud the vision of church leaders to the difficulties being faced by family farmers.

The influence of the World Council of Churches, eagerly followed by prayer and Bible study in countless local congregations at the time of its formation in 1948 and of the Second Assembly in Evanston in 1954, was waning in middle America. This was greatly reversed in the minds of many in the Plains, however, when the WCC Executive Committee elected to hold its meeting in January 1969 in Tulsa, Oklahoma. Invited on the condition that the Committee would build into their agenda time to interact with the community, the week-long meeting was billed by the press as "the most prestigious meeting ever to be held in Oklahoma." A large celebration of the unity of Christ's one Church was held with all 600 congregations invited, and later in the week individual members of the WCC Committee were hosted in individual homes for informal conversation and exchange, organized by local congregations. Recognizing the value of such personal interaction, a series of national meetings was subsequently scheduled in the Plains, including the National Workshop on Christian Unity.

After President Nixon's resignation in 1972, Councils of Churches found themselves in the center of a debate in the denominations. The disagreements that used to exist among denominations were now present within each denomination, each experiencing differing factions who were determined to "get this church under control." Many supported the leadership that university chaplains and Council executives had endeavored to provide; others were convinced that such leaders had been the source of much of the conflict and unrest. "Local control" became the subject of many meetings, and the national leadership that had been responsibly given and gratefully received by Councils was now questioned. "Restructure" was the order of the day, and new patterns of operation, a rewriting of bylaws, and the procurement of new staff marked the life of state and city Councils and even small town associations. Name changes, previously uniformly councils of churches (state or city), now reflected both the plethora of understandings of the ecumenical endeavor and the creativity that had been unleashed: Iowa Ecumenical Ministries, Iowa Interchurch Agency for Peace and Justice, Consultation of Cooperating Churches in Kansas (later Kansas Ecumenical Ministries), Association of Christian Churches (of South Dakota), Interchurch Ministries of Nebraska, Houston Metropolitan Ministries, Metropolitan Inter-Church Agency (of Kansas City), etc. An unintended consequence was the impossibility of easily finding the ecumenical organization in the telephone directory.

Crisis in Family Farming Emerges

Adding to the difficulties was the rapidly accelerating inflation rate throughout the 1970s, which made funding of all aspects of the church, including Councils of Churches, much more difficult and therefore higher on the agenda. It also forestalled until well into the early 1980s the recognition of the growing crisis in agriculture that was developing throughout the Plains States, and indeed in many parts of the country.

In the early 1970s, the organizing of the OPEC nations and its effect on oil production and price was disruptive all over the country, but little press was given to how farms, now fully mechanized, had costs escalating out of control because of the rise in oil prices, causing further disruption to farming, already undergoing vast changes.

Tension experienced in local congregations throughout the Plains alerted Council executives to the growing farm crisis. For a number of years land values had escalated throughout the Plains, and farmers were being encouraged by their bankers to expand their holdings before land prices rose even higher. Cautious by nature, many farmers resisted and watched uneasily as their neighbors' operations grew. With the policies in Washington that broke the inflation cycle, land prices plummeted, and growing numbers of farm families suddenly found themselves facing bankruptcy, their land collateral no longer covering the value of their loan. Small-town independent banks were being pressured to call in the loans of neighbors. As farmers and bankers took their seats in church on a Sunday morning, it was no wonder the pastors suddenly sensed tension.

Denominational leaders, facing serious organizational and financial problems themselves, were reluctant to accept the urgent recommendations of their Council executives that the Church needed to be actively involved in the scenario being faced in rural towns throughout the Plains. The problems were overwhelming. In my own state, Kansas, the unanimous response of the judicatory leaders was negative; the needed funds simply were not available for even the most modest response. Help came from an unexpected source.

Farm Aid

In September 1985, State Council executives in twelve states suddenly received letters from the National Council of Churches enclosing checks (ranging from $5,000 to $10,000) with the explanation that the funds were the result of a Farm Aid concert by Willie Nelson, who had requested that the NCCC simply "get the money out to farmers who needed it as quickly as possible." The NCCC immediately turned to the network of State Councils to distribute the funds. When individual farmers faced loan recalls of up to a half million dollars, how could $10,000 be most helpful in a state? State Councils throughout the Plains formed committees of farmers and pastors upon recommendation of the denominations. Close to the situation in local towns, they quickly put together systems of distribution. In Kansas, the committee recommended grants of a hundred dollars to individual families upon recommendation of a local pastor, the funds to provide for immediate family needs. Names were not requested, only a general description of the scenario being faced by the family to aid understanding. The system was based on trust of local pastors, and the notes that poured into Council offices expressed both the appreciation of pastors who were helped to have a constructive pastoral role to play with desperate families and of the families who told how helpful even this temporary financial assistance was and even more how those funds symbolized that someone knew and cared about what they were experiencing. As they learned more about what the families were suffering, pastors were able to enlist the aid of their congregations in continuing support.

For three years, Farm Aid also provided special funds at Christmas so that farm families were able to be a part of the celebration. The first gift, received on December 22, bore the instructions to "distribute these funds by Christmas." The creativity of committee members immediately interpreted "Christmas" as the Twelve Days of Christmas, and went to work around the clock to contact pastors with the good news.

Throughout the 1980s in each state those initial gifts grew to hundreds of thousands of dollars, not only from numerous additional gifts from Farm

Aid concerts by Willie Nelson, but also from local donations. Deeply moving to Council executives and judicatory leaders alike were the number of farm families who sent in small contributions to add to the Farm Aid fund "so that other farm families can know that someone cares," as one donor worded it.

In the annual report to Farm Aid in 1987, I reported, "Most meaningful for me personally was a call from a group of teenagers, who identified themselves as being from families who had received aid, questioning whether, if they raised money, it could be added to the funds we are distributing. 'We were grateful to get aid, and want to help provide that for others,' they said."

A little-known sequel to this story was that when the Internal Revenue Service ruled that the funds raised through Farm Aid concerts was personal income to Willie Nelson and therefore taxable, gifts poured in to Mr. Nelson from grateful farm families to help meet his federal obligation.

State Council Efforts

The assistance of Farm Aid brought the picture of what was happening in rural communities into stark focus, and Council executives found their judicatory executives convinced that further programs of aid and support must be organized despite financial realities. In Kansas funds were secured to hire a Rural Life Associate, Del Jacobsen, a devout churchman and former farmer who was able to understand, identify, and interpret what was happening far better than I, a native of New York City. Sensitive to farm families and knowledgeable about agricultural needs and governmental policies, Del was a valued colleague during some of the most difficult years for Council executives.

Quickly getting a clearer picture of the crisis, Council executives organized day-long conferences for local pastors to help them understand what was happening and how to recognize the signs of difficulty and respond to them. Telephone hot lines were put in place to counsel farmers who were experiencing impasses and running out of options. Mental health personnel across the states were teamed with local ministerial associations for rapid intervention when needed. Pastors were urged to invite a rural independent bank president from a neighboring town to help local residents hear objectively how caught the local bankers also were in a much larger picture beyond their control; destroying the life of a neighbor was not a task they looked forward to.

Alarmed, Councils of Churches recognized the inherent dangers in one of the ugliest scenarios developing in the Plains States, that of racial and religious hatred and bigotry being fanned by extremist groups looking to gain a foothold by blaming blacks and Jews for the financial woes of farm families. National experts on extremist groups, such as Leonard Zeskind of the Center for Democratic Renewal in Atlanta and Dan Levitas of PrairieFire Rural Action in Iowa, helped Council executives recognize the number and identity of the extremist groups that were at work throughout the Plains offering false solutions to desperate farmers—"phony loan and legal schemes," as Thomas E. Kelly, director of the Kansas Bureau of Investigation, termed it.[2] Meetings were quickly organized to alert pastors to such groups who, using innocent sounding names, were using church properties for organizing and legitimizing purposes. Farmers and townspeople were also helped to see that the "solutions" offered were both illegal and would bring serious legal problems, and that these groups did not hesitate to resort to violence.

In Kansas I was visited by the executive of the Jewish Community Council who was concerned because the banking difficulties were being blamed on "Jewish bankers" where there were no connections.[3] The concern of the Jewish community for the plight of the farmers and for the actions of these extremist groups led to the Jewish community becoming an active partner in the work of our Rural Life Committee.

Personally, I came to understand how dangerous it was for persons to expose these groups through a local farmer who was concerned for my personal safety. As a means of keeping the name of the ecumenical agency before the people of the state, we had arranged for the Council's car to have a personalized license plate using the initials of the agency. The farmer's quiet comment was, "I wouldn't drive that car around Kansas, especially at night, if I were you." I continued to drive the car, but his warning was heard; we arranged for a new license plate.

The scenarios sketched by the local pastors requesting funds for farm families were very helpful in understanding what was happening to farm families. The primary need, we discovered, was for funds for food and utility payments. Unlike the days of the Depression in the 1930s, farm families were no longer growing food for the family in addition to the cash crops. Because of shifting government policies, farmers were concentrating on single crops, or a rotation of two or three crops a year. Leaders in the Plains States were suddenly startled by an article in the *New York Times* in fall 1987 chronicling the severe malnutrition and even starvation of children throughout the area. The poverty rate in the Plains had risen from 9 percent in 1978 to 13 percent in 1986. In addition, the poverty rate for families living on the farm increased in the same period from 12.2 percent to nearly 20 percent.[4] The initial reaction of denial was tempered quickly by testimony from pastors who could document that the story had regrettable validity.

The second lesson from those pastoral scenarios was the extent of medical care needed. Parents often sacrificed to see that their children were cared for medically, but their own needs were often neglected until they became crises. Conversations, begun with local medical clinics about emergency care for these families, met with ready response, but we soon realized that the extent of the need would rapidly outstrip the ability of the medical clinics and the urban hospitals to absorb the cost. In Kansas we were fortunate that the Kansas West Conference of the United Methodist Church had made the decision, recognizing the rapidly changing medical financial realities, to sell their hospital facility in Wichita. The funds realized from the sale were invested in two foundations, one devoted to responding to the changing health care scene. Kim Moore, director of the United Methodist Health Care Ministry, became quite concerned by the findings of the Farm Aid program, and initiated a series of grants to be administered by Kansas Ecumenical Ministries providing funds for desperately needed medical care in amounts of up to five hundred dollars per family, again initiated by recommendation of local pastors.

The scenarios provided by the pastors uncovered needs we had not anticipated. Dental work, particularly for parents, had been neglected. Many local dentists were recruited to help alleviate this need, in addition to the cash grants provided by the Health Ministry funds.

Relationships among the State Council executives, cordial and helpful until this time, became much closer with phone calls crisscrossing the states almost daily. Quickly these executives realized the rolling time lines among the states: Nebraska and Kansas recognized that what they were beginning to experience had been the scenario in Iowa six months before; Oklahoma was three to four months behind Kansas; and Colorado and Wyoming about six months later. David Ostendorf, director of PrairieFire Rural Action in Iowa, an independent ministry designed to call attention to farm problems and influence national legislative assistance, helped all of us understand the larger picture of what was happening and how these events were linked to both the agendas of national and international corporations and to policies being forged in Washington, D.C.

By 1986 Council executives of the states from the Dakotas and Minnesota to Texas had formed the Plains States Rural Ministry Group, and day-long meetings were being held bimonthly to exchange information and lay plans for future efforts. One of the principal goals was that in no state would despair in a farm family result in the suicide of a family member. While regrettably there were a few deaths, thanks to the assistance of mental health professionals who worked closely with pastors and their congregations in local communities that goal was largely realized.

The effect on the confidence and self-image of farmers was devastating. Many were caring for land that had been worked by their fathers, their grandfathers, and many even their great-grandfathers. Their sense of failure, that they were responsible for the loss of a valuable asset of the family, overwhelmed them. Bitter jokes circulated from community to community. "What would you do if you won the lottery? Oh, I'd probably farm until it was all gone," was an oft-quoted example. "You have to be a gambler to be a farmer," was a more serious comment to describe the milieu in which farmers worked. It held truth on many levels: in addition to gambling daily with weather (the night before harvest the whole crop can be lost to a hail storm), the farmer needs to stay abreast of what is happening both in government policy and weather conditions in the countries that may be the buyers of their product. Add to that the policies of the federal government that increasingly favor the productivity of capital over the production of food, and a very unstable situation results for the family farmer.

A large task the executives assumed was helping people in the cities, removed from daily contact with the production of food, to understand what was happening in the rural areas—that federal policies had changed substantially from the 1960s to policies more in line with corporate food production—and what they could do to assist affected farm families. Brochures were developed that pastors were urged to distribute to their congregations. People were trained to meet with groups in the cities to assist in their understanding of the crisis and how it was tied to food production and distribution throughout the world. In Kansas, again the Jewish Community Services Bureau modeled what could be done and how to do it. It arranged for meetings to assist members of the Jewish community to understand the issues and to visit with a farm family, both to help them see for themselves what was happening in rural agriculture and to assure the families that there were city residents that deeply cared about what they were experiencing. It was a gesture that was deeply appreciated by the farm families and an education for families who usually thought of the grocery store as the source of their food.

Deeply moving to those city dwellers, too, was watching the reaction of desperate Plains farmers who, when they learned of the serious drought in the Southeast that threatened cattle survival, quickly donated grain by the trainload to assist those southern farmers.

In Kansas, one of our rural women pastors began to be aware of the complex burdens being carried silently by the wives in farm families. In a class setting in her congregation, a farmer had been sharing his personal story and concluded his remarks by noting that "if I had not had the strong support of my wife, I'm not sure I could have made it." Instinctively the pastor asked, "Where did she turn for support?" The stunned look on the farmer's face indicated he had not thought about that.

Often the wife—the main support system for her farmer husband—worked to provide a calm and safe atmosphere for the children, worked in town to provide the needed cash for the family, and too often was the recipient of the emotional explosions when even small things went wrong. Of increasing concern to Council executives was the number of times such incidents resulted in physical abuse. Brought to the Rural Life Committee, other agency partners were identified, and plans began for an opportunity for farm wives to gather for a long weekend of sharing and support. The Presbyterian Church in Hutchinson, equipped with a large gym and showers, was offered as a place to meet. The women brought bedrolls and meals were provided by the women of the congregation. The women shared their stories and emotions. Relationships began at that first meeting that provided needed support across the state throughout the year as women turned to each other both for comfort and for advice. Church leaders who listened in discreetly on that meeting began to be aware of ways their congregations and judicatories could minister to the needs of these women who were the nurturing force in both their families and their communities.

These weekend opportunities have continued every year since that first meeting, usually held in early November after harvest is finished, the winter crops have been planted, and the demands of the farm cycle have been met. The men have come to appreciate the roles their wives play, have begun to express how they depend on these women for strength and comfort, and are recognizing anew how both husbands and wives are farmers and therefore partners in the farming vocation. The PBS television program "The Farmer's Wife," a program that chronicled the life of a farm family experiencing over a number of years the seriousness of the crisis, dramatized these personal stories with great reality and sensitivity. An interesting sidelight to that program was that the producer, a concerned Bostonian, approached and was rebuffed by the commercial television studios. Finally PBS agreed to produce the piece he envisioned, telling the story of a typical farm family fighting against all odds to continue farming, with whom he lived for more than two years to document the story.

The 1980s were further complicated by the closing of many rural banks by the Federal Depositors Insurance Corporation, affecting countless family farmers whose loans were suddenly due overnight. State executives requested that they be informed in advance so that they could assist the farmers who would be affected. Though the request was denied, we soon realized that the announcement of the closing of a bank always came midafternoon on a Thursday so that the bank could be closed on Friday, providing three days to reorganize the operation, and the bank could reopen on Monday morning under new management. In the states most affected, teams were formed of persons who were knowledgeable about the process of bankruptcy. These volunteer teams stood ready each Thursday for the announcement of which town they were to go to. Council offices contacted the local ministerial association requesting that a location be found and notice circulated about a meeting of farmers that evening and weekend hospitality arranged for the small team.

These meetings prevented panic among affected farmers, helping them analyze what they needed for the meeting with bankers on Monday morning and what their rights and responsibilities were. Knowledge always helps, and farmers went into those meetings on Monday with apprehension but with more calm thinking. In Kansas alone, between January 1984 and September 1989 fifty small rural banks were closed or consolidated with or replaced by banks headquartered elsewhere and staffed by people who had little understanding of food production.[5] Nationwide, the FDIC indicated that 403 rural banks closed, hastening the destruction of countless family farms and small rural communities.[6]

As hundreds of thousands of farmers were forced to leave the land during the 1980s, the need arose to assist them in entering new professional fields. Employment counselors in all of the states volunteered their time to help train volunteer counselors, as well as to work with the farmers themselves. It was quickly recognized that one of the first tasks was to help the farmer, who felt that all he was equipped for and ever wanted to do was farming, recognize the many skills he had to bring to another vocation. (A nagging concern to those who have worked with these farmers is where the international corporations will find the skills, the knowledge, and the wisdom that made the American farmer the envy of the world at midcentury.)

In the late 1980s Lilly Endowment announced the availability of large grants for community vitalization. These were aimed primarily at large cities in the mind of Lilly staff, but Council executives helped them see that assistance was also needed to ensure the continued existence of rural communities to provide continuity of food production and that such grants could be far smaller. "Don't give me a million dollars; I wouldn't know what to do with it. However, a grant of a couple of hundred thousand dollars might save countless rural communities in my State," one executive told them. Planning grants were made to some of the states, enabling them to research what the factors were that caused a town to fold, and how those factors could be reversed. In each state, numerous towns were helped to think through what was needed and to mobilize to provide it. Unspoken but clearly understood, however, was that agriculture was the cohesive factor that held the town together, both in terms of the secondary jobs it supplied and in the sense of community that fostered an understanding of a combined destiny.

As we worked with various communities, it was instructive that the cohesive factors in each was different. For some, residents were convinced that if they lost the high school they would no longer be a viable community. For others it was the local barber shop that served as more than a place to get a haircut. For others it was the local diner, the grocery store, the post office, or the elementary school. Once the town had verbalized what they all instinctively knew, organizing to remain viable became more of a possibility.

Long-Range Causes of the Farm Crisis

With the benefit of hindsight, it is not difficult to see that the crisis in agriculture in the United States was not a phenomenon of the 1980s only but had been building for most of the second half of the twentieth century. After the Depression years, which encompassed the Dust Bowl for the Plains States (an early warning period when low prices forced farmers to abandon conservation practices such as terracing, producing devastating results), and the frightening years of World War II, the mood in the country, including the Plains, was a euphoric one. Few people paid attention to the growing practice of the enlargement of farms, the "adding field to field" recognized by and warned against by so early a prophet as Isaiah. When it was recognized in the early 1980s, it was seen as a result of the almost magical technological advances in agriculture, and as a testimony to the skill of American farmers.

It was not until the late 1970s that farmers began questioning why, if conditions were so favorable, it was increasingly impossible for them to organize farming so that it would allow them to make a reasonable profit, and why so many farmers were being forced off the land. During the period of 1950 to 1980 the farm population in the United States shrank by more than half, from approximately 23 million to less than 10 million.[7] The lure of the city could not account for all of this exodus from farming or for the collapse of so many of the related businesses in rural communities. Farm implement manufacturers were forced to lay off employees, and machinery dealers found few people with funds to purchase new equipment. Small rural businesses, dependent upon these businesses and the farms that used their products, were forced to close. Between 1982 and 1987, A. V. Krebs reported that 60,000 small rural businesses and 2,000 farm implement dealers went out of business.[8]

Even more worrisome, the rapid loss of family farms was resulting in the concentration of land in fewer and fewer hands. By 1991, some 4 percent of farmland owners controlled half of U.S. farm land, and over 40 percent of the more than 830 million acres of private farmland was held by persons or organizations that were not personally involved in farming the land.[9] Most of those who had managed to remain in family farming relied on off-farm income to remain viable, and even with that assistance, a frightening statistic by the U.S. Department of Agriculture showed that 21 percent of those in farming were living below the poverty level.[10]

The high rate of inflation complicated even further the dilemma of the farmer. Holding large loans at the local bank, the farmer found the interest rate constantly rising through the late 1970s and the early 1980s. Collateral for those loans often was the land, whose price had continued to rise artificially in value. Those who entered the 1980s with low loan obligations were in the best position to survive the rapidly changing economic conditions, but the peak in inflation and the collapse of the price of the land caught many farmers in a vise from which they could not escape, and their local agricultural banks found that they, too, were trapped. The policies of the government, both state and federal, focused in the 1950s to assist the family farmer, had subtly changed to protection of capital and to the production of food increasingly being concentrated in corporate hands. Those farmers who were able to continue on their farms saw each year increase their losses, while the profits of the growing food industry were increasing each year. In 1994, PrairieFire Rural Action, using U.S. Department of Agriculture statistics, found that farmers were losing 2.7 percent annually on their equity, while the food and drink industry were realizing profits averaging 17.88 percent return on equity.[11] Something was going terribly wrong.

With memories still fresh in their minds of the Dust Bowl days when ignoring sound conservation practices had produced devastating effects, farmers were becoming knowledgeable and consequently concerned about the role of chemicals in agriculture. Between 1950 and the end of the 1980s, the farm population had decreased by approximately 80 percent, while the use of chemicals had increased during the same period by more than 600 percent.[12] Environmentally aware people in both rural and city settings joined the farmers in this concern, questioning the role of chemicals in agriculture.

As the crisis in family farming deepened in the middle 1980s, it became increasingly clear how government policy, aimed at assisting family farms and ranches in the 1940s and 1950s, was shifting to accommodate the agendas of international corporations. The system rewarded the processors of food products using farmers' crops, and the government made decisions that used food as a tool for diplomacy, overnight affecting and changing the international markets for crops and livestock that farmers depended on.

The horizontal integration of farming by the ever-increasing concentration of land in the hands of a few soon moved to a second tier, the vertical integration of all aspects of the production of grains, beef, poultry, and finally, in the 1990s, pork. Arrangements with financially desperate family farmers were contracted by national corporations, whereby the farmer was guaranteed a price for his product. By the end of the 1980s, A. V. Krebs indicated that two companies, Conagra and Cargill, controlled half of the world's grain trade, with four companies—Philip Morris, Kellogg, General Mills, and Quaker—producing 90 percent of all breakfast cereals in the United States.[13]

Similar corporate integration was taking place in animal production and marketing. In 1994, Jubilee Agriculture Ministries Inc. reported that three companies controlled over 80 percent of all beef production in the United States: Iowa Beef Processors, 32.7 percent; ConAgra, 26 percent; and Cargill, 21.2 percent.[14] In the South, Tyson is a principal example with poultry. In the 1990s the family hog farm was increasingly forced out of business. Large corporate hog production operations replaced them, bringing concerns in many communities about the environmental results of such concentration, particularly in regard to water contamination.

As the new century began, the practice of corporate mergers continued unabated, with a proposal that meat processor Iowa Beef Processors Inc. and poultry giant Tyson Foods Inc. merge. The Associated Press reported that this would result in a single company controlling 30 percent of the beef market, 33 percent of the poultry market, and 18 percent of the pork market. "I am very concerned about this," commented U.S. Senator Pat Roberts of Kansas. "We are losing individual control in agriculture."[15]

As we look back to the 1980s and the 1990s in agriculture in the Plains States from the vantage point of a new century, it becomes clear that not only family farming was radically changed during the last decades of the twentieth century. The very fabric of the United States was altered. The drastic changes in both its urban and rural communities, and its understanding of itself, caused severe transformation that affected all segments of the society and its institutions, including the churches. Troubling Council executives during this whole period of turmoil was the recognition that what was happening in the rural communities was also indicative of what was happening throughout all segments of society. The love affair of the American people with the stock market was rivaled only by the corresponding fascination with state lotteries that were being called upon for an increasing percentage of state budgets. The gap between the wealthy and the poor continued to grow larger, with the percentage of families sinking into poverty growing. The low unemployment rate during the late 1990s masked this disturbing trend, but agencies working with the working poor repeatedly reported increasing needs for their services and assistance. Kansas reflected what was happening across the country: the poorest segment of the population was 9 percent worse off in 2000 than in 1977, while the top income earners were 115 percent better off than they were in 1977.[16] A serious agenda item awaits attention in the new century.

Other Far-Reaching Council Activities

Through all of this period, however, Council executives also continued to address issues concerned with the unity of the Christian Church, particularly through study of the helpful document issued by the Faith and Order Commission of the World Council of Churches, "Baptism, Eucharist, and Ministry." They found themselves concerned about and addressing other issues, such as the economic disparity between the United States and Mexico, and they sought ways for the churches to work together for solutions that would enhance justice and genuine community. Rev. Frank Dietz, executive of the Texas Conference of Churches, organized and led numerous opportunities for judicatory executive and local church leaders to witness and understand more deeply the problems that were growing with the formation of *maquiladoras*, and with increasing illegal migration and the reaction to it by the federal government. Those efforts influenced some national and state legislation, gave birth to some imaginative community programs, and empowered local congregations to become "sanctuaries" for people simply trying to find ways to feed families.

Councils were becoming aware also of a major change in American society. No longer could people even try to pretend that the United States was an exclusively Christian country (if it ever was), since communities large and small were experiencing other living faiths becoming part of their neighborhoods. If it was happening in rural communities in the Plains, people surmised, it was happening all over the United States. The initial moves of city Councils in the 1960s to include Catholic parishes now grew to include congregations of other faiths, such as Judaism, Islam, Buddhism, and Hinduism, into the council structures. This of course raised many questions, but also enabled local congregations to embark on a challenging adventure of learning about other faiths and thinking through anew the relationship of Christianity to those faiths. The adventure resulted in strong, vibrant agencies with a wider definition of ecumenical that included all of humanity. In the Plains this resulted in a few of the strongest interfaith agencies in the country—Houston Ecumenical Ministries, formed in the late 1960s; Tulsa Metropolitan Ministry, formed in 1970; and Interfaith Ministries of Wichita, formed in 1977.

The scope of the ministries engaged in by these interfaith agencies expanded exponentially during this period into such areas as child care for working parents, community corrections, housing and/or day centers for the homeless, social and religious care for inmates, job opportunities and training for young adults, food and feeding programs such as Meals on Wheels, and aid to the growing numbers of elderly. Throughout the 1970s and 1980s both hunger concerns and genuine racial reconciliation continued to be priorities, and the recognition of the plight of low-income families and particularly children in the 1990s has risen to a top concern, uniting congregations of many faiths in new and genuine creative efforts.

In 1981 Interfaith Ministries of Wichita sponsored a national conference of the organized living faiths in the United States, which was attended by representatives of fifteen faiths. Of greatest surprise to the organizers was that some two hundred members of Christian congregations in the area who heard about the conference came to learn, signaling that the members of our congregations were more ready for interfaith contact and friendships than the churches were aware of. The other lesson for many of the Christian participants was that they were the ones who were least prepared to talk simply and coherently about their faith and its meaning in their own lives. The meeting, which came to be known as the North American Assisi, assisted an explosion in councils becoming interfaith agencies in cities and towns across the country.

The New Century

For rural communities, the scenario continues to become more complex and more serious. As we enter a new century, once again a large number of family farmers are facing bankruptcy. The increasing implications of economic globalization as it is presently envisioned has serious consequences for equitable balance of income between the rich and the poor, and food production and distribution for the entire world and is one of the principal dilemmas that will be faced by state Councils and rural communities as the new century proceeds.

Notes

1. From a report of the Commission on Regional and Local Ecumenism of the National Council of Churches, published in the fall of 1984.
2. Groups included the Ku Klux Klan; Posse Comitatus; the Populist Party; the Aryan Nation, the Order; the Covenant, Sword and Arm of the Lord; and the National Agricultural Press Association (*New York Times*, September 21, 1985).
3. *Christian Science Monitor*, November 25, 1985. ABC-TV's 920/209 also did a segment focusing on the role of extremist groups in fostering political extremism and anti-Semitism during this period.
4. From an article in the *New York Times*, quoted in the spring 1988 Newsletter of the Consultation of Cooperating Churches in Kansas (predecessor to Kansas Ecumenical Ministry).
5. From an FDIC report as reported in the *Hays Daily News* (Kansas).
6. A. V. Krebs, *The Corporate Reapers: The Book of Agribusiness* (Washington, DC: Essential Books, 1992), p. 19.
7. "Food and Farm Facts," *Kiplinger Agricultural Letter*, 1994, p. 9.
8. A. V. Krebs, as reported in *Of the Land, For the Land* (Washington, DC: Jubilee Agriculture Ministries, n.d.).
9. Bunyan Bryant, ed., *Environmental Justice: Issues, Policies, and Solutions* (Washington, DC: Island Press, 1991), chapter 12, p. 165.
10. Ibid., p. 165.
11. Corporate Agribusiness Research, PrairieFire Rural Action, March 1994.
12. A. V. Krebs, as reported in *Of the Land, for the Land*, p. 22.
13. Ibid., p 13.
14. Ibid.
15. Associated Press, reported in the *Topeka Capital Journal*, January 11, 2001.
16. Article in the *Parsons Sun*, March 3, 2000, reporting on a project of the Kansas Association of Community Action Programs.

16

STATE ECUMENISM IN MINNESOTA, SOUTH DAKOTA, AND NORTH DAKOTA

Alton M. Motter

Churches, like humans, have histories. And the movements toward greater Christian cooperation, mission, and unity have histories. The record of what happened in local and regional ecumenism between 1950 and 2000 in the states of North Dakota, South Dakota, and Minnesota cannot be written without briefly discussing what took place earlier in these three states.

That earlier record is related to the westward movement of the churches. It was a movement marked by a missionary zeal that grew out of the new England Great Awakenings. This led the Presbyterians and the Congregationalists, in part, to form a "Plan of Union" in 1801. In this plan, the denominations agreed to combine efforts for the winning of the western missionary field. In doing so, each group agreed to recognize each other's ministry and polity.[1]

One aspect of this evangelization was expressed in the organizing of Sunday Schools. As the nation expanded, there was a great need for the training of Sunday School teachers and officers and the best use of available curriculum materials. This led to the formation of state Sunday School associations in many states. Such associations, as well as a number of other developments, paved the way for the rise of the ecumenical movement in these three states. The organizing of the Minnesota Sunday School Association in 1859 led the way. It was followed in 1875 by the South Dakota Council of Christian Education.[2] Similar developments took place in North Dakota in 1890. The basic purpose of these associations was to promote the teachings of the Bible, especially among children and youth, and to lead them to make a personal commitment to Christ, as their Lord and Savior.[3] Through the years, the names of these organizational structures changed as their purposes and functions changed. Today, it is the Minnesota Council of

Churches (1946), the North Dakota Conference of Churches (1970), and the Association of Christian Churches of South Dakota (1971).

What has characterized the way the churches have worked together during this past half century as they have sought to carry out their ecumenical mission locally and regionally in these three states? To answer that question, I conducted nearly fifty interviews. This process included the wide use of written interview forms, telephone interviews, and some correspondence, as well as a number of one-to-one personal interviews during an extended trip to the Twin Cities in 1999. Let me also add that my insights were sharpened by the fact that I began what turned out to be a forty-five-year ecumenical ministry in 1946 when I was called to begin my responsibilities as the executive director of the St. Paul Area Council of Churches. My five years there were extended when I then served for nearly fifteen years (1959 to 1973) as the executive director of the Minnesota State Council of Churches.

As I review this fifty-year period, one impressive event stands out—Vatican II. Called by Pope John XXIII in Rome, Vatican II brought together more than 2,000 Catholic bishops from all over the world for long periods during the three years of 1963 to 1965. The results were far-reaching. When the Decree on Ecumenism was approved in Rome by a vote of 2,054 to 64 on November 20, 1964, it marked a new day in Catholic-Protestant relationships. This document on ecumenism paved the way for the development of new relationships among all Christians, as well as with other religious faiths. One commentator said, "The focus was more on a 'pilgrim' Church moving toward Christ, than on a movement of 'return' to the Roman Catholic Church."[4]

Coming more than a half century after the beginning of the modern ecumenical movement, one could indeed refer to pre–Vatican II and post–Vatican II as two distinct eras of ecumenical history. The contrast was vividly expressed in the Chicago area in 1954, for example, when the late Cardinal Stritch declared that no faithful Catholic should attend the events related to the Second Assembly of the World Council of Churches being held that August in Northwestern University in nearby Evanston. A decade later, that relationship changed radically. Roman Catholic dioceses were becoming members of state and regional Councils of Churches and Catholic parishes were actively involved in city councils, as well as in the various new forms of community ministries. These new relationships were especially dramatized in such areas as Texas and other southwestern states. What happened in some of the upper midwestern states was also impressive.

In the states of North and South Dakota, for example, Catholics had had no previous relationships with these states' ecumenical agencies. Nor did the Lutheran bodies of these states. The Catholic absence was based on the earlier position of the Roman Catholic Church that if non-Catholic Christians wanted a greater degree of unity, all they needed to do was to "return home," for the Catholic Church had it. After Vatican II, however, the new emphasis was, Let us pray and work together in order to discover the will of Christ for the greater unity of his Church. The Lutheran absence was accounted for by the late arrival of various Lutherans from different parts of Germany and Scandinavia who spoke and worshiped in different languages, settled mostly in isolated rural areas, had limited means of communication and transportation, and mostly had pastors who held to inflexible theological doctrines that separated Lutherans from other Christians.

Vatican II broke the ice in these relationships. Consequently, when the North Dakota *Conference* of Churches was created in 1970 to replace the earlier North Dakota *Council* of Churches, Lutherans as well as Catholics became members. The same was true for South Dakota, whose new name in 1971 became the *Association* of Christian Churches of South Dakota. Similar developments took place in Minnesota. While this did not result in formal Catholic membership in the Minnesota Council of Churches, it opened almost unlimited opportunities for greater Catholic participation.

Advance preparation for this increased cooperation took place when two leaders helped pave the way. These were Father William Hunt, a young Catholic professor from St. Paul's Catholic Theological Seminary, and me, the executive director of the Minnesota Council of Churches. I had attended Vatican II as an accredited Lutheran observer and a news correspondent for the *St. Paul Pioneer Press*. Following Vatican II, we two served as an ecumenical team that visited more than fifty Minnesota communities. Both Catholics and Protestants attended these ecumenical community meetings in great numbers, many coming together for the first time in their lives.

As those meetings continued and were reported on, attendance increased. In some communities, no church was large enough to accommodate the anticipated attendance. Meetings were then often scheduled for the communitys high school auditorium. In Minnesota, these were followed by many such events as an intensive statewide conference on racism; the formation of the Joint Religious Legislative Coalition; the anti-Vietnam "Dump the War" Rally attended by some 27,000 people; the Protest Anti-Vietnam March from the St. Paul Catholic Cathedral to the state capital; and the formation of the Tri-Council Coordinating Coalition through which the Minnesota, the Greater Minneapolis, and the St. Paul Area Councils of Churches could more effectively serve the needs of that day. In the words of Pope John Paul II, we, too, believe that "the ecumenical movement cannot be reversed!"

Because the decree said that the "Catholic faithful should recognize the signs of the times and participate skillfully in the work of ecumenism," the faithful in the upper Midwest welcomed it. They actively involved themselves in these five steps outlined in the decree: 1) eliminate past judgments and actions which have separated us; 2) engage in fruitful dialogue; 3) cooperate more closely "in whatever projects a Christian conscience demands for the common good"; 4) share in common prayer; and 5) undertake with vigor the task of renewal and reform. It marked the beginning of a new chapter in ecumenical history.

This was clearly true in the ecumenical history of these three upper midwestern states. Its special significance here was due to the fact that Catholics accounted for a large percentage of these populations. In Minnesota, for example, Catholics represented approximately one-third; Lutherans, one-third; and all other religious bodies, one-third of the religious population.

Thus Vatican II led to membership in the major ecumenical agencies in the Dakotas and to major degrees of new cooperation in Minnesota within the Catholic Church. Vatican II also helped to trigger more positive Lutheran responses. In the period between 1865 and 1900, German and Scandinavian Lutherans accounted for a large percentage of the 13 million immigrants to the United States. Many of these Lutheran immigrants pushed westward and settled in these three upper midwestern states. Unfortunately, however, they remained greatly divided. One noted church historian, Dr. Winthrop S. Hudson, wrote: "As far as influence in the general religious life of the nation was concerned, the Lutheran segment of American church life remained a sleeping giant until after World War I." Dr. Hudson said this had three basic reasons: 1)The overwhelming proportion settled in largely self-contained and self-sufficient rural communities; 2) most were further isolated by language barriers; and 3) there was no way of establishing an organizational unity.

The Lutherans remained badly divided by national origin, place and time of settlement, and deep doctrinal differences. Hudson added: "By 1900, there were 24 different Lutheran groups, with the family tree of most of them so complicated, by constant reshuffling, that it was difficult to chart even their individual histories."[5]

Such was the case until 1965, when the first Lutheran body became a member of the Minnesota Council of Churches and, later, when all of the other Lutheran bodies did the same, with the exception of the Lutheran Church–Missouri Synod. The second most significant ecumenical development during this half century in these three states is, therefore, the Lutheran decisions to be a part of these ecumenical structures. The histories of these three state ecumenical structures indicate that while much was accomplished before this era, the increased participation and support from Lutheran and Catholic resources was a new source of encouragement. In the words of one Protestant executive, "Yes, the coming of the Lutherans has caused us some new problems, but we couldn't do without them!"

In the Dakotas, those ecumenical ministries covered a wide range of developments and services. As in most state ecumenical agencies, these related to the meeting of different needs, as such needs varied from state to state.

North Dakota

In North Dakota, many of these ministries related to a declining rural population, legislative concerns, refugee sponsorships, state prison ministry, chaplaincies, Native American understanding, counteracting racial barriers (Friendly Town Program), New Pastors' Orientations (North Dakota 101), and, in 1999, the production of an educational video, "Stewards of Creation: Stewards of Hope," for use by local congregations. In 1984, a conference on the World Council of Churches' "Baptism, Eucharist, and Ministry" (BEM) document brought more than one hundred pastors from all parts of the state together for study and discussion.

The Rev. J. Winfred Stoerker, who served as the Conference's executive director for the ten-year span from 1972 to 1982, said that those were the pioneer days when "the Roman Catholics and the Lutherans did not know the leaders of their own respective denominations, let alone the leaders of the mainline churches." He reported that, during that decade, the Conference grew and took shape in every respect, "except monetarily." Unable to raise the budget money, at that time about $45,000, Stoerker's term was terminated. It has continued with part-time lay and volunteer executive leadership.

Eunice Brinckerhoff, who recently retired after serving as the Conference office manager/coordinator for seventeen years, said that "without an Executive Director, the interest and participation of all judicatory leaders is required, if we are to be effective. When leaders miss even one meeting, the cohesiveness of the group falls apart. An effective president, however, can make a big difference."

An interesting perspective on North Dakota ecumenism was given by Arabella Meadows-Rogers, Executive Presbyter for the Northern Plains Presbytery in Fargo. She said, "When I moved to North Dakota, for the first time in my life from the geographical center of Presbyterianism and found myself in this 'sea of Lutherans,' the importance of ecumenicity was both tested and confirmed." She added: "Working in this state, where faith survives, even if churches shrivel in size, is a test and an affirmation of the importance of ecumenical work."

An even more pointed conclusion was reached by Dr. Arland D. Jacobson, the executive director of the noted CHARIS Ecumenical Center, located at Concordia College, Moorhead, Minnesota. He noted, "After being requested to organize and conduct an annual retreat for North Dakota's bishops and judicatory executives for fourteen years: There are real signs of hope when leaders can bring pastors together in serious ecumenical engagements in various forms of ecumenical shared ministries."[6]

A most challenging and provocative study of the above shared ministries concept, as it could be applied to Lutheran and United Methodist congregations and possible ways they might work together, is described in "Ecumenical Shared Ministry and the United Methodist Church," by Jacobson and Kerr et al.[7]

South Dakota

When the Association of Christian Churches of South Dakota was officially launched in 1971, the following six priorities were adopted:

- A continuation of work with Indians
- Improved church-community relations
- Increased interpretation and communications through radio, television, and newspapers
- Improved institutional ministries
- Legislative issues related to church concerns
- Continued liaison with CROP–Church World Service

By 1994, a third revision of the association's constitution listed these five purposes:

- To discover and further, through creative forums, the unity we have in Jesus Christ as Lord and Savior
- To make that unity manifest to the world
- To help fulfill Christ's mission in this time and place

- To do those things that we may together do more effectively and efficiently than separately
- To do those things that we ought or must do together

Between these two dates and with their contrasting priorities, this ecumenical association established an amazing record of service and achievement. It did this amid difficulties and hardships during periods in the life of South Dakota's churches and people that tested the very fiber of their souls.

Perhaps some of the greatest tests came during the mid-1980s when massive floods threatened the survival of South Dakota farmers. These floods followed a winter of bitter temperatures, heavy snowfalls, and blizzards, and created dire need among many farmers. A 1985 campaign called "Sow Some Hope" resulted in raising about $37,000, which went to aid some seventy-six families in forty-two of the state's sixty-six affected counties. That assistance included funds to provide wood, electricity, oil, groceries, propane, and even disposable diapers, as well as wheat seed for future sowing.

A decade later in 1994, an even more massive flood swept the state. This affected some eight thousand families in thirty-nine counties and covered more that two-and-a-half-million crop acres. In this effort, called "A Grain of Hope," denominational funds came to the rescue from the national headquarters of Presbyterians, United Methodists, Roman Catholics, and Lutherans, and many individual contributions, totaling $507,167. Assistance was given in the form of hundred-dollar vouchers to purchase any kind of seed from any seed dealer in the state.

During its history, the association was engaged in fulfilling many of its priorities. This included a "Peace Sunday" emphasis in 1981, the defeat of a state gambling bill in 1982, and a strong 1983–1984 resettlement program for some eighty-five refugee families. In 1988, it faced the fact of South Dakota poverty when it recognized that nine of the twenty-five lowest per capita income counties in the United States were in this state, and that eight of the nine included Indian reservations.

Consideration was also given to ways by which many smaller congregations in the state's rural communities with declining populations could establish "yoked" parishes as a means of enabling a church community to survive. An annual report in 1989 said that a yoked parish was defined as "two or more congregations from several denominations who were served by one pastor" and that thirty such parishes now existed among these six denominations: American Baptist, Christian (Disciples), Lutheran, Presbyterian, United Church of Christ, and United Methodist.

In addition, the association maintained relationships with the Shalom Center for continuing education for pastors and laity, the Flandreau Indian School Chaplaincy program, several forms of prison ministry, a Peace and Justice Center, and the Rural Initiative Center (which deals with some of the problems churches as well as family farmers face for survival in rural America). It also issued, in 1995, a set of Suggested Marriage Guidelines signed by leaders of nine denominations.

According to the Rev. Norman D. Eitrheim, a former bishop of the South Dakota Synod of the ELCA and a former association president, "a decline in Association financial support was due primarily to tighter budgets in congregations, and consequently councils of churches were impacted together with all other ministries beyond the congregation." This led to the decision to terminate the full-time services of Bruce Gray in 1991, who had served as the association's executive director for nearly a decade. Its work was then continued by volunteer executive leadership, assisted by Pat Williard, who serves as secretary/office manager. The president of the association, the Rev. Richard W. Fisher, a United Methodist, said in his 1999 annual report that "Pat Willard is the glue that holds things together, helps people find answers to questions, and calls events and concerns to our attention." He expressed his ecumenical philosophy in these words, "When we face paths we do not wish to go, we must be open to the power of the Holy Spirit to lead us."

Minnesota

Minnesota has three of the strongest ecumenical developments of any state in the nation: the Minnesota State Council of Churches, the Greater Minneapolis Council of Churches, and the St. Paul Area Council of Churches.

The Minnesota Council of Churches

Much of the credit for what has happened in Minnesota goes to the leadership of Hayden L. Stright. For forty-two years between 1922 and 1964, Dr. Stright paved the way for what was to follow. The climax of his outstanding ecumenical leadership came when, after five years of intensive planning and fund-raising, the new six-story, two-million-dollar Minnesota Protestant Center was dedicated on March 4, 1964. Occupied by seventeen denominational and interdenominational agencies and their nearly 150 staff members, it became "Minnesota's Spiritual Nerve Center." With increased participation by both Roman Catholic and Eastern Orthodox leaders, the Center was renamed the Minnesota Church Center in 1968.[8]

The decades that followed were marked by dramatic developments. I followed Dr. Stright's long administration, and when I concluded my nearly fifteen-year tenure in 1973, I listed these six developments:

- The reception of four out of five possible Lutheran bodies, which more than doubled the membership of the councils' 18-member church bodies
- Ever-widening circles of Roman Catholic leadership and participation
- The strong response to meet many social needs and causes during the socially sensitive 60s
- The expansion of an Indian Ministry resulting from a rise in the spirit of self-determination and responsibility among Native American Indian people themselves
- The formation of the Tri-Council Coordinating Commission (TCC) in order to provide for a greater coordination of staff, program, and resources with the Minneapolis and St. Paul Councils
- A continuous restructuring process for greater flexibility and effectiveness in order to meet the changes taking place in the culture of that day

In closing my final 1973 report, I wrote: "I do not believe the ecumenical movement is dead, or is dying. Christians can never escape our Lord's prayer for greater 'oneness.' These days of ecumenical transition call—not for fair-weather ecumenists—but for ecumenical pilgrims and pioneers of deep commitment and courage."[9] Changes continued to mark the life of the Minnesota Council. During the 1985–1995 decade, when Margaret J. Thomas served as the executive director, she reviewed these significant developments:

> The creation of two new categories of membership: 1) Corresponding, for eligible communions, who could not choose now to become full members; and 2) Observer, for non-Christian religious faiths.
>
> The establishment of a Commission on Unity and Relationships to facilitate the way the above categories operated, as well as other bilateral and multilateral ecumenical conversations such as COCU developments. This emphasized a greater concentration on Christian unity developments.
>
> The developing of ad hoc coalitions to address ongoing and emerging issues like migrant workers, domestic violence, the farm crisis, racism and clergy sexual malfeasance
>
> The expansion of the ongoing Joint Religious Legislative Coalition (JRLC), which included Catholic and Jewish participation.

In addition, the Council became a major proponent in securing more than $2 million to enable nonprofit agencies to plan strategically how to assist those whose social safety net was being withdrawn. Since 1995, under the executive leadership of the Rev. Peg Chemberlin and a full-time support staff of sixteen and operating within a total operating budget of $1,547,770 in 1999, the Minnesota Council's program has continued to expand. To review its total ecumenical ministries within the limits of this chapter is impossible. It has included such events as an annual two-day Ecumenical Summit Meeting of the heads of the Council's nineteen member denominations and thirty-one judicatories, as well as heads of nonmember denominations; the resettling of some three hundred refugees; a reorganized focus for its State Fair Chaplaincy; the development of dialogues with Jewish, Muslim, and Hindu leaders; the providing of a wide variety of services to more than two hundred migrant families each year; and the expansion of its Minnesota Indian Ministry to include transitional housing for women from nearly all of Minnesota's reservations, which involved a $300,000 remodeling project.

The high quality of the ecumenical thrust within and around the vibrant Twin Cities area was made possible through the cooperative efforts of the Tri-Council Metropolitan Church Commission. The combined efforts of the strong Minnesota, Greater Minneapolis, and St. Paul Area Councils provided for an unusually effective ecumenical witness. The most recent major project (1998) resulted in the creation of the Minnesota Churches Anti-Racism Initiative (MCARI). This was launched when nearly seven hundred persons, including thirty-seven staff and board members of the three sponsoring councils, participated in intensive antiracism training. This was followed up with trained leadership teams in nearly forty local congregations and religious communities.

The Greater Minneapolis Council

During this half century, the Greater Minneapolis Council of Churches was shaped by the Rev. David Witheridge (1951–1979), Dr. Thomas Quigley (1980–1988), and Dr. Gary Reierson, who began his duties in 1989. This Council could well be the largest metropolitan Council in the nation. Operating within an annual budget of $4,158,871 (1998) and with a full-time professional staff of forty-one, one of the Council's major developments is its Division of Indian Work, which alone has a budget of $1,215,924. A high point in that work came with the dedication of a new Native American Indian Center in 1995 into which the Council moved its own offices.

The Indian Ministry includes the provisions for job training and finding jobs for unemployed Indian people, as well as programs related to family violence, teen Indian parents, and an Indian youth leadership development program.

Among its most dramatic program is its metro Paint-A-Thon. This is a project in which youth and other volunteers help to paint houses for low-income elderly and disabled homeowners. In 1998, 240 painting crews spruced up 228 homes. Since 1984, Paint-A-Thon volunteers have painted more than 4,500 homes across a seven-county metropolitan area.

Another major intercouncil and interfaith partnership event was the Minnesota FoodShare project, done in cooperation with other agencies, which raised some 4.4 million pounds of food and supported a number of other major public food policies.

As the Council's record was reviewed, two voices spoke. The first was Hallie B. Hendrieth-Smith, a retired Minneapolis African-American public school teacher:

> My experience with the Greater Minneapolis Council of Churches' weekday Released Time religious education program provided opportunities for me, as an African American, to share with other Christians. Their welcome to me was both warm and caring, which was surprising to me. It took several meetings, and we were communicating as one staff, rather than as representatives of different denominations.
>
> After I served as the first and only African American woman as President of our Council of Churches, other women have been elected to that position. I feel that my leadership involvement opened the minds of others to realize that people of other ethnic backgrounds have contributions to make. To do this, sometimes you have to be bold. This became my greatest Christian milestone, for I was a strong no-nonsense woman, outspoken on many moral issues, and came to be respected as a leader by my colleagues.

The Rev. Bill Smith, president of the Minneapolis Interdenominational Ministerial Alliance, pastor of African Wellsprings Ministries, and a member of the Minneapolis Council's Board of Directors, is an African American pastor who has filled a wide variety of leadership roles at different levels of society for some thirty years. Among many other positions, he was the editor, during the 1960s, of the African American publication, "The Spokesman." His strong spiritual leadership among the African American churches led him to be recognized as the natural leader of the Minneapolis Interdenominational Ministerial Alliance, which has a membership of thirty-four members and meets monthly with an average attendance of twenty. The Alliance provides a means through which African American pastors of various denominations are able to strengthen their morale and unite in supporting projects to meet common needs among their people.

Leaders of the Alliance expressed appreciation for the work of the Greater Minneapolis Council of Churches, but said that its members have felt a need for more intimate and personal relationships than the Council can provide. They felt that such a warmer relationship did exist under the leadership of the Council's former executive director, the Rev. David E. Witheridge, who seemed to give the Council's relationship with the black churches a higher priority. This relationship was probably harder to maintain, as the Council's total program later expanded greatly.

A major ecumenical thrust was a project aimed toward a greater employment of blacks. This became an interfaith movement, which gained the support of the city's mayor, Chamber of Commerce, business leaders, and firms like Honeywell, as well as the backing of some of the city's major churches.

Another project was MANNA (Ministries, Anointing, Neighborhoods, Now, Accountability). Its purpose was to improve some of the population centers where African Americans lived. It also included a plan to provide more specific support for additional educational opportunities for African American pastors.

In my personal interview with him, Smith felt that "if black churches and their leaders were to get more involved in the total ecumenical movement, white leaders and their churches needed to establish more intimate relationships. Without that personal and warmer relationship, each will tend to go their own way."

Dr. Reierson's conclusion is that throughout its history the Minneapolis Council of Churches has been "meeting human needs and [that] seeking social justice has been at the core of our mission."

An Evangelical from the Upper Midwest Looks at the Ecumenical Future

A still different voice came from Joan Magnuson, a conservative charismatic member of Hope Presbyterian Church in Richfield, Minnesota, in an interview from June 23, 1999, in Minneapolis. During her college days, Magnuson was involved with the Campus Crusade for Christ. This led her to accept a very conservative view of the Christian faith. In a strange set of circumstances, she later married a member of the Lutheran Wisconsin Synod, who became a Lutheran charismatic. A highlight of their marriage came in

1972, when they attended a national Lutheran gathering on the Holy Spirit, attended by some 6,000 persons, including many Roman Catholics and others of many different Christian backgrounds.

She sought what she called a "high view of the Scriptures," which would include a "broad view of human relations." She found this, almost by accident, in a conservative Presbyterian Church. Magnuson strongly promotes "Bridges for Peace" as a way to establish closer ties between conservative-minded Christians and Jews. This has led her to make forty-five trips to Israel with others who believe that Israel is indeed God's Holy Land. The Bridges for Peace world headquarters is in Jerusalem. Her support for this program also includes a number of supportive charitable projects for Jewish people.

When asked in this interview, "Do you consider yourself a 'born-again' Christian?" she replied, "Oh, yes." "When did that occur?" She said, "Oh, 2,000 years ago!" She feels that the ecumenical movement cannot move forward until all Christians are willing to remove the stereotypical concepts we have of each other who are different from ourselves. She reports that she has had more success in doing this with the ecumenical churches than with other Christian evangelicals. In her mind, evangelicals tend to compete with one another, often in very negative ways.

Magnuson agreed to share some of her experiences as a "conservative evangelical Christian." First of all, she is not typical in that she has experienced a series of unusual religious and ecumenical involvements. This included a relationship with the Minnesota Council of Churches when she agreed to serve on the council's Christian/Jewish Committee in 1992. In that relationship, she gives great credit to the Rev. Lydia Veliko, a Council staff member, who also became a colleague and a friend. Magnuson said: "Lydia's personal spiritual depth, her sensitivity to conservative Christians, and her honest efforts to bring Christians together across lines that have long divided us has been one of the highlights of my spiritual pilgrimage."

It is significant to note that the role filled by Veliko, a Council staff member, helped to shape Magnuson's attitude toward the ecumenical movement. After nearly a decade in this relationship, it is also significant to hear how she sees the challenges facing the ecumenical movement's new century. She wrote:

> As an evangelical, I hope the Christian community at large can begin and continue broad opportunities for dialogue, and I hope that will in-

clude tough dialogue, about issues that seriously divide us. The conservative community, where I spend most of my time, needs to talk to those they regard as opponents. The liberal community also needs to listen to the conservatives and to respect the concerns of those who fear that wider fellowship will cause us to weaken and possibly lose the distinctive beliefs of biblical Christianity.

As we face issues in the future not only of greater Christian unity, but also of greater interreligious unity, Magnuson had this to say:

> I think interreligious work should be pursued while Christian unity needs to be a continuing priority. For instance, to involve Evangelicals in dialogue, I've found it does not work well to try to do Jewish-Christian dialogue by bringing Evangelicals into groups of Jews and liberal Christians. The two Christian groups have too many undiscussed differences between themselves, and the Jews either try to arbitrate or are left wondering if they have wandered into a theological ping-pong match.

In my fairly intensive interviews of nearly fifty persons in the three states of the upper Midwest, I found Magnuson's responses to be among the most discerning.

St. Paul Area Council

Under the very capable leadership of the Rev. Dr. Thomas A. Duke since 1988, the St. Paul Area Council of Churches has also greatly expanded during this half century. Operating with a professional staff of twenty-five and within an operating budget of $1,167,893 (1999), the St. Paul Council devotes the largest share of its budget ($172,609) to Indian work. This includes an American Indian Parenting Program, a Youth-Enrichment After-School Program and a Youth Summer Enrichment Program, as well as a wide variety of emergency Indian-related services.

A major aspect of the Council has been its unique work with African American and Indian children. This program, involving some 35 volunteers, operated in four program sites in 1998, with some 145 children, in what was called the Waging Peace Initiative. This involved learning holistic concepts of peace beyond conflict resolution, and included interpersonal relations, physical safety, economic security, personal development, and the importance of relating to the community. Another aspect of the program included steps to counteract child abuse and to develop actions that would create families and communities where the child is valued and loved.

The Council has also developed ways to assist low-income families and people moving from welfare to work and has provided a support and shelter program for homeless families, recruited volunteer police chaplains, and provided leadership to counsel with prison residents. Among its fairly recent developments was the completion and dedication of its greatly expanded offices, meeting rooms, and headquarters, at a cost of about one million dollars.

When looking to the future, Arthur Sternberg, a Presbyterian layman, retired law book publishing staff member, and a long-time Council supporter, said that we need to "face the growing disparity between the haves and have-nots. In this country where everyone knows how the other half lives, the ecumenical movement must have some answers, or face the charge that the church is out of touch with reality. Find ways of relating and cooperating with other religious faiths. And emphasize our similarities, rather than our differences."

An interview with another of St. Paul's conciliar leaders shows the complexities of the ecumenical life for a prominent layperson. J. Stanley Hill, of White Bear Lake, said that as a young man he became interested in the teachings of all religions. Gradually he leaned toward the Unitarian-Universalists. His wife, Doris, remained a Lutheran, and they now attend an ELCA Lutheran Church. About 1945, he agreed to serve on the board of the St. Paul Area Council of Churches, led its annual fund drives, served for four years as chairman of its Finance Committee, and later became for two years its board chair. Yet, he has traveled widely and has related to many other religious faiths. He looks upon the intricate religious affiliations of his family as a symbolic case study of the broader ecumenism: His youngest son's wife, Satoko, from Japan, is now a Christian but was a former Buddhist. His youngest daughter married a Roman Catholic. Two of his five children are "born again" Christians, who are convinced that "he will go to hell!" In spite of these great differences, he has maintained a loving relationship with each. Mr. Hill went on to reflect on his personal religious beliefs:

> I believe that our Creator gave us the capacity to love, understand, and have compassion for all fellow human beings. Doris and I have both found our philanthropy and our extremely active community service to be deeply spiritually rewarding. I find myself in tune with much of the writings of Bishop John Spong in his *Saving the Bible from the Funda-*

> *mentalists* and *Why Christianity Must Change or Die*. As a young person, I found it difficult to understand the teaching that it is more blessed to give than to receive. Now by experiencing that blessing many times, I have come to believe it with a whole heart. I am a deist, and as a result, find myself in a "self-imposed" exile from all established Christian Churches. My attendance with Doris at St. Andrew's (Lutheran) is a sort of unspoken compromise. My deep belief in a Supreme Being and the importance of doing God's will and exercising love, compassion, understanding, and forgiveness form the essence of my faith. This has enabled me to free myself from all negative emotions. The rewards have been tremendous. Life continues to be a wonderful journey, each day brings its own joys and opportunities to serve and learn.

Perhaps Stanley Hill and many others have chosen to give leadership in ecumenical arenas because they do not quite fit in most local Christian Churches. In commenting on the way St. Paul's 166 member congregations from 22 denominations cooperate to fulfill the Council's mission, Dr. Duke said, "Our task is to build a life-giving, just, and anti-racist community for all people in the East Metro Area of the Twin Cities."

Some Ecumenical Observations for the Upper Midwest

Following this brief survey, it seems logical to ask, What were the most significant ecumenical developments during this half century in these three states? Let me try to list eight:

1. This half century was marked by a shift from a Protestant-centered emphasis on Bible study to a wider and deeper emphasis on the ways the churches should try to meet the broader needs of a changing culture. In 1950, for example, the major emphasis of the St. Paul Area Council was on its extensive program of weekday released time classes of Bible study. Some 1,500 children from grades 4, 5, and 6 from 32 public schools met weekly in 21 church centers under the guidance of a Christian Education director and 17 qualified, paid teachers. That program accounted for 55 percent of the Council's budget of approximately $25,000. In a list of the Council's 18 involvements, the above religious education program was number one. Number 18 was "works

for civic and social righteousness." That's quite a contrast to today's involvements of the St. Paul Council!

2. Another very significant development was the broadening of the ecumenical base in all three states. Prior to about 1950, Lutheran Church bodies, for example, were not official members of any of these three state councils. After 1965, nearly all were, except for the Lutheran Church–Missouri Synod. That was especially significant in view of the unusually large Lutheran population in these three states. It also included the Eastern Orthodox.
3. The actions of Vatican II (1962–1965) probably had the most profound effect upon ecumenical developments during this half century. This influence was felt everywhere. It resulted in state membership in North and South Dakota and greatly increased participation in Minnesota. It was especially beneficial for local councils. Eight Roman Catholic congregations became contributing members of the St. Paul Council, for example, while that number increased to fifteen with the Minneapolis Council.
4. There was also a stronger emphasis on the meeting of human needs and for social justice. This was especially pronounced in each of these three states in Indian Ministry. It became a highest priority, not only for the three state councils, but for the two local city councils as well. In St. Paul, for example, 18 percent of its 1999 budget went for Indian Ministry, while in Minneapolis, this percentage went to 25 percent. These were relevant challenges in view of the large Indian populations in each state. Strong concerns were also supported for ministries related to the farm crisis, racism, poverty, homelessness, local and world hunger, sexual abuse, violence, correctional care, family life, and refugee sponsorships.
5. There was also a greater interest and willingness to become legislatively involved. While such steps were taken in each state, the strongest example was the interfaith Joint Religious Legislative Coalition centered in the Twin Cities. With full-time staff leadership, this became an effective ecumenical arm to deal with the Minnesota legislature on such issues as child care, affordable housing, education, tax relief for farms, and stopping state-authorized casino gambling. This included the development of congregational leaders and a statewide network of more than 7,000.
6. While nearly all of the persons that I interviewed were receptive to the need to establish lines of communication with non-Christian faiths,

there was almost complete agreement that their councils should continue to be based upon a Christ-centered foundation. Margaret Thomas, former executive director of the Minnesota Council, said it this way: "All of us face the challenge of increasing the size of the table so that people of all faith traditions can be in conversation with one another. But we must do so without losing the distinctiveness we each bring to the table."

7. One of the most impressive changes during this past half century is the way local and regional ecumenical agencies have been financed. In most cases, state councils of churches were financed by their member denominations. Local councils were supported by their member-congregations. In many, many cases, this is no longer true. This former method seems to be true for North Dakota and South Dakota. But it is no longer true for Minnesota. The Minnesota Council's budget support for 1998 showed that only 23 percent came from denominational contributions. Support from the approximately 100 congregations to the total St. Paul Council budget was 9 percent, while such support for the Minneapolis Council's some 150 congregations reached only about 5 percent. How can this state and two city councils carry out their strong, vigorous ecumenical ministries with such a small percentage of support from their congregations?

   The Minneapolis answer is to be found in the other major sources of income: foundations and corporations, 36.9 percent; individuals, 21.4 percent; government sources, 10.0 percent; United Way, 8.7 percent.

   Other major sources of income for the St. Paul Council are foundations and corporations, 53 percent; government contracts, 11 percent; United Way, 9 percent; the council foundation, 7 percent; individuals, 4 percent.

   This shift in the basis of support for ecumenical agencies calls for greater in-depth reflection and discussion. As we look ahead, how should we try to answer these questions: Do our ecumenical leaders envision too much? To what degree can our congregations and denominations increase their financial support? Do the large contributions from secular firms, corporations, and foundations hamper the prophetic role that many councils have fulfilled? In what way do government grants affect the principles involved in the church-state separation issue?

8. As one studies these expressions of local and regional ecumenism in the upper Midwest, one additional fact becomes quite clear: There is a great dependence upon the depth of an ecumenical leader's commit-

ment, the quality of such leadership, and the length of such service. A number of very difficult factors account for the variations of such leadership in North and South Dakota. Among them are the earlier absence of Lutheran and Roman Catholic participation, the farm crisis, declining populations, and a faltering economic base.

On the other hand, Minnesota fared differently. The state and two Twin City councils were led for the most part by full-time men or women ecumenical executives. Most served for ten years or longer. They were able to recruit ecumenically committed clergy and laity who held key positions in the life of the churches as well as in wider circles of the culture, both of which have been marked by expansion and growth. If it is true that most institutions are but the lengthened shadows of their leaders, it is perhaps even more true for the institutional forms of the ecumenical movement. Too often, local ecumenism has been an entrepreneurial endeavor on the part of leaders who have a vision.

How Do We See Our Ecumenical Future?

We asked the question in our interviews, How do you see our ecumenical future? The answers to that question varied widely. Most were cautious. A few were pessimistic. Yet many more of the respondents held strong hopes. Nearly all recognized that the ecumenical movement was now in a stage of transition. It began, of course, with Christ and his prayer in John 17. The central theme was supported and expanded by the Apostle Paul. But, after centuries of separation and division, the modern ecumenical movement did not really take on world dimensions until 1910. Nor did it truly expand on the world scene until 1965. At the end of this "ecumenical twentieth century," where do we go from here?

North Dakota Voices

One of the clearest answers came from Dr. Arland D. Jacobson, a Lutheran and executive director of the CHARIS Ecumenical Center located in the twin cities of Grand Rapids, North Dakota, and Moorhead, Minnesota. Out of his extensive ecumenical experiences, he said:

> Our first challenge is to face the fact that too much of what passes for progress in ecumenism is simply a tolerance based on indifference. At the ecclesiastical level, we have focused too much energy, in my view,

on high-level negotiation of institutional differences, without a corresponding effort at the grassroots level. I do not want to diminish the value of theological conversations, but I think that our agreements are so often greeted with either yawns or anger and reveal the failure of our usual approach.

Our second challenge is that of overcoming the sectarianism built into American denominationalism. I realize this, too, is peculiarly American, though we have spread our disease around the world. By sectarianism, I mean the arrogance of assuming that a particular "we" (Lutherans, Anglicans, some other denominations, some congregations, megachurches, etc.) can exist in complete indifference toward and ignorance of other Christians. This is the greatest heresy of our time, and far from being recognized as a heresy, it is a condition that is celebrated with a great spirit of independence and pride. This must be challenged theologically and unmasked for what it is.

There are real signs of hope when leaders can bring pastors together in serious ecumenical engagements in various forms of ecumenical shared ministries.

We need to continue our ecumenical vision of the Church, not merely as a nice pragmatic goal or ideal, but as a theological and ecclesiastical necessity. This means that we must articulate the necessity of Christian unity in fresh ways, and in uncompromising terms.

A North Dakota voice, also with long ecumenical experience in that state, came from Eunice Brinckerhoff, who, after seventeen years, retired recently as the office manager/coordinator of the North Dakota Conference of Churches: "North Dakota is predominantly Lutheran and Roman Catholic. Without their participation, the conference would be unable to continue. From my seventeen years, I have learned that listening and learning from one another in an atmosphere of mutual respect is the heart of the ecumenical movement."

From his years as the bishop of the Eastern North Dakota District of the former American Lutheran church (ALC), Bishop Wesley N. Haugen, Fargo, said: "My ecumenical journey leads me to believe that we must increase our support for our local ministerial associations, as well as our state Councils of Churches. Their task is to build more effective ecumenical bridges. Then, we must provide more responsible and effective religious leadership at all levels. This we must do, even amidst conflicting voices, and at a time when trust in much of our political leadership is eroding."

South Dakota Voices

An unusually discerning voice came from the Rev. Jerry L. Folk, the former director (1976–1987) of the Shalom Center, an Ecumenical Center for Continuing Theological Education in Sioux Falls, South Dakota. Since 1993, he has served as the executive director of the Wisconsin Conference of Churches:

> As we look to the future, our greatest social challenge will be to resist the continuing depersonalization and atomization of society. Under the pressure of technology and the market, the human person is being more and more reduced to his or her ability to contribute to the production or the consumption of goods and services.
>
> A second challenge is the increasing extremes between the very rich and the very poor. There is a need for a radical economic reform that will reduce this discrepancy.
>
> The third challenge is the persisting ethnic and ideological hatreds that motivate the enormous cruelties and abuses of our time.
>
> To do this, the Church must get out of its self-serving, institution-centered, corporate-grown mentality and articulate a vision of the Gospel that has the power to wean humanity away from the nihilistic and destructive forces of our time. This is required if we are to prosper and, perhaps, even survive the third millennium.

Another South Dakota voice came from the Rev. Norman D. Eitrheim, Sioux Falls, who served earlier as the bishop of the South Dakota synod of the ELCA. Bishop Eitrheim said:

> As a bishop for 15 years, I was very involved with the Association of Christian Churches in South Dakota. Close relationships and joint experiences with other judicatory heads provided the mortar that held the Council together, despite the decline in financial support due primarily to tighter congregational budgets. Major issues in our society, such as the Vietnam War, were of such magnitude that churches were pushed to respond jointly. Guilt over actions and past misunderstandings motivated efforts to understand and accept each other. Lay people encouraged openness toward their neighbors who belonged to different churches.
>
> As we look ahead ecumenically, it is imperative that we must continue to look to the biblical injunctions for greater Christian unity. De-

> clining rural populations, and therefore declining church membership in rural areas, will result in more yoked parishes. This may mean that loyalty to denominations will continue to decrease. The growth of non-Christian religions in our country will undoubtedly move Christian ecumenism toward greater cooperation with other religious faiths.

Still another South Dakota voice came from the Rev. Richard W. Fisher, a United Methodist and the current president of the Association of Christian Churches of South Dakota:

> As we face a new century, I believe we need to do more to empower the laity in ecumenical matters. We also need to do more to place Christ at the center of our theology. I feel keenly about this after my being excluded on some occasions from the Lord's Supper for some theological and ecclesiastical reasons. We need to remember that there is more grace in the heart of God than there is sin in us. Let us seek to be responsive to the Holy Spirit, who frequently leads us to walk in paths where we did not intend to go.

Minnesota Voices

There was a greater variety in the voices of Minnesota. This may be because the ecumenical scene in Minnesota had developed in many different ways and in some respects was more complex. In any case, the voice of the Rev. Sally Hill, Presbyterian and former long-time director of the Tri-Council Metropolitan Church Commission of St. Paul–Minneapolis, was noteworthy:

> In facing that future we must be aware of the failure of most mainstream denominations to grow; the evangelical boom; the development of megachurches; the hot growing interest in spirituality; the severe stresses (some call them "wars") within denominations on the ordination of homosexuals and biblical interpretations, which could cause denominational splits and the formation of even more denominations. This does not bode well for traditional ecumenical organizations. But social issues will not go away, and it will still take ecumenical coalitions to provide help and advocacy. This means that in view of the growth of the non-Christian landscape in the United States, we need to make interfaith dialogue a high priority. The nation and the Church has to better live with diversity.

An equally challenging voice for the future came from Dr. Margaret J. Thomas, Synod Executive of the Synod of Lands and Prairies of the Presbyterian Church (USA). She said:

> Ecumenical entities will need to be more focused and more efficient in our efforts. The denominations and member congregations are demanding a higher standard of accountability, so that scarce resources can be deployed where they will advance the missional needs of the participants.
>
> We are also faced with a greater degree of theological and ecumenical illiteracy. This will call for clearer expressions of why we do what we do.
>
> All of us also face the challenge of increasing the size of the table so that people of all faith traditions can be in conversation with one another—without losing the distinctiveness we each bring to the table.
>
> We are encouraged by the increased degree of cooperation and participation of Roman Catholics, Eastern Orthodox, and Conservative Evangelicals, which has taken place in the past 30 years. Is this a hoped-for possibility with the Christian Fundamentalists?

An even more challenging note came from the Rev. Willis J. Merriman, a United Church of Christ pastor, who, in earlier years, served ecumenically in Minnesota, Wisconsin, and Pennsylvania:

> The ecumenical movement is, in my opinion, no longer a movement. It has few lay people involved, is primarily concerned about survival, and has become politically correct. It is in its period of denominational captivity. I am still a student of ecumenism, but I am convinced that present ecumenical organizations are not the spiritual inheritors of the movement that earlier gripped my soul, heart, and mind. If ecumenism is to survive the next century, it must once again regain its birthright.

As we look to the future, let us be reminded of these lines in my book, *Ecumenism 101*: "As long as there are living Christians, there will be an ecumenical movement."[10] Our responsibility is to receive this Christ-given gift and to help shape its course for greater mutual cooperation and visible unity.

Notes

1. Sydney E. Ahlstrom, *A Religious History of the American People* (New Haven: Yale University Press, 1973), pp. 455–471.

2. Jeanne Richardson, *The Association of Christian Churches of South Dakota: The First 25 Years, Sioux Falls, SD* (n.p., 1971–1996), pp. 1, 132.

3. Alton M. Motter, *Ecumenism 101: A Handbook about the Ecumenical Movement* (Cincinnati: Forward Movement, 1997), pp. 12, 53.

4. Walter M. Abbott, S.J., editor, *The Documents of Vatican II* (New York: Guild Press, 1966), pp. 346–355.

5. Winthrop S. Hudson, *Religion in America* (New York: Charles Scribner's Sons, 1965), pp. 237, 260.

6. Most of the quotes that follow in the text below are drawn from the audio and written interviews done by the author. These materials are deposited in the project archives at the Library of the Christian Theological Seminary, 100 West 42nd Street, Indianapolis, IN 46208.

7. Arland D. Jacobson, Judith P. Kerr, et al., "Ecumenical Shared Ministry and the United Methodist Church" (Moorhead: CHARIS Ecumenical Center, Concordia College, Moorhead, MN 56562, 1995), 67 pages.

8. Hayden L. Stright, *Together: The Story of Church Cooperation in Minnesota* (Minneapolis: T. S. Denison, 1971), pp. 210–214, 265–270.

9. Editorial, "Minnesota Panorama," in *Minnesota Messenger*, news publication of the Minnesota Council of Churches, spring 1973.

10. Motter, *Ecumenism 101.*

17

THE SELF-DISCOVERY OF TEXAS ECUMENISM AS A COUNTERCULTURAL MOVEMENT

David Bos

"We didn't have to be radical to be radical." These words of an Episcopal priest as he looked back upon several decades of ecumenical and interfaith involvement in Houston epitomize those involved in local ecumenism in Texas in the second half of the twentieth century—from people like nonagenarian Harold Kilpatrick, the layperson who founded the Texas Conference of Churches as the first statewide ecumenical body in the United States to include all the Catholic dioceses within its boundaries, to the young David Davis, associate director of the Austin Metropolitan Ministries (and former director of the Hill County Community Ministries), who speaks of a movement away from denominational authority, going with technology and embracing chaos and organizational reinvention as an ongoing thing. "Radical" may be too strong a word when viewed against the backdrop of the entire United States; yet, ecumenists in Texas bore the stamp of "radical" courageously and modestly. They became a cultural, political, and religious avant-garde in Texas. Their story is one of finding themselves again and again in the midst of "dangerous business" (as Clifton Kirkpatrick, former director of Houston Metropolitan Ministries and now Stated Clerk of the Presbyterian Church, USA, referred to it), as they engaged in struggle after struggle in the cause of social justice, following the mandates of their faith and their conscience and doing so in an ecumenical and interfaith way.

Frank Dietz, who was the executive director of the Texas Council of Churches in the middle of our period of study, speaks of a "radical Christology" that describes the experience of Christ as "barrier breaking rather than fence building." Such a concept of Christ became useful, then, in interfaith as well as in ecumenical relationships. This is his explanation of why Texas was in the forefront of both Catholic-Protestant and interfaith relations from 1950 on. The ecumenically minded Christian communities professed a faith in Christ that expressed itself in ways that made them a countercultural force.

These ecumenists needed each other—not only because of the need for cooperation in striving for their "barrier breaking" goals, but also because they needed the support of one another in prayer and theological reflection in a context in which prayer and theology were considered the preserves of right-wing ideologues. Thus Dietz cites the Roman Catholic bishop, Charles Grauman, who, upon arriving in Dallas from a rural diocese, feeling the social challenges of the change in scenery, introduced himself to the area by initiating one-on-one discussions with leaders of the various religious communities on the subject of prayer!

Dietz deserves our special attention because he bears the informal title of Mr. Ecumenism in a state that was already known for ecumenical activity before he arrived there. It is both instructive and illustrative—so many of Texas's interfaith and ecumenical leaders have come from outside the state—to note that he grew up in New Orleans, where just to be a member of the United Church of Christ was to define oneself as a countercultural religionist. Then, also to become involved, as he did, in the Church Federation there, was to receive the stamp of radicality. He remembers Congregational and Evangelical and Reformed youth (before the merger that was to bring them together as the United Church of Christ) discussing what it would be like to make the transition from a segregated to an integrated society. Right from the beginning and continuing into the present, Texas ecumenism took its cue from leaders such as Dietz for whom the very nature of the faith into which they were born put them into a disjunctive relationship with the surrounding culture. Thus, the Texas Conference of Churches and many other ecumenical/interfaith configurations were in the forefront of the civil rights and peace movements in a way in which most of their counterparts in other states were not.

The position of Texas ecumenism and its constitutive denominations on the periphery of religious culture suited and encouraged the participation of those who came to the state predisposed to a prophetic expression of faith. One such, Carl Siegenthaler—a pacifist and a product of Yale Divinity School, the World Student Christian Federation, the Protestant Council of New York City, and the Urban Misssion Institute (Chicago), and director of the Urban Mission Training Center in New York City—was called to lead the Austin Urban Council and to teach at the Austin Theological Seminary. Siegenthaler brought with him the values of nonviolent direct action and community action in the days before Martin Luther King Jr. and Saul

Alinsky. As such, he (and others) coming into the state from the upper Midwest and Northeast gave impetus and momentum to Texas's special brand of ecumenism and interfaith relations—even as he expanded the circle of ecumenical relationships in Austin. Under his leadership, the Austin Urban Council eventually became the Austin Metropolitan Ministries, which came to include Catholics as well as Protestants, and Jews and Muslims as well as Christians.

In Carl Siegenthaler, the Texas ecumenical movement, which from the beginning was accustomed to being somewhat subversive of the prevailing cultural norms, met the essential subversiveness of the worldwide ecumenical movement, which was born in the matrix of resistance to European fascism. Siegenthaler's ecumenism was forged in the crucible of the beginnings of the World Student Christian Movement, including attendance at the landmark meeting in Oslo in 1947 and the formation of the Student Christian Movement in the United States. Siegenthaler tells of a WSCF meeting in the tower of Riverside Church in New York City, and of listening to Hans Hoekendijk and others tell stories of the Resistance while a near hurricane-force storm raged outside. Somehow the weather seemed to fit both the momentousness of the occasion and the World War II struggle that was being described. He recalls being influenced by Visser't Hooft, the first General Secretary of the World Council of Churches, and Phillip Potter, the first General Secretary of the WSCM.

Remembering those days and subsequent involvement within radical ecumenical frameworks before coming to Texas, Siegenthaler recalled the concept of "hidden Christians," which had much currency in post–World War II days. This concept would have reinforced the countercultural nature of Texas ecumenism. It downplayed the ultra-visible popular faith of the region, emphasizing instead the notion that even those who did not publicly confess Christ might be "hidden Christians" in the sense of being allies in the project of transforming society. The essential thing was not what one said one believed but how one acted in the moment of truth—"by their fruits you shall know them."

If one seeks a reason in the pre-1950 years for why Texas ecumenists were so open to the countercultural leadership of persons such as Frank Dietz and Carl Siegenthaler, it might be found in the testimony of Harold Kilpatrick, the Texan with the longest history of ecumenical involvement there. Kilpatrick, himself a Presbyterian layperson, stresses the importance of lay training and participation in Texas ecumenism. He reports that his selection as the first executive of the San Antonio Council of Churches and then as the first executive of the Texas Council of Churches were both "mystifying experiences." As a layperson he at first felt unqualified for the positions. In both cases he later came to think that not only had he been qualified but that it was important and salutary to put laypersons in the "top jobs." He meant that lay leadership broadened the ecumenical movement's constituency and made it more relevant to the average church member. To him the breakthrough of putting laity into positions of ecumenical leadership was more important than the event of Roman Catholics coming into the movement. (Under his leadership Texas was the first state in which all the Catholic dioceses joined the state ecumenical organization—which then changed its name to the Texas *Conference* of Churches.) It was of the highest importance for him to see to the constant nurturing of the annual Faith and Order Conference, which was an ecumenical training ground for laypersons.[1]

An essential element in the subversive potential of the ecumenical movement in the second half of the century was its emphasis on the ministry of the laity and on the training of the laity to assume roles in ecumenical and interfaith mission that were at least equal to if not more significant than clerical roles. This innovation was particularly influential in places like Texas where exclusively male Protestant preachers and Catholic priests had represented the religious majorities when they interfaced with the civil order or with other faith groups. Now they found themselves dealing with lay women and men in connection with civil or ecumenical ceremony. Also, the employers and elected representatives of the newly empowered laity found them to have a faith-inspired, critical perspective on what they—the employers and elected representatives—were doing.

Thus, Texas ecumenism began to benefit from the talents of laywomen such as Ethyl Dunbar (Metropolitan Ministries of Houston), who, upon moving from Pittsburgh where she had been the first president of an ecumenical youth group, helped to activate Church Women United and eventually directed the Leadership School of the Council of Churches of Greater Houston in the 1950s. She was also an organizer of the Christian Education Directors' Institutes there. She remembers these training events as reaching a wide constituency and having, therefore, a major impact on the churches, the community, and the ecumenical movement itself. When I asked Clifton Kirkpatrick, former director of Houston Metropolitan Ministries, about the greatest impact of that organization, his answer was in the development of strong lay leadership—although he could have cited many other projects and activities, especially in the field of social ministry. The fact is, and perhaps this was the point intended, HMM could not have had the impact it did have—in countering police brutality practices, for example—if it were not for the support of lay leadership. So the lay ministry movement, which was a major emphasis of the National Council of Churches generally in the early part of the period under consideration, was a foundational influence in making Texas ecumenism a countercultural force.

James Tucker's words, "We didn't have to be radical to be radical," really carry a double meaning. First, in the general sense that was discussed above; and second, in the specific case of the civil rights movement that led, in turn, to crucial participation in the peace movement and the women's movement. First, in the sense that most of the time, the ecumenically minded people did not know how radical they were just by virtue of being ecumenical; and second, in the sense that at a certain point (in the civil rights struggle) they realized that that they were indeed, by the grace of God, "radicals."

The civil rights movement was both a culmination and a beginning for ecumenical and interfaith relations in Texas. It galvanized the people of faith as no other event has during the fifty years from 1950 to the present. According to the testimony of everyone that I heard speak on the subject in the course of some seventeen interviews, the civil rights movement was the greatest recruiter and reinforcer of ecumenical and interfaith commitments that Texas had ever seen. Tucker refers to the spirit of those times as a "marching together," both literally and figuratively. Bruce Teunnison, who directed ecumenical organizations in Philadelphia, Tulsa, Houston, and Dallas, said that cooperation in the civil rights movement was the cause of the greatest expansion of ecumenism in the period under discussion.

Ouida Botdorff-Teunnison is a case in point since she came into the ecumenical movement through her convictions and activities on behalf of the cause of civil rights as a recent college graduate in Tallahassee, Florida. Then she found that she could pursue the agenda of the women's movement within the ecumenical context. In 1972 she joined the staff of the Greater Dallas Community of Churches where she fostered the growth of neighborhood community ministry—"ecumenism at the most local level possible." While in her capacity at Greater Dallas Council of Churches (GDCC), she formed Block Partnership, a community organization formed to facilitate school desegregation. She also was a founder of the Dallas Women's Foundation. For her and countless others, Texas ecumenism provided a means to put faith into action and to let faith be informed by action in a number of causes.

But note that in Botdorff-Teunnison's case, the point of entrée was the civil rights movement and that Texas ecumenism's struggle against racism did not end with the fading of the movement. To a person, these people say that one of the most important unfinished agendas for the ecumenical movement is the elimination of racism. At GDCC, John Stace, who has held the position formerly held by Botdorff-Teunnison from 1989 until the present, inaugurated a Dismantling Racism Program through which an attempt is being made to understand and combat racism in its most recent manifestations. When asked what he most values in his experience of ecumenism in Texas, Stace says that it is "a deeper understanding of the Gospel call to combat injustice." After speaking with a number of former and current Texas ecumenical leaders, I was not surprised at this answer. If fact I think that it serves as a kind of summing up of this story of self-discovery.

Stace's efforts and that of other younger staffers in the metropolitan and community ministry ecumenical organizations throughout Texas demonstrate that much of that countercultural energy still remains from that earlier time of marching together. Yet, there is an almost unanimous expression of disappointment at the current scene. In Stace's words, "There seems to be as much interest in responding to funders as in pushing for systemic change." And, in the dozens of ecumenical community ministries that have been started in the last thirty years, there is a trend toward service projects, as opposed to working for justice. There was a coming together, then a marching together, and now, it seems, a fading together.

Note

1. Richard Grant, former executive director of the Lancaster, Pennsylvania, Council of Churches, emphasizes the importance of the lay training projects of the NCC in providing leadership for the ecumenical movement across the country. He singled out NCC staffer Cameron Hall—his *On the Job Ethics* project and book (1963), his *Listening to Lay People* project and book (1971), and his *Lay Action: The Church's Third Force* (1974). There were other significant lay ministry training efforts in the 1960s and 1970s, such as the Metropolitan Associates of Philadelphia and the writings of its director, Richard Broholm, and of the institute on the ministry of the laity that he founded at Andover-Newton Divinity School. One thinks also of developments in lay ministry in the Catholic Church after Vatican II.

18

STATE ECUMENISM IN THE SOUTH: VIRGINIA AS A CASE STUDY

Judith Bennett

Virginia is a place where tradition is honored and friendships run deep. It is also a place where change happens slowly. Both of these forces—the valuing of tradition and friendship and the pace of change—have been played out in the ecumenical life of the Commonwealth of Virginia in the past half century, a time of impressive advances in Christian unity at the local and regional levels. The story of ecumenical life in Virginia is the story of judicatory leaders who took risks because they trusted one another. It is the story of power struggles that, for all their gentility, wounded some and liberated others and left the major players able years later to express love for one another. It is also the story of a core of foot soldiers in the trenches—laity as often as clergy—who glimpsed visions of new ways of being together and committed themselves to the hard work of making the visions happen.

While not the only form of ecumenism to be found in the Commonwealth, the Virginia Council of Churches (VCC) has clearly been a major force since its inception in 1944, at the close of World War II. As was the case in many other states, the VCC emerged from the Sunday School Movement, itself a response to a call from another century to address the religious education needs of a population regarded as spiritually illiterate. Those who gathered for the first Virginia Sunday School Convention in 1875 were the forerunners; by 1882 the Virginia Sunday School Union was organized and hired its first paid executive. While it arose to address a particular need, it contained within it an early form of interchurch cooperation that would take many forms through the decades to come. By 1891 it was reorganized as the Virginia Sunday School Association, and by 1928 it became the Virginia Council of Religious Education with, for the first time, denominational judicatory membership.

While the Council's work was devoted primarily to Sunday School work and the formation of Weekday Religious Education programs, interest was growing by the end of the 1930s in greater cooperation among denominations. By 1941 a committee of thirty-one persons had been named to draft a proposed structure, constitution, and bylaws, and by July 1944 the Virginia Council of Churches had been formed. Joining the Council were several other agencies that manifested other forms of ecumenical cooperation through ministries of service and justice: the Virginia Commission on Interracial Affairs, the Rural Church Board, and the Church Conference on Social Work.

The 1928 stated purpose of the Virginia Council of Religious Education was "fostering religious education" through those "means which the cooperating denominations may agree upon." With the adoption of its new constitution in 1945, the purpose of the Virginia Council of Churches is considerably broader: to "more fully manifest oneness in Jesus Christ as Divine Lord and Savior." The earlier concerns for racial justice and meeting needs across the Commonwealth were continued, and, with massive needs to be addressed in Europe and Asia following the close of World War II, new programs came into existence.

The work of conciliar ecumenism in the last half of the twentieth century was led by three men. It is perhaps reflective of Virginia's valuing of tradition and friendship that two of those men, Minor C. Miller and Myron S. Miller, were father and son. Minor C. Miller served from 1923 to 1958 and Myron S. Miller succeeded him, serving from 1958 to 1982 as executive, continuing until 1993 on staff. Thus, from 1923 until 1993, a Miller served on the Council's staff in one capacity or another. The third, James F. McDonald, came to the position in February 1988 as a known quantity, adept at navigating in ecumenical waters. He had served as campus minister at the University of Virginia for twenty years and emerged from the campus ministry network that had a long history of working together across denominational lines.

Twenty years after the Council's founding, Vatican II was under way and ecumenism took on new momentum. Virginia's first faith and order conference was held in 1967, and by the mid-1980s had redefined "faith and order" and restructured itself to address the churches' interest in exploring unity that moved beyond cooperation in ministries of service. At the same time, this restructuring reined in both membership and participation in the Council. Areas of work brought into the Council at its beginning, through formerly freestanding agencies, became "concern areas" whose membership must be named by judicatories and, as a byproduct, became primarily clergy—a far cry from the early Sunday School Movement, which was a largely lay-led phenomenon. Moreover, with the new focus on faith and order issues, Virginia began to experience an underlying tension between those who saw needs to be met in Christ's name and those who took seriously Christ's prayer that "all may be one."

It must be noted that while the Virginia Council of Churches embodied the broadest denominational representation within its ranks, there were other forms of ecumenism flourishing in the Commonwealth. Through the entire fifty years covered in this chapter (and before), the women of Virginia churches consistently stepped out into the ecumenical arena, whether as teachers in the Commonwealth's large weekday religious education program, as members involved in the work of the Virginia Council of Church Women or its successor, Church Women United, or as part of the effort to work across the racial divide in local communities.

Clearly the original Consultation on Church Union (COCU) had an impact on the churches and led to the formation in 1972 of the Richmond Ecumenical Parish, one of a small number of such congregations formed as a part of COCU's interim eucharistic fellowship emphasis. The experiment lasted for nine years and is warmly remembered by its former members. Another parish of an altogether different sort, Holy Apostles in Virginia Beach, one of an even smaller number of Anglican–Roman Catholic parishes, is still in existence. "A Call into Covenant," issued to their people by Lutheran, Anglican, and Roman Catholic bishops of the Commonwealth of Virginia, led to the formation of the Lutheran, Anglican, Roman Catholic consultation (LARC) in 1990. LARC has been the impetus for regular gatherings at state and local levels since the signing of the Covenant.

Other ecumenical agencies are also on the scene, chief among them Chaplain Service of the Churches of Virginia, which addresses the spiritual needs of those incarcerated in Virginia's prisons, and the Virginia Interfaith Center for Public Policy, which is the legislative advocacy representative of a number of religious bodies.

Ministries Remembered

Myron Miller grew up with ecumenism in his blood. He also grew up, he says, "not knowing where my father was—I just knew he was somewhere speaking at a Sunday School Convention or a meeting." He remembers his father saying that there were seventy county, town, or city Conventions and another forty district Conventions, and that he had spoken in most of them in the past year. The younger Miller had vowed not to follow in his father's footsteps because "my father was always traveling, money was always tight, and I thought he worked awfully hard," so he chose another path. He went to work for the Church of the Brethren, serving as the southeastern representative for their Service Commission, organizing work camps, doing peace education, and piloting the first year-round volunteer program in a Florida migrant camp. This was his first encounter with migrant farmworkers, and this experience led him to begin a degree in social work, then to attend seminary, and finally to accept a position as Minister of Education at a Presbyterian church in Charlottesville in 1956. By 1958 he was elected the Council's second executive secretary, following, after all, in his father's footsteps.

Miller's long tenure with the Council was filled with numerous programs of direct ministry, meeting the needs of migrant farmworkers and their children, disaster victims, refugees, and needy Virginians in the state's poorest southwestern counties, as well as schoolchildren, youth, and college students. There were years of Church World Service relief work, the United Clothing Appeal, and Thanksgiving Hunger Offerings, until the opening of the Virginia–North Carolina CROP office in 1973. From 1966 to 1981, when CWS trucks came to pick up clothing at centers across Virginia, they also brought clothing to Wise County, where it was distributed to four other poverty-stricken counties in southwest Virginia, serving hundreds of children.

The Council had begun a ministry of pastoral care and recreation with migrant farmworkers in 1948, serving families on the Eastern Shore, in the Winchester area, in the Shenandoah Valley, and in the Roanoke area. By 1966 recreational staff were employed, offering movies, volleyball, and craft programs. What touched Miller deeply during those years, however, was the plight of the children, even infants, deposited on the fringes of the fields while their parents worked. His concern led to the first day-care centers, which improved and expanded over the years, eventually becoming a part of the East Coast Migrant Head Start program, a network of centers providing coordinated services for young children wherever in the eastern United States their parents travel to find work. From 1956 to 1966, until Title I began in 1967, the Council ran Day Schools for children who had missed so much school they were lacking basic skills. Some camps, Miller recalls, were filled with children with nothing to do all day.

Children and youth in Virginia's churches, and the leaders who worked with them, were not forgotten. Under Miller's leadership major Christian education events were held that drew large attendances and brought nationally recognized leaders like John Westerhoff to Virginia. He launched the first Joint Meeting of Virginia Ecumenical Commissions, which brought together the denominational personnel with responsibility for Christian unity; it has continued as an annual event. He also called together the first church planning consultations, including the one that formed Richmond's Brandermill Church, a Presbyterian–United Methodist collaboration. Other efforts included cooperative ministries such as the Green Run Cooperative Ministry, Roanoke Area Ministries, and ACRE (Appalachian Christian Resources in Education) at Emory and Henry College.

The Church Disaster Response Network was formed, a program that ties church volunteers into the larger state and Red Cross disaster response team. Later this program became Virginia VOAD (Voluntary Organizations Active in Disaster). The Council's ongoing Refugee Resettlement program followed the earlier "Flight to Freedom" program that brought Cuban refugees to Virginia. Myron Miller is not a man who finds it easy to claim credit for the work accomplished during his term as executive secretary. All of it, he says, was better, stronger, more creative because "when you put a group of people together they always arrive at solutions that are better than they could have come up with individually." Being a part of it, of "the exciting, creative experience of sitting with those people around that table," is something he says he will always remember.

Race and the Churches of Virginia

There is also another side of Miller's years with the Council, a darker side that haunts him yet. It is the heritage of racism that is a part of Virginia's history. The Council, Miller holds, was interracial from its beginnings. Its predecessor organizations, the Sunday School Association and the Virginia Council on Religious Education, had involved historically black denominations in their work of Christian education, youth ministry, and leadership training programs. Indeed, black denominations were among the founding members of the Virginia Council of Churches.

But if he remembers the presence of African Americans in Council programs, he also remembers the accommodations made to white racism. One of the first events of his tenure was a major ecumenical youth conference with some three thousand young people attending. It was planned by a committee that included black denominational representatives. The conference was held in a hotel and because of local segregation practices "we couldn't house the black youth," he said' "we had to bus them to Virginia Union University, but at least we were together for meals and everything else." Consistently, he recalls, Council events sought to be interracial and were usually the only place blacks and whites could at least have meals and fellowship together. Miller always hoped for more. He was counseled by Dr. C. L. Evans, president of the Baptist Allied Bodies (predecessor of the Baptist General Convention of Virginia) and the first black elected leader in the Council. "Myron, you can do what you want to do and lose your shirt, and the Council, or you can be satisfied with doing a little bit, and maybe we can do a little more next year."

Leaders from Virginia's black churches also provided leadership in the Virginia Council of Churches: Dr. John M. Ellison, then president of Virginia Union University; the Rev. C. L. Evans, Executive for the Baptist Allied Bodies; Dr. J. Oscar Lee, Baptist pastor and professor at the School of Theology at Virginia Union University, who later left Virginia to join the staff of the Federal Council of Churches. Noted preacher Dr. Samuel DeWitt Proctor was a frequent speaker at Council events.

The Rev. Robert Taylor, known informally as the dean of Richmond's black pastors, is now approaching eighty. He has pastored Baptist churches, large and small, and for decades has worked tirelessly for justice for his people and for unity in the church. As early as the mid-1940s Taylor was actively involved in the Council. He remembers he was initially drawn to the Council when the Rev. Henry Lee Robinson was the executive secretary and the Council was involved in an effort to see the first African Americans on Richmond's police force. Eventually four African Americans were hired, "the first I had ever seen," Taylor recalls. "Of course, they had some restrictions on them about who they could arrest. They wore the same uniform as the other Richmond police, but they had to walk their beat, couldn't drive a police car." Nonetheless, he says, "from then I was involved in the Council—in my experience, this was a new thing for a white group."

In those days there was little contact between black and white clergy, and no interracial clergy organizations. Only on an individual basis did such contacts occur. A few African Americans, according to Taylor, joined the Council because they dealt with racial issues. "The VCC was a pioneer group," says Taylor, "more open than clergy groups." It was also the organization that offered ecumenical contacts, as there was little interdenominational activity among the black churches themselves. Robert Taylor has a wealth of memories that include making his way from Richmond to Baltimore under curfew in order to get to the funeral of Dr. Martin Luther King Jr., the interruption by black leaders of the Sunday morning service at downtown Richmond's Second Presbyterian Church, and "reparations time with white folks doing a lot of confessing." A high point for him was when, as coincidence would have it, both the black Baptist General Convention of Virginia and the white Southern Baptist Convention were meeting in Richmond the same week. Taylor approached both judicatory executives about having a joint service that would include Holy Communion, with a mass choir and mixed usher boards. They approved the idea and the service took place at the Robbins Center at the University of Richmond and drew "one of the largest interracial meetings in Richmond other than the Graham Crusades." Says Taylor, "People began to say, if we can meet together in the Robbins Center, why can't we do it in our churches?" Robert Taylor was honored by the Virginia Council of Churches with its 2001 Faith in Action Award. "Every chance I had to improve race relations," he said, "I tried to do it."

Myron Miller is grateful to the black leadership that worked with the Council. "Whatever we did in the area of race," Miller recalls, "we did with the black churches, and their leaders were involved in the decisions." By the time the Supreme Court ordered the desegregation of schools, the Council had a track record of offering its Institute on Race Relations, which brought Virginians together to discuss such topics as the church and race relations, education in a biracial system, race and the problem of earning a living, and citizens in a democracy. In anticipation of the Supreme Court ruling, the Council began organizing, calling on churches and pastors to prepare for it. In 1956 it adopted a resolution declaring the decision "in accord with Christian principles." An anonymous donor gave the Council one thousand dollars to begin a series of interracial clergy retreats. "It was only seed money," Miller remembers, "but money went farther then!"

When Virginia closed its schools, Miller says, "we didnt really know what to do, what we could do." There were "all kinds of meetings to try to save public schools," including a VCC Annual Meeting that passed a statement about race relations in Virginia. It was mailed out to denominational leaders but "when it came up for approval we couldn't get the denominations to approve it." A couple of denominational heads balked, so the rest said "it doesn't speak for us" and that was the end of it. Miller remembers the hours he spent traveling the state to visit pastors, both black and white, who spoke out on the issue and were ostracized or endangered because of it, in an effort to provide encouragement. One white pastor, the Rev. Paul Stagg of

First Baptist Church in Front Royal (later to become executive of the New Jersey Council of Churches), spoke out against the school closing. He told an inner circle of progressive pastors at a fellowship breakfast, "In those dark days when schools were closed, who was it who came to see me? It was the Virginia Council of Churches."

Looking back on those days, Miller says, "We didn't do many things, but it wasn't very easy to do what we did do. It seems now that it was so little. We were concerned but we couldn't do a whole lot more." At least, he says, "we kept lines of communication open and gave people the opportunity to be together, and to talk together in ways they hadn't done before."

Winds of Change

The earliest Virginia Council of Churches programs to take legislative issues into account were the Churchmen's Seminar on State Government in 1962, to be followed in 1973 by the Legislative, Information, Education and Witness Program. The Churchmen's Seminar was a program for laity that sought to educate about "issues facing Virginia and the responsibilities of Christian citizenship," according to the Council's 1966 Yearbook. The second program modestly broadened the work, but that expansion was insufficient to answer the challenges that lay ahead.

There are competing versions of what happened several years later. Some say radical leaders who wanted to move too fast staged a takeover that forced Myron Miller out of his position as executive. Others say the Council was ducking its advocacy responsibilities and dissipating its resources in a myriad of programs that accomplished little of significance. One thing that is clear from Council records and newspaper accounts is the steadily growing effort to move the Council out into the public policy arena.

The Rev. James A. Payne, a Presbyterian minister and native Virginian, joined the Council staff in mid-1977 as associate executive secretary. He had been the executive for the former Synod of Virginia and then of the newly created Synod of the Virginias (a merger of Virginia and West Virginia). Tired of years on the road and administrative tasks, with no time for the justice and peace issues he cared about, he felt called to "really do something in public policy." He had become friends with Myron Miller and found a responsive chord in his friend. On a sixteen-month sabbatical from the Synod, Payne came to Richmond in January of 1976 and, on a token stipend from the Council, the Catholic Diocese of Richmond, and the National Conference of Christians and Jews, developed a proposal for a research project on "the nature and quality of the relationship between the religious community and government." He spent the year talking with church leaders across the Commonwealth and nurturing a network of those interested in developing a cooperative legislative witness. He took the results of his research to the Council in the form of a program proposal; the Council accepted it and voted to adopt and implement it as its own program of education and active witness. He was soon offered the staff position that would enable him to implement the program.

Assessing the scene when he assumed the office, Jim Payne described "not a whole lot going on because there was little addressing of public policy, and not much examining of the theology of church-state relations (despite the Council's large in-school Weekday Religious Education program) or the corporate ethics of the churches, in contrast to what was happening around us—the civil rights movement, the Harlem riots, the death of God theologizing." Virginia, he said, was "pretty much struggling." He admired much of what Miller was doing, but the Council was "not addressing a wide spectrum of other issues." With a job description that appeared to offer an openness on the part of the Council to develop an advocacy network among Virginia's faith communities and to move into active advocacy, he began to encounter difficulties, the same difficulties that had discouraged two predecessors. He credits the Rev. George Williams who, in the late 1960s, had done "some good work but it was purely informational because the Council wasn't supposed to do any advocacy." Neither did many of the denominations, he says, "because they didn't want to upset anybody." Williams was followed by the Rev. Carl Howard, who established relationships with legislators and spent time in subcommittees helping to write legislation. This was viewed as problematic because it was neither owned by, nor accountable to, the Council.

Hopes for a new start were high, and nowhere were they higher than among the Presbyterians. The Rev. H. Davis Yeuell, who had worked as Payne's associate in the Synod of the Virginias, succeeded him as its executive. The new Synod of the Virginias was formed with "a high commitment to ecumenical and social ministries," according to Yeuell, and his new position put him on the Council's Governing Assembly and its Executive Committee. As time went by, Payne gained a fuller understanding of what he perceived to be a gap between the Council's stated intentions around legislative advocacy and how its staff time and funds were actually deployed. His "Presbyterian sense of order" led him to see things he had not seen before, and in March 1980 he presented to Miller a recommendation proposing a comprehensive study and evaluation calling for: 1) the Council to establish priorities for the development of programs and the deployment of funds and staff; 2) the Governing Assembly to initiate an assessment and evaluation of the manner in which all funds and staff were currently being deployed; and 3) the Governing Assembly to adopt the organizational goal of maximum and effective involvement by judicatory representatives in the various VCC program units.

Payne's proposal was taken to the Executive Committee a month later, where it was approved, and a special committee was formed to accomplish the study. The committee accomplished its work in three meetings held between July and October and brought their report and recommendations to the Governing Assembly in mid-October. The report indicated two areas of concern: 1) inadequate involvement of participating judicatories and issues of ownership of Council programs; and 2) lack of a comprehensive and intentional planning process that shapes expenditure of funds and deployment of staff. The Committee further recommended that "in order to address these problem areas a major consultation of judicatory heads be held to review the existing situation and to consider directions for the Council's program in the 1980s."

The Executive Committee adopted the report of the special committee and voted to ask the Spring Governing Assembly to direct the four Concern Areas (Church and Society, Direct Ministries, Educational Concerns, and Ecumenical Relations/Faith and Order) to conduct their own self-evaluation, reporting by mid-October on their conclusions in light of their assigned mission responsibilities, including a review of direct and indirect funding of each activity and of staff time involved. The evaluation was to include a recommendation on the continuation or discontinuation of each of their activities. The Executive Committee was directed to bring the results to the Fall Governing Assembly, while the Budget and Finance Committee, in consultation with the executive secretary, was to prepare and present to the Fall Assembly a proposed budget for 1982 compatible with the recommendations of the Executive Committee, together with an alternate proposed budget assuming continuation of all present programs, as well as projected budget proposals for 1983 and 1984. Other issues to be addressed were the establishment of a special committee on Interpretation and Mass Media to plan for use of the media for mission and for interpretation of Council activities, a special committee on Participation and Ownership charged with implementing a priority for broadening participation in the life and work of the Council, and an overnight retreat for heads of judicatories, officers, and Concern Area chairpersons to be scheduled in December 1981. The Executive Committee sent all to the April Governing Assembly, where it was adopted without change.

By this time, Payne believes, the process was uncomfortable for Myron Miller, who began to view it as a leadership conflict. In early October the Personnel Committee conducted the evaluation of Payne called for at the end of the third year of his four-year term, although that term had already expired on August 31 of that year. In that evaluation session, Payne indicated that his willingness to continue beyond December 31, 1981, would depend upon the progress of the evaluation process and any modifications in his job description that might result. Davis Yeuell recalls that there were clear signs that Payne's relationship with Miller had begun to deteriorate.

Meanwhile, the Concern Area on Church and Society made it clear in their self-evaluation that their desire was "to do much more," recalls Payne. They wanted "to be more inclusive, and they recommended formation of an office on governmental affairs rather than an executive secretary working under Miller." That separate office was to be open to more than those judicatories participating in the Council. Payne also recalled that Bishop Walter F. Sullivan of the Catholic Diocese of Richmond, known for his commitment to both ecumenism and social justice, had danced around the issue of diocesan membership in the Council, although he supported many of its programs. Payne believes a part of Sullivan's reluctance to bring the diocese into Council membership was tied to its reluctance to step out on public policy issues.

When the Executive Committee met on October 15, 1981, to receive the report of the Special Committee, the lines were already drawn. Layperson Charles Shenberger, assistant to the Lutheran bishop, spoke for the Concern Area on Church and Society, voicing support for greater emphasis on advocacy by establishing an Office of Public Affairs responsible to the Council. The recommendation failed, which led the Lutherans to sign on as early supporters of a completely separate organization to do the churches' advocacy work. A special meeting of the Executive Committee was set for November 23 to prepare a report on the evaluation and its mandated actions for the upcoming meeting of the Governing Assembly, now rescheduled for December 11.

At that special meeting, Davis Yeuell presented a Presbyterian proposal for establishment of two distinct programmatic emphases: 1) ecumenical relations and partnership ministries; and 2) public policy and social witness. Also recommended was redeploying staff by assigning Myron Miller to the first, Jim Payne to the second. At this point, some say, the Executive Committee waffled; it rejected the Presbyterian proposal and established another special committee to look at the Council's structure in terms of staffing and report to the Governing Assembly in spring 1982. When the Governing Assembly met in December, with Davis Yeuell as its newly elected chair, it received the report from the Executive Committee. Then another proposal came from the floor to establish the two distinct program units and staffing pattern proposed earlier by the Presbyterians. A substitute motion prevailed, directing the Executive Committee to reconsider the matter and bring a new recommendation on program and structure to the spring 1982 Governing Assembly, by a 27 to 21 vote.

At that point, Jim Payne gave up; he submitted his resignation on December 18, to be effective at the end of March 1982, followed three days later by Davis Yeuell's resignation. Presbyterians and Lutherans already had a history of doing advocacy work together; they had Catholic support and the interest of members of the Jewish community who wanted to work on an interfaith basis. In Davis Yeuell's memory "the initiatives we wanted to take were being blocked" because they lacked Miller's blessing. His decision to resign less than a month after his election as chair of the Governing Assembly, he says, "was partly my recognition that the situation between us had deteriorated to the point [where] it wouldn't be fair to Myron because of our disagreements." Drawing on his own experience as a Synod executive, he said, "I really respected the man, but I felt I couldn't give him the help an exec deserves. I knew you needed to have staff who supports you, at least most of the time." Payne recalls the December meeting as the moment when he became personally convinced that, given the prevailing dynamics of Council leadership, providing leadership in the manner he felt called to do would be impossible. With the support of Shenberger, Yeuell, Sullivan and others, he "felt the need to try going separately as an interfaith center—but it was a lonely, lonely time for me."

It didn't help the situation when Presbyterians redirected $10,000 of their funding to establishment of a new advocacy agency. It did even more damage when the religion reporter of Richmond's daily newspaper, with a bent for airing church-related conflicts, picked up the story. What had been a call for tighter controls on deploying funds in relation to established Council priorities became laden with an implicit challenge of Miller's leadership. "Nobody questioned Myron Miller's integrity," says Jim Payne; "not one of us would have considered Myron capable of malfeasance." While sizable federal funds were going into the project closest to Miller's heart, the

East Coast Migrant Head Start Program, says Yeuell: "that wasn't big on my screen, or anybody else's that I know of; it was a struggle over the public witness arena—that was what we cared about." Another factor was the reluctance of United Methodists to change the Council's structure. They were, and remain, the Council's major funder. Yeuell and the United Methodist leadership found it difficult to work together. "We just weren't on the same wave length," says Yeuell; "we were at genteel loggerheads."

Following the stormy meeting and two pre-Christmas resignations, there was no "peace on earth" in the Commonwealth of Virginia—nor for some months to come. More meetings followed, more special committees and studies, a second round of consultation efforts by the Rev. Joan Brown Campbell, then head of the National Council of Churches of Christ in the USA's Commission on Regional and Local Ecumenism (CORLE). By the time dust settled the following spring, the Council had adopted a new structure calling for three leadership positions that it could not raise the funds to fill. It settled for an eighteen-month interim general minister who was charged with the task of assessing the feasibility of three full-time staff positions and initiating a process for the continuing evaluation of Council operations. David Wilson, a U.C.C. retired military chaplain, became the interim general minister. Myron Miller continued as associate director of programming, and a Southern Baptist, the Rev. David Bailey, was hired to advise the Council in legislative matters on a part-time basis. By the following Christmas the newly formed Virginia Interfaith Center for Public Policy was in operation, with Jim Payne as its executive director, and significant judicatory support. By the mid-1980s the Rev. David Isch was selected to be the general minister. Isch brought great energy to his assignment, with visions for a highly centralized organizational structure. It is also significant that Isch was given major responsibility for public policy advocacy, an assignment that suggested that the Council and the Interfaith Center were competing advocacy agencies. Isch's tenure was brief, providing insufficient time for implementing any significant or enduring change.

Building Bridges

Much of the 1980s had been dark days for the Virginia Council of Churches, with much dissension and several failed attempts at reorganizing. By 1988 when the Rev. James F. McDonald stepped into the role of general minister, the search committee had looked, not for an administrator, but for a bridge builder. McDonald learned the first week that administrative skills were essential, but he also learned quickly that he didn't need to do all the bridge building himself. Council leadership was "ready to put the dark days behind and to work with him to move with understanding, charity and clarity into a more effective ecumenism."

The same religion reporter who covered the earlier conflict reported on McDonald's selection by suggesting that his "social activism made him an unlikely choice." On the other hand, when the Rev. Dennis Schultz, a member of the search committee, spoke the first words to him after informing him of the vote affirming him as their choice, he advised, "Concentrate on faith and order—it may well be that the lead on social justice issues can best be taken by the VICPP [Virginia Interfaith Center for Public Policy]." One of McDonald's first moves after taking office was to join with Jim Payne in establishing the center as the Council's primary advocacy voice. That step provided an important sign of healing. McDonald joined the center's board and remained actively involved in the center throughout his tenure at the Council.

As a campus minister, McDonald did have a history of involvement in social justice issues; however, it was also campus ministry that groomed him for ecumenical leadership. Brother Cosmos Rubencamp, campus ministry staff for the Catholic Diocese of Richmond, "opened the door into Catholic life for so many of us," McDonald said, "and he did it with intentionality and integrity," enabling a new dimension for the ecumenical Campus Ministry Forum. Not long on the job, he realized that there were three important elements in ecumenism: Christian unity, cooperative ministry, and social witness. "In my mind, I understood that the greatest of these at that time needed to be Christian unity," he recalls," and as I look back over my watch I find that we certainly paid attention to that but were often distracted, perhaps appropriately so, by the other two legs of that triad."

The very fact that he had a history of involvement in social justice issues, as well as the trust of those for whom social justice was not the first order of business, helped him to build alliances quickly in various camps. "I never became identified with one part of the triad to the exclusion of the others," he believes, "and I could move easily in all three." Relational by nature, McDonald says for the first several years he never closed his office door, as he set about fostering healing.

There were a number of notable accomplishments in the last twelve years of the century under McDonald's leadership. The introduction of *Bridges*, the Council's primary publication, established the Council as "something other than shared ministry with migrants and refugees. It reflected thought, not just cooperative ministry, and was designed to be a thoughtful piece for the entire state, and it described what we were about, our first order of business." Other bridge-building programs included Ecumenical Evenings, "an effort to go local with the thought process." McDonald and I, as associate general minister, traveled the roads of Virginia, meeting for conversation with local gatherings of church members from various denominations. It was a labor-intensive undertaking but, McDonald remembers, "it was one of my greatest joys to help folks appreciate both the things they shared in common and the differences that added to the big picture."

McDonald served on the board of Richmond Hill, "one of the most exciting ecumenical ventures in the Commonwealth." Richmond Hill is a unique ecumenical retreat center and resident community headed by the Rev. Benjamin Campbell, an Episcopal priest. While it is not a congregation, McDonald noted, "it is definitely a community, and has reached across theological and racial and social diversities in ways that are exemplary." He views his service there as a gift to him, where he could be a part of "some of Richmond's best work around racial issues." Most of greater Richmond's ecumenical leadership, black and white, finds its way to Richmond Hill on a regular basis.

Other programs that contributed to the task of building bridges included the annual Executives Retreat, designed not as a place to do business, "but a place to be together in a confidential and pastoral setting." McDonald describes it as "a rich experience, like a wonderful garden for nurturing trust and understanding." Judicatory executives also gathered on an ad hoc basis around Catholic Bishop Walter F. Sullivan, as he would invite them to his home for breakfast and the opportunity to join together to address a critical issue. The group was unstructured, but "a very useful vehicle for giving voice to issues of concern." The relationships built there "were very useful when an issue arose around which momentum was needed." The Council could then play a facilitating role. Sometimes that role was played out in major programs, such as Justice and Mercy: Alternatives to Incarceration, Searching for Light: A Study of the Death Penalty, Walk with the Poor, and the Jubilee celebration in May 2000. Sometimes it occurred in ways such as connecting the resourcing gifts of Dr. Stephen Colecchi, director of the Catholic Office of Justice and Peace, with the need for advocacy education in other Virginia judicatories. Within an atmosphere of trust, McDonald said, "we provided much of the needed connective tissue that linked the extensive resources present in each of the denominations."

In May 1996, the Council joined with the Catholic Diocese of Richmond to host the National Workshop on Christian Unity. This was Richmond's first experience in hosting the event, and only those who have also hosted it can fully appreciate the complexity of the task. Says McDonald, "It was a feast of trouble and nourishment for us." While listing it as a highlight of the century's last decade, "it required more energy than was humanly available." The opening service at the Cathedral of the Sacred Heart was moving, he recalls, one "not soon forgotten by ecumenical folk in Virginia and across the nation."

There were other highlights: welcoming the Catholic Diocese of Richmond and the Armenian Orthodox Church into Council membership; conversations with the Latter Day Saints, "which introduced some conflicted thoughts, to be sure, but enriched our understandings of each other, about Mormon life and what it means to be in relationship to other denominations, and mutual understanding of boundaries, the things we could not, or will not, do together." Discussions in various groupings around the Commonwealth of the World Council of Churches document "Baptism, Eucharist, and Ministry" enriched ecumenical life. A special opportunity to bridge racial barriers came in 1992 when the Council moved its offices into the newly constructed state headquarters of the Baptist General Convention of Virginia, the state's largest African American judicatory. The move sent a clear message of inclusiveness and "became a very important touchstone for our identity," according to McDonald.

Relationship was as important in the 1990s as it had ever been in Virginia. McDonald and I both take pride in the opportunity the Council provided us to work as a team, providing a model for judicatory and congregational staffs to move beyond gender-related tensions and work in collegial relationships. "The team relationship was very important," according to McDonald; "it was an opportunity for shared leadership that was well-informed and competent." Both of us brought special abilities to the mix but, perhaps more important, these brought complementary perspectives. While both of us are United Methodist, McDonald describes himself as "a product of old Virginia," and I am a transplanted Yankee, having come to Virginia in 1989 from New York. My presence on the staff accentuated the general absence of women in leadership positions in Virginia judicatories. It also ensured that issues affecting women and children stayed in the forefront of the Council's agenda through such programs as Bread and Stones, Friends of Incarcerated Women, and the Elizabeth Project, a mentoring program for pregnant teens. In collaboration with Dr. Kathleen Kenney, Associate Director of the Catholic Office for Justice and Peace, activities marking the Ecumenical Decade: Churches in Solidarity with Women were held across the state.

McDonald and I see our friendship and our ability to work as a team as connected to the very heart of ecumenism. "There is incredible diversity in the ecumenical world," according to McDonald, "and one organization, one way of staffing, one way of doing things that is acceptable to everybody is just impossible." He believes that flexibility in structures that allows people to invest their limited time and funds in what is important to them, in step with their denomination's interest and understanding, could bring new vitality to ecumenism. That is why, in a "white paper" he wrote for the Council's Long Range Planning Committee shortly before retirement, McDonald proposed consideration of a restructured Council, creating four "centers" for Christian unity, ecumenical ministries, advocacy, and resourcing. Needed above all, he is convinced, are structures that allow denominational groups to function, not in isolation, "but in cooperation with each other and in nurturing relationship with each other."

Season for Doxologies

The front page of *Bridges*, the Virginia Council of Churches' publication in the 1990s, heralds the reception of the Catholic Diocese of Richmond into membership in the Council:

> It was a day for enthusiasm and applause, for hugs and for handclasps, and for smiles—lots of smiles. Most of all, though, it was a day for doxologies, a day when "Praise God from whom all blessings flow" rang out in Richmond's Fifth Baptist Church, sung by an ecumenical chorus with all the joy that great paean of praise deserves, sung to welcome the newest member of the Virginia Council of Churches. Annual Assembly, November 9, 1990, marked the formal reception of the Catholic Diocese of Richmond into our midst.

The article notes that the celebrative moment arrived

> after a careful and deliberate process, after lengthy and thoughtful negotiation. Letters were written, phone calls made, meetings held—and there was discussion upon discussion. Real differences were never glossed over, every "what if" was given serious consideration. It was not as if the two parties—the Diocese and the Council—were strangers to one another. There has been a long history, both of cooperation on particular projects and of strong participation in the Council itself. Still, protocol must be followed, propriety must be observed.

In the end, of course, it came down to something far more personal than protocol. It came down to one Catholic bishop's commitment to ecumenicity and his trust in the Council's new general minister. Asked eleven years later what tipped the balance for him in his decision to join the Council, Bishop Walter F. Sullivan responded instantly, "Jim McDonald." McDonald had moved into the leadership of the Council in 1988, following the conflict of the early 1980s and a period of interim executive leadership.

Sullivan sees McDonald's leadership as a sign of the Council's broadening of its mission, "reaching out to others where, I think, it was previously more focused on the wishes of the judicatories." Known for his passion both for ecumenism and for justice and peace, Sullivan saw the Council previously as "afraid to take stands that were very important to me, because they had to have the consent of their membership." Referring to the conflict now nearly two decades in the past, he added, "When we found we had a hard time going through the Council we decided to bypass it and establish an interfaith group for which these issues are very important." The new organization was, of course, the Virginia Interfaith Center for Public Policy, which grew out of the conversations of a group that shared Bishop Sullivan's concerns. "There was a tremendous bond of friendship that developed," he explained, "because we met monthly to discuss the death penalty, welfare rights, the poor, open housing."

Bishop Sullivan's ecumenical vision was in evidence years earlier, in the 1960s when he was Rector of Richmond's Cathedral of the Sacred Heart and became friends with the Rev. Richard Baker, rector at neighboring St. James Episcopal Church. Together with other pastors in the area adjacent to the campus of Virginia Commonwealth University, he helped form Stuart Circle Parish, a cooperative effort by six to eight churches that launched a social service center called Grace House, held joint Lenten services, pulpit exchanges, and a number of other activities. Friendships with his colleagues matter a great deal to Bishop Sullivan. When asked why ecumenism was so important to him, when it was not a priority for other Catholic bishops, his explanation was a simple one—"my own experience in areas where the Roman Catholic population is rather low." In such cases, he continued, "you automatically are open to other groups, you have a fundamental need to be in contact with others, not like places where there are large Roman Catholic populations and are very self-satisfied." If you are a minority, he added, "you automatically interface with interfaith and ecumenical endeavors, and it's very rewarding." He speaks warmly of his long friendships with brother bishops, but also of those with Richmond's Jewish community, which led to a Holocaust memorial sculpture on the Cathedral grounds, and with the

Rev. Nicholas Dombalis, leader of the Greek Orthodox Cathedral of Saints Constantine and Helen.

The fresh air coming through windows opened by Vatican II, and his friendships with other leaders, led Bishop Sullivan to venture into partnering with Bishop David Rose of the Episcopal Diocese of Southern Virginia in founding the Church of the Holy Apostles, an Anglican–Roman Catholic parish in Virginia Beach in 1977. The church was, he says, "founded on rocking chairs overlooking the James River," as he and Bishop Rose realized they were both looking for a piece of property for a new church and concluded, "instead of being separated let's do it together—and be together in everything we could." Co-pastored by both a Catholic and an Episcopalian, that being "together in everything they could" led to the development of a Sunday liturgy that keeps the Eucharist at the center of their life. The congregations participate together through the "pre-service" part of the service, moving to different altars to continue the rites of their own traditions. While parishioners own that there is a bittersweet quality to this together-but-apart liturgy, as the only instance in this country where the two groups can worship together on a weekly basis, Holy Apostles provides a haven for interchurch families.

Bishop Sullivan also lists several Lutheran bishops among his friends, which led him to become a supporter of Virginia's LARC (Lutheran, Anglican, Roman Catholic) initiative. "It started with a conference including people from the three churches at our retreat house in Hampton," he said. A Lutheran theologian was the keynote speaker and "the experience was so good we decided we needed more." After several years and several more conferences, they developed their own covenant, which was signed on All Saints Day 1990 by two Lutheran bishops, five Episcopal bishops, and three Catholic bishops. The Covenant contains a list of twenty actions the judicatories agree to do, the twentieth being "to celebrate the renewal of this Covenant annually at the statewide LARC Conference," an event looked forward to by the many laypersons who attend each year, staying in each other's homes and forming friendships that deepen through the years.

Bishop Sullivan points with pride to the development of the Diocesan Ecumenical Commission, even as similar groups were flowering in other denominations. These commissions eventually began to gather annually in conjunction with the Council's annual Faith and Order Conference. Remembering some of those joint meetings, Bishop Sullivan spoke of the close ties that were formed: "How little at first we knew of one another, but then the deep spirituality in others dawned on us."

Standing beside Bishop Sullivan in some of his greatest ecumenical triumphs was Brother Philip Dougherty, an Xavierian brother from Baltimore. Brother Phil, as he was known to the many of all denominations who loved him, shared Sullivan's twin passions for ecumenism and social justice. Brought to Richmond in 1976 to found its Ministry Formation Program, a program for laity of the Diocese, Brother Phil became theological advisor to the bishop in 1984, at the age of sixty-eight. His love for reading was legendary, as was his theological acumen, his championing of the leadership of women in the church, and his conviction that God was calling Christians to new ways of being church. When Brother Phil died at the age of eighty-two, Bishop Sullivan wrote in the *Catholic Virginian*, "We looked up to Phil not because he was the elder in our midst but because he was younger at heart than most of us."

Christian Unity in the Trenches

Phebe Hoff, an Episcopal laywoman, has been witness to, and participant in, extraordinary movement toward Christian unity in Virginia, indeed in the nation, for more than half a century. A British immigrant who still retains the citizenship of her birth, Hoff is now ninety-one years old—but younger at heart than most of us. On January 25, 2001, she was awarded the Christian Unity Award on a unanimous vote by the Vestry Council of the Church of the Holy Apostles. She has won numerous awards through the years, but surely none meant more to her than this one. In presenting the award for her lifelong witness to the cause of Christian unity, the church's Episcopal co-pastor noted that the letters "St." were missing from the award's inscription, since he was certain that she was one of the "Saints of God."

Active in Church Women United, beginning with its predecessor United Church Women, Hoff moved through the ranks, providing local and state leadership and eventually moving beyond the women's organization (though never leaving it behind) into the larger ecumenical arena. She remembers well that black and white churchwomen in Virginia moved out ahead of the churches in coming together and working together. There were, for instance, the CWU-sponsored Leadership Schools for many years, "geared to building the leadership skills of black women, but not limited to them by any means, because a lot of us went and enjoyed it." The Monday to Friday schools offered many courses but, more important, "we developed relationships by staying together, eating together, so it had a positive and lasting impact."

Later, other relationships began to be formed as the Consultation on Church Union began to take shape and, in the wake of Vatican II, as Roman Catholics reached out to other Christians. It was an exciting time, recalls Hoff, because all the churches were stimulated by what was going on at Vatican II, which had a tremendous impact on the whole ecumenical scene. Together with her husband, Dr. Ebby Hoff, M.D., she was one of the founding members of the Ecumenical Commission of the Episcopal Diocese of Virginia and early on she was appointed as the Diocesan representative to the newly formed Ecumenical Commission of the Catholic Diocese of Richmond, prior even to Bishop Sullivan's appointment to the episcopacy.

Already a friend of the Rev. Paul A. Crowe Jr., an early COCU executive, Hoff found herself called into participation in that movement at local, state, and national levels. "That was the period when everything was boiling up in COCU," she remembers. "We had the Theology Committee, Generating Communities, and Interim Eucharistic Fellowships, where we were trying out stuff all around the country, to see what would happen if we had a uniting church." There were, she says, "clusters of churches working together and trying to do all the things we could do together, and the eucharistic fellowships where we shared the Eucharist and studied together." The one in Richmond was one of the most active in the country and lasted for seventeen years, longer than most. The Richmond IEF planning committee had all the COCU partners represented, both black and white. Meetings, which began with a potluck dinner, moved among the participating churches, originally using the liturgy of the host church but, when the COCU liturgy was developed, it was used. Once, at the invitation of Bishop Sullivan, the group met at the Cathedral of the Sacred Heart, where Sullivan officiated at the Eucharist. "Of course," says Phebe, "we couldn't share in the Eucharist so when the time came, only the Roman Catholics went up." Asked how she felt about that, she replied: "Just fine—because do you know what Walter did next? He invited the rest of us to come, and he personally gave each of us a medal, so that everybody didn't get the real thing, but we got something—and it was a symbol of where we hoped to be, and it was an exciting occasion."

COCU's impact in Virginia, Phebe Hoff believes, did not involve large numbers, but deeply impacted those who were involved. Interim Eucharistic Fellowships were one manifestation; Generating Communities were another. The Richmond Ecumenical Parish had just begun its nine-year experimental life span when invited by COCU to join with the local IEF to form a Generating Community. COCU had developed a list of nine "marks of wholeness," which characterize church unity. Together the two entitities embodied all nine marks of wholeness, and they covenanted together with COCU to maintain communications for a three-year period, "to listen to what is there being learned, to share what is being learned elsewhere, and to be an enabling and encouraging partner in our common mission."

Richmond Ecumenical Parish, while never a large group, remains a key experience in the lives of those who were a part of it. Supported financially by several judicatories (originally five, then a sixth), it also received staff time and encouragement from the Virginia Council of Churches. The Rev. Dodie Rossell, a pastoral counselor, was the parish's last pastor, overseeing its closing in June 1981. She had been a Presbyterian campus minister at East Tennessee State University and pastor of a hundred-member ecumenical house church in Johnson City, Tennessee. Rossell remembers the parish as "a rich experience," a unique blend of interactive worship and urban outreach. Essentially a house church, the parish's worship style was innovative and there was a high degree of lay involvement. Dorothy Thomason, now an elder at Richmond's Second Presbyterian Church, was a member. Finances, she recalled, "were always problematic because the promised denominational funds did not always appear, and we were expected to become self-supporting in three years." Pastors were always part-time and had to hold other jobs. Despite its problems, the parish, which had many members of the local seminary community and a number of clergy involved, pioneered intergenerational Christian education, sponsored two refugee families and two foreign students, developed Richmond's first fund for emergency fuel grants, and engaged in various other outreach ministries.

Phebe Hoff was a member of the Council's Richmond Area Church Planning Committee, which met for a period of two or three years and developed the proposal to form an ecumenical parish. The result was the Richmond Ecumenical Parish. The way Phebe Hoff sees it, ecumenism is meant to be lived, not just discussed. Her passion for Christian unity led her also to be an important participant in the LARC process. Having already begun as ARC (Anglican/Roman Catholic), participants were challenged by Vatican II and decided "we really could work together." Meanwhile, LED (Lutheran/Episcopal Dialogue) was also under way, and the Episcopalians began to realize that "we had the same people, we were all talking to each other wearing different hats, so why not bring us together." Thus, LARC was born. In the early days, Hoff recalls, the Missouri Synod Lutherans in Virginia were involved and "there was much discussion about signing the Covenant, which the executive for the East Coast area was willing to do, but was told not to do so by someone higher in the chain of command." Still, however, there are individual Missouri Lutherans that participate.

Despite her name recognition in national ecumenical circles, Phebe Hoff is no more comfortable with accolades than Myron Miller. Nonetheless, her gentle mix of theological acumen and her passion for Christian unity, combined with her ability to form first-name-basis relationships with bishops and other judicatory leaders, provided a model that encouraged and inspired other laity. How did she do it, given the perception of women's place in the church in those years? "Bishop Gibson got me involved and he supported me—and I just barreled ahead and did it." She also expresses gratitude for the Rev. Jerry Boney's encouragement—a Presbyterian theologian who taught at both Virginia Union School of Theology and Union Theological Seminary in Virginia and was deeply immersed in ecumenical affairs, including the Richmond Ecumenical Parish, and as Assistant General Secretary for Faith and Order in the NCCC/USA until cancer claimed his life in his early forties. "Jerry deserves," says Hoff, "to be remembered and honored." So, too, does her contribution to Christian unity in Virginia. For her, "ecumenism *is* the Gospel, and that means more than people doing their nice things in their nice churches."

Conclusion

This history of ecumenical life in the Commonwealth of Virginia in the last half of the twentieth century records some things and omits others. What is included is the broad stroke picture: conciliar ecumenism and other manifestations of Christian unity that were statewide and that involved several denominations and significant numbers of people. What is not included is the finer detail and narrower scope of local manifestations—the array of ministerial associations, direct service agencies, and ad hoc ecumenical or interfaith groups that bring people together for a time, around a need or an issue, and then fade away. In a state the size of Virginia, they are innumerable.

Certain underlying themes are evident in this narrative, some of which will be found in many, if not all, regions of the country. Others are especially characteristic of the Old Dominion or, perhaps, of the South in general. Two underlying themes may be omnipresent, given the precarious nature of funding for ecumenical agencies. First, when funding comes from judicatories it is dangerous to get out ahead of those judicatories and to be prophetic. Dependence breeds caution. Second, missional needs and opportunities far outstrip resources. For most of the past fifty years, the Council has struggled to respond to the cries for help, staff has been pulled in many directions, and hard decisions have been made.

The other theme, which may be peculiar to Virginia, has to do with relationships. On the surface, the impressive achievements in Christian unity appear to be the work of a relatively small number of larger-than-life personalities, but on deeper scrutiny it is clear that it was the deep and lasting friendships with one another that made things happen. That they were, with the exception of Phebe Hoff, a gentlemen's club in the characteristic Virginia mold goes without saying. For some, their individual perspectives on their style of operation have shifted dramatically in recent years. It must also be said that their accomplishments as a group are consistently toward greater unity.

If it was campus ministry that groomed some for ecumenical leadership, it was also the friendships formed there that were carried over into later work on behalf of Christian unity. It was the friendship between bishops and other judicatory leaders that led to the formation of the Church of the Holy Apostles and several other lesser-known interchurch congregations. It was friendship that produced the LARC Covenant—first the friendship between the bishops and then among the working committee that met in the home of Phebe Hoff, writing the text of the Covenant around her dining room table. It was friendships born of long hours of working on committees together, traveling the state together, that made more happen under the COCU banner than happened in many other places.

The entrance of the Catholic Diocese of Richmond strengthened the life of the Council enormously, in part because it broadened and solidified working relationships, connecting a number of networks that had operated more or less independently of one another—another way of saying friends could now work together more easily. Adding commentary on what happens when friends can work together, Jim McDonald cites the example of the opening service at the National Workshop on Christian Unity held in Richmond. The team that designed the service was assembled, of course, on the basis of gifts and skills, but also with predictable bureaucratic concerns in mind, i.e., was it inclusive in terms of race, gender, denominational affiliation, age, and geography? But, points out McDonald, that only laid the groundwork for an adequate product, not necessarily an inspired one. The final product, he believes, "was not accidental"—there was something that preceded it, a level of trust and commitment in the committee that enabled them to write with brilliance. That "something" was the relationships that already existed among team members, friendships formed by having a history of collaboration within the Council. Ecumenism, where there are "opportunities to think, rather than just do," in McDonald's words, "invites people to invest their heart and mind in reflective ways that become creative."

But if friendships run deep, how does that affect the way in which conflict is resolved? What happens when competing visions collide, as in the early 1980s when the Virginia Interfaith Center for Public Policy was born? Virginia's combination of the power of friendship with the hallowing of tradition begs the question, How does change happen? Jim Payne said it best: "The bane and the curse of the Southern way is that we're so genteel we usually never really confront issues. When we gathered around the table as Virginia gentlemen are wont to do, sometimes a bomb was dropped, but mostly we were genteel. Friendship is both a curse and a blessing. It is the mud that mires and the glue that bonds, enabling the taking of risks." While one rarely sees in Virginia ecumenism "a *kairos* moment when the flag is raised and everybody marches off together, if you don't have a rupture, eventually things move. Change may come more slowly in this tradition-loving Commonwealth, but it does come."

The power of deep friendships was articulated in words that struck a resonant chord in the hearts of many during the funeral liturgy held at the Cathedral of the Sacred Heart for Brother Phil Dougherty. Seated in the packed church was Phebe Hoff, together with a large delegation from the Council. His fellow Xavierian brother Arthur Caliman spoke of Dougherty's "gentle, but firm, kind of inclusiveness" manifested in his concern for women's issues and his strong friendships with strong women. Caliman described his last visit with Brother Phil in his hospital room:

> On the night he decided he would die, when we asked if there were any more individuals he wanted us to contact, he said he had one final message for his friend Phebe Hoff, with whom he served on the Faith and Order Commission of the Virginia Council of Churches. I can remember his words distinctly: "Tell her I look forward to greeting her and welcoming her into the unified church of Christ in heaven that she and I worked so hard to try to bring about on earth."

It is hard to imagine more eloquent testimony to the power of friendship. It is not at all hard to imagine the rejoicing on high when, one by one, those now working to bring about the church's unity on earth go to join Brother Phil in the heavenly church.

PART FIVE.
MEMOIRS OF A FIFTY-YEAR ECUMENIST

All our stories are about the lives of real people trying to live their values and dreams, day to day. These have been stories told largely from the big picture—the macrocosm. But the local ecumenical story is also the story of thousands living their ecumenical dreams by making it their lifetime vocation—stories of faithfulness, of using their capacities to lead states, cities, counties, and places across America to greater unity, justice, and caring. In the following pages the lifetime path of one faithful ecumenist is chronicled, along with the stories of larger networks that nurtured his ecumenical vision. It is only one story of the thousands that might be told, but it is the story of one person whose ecumenical career exactly spans the fifty years of this study.

Meet the Rev. Robert Grimm, ecumenist.

19

ONE ECUMENICAL JOURNEY, 1950–2000

Robert Grimm

Local and regional ecumenism in the last half of the twentieth century is indebted to hundreds of people who made ecumenical ministry their career. Each person's career has been an ecumenical journey, highlighting the events of their past years. I hope the events of one ecumenical journey, my journey over fifty years, will cast new light on many past journeys and journeys still in the making.[1]

This one ecumenical journey had many challenging highlights—the 1977 Love Canal crisis for families in the tourist and chemical industries of Niagara Falls; the 1965–1970 Syracuse racial revolution as played out in its anti-poverty agencies and the responses of the religious community; the response of a Catholic bishop in Erie, Pennsylvania, to Pope John XXIII, who opened a window, in involving his and the Protestant community. It all began when a seminary graduate, just four years out of the Navy, found himself called to a place far removed from Rochester, New York, to serve as the pastor of a community church in a South Dakota town created by army engineers who were building a Missouri River dam. I was that pastor, and the story of my ecumenical journey follows.

It began at Colgate-Rochester Divinity School (CRDS), after World War II service as a Naval officer. CRDS trained young men for pastoral ministry and paid little attention to other options. I recall only one ecumenical event during my seminary years: a trip to Philadelphia with four other seminarians for a meeting of the Inter-Seminary Movement discussing themes of the 1948 World Council Assembly. Our class graduated in 1949 and spent the early months of that year seeking pastorates. My future was uncertain, as I had rejected the option of being ordained in the Methodist church of my family and youth. A different choice arose in the person of Arthur Schade, a former German Baptist professor who was then executive secretary of the South Dakota Council of Churches. He said: "I'm looking for someone to serve a Community Church in a town still being built by Army Engineers to house workers on a large Missouri River Dam. Will you come to South Dakota and be their minister?"

South Dakota? My wife and I scarcely knew where it was, but we talked it over and took the plunge.

Thus, after graduation and ordination by Congregationalists, we set off with our two children on our first great adventure, after saying good-byes to our families in Cleveland and Evanston. The drive took us twelve hours, and we arrived at our new South Dakota home on July 1, 1949.

The Early Dakota Days

South Dakota was very different from the Great Lakes and northeastern cities in which we had grown up. It is a small population state, with rural small towns in its eastern half and even smaller towns in its Great Plains desertlike western half. Distances between towns were great and marked by unending, flat, treeless expanses. Too much of the sparse water supply flowed through, which was one reason the Army Corps of Engineers was building a series of main-stem dams on the Missouri River[2] to provide power and create a series of huge lakes extending from Montana through North Dakota and South Dakota. The Fort Randall Dam was the key southern dam in the series and promised to change the lives of these small towns and their people in the near future.

The engineers had built a complete separate town to house the 3,000 or more contract workers on this dam. This was Pickstown, named for a General Pick of World War II fame, six miles from the nearest farm community and complete with the amenities of government-style housing, schools, a hospital, a small shopping center, a community building with bowling alleys, and an army-chapel-style church with a revolving altar to accommodate Protestant, Catholic, and Jewish worship. The Protestant Church was the only one with a resident minister. Catholics and Lutherans sent in the nearby priest and a visiting pastor to serve their communities. We were the only clergy in town and remember fondly our effort to minister to all there as well as finding a welcome for all the widely divergent Protestants who would be part of our Community Church (we once counted our people and found twenty-two traditions represented). Nurses in the hospital who were staunch Catholics insisted on calling upon this resident clergyperson rather than the Catholic priest in the town six miles away when patients needed spiritual aid. Tourists would sometimes demand to see the revolving altar in action, which meant putting my shoulder to the mechanism to push it all the way around. Only one Jewish family lived in Pickstown. The Jewish altar space was never used for worship. My talented wife sometimes used the space for her first liturgical dance group, and once the Holy Family appeared in this space as part of a Christmas pageant.

The church experience was local but soon broadened out. A drive to collect grain or cash for CROP, then called the Christian Rural Overseas Program, introduced me to county farmers. CROP was begun by Mennonite and Brethren people in Indiana and was then active in a number of midwestern states. It continues today across the nation as one visible arm of Church World Service, a major unit of the National Council of Churches of Christ until the year 2000, when it became largely independent of NCCC.

Outside contacts continued and grew through association with the State Council of Churches. It was difficult to relate to fundamentalist churches. Lutherans, who were the majority of Protestants in the state, kept to themselves. Many were in rural areas settled exclusively by Lutheran families. Their pattern of isolation continued as they moved to the cities. This was all before the many Lutheran mergers, and some were as separated from one another as they were from other Christians. Despite local contact with the priest six miles distant, Catholics and Protestants just did not relate to one another in those days.

This left cooperating Protestants—American Baptists, Congregationalists, Episcopalians, Methodists, and Presbyterians—as Council of Churches members. They were the state ecumenical movement, a minority amid all the Catholics, Lutherans, Fundamentalists, and other Protestants. Our Community Church was developed with the consent of the State Council member churches, and we looked to the Council for primary relationships to the religious world beyond our community.

This relationship became more primary less than two years into the pastorate. The Council executive resigned to develop a statewide Hospital and Home Association. He had never been able to enlist more than nominal support from any of its five member denominations, and his efforts to develop visibility and program were not received kindly by some church leaders. It was time for a change, yet the Council itself, receiving but $ 1,500.00 annually from all its member groups combined, was in no position to seek or pay for new leadership. The Council asked me to give part-time temporary service, in addition to serving my church, to keep its image and programs alive.

Many relationships were already developed with South Dakota church leaders. Such contacts widened with my introduction to a world of 1950s ecumenism by ACS, the Association of Council Secretaries, at the invitation of one of its staff leaders, Jack Ketcham, who headed the National Council of Churches Office for Councils of Churches.[3] Thus, my first visit to Conference Point, Lake Geneva, Wisconsin, became a search for a possible replacement executive. None wanted to even consider such an iffy job prospect. ACS leaders seemed to have much more responsible and well-financed Council of Churches positions. That first ACS meeting, in 1950, led to a great many more. It also led to the beginning of my professional ecumenical career.

After two years of part-time service to a Council of Churches in serious question of its continuing life, a meeting was scheduled in the Black Hills in the western area of the state. All the leaders of the State Council member denominations, plus the president of the largest Lutheran group, attended this meeting called to consider the future of the State Council. Dr. J. Quinter Miller, an Associate General Secretary of the new National Council of Churches, whose portfolio was the local and regional Council movement, was invited to the meeting. Dr. Miller told of national church commitments to ecumenical cooperation, and then challenged these church executives to strengthen support of their Council and make it a full-time enterprise. Their answer was positive on condition that their present part-timer would accept the full-time position. They asked what it would cost to begin a new Council operation, and eight thousand dollars over what they had given before was agreed upon. After prayerful consideration of what it would mean to me and my family to leave pastoral ministry, the offer was accepted. We moved to Huron on July 1, 1954.

Much adjustment lay ahead. A new house-office combination had to be found, a good office manager was needed to enable the executive to be on the road and develop program and contacts. New enthusiasm, new contacts, programs, and ecumenical excitement were needed. The new NCCC Office for Councils of Churches helped us in many ways.. Many national staff came to aid us in our efforts to make church and community life in our state aware of the Council movement.

We first introduced the Revised Standard Version of the Bible in a series of community celebrations. We then set up National Christian Teaching Missions to join churches in community-wide educational and evangelistic efforts. We held many stewardship institutes across the state, with one series interrupted by a blizzard stranding us forty miles east of Rapid City.[4] We scheduled outstanding speakers for interchurch community meetings. One notable week featured Rosa Page Welch, a nationally revered speaker-singer of African American heritage. The already operating Rapid City Community Services Center, directed by a Lakota Indian couple, begun through the Indian ministry of the NCCC, received greater visibility and support through our offices.[5] Our most rewarding program developed in cooperation with national leadership was an annual UCYM (United Christian Youth Movement) camp planned by the leaders of our state youth fellowships, plus some Native American youth. Don Newby, director of the national UCYM, joined with me as staff of this unique ecumenical youth camp experience.

Visits with state church leaders helped us rebuild state ecumenism. An early visit to the city of Aberdeen, where the Council president served an Episcopal church, is well remembered.[6] We talked ecumenical theology all evening, then I received the Eucharist at his morning Lenten service, even though this brought his high-church convictions into conflict with his equally strong ecumenical convictions. Many other visits to local clergy and church leaders across the state helped the cause.

Our state ministry included work with Dakota Indian people, especially in Rapid City and through a pioneer teaching mission venture on one reservation. We made the state CROP office a part of our total outreach. We developed a church presence at the state fair and found ways of making our presence known in major cities of the state. Press and media opportunities were used wherever possible. The "Church of the Plains" became a long-running radio program in Huron, and local pastors produced cooperative programs in their communities. We pioneered public service television through a new station just built in a potato-farming area between the three larger communities of Aberdeen, Huron, and Watertown. The daily newspapers in Huron, Rapid City, and Sioux Falls granted credentials for our attendance as press at the World Council Assembly held in Evanston, Illinois, in 1954. Daily stories on this monumental event in the Christian world were filed, and most were carried in each paper.[7]

Christian education and mental health workshops were presented at least once each year. A lecture series in Huron featured Harry and Bonaro Overstreet, famous writers and speakers on mental health. Another, in cooperation with the State Mental Health Association, featured a prominent pastoral leader of the day, Dr. Roy Burkhart of First Community Church in Columbus, Ohio. We shared with others in bringing Eleanor Roosevelt to South Dakota. She addressed an audience of over fifteen hundred in Huron on behalf of the United Nations Association. We helped bring a wider world to our state.

Finally, we renewed the ministry of our churches to state government, in both its executive and legislative branches at the state capital in Pierre. A close relationship developed with the Lutheran legislative representative, as we agreed that the best road to ecumenism was in sharing a cup of coffee.[8] Together, we influenced the state mental hospital to provide resident Catholic and Lutheran chaplains and successfully urged the legislature to appropriate funds for a chapel that would make their ministry more effective.

It seems amazing, looking back, that so much ecumenical ministry took place with such small resources. Our relationships were direct and frequent despite long distances traveled by church executives. Our Council worked in spite of the small number of supporting communions. We were able to survive, even without Catholic and Lutheran support (though Lutherans were unfailingly friendly, and both became full participants many years later). We learned to care for one another ecumenically.

During those South Dakota days, this young minister turned ecumenical executive was introduced to a host of colleagues on the local, state, and national ecumenical scene. These came through meeting folk like Hayden Stright and John Wilson of the Minnesota Council of Churches and the annual gatherings of Midwest Council executives. They came through regular attendance at ACS, then always held at the Lake Geneva, Wisconsin, Conference Point Camp. They came through visits of National Council staff, or meetings at which rural church leaders and others spoke. They came in renewing a relationship with Howard Thurman, who invited me for a week of ministry with the church he was leaving, Fellowship Church of all Peoples in San Francisco.

Such contacts confirmed the ecumenical nature of this ministry. Even more, the mentoring roles of Jack Ketcham and Quinter Miller of the National Council of Churches were keys to my future. Quinter gave me opportunities to attend ecumenical leadership sessions at the Bossey World Council Institute and at Boston University with Walter Muelder and Union Seminary with Ralph Hyslop. All were regretfully turned down because of the strain it would put upon my family and work. Opportunity to spend a year of study at Union was opposed by my board chairman, who said that a year's leave of absence would only lead to separation from the South Dakota ministry. His words later proved prophetic when an invitation came to return to Erie, Pennsylvania. The prospect of a larger responsibility in a city, which would mean less travel and more time with a growing family, as well as the chance to renew a close friendship with the liberal and ecumenically minded pastor of its First Baptist Church, Roger Sharpe, his wife, Dorothy, and family whom we had known since college days was irresistible.[9] We accepted the invitation and moved to Erie in the fall of 1957.

A New and Different Community

Erie was a smaller industrial city on Lake Erie whose surrounding county of the same name contained 250,000 people—one-third of the population of the whole state of South Dakota. Hammermill Paper and General Electric were its largest plants. GE had just about completed the downsizing of its work force from a high of 20,000 to a 1957 total of about 8,000. A parsonage awaited us, made available some years before by the Erie Foundation, located near the peninsula and beaches of Lake Erie. The Council of Churches offices, and its executive minister, were downtown at the YMCA.

Like many other northeast cities, Erie's religious population was predominantly Roman Catholic. An old but vigorous and respected bishop headed the Diocese of Northwest Pennsylvania.[10] Two Jewish temples and a number of small, ethnic Orthodox parishes provided variety for the numerous Protestant churches belonging to the Council of Churches. A Sunday School Association was another interchurch group in the county. It had never become part of the Council and went its separate ways. Black churches only nominally related to the Council. Compared to South Dakota, which had very few African American people, the black church community seemed large, though their size and influence was relatively small compared to other northeast cities.

This smaller northeast urban area was different from the South Dakota we had recently left, though its church life was different only in the way it lived in community, much closer together than the vast expanses between the very small towns of a rural and ranching state. We often thought of the quip shared by the Episcopal Missionary Bishop of South Dakota[11] who reported the reaction of his key layperson to a national Episcopal Convocation, saying in amazement at the gathered crowd: "I never knew Episcopalians were so dense back East!"

The Protestant community around its Council of Churches had United Methodist and Presbyterian executive leadership and a local Episcopal bishop committed to ecumenism. About half of the area Lutheran congregations were members of the Council, as were most all Presbyterians,

United Methodists, American Baptists, Episcopalians, Reformed, and others. Many of the fifty-five member congregations were located in or near the downtown area of the city, all still comparatively strong. Most felt the Council was a useful adjunct to their ministry, giving greater visibility in the city and county and providing a way to face community issues.

The Council had a board of directors meeting monthly. Quarterly meetings of its member churches were well attended, and a list of supportive lay people could be counted on for leadership and financial support. One of its key thrusts was communication in news and broadcast media, augmented by the monthly publication of a printed newspaper called the *Erie Churchman*. This was printed at a shop owned by a committed lay supporter, and its circulation was about eight thousand per issue.[12] The Council executive was its editor-writer, and editorial policy was determined by a special board composed of prominent downtown clergy and a few others. The monthly meeting of this group proved to be an invaluable resource for the Council and its executive.

One Council program was a summer migrant ministry to Hispanic workers along the Lake Erie grape belt. Each year we would recruit a chaplain, usually Hispanic, and help him set up relationships with the grape growers and their workers in camps nearby. Annual Christian Education Institutes and workshops on important personal and social issues were part of the regular Council program, as well as special media training. Chaplains, clergy serving part-time, met as a department set up to guide their work in hospitals and institutions. The Council had a second staff person, a Baptist minister who served as associate, and two office secretaries.[13] The Erie Council of Churches had good programs and was accepted in the wider community, at a time when Councils were the ecumenical norm.

One major community problem was the relationships among Catholics and Protestants. General Electric had published a Community Evaluation report in 1957. It highlighted separation and misunderstanding between religious groups as a negative factor for community relations. This affected the GE plant's view of the community. It should also have affected religious institutions, but few knew what could be done about it. I, knowing that my predecessor had been seen as anti-Catholic in his zeal for separation of church and state, was concerned. It was clear that the Council image was negative on the issue and was regarded as a significant part of reported religious enmities in Erie. Of course, the problem was not peculiar to Erie but had began many years ago in northeast cities when Protestants established their businesses and hired Catholic immigrants as workers. How could such a deep problem be addressed? It seemed that the best way was to be open and welcoming and work at breaking down barriers, doing whatever possible to make the Council image pro-Christian rather than anti-Catholic.

So we tried to be positive by getting to know as many church and community leaders of all faiths as possible. My memories of contacts and friendships made remain warm over the years. These included the mayor and other officials, Orthodox priests who gathered for a meeting only to find that none of them knew the others, rabbis and lay leaders of both temples, social service and United Way staff and leaders, directors of Catholic and public hospitals, schools, and institutions, and Catholic priests and diocesan leaders wherever possible..

The publication of the *Erie Churchman* helped its editor open other doors. The daily newspapers, whose publisher and editors were all Catholic, invited this church editor to produce a weekly column entitled "The Church: Here, There, Everywhere."[14] The column continued until we left Erie, featuring religious news, including national and world ecumenical events and religiously oriented views on news of the day. The press seemed more open to religious news then than it has been since.

The news and opinions presented were not always received in a friendly manner. Some of our critics on the conservative side were in our churches, voicing objections to what they saw the National or World Council of Churches doing. This was also true in terms of early reactions to Martin Luther King Jr. and the civil rights movement. We secured industrialist J. Irwin Miller, then National Council of Churches president, to fly into Erie and speak to a select gathering of community leaders. His calm authority would reassure where no local voice would be heard. A top executive of Hammermill Paper Mill and head of the Episcopal cathedral vestry, was very critical of Dr. King until he read his "Letter from the Birmingham Jail" and gained a new insight into what was going on.

Perhaps the greatest benefit of our press and writing emphasis was a warm friendship developed and sustained with the editor of the Catholic diocesan weekly, Father James Caldwell. We shared much from our similar positions and sought to be sure that neither of our publications would carry material unfair to the other, while exploring our differences and agreements. His friendship was in stark contrast to the hostile tone of his predecessor and was appreciated.

All this led up to the Catholic community outreach on Memorial Day 1963. Our bishop had been to Vatican II and wanted to share the spirit of Pope John XXIII and Vatican II with his diocese and community. He remembered his episcopal motto, "That you love one another," and decided to show love to his total community, including us, the separated brethren. He sent a priest from his local Gannon College to our Council office with two requests: "The Bishop wants to hold a big banquet inviting all area Protestant clergy, along with community leaders, and hopes the Council can provide lists for mailing the invitations. Secondly, he would like you, the Council Executive, to be the main speaker." The answer to both requests was a most surprised Yes.

The big day arrived and began with a morning Mass to which many of us were invited. The newly arrived Reformed Rabbi and I sat together. We were both amazed to hear the organ peal forth with "A Mighty Fortress Is our God." During the Mass, honors were given to a Jewish Supreme Court justice and our Episcopal bishop.[15] The evening affair, held at the Gannon College gym, included over thirteen hundred invited guests. One ecumenical gesture came as the invited Protestant clergy, who did not feel it proper to drink alcoholic beverages in public, offered their glass of wine to the priest next to them. It was only one day and one community banquet, but this night was truly "different from every other night," made more special by the illness of the Pope, whose portrait overlooked the podium and was flanked by church and ecumenical banners. Eight months later, we were able to get the Catholic bishop to host the first Week of Prayer for Christian Unity, an ecumenical gathering bringing together over one thousand Catholic and Protestant folk. The diocese did not join the Council of Churches, but the day its bishop gave to Erie marked the beginning of a significant change in Catholic-Protestant relationships.

In another area, the Council was able to expand its hospital chaplain program. The opportunity came when the associate executive resigned and was replaced by the Rev. Carey Mumford. His presence and drive enabled us to begin a significant full-time ministry in one of our two major hospitals. Previous chaplains had been only part-time voluntary extras in the portfolios of some of our pastors. Carey took up residency at the Hamot Hospital emergency room for six months and made the chaplain's role needed in that setting. He began voluntarily, his salary paid by the Council, and ended up with the hospital paying for his full-time services, which included providing better access to clergy as they visited their parishioners. He went on to complete his chaplain's certification, and the program continued for many years following.

Our Council featured annual assemblies with outstanding speakers and invited guests from the community. One speaker, Dr. Edwin Dahlberg, a former National Council of Churches president, completely charmed the guest sitting next to him, our Irish Catholic newspaper publisher, with stories of Swedish immigrants. Other speakers included the Hon. Charles Taft, Mrs. Harper Sibley, and Dr. Gardner Taylor, preacher par excellence. An early annual meeting featured the director of the Detroit Council of Churches, Dr. Merrill Lenox, who told all present to "Pray and Pay for Ecumenism."

The early sixties, our final Erie years, were marked by the rise of the civil rights revolution. We did little more than write about it, and the community we were in touch with seemed to treat it as something happening elsewhere. This Council executive didn't do much either, even though I was on the boards of the Booker T. Washington Center and the Erie Human Rights Commission. Our efforts to develop meaningful relationships with the black community and its churches were too little and too late.

While participation in the wider national and ecumenical scene was limited in the years in Erie, some significant events were covered with the help of local press credentials. Not included was the March on Washington and the King "I Have a Dream" speech, due to a flu bug hitting at the wrong time. Many National Council of Churches meetings were attended, where news of involvement in southern voter registration drives and other events were shared. Bob Spike, who had been a college classmate, was the key relationship person from the national church to the civil rights groups. Andrew Young was leaving the National Council UCYM to become a lieutenant to Dr. King. An Erie product, Robert Pierce, was involved with both the National Council Youth Movement and the civil rights revolution. Bob presided over the planned demise of UCYM in the 1960s, due to the collapse of national denominational youth groups. He later went on to a significant local ecumenical career in Schenectady, New York, and Long Island. The final president of the Erie Council of Churches during my tenure was a fine young attorney named Robert Kilgore, who also became the general counsel for the Hammermill Paper Company. Hammermill may be remembered as the firm that opened a new plant in the city of Selma, Alabama, just as critical events in the career of Dr. Martin Luther King Jr. and the Southern Christian Leadership Council were beginning to happen.

The Hammermill-Selma coincidence happened just before we left Erie on March 1, 1965, and the SCLC March over the bridge occurred within three weeks after moving to Syracuse, New York. It was a reminder that new challenges awaited our move to a new city and region.

Introduction to New York State and Syracuse

What awaited us in Syracuse? A metropolitan area twice as large as Erie, highlighted by a university and multi-hospital complex. Southeast of the city were many glacial hills called Drumlins near the suburb of Dewitt, where we were to find our home. There seemed to be a greater diversity of people, enhanced by Syracuse University and the hospital complex, which was located southeast of the city center. The society seemed more sophisticated, with its bankers and business movers, students and professors, clergy chaplains and radicals trying to relate to one another while conscious of what seemed to be a much more conservative society and religious community.

My role was executive director of the Syracuse Area Council of Churches. It shared offices with the New York State Council of Churches, larger and more significant in most views than its local counterpart. Their priority was to complete the fund-raising and break ground for an Interchurch Center to be opened two or three years hence. Our Council had to decide whether it would move its offices to that new building and share space with the State Council and a number of denominational offices. The decision was not difficult given the visibility and influence of the State Council and its leaders, Ken Roadarmel and Ted Conklin.[16]

The local Council did have quite a bit going for it. Its staff included a Social Services director and a highly competent chaplain to Family Court and the Detention Home for Youth; two Christian Education persons, one of whom ran a very successful summer Day Camp owned by the Council; a part-time Public Relations person whose main role was to publicize a long-standing noonday Civic Lenten series; and three full-time secretaries.[17] There was also an Urban Ministry department, seeking to be part of the Urban Ministry response in the churches to the civil rights scene of the day.

They would later become a key part of how our Council sought to help the churches respond, though in 1965 there were some on the Council board who were not at all sure the Council should be in Urban Ministry. Later on in 1965, Urban Ministry found resources to engage a full-time staff person and affirmed its independence of but continuing relationship to the Council. Area church and denominational support for the Council was fairly good, though some questioned why both a local and a state Council of Churches were needed..

In March 1965, two radical professors associated with the local chapter of the Congress of Racial Equality (CORE) expressed the turmoil of the sixties. Their radicalism expressed itself with humor, as they renamed the Syracuse daily newspapers "The Sub Standard" and "The Sterile Journal." Later they led a protest against discrimination and chained themselves to a gate in front of the downtown utility company. Another but unrelated incident of the month was the takeoff of a chartered plane crowded with clergy on their way to join the King forces crossing the Bridge in Selma, Alabama. There was no way of getting a seat on that plane. This newcomer could only see its passengers off.

These incidents and others illustrated the gathering storm of the civil rights revolution with Vietnam in the background. Racism, poverty, and an unjust war were the issues. Some great people were trying to deal with these issues, in society and through their churches. One was Charles Willie, a sociology professor who was a respected Episcopal churchman nationally. He belonged locally to Grace Church, the only integrated Episcopal church in Syracuse. Its rector, Walter Welsh, was a determined presence in most of the protest marches of the day. Both Willie and Welsh were leading figures in Council efforts to be relevant. Still another was Ruth Colvin, a laywoman who founded a great program known as Literacy Volunteers. These are but three of the many, in and out of the Church, who tried to recognize and deal with the problems of a society coming to grips with its racism, class divisions, and violence.

A number of factors complicated the Syracuse efforts to deal with racism and poverty. One was that Syracuse University, through a vice-chancellor, had obtained a special grant from OEO (Federal Office of Economic Opportunity) to work at community organization. This grant came before the appointed anti-poverty group had received its OEO funds, and one community reaction was shocked anger. In response, an old-style editorial writer produced some vitriolic opinions on the dangers of this development. But the Alinsky program went forward, headed by trained organizers who taught students how to do community organization. Saul Alinsky came to town once a month only, receiving a lot more bad publicity than his infrequent visits should have warranted. The Episcopal diocese ignored the alarmists and gave a ten thousand dollar grant to the university program, signifying that it supported this kind of effort.

Meanwhile, the Council of Churches was trying to decide what to do about its Urban Ministry. Many on its board were hesitant to have the Council involved in such a controversial issue. But a motion was passed committing the Council board to its possibly controversial department as an independent unit of the Council. Urban Ministry found and hired a staff member who began to develop relationships and program in the midst of this turmoil. He found support in his role from the Council and others doing Urban Ministry, including Catholics, in and beyond the department.

Another effort to combat racism and poverty came from an interfaith leadership group formed in response to Matthew Ahmanns national Interfaith Commission on Religion and Race. About eight people met regularly in search of an appropriate cause. They included an older priest to the poor, a lay worker for Catholic Charities, a younger priest who shared with the Council Urban Ministry, a Reformed rabbi, an Orthodox Church in America priest, an Episcopal layman, and the Council executive.[18] This group finally found a worthy project and purchased fifty older homes through a large loan from the State Housing Administration (unit of FHA). It rehabilitated the properties and rented them out to poor families. Efforts to add a training component for minority workers did not work. In spite of valiant efforts and the investment of some personal funds, the project went bankrupt in a little over eight years. This was the first organized interracial and interreligious effort in Syracuse area ecumenism, whose name became the Syracuse Area Improvement Corporation after it got into housing.

Back to the antipoverty movement. While the University effort was quietly training organizers, one with this kind of training became director of the OEO effort. He was James Tillman, a man who felt that power to the people was the only way to run an OEO antipoverty agency. He led the agency, which called itself the Crusade for Opportunity, to be independent of its community board and even of its state and regional OEO offices. Finally, in spring 1967, the regional office put a stop to this independence and determined to select a trustee who could control the movement by withholding funds until things could be straightened out. I was asked to be that trustee and refused on the grounds that there ought to be at least three trustees headed by a respected person from the African American community. The latter happened, and the Council survived a three-month leave of absence and then seven more years of trying, with the two other trustees, to straighten things out.[19] During those years, OEO changed its definition of "maximum feasible participation" from a majority of poor people to a one-third, one-third, one-third definition. The Power to the People organization that Tillman had fostered (he resigned as the trustees took over) was superseded by another board conforming to the new OEO guidelines. Withheld money was restored, and a new antipoverty group that called itself PEACE, Inc., instead of the old name, Crusade for Opportunity, took over after the years of trustee control. PEACE continues as the antipoverty organization in the Syracuse area.

During the OEO crisis an independent community organization was formed out of efforts of some of the university program trainees and other advocates, including our Urban Ministry. Seeking to bring together a number of neighborhood organizations, one of which had been nurtured by the Council Urban Ministry, it called itself O of Os, or the Organization of Organizations. Finally, in 1969, it got its act together and held a Congress to help establish it as a community advocacy presence with power. One way to power, the organizers thought, was to discard the old O of O name for one called POWER, People Organized to Win Equal Rights. The Congress actually voted in the new name, but then a minister in the group gave a long speech or filibuster, and moved to rescind the previous motion. The motion passed, POWER went back to O of O, and the organization, despite some valiant efforts, faded away after a few more years.

During these turbulent times, other Council of Churches programming went on. The Family Court and Detention Home Youth Chaplain continued his effective service. Its Social Services program lost support, and its director resigned. Later, both staff positions changed with some loss in effectiveness. Christian Education programs received fewer and fewer calls for the services of its director. The Day Camp continued effectively for many years, as it survived the retirement of its staff director and found a capable replacement. But the Civic Lenten series, which once had seen noonday worshipers numbering over one thousand per day three days per week, began its precipitate decline in 1966. Despite many efforts to use the talents of the visiting preachers, participation dwindled until 1970, when the series was stopped. A luncheon tribute to Ralph Sockman, the most popular "Prince of the Pulpit" of this long series, was its swan song. This was a good traditional Council for its day, but one fast losing its power to influence community or keep the local church and lay support necessary for its existence.

Many felt that the Council must change to become more inclusive, especially of the Catholic and Jewish communities, with Urban Ministry as its major activity. Such goals were expressed often in the late 1960s. Finally, in 1970, a select group was gathered for intensive planning sessions. Included were some key people from the Council board, the chancellor of the Catholic diocese, Protestant church leadership, Rabbinical Association and Jewish Federation representatives, and black church leaders. Two process-oriented people from Syracuse University led the session.[20] A new group to be called the Metropolitan Church Board (MCB) was proposed to replace the Council of Churches. Key judicatory leaders, including the Catholic bishop, approved, and the proposal was voted by the Council board, presented to its assembly, and unanimously adopted. This new form of ecumenism began in early 1971. Staff additions included a fine Catholic priest[21] who had more training in urban life than any other in the diocese. Major financial commitments came from the Catholic diocese, Protestant judicatory bodies, and the Jewish community. We began our new life full of hope.

However, in a few short years, hope began to turn sour. Some local churches cut back their support, leaving it to their denominational judicatories, and two judicatories cut back on the strong support given when they had entered MCB. A series of staff changes was another indicator that all was not well. Another factor, perhaps the one underlying all the above, was shared later by Harold Garman. Hal, who got his urban ecumenical education under Walter Muelder at Boston School of Theology, had come to Syracuse in 1967 to be the United Methodist urban minister. He soon found a waning interest in this priority in the churches and developed responses outside the life of the church. One was Priority One, a metro citizens group that enlisted community-oriented people to deal with racism and related issues. Looking back, Garman felt, people had changed from 1969 to 1971. Both society and churches turned inward and were no longer interested in the problems of other people. Suburban people lost interest in the poor and the city itself. Priority One and related forums fought a valiant battle against indifference to city problems. Urban Ministry, however defined, lost a great deal through this attitude change. And looking back, MCB may have begun as a lost cause because the issues it was trying to address were not being responded to by the churches at the time of its beginning. Or it may have been superseded by a new agency because its executive was unequal to the task of adjusting to yet another change.

By 1975, a new Committee was at work to create another new ecumenical agency. It came up with a slightly different plan, creating two new agencies to replace MCB. One would be Protestant Community Ministries to deal with distinctively Protestant concerns; the other would be an Interreligious Council to deal with interfaith matters. The new creations were ratified in the spring of 1976, and I felt it best to resign and make way for new leadership. The two newly created agencies struggled for two years until Dorothy Rose came on the scene,[22] made the two again one, and helped build what became one of the truly strong Interreligious Councils in the nation.

During all of the latter years of my sojourn in Syracuse, from 1970 to 1976, interest in national ecumenism was renewed. A six-year term on the NCCC governing board began in 1970, along with service on the Commission for Regional and Local Ecumenism (CORLE). During this time, a strong friendship developed with Richard Norman Hughes, an ecumenical colleague in Rochester, a city that had gone through a much more extensive civil rights and community organizing struggle than had Syracuse. Dick and I attended together the Detroit NCCC Assembly in 1969. It endured a massive number of protest groups and challenged the racism within the church. We shared governing board meetings from 1970 to 1976, he with the Presbyterian delegation, I with the United Church of Christ delegation. We shared concern for Israel and its treatment within NCCC and member denominations, prompted by Rabbi James Rudin, an observer to the NCCC board from the American Jewish Committee. We both went separately to Israel during that period. My wife and I also joined a study tour of church life in Amsterdam, Netherlands, organized by local United Methodist pastors and professors.

What about the state of local ecumenism in Syracuse from 1965 to 1976? First, a traditional older-style Council lost its way and tried Urban Ministry as its new priority. Second, Urban Ministry was rejected by the innate conservatism of the church community, or left to be done by specific denominations. This also happened to other programs, such as campus ministry. Third, the attempt to place primary responsibility for ecumenical life in the hands of denominational judicatory leaders lost some local church and lay support. Fourth, continued Catholic and Jewish participation assured that an interreligious style would be its ecumenical future. The Syracuse leg of the journey over, the Grimm family . . .

"Shuffled off to Buffalo" and Western New York

The Buffalo area religious community had begun its most recent series of ecumenical crises in 1972. Carl Burke, a long-time Baptist pastor and county jail chaplain who had become Council executive in the mid-1960s, resigned his Council position to return to parish life. A search committee began work but suspended its search to await the results of an intensive study of interchurch life to be financed through a grant from the Margaret L. Wendt Foundation. A key trustee of Wendt was the Rev. Dr. Ralph Loew, the long-time pastor of Holy Trinity Lutheran Church and a past Council of Churches leader.

Alton Motter, recently retired from the Minnesota Council of Churches, led the study. Motter spent over a year doing interviews with church and community leaders and produced a 75-page report. It found the Buffalo area religious community ready to come together in a more inclusive way to respond to quality-of-life issues such as racism and its social and economic consequences. The report recommended the formation of a new organization with an inclusive membership of religious groups, and suggested that the Council of Churches needed to evaluate its future in light of the new reality. Area judicatory leaders, including Catholic diocese representatives, formed Buffalo Area Metropolitan Ministries (BAMM) in 1975 and called Max Glenn to be their first executive. Max arrived in April 1976, just after a federal court judge had ordered the Buffalo public school system to begin immediately to desegregate its public schools. Response to that order became the first order of business for Max Glenn and BAMM.

The Council board and supporters also responded to the Motter report by affirming its continued role in the religious community and by initiating a process of study of its programs. It also renewed its search for a new executive director and found me in search of a new position. The call was accepted, and my work in Buffalo began in September 1976. Council offices were in a magnificent Delaware Avenue mansion (a 1941 gift to the Council from a prominent Buffalo family) shared by area offices for three Protestant denominations. Within this headquarters on Delaware Avenue, there was a Council in need of restored mission and confidence. This was true of its staff, of its programs, and among the local churches, its primary supporters. One characteristic of this Council was its memory of the programs, including Church Planning, Campus Ministries, Christian Education, Social Services, which had begun under its auspices and had died out or gone their independent way. Board and committee heads had to evaluate what remained, remembering or imagining what had once been.

Still-viable programs included a strong Radio-TV Department with a number of well-produced public service offerings on local media; a pioneering Food Pantry with an interest in expanding service to people caught in welfare problems; an active Church Women United unit; a Literacy Volunteers chapter that was later to go out on its own; a Church Supply Agency; chaplains services in local hospitals and institutions; and management of the headquarters building, along with an apartment complex that the Council owned. The Council published "An Ecumenical Wind in Buffalo," written by former Council executive Harlan Frost in 1977. A staff of seven, who needed leadership to affirm and give direction to their efforts, handled these activities. Added to this was the need to visit the many related ministerial and neighborhood community groups, take part in the BAMM Board and Religious Leaders Forum activity, and interpret our ecumenism to the wider area community. There was a lot for this new arrival to do.

Program evaluations soon gave way to community issues and needs. School integration was dealt with primarily by BAMM. Pastors guarding against possible outbreaks of hostility stood guard at school entries and on buses. A weekly conference of community religious and civil rights leaders took place in a city hall room. Nothing serious happened, but the religious community was present to help relieve tensions. BAMM, through Max Glenn, had received funding for a school desegregation monitoring group called the Coalition for Quality Education (C4QE). Participation in this effort was a most important plus for BAMM and the whole religious community.

Then in 1977, after one of the biggest blizzards in Buffalo area history, another more insidious kind of natural disaster came to our attention in the neighboring city of Niagara Falls. In a place known as Love Canal, on that city's eastern edge, chemicals had been dumped over thirty years before. The chemicals had been covered over. A city school surrounded by moderate-income houses had been built at its center. Toxic chemicals had been seeping into basements. Cancer, other diseases, and babies born with birth defects were being noted in alarming rates. There were many suffering families. The first government action closed the school and razed homes in an area three blocks wide and six blocks long. A high chain fence was placed around the area. Those whose houses were inside the area were relocated, but chemicals borne by underground swales continued to seep into homes outside the fence. Neighbors began to petition, but were given reports of false assurance and denial by government and other authorities. Leaders among them formed the Love Canal Homeowners Association. One of these, a young housewife named Lois Gibbs, stuck with the problem and heads to this day a national movement called Center for Health, Environment, and Justice (CHEC) based in Falls Church, Virginia.

Religious response to this emergency began in 1977. One homeowner spoke at our Council Annual Meeting, and in a later response our board affirmed its desire to help. The Presbyterian pastor from nearby Lewiston and two of his lay members were busy organizing a local church coalition in Niagara Falls. It held its first organizing meetings at a United Methodist Church, located just outside the fence. It would later be closed. Area judicatory heads were enlisted to communicate with their national mission and relief arms to pry loose some disaster relief funding. There were no precedents to provide this kind of disaster relief, but funds were produced. Church World Service was a coordinating aid and went beyond funding to provide the coalition, the Ecumenical Task Force, with a director in the person of Catholic Sister Marjeen Hoffman.[23]

Before Sister Marjeen took over, a number of volunteers came forward to provide support for families living temporarily in motels, or counseling with early family health and other crises. Later, our director and two dedicated women from the affected Love Canal area took over this comprehensive pastoral role.

From the beginning there seemed to be a crisis per week, either in seeking to answer false public relations from official emergency control sources, or in supporting scientific and health studies that would prove the case for better remedial action, or in putting pressure upon legislators to get government to do what it needed to do, or to enter a court case as amicus curiae dealing with the claims of dispossessed homeowners, or of health emergencies. It must be said that government was a very hesitant respondent to this emergency and that its efforts seemed more directed toward fixing blame than helping hurting people and making sure the environmental disaster would be removed at Love Canal and prevented from ever happening again, here or elsewhere. The Love Canal area was finally covered over and a Superfund established to deal with future toxic waste problems. The city of Niagara Falls seemed mainly concerned with rebuilding to restore its tax base in the area, and so the sore remains not completely healed.

At first, local churches with members in chemical industry executive positions were hesitant to have anything to do with the crisis. But some did come forward during the life of the Ecumenical Task Force, especially two Lutheran pastors. Before their time, the task force met weekly at an early hour, first in a Catholic school near Love Canal and then in a Catholic parish rectory downtown. Well remembered are those who began at the outset and stayed to provide both aid for the hurting and advocacy. Two who began Love Canal advocacy have continued advocacy in other causes during all my Buffalo area years. They are Roger Cook, now the director of the Western New York Council on Occupational Safety and Health, and Sister Joan Malone, who early on stood up to Armand Hammer at a meeting of Occidental Chemical Company in her role with Love Canal and the Interfaith Center for Corporate Responsibility.

Love Canal was very important in the life of the Council of Churches. Its integral programs went on fruitfully during these years. Church Women United provided leadership for many Council activities as well as sustaining its series of Celebrations: World Day of Prayer, May Fellowship Day, World Community Day, and its annual Advent celebration. Others included a continuing series of workshops for church leaders on various subjects; participation in clothing and Church World Service drives; daily attention to its Food Shelf clients; weekly attention to producing its regular public service radio and television programs, which numbered thirteen in all; and the inauguration of an Appreciation Dinner inviting churches to honor one of their members for ecumenical service. This dinner became an annual event attended by an average of six hundred people and continues today as the only large event attracting an equal number of black and white church participants.

BAMM did important social action under Max Glenn's leadership. Its response to the school desegregation crisis was outstanding. It helped make ecumenism a player in the local search for economic and social justice on a broader base than had been possible with the Council. After three years, Max developed a proposal for area economic development through cooperation of the BAMM religious bodies with university development groups. The proposal did not bring the desired response from religious leadership. Whether or not this had any bearing, Max soon after resigned and left Buffalo in 1979 to return to his home state of Oklahoma for other ecumenical work.

BAMM then sought and found an executive from California, the Rev. Charles White. Chuck White sought new social ministries related to the downsizing and exodus of Bethlehem Steel from the area, but neither this nor other social action efforts bore fruit. He then began to explore a broader base for BAMM and helped it become more fully interreligious with the entry of Muslims, Hindus, Buddhists, Baha'is, and others to supplement its Catholic, Jewish, and Protestant membership. Two events planned by White and held in Buffalo were the 150th anniversary celebration held downtown in 1982 and a regional gathering of the North American Interfaith Conference held in 1991. The social justice quality of life emphasis that had originally given BAMM birth waned as neither the resources nor the energy were to be found in its supporting church bodies. Chuck White left the Buffalo area in 1992 to return to California and was followed on a part-time basis by an Episcopal priest, Cynthia Bronson.

I reached retirement age in 1987 and determined to do just that in hopes that the Council could find new leadership and energy. During my eleven years with the Council, relationships between it and BAMM remained a priority. Despite three serious efforts to bring the two together, conditions upon my retirement did not seem ripe for any positive joining of ecumenical forces.

A year after my retirement, the Rev. Stan Bratton became the new Council executive. He held it together under more difficult conditions than experienced previously and developed the theme of looking forward to the Year

2000. During his ministry, radical Right-to-Life advocates visited Buffalo. But the Council had begun an innovative response to that kind of confrontational situation, a local unit of "Common Ground" that fosters dialogue and conversation in search of places of agreement. This, plus solidarity in the local religious community, helped the "Spring of Life" demonstrations come and go without much impact, and at least one local Right-to-Life leader began a fruitful public dialogue with a Right-to-Choice leader.

After Cynthia Bronson's tenure, another capable part-time director, the Rev. Father Francis (Butch) Mazur took over BAMM in addition to his parish duties. Butch was a committed ecumenical leader and gave BAMM renewed ecumenical direction. By this time, new leadership in area churches, including a new Episcopal bishop who wanted his diocese to cooperate with both ecumenical groups, made it more possible to renew conversation between BAMM and the Council. For the first time, strong efforts were made to ensure that the programs and emphases of both organizations would not be lost but included in a new and more inclusive organization should it come to be. With this assurance, an inclusive set of committees began planning in 1997. Out of their efforts, ratified by the board and member bodies of BAMM and the board and Assembly of the Council, the Network of Religious Communities was created with shared offices in the old Council of Churches building now simply named "1272." It began operating January 1, 1999.

Much of the credit for this new creation goes to Stan Bratton and Butch Mazur, who continue as Network codirectors. The priority task for the Network would seem to be one of dialogue to enhance understanding and cooperation between all the religious communities of western New York and to face the issues that divide in the spirit of a mutual search for understanding and peace with justice. The first president of the Network Board of Governors was a minister of the Church of God in Christ who pastored a church and served many years as Protestant chaplain at the Attica Detention Center (Prison). His irenic spirit served the Network well in its first real crisis, facing a division between Evangelicals not in the Network who sponsored a Day of Prayer in front of City Hall in exclusively Christian terms, and those in the Network who felt this prayer day excluded many and possibly violated separation of church and state principles. The Network president, Jeff Carter, was firmly on the side of black clergy who felt it imperative as a matter of faith to participate in this day of prayer, yet he listened to others in the Network and helped them and his brothers and sisters work toward reconciliation.

That closes the western New York ecumenical story in terms of its official ecumenical agencies, now one Network. But it does not include the many other ways in this region that ecumenism is being practiced. Activity in community groups acting outside of the Network became a primary way in which my ecumenical journey continued since 1987 in retirement years. One such group was previously described in the response to the Love Canal crisis. Groups other than the one ecumenical agency, the Network, are described because they seem to be authentic ecumenical expressions, even though some avoid any religious identification or relationship.

First is CEM, an acronym for a group whose full name is Concerned Ecumenical Ministry to the Upper West Side of Buffalo. It began over thirty-five years ago with a "Lots of Summer Fun" program for youth designed by some of the churches in that neighborhood. Other churches and a local college campus ministry made it a continuing community ministry agency, with three Catholic parishes, twelve Protestant churches, a Catholic college ministry, and a Reformed Jewish Temple represented on its board. Since it converted a former Baptist church into its main site, it has become a multi-service community center.

CEM supports the work of six senior caseworkers reaching homebound elderly people and aiding them in keeping up their property and in health and other welfare issues. Its senior activity center reaches well over a hundred more active elderly people with a varied program in-house and beyond. Its youth programs reach over fifty youth during after-school hours in addition to continuing the summer program. Its dining room is called "Loaves and Fishes" and serves about one hundred and fifty, five noondays per week. A Care shop providing free clothing is open one day a week. Finally a "Mosaic" program gives counseling and other aids to refugees living in the community. Special events take place regularly in the community center. My activity with CEM and its board began in 1977 when it struggled to make ends meet with a staff of three. Now its staff numbers over fifteen, and while it continues to struggle like all social service agencies, its budget is more than a half million dollars per year, enhanced considerably by local government and United Way funding.[24]

Another special agency is called VIVE. It began in about 1985 under the inspiration of a former Catholic sister, Bonnie Butler, who had been associated with the Center for Justice, a group of six Roman Catholic orders formed to deal with education for social justice in the church and community. She saw a need to provide housing and other services for refugees reaching our area with no U.S. immigration backing and seeking entry to Canada. VIVE has grown from its early rectory home for sisters into a much larger facility that provides housing and food plus legal and other assistance for a daily average of one hundred people. Its first residents were mostly from Central and South American, explaining its Hispanic name, but they now come from crisis areas such as Africa, Asia, and Middle Eastern and Balkan countries. VIVE is continually challenged by the changing regulations from U.S. and Canadian immigration authorities. Its staff includes some former refugees and was guided by an executive director, a Presbyterian minister named John Long, who retired in 2001 with his successor in place, a Methodist minister with previous social service experience, Chris Owens.

CEM and VIVE came into being with the blessing and support of ecumenical agencies—CEM with the Council of Churches and VIVE with BAMM. Both began and remain fully independent, developing support on their own. They have been able to function better on their own rather than being part of some ecumenical umbrella. Whether such independence is peculiar to western New York or part of a trend is not established. What is certain is that such groups are important parts of local and regional ecumenism.

Another such group is the Western New York Peace Center. It began as a local chapter of Clergy and Laity Concerned during Vietnam War days and was first sponsored by an area United Church of Christ congregation. However, it began and has remained independent of any religious affiliations. For the past twenty years it has been led by James Mang, a former Catholic priest, and his wife, Audrey, who has pioneered in developing one Peace Center program, Alternatives to Violence, which began nationally under auspices of the Society of Friends. The Peace Center functions as a coalition of committees dealing with specific peace and disarmament issues, and under Mang's leadership has included area social and economic justice issues, including the also independent Coalition for Economic Justice. Its AVP program developed by Audrey Mang began with prisons and has expanded to two-day sessions with selected groups in public schools. This is an individual membership–based coalition and will continue after the retirement of the Mangs, as a young couple with great connections to the local advocacy community now directs both the Peace Center and the Coalition for Economic Justice.

This Coalition, called CEJ, began in 1985 in response to a local economic crisis. A long-time Buffalo firm, TRICO, manufacturers of windshield wiper blades for the auto industry, announced its intention to move most of its production to a plant on the the Texas-Mexico border using *maquiladora* workers. The leader of the TRICO labor union asked some activist clergy for help. Others from area labor and education groups joined in. A process of seeking facts and preparing alternative solutions helped to form a Coalition. Allies from the religious and education communities were sought. A key organizer aiding the coalition was Roger Cook, previously active in the Love Canal crisis response. The leader was Rev. Robert Beck, now deceased, then the long-time pastor of a small United Church of Christ congregation in downtown Buffalo, whose main ministry was social justice activism. Others involved early on were from the Labor School of Cornell University located in Buffalo and from New York State economic development offices. The dozen or so activists who founded it tried to gain significant support from the Religious Leaders Forum, a unit of church heads related to BAMM, but got very little encouragement from that source. As a coalition, they developed relationships with others in similar situations and relating to church and economic life issues. The main battle was but partially won. TRICO now does most of its manufacturing in the Mexican border city of Matamoros.

The TRICO event gathered a growing number of justice advocates. It has since led the way in dealing with economic justice issues and has attracted the growing support of organized labor unions in the area. Its first director was Joan Malone, also a Love Canal activist. Malone strengthened relationships with labor, particularly in health and nursing fields, and became a key lead organizing person for social and economic justice causes in the area. She parted amicably with her Order during her tenure, and has recently left CEJ for Jobs for Justice, a national activist group. Joan's CEJ involvements included many successful hospital actions; Justice for Janitors campaigns; adoption of an agreement with the international ownership of a large supermarket chain in the area; and adoption by the Buffalo Common Council of a living wage ordinance to be applied to city employees and contractors for the city. CEJ held a fifteenth anniversary dinner in 2001 and gave Joan Malone one of its three awards for meritorious service in the search for economic justice. CEJ and the Peace Center, sharing the same office center and now with two outstanding young persons directing each, are examples of the way the search for justice can move from religious to community involvement.

One final example is VOICE. Some might call it a new style of ecumenism more related to local congregations. Others might call it a new kind of advocacy, born in the sixties and adapted to today. VOICE calls itself faith-based community organization. It has adapted the Alinsky style of the sixties to center on the life of local congregations and, through them, to build up a base of support for advocacy on issues that affect quality of life. It began out of the concern of a few pastors, extended to a prayer group on Buffalo's west side, and now is citywide and beyond. The Gamaliel Foundation in Chicago was engaged to provide an Organizer to lead and motivate the twenty-seven-plus member congregations. VOICE has developed Core Teams in these congregations, has trained leaders, and has held monthly meetings that have developed hardworking committees to deal with issues such as Housing, Crime and Drugs, City River Walk Development, Rats in Neighborhoods, and Education. It has held Congresses that have attracted 1,000 to 1,500 people, including the mayor, the county executive, and other officials and has held them accountable for their cooperation in solving such problems. It has developed a prayer life and a discipline and research on issues that makes it listened to by decision makers, and its training has provided new enthusiasm in many congregations. VOICE is ecumenical. Catholic and Protestant and black church congregations join to form responses that can make a difference. As this is written, VOICE seems to be the most alive kind of ecumenism at work in western New York.

The journey continues through voluntary participation and, representing my local church, in the Network of Religious Communities and in the kind of groups described above. A lot has changed over fifty years. Once the National and World Councils of Churches seemed to embody ecumenism and were the bodies to give encouragement and strength to their local counterparts. Now all ecumenism is local, even that performed by national and world groups. It seeks to help all religious communities in any area relate to one another with respect for the varieties of belief and culture represented in each, or it seeks ways of dealing with the issues that arise in any community, local or wider. It can be sponsored by church agencies or become separate from them. But it seeks to apply some kind of faith to building communities of justice and caring for others. All this seems confusing to some. It does seem a far cry from the neat ecumenical movement I entered fifty years ago. We recall that Jesus came to bring a new abundant life to all. We try to relate to that in ecumenical organizations and in coalitions of various kinds. While we still believe, we think it more important to understand and work with those who believe in other ways or do not affirm any belief. Our goals are reconciliation and peace with justice. It is our hope that ecumenical organizations may help these goals be realized. The ecumenism I discovered fifty years ago may have led to the diversity we now experience. Grateful for our past, we hope for a renewed ecumenism and new life in days ahead.

Notes

1. This story is composed almost entirely of personal recollections. Personal references in the story remain only where it was felt necessary, as I tried to make the whole illustrate a typical ecumenical journey.

2. *Cadillac Desert,* by Marc Reisner (New York: Penguin Books, 1966), is a comprehensive review of the dam-building period in our nation. It is critical of some of its rationale and highly critical of the competition between the U.S. Army Engineers and the Department of Interior Bureau of Reclamation.

3. Jack Ketcham, who became a mentor and friend, had come to NCCC from the International Council of Religious Education, one of the many national agencies that had merged to become NCCC. He and Dr. J. Quinter Miller were the NCCC staff most involved with local and regional Councils of Churches.

4. Leroy Brininger helped us set up the many Revised Standard Bible Celebrations across the state. Alva Cox led a National Christian Teaching Mission in Rapid City. T. K. (Tommy) Thompson was the national staff stranded forty miles east of Rapid City. Three days before, the temperature had been 70 degrees.

5. Russell Carter headed the NCCC Indian ministry and helped establish the Rapid City Center.

6. The Rev. Standish McIntosh was my first Council board president. A most amiable man with Scottish and Anglican ways, we attended the first Assembly of NCCC together in Denver in 1952.

7. The WCC Assembly was in the city of my family home, providing me with lodging. Upon my arrival, my father showed me a copy of the *Chicago Tribune,* which headlined the ban on WCC meetings for faithful Catholics by the Cardinal. He said his Catholic friends were calling to ask, "How can we get tickets?"

8. My Lutheran colleague at the state capitol was Pastor Otto Bergeland.

9. Friendship between the Grimm and Sharpe families went back to Cleveland Heights High School for Roberta and began in college for me as the four of us shared a date and later our families.

10. The Most Rev. John Mark Gannon had been awarded the title of Archbishop though his diocese was small. He was in his 80s when I arrived in Erie and died with his boots on in his 90s.

11. The Rt. Rev. Conrad H. Gesner was a very supportive mentor and friend. His Missionary District included only fourteen self-supporting parishes, plus about thirty white and over fifty Indian missions.

12. Roy Hackenberg, whose print shop was a block from Council offices, published the *Erie Churchman.*

13. Dr. Charles Hough was the associate. Martha Hawley and Marlyse Blanchard were secretaries.

14. Publisher of the Erie newspapers was George Mead. Executive editor was Joseph Meagher.

15. The judge was the Hon. Samuel Roberts. The Episcopal bishop was the Rt. Rev. William Crittenden, ecumenically committed, who had been a panelist at an ACS meeting and later was on the NCCC Board.

16. Ken Roadarmel came to the State Council after years as a state Baptist executive. Ted Conklin spent much of his time in Albany, where he represented the Council at Executive and Legislative offices.

17. Secretaries were Alberta Cromie, Janet Pavlus, and Betty Cottrell. Staff included Wayne Balcom, Social Services, Harlan London, Family Court Chaplain, Elizabeth Reed and Margaret Cole, Christian Education, and, later, Herbert Talabere, Urban Minister. Over six years of the Civic Lenten Services, three part-time

persons did the publicity. Only Alberta Cromie continued through my eleven years of service.

18. Key people in this first interreligious group were Fr. Charles Brady, William Chiles, Fr. Francis Woolever, Rabbi Theodore Levy, Fr. Alexander Warnecke, Donald Pomeroy, and me.

19. Other OEO trustees were Sidney Johnson, chair, later a Syracuse School superintendent; and Robert Sedgwick, a University economics professor. Our attorney was Benjamin Carroll. We called ourselves Federal Grantees.

20. These were Dr. T. William Hall, who chaired the university religion department, and Dr. Augustus Root, professor of educational development.

21. Fr. John McCrea became my MCB Associate, as nominated by the Chancellor of the Diocese, Msgr. John McGraw. McGraw and Auxiliary Bishop Thomas Costello were influential in MCB.

22. Dorothy Rose should be given great credit for, after my departure, reuniting an Interreligious Council and staying with it until her 1999 retirement, as it became one of the top such agencies in the nation.

23. The Archives of the State University of New York at Buffalo contain a collection of materials relating to Love Canal. Included are government records and records of related groups such as the Homeowners and the Ecumenical Task Force. It is named in honor of Pat Brown, a former area homeowner and ETF staff worker until her untimely death from cancer, probably due to Love Canal chemicals.

24. My role with CEM has included over twenty-two years of service on its board, a term as board president, and interim service as executive director. The present executive director is the Rev. Cathy Rieley-Goddard.

20

GATHERINGS AND ASSOCIATIONS THAT KNIT LOCAL ECUMENISM TOGETHER

Robert Grimm

In all of the fifty years covered by these stories of local and regional ecumenism, a special group has gathered—ecumenists employed as staff of ecumenical groups created and sustained in states, cities, and regions of our nation coming together for fellowship, inspiration, and ecumenical nurture.[1] In 1950, the name of this group was ACS, the Association of Council Secretaries. In 1972, its name became NAES, the National Association of Ecumenical Staff, and in 1991 the word interreligious was added to its name. Why did the name and the style of ecumenism change? Who were some of those involved? What follows is a memoir of my fifty-year experience with ACS-NAES-NAEIS—how it was in the beginning and how it evolved over the years. Indeed, its evolution is a reflection of the changes that were taking place in local ecumenism.

My early experience, outlined in more detail in the previous chapter, can be summed up briefly: college; three years in the Navy during World War II; three years in seminary with no definite direction to my Christian commitment; minister of a Community Church related to the South Dakota Council of Churches in a construction town built by the Army Corps of Engineers; and voluntary involvement with that Council leading to a part-time and then a full-time position, during which came my first definite ecumenical experiences. All this is said because a great many professional ecumenists, or council secretaries as they were then called, had similar entry experiences. Many of those I first met at ACS were very creative people, mostly ministers, who did not perhaps fit in as pastors of the churches of their denominations. Many found a role more suited to their theologies, entrepreneurial skills, or lifestyles in ecumenical work. Most successful ecumenists of the 1950s considered themselves to be on the cutting edge of the life of the Church in society.

In June 1950, an invitation to attend ACS, then held each year at Conference Point Camp, Williams Bay, Wisconsin, was received and accepted. This was my introduction to the group that felt it was part of a more involved Christianity than perhaps existed in separate local churches and denominations. It also introduced me to the local expressions of a group that was more familiar, the National Council of Churches in process of formation.

It seemed important to attend the NCCC Constituting Convention to be held in Cleveland the following December. It was a long way from South Dakota, and a snowstorm paralyzed the city and made entry difficult for all delegates and visitors.[2] But it was a great event. The hall was packed for a plenary session that was to hear the president of the United States address this expression of a united Protestantism. Alas, he was prevented by the looming Korean crisis from attending. So Dr. O. Frederick Nolde, who represented the Church Commission on International Affairs of the World Council of Churches at the United Nations, substituted with a calm and grave summary of this world crisis. His words were measured and reassuring. More important, they set the scene for the importance of this new entity in our nation. Those folk in summer casuals whom I had met the previous June at the ACS seemed to be part of a great and hopeful movement that would transform the Church into the mighty army, sung of in a youthful hymn but built upon the foundation of Christian unity. And the work of local Council secretaries would be aided immeasurably, or so it seemed, by the great number of NCCC staff who were installed in office at the Cleveland gathering.

It just might all come together, or so this youthful dreamer felt, in South Dakota. So, this volunteer became part-time, then full-time, as a Council executive. And each year after, those early dreams were sustained, sometimes given a dose of reality and informed by attendance at the annual gatherings of ACS and the midwinter regional gatherings of secretaries in the midwestern states. A career was begun. Colleagues were met. Friendships were begun and sustained. The Church Ecumenical became real, with all its possibilities and problems. Here is what it was like in the beginning and in the years following.

Introductory Ecumenism—ACS in the 1950s

Conference Point Camp[3] seemed an ideal setting for a professional church gathering, with its beautiful lake and adequate recreational and meeting facilities. Varied living accommodations, including old-style green cabins with bunks for younger men or families, were clustered around two or three meeting and assembly buildings and a central dining hall. Each breakfast featured a morning devotional led by the Rev. John B. Ketcham. His deep, vibrant voice and meaningful stories were a very impressive introduction to ACS. After breakfast and socializing times, all went to the main assembly hall for the morning devotional and lectures. These features were followed by a series of meetings of executives in similar-sized Councils or regions, educational and sharing in nature. Afternoons usually meant recreation and evenings brought more programs.

ACS brought the realization that most all the states outside of a few in the South and most of the larger cities of the nation had full-time Councils of Churches (usually but not always the name). About 150 of the executives of these Councils attended each year. Their schedules were full: in-service training, hearing inspiring speakers, sharing with others on events and policies in their own Councils and in the new National Council of Churches of Christ in the USA (NCCC). It was a busy time for all. A good number of NCCC staff attended for their own stimulation. In those early days, NCCC was doing a lot of its work "out in the field" using many state and local Councils to help set up the workshops or other events they ran. But the main contact with NCCC came through Jack Ketcham of the Office for Councils of Churches and Dr. J. Quinter Miller, the NCCC Associate General Secretary for Local and Regional Ecumenism. Both were at the center of what went on at ACS, a gathering place for working out what we then called the Council of Churches movement. Their roles were to build up ACS as a professional association and to encourage its members to relate to NCCC as the center of a strong and dynamic united Protestantism.

Those early ACS meetings expressed the conviction that we were on the cutting edge of church life. Neither local church nor denomination seemed to those who gathered relevant to what were felt to be the real needs of our day—in education, in supplying chaplains to institutions or for ministering to migrant workers, or in speaking truth to power with a united voice in the city and county halls or state government offices, or in serving refugees and returnees from World War II and those on colleges and university campuses, or in reaching out to the minority communities and to Native Americans. All this, and more, formed the agenda of those gathered, and we felt the Church could do a much better job of addressing these agendas through cooperation and through the Council organizations they served.

Gathering at ACS was a time to share all this, as well as what we were doing, or hoped to be doing, back home. It was also a time for ecumenical stimulation. ACS programs provided a steady stream of speakers. Two stand out in my memory. One was Roswell Barnes, the top Associate General Secretary of NCCC during the period of the McCarthy hearings. Referring to the congressional hearings then in session, Barnes produced this one-liner: "Not since the days of Samson has a whole army been put to flight by the jawbone of an ass."

Another speaker of memory was Dr. Ronald Osborne, professor of American church history at Butler University School of Religion in Indianapolis (now Christian Theological Seminary). Osborne delighted his audience, especially when he said, "Council Secretaries ought to be the real Bishops of the localities where they serve." The remark brought down the house, but it did not please my Erie, Pennsylvania, Episcopal bishop, whom I had been instrumental in inviting to attend ACS that year as a panelist to respond to the main speaker.

These stories express the spirit of the times at ACS in the 1950s. My first meetings introduced me to a top concern of the ACS executives. Before the National Council of Churches was formed, sometime during the 1940s, many who had experienced the local and regional Council movement and other groups felt strongly that the new national agency should be a Council of Councils, represented and controlled on a territorial rather than a denominational basis. One leading executive, Hayden Stright of Minnesota, was a leader in this concern. Stright had even written a book advocating this point of view. The cause was lost by 1950. What remained was a strong concern for the role of local and regional Councils and their influence at NCCC and in the nation. This was often expressed at every ACS meeting through the 1950s.[4]

Of course, the answer to these concerns from the new NCCC was Quinter Miller's role as Associate for Local and Regional Ecumenism and the Office for Councils of Churches headed by Jack Ketcham. This office and Jack really acted as staff for ACS. It was also the office helping Councils to find new staff leadership and Council staff who sought new positions, as well as helping to connect local Councils to other resources within and beyond NCCC. A part of their role was to offer ecumenical education and in-service training opportunities for present and potential Council executives. Some of this happened at the Boston University School of Theology under its dean, Walter Muelder. More happened at Union Theological Seminary with Ralph Hyslop, and still more at the new Bossey Ecumenical Institute of the World Council of Churches in Geneva, Switzerland. Quinter Miller promoted all these ecumenical educational opportunities, urged ACS to include them as important concerns, and continued to explore new educational possibilities. In the mid-1960s, Miller and Cynthia Wedel arranged a series of three-week seminar sessions in North Carolina and other places that gathered ecumenical and denominational executives for midcareer human and organizational development.

The executives who gathered at ACS are too numerous to provide a complete list. Just a few names and places can give an idea of who came to ACS in the early 1950s: J. Henry Carpenter of Brooklyn and Dan Potter of the Protestant Council of the city of New York; Jennie Dodge elsewhere in the New York area; Hugh Burr of Rochester; Bill Powell of Philadelphia; Jesse Reber of Pennsylvania; Forrest Knapp of Massachusetts; Ross Sanderson, who wrote an earlier history, *Church Cooperation in the United States,* and edited an ACS journal in the 1960s; Harlan Frost of Buffalo; Ken Roadarmel and Ted Conklin of New York state; O.Walter Wagner of St. Louis; Jon Harms of Chicago; Burt Bouwman of Michigan and Merrill Lenox of Detroit; Forrest Weir and Abbot Book of Southern and Northern California; Gertrude Apel of the state of Washington (who seldom was able to come but was often spoken of as a respected woman executive); Virgil Lowder of Washington, D.C.; Henry Shillington of Ohio; John Wilson, later of Ohio, but early on an associate of Hayden Stright in Minnesota; and Dave Witheridge of Minneapolis.

One of this early group was Stanley Stuber of Kansas City (later of Albany, New York), an outspoken advocate for peace in the world and justice at home. He was defamed by local radio, and other attacks were made on his rumored Communist ties or influences. The McCarthy era affected Stuber and many others in those days. Alton Motter was at the Chicago Sunday Evening Club but followed Stright in Minnesota and stayed until after retirement to be the longest serving ACS member, still going to NAEIS and other ecumenical meetings as this is written. Alton recently published an educational book on the ecumenical movement entitled *Ecumenism 101.*[5]

Another ACS leader, serving from 1946, was Grover Hartman, who came to be the soul of ACS in the 1950s and 1960s and the ecumenism of NAES after the 1970s. Grover was a United Methodist layman, with a Ph.D. from American University in peace studies, who chose the ecumenical movement as his calling and spent his career in Indiana. As the long-time director of the Indiana Council of Churches, he was able to foster good relations with other local, interfaith, and issue action groups, as well as the church leadership of that state. He was a United Methodist delegate to NCCC for many years. At ACS, Grover became the compiler of citations for those who had passed on during the year and those to be honored for years of service. He prepared certificates and presented them for five, ten, fifteen, twenty, and up to forty years of service. Grover read these in a solemn manner that conveyed their importance and the importance of every career. His almost childlike sense of uproarious good humor and friendliness made him the one who rose out of his youthful times in the 1950s to be carrier of the old spirit into the new and an exemplar of quiet but strong ecumenical leadership. Grover passed on in the 1980s after forty years of ecumenical leadership in Indiana, in our ecumenical gatherings, and in the nation.

Two others around in the 1950s became, with their wives and families, close friends and ecumenical colleagues into the sixties and beyond until their passing. Bob Kincheloe began his ministry as a pastor in the Greenbelt, Maryland, community, then moved to new Council positions in South Bend, Indiana, and in Pittsburgh for a long career, then to Detroit and retirement. Richard Norman Hughes moved from Councils in Bay City, Michigan, to Albany, New York, then to Rochester during the sixties and the racial revolution, and finally to Portland, Oregon, where he died from an angina attack before his sixtieth year. Dick was a close colleague in upstate New York and shared governing board meetings of NCCC with me in the 1970s. Both Bob and Dick were to me outstanding examples of ecumenical people, each seeking in different ways to make faith relevant to their society. So, with them and many others in mind, let us trace how the Council of Churches movement responded to the changes to come in the sixties.

The Revolutionary Sixties and NCCC

In December 1969, the National Council of Churches held the last of its three-year cycles of Assemblies in Detroit. It was a wild and wooly time. Neither President Arthur Flemming nor General Secretary Edwin Espy knew quite what to do with the outpouring of protests that marked each day of the Assembly. Ketchup, signifying blood, was poured on the presiding table, and a coffin was paraded up and down the aisles. Every advocacy group of the sixties was there to tell the church establishment how far short of justice and mercy it had fallen.[6] This Assembly was the outward sign that a lot had been wrong with society for a long time and that payback day could lie ahead. A bit later James Forman challenged the NCCC (by occupying its eighth floor offices for more than a week and emptying files until they covered the floors), prominent denominations, and the Riverside Church in New York City, demanding monetary reparations to pay for institutional racism. The effects of both racism and the Vietnam War were to challenge the old order of ecumenical life in the churches throughout the 1960s and continuing for a long time afterward.

It is impossible to understand the Council of Churches movement and other aspects of local and regional ecumenism without taking into account their symbiotic relationship with NCCC, especially into the 1960s. Some parts of this relationship happened at ACS. More came about through ecumenical executives, members of ACS but independent of its gatherings. A key role was played by NCCC staff and local and regional ecumenical agencies to aid the southern voter registration movement. The priorities of both local and national ecumenical staff people converged in their response to the racial crisis in the 1960s more fully than ever before or since, as they sought to respond to key actors in the civil rights movement. Two who served on the NCCC staff and later in local and regional ecumenical agencies illustrate these relationships that developed in the sixties and have shaped changes in our roles since then—Jon Regier and Bob Pierce.

Jon Regier[7] graduated from McCormick Seminary in 1947 and began ministry in Detroit as a neighborhood organizer, influenced by *Reville for Radicals,* authored by Saul Alinsky, who was the prime proponent of "in your face" community organizing begun in Chicago through the Industrial Areas Foundation (IAF). Jon went to Howell Neighborhood House in 1949 and stayed until 1958, when he moved to National Missions and Life and Work desks of NCCC. There he found himself the disgruntled young man in a bureaucracy involved in producing study papers and traveling to national assemblies of various church bodies. Jon needed support from national mission groups of such church bodies as the Presbyterian Church and United Church of Christ. With these, including David Ramage, Presbyterian, and Robert Spike with the UCC, and later working at NCCC with Jon, contacts were made with early civil rights leaders. John Lewis of SNCC challenged them to organize a ministry in Mississippi in support of what was already going on there with Robert Moses and other voter registration leaders. They did and formed the Delta Ministry. Jon remembers his NCCC years as a time when church leaders were given a challenge to act and accepted it. He saw this as the key to ministry rather than ecumenical structure or theology. He resigned from his NCCC post in 1972, in part because the hierarchical model of NCCC reorganization did not provide his unit, which was in contact with change movements of all kinds, the funding and other support needed to meet the demands upon it from students, minorities, and others.

After his NCCC experience, Jon wanted to find a place in the cities where he felt the action was. He hesitated but finally accepted an offer to lead the New York State Council of Churches in Syracuse, where he stayed after retirement, continuing to be active in local ecumenical agencies there and in the state. His career from its beginning has been one of urging action on behalf of people where they live, in terms of issues such as race, poverty, welfare rights, criminal justice, student power, and more. His story highlights the importance of direct action and networking that took place in the civil rights movement and in other revolutions of the sixties. This has shaken the bureaucratic foundations of our national church bodies and ecumenical structures, national and regional and local. Jon has been and is an ecumenical networking pioneer, from ACS to NAES and NAEIS, and beyond.

Bob Pierce's[8] youth and college and seminary careers were marked, up to and around 1960, by active response to the civil rights movement based upon the reasonable and active faith he had grown into, and through contact with leaders in the black community. His first job out of seminary was at the Valley Forge American Baptist headquarters. He left that after a short stint, marked by his feeling of its unreality, and moved to the National Council of Churches as an administrative assistant with its Youth Department and the United Christian Youth Movement. UCYM was supported by denominational youth groups and had its own network of ecumenical youth groups across the nation. There he joined long time ACS-NAES ecumenists Don Newby, John Wood, Dorothy Berry, and Andrew Young, who became a key lieutenant in Martin Luther King Jr.'s movement, later a Carter administration U.S. ambassador to the United Nations, then mayor of Atlanta, and, at the turn of the twenty-first century, president of the NCCC. At NCCC, Bob shared a bit of the vision of Jon Regier and others, that NCCC could somehow be that force to reshape and lead the Church in building a new and better society. He shared in the contacts with civil rights leaders. In summer 1964 the Youth Department had staff people in Mississippi to help train those doing voter registration. The end of his seven years saw him become the final UCYM head presiding over a planned phasing out of UCYM, due to changes in the realities of youth work and society. The civil rights movement achieved early success, the previous generation of youth had cycled out and moved to other things, denominational youth work became more protective of its own, and there seemed to be no place left for UCYM. These things also happened to other student movements. People like Mark Rudd at Columbia University were saying: "We will be participants in institutions, and we will hold you accountable." Those in power were having apoplexy at the apparent cracks in their power in all aspects of society, not just of students and youth.

In 1968, after his NCCC years, Bob moved to a community ministry in Schenectady—Schenectady Inner City Ministry (SICM), which had been set up as a response of local churches to the civil rights and poverty movements of the time. There he led organizing and other movements to meet the needs of those most in need in a city facing the downsizing of its major industry, General Electric. After seventeen fruitful years there, he moved to the "ultimate suburb," Long Island, in 1985, where he ended his career in 1998. From national to local to regional ecumenism, Bob Pierce has been on the cutting edge of where the Church and the ecumenical movement ought to be. He and Jon Regier, along with many others, both local and national, embodied ecumenical and issue-oriented movements of the sixties in new styles of ecumenical gathering.

How ACS Became NAES

The challenges of the sixties brought a new style of ecumenists to Conference Point Camp. The Office for Councils of Churches at NCCC was itself changing. Conrad Hoyer, a Lutheran, came on board to assist Jack Ketcham and to share with local Councils his expertise in church and community planning. Jack began the retirement process, as did Quinter Miller, and was replaced at NCCC by an energetic young local executive from Columbus, Ohio, Nathan VanderWerf. Nate became an influential advocate for local and regional ecumenical units at the National Council of Churches. He developed the image of weaving together a varied garment to describe ecumenical life, trying to assure those who gathered at ACS that they and their agencies were important parts of a whole, an ecumenical church responding to poverty, race, and other aspects of American life.

But as he reassessed ACS, he became convinced that it must change, that new personalities and styles must replace the old order of ecumenical professionals. The annual meeting planning committee brought Robert Bonthius and Joan Campbell from Cleveland as leaders in a new style of ACS program. It included a series of consciousness-raising sessions, including fishbowls, to help ACS face what it needed to be in a changed society with different and younger membership. It was a heady and disturbing conference that year. The next year, First World and Third World disparities were dramatized by having the whole conference assume and act out the roles. Situations were set up that brought attendants into conflict. In one situation, both a conference participant and a young camp staffer took accidental, but bad, falls.

Out of this turmoil in ACS from 1969 to 1971, a new organizational style and name were created. ACS became NAES, the National Association of Ecumenical Staff. Cliff Kirkpatrick (later the Stated Clerk of the Presbyterian Church in the USA) became the first president of NAES. The other happening was the move from Conference Point as the annual gathering site. Beginning with meetings at Bethany College in West Virginia, the group began to select other sites across the nation, some in other conference settings such as Ghost Ranch in New Mexico and YMCA camps in the Colorado Rockies; some in college settings such as St. Olaf in Minnesota and the University of Puget Sound in Tacoma, Washington; and still others in more urban settings such as Washington, D.C. We did return to Conference Point one year for sort of a reunion meeting, but the older chain had been broken. Later, NCCC transferred Conference Point, which now operates and is governed as a regional conference center of the churches.

Nate VanderWerf came as the first executive of a newly constituted unit that was part of structural changes taking place at NCCC. When the going got tough for the NCCC in the 1960s, General Secretary Espy engineered two astute strategies to "drive the conversation upward" through a new Faith and Order Commission and to drive the roots deeper, changing the Office for Councils of Churches into the Commission on Regional and Local Ecumenism (CORLE). This gave local and regional ecumenical people a recognized voice in the NCCC structure. Also, ecumenical delegates to the NCCC Governing Board were once again possible, in addition to slots open to state executives. Both categories of ecumenical representation were made ecumenical members of their denominational delegates by a process of nomination that went through VanderWerf and CORLE.

After the series of confrontations that turned ACS into NAES, the meetings went on with roughly the same format (speakers and group sessions of various kinds) as in previous years. Those who attended seemed different than in the 1950s, more attuned to the Urban Ministry style of expecting church efforts to be part of making needed changes in society. Most local or metropolitan Councils went through their own transformations. Some developed direct Urban Ministry programs. Others confronted racism and poverty in their own communities, or supported the civil rights and advocacy movements led by African Americans and others in and beyond the Churches. Some older programs such as Civic Lenten Services, Released Time programs in or related to public schools, and ecumenical church research and planning were cut drastically, or died. All this and more was reflected in NAES meetings.

NAES itself got involved in a lot of things beyond its former role. It developed its Women's and Black Leadership Caucuses. It aided CORLE at NCCC to establish a program called PIE, Partners in Ecumenism, whose goals were to develop greater black church participation in ecumenical life and to encourage the entry of black church leaders into local and regional ecumenical organizations. This was one of the many things that Marvin Chandler, who had been an associate at the Rochester Council of Churches during its days supporting the Alinsky FIGHT organization, did for the wider ecumenical scene. And this was one of the key efforts of Donald Jacobs, an AME minister who had become director of the Cleveland Church Federation, and Joan Campbell, associated in Cleveland, who had helped direct the previously mentioned consciousness-raising sessions changing ACS to NAES. Campbell became president of NAES in the early 1970s, from where her varied ecumenical career began. Other NAES events worthy of mention were the trip to Delano, California, by a good segment of the membership in support of Cesar Chavez and United Farm Workers, and a later series of special NAES trips, two to Middle East sites, for members.

NAES to NAEIS and to Now

During the 1970s and 1980s the process of change in local and regional ecumenical agencies and staffs continued unabated. Many Councils were involved in change; some died, sometimes to be resurrected in new forms. And so, at ecumenical gatherings, there were always a lot of new folk and some of the older folk to tell new stories, or to share information on how to respond to new situations back home. In the late 1980s, Grover Hartman suddenly passed from us, his voice and quiet leadership stilled at our meetings, even though his equally warm and talented wife, Annabelle, came by from time to time. A new person arose to symbolize continuity at NAES. He was Skip L'Heureaux Jr. from the Queens Federation. Skip became and remained Registrar and Treasurer for a long period, the Registrar part continuing to the end of the century. His early skill with computers helped, and he also put that skill to use by helping introduce NAES to modems and other modern communication tools.

Each year for a long time both ACS and NAES have elected presidents for a year[9] and have continued the practice carried on so long by Grover Hartman of recognizing lengths of ecumenical service and those who had passed on. One of the presidents was Lee Hicks, who had succeeded Bob Kincheloe in Pittsburgh and led that Council to become regional—Christian Associates of Southwest Pennsylvania. Lee was a strong and steady voice at NAES until he left to go into full-time church fund-raising.

Another was James Webb, now retired. Jim had attended the Boston University Ecumenical Institute in 1963 before his first post and before beginning an ACS-to-NAES relationship in 1964 with the Connecticut Council of Churches, an early judicatory-based state council in the United States. Jim worked on the changes in the 1960s there. After he left in 1973 it became CRISCOM, an organization of church executives, with most of its earlier style of ecumenical organization gone. He then went to Rhode Island, with his tenure cut short by controversy over an application from the Metropolitan Community Church for Council membership, then to the Illinois Conference, another consortium-style organization with Roman Catholic dioceses in full membership and social justice and legislative concerns. Jim retired formally in 1985 but became a part-time executive of the Council of Churches in Cape Cod, where he went to live. His was a steady and friendly ecumenical voice at NAES and at NCCC meetings.

Still another ecumenical voice was that of William Cate. Bill was an early leader who pioneered in relating the Councils of Churches he served to the issues faced in community and society. His ministry included Bedford, Massachusetts, and then Portland, Oregon, where he helped developed a state and metropolitan Council serving the two areas under one organization. Later, he came to Seattle where his service was long and creative until his retirement. He has published more than one book on ecumenism. One was inspired by the World Council Assembly in Nairobi, Kenya, where a new definition of ecumenism emerged. It stressed the ecumenical goal as happening to "all in each place." Bill's book, *Ecumenism on Main Street,* translated World Council theology into local realities.[10]

Wallace Ford of New Mexico has been another ecumenical voice in an area that included many church bodies in the New Mexico Conference of Churches. One of the earmarks of that ecumenical group in the Southwest has been its connection with Native American and Hispanic groups. Among the long-active members of the New Mexico Conference are Roman Catholic dioceses. Beginning in the 1990s and continuing has been the entry of many Roman Catholics into the formerly mainline Protestant Councils. ACS and NAES remember the wonderful work in this respect done by Father David Bowman, who was, as a Jesuit on the NCCC staff, related to CORLE for a time. Dave Bowman also pointed us toward Protestant and Catholic reconciliation efforts in the unending Irish political-religious crisis.

Issues such as those related above were more and more the center of NAES life and discussion. Some members tried to steer it as a group toward greater involvement in the issues of the times. Others were content merely to discuss these issues and their effect on their home organizations. And during this time, it seemed that the relationship between NAES members and the NCCC, despite having some members on the NCCC Governing Board and having the Commission on Regional and Local Ecumenism (CORLE) as a unit of NCCC, slowly but surely diminished.

Things at the "Protestant Headquarters on the Hudson" in New York City with NCCC also continued to change. Nate VanderWerf left NCCC and went to a group sponsoring self-help in world missions. After a year-long interim by Arleon Kelley (who had been an associate in CORLE and who had staffed NAES during most of VanderWerf's tenure), VanderWerf was succeeded at CORLE by Joan Campbell. She spent a number of years as our liaison with NAES, then went on to serve the U.S. Office of the World Council of Churches, and then moved back to NCCC for two terms as its general secretary. These terms concluded in January 2000, and Joan now directs religious programs at the Chautauqua Institution in western New York.

Joan was succeeded at CORLE by Kathleen Hurty, a Lutheran with a wonderful educational and ecumenical background. During her tenure, CORLE became Ecumenical Networks in still another NCCC reorganization. Kathleen related to NAES and all in a friendly and affirming way and was missed as she moved to become director of Church Women United in 1996. Because of budget cuts, there was no full-time replacement for Kathleen, and Barbara George, from Ecumenical Ministries in Oregon and then as staff of the office for the general secretary, served CORLE on a part-time basis. Finally, after Joan left NCCC to be succeeded by Robert Edgar—whose priorities had to be the serious NCCC financial crisis—there now seems no place at NCCC for local and regional ecumenism. So goes the ever-shifting and changing life of national ecumenical structures.

During the late 1980s, as a number of local and regional agencies expanded beyond their Roman Catholic participation and membership to welcome members from other faiths, NAES began serious conversation about the implications of the interfaith movement for its membership. Some of the issues were the history of the association and its Protestant roots; the relation of NAES to the ecumenical movement, which, including Protestants and Catholics as full participants, had a distinctly Christian cast with Christian justice objectives; and the existence of some ecumenical groups committed to the Christian unity aspect of their life. One of these, with a long history of commitment to the Christian unity movement as a primary reason for its being, was the Massachusetts Council of Churches (MCC) headed by Diane Kessler.[11] The MCC, and others with similar views, felt no objection to having interfaith relationships but a real hesitation at opening its membership outside of Christianity because that would be a hindrance to its concentration on Christian unity and working out programs and contacts with churches on that basis. The document that this Council still uses to describe its purposes and goals is entitled "Odyssey toward Unity: Foundations and Functions of Ecumenism and Conciliarism," published in 1978. Diane Kessler has been an outstanding ecumenical unity scholar, with publications on related topics, including a compilation in English of the proceedings of the World Council of Churches Assembly in Harare, Zimbabwe.

Proponents of a name and style change came mostly from agencies that had become interfaith or interreligious. Examples included Washington, D.C., Wichita, Kansas, Tulsa, Oklahoma, and Syracuse and Buffalo, New York, each being created out of older Councils of Churches.[12] These groups responded to the growing pluralistic character of society, especially in urban areas, and sought to give more emphasis to the goal of including all in the religious community as one more responsive to the times than the exclusive concentration upon Christian unity. Partly because NAES perceived itself as a professional association and not as a church-related body, the inclusive proponents prevailed, and NAES voted in 1991 to become a slightly new creation by virtue of adding one word, but a most important word, to its name. And so now those gather as the National Association of Ecumenical and Interreligious Staff (NAEIS).

A recent meeting of NAEIS was held at a hotel in Rock Island, Illinois, in July 2001. The list of NAEIS officers and program planners for that meeting tells much about the present nature and diversity—geographical, vocational, and religious—of the association. President is Jay Rock, the director of Interfaith Relations, National Council of Churches, in New York City. Vice president is Julia Sibley of the South Carolina Christian Action Council. Secretary is Sr. Paul Teresa Hennessee of the Graymoor Ecumenical/ Inter-religious Institute. Treasurer is James Robinson of Tulsa Metropolitan Ministry. Other principals include David C. May of the Grand Rapids Area Center for Ecumenism; David Leslie, Ecumenical Ministries of Oregon; Janet Leng of Tacoma, Washington; and Barbara White of the Interfaith Conference of Greater Milwaukee, Wisconsin.

Speakers for the meeting tell us about NAEIS concerns. They include Marian Wright Edelman, founder and president of the Children's Defense

Fund; Michael Kinnamon, professor of Mission and Peace at Eden Seminary in St. Louis and general secretary of the Consultation on Church Union (COCU), who served previously on the World Council of Churches staff and has coauthored *The Ecumenical Vision* with the next speaker, Diane Kessler of Massachusetts. Also listed are Sharon Daly, vice president for social policy at Catholic Charities; Gustav Niebuhr, religion writer for the *New York Times;* Kim Bobo, founder and executive director of the National Interfaith Committee on Worker Justice; and finally, Sandra Kaye Rana, a member of the Islamic Society of Tulsa, Oklahoma, and a private consultant who has served as president of Tulsa Metropolitan Ministry.

Finally, the program lists learning track topics for the Conference: Hunger in the Heartland, a look at hunger in the midst of plenty; Environmental Stewardship and Justice; Economic Development and Justice; Community and the Ecumenical and Interreligious Movement; and Responding Responsibly to Diversity. These were the titles of the formal small group discussions and learning sessions. So, once again, those in local and regional ecumenical callings met and sweated and toiled to make sense out of their ecumenical calling. That they did and will continue to do so is perhaps the key to the meaning of local and regional ecumenical gatherings.

Notes

1. All incidents in this chapter come from the author's personal recollections. Thus, it does not pretend to be a comprehensive history of ACS-NAES-NAEI or of the National Council of Churches.

2. My family, including our six-month-old baby and our two other children, both under six years, somehow made it from the airport, aided by an intrepid cab driver, to my wife's family home. Meetings were downtown, with bus and streetcar transportation the first day taking over three hours.

3. This campsite was then owned by the International Council of Religious Education, one of the national cooperative agencies that merged into the National Council of Churches.

4. *Editor's note:* The issue Stright was addressing was a controversy dating back to the turn of the twentieth century. When the Federal Council of Churches was being formed, the local council executives had argued that the Federal Council should be composed of denominations and the denominations had argued the Stright point of view. More than forty years of the Federal Council experience caused the argument to be reversed.

5. Alton Motter, *Ecumenism 101: A Handbook about the Ecumenical Movement,* was published in 1995 (Cincinnati: Forward Movement). An earlier practical review of how local Councils worked or should work was "Growing Together: A Manual for Councils of Churches," published by the NCCC in 1955. It contained a brief history of the movement and chapters on organization written by local executives.

6. As ecumenical visitors, Dick Hughes and I were approached by early represen-

tatives of AIM, the American Indian Movement, who sought our influence and financial help in getting them a hearing.

7. See my written summary of a taped interview in the History Project Archives at the library of the Christian Theological Seminary in Indianapolis.

8. Ibid.

9. The presidents of ACS, NAES, and NAEIS have included the following from 1940 to the present:

Association of Council Secretaries

1940–41*	O. M. Walton, Cleveland, Ohio
1941–42*	John W. Harms, Maryland-Delaware
1942–43*	Hugh C. Burr, Rochester, New York
1943–44	J. Burt Bouwmann, Michigan
1944–45	E. C. Farnham, Los Angeles, California
1945–46	No meeting (all officers carried over)
1946–47	J. Harry Carpenter, Brooklyn, New York
1947–48	Willis R. Ford, Maryland-Delaware
1948–49*	Henry Reed Bowen, New Jersey
1949–50*	Gertrude L. Apel, Washington
1950–51	Hugh C. Burr, Rochester, New York
1951–52*	Harold C. Kilpatrick, San Antonio, Texas
1952–53*	Hayden L. Stright, Minnesota
1953–54	William D. Powell, Philadelphia, Pennsylvania
1954–55	O. Walter Wagner, St. Louis, Missouri
1955–56*	Forrest C. Weir, Los Angeles, California
1956–57*	Harlan M. Frost, Buffalo, New York
1957–58*	Virgil W. Lowder, Houston, Texas
1958–59*	Forrest L. Knapp, Massachusetts
1959–60*	Harvey W. Hollis, Denver, Colorado
1960–61*	G. Merrill Lenox, Detroit, Michigan
1961–62*	Grover L. Hartman, Indiana
1962–63*	Robert L. Kincheloe, Pittsburgh, Pennsylvania
1963–64	David E. Witheridge, Minneapolis, Minnesota
1964–65*	Jesse D. Reber, Pennsylvania
1965–66	Donald F. Bautz, Rock Island, Illinois
1966–67*	Cynthia Wedel, New York, New York
1967–68*	Vladimir Hartman, Albany, New York
1968–69*	Alexander H. Shaw, New Jersey
1969–70	B. Corterz Tipton, Bridgeport, Connecticut
1970–71	Earl N. Kragnes, Oklahoma

National Association of Ecumenical Staff (Presidents)

1971–72	William B. Cate, Seattle, Washington
1972–73	James H. Webb, Providence, Rhode Island
1973–74*	Horace N. Mays, Los Angeles, California
1974–75	Clifton Kirkpatrick, Houston, Texas
1975–76*	Richard N. Hughes, Oregon
1976–77	Joan B. Campbell, Cleveland, Ohio
1977–78	Joan B. Campbell, Cleveland, Ohio
1978–79*	John T. Frazier, Columbus, Ohio
1979–80	W. Lee Hicks, Pittsburgh, Pennsylvania
1980–81	Dorothy G. Berry, Kansas

1981–82	Donald G. Jacobs, Cleveland, Ohio
1982–83	Loren Arnett, Washington
1983–84	Martha Miller, Dutchess County, New York
1984–85	Melvin Hoover, Stamford, Connecticut
1985–86	Thomas Quigley, Minneapolis, Minnesota
1986–87	Margaret Koehler, Atlanta, Georgia
1987–88	Sylvia Farmer, Minneapolis, Minnesota
1988–89	Larry Witmer, Rochester, New York
1989–90	Sr. Sylvia Schmidt, Tulsa, Oklahoma
1990–91	Wallace B. Ford, Albuquerque, New Mexico
1991–92	Debra L. Moody, Columbus, Ohio
1992–93	Mel H. Luetchens, Lincoln, Nebraska
1993–94*	Dorothy F. Rose, Syracuse, New York

National Association of Ecumenical and Interreligious Staff (Presidents)

1994–95	Arleon Kelley, Albany, New York
1995–96	Thomas Van Leer, Minneapolis, Minnesota
1996–97	Peg Chemberlin, Minneapolis, Minnesota
1997–98	David T. Alger, Tacoma, Washington
1998–99	Arthur Lee, Seattle, Washington
1999–2001	Jay T. Rock, New York, New York
2001–2003	Julia Sibley-Jones, Columbia, South Carolina

* Denotes those known deceased.

10. Publications in the 1960s included Ross Sanderson, *Church Cooperation in the United States* (ACS, 1960). Later periodicals were *ACS Journal,* edited by Ross Sanderson and Robert Grimm, and "On Location," a series of articles published by CORLE and edited by Arleon Kelley and Dorothy Berry. CORLE's executive director was Nathan VanderWerf.

11. See taped and written summaries of interviews with Diane Kessler in the History Project Archives.

12. See Chapter 6 by Charles White on the interreligious movement and the oral histories in the History Project Archives.

PART SIX.
REFLECTIONS

These are stories of hope—stories of faithfulness to a vision of unity, justice, service, and community. Sometimes these are stories of disappointment and defeat but more often of transformation. Indeed, these are stories of God doing a new work—creating anew in the midst of the communities of America.

What are we to make of these stories? What are the theological rumblings? What are the sources of hope for the future? What will be the future of local ecumenism? The Story can be constructed from our history. And the theological underpinnings can be deduced. However, we can only speculate about the future, because so many variables in our world will be instrumental in shaping the timely vision that will capture the ecumenical imagination of next generations, as they live out unity, justice, service, and community in their lives.

21

THE BODY OF CHRIST AND THE FAMILY OF GOD: A THEOLOGICAL REFLECTION

Arleon L. Kelley

The interwoven textures of the rich cultural and religious tapestry of local ecumenism create a panorama, beautiful to behold. These scenes are not isolated events but integral to the larger faith story in American life. They are tales that reflect the long-term faithfulness, momentary triumphs, and sometimes frustrations of ecumenical life—testament to the faith and theological underpinnings of tens of thousands of people. Sometimes this theology is expressed, but most often not. The theology that underlies the life of local ecumenism must often only be deduced because the life and action has far outstripped the stated theological formulations.

Yet, theology is the strength that holds the local ecumenical fabric together. And shared work gives new texture and meaning to that theology. Together, ecumenical people are continually weaving a new tapestry of beauty and value, pulling and tugging their larger communities to new life and purpose. That is one role of beauty—to challenge the soul of the community. In this chapter, I will reflect on this theology, first from the Body of Christ perspective, focusing expressly on the unique marks of an ecumenical Christian and on ecumenical life as we find it embedded in the stories that have been told. Then we will explore how ecumenical Christians might understand the Family of God and attempt a rationale for how the Body of Christ is a full member and participant in the Family of God.

THE BODY OF CHRIST

The Story

Ecumenism is in the world in a unique and hopeful way. These chapters give us clues that an ecumenical life orients around a worldview that includes multiple dimensions, including one world, hope, justice, service, community, and unity. The ecumenical worldview has evolved considerably in the fifty years of our concern. Ecumenism up to 1950 had a "one world" view that was mechanistic. It saw the world as whole, but made up of discrete parts, like nations, geographies, economies, technologies, and cultures. If the parts could be fit together in the right ways and kept oiled, then the whole world mechanism could work. Mechanical things do not have life. They work, or break down. And it often seemed, through two world wars, the Korean conflict, and the Vietnam War, that the better we were at fixing things the worse the mess became. By the late 1960s a bifurcation in worldview began to emerge. Ecumenical Christians began to see things in life or organic terms. Each of the parts was not discrete, but living, connected, and interdependent. And together, they became more than their sum. We began to understand that as one cares for the whole one also cares for the parts of the body and vice versa. When seen organically it becomes a body that is alive and has vitality. The New Testament imagery of the Body of Christ takes on new meaning. Relationships take on new significance. The world is composed of diverse parts. Each part has gifts to share and needs to be met. When interdependence is understood this way the markers of the ecumenical vision and vocation begin to look quite different.

Yet, the vision of globalism taught by ecumenical giants like John R. Mott has not been realized. Multinational capitalism has molded globalism to benefit the few at the expense of the many. What was envisioned as a globe at peace, cooperating for the well-being of all, has become a global competitive marketplace. The resources of the Third World are being usurped, often by economic or armed force. Distributive justice has been diminished. Enmity builds, both at home and abroad. Hopelessness abounds, with terrorism one result.

We see our culture and even our religious expressions move from personal relationships and individual participation to a mass media and spectator society. Secularization has become rampant. Primary relationships and caring for one another has diminished as concern for one's own self and safety emerges as a principal way of being in the world. The care of the community, and its institutions, in all spheres from local to national has often given way to a sense of helplessness, if not despair, on the part of many. And many denominational churches have not coped well. Denominational church membership has diminished, as has attendance. As the saying goes, "The largest alumni association in the world is those who were once in the churches."

By the end of the twentieth century, the mainline churches and the numbers of people that participated in the life of these churches were diminishing. At the same time the Church was denominating in new ways. The spectator society began attending megachurches that put on a multimedia show each Sunday. Liturgy—the celebration of the work of the people—gave way to entertainment and twelve-step groups to save us from our addictions. Salvation was being mediated in a new way, and at the same time these approaches were only providing a tertiary sense of community—the historic basis for Church. In megachurch expressions of Church, many fundamental things are lost. An authentic community of caring is one. The liturgy of community life is another. And another is often the prophetic witness, especially the commitment to witness, beyond the doors of the known. Individuals may be transformed, but the concern for the transformation of the society and culture is not a blip on the radar screen. And when it is, the focus is almost always on gaining political power for a reactionary or conservative social agenda that will not transform society but rather force conformity.

The Markers of Local Ecumenism

There are eight theological facets one can discern from the stories in these chapters that I believe dramatize local ecumenism as a manifestation of the Body of Christ—a sacrament if you will, mediating and pointing all to God's intentions for the creation. These facets are each different dimensions of the same truth and are evident in most local ecumenical manifestations. Local ecumenism is

Creative;
Inclusive;
Brings renewal in the midst of the struggle between good and evil;
A prototype of community, prophetic and caring;
A servant of the needs of people;
A manifestation of unity;
An ecclesial manifestation of Church; and
A source of transformation.

We will explore these theological implications and reflect upon how they interact in places across America to become a sign and symbol, even a sacrament for their communities of service.

Perhaps the most significant theological insight embodied in local ecumenism's growing understanding of the Church as the Body of Christ is that it is a sacrament in the corporate and cultural sense. More about that later.

Local ecumenism is creative. In the middle of the twentieth century, U.S. Christianity was a vibrant force and led by denominations. In this context the ecumenical role of sacrament emerged. The modern local ecumenical movement in the United States can be viewed as a faith-rooted alternative response or a sacramental response to the dysfunctions of this enlightenment-mechanistic cultural cycle, pointing the culture beyond itself to universal truths. Indeed, ecumenism, as it developed in the United States, became almost a sacramental precursor for a different understanding: calling the fragmented discrete parts of the machine to a new sense of holistic organic relationships (unity); denouncing the excesses of the dysfunctional mechanistic fragmentation of people and building network relationships (community); challenging the creation as object-to-be-(ab)used and people-to-be-used view of the world (justice); and providing a cup of cold water for those who are being harmed by the excesses of that dysfunction (service). It is in local ecumenical arenas in many communities across America where hopelessness and helplessness gives way to hope; where preoccupation with the past gives way to concern for the future; where conformity is challenged by the possibility of transformation; where fragmented diversity confronts a vision of unity borne of complementary diversity; where those who are all alone are invited into caring community relationships; and where malaise that can come from the sense of chaos all around us can be turned into creativity. When this happens, local ecumenism, although a remnant, becomes a sign of hope, pointing to the possibilities God intends for all creation. Local ecumenism becomes what Arnold Toynbee calls a "creative minority." And he argues that it is the creative minority that breathes life into a stagnant majority—sometimes replacing them, but more often infusing the dominant culture with new vision, values, goals, and life. That is the way local ecumenism becomes sacrament. It points to life!

The creativity that emerges from chaotic situations and the prophetic stance that results is a marker of the ecumenical vocation. Wallace Ford shares an imagery descriptive of what creativity of ecumenism is in each place. He says:

> Living west of the 98th meridian for almost an entire lifetime . . . where rainfall drops precipitously below 20 inches a year, aridity is a fact of life and anything about water is always fascinating. . . . The Bay of Fundy that separates New Brunswick and Nova Scotia is noted for its extraordinary high tides (and the tidal Bore). . . . On this particular day, the Bore would occur at 12:25 P.M. At that moment, slowly mov-

ing around the bend of the river, was a 4-foot wall of water pushing upstream. What was minutes before a broad sandbar stretching across the valley below me with streamlets coursing through it now became a lake of water moving against its source. As the Bore (the name of the actual first wave of the rising tide) moved along, encountering the river currents (pushing downstream), whirlpools were created, spinning wider and wider until finally absorbed in the broad expanse of water. . . . What I saw happening before me became a visual symbol of God's Spirit moving over the face of the deep, creating, in Marjorie Suchocki's terms, the whirlpools between God announcing "Behold I make all things new" and "our glorias" . . . as it was in the beginning, it is now and ever shall be. . . . These whirlpools are also images of the ecumenical movement: God's Spirit bringing forth the new and our cherishing the vessels in which we have held the treasures of the Gospel; God's creating new possibilities which invite us out of our comfortable satisfactions."[1]

Local ecumenism, at its best, is the whirlpool formed when chaos churns as the fresh and new comes up against the old and comfortable. It is the rustling of the Spirit as the wind moves the dying leaves of a tree in the fall. Local ecumenism is a renewal movement challenging all that fragments community, all that is unfair and unjust, and all in the community that denies humankind's God-given dignity.

At the same time, local ecumenism is often beholden to denominations or congregations. To be healthy, local ecumenism has found it must almost always be in tension with its constituency, creating a bit of discomfort, if not chaos, among its constituents, as well as its community. In that sense, vital local ecumenism is prophetic. This creative tension, as we have seen in the Northern California story, is sometimes successful from one generation to the next; or for a couple of generations as in the East Harlem story; or, as in the Youngstown steel story, as a necessary prophetic response that is ultimately overwhelmed by corporate America. But, in every case, the ecumenical worldview is organic and creative. It has little vested interest in the past, as do the denominations. It is about being the means through which God is "doing a new thing"—giving life and vitality, in the midst of the powers of destruction, decay, and death.

Local ecumenism embodies inclusiveness. Local ecumenism has long embraced the unity that flows from complementary diversity and inclusiveness, and is the way that stance is implemented. In the survey, one of the underpinnings of this project, it became evident that local ecumenism has worked to implement its own organizational life as inclusive. Most ecumenical bodies across the country have worked hard to equalize the number of males and females in staff and decision-making positions. They have worked hard to include ethnic and racial minorities and people of all sexual preferences. These actions have led to small transformations in organizational style and mission. Yet, there is valid criticism that the organizational culture of local ecumenism has not, for the most part, been transformed enough from its traditional white, middle-class, male roots. At the same time, however, these acts of inclusiveness in ecumenical organizational life have often led the way among the churches and other community organizations.

Thus, it is the vocation of local ecumenism to include all—not just the denominations, which are largely unique to the American scene—but all, including all races, genders, sexual preferences, denominations, ideologies, theologies, classes, geographies, and cultures. Denominational congregations have not been good at this. They are good at de-nominating, i.e., at building walls and defining who can be in and who is out. Congregations often use their theology mixed with prejudices and ideologies to do this. They have experienced the struggle because of racial divisions. Some have sworn that the Bible ordained it. It does not. Most everyone has seen the struggle of women for equality. Some swear the Bible insists on women's subsidiarity. It does not. All Americans have had their consciences pricked by the struggle of the poor in our midst. Some say the Bible insists we will always have the poor among us. It does say that we are to serve those who are marginalized. However, we live in a society that largely has ignored the needs of the poor. We live in a time of selfishness and greed. Some support this selfishness and greed by saying that "my prosperity shows that I am living in God's favor." The Bible does not say that!

Geographic inclusiveness is an unsung difficulty for the Church. The East Harlem story dramatizes what happens when the congregation devolves to a voluntary association of self-interests. There, as in almost all inner cities, when a congregation's members leave a neighborhood, so do their congregations. Thus, in order to be geographically inclusive, an ecumenical approach becomes essential—to give courage and to pool the spiritual and monetary resources necessary for reentry into the turmoil once left behind.

Inclusiveness does not come without cost, because the value of inclusiveness has become one value those in opposition can organize against. Indeed, the sources of the new Protestant denominationalism no longer are deeply rooted in faith or doctrinal issues but rather in stances regarding the participation of women or of gay and lesbians, and occasionally that of people of color in the life of the Church.[2] Indeed, controversial social issues, like abortion, peace, the death penalty, or guns, are often the source of new divisions, not unlike abolition, suffrage, and temperance/abstinence were in the mid-nineteenth century. But local ecumenism values inclusiveness, sometimes almost to the exclusion of its prophetic witness on some other society-dividing issues. And it often leads on these issues, more often by example than by prophetic utterance.

A caring presence is bound hand-in-hand with local ecumenism's inclusiveness. These stories show that churches together can develop ministries of hopeful presence in places where individual congregations cannot survive. In Newark, on the farms of the Great Plains, and in the mountains of Appalachia more can be done together than one denomination can do by itself. This is more than cooperation. It is faithfulness to the Gospel. The parts of the Church transcend self-interest to become the Church in mission—prophetic, caring, serving, and reaching out. It is then they are truly ecumenical. These experiences may not be churchly as in the traditional sharing of bread and wine in the congregation's weekly liturgy, but they are sacramental in the broader sense that God intended the Church to be sacramental, in the liturgy of its work amid the powers and principalities. These ecumenical responses point to hope and caring. They point to the importance of community. They point to the truth about the love of God and the purpose of God's creation—that all might be one. The ecumenical worldview is inclusive. Local ecumenism keeps our need to be inclusive and caring alive in their communities.

Local ecumenism is marked by signs of renewal in the midst of the struggle between good and evil. The re-denominating can bring either renewal or destruction. When divisions occur as a means to go back to past values, mores, ideologies, or forms, evil almost always results. On the other hand, renewal is what happens when the new confronts the comfortable and old and something new and creative results. Renewal draws on the past but re-mythologizes those values and structures in response to the present situation to create something new. Destruction happens when an obsolete idea, form, or value becomes an end in itself to be worshiped. It then becomes the incarnation of evil. Over the past few decades healing toward unity has been taking place among the churches in many communities across America. Because of the work of the bilateral and the multilateral relationships developed in ecumenical bodies, like the historic Consultation on Church Union, many churches developed covenantal relationships, only to see the denominations and their local churches re-denominate, or re-fragment, around views about sexual orientation, political ideology, theology, race, or culture, but in the end, mostly about power and who should be in and who is to be excluded. This attitude makes the agitator the god. For you to tell me that I am not as good a Christian as you, or your faith is the only true faith, is to judge me. And judging the other is almost always a harmony breaker. Mark Twain told a fable:

> I built a cage and in it I put a dog and a cat. And after a little training I got the dog and cat to the point where they lived peaceably together. Then I introduced a pig, a goat, a kangaroo, some birds and a monkey. And, after a few adjustments, they learned to live in harmony. So encouraged was I by such success that I added an Irish Catholic, a Presbyterian, a Jew, a Muslim from Turkestan, and a Buddhist from China, along with a Baptist missionary that I captured on that same trip. And in a very short while there wasn't a single living thing left in the cage.[3]

The missionary believed only (s)he had the truth. And it destroyed all. All that builds walls in religion is a denial of the essence of the Christian faith.

Trying to stand alone makes room for new divisions. It makes people very anxious and judgmental. Most of the new divisions in the church are rooted in judgments of who and what these groups are against, rather than what they are for. Still others are rooted in an imagined past they wish to recapture and force all to accept, when often it never existed other than in their imaginations. For example, some long for a return to an American government and way of life that is "Christian," even though that memory is mainly false. Our nation was founded largely by Deists. These movements back to an imagined past become destructive. They are evil in the sense that they impede creation's struggle for wholeness and life and the Church's sacramental role as a sign of hope and life in that struggle. They have gotten the "evangelical principle" wrong. They believe that "it can't happen through you until it has happened to you. You must be Christian like I am a Christian. If you do not fit into my parameters, I can't be in relationship with you." Such ways of being in the world immerse us all in the destruction and death we are all too often seeing within the churches. Rather, I believe the evangelical principle should be, Where there is creativity, hope, community, and vitality there is the Body of Christ regardless of its name. Go and give your life to it. The ecumenical worldview is hopeful, life-giving, and future-oriented. On the other hand, where there is weakness, little life, and no hope there is often fragmentation. It is always easier to tear down than to build up. The reactionary view is an almost exact opposite to an ecumenical view.

Local ecumenism's experience knows that good, grounded in love and justice, is very real. But the wisdom of our experience also knows that evil often embeds itself in our social and religious systems by replacing love with self-interest, greed, and malicious intent.

The struggle between good and evil is a sign of God's work in our midst. This is one of the things that becomes quite apparent in the stories. There is a very real struggle going on in many places between good and evil. In the stories of the Farm Crisis in middle America and in the Youngstown struggle we can see the dramatic struggle among the farmers'/workers' need to provide a livelihood for their families, the need of a community to maintain its economic base, and the corporate drive for profit quite apart from who is hurt. These are stories of David and Goliath, stories of powers and principalities that are not accountable or responsive to the basic needs of people and human community. They are stories of evil, but also stories of tenacity and resiliency where what is evil is oftentimes turned to good. The same struggle between good and evil is also often evident in local ecumenism's stories about struggles of ecumenical agencies to overthrow the death penalty, to get rid of draconian drug laws, to advocate for the use of some of our society's vast resources to provide health care for all, and to protect the rights of those who have been marginalized.

The stories of local ecumenism are often stories where that which is not good carries the day. Evil often seems to win. One might ask with Job and so many of the ancient sages, How is God at work in the midst of this oppression? It seems that many professional ecumenists have either purposely or inadvertently become process theologians. They tend to find a silver lining each time the powers and principalities send another blow of defeat and then proceed to create new possibilities for good. Every situation, no matter how bad, always presents anew to them three possibilities: the possibility of new creativity, the possibility of the status quo, and the possibility of accepting defeat and the destruction that comes with it (which is usually intolerable). The faith embedded in most ecumenical life causes ecumenical leadership most often to opt for the first possibility—new creativity—probably because local ecumenical leaders seem to be essentially hopeful people.

For example, after the defeat in Youngstown, leadership emerged that found other alternatives for economic survival. These were not always good solutions, because one solution was to build a for-profit prison. But there were other solutions that brought some small industry and business. These latter were more creative and health-giving to the community than a private prison. At the same time, the crisis of losing an old industrial plant meant that in the struggle many other issues came to the forefront and were addressed in Youngstown, like a race problem and the poor quality of its education, its university, its police, and its infrastructure. To be attractive to new enterprises these things had to be addressed. The faith communities through the Mahoning Valley Council of Churches continue to faithfully play a cohesive and creative role, along with other community organizations, in sustaining the drive toward new creativity.

Similar stories of tenacity, that turn evil into something good, are evident in the Farm Crisis. The crisis began with the oil embargos of the 1970s and to a lesser degree the return of Vietnam veterans. Farmland had been highly valued and farmers had been encouraged to buy more of everything by taking mortgages on that high valuation. With the increase in the cost of fuel and poor crop prices, the price of land plummeted. The cost to raise crops was more than the income that could be realized when crops were sold. This dilemma made cropland less valuable. Mortgages and loans could not be repaid and banks foreclosed. Communities and returning veterans saw their dreams and their economic foundations crumble. Every sign of community distress became evident. Suicides, divorces, and loss of farms were only the tip of the iceberg. Hamlets, villages, and towns were in turmoil. Community institutions failed. Friends became enemies. Corporations were busy buying up the best land at foreclosure sales in a strategy of vertical integration—or making deals with farmers that farmers hoped would let them continue, only to find they were now held economic hostage on their own land and losing the land in the end.

Ecumenical organizations—mainly state councils—often became the mediating influence between good and evil. When the Willie Nelson Farm Aid concerts generated millions of dollars, these state councils became the conduits to get the money to desperate farmers. Councils mobilized mental health and health facilities. They created dialogues among the contending parties, bankers, local businesses, and farmers, all people who sat together in the pews on Sunday. Much was lost in the nearly thirty years of distress in the heartland, but some radical restructuring of American agriculture and institutions in rural communities also occurred. Some was not desirable, because it brought vertically integrated corporations to the fore. Yet, much of it was positive, because among the surviving community institutions, alliances and stronger bonds were created. A just outcome? For many it was not. Yet, as the restructuring of rural life continues, new boundaries have been set, new institutions have emerged out of the old, and there is vitality in the remaining centers of most of the affected rural counties. To some extent, churches, themselves institutions requiring restructuring and consolidation in these rural communities, were able, through their ecumenical organizations, to play a generally positive mediating role, making the unpalatable move toward some creative outcomes. They were signs of renewal.

These, and the many other stories told in this book, make it clear that evil is real and pervasive. The sin that is dealt with most often in the ecumenical context is not personal, but rather the evil that is imbedded in institutional inertia and complex systems. These stories remind us that all institutions and systems of institutions are more than the sum of their parts. And even though the original sin embedded in them may lie in someone's greed, avarice, pride, or jealousy, when it becomes embedded in an institution, i.e., becomes a part of the institutional or system culture, the bad becomes a way of being for the institution or system. This is true in the corporate culture of greed that closed still-profitable factories in Youngstown only to use their capital to build elsewhere, or invest elsewhere for greater profits. In this case, greed was institutionalized. The same was true of Midwest banks foreclosing on farms. Many of those bankers, as well as the farmers, could not live with the contradictions. When they had the option, many bankers retired rather than hurt their friends. Others with no options fled the area or even committed suicide. The future will require sophisticated understandings of the nature of evil by institutions whose mission is to transform that evil into goodness. Local ecumenism is in position to be a part of this transformation.

The denominations are caught up in this struggle. They are fragmenting. Many of the ecumenical bodies have enough life to transcend this—at least for a time. Gary Peluso posits that, in the end, the denominations may indeed have birthed a more perfect interim form of Church in the ecumenical agencies than exists in the denominations. I believe that local ecumenical experience over the past fifty years may bear that out. Unity is good. It is manifested in ecumenical organizations. It is an ecclesial sign. Destructive fragmentation can be evil and is a contributor to the decline of the denominations.

Local ecumenism is a prototype community. Community is another theological mark that emerges from these stories of local ecumenism. Local ecumenism at its best is both real community and prototype community—by prototype I mean a community that is living out all its struggles for the whole world to see. As it succeeds, it becomes a hopeful sign—sacrament—for the broader community to emulate. Community building is the work of the Spirit and is always fragile and always in progress. One story from an oral history interview illustrates the point. One of the state conciliar bodies had worked for more than five years to re-mythologize what they were called to be in the ever-growing secular, media-oriented culture. Denominational voices were not being listened to by the dominant culture. Over months and months of study and prayer the denominations discerned that in their common baptism, they were all of Christ's household. And they began to see themselves as constituting the household of Christians in that place. The Spirit was working in their midst. Indeed, the various denominations were coming out of their rooms of separation in their common household. They were throwing open the windows and opening the doors into the hallways. A cleansing breeze was beginning to blow throughout the whole household. They were finding themselves drawn together around the hearth for conversation and in the dining room to break bread with one another. In their conversations they found they all shared the same baptism and hence the same allegiances to Jesus Christ. And in the end that was what really mattered. That allegiance to Jesus, the Christ, was more important than doctrine or even practice. Many of the church's leaders began to think of themselves differently—as brothers and sisters in the household rather than as isolated competitors. Membership and denomination were less important. If you named the name of Christ as yours, you were included. Many were finding ways to take mutual responsibility, to communicate their plans, and to give over some of their previous illusions of sovereignty to the whole community.

However, there was one denominational leader who held himself aloof from the process even though the others from his denomination were excited about the possibilities. It seemed his ego and identity were so entwined with his own denomination and his place in it that he apparently could not stand to see this strong new form of Church emerge. He came into the semiannual meeting where the transformation was to be made official and made what proved to be unfounded charges of fiscal impropriety. It took the next year to investigate and prove there had been no impropriety, but the damage was done. He had successfully sidetracked and scuttled this fragile new experiment of ecclesial community. And the result has been that each of those family member denominations has continued to lose strength.

Even though this experiment did not succeed, the formation of communities of interdependence, communities of hope, and communities that can deal with the new realities emerging in our social context is the work of local ecumenism. It is central to an ecumenical worldview. We work for it always and sometimes we succeed. Yet, what is the nature of this community we seek in each place across America?

Local ecumenical organizations are not only rooted in community but are among the cohesive forces that help maintain and sustain community in each place. Indeed a vision of community wholeness is the driving force for many local ecumenical organizations. Most religion is communal. Christianity gathers in community weekly to celebrate its faith. All religions sustain themselves through familial and communal acts. In places where families and communally affiliated groups of several different religions are present, the ecumenical task is often more difficult, because that which provides cohesion and community for one group can become a bone of contention when two or more different religious groups are present in that place. This is equally true when these groups are denominations within the same general faith tradition. For example, Methodists, Presbyterians, Baptists, Jehovah's Witnesses, Mormons, Ukranian Orthodox, and Roman Catholics sharing the same community of place may have almost as many disparate views as one would find between Christians and Jews or Christians and Muslims who share the same city of residence. Each tends to build a wall around itself—for both good reasons like creating identity, but also for reasons rooted in the fear that the other might harm them in some way or that some of their number might stray from their community. It is the ecumenical task to bridge these differences so that the many gifts each has to offer can be offered for the benefit of the whole community. That involves education, cross-religious experiences, and the involving of all in common work.

There are many values and views that undergird the overarching value placed on community in each place. These are evident in the stories of local ecumenism. Perhaps first and foremost is the value that the community must be *responsible or just.* Walter Muelder, dean emeritus at Boston University School of Theology, coined the term "the responsible society" in a study book for the Uppsala Assembly of the World Council of Churches. He argued for a just and righteous community where each is treated with respect and equality and where relationships are right and whole. This requires that the strong care for the weak and that all have a voice in community decisions that affect them.

Of course, this view of community had other underlying theological values—foreign neither to the communal idealists of the nineteenth century, the social gospel, or to Muelder—namely its perfectability. Local ecumenism values *the perfectability of the community,* that is to say, there exists a common belief in local ecumenism that communities can be perfected in the sense that they can be made into places where all can have quality of life. Thus CORA invests much of its resources in empowering all in a community to participate in making the community a just and wholesome place to live. And those in Newark or Youngstown join together to quell riots or rebuild the economic base in these distressed cities. So many from so many sectors joined together to deal with the Farm Crisis. All these believed that they could perfect their communities to be more just and wholesome places to live.

Still another value of community is *solidarity*—standing together in the face of injustice. Solidarity is usually the product of grassroots organization among those unjustly treated. It becomes a powerful force in righting the relationships of inequity that so often prevail and which are so destructive to community. Grassroots organizing in order to build solidarity is a strategy frequently employed by local ecumenism in order to pursue its concern for just, responsible communities.

Interdependence is an integral component of community. No one part of the community or one part of the creation can sustain itself, by itself. All parts are organically related to all other parts. The sulfur- and nitrogen-laced smoke from midwestern coal-fired electric plants affects the ecosystems in the Northeast. Corporate actions in New York that close factories in Dubuque, Waterloo, or Des Moines affect the community life and the social contract that these communities had with the industry when they agreed to provide the industry with water, sewage service, protection, and an educated workforce. Similarly, one church's self-interest can affect the ability of another to sustain itself. And the list could go on. But one of the basic truths of local ecumenism is that all is related to all else. Science has known this for years. The Church has had the theology of the Body of Christ, but the churches have not always lived this theology. Local ecumenism has been one place that the organic relationship of the Church as a sign or sacrament of the organic relationship of all creation has been valued.

Another value underlying community is the importance of *place.* The globalization of society and the needs of global economic institutions have greatly diminished the importance of place. Mobility has diminished the importance of "blooming where you were planted." Higher education and the job market have caused significant brain drains for some communities. Local ecumenism has been a witness to the importance of place through its work to make neighborhoods, communities, and cities wholesome places for families to put down roots. It is a countercultural witness to the importance of place, as the Love Canal work in New York, the work in the Farm Crisis, or the work in East Harlem will testify. It is immoral to ravish and pillage places in America for profit.

These values are implemented when local ecumenism creates a means for the disparate parts of the community to collaborate and cooperate. And the wisdom of ecumenical experience is that such collaboration is usually the source of a community's roots and fabric.

Local ecumenism is a servant giving a cup of cold water to the thirsty. Another theological mark of local ecumenism is its ministry of giving service to the needy, often where local ecumenism began. Societies were created to teach children and the illiterate to read and write, care for the ill, address social evils, and help the addicted. The interviews and the stories tell us that this is what local ecumenism does best. There are the food pantries to feed the hungry across Minnesota. There are myriad hunger programs among the Community Ministries. There are programs to aid those on welfare. There are programs for those with AIDS. There are programs to fix up houses and to build housing for the elderly and the homeless. Indeed, caring for those who have needs is probably the greatest single work of local ecumenism. Whole segments of local ecumenism are dedicated almost exclusively to this work. It is the principal work of Community Ministries.

Local ecumenism is a manifestion of unity. Another sign of the Kingdom of God in our midst is the struggle for unity. A synonym for unity might be the Hebrew word *shalom*—all is at peace because all the diverse parts are of the same fabric complementing one another and living in right or just relationships with one another.

Ecumenical organizations have an underlying concept of Christian unity and interreligious organizations a concept of the unity of humankind and all life. Unity should not be confused with uniformity or ideas of a superchurch or a superreligion. Local ecumenical organizations pursue a vision of what people of faith can accomplish when they work together. They have a vision of the unity of the Church as a sign of the possibilities for the unity of all humankind and for the unity of all creation. Indeed, broken communities like those chronicled above are vivid illustrations that ecumenical and interreligious forces are hopeful enough that unity can be achieved that they will give their life working for it. In these communities it often proved true that the ecumenical vision and the motivating energy that flows from that vision are sacraments. This struggle for unity points the whole community toward the hope for wholeness—unity we all share.

Ecumenical bodies have ecclesial significance. These marks and the numerous transformations that have taken place because of the presence and work of local ecumenical bodies are indicators that these bodies have ecclesial significance. In the United States, they are often a more complete interim manifestation of Church than are the historic fragmented denominations. They are another step along the path toward the reintegration of the Church as true sacrament for creation. They embody the good news, they are prophetic, they have unique ministries, they are places of renewal, and they are often a living faith community with great times of celebration. Their organizational life is a liturgy. As noted earlier, even though they do not give the sacraments, they are sacramental in the best sense of that term. In that and in many other ways they embody the marks of Church.

Many in the local conciliar movement, as well as in the Faith and Order arenas, have argued vociferously that ecumenical bodies have no ecclesial significance. But I have argued for forty years, in those same circles, that ecumenical organizations are often a more complete manifestation of the Church than most all denominations I have known and worked with. I believe that can be borne out by the stories shared in this volume, by the marks of local ecumenism reviewed above, as well as by research.

In the late 1980s, Dr. Gary Peluso, now dean of Phillips Theological Seminary in Tulsa, Oklahoma, did an intensive study of state ecumenism. In a paper given in 1995[4] he argues that congregations and denominations do not own state councils. He observes that they are usually broader in membership and geography than their member denominations and that there is a more complete reflection of the Church than in any one of its member parts. He suggests that Christ owns state councils as well as other local ecumenical organizations. Yet, the paradox is, they could not exist in the short run without the always declining support of denominations. This is to say, the ecumenical organizations are not corporations that are an extension of the denominations. Rather, they are organic, and the denominations are midwives to a form of church that is related to them but at the same time distinct of them. They are something of the Church in their own right. Councils are not corporate agencies, but have some, although not complete, independence, similar to the way a denominational form of Church is related to, but distinct from, the congregation.[5] They are a form of the healing of the churches. Such healing is a dramatic statement in a fragmented and evil world. Michael Kinnamon says: "So one thing that works against a proper rooting of state [local] ecumenism is a distorted ecclesiology in the churches. Another is a distorted understanding of ecumenism itself. Ecumenism . . . is not synonymous with tolerant cooperation, indeed it might be the antithesis, since tolerance[6] drains off the passion for renewal. Councils exist not because Christians need to learn to get along, but because we need each other and are given each other in order that through one another we might become more fully the Church God wills."[7]

In the end we need ecumenical expressions of Church because the world needs to see what Christianity living in harmony looks like. We live in a world of many religions, indeed many historic world religions. We live in a world that has selective hearing at best and which usually chooses to not hear the churches, the Church, or most religious voices. We live in a world that largely gives credence only to what it has seen. The world may come to see the Church if it can live together in harmony. As that happens the ecclesial significance of local ecumenical expression becomes clearer.

So, what can we say about local ecumenism as the Body of Christ in each place? It is quite clear from the stories that an important part of the ecumenical vocation is to be the hopeful sign in the midst of fragmentation and despair, because each part has something of value that we all need. At its best, local ecumenism is an important manifestation of Jesus' prayer in John 17: "We might all be one, as my Father [parent] and I are one." Denominations, by themselves, are not very helpful signs of hope for creation's wholeness, because they are, in themselves, reminders of fragmentation. But together in ecumenical or interreligious linkage, they become powerful community symbols of hope for those who live daily in fragmented communities. In them something of the wholeness of the Body of Christ is manifest.

When we get beyond the foundational constitutions and bylaws of ecumenical and interreligious organizations and read the stories of their activity, we can say that local ecumenism, in large part, is built around an immanent and hopeful theology that all may be reconciled so unity may one day prevail as a sign that one day humankind may also be in harmony. This is evident because local ecumenism operates mostly from a positive view of humankind's possibilities and with a strong sense that God is actively involved with God's Creation. There is a strong current running through local ecumenism that the Kingdom of God is at hand. One can almost hear local ecumenism's leaders saying, "We have only to work with God to liberate our community from evil. We have only to work with God to be liberated from the powers and principalities that oppress and bind so many and so much of God's Creation. We have only to work with God to see the brokenness and fragmentation made whole."

Transformation. The dimensions of ecumenical life, when working together, often result in the final indicator that a work is of God—transformation. Transformation is that miracle which happens when all things work together for the benefit of all. It is when all take on new life, to become a new organism, alive, vibrant, and glowing. It is when the God dimension is really added that it becomes more than the sum of its parts. Transformation is when all things are made new. And that is what gives local ecumenical life both sacramental and ecclesial significance.

Yet, there is much religious life beyond the churches and the Church. This means that we live in a world that must be interested in dialogue among the historic world religions. Some years ago an Episcopal Church diocese invited some of the world leaders of Buddhism to come to their city for a dialogue. The Buddhists arrived for the first plenary meeting, and when they found that there were only Episcopalians present they protested. "We have come for a dialogue with Christians, not Episcopalians," and promptly walked out. The message was clear. Episcopalians are Christians, but they are not the Christian Church. World Buddhism will only talk to world Christianity. The global dynamics are demanding a common voice from Christians. A common life, a common community, and a common vision to go with the common voice sounds like the stuff of ecclesial import, and that leads us to the second part of this chapter. How does the Body of the Universal Christ fit into the Family of God?

The Family of God

Local and regional ecumenism seems to be engaged in a project that understands Christ in more universal terms, quite in contrast to many of its participating Christian denominations, which in some cases are interpreting the Christ event in ever narrower terms. The culture and worldview of Americans has changed dramatically and with it the place of religion. Particularistic, narrow Christianity provides identity in the midst of cultural chaos; yet for many it makes little sense, given the kind of interconnectedness we are experiencing every day in what some have called the "green" or "sheen"[8] era, i.e., the postmodern era. The postmodern era is marked by its leveling of the philosophies, theories, myths, and "scientism" that had sustained the machine era. This emerging era views all as an interdependent and whole organism, connected to the very origins of creation itself. In this worldview, the earth is alive, not a machine with rusty discrete parts, always requiring oiling to keep running. We now know that atoms are not inert but rather patterns of energy—as are all living things. Chaos is honored as the necessary condition for creation, and with it the processes of spontaneity and freedom that serve the creative processes. In this cosmological worldview, God is feminine as well as masculine, and instead of being apart and elsewhere from ourselves, the Divine is understood as within all things.[9] Humankind exists to sing praises to the Creator and the Creation. We know that all matter and energy are sacred. "Atheism melts before the astonished minds of scientists, as they rediscover the dignity of their vocations in the newly found wonder of time and space."[10] Particularistic religion also disappears when one realizes all is connected. Indeed, this worldview sounds very similar to many of the ecumenical documents one might read, and it certainly is the basis of much of the interest in a broader understanding of world religions.

This story of the transformation that is emerging is dramatic. What is being born is rooted in the new understandings of cosmology and human relationships within our unfolding understanding of our place. With the threats the machine-era worldview presents to our world, it is no accident that prophetic ecumenism is coming to understand anew and describe itself as the Body of Christ, connected, relational, organic, universal, and global within the Family of God. And it is no accident that much of the work of modern maxi-ecumenism[11] has been rooted in issues of justice raised by the machine worldview—like patriarchy, racism, super-patriotism, misused power, unemployment, income distribution/poverty, and ecology—all dysfunctional aspects of the machine-era worldview. It is solidarity with the victims of these injustices that has become the focus of our larger or maxi-ecumenical impulses to be with and, at the same time, serve, the needy—the poor who can't get or hold jobs, the uneducated, families broken by the addictions and pressures of materialism and consumerism, refugees from nation-statism, and many others. And even more recently this maxi-ecumenism has taken the lead in building bridges of discussion and shared work with the many living faiths—a testimony to the common roots of all faith in the awe and wonder of life. All of this work is a part of the same creative work that is transforming the consciousness of our culture and our view of all the world's living faiths.

Anthropologist Arthur Geertz says, "The modern world is a place in which no one will leave the other alone ever again."[12] Even though nation-states are busy every day trying to build new boundaries, they will be ever more porous. We will transcend these new boundaries because the Internet and other forms of communication and rapid transportation mean that no member of the human race can remain isolated for long. Now, unlike in the past, people can know what is really happening, and the people will be heard. In the end, in spite of what great governments and great institutions like education, newspapers, television news, and even religion say, the people will find the truth because they can bypass these mediating institutions and get to the unvarnished source, often via the Internet. Unless all humankind is nearly destroyed and we are thrown back to the Stone Age, we will never be left alone again, nor will we be left only to what we are told by our institutions. We live in a world that has its own nervous system. It is the *ghia*, "the world as a living body," envisioned by the French Jesuit priest Teilard d'Chardin, some two generations ago.

At the same time that these paradigmatic shifts are taking place, we must remember that a struggle between the old machine-era ways and the new ways is also under way. The reasserting of individualism and economic and political imperialism in the 1990s, with its possibilities of setting East against West and North against South, are all reactionary responses to a wholistic vision of humankind and creation. And the jury is still out. Yet I believe it is the work of ecumenism to develop the larger vision at the same time it mediates between old and new and meets the need of those unjustly treated because of the struggle.

What might be that larger vision? It must include a rethinking by Christians about who we are in relation to the rest of God's family.

Toward a Creation Theology: A Rationale for Christians Participating in Interfaith Activity

These questions within the Christian community and the emerging worldview of local ecumenists described above have been enabled in part by the Christian ecumenical vision. That vision of "one world" has moved humankind beyond its uneasy tension with the sacred to a more integrated view. This new worldview, along with the wonder and awe one experiences when viewing the magnificence of the universe, are the basis for the sacred. It has come about for some Christians because of a new and deeper understanding of their faith in the light of the nature of Creation. This insight came about in a strange way for me and was some thirty years in the making. But by the 1980s I had come to understand my theology in such a way as to be inclusive of all faith traditions. Here is how it began and developed.

I believe that for each of us there are times when we feel the mystery and awe of being at one with the creation. We see God breaking in! But we don't often think about what it means for our relationships with the "others" of faith. I began to think about it when I was a freshman in college. My assigned roommate was Kan Ori from Osaka, Japan. The first day we met in our dorm room, in my then "in your face" evangelical fashion, I asked him if he was saved. He said yes, and in my brazenness I asked him to tell me about how it happened. He told me a story that was forever to transform my life. It was a story that made me ask new questions of my then-narrow Christian faith. His answer was mind boggling:

"When I was twelve years old my father died. I was an only child and I couldn't bear it. I ran away and climbed up on the hills on the east side of Osaka and cried my heart out for hours and hours. Then, as the sun was setting over the city in the west, all of a sudden I felt at total peace—at one with the creation."

I scratched my head and then blurted out, "Well, where does Jesus come into this picture?"

"Well," he said, "that happened four years later when I was sixteen. One day a fellow student invited me to go to a Bible study with her. I arrived to find a Canadian Presbyterian missionary talking about Jesus and what he could do in a person's life, and I knew that is what had happened to me on that hillside when I was twelve!"

Could it be that God reveals God's self in the very creation—if we but have eyes to see? Could it be that my vision of God in the world was far too small?[13]

What this event eventually taught me, when I had the faith maturity to accept it, is that God and God's transforming power are universally revealed in the very nature of the creation itself. All one needs to do is be a close observer and then believe what you observe. Slowly, I began to understand my Christian beliefs and myths in new ways. It began a new understanding of John 1:1–5: "When all things began, the Word already was. The Word dwelt with God and what God was, the Word was. The Word, then, was with God at the beginning, and through him all things came to be; no single thing was created without him. . . . the light shines on the dark and the darkness has never mastered it."

With the new eyes God had given me to see with after the encounter with Kan Ori's faith story, I came face to face with the Universal Christ. It was the bridge between my Christian tradition and meeting other faiths. I came to understand that God is primarily Creator. The Word is the Christic creative and transforming dimension of God. The Word is love, by which I mean the attraction, that pulls all toward the other. That is where creation begins. It is this force of attraction that continues the ongoing Creation process and it is the means of continually renewing or transforming the Creation when the darkness seeks to creep in and push all things apart and back toward the nothingness from which it came. Thus, the Word and the Christic are synonymous and are the sources of the initiating, life-giving, and sustaining of the continuing creation process—love.

Earlier ecumenism was clearly rooted in orthodox statements in the organizational document's preamble about the divinity of Jesus, the Christ, as God's only Son and often connecting him to the only means of salvation. During the years since World War II there has been an evolution in the understanding of the Christ event in history. As local ecumenism became increasingly a creature of the denominations rather than a largely voluntary association in which denominations participated, significant changes emerged in how one could be a member. For example, when the Lutheran Church in America participated in local ecumenism in the 1950s and 1960s, its president, Franklin Clark Fry, ruled that they did so on two principles: the Evangelical Principle and the Representative Principle. The first required that the ecumenical organization have an orthodox Christo-centric purpose and be composed of member denominations or congregations that subscribed to that purpose. It built high boundaries. It made local ecumenism an exclusive Christian club. The second principle required that the governance entity of the ecumenical organization be named by sovereign denominations, usually on the basis of communion size. That is, governing boards should not include any persons not delegated by a member denomination. And the bigger the communion's membership, the more delegates they could have. In earlier ecumenical configurations, including the NCCC/USA, a portion of governance membership had been nominated by local and regional spheres of ecumenical life. But this principle forbade that. It implied that the authentic Church was only manifest within a denomination, and a narrowly defined understanding of the salvific role of Jesus Christ in the world could only be mediated through a sovereign church.

However, as the culture changed, with many immigrants from eastern non-Christian cultures, the nature of the community of work and the pluralism of residence communities caused local ecumenism to struggle with its narrow orthodox understanding of the Christ event. By the 1970s many local ecumenical expressions were living their way into new understandings.

The evangelical principle was often bypassed, if not conveniently forgotten, so that rich faith diversity could be embraced, while not denying the central role of the Christic in creation or in salvation history.

For example in the Syracuse story, after nearly two years of being hung up in the formation of a new, broader interreligious organization, because of the Evangelical Principle, the leading Lutheran pastor participating in the discussion suddenly caught a new insight about faith, faithfulness, and community. He reversed his stance, and almost immediately all the faith communities in the Syracuse area joined to form a new, strong, and dynamic Interreligious Council of Central New York. This transformation of a pastor's thought and willingness to join with others happened in the context of a group process exploring the questions, Who is my neighbor? and What is required of us to be faithful to this neighbor?[14] This sort of thing happened in varying degrees in so many of the histories and stories we collected. So it is not difficult to speculate that a new theological formulation about the nature of Christ and the Church has been developing and coming into wider acceptance over these fifty years. These formulations are rooted in the theological work that has been done on the relationship among Church, Faith, and Creation and the related development of new insights about the nature of the Christic[15] in our midst.

Indeed, the Christic might be said to be the source of the transformation of the above-mentioned Lutheran pastor's views. He moved beyond rules and regulations to a broader and deeper understanding of a deeply held belief in the transforming power of Jesus the Christ, to an understanding that perhaps other traditions may also share similar views, because transformation is embedded in the very nature of creation itself. These transformations are the "new creations" Jesus talked about. They are the Word that Jesus embodied. These kinds of radical shifts in thinking are not unusual happenings in local ecumenism. There are many such instances embedded in the stories and information we collected. When people from various deeply held theological traditions come together around various issues of global import—saving the environment, racial, social, or economic justice, and ways to provide a cup of cold water to those who are suffering—the dialogue will either bring theological transformation, which releases tremendous creativity, meaning that God is still being revealed, or the status quo will prevail, which often becomes past oriented, self-serving, and deadening, if not destructive, because it assumes, at its extreme, that God does not continue to be revealed. All we will ever know about God is codified in the scriptural revelations of old. God is dead!

In a real sense this distinction between transformation and status quo was the source of the greatest cleavage in the Protestant church—a cleavage that has had serious repercussions throughout the period of our study. One believes God is still actively revealing God's intentions for the creation and the other insists that we live with past formulations.

The work of Walter Rauschenbusch and other liberal theologians was one source of the new stories of the faith that led Christians to new understandings of Christ. Their work, of course, engendered a violent debate among traditional and reactionary theologians. Rauschenbusch defined evangelical Christianity's social responsibility in terms broader than personal salvation. Christians and Christianity's project was also to transform not only persons, but their institutions and systems of society as well. This view was also fueled by the liberal philosophical projects, which in turn initiated a whole series of other late-nineteenth-century theological endeavors, like the quest for the Historical Jesus, or the attempt to bring Christianity and science into a closer relationship. Yet, scriptural conservatives who believed in the inerrancy of the Bible believed it wrong to try to reconcile biblical and scientific knowledge. They could not accept the Bible as myth or as salvation history. They believed every word had been dictated by God. You do not do theology from myth, textual tradition, experience, or observation. And this fundamentalist schism still is the source of fragmentation. Reactionary and conservative Evangelicals (Fundamentalists) have caused social gospel advocates and theologians to struggle anew with the Christ concept in the last quarter of the twentieth century, and as we have struggled, we grow farther apart—particularistic on the one hand and more universal on the other. Ecumenical theologians are trying to understand Christ in the culture and creation, while fundamentalists argue Christ is apart from culture and creation.

As American culture has become dramatically more pluralistic during this fifty-year period, the experiences of Christians in settings of religious pluralism, whether in the United States or in missions to Asia, caused a great deal of the theological ferment on the nature of Christ. Indeed, this discussion in the United States is embedded in the experiences of local ecumenism. It is the environmentalists, religious pluralists, and social activists, more concerned with the community than personal salvation, who are often active in local ecumenism, and it is these same people who are the proponents of a broader view of Christ. Essentially the story of the new more radical liberal perspective became this: Every time a new transformation takes place, in any sphere of life, it leads to a more universal understanding of the Christ, i.e., the Christic in creation. At the same time there was always a backlash from those who wish to keep status quo.

A Theologically Pragmatic Foundation for Interfaith Work

So how are we as Christian ecumenists to deal with this? Theology seems to be divisive. Yet when you meet with and work with a person of another faith, pragmatism begins to inform. Charles White's chapter on the emergence of interfaith life in these United States so vividly illustrates how our action leads us into new understandings. When the overarching faith concern becomes the care of the community and the care of the earth, it only makes sense that it cannot be done on a religion-by-religion basis. All faith traditions have ethical systems that concern themselves with justice and all have teachings about how to live responsibly in the creation. And a common table makes it possible for these faith traditions to find shared ways to work on common concerns in the communities where they live side by side.

We are curious about our new neighbor's faith and we want to talk with these neighbors to learn more about their faith traditions. In the process our communities often have developed a whole new theological point of view—a point of view that a large proportion of the population, especially those who have left the churches, cannot articulate, but nonetheless are now quite comfortable with. This was expressed so well by Hal Garman in chapter 6. When asked to reflect on the spiritual foundations of the Interreligious Council of Central New York, Dr. Garman said that the IRC

> demonstrates that there is one divine source of all, and in our particular ways and faith traditions we are choosing to relate to that same divine source. The IRC as a community symbol suggests that all relate to one God and we are all Children of that God. We need to realize we are one people with one spiritual source. This then drives all the concerns about poverty, economic and racial justice. It drives us into concern for our multicultural, multiracial and multifaith diversity work . . . to toleration and then moving beyond that to living together in community . . . to get beyond the barriers that tear down community and all the "isms." IRC sets an ideal, as a standard and a path. It is much preferable to just an ecumenical or just a Protestant organization. We have grown beyond that even though we may not know it. At the same time, one divine source drives all the ethical issues. The ethical challenge is to remove the barriers and to find a way to enable this economic system to serve all the peoples at the margins so they become mainstream. IRC is the basis for this vision in Syracuse and surrounding communities.[16]

This is about as solid a theological rationale as we heard anyplace in our research on the interreligious phenomenon. It is pragmatic in that it has grown out of experiencing the other and finding that we share so much. The most interesting thing is his statement, "It is much preferable to just an ecumenical or just a Protestant organization. We have grown beyond that even though we may not know it." Why would a well-educated urban pastor who is baptized into Christ and who affirms Christ as Lord say such a thing? Because it is true! We may not have the theological categories developed to clearly describe it, but from all we know, deep down in our heart, there is one divine source. And this source drives our religious and ethical systems. And those ethical systems concern themselves with justice, community, and creation.

What are doctrinaire, confessing Christians to make of this viewpoint? Many will reject it out of hand, but it is a leading edge in Christian theological thinking. And the exploration of the Christian scripture shows that churches need not be so narrow. "In my Father/Mother's house are many mansions. If it were not so, I would have told you" (John 14:2). "And other sheep I have, which are not of this fold: them also I must bring" (John 10:16). Or, "For the created universe waits with eager expectation for God's children to be revealed . . . yet always there was hope, because the universe itself is to be freed of the shackles of mortality and enter upon the liberty and splendor of the children of God. Up to the present, we know, the whole created universe groans in all its parts for its fulfillment, as if the pangs of childbirth" (Romans 8:19–22). Many mansions? Other sheep? The children of God? The whole creation is to be freed of the shackles of mortality? The whole created universe groans in all its parts for its fulfillment? These testimonies, and many more one might identify throughout the Bible, allow, and indeed almost force, Christians to ask new questions about how unique Christians really are. Could it be that Christians must evaluate how particularistic and unique Jesus whom we believe to be the Christ really is? Could it be that Jesus did not come to create a Church, but rather to draw out a remnant of people who would be a universal symbol of God's work in creation for all people? Could it be that some of those same truths also reside in other faith traditions? After all, they too have been resident in this world for hundreds of generations, and they too have observed the creation and figured out something of the Creator's intention for both creation and humankind.

Yet, many Christians do not want to think these new thoughts. They do not want any new means to deal with other faiths. But we do have the means. It is rooted in one of the earliest Christian Council's teachings. I came to understand this when I was once a part of a teaching team for a course at Harvard Divinity School sponsored by Boston's Theological Institute. Ethicist Max Stackhouse was a part of the team. He observed one day in class that the Council of Nicea in 325 A.D. defined the Trinity for very pragmatic reasons. He said that the issue was, How does a Christian minority know how and where to participate in the larger community's life without compromising themselves? He said that the teaching of the Council was, Wherever you see creative things happening in the community, go join in. That is God the Creator at work. Wherever you see transformation breaking through, go and join in. That is Christ—the Christic—at work. And wherever you see community being formed and strengthened, go and join in. That is the Holy Spirit at work. Christians have a long history of participation and interaction with the "whole inhabited earth." If we are creating, if we are transforming, or if we are developing community, that is God's work regardless of the context—secular, interfaith, or Christian. Whether we do it with Hindus, Muslims, Jews, Buddhists, Sikhs, Animists, or people of any other religion, it makes no difference. We are participating with God in the ongoing creation process. And it is then that we are manifesting our place in the Family of God.

When one looks closely at the creation, the same cosmic struggle and its general revelation of God's purposes is evident. Both the plight and common task of the family of God becomes evident. Creation's light is not an assured thing. Creation is always confronting the forces of darkness in the decay, disintegration (fragmentation), and death that is seen all around. Yet, the hopeful image of the ongoing creation process is creating light in the midst of the darkness, that is, a transformation that makes all things new. It is a cycle: Chaos, creative ordering, life, struggles with decay and death, which ultimately, if we work with the purposes of God in the Creation, results in creating more life and life-giving elements, capped ultimately with our death and return to the bosom of the Creator and Creation. Ideally, it is an upward spiral with each succeeding generation moving all further toward Creation's fulfillment. On the other hand, if a person, a generation, or a people fail in their struggle with the powers of decay and death, they impede the hope of God for Creation's fulfillment.

At the same time, most world religions and certainly Christians already believe humankind is created in God's image. We, as the most sentient of beings, have the high honor of being born to be intentional participants in this ongoing Creation process toward wholeness. The Creation is "groaning for its fulfillment," i.e., when all things work together in harmony—in unity. At a minimum we are called to care for the Creation while living in it and from it. Beyond that, we are called to be keen observers of Creation's purposes. And finally we are called to add our life forces—our hands, minds, and feet—to the creative tasks in our time (because they are different in every time span) of overcoming the evil and giving the Creation ever new life. In the words of our ecumenical colleague Wallace Ford, "We are here to sing praises to the Creator and the Creation." We will know we have done well if we leave the Creation more whole and more vital when our work is done than when we were born into it. All living things have a role to play in this process, but humankind, in this span of history, has been given the key role. If we succeed in our work of finding harmony with Creation's purposes, then shalom or harmony can be realized. If humankind fails, and we destroy ourselves through some global holocaust, or death overtakes us in some other more insidious way, our role in God's history will be a failure. Then, I would posit as a faith statement, God will have faced a setback in Creation's move toward fulfillment and probably would raise up a new species of God's children to be given an opportunity to fulfill the task.

Indeed, I have come to believe that humankind is playing in a great drama on one of Creation's stages. It is a liturgy. And Christians have one model for participating in that work. But so do all other faith traditions, because all have understood the general revelation we garner from seeing the dynamics of Creation. In fact, all the world's religions are themselves continuously living through the same cycle of birth, life, struggle with the dark forces, and then either renewal or stultifying death, that can lead to new birth.

Local ecumenical experience has come to understand that. Many of the Christian ecumenists have come to understand that the creative, the Christic, and the communal is embedded in the very nature of creation. The vitality of all faith formulations is rooted in some dimension in this truth. We are all God's family. Such an understanding is humbling and demands a Christianity that is not triumphal and that will take its place as a responsible world religion. It calls us to first to be Christians, and then it calls us to bring our gifts to the table being set for the whole Family of God. To do otherwise is to shirk our responsibility.

Conclusion

Some have said ecumenism is just a slippery slope to universalism. That is both false and true at the same time. Ecumenism helps us transcend our religious tribalism and understand the salvific activity of God in new ways. It provides the opportunity for us to be with the other and find what we share. It provides the opportunities for diverse parts to work together in harmony, thus enriching each of the parts. But ecumenism provides another element. For the diverse Christian community it provides the arena for Christians to find their common voice. And this secular world, and the other faith traditions, need to be in dialogue with a common Christian voice. So there is need for both Christian ecumenism and for interfaith or maxi-ecumenism. In the end we need each other for our own salvation to be complete as well as for creation to be completed. And in the end all faith traditions will need each other in order to have an impact on the competing global corporation–rooted culture. We are the family of God! And God needs all the siblings in that family in order to do God's work in the Creation!

Notes

1. Wallace Ford, excerpt from "A Brief Overview of the New Mexico Conference of Churches," in proceedings of the *State Ecumenism Consultation*, February 2 to 5, 1995, in New Orleans, p. 59. A copy is in the Local Ecumenism History Project archives in the Library at Christian Theological Seminary, 1000 W. 42nd St., Indianapolis, IN 46208.

2. Richard Niebuhr and others have long argued that most all denominational schisms were deeply rooted in societal dynamics. I largely agree, but by the time that many of these denominations reached the Americas, they had developed strong theological rationales for their differences and often had made them matters of faith. It was these faith statements that have been used most often in the American scene to differentiate them from others. Now those faith statements are less important, and the new social differentiations are cutting across all the Christian denominations, denominating them in new ways.

3. Conrad Hyers, "The Comic Vision in a Tragic World," *Christian Century* 100 (April 20, 1983): 363–67.

4. Gary Peluso, "State Ecumenical Organizations: Who Owns Them?," pp.17–28, in Report, "State Ecumenism Consultation: Revisioning, Reconnecting, Rerooting, and Rejoicing," National Conference of Catholic Bishops and the Ecumenical Networks of the National Council of Churches in the USA, February 2–5, 1995, New Orleans. This report is available in the History Project Archives, Library, Christian Theological Seminary, Indianapolis.

5. Ibid., p. 19.

6. I have often defined tolerance as the most sophisticated form of hatred.

7. Michael Kinnamon, *Breaking New Ground: Re-Rooting State Ecumenism*, p. 36.

8. Brian Swimme, *The Universe Is a Green Dragon: A Cosmic Creation Story* (Santa Fe: Bear and Co., 1984). Sheen refers to the luminosity of the atom and energy generally.

9. This new perspective of the Divine Being in all things is very similar to the beliefs of Animist tribes that we worked with in northern Bangladesh, who believe that God is in every living thing and created object.

10. Matthew Fox, *The Reinvention of Work: A Vision of Livelihood for Our Time* (San Francisco: Harper San Francisco, 1995), p. 88.

11. "Maxi-ecumenism" is a term I often use to distinguish the broader interfaith relationships from the narrower Christian ecumenism. The term "ecumenical" means the whole inhabited earth but has been largely co-opted by Christians to describe what Christians do and commit to one another. Therefore maxi-ecumenism is what the various world faiths do and commit to one another.

12. Peluso, *State Ecumenical Organizations*, p. 28.

13. This is a true story that was life-changing for me. I have told it many times in many contexts, including in an article published in 1990 by the Interfaith Dialogue Office of the World Council of Churches, as well as in several sermons. Kan Ori went on to earn a Ph.D. at the University of Minnesota and then to become a professor of peace studies at the Jesuit Sophia International University in Tokyo and an advisor on peace concerns to the Japanese prime minister.The last time I talked with him, before his untimely death, he had just returned from leading an official Japanese peace delegation to the Soviet Union and Helsinki, Finland.

14. From my design and process work in Syracuse.

15. Christic is the transforming nature of God's activity in history. That which Jesus came to dramatize in the lifetime of one man is endemic in the very nature of creation itself. Death and resurrection—transformation—is the stuff creation and history is made of. This view does not take away from the efficacy of Jesus as the Christ; rather, it universalizes it.

16. From an interview with Hal Garman. Garman holds a Ph.D., completed with Dean Walter Muelder of Boston University. He dedicated all his career to being a United Methodist urban minister and a central city pastor in Syracuse. This videotape is available in the Local Ecumenism History Project archives in the Library at Christian Theological Seminary, 1000 W. 42nd St., Indianapolis, IN 46208.

22

HEADLINES OF AN ECUMENICAL FUTURE

Peg Chemberlin

Ecumenism in the twenty-first century is at a turning point, as happens in every generation, and there are at least three central questions that will need to be resolved. The first is the question of the movement's and organizations' value to the world context as it emerges in the twenty-first century. The second is the question of the relationship of ecumenism to other expressions of Church: congregations and denominations. The third is the dilemma of focus and organizational viability. The resolution of each of these dilemmas has an impact on each of the other dilemmas. What follows are some hypothetical headlines from this future.

"The Ecumenical Worldview Challenges Cultural Assumptions and Awakens New Hope"

This headline foresees the possibility of the ecumenical worldview of relatedness and mutuality offering a counterresponse to a renewed quest for global domination.

A few years back, after the Berlin Wall had fallen, the first George Bush was talking about a new world order. The National Council of Churches of Christ decided that the Church should be in on this discussion and held a conference called "A World Made New" in downtown Indianapolis. Central Indiana is not known for being a place of liberalism, either politically or theologically. The meetings were held in the Episcopal Cathedral. Attending that meeting was William Sloan Coffin, a well-known, self-avowed, practicing liberal leader in the Church. One morning he walked into the Cathedral, past a small crowd gathered outside holding signs that said things like "NCC is the anti-Christ" or "NCC=666." One young ecumenist turned to him and said, "Well, Bill," and then repeated those well-known words of Ephesians, "one Lord, one faith, one baptism?" Coffin turned and, scowling over his glasses, looked at her as if she had just asked the most annoying question. Then he lifted his glasses up onto his forehead, turned and looked at the crowd, and pondered. She waited for insightful words from the great orator. He lowered his glasses, turned to go in the doors, shrugged his shoulders, and said, "That's what they tell me." Since its inception the ecumenical movement has been one that speaks of this relatedness, and certainly a conference called "A World Made New" in response to the political call for "a new world order" was within the scope of the movement. But it was perhaps this simple interchange outside the cathedral that captured the hope the ecumenical movement presents.

We are related, that's what they tell me. The central Christian experience of reconciliation with God through Christ had led many to urgency for reconciliation with others. They say, "This is the witness that we know we have when, in Christ, we are welcomed back to the heart of God—we are related." The Body of Christ image has been a predominant one in the ecumenical movement. That sense of oneness, even as the Son and the Father are one, is believed to be a gift of unity already given in Christ—not based on denominational agreement, or even affinity, but on the gift already given by Christ. "The gift precedes the vision of the gift," Michael Kinnamon repeatedly reminds us. "Like families of origin, perhaps even more than our families of origin, we don't associate with each other because we like each other but because we're related. If we like each other it just makes it more fun."[1]

Since that moment outside the cathedral in Indianapolis a new George Bush has come to the White House and a new more blatant vision of world domination is seen. Karl Rove, often believed to be the architect of George W. Bush's election and, to some extent, foreign policy, is a student of the McKinley era and, according to Bill Moyers, is intent on replicating its oligarchic approach to both domestic and foreign policy.[2] Under the McKinley administration, the United States acquired Guam, the Philippines, Puerto Rico, Hawaii, and islands in the Samoan group. When the Philippines revolted, McKinley said, "There is nothing left for us to do but to take them all, and educate the Filipinos and uplift and civilize and Christianize them."[3] McKinley couched his foreign policy in economic terms. He moved the country onto the global scene primarily for economic reasons. In a speech to the Pan-American Exposition in Buffalo shortly before he was assassinated he said, "By sensible trade relations which will not interrupt our home production, we shall extend the outlets for our increasing surplus. . . . The period of exclusiveness is past."[4]

That policy of global domination provided the context for the emergence of a countering vision, one of global mutuality—the ecumenical worldview. Today's renewal of the McKinley approach carries the possibility of religious (transcendent) meaning. In the twenty-first century will the ecumenical worldview again offer an alternative framework as it did in the early twentieth century?

When the Vatican released the document *Domine Jesu* in 2000, it was thought that perhaps old perspectives were being renewed, particularly ones about other Christian groups and other world religions. Many viewed the statement as an attempt to diminish the power of Vatican II. But one Roman Catholic bishop said that this was the last gasp of the old worldview and that the statement had little authority.

Are we seeing the last gasp of an old worldview inside the Church and in the world? Some would contend, as the bishop did, that the prevailing worldview is changing, and that these are just the last gasps of a passing era. They say that documents and worldviews that deny the global connectedness are reactionary and antiquated and will increasingly be discounted by more and more of the world's leadership. Certainly, on a worldwide scale we have seen broad worldwide opposition to George W. Bush's foreign policy. But which perspective will be embraced?

Among the most important images of the last half of the twentieth century was that first picture taken from the moon, of the earth rising. It was a new view of the world and indeed it was a new worldview. It was a worldview of the whole inhabited earth, what the Greeks call the *oikoumene*. To see that wholeness put a new claim upon us, and we came to regard our planet home with new wisdom and to hear old phrases in new ways. We could see what Buckminster Fuller and some others had been preaching—we could see the oneness, the organic unity of the planet.

These themes were being repeated inside the Church and in the broader religious community, as well as outside. For instance, theologian Letty Russell says that God calls us primarily to join the Holy One in the mending of the world. The emergence of the *Tikkun Olam* magazine and movement is another striking example. "Tikkun olam" means to heal and repair the world. This new worldview will relativize all claims of sovereignty. In the future neither nation nor denomination can carry a claim apart from this whole earth image. The new view of the earth rising called us to hold the earth in all its diversity as a single entity, whole, connected. This is indeed a worldview that many embrace with vigor—but is it emerging as a worldwide value?

In the meantime we struggle with a world in deep need of a new vision. Our community—that is our congregations, our neighborhoods, our cities, our state, our country, our world—our community—will continue to shatter into special-interest shards that cannot carry a commitment to a common good. Nor will those shards envision, much less build, that commitment. Our community will continue to feel the social earthquakes of deep-seated mistrust, vitriolic slander, and broad apprehension about any common ground from which to seek the common good. In a vision of the future, we seem inextricably drawn into adversarial finger-pointing and blaming that holds no one accountable for the necessity to act on behalf of the whole. There are few places that provide an articulation of a vision of an inclusive, worldwide common good, built on a shared relationship.

A vision of relatedness is a vision that this world will desperately need. Today we hear accounts and see the images of fragmentation, alienation, and isolation. We're alienated from one another and from our institutions. We're alienated from the institutions needed to form a society. We don't trust those fundamental institutions of governance, culture, education, health, business, and faith. A group of young professionals, who have each identified that they have a vocational calling to lead in their communities, also say that they are unclear about how to do that in this day. One of the brightest in a very bright group recently said: "The older generation did a great job of deconstructing public institutions, for good reasons in most cases, but you've left us to reconstruct them without a blueprint." He's right; the generation now in charge saw the problems with centralization, big government, big business, and big religions and called for a new grassroots movement. We have successfully created a culture of suspicion toward all institutions and the values perpetuated by them. The challenge of reimagining and recreating institutional life looms large on the horizon.

In the 1960s we stepped across the threshold of pluralism and will never be able to go back. As a culture we went from one right way to do things to seeing the legitimate call for the embracing of our multicultural world. In addition we began to see the organizing among those who had a shared sense of victimization and who, from their organized base, could call for a new analysis that looked for the systemic causes of victimization and required the culture to quit blaming the victim. But that movement was one of advocacy. In the religious world we called it "speaking truth to power." As if we had no power, as if power were out there somewhere, only to be confronted. As if the hierarchy was the only place of power. And then we became the hierarchy and we still felt we had no power.

Leadership will need to be renewed as a function of authority and accountability. The twenty-first century will require new articulations and practices to be developed, tested, and evaluated. Today we're fully ambivalent about our leadership. At the time of the election of one president of NAEIS, the job was described as "herding cats—wild cats—to get this very independent group to do anything together." Another colleague said, "We want you to lead us, now just try." One newly elected leader of a state ecumenical agency set off to meet with the leaders of the member communions. The number one issue, across the board, was the ambivalence they felt about their roles and authority—their own ambivalence and that of their constituencies.

The sixties was a very important time for us to test our power analysis, which saw the systemic causes of problems. We learned how important it was not to blame the victim but to look at the systemic causes of victimization. We learned to rally victims to create new power bases. But that has left us with a special interest politic. Everywhere our communities are divided into special interest groups, none of which can carry a commitment to the common good.

We mistrust our political leaders and our political lobbyists. Yet we see them as service providers to We, the Taxpayers. We rarely see ourselves as partners in the civic enterprise. Our government leaders laud the private citizen and we bow in honor as if there were such a thing as a *private* citizen. An ecumenical staff person met with a group of college students at a state university to talk about the public role of the church. In that discussion he asked, "How many of you think of yourself as an obligated citizen?" No one raised his or her hand. When he changed the phrase to "responsible citizen," a few, but only a few, raised their hands. Who does the next generation think is going to lead them?

If present trends hold, in the world to come we will grow in our alienation and fragmentation. We will work in one place, live in another, socialize across town, vacation around the world, and if we worship at all, we will worship in another neighborhood completely. Our friends will not be the parents of our children's friends; we won't run into our children's teachers in the grocery store. We won't know the precinct captain even if we see her. We will get our personal care and health care from team members who have never met each other. Our banker won't know our real-estate agent; we will have no ongoing relationship with most of the professionals in our lives. We will be more likely to know the guy at the desk next to us than we will to know the fellow in the house next to us. You have heard it said that it takes a village to raise a child. But in the future there will be no more sense of village in which to raise our children, in which to develop moral integrity, in which to find coworkers to solve community problems together.

We'll be even more mobile than ever and more isolated as well. People will tell how their best friends live across the country or how they've never had a best friend. We will consume entertainment as if that were real relationships. The private lives of public figures will be more important to us than our own public lives. We will commodify our most intimate relationships. There will be an increasing difficulty in differentiating real relationships from the relationships of entertainment.

The culture will hold out a number of responses, some more hopeful than others. One response to fragmentation will be to become the dominant fragment, to do those things that puts one in charge enough to control the decision making, the resources, the values, the enforcement institutions in a community. This is the worldview of the McKinley era. A second response will be to try to secure oneself against the other fragments. Walled communities, increased security measures, expansion of conceal-and-carry gun laws, and a preponderance of larger and heavier SUVs are signs of this response. And the culture will hold up, as it often does, advanced technology as a possible salvific response. More and better communication tools will be touted as a hopeful sign but will leave us with more anonymous communication, not more actual community relationships.

Pay-per-minute relationships on telephone 1-900 calls to strangers is a growing enterprise. Real relationship or not? Springer guests, real or not? Tabloid news stories, real or not? Home videos sent in to win big prizes, staged or not? So called reality television, video voyeurism—real relationships or not? Relationships, supposedly real relationships, have become valuable commodities. In a world where communication technology has never been more advanced, anonymity seems to be winning out. And a sense of being related to anyone drops from sight. Alienation, fragmentation, commodification, isolation are on the move among us.

This lack of relationship leaves us without structures of accountability. Whom are we accountable to? How do we hold each other accountable in an anonymous universe? And how will the largest problems of society get solved by people who are anonymous to each other? Without structures of relationships, networks of capacity working together, how can we solve large-system problems? Without community structures to which we will allow ourselves to be held accountable the fabric of community will continue to unravel. In the future, accountability will also become a commodity—that is, accountability will be bought and sold. Our only relationships of accountability are likely to be with the ones who sign our paychecks.

It is not only accountability and intimate relationship that will become commodities; even our notion of church is being commodified. Increasingly, congregants will think of themselves as consumers of church and not producers of church. And increasingly congregations will think of themselves as consumers of denominations and not producers. And increasingly denominations will think of themselves as consumers of councils of churches, not producers. As in our public life, we will all too quickly think of ourselves as taxpayers, read consumers, first and obligated citizens a far second. This self-identification alienates us from the civic fabric and unravels the social capital—inside the church as well as out. And we will be left with little capacity to act together for the common good.

Many in our world now dare not even hope that we can solve the problems that plague us. Increasing numbers will give up the hope that all our children can be fed, or health epidemics controlled, or housing built so that none go homeless. A neoconservative agenda that is now showing itself on most social issues at local, state, and national levels will push to become the agenda of the majority. The agenda carries a proclamation making individual economic freedom the top value. The agenda has little regard for the common wealth, only for the private wealth, as if those two are independent of each other. The transcendent value given to the individual and his or her capital will encourage the followers to denounce all other realities, thereby appearing to have a mandate to perpetuate itself.

If this agenda succeeds in capturing the loyalty of a majority of Americans, increasingly the churches will need to post the request that no guns come into that space. Social programs will be cut. In a country that has long been lifted up as a place of excellent health care and education we are likely under the new conservatism to continue to have one of the worst records in health and educational disparities along racial and economic lines. Business giants will continue to threaten bankruptcy and loss of jobs without tax cuts while executives get million-dollar bonuses and union members are asked to take double-digit percentage cuts. Charges of class warfare will continue to be leveled in the tax debates whenever the opposition calls for economic justice. And military excess will continue to be touted as a redeeming feature of the society and the cure for fear and anxiety. And those who raise questions about a policy of war are branded as unpatriotic and even traitorous.

It is a great challenge today and in the future to be the whole Church, the One Body, in all its very complicated diversity. But this is the gift we have been given and a gift that is intended for the whole world, a gift that will reveal itself more fully in the century to come, and a gift that is deeply needed. Our relationships with each other are meant for the redemption and reconciliation of the whole world. How desperate the world is to know this witness. It is the witness to the promise of God's reconciling power for the church and the world. It demonstrates a community that values each member, makes decisions that honor diversity, and is able to hold each other accountable while building up the community. We are in desperate need of models of community in which there is an expression of relatedness beyond agreement on issues.

In the coming century perhaps more than ever before we will need to renew our conviction that we are related in the Church to Christ and through Christ to one another. In the second person of the Trinity we are knit together into an extraordinary oneness. And the eye cannot say, "I have no need of the hand." And the hand cannot say, "I have no need of the foot." And the foot cannot say, "I have no need of the ear." Each part of the Body of Christ is needed to know the whole Body of Christ. To be the church is to be the church with others, to be out of fellowship with any part is to be missing a part we need in order to know the whole body.

In the same manner as we move into the twenty-first century we cannot avoid, nor should we, the call of the unity we have with the whole world in the first person of the Trinity. We have a witness to bring together; it is a witness to the *oneness* of this creation. For the earth is the Lord's and the *fullness* thereof. It is not just a few who are held in God's hand but *the whole* world, the fullness of creation. Every man, woman, child, rock, tree, and mosquito belongs to God. And if the world is hell-bent on splintering itself into more and more pieces, if the culture all around us continues to praise the individual and divide the community, if the whole creation groans under the divisions among us, then we have a different message to tell.

We have a different word, a word of hope to speak. In the face of fragmentation we proclaim that we belong to each other. The left hand cannot continue to ignore the pain of the right hand. Nor can the imaginary lines of national sovereignty blind us to the created oneness of the whole *oikoumene*. (The word ecumenical, of course, comes from this Greek word *oikoumene*, which means the whole-inhabited earth, or the whole earth household.) The twentieth-century picture taken from the moon of the earth rising puts a new claim on us. The ecumenical Christian is also called to an ecumenical worldview that presses us beyond the confines of a Christo-centric understanding of ecumenism to include a Creator/creation-centric revelation.

Sometimes other Christians accuse ecumenists of relativizing the faith. Michael Kinnamon answers a firm "no" to that accusation, saying, "What I hold to be true about God and life, is not other than what is revealed in Jesus Christ. But precisely because of what I have come to know about God in Christ, I know that God's truth is far greater than any of my particular conceptions of it. And, perhaps of most importance, precisely because of what I have come to know about God in Christ, I believe that God's abundant love extends far wider than my particular community. The Christian understanding of God's love is a universal understanding. That is, God's love is intended for the whole world."[5]

So tradition shows the way to live into love. It also shows the value of diversity. From the ecumenical worldview we affirm that God has brought into existence a single human family of great diversity, and that diversity is a gift to the creation and constitutive of that creation. Joan Brown Campbell, former general secretary of the National Council of Churches, tells the story from her years at the NCCC. A number of religious leaders were called into a meeting at the White House to talk about life on Mars. Most of those in attendance were scientists, physicists, and astronomers. In that conversation the word "ecumenical" came up a number of times but it wasn't the religious leaders that were using that word, it was the scientists who talked about the ecumenical nature of the foundation of life, meaning that diversity is required for life to exist. That great earth rising is a tribute to the processes of diversity that undergirds the very fabric of life. Diversity is constitutive of life itself.

The fundamental task of the ecumenical Christian in the twenty-first century will not be to ignore diversity or move to sameness, nor is it to "whitewash" the diverse character of our being, but rather to act and see that diversity as a gift. Christians will need to understand that diversity needs freedom to flourish. That is true for the biology of the planet, it is true in the journey of every human, and it is true of the political system with which we all struggle.

Finally, this love and this embrace of diversity propels us toward at least three practices for our life together in the twenty-first century: the Comparative, the Cooperative, and the Appreciative acts. We must sit and compare what we think, feel, and believe. We need to have more straightforward heartfelt conversations about what it is in our own tradition that is of transcendent and ultimate value and why we are each willing to risk everything on that faith or belief system. In so doing, we will grow in faithfulness to our own tradition. We must know our tradition as a first step in knowing the "other" in our midst. We must cooperate to build communities of love, justice, and peace and push one another to be true to each chosen tradition, and then find where values are shared. And we must learn to appreciate and celebrate the wonder of our diversity as a gift to the whole creation, the whole world household, never overlooking the differences, but always embracing them as gifts enriching all of us.

We may start from different points and, perhaps, end at different points, but there's a great deal of common value and concern in between. We may not agree on who or what—or if—God is. Or where, when, or how we arrive in the godly presence or at the point of liberation or enlightenment, but among the historic world religions we do agree that love, in it's many forms, is the prime directive. And there seems to be plenty of space in between the first and the last moment in which to live into those shared values.

As we recall that picture of earth rising we see for a moment a hope, a vision of connection, a new worldview. Let's join the farmer and poet Wendell Berry, who said, "The divine love summons the world toward wholeness."[6]

"Denominations Renewed by Ecumenical Movement"

This section will focus on the ways in which denominational and congregational life need the ecumenical worldview. It will also consider the implications for the ecumenical movement if the denominations are not renewed in this way.

If diversity is constitutive of life, what does that mean for denominational identity and perceived sense of solidarity? Identity functions to position Christians in relationship to the world. The definition of identity will formulate mission to/with the world. Choosing a Christian identity, which understands itself to be in relationship to the rest of the world, gives one a basis for ecumenical work and practices but also offers a word about mission and the body politic. Can the ecumenical identity offer meaning in the identity struggles that individuals, congregations, and denominations are going through? Can an identity of inclusivity—understood as having a given relatedness—be embraced in the future?

In every age the Church has asked, "How shall we live as a holy people, a redeemed people? How can we be encouraged in that effort?" Often the models of community that have been attempted to answer those questions have required a coming out from the world. Sometimes that happens as a complete rejection of the world. Sometimes it happens in more subtle ways like a denomination's fight about who is in and who is out and how we protect the purity of the faith. To the degree that the posture toward the world is rejection, then the world could only be engaged as that which is to be converted and brought inside the particular version of Christian identity. This kind of community holds to a sense of being other or alien to the culture or cultures around it. These models rely on an assumption of identity that is, in part, based on being "not them." The definition of identity will formulate mission to/with the world for the ecumenical movement but also for congregations and denominations. If the Christian is called out of the world into a protective environment, what is the inherent theology about God's relationship with the rest of the world? And about the identity of those who are "not us"?

Often this "setting apart" takes place because of our need to be nurtured in the faith, to be encouraged in the calling of God, to be held to the spiritual disciplines; these can all be gifts of a community of shared identity. On the other hand, that kind of setting apart can easily slide into an inherent rejection of the rest of God's creation. This is a particularly inviting posture in a world where so much seems to be foreign to the will of the God of love. But an identity that is built on who we are not, built on a rejection of the other, will need to be replaced in the twenty-first century with an identity built on an acceptance of relatedness with the other. We must no longer find our identity in that which we are not. There are at least three reasons this is true:

1. We know each other too well. Building identity on that which we are not may have worked in a context of religious isolation, but we're too close these days. Living in a religiously pluralistic world dramatically increases that closeness. Building one's "I-ness" on the other's "otherness" requires a distance we no longer have.
2. Secondly, we've crossed a threshold: A critical mass of Christians no longer believe that other Christians are outside the fellowship of the body of Christ just because they are different. We have begun to see some of the gifts of differences.
3. But the third reason may be the most compelling. Pope John Paul II reiterates the Vatican II decree in ecumenism when in *Ut Unum Sint* he says, "Division openly contradicts the will of Christ, provides a stumbling block to the world and inflicts damage on the most holy cause of proclaiming the *good* news to every creature."[7] If we preach a

> gospel of reconciliation but we do not model that gospel then our division diminishes our proclamation. For the sake of the proclamation we must find ways to give up claiming a denominational identity over and against another Christian denomination.

Have you ever had to list your faith, for instance, when you check into the hospital? If one puts "Christian" they will tell you that you've done it wrong. They are asking for faith but mean denomination. But our first identity must be as Christian, as a member of the Body of Christ. To do otherwise is to practice a certain form of idolatry. Given that, what is the role of the denominations and denominational identity? It has to do with being the bearer of a tradition of certain gifts that the whole Body of Christ needs. Why? Because each part of the Body of Christ is needed to know the whole Body of Christ. To be out of fellowship with any part is to be missing a part we need in order to know the whole body. Because this body is the Body of Christ, the one, we must pay attention to each other, each part revealing a deeper understanding of the whole Christ. Michael Kinnamon has spoken repeatedly of the ways in which each reforming movement has seen itself as an attempt to recover some aspect of faithfulness that it saw as missing in the Church at the time. Our ecumenical discipleship, that is, our efforts to know and live with each other, are, at their center, efforts to more fully know the one we call Christ.

That definition of identity will formulate mission to/with the world in very different ways. Can the denominations find an identity in the inclusive worldview? Or is it only the stewarding of the identity that has been such a powerful institutional tool for separateness? Is it possible to have an identity that leads us to a bridging posture? Is it possible that the new, emerging identity, which needs to be central to the Christian church, is that of being ecumenical? That is, to be a Christian is to be one who has a deep sense of the relatedness of the creation and to every local community, and to be a Christian means to learn and practice a worldview within one's own faith community in order to practice it in the larger faith community. The church then becomes increasingly the clinic, the lab, the staging area that both prepares us for engagement with the larger cultural and its values and practices attempting to find a common ground out of which we can act in accountable ways for the common good.

Is it possible to see a relationship through God's given gift of personhood whether or not one assents to the creedal statements of the faith community? Can we look to two levels of community mandated by our relatedness? While that relatedness has an additional quality to it within the identity of the faith, if that identity is primarily understood as relatedness, as gift of God, then, perhaps, that postures us toward the world in ways that are different from any of the models of the past.

If our first identity is as a Christian and we claim relatedness to all who are baptized and confess Christ, then there has to be a place to work out that relatedness. We don't marry and then live in separate houses on opposite coasts and never talk to each other. If we're related then we have a household to tend to. Ecumenical discipleship is the working out of those relationships, and each Christian in every place is called to some aspect of tending the ecumenical relationship, to bring the gifts to the household. That is true for the denomination as well (and each judicatory within a denomination and each congregation)—every level has an ecumenical discipleship to be lived out, and that discipleship has to do with bringing individual gifts.

It is also the role of denominations to be structures of accountable relationships, to knit together a more tightly woven whole. Not every Christian can engage with every other Christian. In denominations, congregations are related structurally to other congregations. And in state councils of churches, denominations are related structurally to other denominations. There are great questions these days about the future of denominations and therefore ecumenical activity built on denominational structures. Denominations are reinventing themselves to be more accountable to congregations, but doing so using a commodity model as if the only leverage of accountability is in withholding the fair share offerings from the congregation to the denomination. The reinvention of the future will have to design more mutuality and reciprocity in the relationships in order to weave a unified fabric as the foundation for the tapestry of God's work in the Creation.

Other issues in the lives of denominations will be played out on the ecumenical landscape as well. One set of issues is being raised across denominations by the neoconservative segments within denominations that have been the ecumenical stalwarts over the years. There are three primary issues: What is the authority of scripture? Is there salvation apart from Christ? What shall be the Church's response to the presence of gay, lesbian, bisexual, and transgender persons, or any other person who is perceived as different? This language is not necessarily the language of the neoconservatives, but these are the issues.

The authority of leaders and the authority of community are related to the above questions but are only now emerging in the conversation as fundamental with the so-called Evangelical community. These issues have long been at the center of dialogue in and with the Roman Catholic Church, however, and will be clearly focused on in the discussions with the neoconservatives. The issue of authority will be at the center of the denominational crisis, which will become an identity crisis. Who are we as a denomination? Who is the "we"? How do we organize our relationships? What authority do we have? Do we lead, or provide service to congregations, or both, and who decides? This crisis will have a direct bearing on the health of middle judicatory-based ecumenical and regional ecumenical organizations that will have to ask similar questions. Who are we to one another? What authority do we have? Do we exist to lead congregations or to serve, to speak to or to speak for? American ecumenism has never really been carried by the denominations. In fact, ecumenical leaders have often carried a vision that was critical of the parochialism of the denominations.

The diminishing membership of youth and young adults in mainline denominations is a related critical issue. This has, of course, financial implication for the denominations and those ecumenical organizations that are judicatory-based. But there is a greater question. To what degree is the diminishing membership in mainline denominations indicative that the denominations are not relevant to youth and young adults? And to what degree is that irrelevance due to a too-narrow worldview?

Karen Armstrong writes, in *A Battle for God,* that "there is a self selection process going on in American religion." The Fundamentalists are more serious about that battle than are the old-line denominations. At best the youth of the mainline churches are pursuing their Christian vocations outside the churches. At worst, they have given in to the Fundamentalists' argument—even though they may not really believe it. The re-sectarianism of American religious life will mean that the ecumenically oriented denominations will feel pressed to either join the more fundamental identity or lose strength."[8] Will ecumenism be a forerunner of a renewed Church with a vision for mission based in a vital worldview, or is ecumenism the canary in the mine of the denominations' demise?

In the future, if denominations are too focused as stewards of the institution, if they do not have a motivating vision or mission, and if they are turned inward, the decline will continue. Only organizations that are turned outward will thrive. And only organizations that are about community can meet real needs in a secularized society. Most denominational leaders have had their roles defined as steward of what is or has been, a valuable role to be sure, but not a leadership role. Leadership is about past, present, and especially the future. But given the ambivalence we have toward authority and leadership, a renewal of those roles will have to be part of the solution. To have dynamic leaders rather than managers of decline will require a renewal of the whole set of assumptions, authority, and rewards for denominational leaders. Can ecumenical organizations survive linked to that dilemma? Managers of decline have very little motivation for having a compelling vision or to be very ecumenically minded.

Gary Peluso, in a study on local and regional ecumenism for Lilly in 1995, has said that "many peoples on this planet are ready to observe groups with differences [as they] learn how to discover, speak, and live the truth in love together."[9] Here is perhaps a vision that could capture the attention of the generations of the twenty-first century. What better place than in the ecumenical movement to respond to the world's need. But it takes enormous effort to build those kinds of relationships—to know each other and engage each other and reweave each other into the kinds of communities that can deliberate in differences and still find a common ground, the kinds of communities that can act together on that common ground for the common good, the kinds of communities that are so knit together that we find we can hold each other accountable and be held accountable. Can the Christian ecumenical vision and practice of relatedness offer a different transcendent meaning to the world of our future?

As we weave the repairs to the fabric, or build the new stained glass window, we will be successful only as we engage in this work together, for it is precisely in the witness of our ability to work together that a witness to the common good can take shape. And when we do it together our achievement will exceed our resources. Our work must be marked by the repairing of small rips and tears that divide us, so that our work and witness *together* might be made strong for the building up of the new art of community, for the repairing of the vast fabric of our lives.

In 1990 the World Council of Churches said: "Now is the time when the ecumenical movement [and I would say, the Church as a whole] needs a greater sense of binding, mutual commitment and solidarity in word and action."[10] Can the Church reclaim its call to be an arena for moral deliberation and discernment on behalf of the public good. Such a calling requires us to provide models, guidelines, resources for the development of those opportunities in local congregations and communities, but must also be modeled in our life together. Such work of reconciliation will require the repairing of the breach *within* the Church as well. In the WCC document *Costly Unity*, the authors write, "Are the different communions ready to see that communion between them—koinonia—whether in matters of faith or of ethical responsibility, calls for steps toward structures of mutual accountability?"[11]

By coming together we not only share our diverse gifts but *receive* gifts as well. That's a very important statement. It implies mutual accountability, an assumption that by our coming together we will be changed and through our interaction with each other we will move toward becoming the Church God calls us to be. The nature of what it means to be church is wedded to our life together as *the* Church.

But how to do that? What are the signs of such accountability? Let's take a look at what that might look like for those councils of churches that are constituted by denominations. The following is based, in great part, on the Ecclesiology Statement of the NCCC 1997, a vision which has yet to be practiced. We have said relational ecumenism is based on the conviction that the Body of Christ is One and that Unity is a gift of God already given in Jesus Christ; the gift precedes our vision of the gift. Therefore it precedes any efforts we may make to be faithful to that gift. It is not a result of either our agreement or even affinity. As a gift already given, denominations receive the ecumenical calling as essential to their own denominational identities. Our life together serves first of all to manifest this gift in the fellowship *among* the member churches. Identity comes from this relationship, not from agreement on mission. But rather the identity propels the mission.

In the future it may be that denominations do not pursue their life and mission independent of the other churches, but rather attempt to discern together what builds up all parts of the Body. In the future we may find that we commit to pray for each other not just in our work together but in our seemingly separate endeavors, knowing that we pray for ourselves. We may recognize that we are a part of the one ecumenical movement and demonstrate the oneness of the ecumenical movement through relationships with local, national, and ecumenical bodies and movements. In the future our life together provides space for continual conversation about the nature of our fellowship and the impact on our denominational ecclesiologies.

The future also holds an expansion of the traditional ecumenical membership. The Body of Christ is not limited by membership; therefore a council will always seek to expand the ecumenical conversation. We see evidence of that in the Churches Coming Together in the USA at our national level and in the Forum at the international level. These are judicatory-based/denomination-based initiatives, but with many more judicatories and traditions coming to the table. Some states are seeing that expansion as well. Minnesota has a quarterly meeting of heads of communion from a very broad

Christian spectrum. The meeting's agenda is to hear the stories of each other's faith journeys and to share information about cooperative ministries.

We have seen that diversity is also understood to be a gift of Christ within unity and therefore an opportunity to more fully understand the One who does the uniting. Encountering diversity within the unity, then, is a means of the Spirit's renewal for the whole Church. Councils could be places for diversity to be lifted up. We should expect to be surprised and changed by the Spirit in this life together. The fellowship of a council of churches is not something static but instead is dynamic. That is, fellowship experienced in councils is not only rooted in what the churches *are* but in what they are called to *become*. Because every member denomination is part of the Body of Christ, every member denomination is an equally valued contributor and each point of view is understood. Each member looks to see what new understanding of Christ the other has to reveal.

The ecumenical fellowship of the Body of Christ is not based on agreement, but holds *within* the relationship both agreement and disagreement. Dialogue then includes examination of the convictions that *separate* us as well as *unite* us and looks for the Spirit's power in overcoming barriers that divide us. We structure opportunities for mutual admonition as well as affirmation. Admonition, in relationally based ecumenism, is first of all a challenge to understand and to be understood rather than to come to agreement or win a vote. We expect to be challenged and to be understood. We expect (demand) to be challenged to deeper and deeper and more costly ecumenical commitment.

The gift of Unity given in Christ, sustained in the Spirit, is intended for the well-being of the whole earth community and is also a gift given by God the Father and Mother of all in creation. Council life witnesses to the promise of God's reconciling power for the church and the world. It demonstrates a community that values each member, makes decisions that honor diversity, and is able to hold each accountable while building up the community. In the future, therefore, councils must seek multisector collaborations that also strive for the well-being of the whole earth community. And internal structure and processes must also be relational, have integrity with, and embody the above principles.

"Ecumenical Organizations Solve the Dilemma of Organizational Focus"

Here we will seek to explore how the question of focus in organizational life will need to be attended to in the future.

The final significant dilemma is the one of focus of local ecumenism. Organizational development consultants say that an organization's viability depends on being focused. But focus can result in a truncation of the ecumenical calling. Prior to 1995 Gary Peluso interviewed many local and regional councils of churches and community ministries. He concluded that there are four spatial metaphors that describe the location of local ecumenical organizations. They are the center, at the margins, in the gap, and on the horizon. These spatial metaphors offer a starting point for thinking about the focus of ecumenical work of the future.

Peluso reminded us that some elders can remember when "a council's powerbrokers could hardly be distinguished from the business and political kingpins of a locale."[12] Peluso suggests that few organizations see their role in that way today. He notes that few are actually in the center of society, but many still have access to the power centers of community life. An ecumenical organization being at the power center is an image of councils in the 1950s.

The image changed dramatically in the 1960s, as we have seen. Peluso typifies the next role with the metaphor of the margin: "Many desired . . . a solidarity with persons on the margins of church and society." He notes that organizations are margin organizations if they are constituted by those individuals who were on the margins of the Church's theology or practice, or if they are seeking primarily to relate to those on the margins. But he also notes that ecumenical ventures are themselves on the margins of congregational and denominational life.

Peluso says that ecumenical efforts have often been focused on filling the gaps of society, particularly in providing needed direct services that government seems unwilling or unable to provide. In turn there have been times when the larger society, including government, has looked to the faith community, through ecumenical or interreligious organizations, to provide moral guidance in moments of crisis.

Finally he names as his preferred spatial metaphor for ecumenism, the church on the horizon. "Horizons are places of meeting, of encounters, of looking ahead while seeing what is now."[13] He places ecumenical organizations at the place where the church and the world meet.

There are some parallels between this Peluso description and our understanding as expressed in the previous chapters of the aspects of local ecumenism's foci of service, justice, community, and unity. Much of the justice work is conducted at the margins, although leadership sometimes longs to be more at the center of such decisions. The service work of organizations is often the gap work that Peluso speaks of. But unity does not appear to line up clearly with any of these metaphors unless it is molded from a common focus on the horizon. A horizon pulls all forward. And, indeed, among the ecumenical organizations he studied, unity had relatively lesser play.

Local ecumenism has provided housing programs, after-school mentoring efforts, AIDS ministries, soup kitchens, and chaplains, has educated young people, launched antiracism efforts, fought for the common good, lobbied, convened discussions resulting in new acceptance of racial and religious diversity, held living room dialogues among various Christian faiths, and supported interfaith conversations. The list goes on and on. In this volume, we have seen the role that service, justice, and unity have played in ecumenical life because together they have been dedicated to building community. Keeping all three going at the same time is a rare accomplishment. Some would say that trying to keep all three in play causes a lack of focus that will eventually diminish the viability of the organization. Others would say that to neglect any one of them is to diminish the ecumenical vocation and the movement. One dilemma to be resolved in the future of ecumenism is how an organization will respond to the question of focus. Will it focus on one of these primary areas or attempt to keep some sort of balance among them?

Some local ecumenical organizations focus on service. The questions that are primary in that focus are, What can we do together to support our community and how can we make that happen. Community ministries often fit this category but can be complementary with ecumenical organizations so that across the spectrum, say of a state, all dimensions of ecumenical life are manifest for the benefit of community. In Minnesota, for instance, many community ministries have initiated and supported food shelves for two decades, since the early years of the Reagan administration's cutbacks. The statewide interfaith FoodShare campaign, whose sponsors include metropolitan and the state councils of churches, raises almost eight-million pounds of food each year for those food shelves. This complements what other ecumenical partners are doing.

The advantages of focusing on service are many. First, the work is less controversial—there is a broader acceptance of the appropriateness for the church's involvement in this work. Second, it is more easily funded, partly because of the broad appeal of the work and partly because funding streams seem to be more plentiful. Public funds are often available for this work.

Justice work has tended, as Peluso notes, to draw those who are on the edges of the church institutions and is focused on working with those who are on the edges of the larger society. The primary question here is how

God's will is being manifested or not, vis-a-vis the larger community. "Edge work" funding is always harder to come by, and criticism is stronger and acceptance weaker in the larger community. But those who do this work have an intense sense of purpose and meaning in the work.

Unity work probably receives the least attention. Its value seems not to be as readily apparent even to those within the Church. To the outside world it appears to have nothing to do with their agendas or concerns and seems even at best like "internal" business and at worst like pointless naval-gazing. But unity work is the foundation of community. And unity work among the separate entities of the Church is work to receive a gift already given, so that the churches can manifest the Church, demonstrating the possibility God yearns for in the whole human community, if not Creation. Yet, funding is difficult to find and leadership has tended to be found primarily in those with a significant bent for theological reflection and academic routine.

The way to approach this dilemma is to see the work as continuous rather than discrete. When one organization embraces one aspect of the work at one time and another organization another aspect at another time, when seen together and understood as a whole, the broader ecumenical calling of the movement's vocation is being fulfilled. As we look at the future of ecumenical relations we should remind ourselves, as some of our ecumenical elders have in the past, that interchurch relationships can be found on a wide spectrum over the years: Oppression/condemnation/isolation/competition/mutual assistance/internal cooperative ministry/external cooperative ministry/unified witness/full communion/merger.[14] (There is a shift to a positive basis of engagement between competition and mutual assistance. And structural merger is rarely seen as the goal anymore, being replaced with full communion. The term "full communion" itself will need to be clarified in the future and the communions and communities will need to achieve some convergence of understanding in order to achieve whatever it is decided that that means. Nevertheless, there is an image of structured relationship imbedded in the concept, which seems to have caught the attention of the ecumenically minded leaders.)

If we tie these positive ways of engaging (excluding merger) to the functions of church, we may see new opportunities for work in the future. Theologians have long identified the five functions of church as:

Kerygma, which is the *proclamation of the Gospel*
Leitourgia, which is the community's *worship of God*
Koinonia, which is the *community/solidarity among believers*

Diakonia, which is *service to others in the name of Christ*
Paideia, which is the *formation of believers in discipleship.*[15]

A MATRIX OF THEOLOGICAL FUNCTION AND RELATIONAL STYLE

	Mutual Assistance	*Internal Cooperative Ministry*	*External Cooperative Ministry*	*Unified Witness*	*Full Communion*
Kerygma	Evangelism pamphlet	Yoked	Evangelism follow-up	Shared public statement	Common statement of faith
Leitourgia	Shared sanctuary	Baptismal presence	Nursing home services	Thanksgiving services	Full sacramental fellowship
Koinonia	Shared fellowship hall	Shared youth group	Ministerial association	Shared pastoral counselor	Discernment and accountability
Diakonia			Food shelf		
Paideia	Buying Sunday School materials	Combined VBS		Formation groups	Mutual recognition of gifts and traditions

Remembering that we need to hold to a principle of subsidiarity (doing what must be done at the "lowest" possible level), we therefore remember that some of the expressions of the above elements must only be done in the congregation, while some expressions are better done in the national denominations, global fellowships, or ecumenically at one or more levels. Having said that, putting these two sets in a matrix offers some help for imagining new opportunities for the future. We have also added a line for the miscellaneous aspects of shared life, none of which are required ecclesially to be church but which may be helpful. We will explore the work in this instance from the context of local ecumenical life as constituted by congregations, but the same format works to consider statewide ecumenical work.

An example of *kerygma* in the mutual assistance column would be the shared evangelism brochure. A set of congregations who wanted to offer mutual assistance to one another in the area of *kerygma* might choose to develop an evangelism brochure that would express the particular gifts and styles of each congregation, urge people to choose from among their congregations, and have all of their worship times on it. They would together develop a strategy for shared distribution. This effort is much like what the communities in resort areas do now in their efforts to distribute posters of worship times.

An example of *leitourgia* in the mutual assistance column would be two or more congregations that decided to build a new worship space together with both using it at different times. We see examples of ecumenical ministry for the internal life of congregations. Work in this column takes a greater commitment to each other, requires a new level of accountability and agreement, and offers a greater witness to the community, as well as providing more opportunity to know each other more deeply. An example in the *kerygma* column might be entering into a pastoral yoking of the congregation. *Leitourgia* might include a commitment to be present at each other's services of baptism. And *paideia* could include sharing a vacation Bible school.

The third column indicates work done together on behalf of the larger community. For instance under *kerygma* we find the example of shared strategy for follow-up of the evangelism brochure distribution, including pairs of visitors who come from different congregations. *Leitourgia* might be expressed in shared nursing home worship services and *diakonia* in the shared running of the food shelf.

The fourth column indicates the work we do together because it cannot be done, by definition, without being done in a united fashion or without clearly intending an ecumenical outcome—not simply a cooperative one. For instance, ecumenical worship services cannot be ecumenical if they are done by only one group. It takes an ecumenical group to be ecumenical, to bring an ecumenical witness. When a public statement of Christian leaders is made and the delegation is intentionally composed of representatives of different groups, this is an example of ecumenical proclamation or *kerygma*.

Full communion engages all aspects of ecclesiology and will require some alignment with the larger denomination's efforts, but given that, we can imagine that under full communion local congregations could live out ecumenical *kerygma* in making a shared statement of faith, in *leitourgia,* by full sacramental fellowship. *Koinonia* means fellowship. But more than that, it means solidarity and mutual accountability. *Koinonia* under the full communion column might mean including representatives of each other's congregations in regular mutual interaction, perhaps including being on each others' boards.

This has just scratched the surface of possibilities for ecumenical life in the future. Now we must examine the church's identity in the larger world.

Many Issues and Trends Threaten the Ecumenical Horizon

There are many other issues and trends inside the church and in the culture that will affect how ecumenical work is pursued and even whether ecumenical work is pursued. The Evangelical middle will increasingly see value in the ecumenical worldview and will look for the history needed to advance the relationships or will reinvent the ecumenical wheel out of its own experience. The ecumenical and Evangelical camps will continue to fight about the importance of personal morality versus the morality of the systems of our shared life.

The historic black churches will continue to advocate for the ecumenical agenda, focusing in the justice areas. In recent years, racism has been defined as as much a church-dividing issue as differing perspectives on the Eucharist. The work of Churches Uniting in Christ will bring that concern into a fuller view as a matter of multilateral conversation. But it isn't a new issue, and work to dismantle racism and for civil rights will continue to gain energy. New immigrant and language groups will expand that conversation, adding value in the diversity and posing new tensions as well.

Economic disparities will continue to grow unless some kind of major long-term organizing comes into existence. These issues and their concurrent issues of education, housing, health care, and criminal justice will continue to be on the forefront of ecumenical life in local and regional ecumenical organizations. Faith-based organizing will continue to grow, and more traditional ecumenical organizations will either find ways to collaborate, which will not be easy, or adopt some of the tools of the faith-based organizing movement—or the groups will polarize and the common good will be weaker because of that lack. At the same time the agenda for ecumenical expressions of ecclesiology will be diminished if faith-based organizing does not acknowledge the relatedness within the church—even in what are sometimes viewed as "enemy camps."

There will continue to be the split between traditional Faith and Order and Life and Work arenas and approaches. And there will be a tendency to define ecumenical solely in terms of cooperation on peace and justice issues. Collaboration between and among ecumenical, interfaith, other faith, other nonprofit, and other sector organizations will increase not only for the sake of efficiency and effectiveness, but also as expressions of the emerging worldview of relatedness. Bilaterals and multilaterals will change the ecumenical horizon, but probably only if there is a generation of successful practicing of the new possibilities.

We conclude with one other trend in the culture to which the ecumenical movement is called to respond for the renewal of the Church as well as the world. As we have said, Christian theology of relatedness will eventually press the question about our relationship to the larger society and world. If we're related, how shall we be in life together? How shall we choose to make decisions and act together? It is our relatedness that compels us to recognize that self-interest is served in our attending to the interest of the other as well, for they are related interests. Democracy, at its best, understands self-interest in a context of other selves, who, when they know their relatedness, see the truth that the interest of the other is my interest and know the need to moderate self-interest for the common good. Democracy will be challenged in this coming century not from without as much as from within.

The tenets of democracy, like the Christian theology of community, will be increasingly threatened by the service-oriented, market-driven paradigm in its current incarnation. Voluntary association, a political necessity, can heighten the effects of a marketplace assumption. Together these can deny God-given relatedness and assume that one may choose whom one will relate to. Such a cultural context increases the separation from the larger community and denies the relatedness of self-interest to common good. The ecumenical vision can contribute to democratic renewal in the twenty-first century.

The market-driven model of community will increasingly typify internal church community, contributing to the Church's decreasing relationship to the larger community. The tendency for congregations to focus upon therapeutic and private concerns will reduce religion to the private sphere, and congregations will be understood solely as extended families and/or community marketplaces rather than also serving as places where public argument, resolution, and actions are formulated.[16]

With the lack of public culture within churches comes an inability to talk about important issues without fear of polarized conflict. Diversity becomes a problem rather than a source for insight and growth. Too little importance is placed on the congregation as a place to learn and develop deliberative skills, community witness, and faithful citizenship. As a result, many members feel diminished as participants in the public square. The spiritual call to public work requires new learnings, new expressions, and new connections. Community behavior within congregations reflects the larger service society's orientation toward passive or narrow participation as citizens."[17]

Because we are related we must deal with the whole community, not just those with whom we agree. Personal self-interest is best served in dialogue with the others' self-interests. The internal culture of the Church will be renewed as we renew our relationship with the rest of the community and vice versa. Perhaps Christians with an ecumenical identity are in an extraordinarily gifted place to reclaim community both inside the Church and in the wider community in the years to come.

In the world to come, the Church—in its denominational, ecumenical, and congregational forms—must increasingly become a place that transcends the common practice, the common culture, to become an arena for moral deliberation and discernment for the common good and a place where we act upon that which we say is valued. This will mean creating new patterns of relatedness and mutual accountability both within the Church and as the Church in relationship with the rest of the community.

Conclusion

Will this radical vision of relatedness offer anything of transcendent meaning to the world of our future? Does this ecumenical worldview have anything to offer the world coming at us? Can this ecumenical theology rooted in the Oneness of the Body of Christ of the second person of the Trinity and the Unity in creation based on the first person of the Trinity offer a worldview that can sustain the community and renew the Church?

Like the world of Isaiah we will live in an increasing time of fragmentation and alienation. In the midst of this rending of the fabric of society are we called to be repairers of the breach? In such a time we hear again the words of Isaiah (58: 9b–12):

> Then you shall call, and the Lord will answer;
>   you shall cry, and he will say,
>   Here I am.
> If you take away from the midst of you the yoke,
>   the pointing of the finger, and speaking wickedness,
> If you pour yourself out for the hungry
>   and satisfy the desire of the afflicted,
> then shall your light rise in the darkness
>   and your gloom be as the noonday.
> And the Lord will guide you continually,
>   and satisfy your desire with good things,

and make your bones strong;
and you shall be like a watered garden,
like a spring of water,
whose waters fail not.
And your ancient ruins shall be rebuilt;
you shall raise up the foundations of many generations;
you shall be called the repairer of the breach,
the restorer of streets to dwell in.

Notes

1. Michael Kinnamon, address to NAES Conference, "Contending for the Soul of the Nation," July 11, 1996, Lexington, Kentucky, unpublished notes.
2. Bill Moyers, America's Future Conference, Washington DC, Omni Hotel, June 4, 2003.
3. World Book Encyclopedia, McKinley, Vol. M, pp. 274–275.
4. Ibid., p. 276.
5. Kinnamon, address to NAES Conference, July 11, 1996, Lexington, Kentucky.
6. Ibid.
7. Pope John Paul II, *Ut Unum Sint,* CNS Documentary Services, June 8, 1995, p. 52.
8. Conversation with Arleon Kelley, 2003.
9. Gary Peluso, "Life on the Church's Horizon: Ecumenical and Interreligious Organizations in the United States Today," unpublished study funded by the Lilly Endowment, Aug. 1995, p. 188.
10. Thomas F. Bert and Wesley Granberg-Michaelson, eds., "Costly Unity, Koinonia and Justice, Peace and the Integrity of Creation," World Council of Churches, Geneva, 1993.
11. Ibid.
12. Peluso, "Life on the Church's Horizon," p. 7.
13. Ibid., p. 8.
14. Wallace Ford, "Towards Full Communion with One Another: Evaluating Where the Member Churches of the New Mexico Conference of Churches Are on the Journey," New Mexico Conference of Churches document, 1997.
15. Ibid., quoting James Fowler, p. 4.
16. "Renewing the Public Church," working document, Minnesota Council of Churches, 1998.
17. Ibid.

AFTERWORD: SOME FINAL REFLECTIONS ON THE STORY

Arleon L. Kelley

The first chapter of this book ended by raising a series of concerns about local ecumenism and its future. We anticipated that the stories from the last fifty years would raise questions about current and future local ecumenism. These were the following:

As Public Church

Local ecumenism has been the public face of the Church in many places across America. With the growing privatization of religion and the secularization of our culture, how will the Public Church be expressed in the future—or will it?

Theologically

Has local ecumenism embraced fundamentally different theological worldviews than those prevalent in more traditional Christian settings?

Has local ecumenism developed an underlying organic theological understanding based in the Body of Christ image? We suggested that such an image, when tied with creation spirituality, sees all as sacred and all as connected. This view also diminishes the separation between sacred and secular. God is not separate from any part of the creation.

We wondered, if these theological directions were borne out, would they be in striking contrast to underlying denominational theological assumptions that have historically differentiated one from the other and which have been the basis to argue for denominational sovereignty?

We were also curious about the role of local ecumenism in transcending the boundaries between world faith traditions.

In the Culture

We wondered if local ecumenism has enabled people of faith to transcend traditional boundaries of gender, race, patriarchy, super-patriotism, unemployment, income disparity, ecological degradation, misuse of power, and the so-called dysfunctional aspects of the machine era.

We wondered what local ecumenism's role has been in moving insular and triumphal Christian positions to become more open to dialogue, interaction, and shared service in the community.

We wanted to reflect on the question of how the ecumenical worldview can help us deal with the emerging imperial worldview of economic and political dominance. Many across the world believe that as Americans we are in the "belly of the beast" dedicated to world domination. If so, what is the creative mediating faith worldview that can be sacramental for the future of humankind—in communities across America, in our nation, and beyond?

And, finally, what is the future of local ecumenism?

Following are a few observations drawn from the stories related to these questions. These observations may point to the essence of the story of local ecumenism today and into the future.

The Public Church

Ecumenism has historically been an important way for pluralistic Christianity to weave a tapestry of common means to serve, witness for justice, and symbolize unity in the communities of America. Over the fifty years of our focus we have seen the culture privatize and marginalize religion. It seems that the interpretation of the U.S. Constitution has moved from protecting the rights of all to practice the religions they prefer to a current view of protecting society from the claims of any religion. I see that the positive voice of religion as value and hope-giver in our culture has been muted. Indeed, the religious views most visible in the public arenas are typically those against progress and justice. They are the naysayers and practitioners of reactionary and conserving theology. Local ecumenism's more prophetic and progressive theology is less frequently the voice of the Public Church than it was even forty years ago—if indeed there even is a Public Church today.

Theologically

Ecumenical theology has evolved over these fifty years to become more holistic. At the same time, denominational theologies have been increasingly challenged to defend their historicity and uniqueness to satisfy reactionary and conserving forces within their boundaries. As a result some denominational theologies have been forced to make the tent smaller rather than larger and more inclusive. And of course, Fundamentalist theology seems to have had a renaissance during the latter half of the fifty years under consideration.

Our stories tell the Story of how ecumenical theology has been in dialogue with the creative parts of the emerging culture. Globally this is typified by the historic conference, "Faith, Science, and the Future," sponsored by the World Council of Churches at MIT in the mid-1970s. Representatives of local ecumenism participated. Our stories are also ones of local ecumenism's dialogue with the environmental movement; with those philosophically inclined toward the *ghia* principle (which sees the earth as a living entity); with those who have been marginalized—by politics, gender, sexual preference, race, class, wealth, poverty, or religion—in our world's cultures; and with creation spirituality. In other words, local ecumenism has been probing the growing edges and the tender shoots of creative inquiry in the contemporary world. Ecumenical theology has grown and been moved toward greater relevance by these dialogues. Yet, in so doing, I believe that we are seeing an even greater bifurcation between ecumenical theology and traditional theology. That bifurcation has become, in Karen Armstrong's words, a "Battle for God" in our culture. It is a serious enough rift that it may be leading to a new "re-formation" of faith in American life.

Ecumenical theology is increasingly being organized around images of the Body of Christ and the Family of God. This means it is open to the new understandings of creation spirituality; it is open to exploring what it means to be a part of the Family of God; and it is coming to understand the salvific acts of God in the creation in new and broader ways. These tendencies, even trends, in ecumenical theology, are in marked contrast to such theologies as proposed by groups such as the Presbyterian Laymen, the Good News Movement, the Institute for Religion and Democracy, and the various groups in the Lutheran, Disciples, Baptist, Roman Catholic, and other denominations seeking a return to seventeenth-, eighteenth-, and nineteenth-century theology and practice.

Why has local ecumenism moved in these theological directions? Historically, local ecumenism has been more rooted in the Life and Work or Missional areas of ecumenical life, and its theological work reflects the struggle with issues of day-to-day life and justice. At the same time Faith and Order work has been largely focused on resolving the historical differences among the Christian faith traditions—especially during the first three decades of the period under study. More recently, the Consultation of Church Union (Christ's Church Uniting) has struggled with some life- and faith-dividing issues, like racism, gender justice, and economic justice, as has the Faith and Order Commission of the NCCC/USA. Even so, there is a difference in the way local ecumenism and Churchly national ecumenism does theology.

At best, local ecumenism does "situation, reflection, action, and then again reflection theology" from the bottom up. It is more deductive than inductive. It asks many questions. From this situation, what is God saying? Because local ecumenism is often on the front line with other world faith traditions it asks different questions about interfaith relationships than do many academic ecumenists. In such situations in the local community, for those of other faith traditions, the local ecumenical entity often is the Church. What does this say about local ecumenism's ecclesiological significance? Local ecumenism has learned that it must relate to all world faith traditions that are not Christian out of hospitality. It must accept the validity of the other's faith before dialogue can begin. Local ecumenism is learning the relationship between this creation that has put us here together and how we are all related to the Creator. It is learning anew how we are to relate to the Creation.

At the same time, local ecumenism has experienced emerging needs for community justice, in the context of globalization. This is illustrated in Charles Rawling's Youngstown story, which raises new questions about the nature of powers and principalities in our culture. We have few values or local-global institutions for mediating the conflict between a community's long-term investment required to host an industry and a corporation's sometimes capricious action to move elsewhere, in this case investing profits made in steel in a different industry elsewhere. This story raises new questions: What is the relationship between capitalism and community? How do local communities get justice in a global economy? Why are there so few democratic global political structures in place to regulate the appetites of profit-driven corporations? And what can local communities expect in the ways of justice? Indeed, local ecumenism is a rich context in which to do theology. And the answers are often a bit different than in other approaches to doing theology, because they soon move one into economic and political justice issues.

In the Culture

The Story is that ecumenical Christians are unique in our culture. Rooted deep in Christian tradition, they often transcend that tradition to be inclusive of great differences, with a worldview that is holistic and concerned for universal human, economic, and environmental justice. They are often the advocates for peaceful solutions to intractable conflicts. They advocate servanthood more than power. They are as concerned for the positive transformation of the cultural systems and the culture itself as they are for the salvation of the individual. Ecumenical Christians are open to new understandings of their relationship with the world's major faiths. They are accepting rather than judgmental of the other.

Yet, the Story at the beginning of the twenty-first century is also that ecumenical Christians, at least within the churches, seem more and more a remnant or a counterculture species. The ecumenical worldview seems increasingly a minority view because it largely stands in contrast to a predominant worldview of profit, conquest, violence, and domination. It is countercultural, as David Bos suggests in his memoir on Texas ecumenists, because it is open to dealing with community needs and global environmental, economic, and political justice issues more than national or personal interests. Ecumenical Christianity is a remnant because it accepts the value of the other's position. It does not impose its way on others. It gives because the other has need, not because it wants to dominate the other. Ecumenical Christians see their role as sacramental, pointing to the possibility of wholeness, rather than preemptive and triumphal and assuming its way is best. The ecumenical Christian is in the culture, as yeast is in the bread dough. The ecumenical Christian is not "set apart" from the culture or set against the culture.

The many stories told here demonstrate over and over again that local ecumenical life is dedicated to the proposition that all can be transformed by love rather than by power. Work for justice is a work of love. Work of *diakonia* or service is an act of love. And acting to receive the gift of unity is an act of loving faith. This work becomes a sacrament in the communities of America, pointing to the hopeful possibility that all can be whole.

This witness is in contradistinction to the cultural Christianity embedded in and supporting the triumphal American nationalism. This cultural Christianity wraps itself in the flag, supports reactionary and conservative political causes, and perpetuates false cultural myths about our manifest destiny to rule the world as the new Israel. Cultural Christianity is exclusive—often male, white, rich, and powerful. Too often this narrow triumphalism has become the most public face of religion, albeit not the majority of religion in our culture.

The ecumenical, which if clearly enunciated, is appealing to thinking, historically and scientifically sophisticated people, who appreciate beauty and hate injustice, and who have a balance between "head" and emotion. They are global citizens, open to God's continuing revelation. For ecumenical Christians, God is alive. On the other hand, we have reactionary cultural religion that appeals to those who live more in their emotions and fear, have a weaker sense of self-worth, and who need identity with a tribe more than with the whole world. For them God's revelation is in the past. God is dead. It is not surprising that the two have difficulty with any efforts toward reconciliation. They are like fire and gasoline. At this time in history, when put together they cause a great conflagration.

Learnings Useful for the Future of Local Ecumenism

The Story is that there are a lot of pragmatic dynamics that local ecumenism is facing that will determine its future. Peg Chemberlin has outlined the many issues that local ecumenism will face in the future. I have come to believe a basic one may be related to ecclesiology. Grand Rapids, Minneapolis, Indianapolis, and numerous other communities have developed an ecumenism with the signs of proclamation, service, justice, and community that give them churchly significance. Rather than giving the sacraments, they are becoming a sacrament pointing to the possibility of wholeness in the midst of brokenness. Why? Because often the media and the halls of power see them as the Church in that place and will not deal with the churches.

Certainly local ecumenism's support is increaslingly not from the churches. As Alton Motter pointed out, most local councils were formerly funded by the member churches and most state councils by the member judicatories. That is no longer true. At the time of his research, 23 percent of the Minnesota Council's budget was from denominational contributions. Congregational support of the St. Paul Council amounted to 9 percent of the annual budget, while the Minneapolis Council's congregational support amounted to about 5 percent.

These patterns raise a lot of questions. For example, how does this shift affect the justice and prophetic message or the connection of ecumenical organizations with the churches? Judith Bennett, in her chapter on Virginia, notes: "When funding comes from judicatories it is dangerous to get out ahead of those judicatories and to be prophetic. Dependence breeds caution." And perhaps most important, as the middle judicatories let their role be redefined from being the "means for all of us to support one another and to share the broader mission of being Christians, to merely being service agencies for their local congregations," what is the future of middle-judicatory-based ecumenical organizations? With the withering of the middle judicatory, judicatories are no longer a stable source of funding. They are also less than able to be faithful partners in the ecumenical vocation. When funding no longer comes from judicatories is there really more freedom or is local ecumenism then beholden to new masters?

Similarly, in congregational-based ecumenical life, when congregations choose to support only appealing and feel-good service projects, how do the less-appealing and hard unity or justice issues get addressed in the community?

Could it be that, in the future, state and city ecumenical councils will be called to declare their ecclesial significance and become the vehicles for sharing and doing the broader mission of being Christian in that place and around the world, receiving financial support from a host of sources? Heresy? Perhaps. Yet, that is what is happening. Why? I am convinced that being ecumenical is embedded not only in the nature of the Gospel, but in the very nature of creation itself. It will find outlets, in spite of the churches, if need be. Indeed, the future of local ecumenism will be exciting and probably tumultuous, and holding the churches accountable to their mission of service, justice, and unity may be one of its most important mission fields! Or the temptation may be to just get on with the work.

There are numerous lessons from the past Story that will contribute to the future Story of local ecumenism. For example:

- East Harlem found that there were three dimensions to its ministry: identification, presence, and witness. This is basic ecumenism.
- Virginia, Newark, the Farm Crisis, CORA, and state ecumenism in general give credence to the generalization that missional needs and opportunities far outstrip resources, given the way the church presently organizes those resources. It has probably always been true; but with different ecclesial arrangements, it need not be true in the future.
- Relationships are key to ecumenical success. Judith Bennett observes in her chapter on Virginia: "On the surface, the impressive achievements in Christian unity appear to be the work of a relatively small number of larger-than-life personalities, but on deeper scrutiny it is clear that it was the deep and lasting friendships with one another that made things happen." Trust is essential among leaders in order for relationships to develop and an ecumenical spirit to be sustained.
- Ecumenism is universal, but must be responsive to its cultural context. Hugh Wire writes: "The story of the perspectives and work style of the generations suggests how changing times shaped the different role each

would play in the same institution and its successors. The extent the institution could mobilize the ecumenical impulse in different times is made clear by looking at this changing role in one family."

- Professional and lay leadership are key to successful ecumenical organizations. Wire, the Grimms, Hurty, Motter, and others observed that charisma, character, and achievement are the hallmarks of a successful ecumenical executive. The depth of the leader's commitment and the quality of leadership, as well as the length of service, are often determinative of an ecumenical organization's success and credibility. The rapid social change over the last half of the twentieth century favors the entrepreneur and the start-up executive over the manager. For example, newer organizations continually surpass the older in California and perhaps elsewhere.
- There is notable tension in many cities between traditional ecumenical organizations and church-based community organizing models. Community organizing is a method for marginalized people to gain power in their community. Hence even church-based community organizations are not ecumenical in the traditional sense but utilize the churches primarily as a source of financial support and for credibility. Local ecumenism has a good record of paying attention to and advocating for the marginalized; but it is one of many agendas that must be cared for, and it is doing something "for" not "with" the affected people. Community organizing is a method of gaining justice by those affected by the injustice. Most ecumenical organizations have little quarrel with that. It appears the tension comes largely from competition for church support funds.
- In the end, hospitality toward any community, along with focused action on achieving a particular human good, is sustainable—but it requires intuitive leadership.
- Finally, both David Baak and Hal Garman observe that faith today seems to assume unity. We are all one, whether Hindu, Muslim, Christian, Jew, or Buddhist. Yet, this observation, if true, raises new questions for the future. For example, why is fragmentation so prevalent and the need for reconciliation so great? And to what is an ecumenical organization called to do, in everyday local terms, especially when that agency has a vision for demonstrating the kingdom and inviting all into greater reconciliation What is the relationship of the Grand Rapids Area Center for Ecumenism or the Interreligious Council of Central New York to the Church, the churches, and other world faiths?

With all of our authors, we ask, one more time, What can we learn from the past to help us as we move into the future?

In the end, we believe that the Story is that the ecumenical impulse is embedded in the Gospel and in the very nature of creation itself. Local ecumenism has woven a multidimensional tapestry that has released that impulse. This impulse has found and will continue to find outlet, in spite of human propensity for selfishness and, yes, even in spite of the churches, if need be. Local ecumenism has demonstrated tenacity. Indeed, the future of local ecumenism will be exciting and probably tumultuous. The stories well illustrate that the ecumenical vocation is for the brave of heart.

The Story of local ecumenism is one of hundreds of thousands of faithful and courageous people coming together, community by community, to pray, teach, act, and celebrate the faith they share for the sake of their community. It is the Story of thousands of little and big transformations in communities across the nation. It is the Story of God's people doing God's work in God's Creation!

CONTRIBUTORS

THE REV. DAVID P. BAAK is a member of the Leadership Team of the Grand Rapids Area Center for Ecumenism (GRACE). He served as its executive director from 1983 to 2002, worked in pretrial alternative programs in the criminal justice system, and served congregations in Flint, Michigan, and New York City. He is ordained in the Reformed Church in America and is a member of Central Reformed Church in Grand Rapids. He is a graduate of Calvin College and Seminary in Grand Rapids and studied at the University of Detroit and Western Theological Seminary in Holland, Michigan. He resides in Grand Rapids.

THE REV. DR. JUDITH BENNETT, Ph.D., served as pastor in New York City before moving to Virginia to be Associate General Minister of the Virginia Council of Churches from 1989 to 2000. A retired elder in the Virginia Conference, she is executive director of the Center for Congregational Ministry in Richmond, a member of the adjunct faculty at Virginia Union University School of Theology, and a free-lance curriculum writer for the United Methodist Publishing House. She resides in Richmond.

DOROTHY G. BERRY has served in executive positions at the local, state, national, and world levels of ecumenism. A native of Brooklyn, New York, she is an active leader at the national level of the United Church of Christ and also served as vice president of the National Council of Churches. Before her retirement she was the executive director of what is now the Kansas Ecumenical Ministries. She lives in Topeka, Kansas.

THE REV. DAVID BOS is founder of the Interfaith Community Ministry Network, former executive director of three such ministries, and author of books and articles on community ministries, including *A Practical Guide to Community Ministry* (W/JK, 1993) and *The Neighborly Congregation: Theology and Practice of Community Ministry* (Pilgrim Press, forthcoming). He is a Presbyterian (USA) clergyperson and resides in Louisville, Kentucky.

THE REV. PEG CHEMBERLIN is the executive director of the Minnesota Council of Churches, ordained in the Moravian Church, on the NCCC/USA Executive Board, and chair of the Standing Committee on Ecumenical Relations. She has served as president and program chair for NAEIS. She received the N.O.V.A. award for peace and justice, the Angel of Reconciliation Award, and the Governor's Award for Women of Excellence. She graduated from United Theological Seminary in the Twin Cities, where she was awarded the academic prize for historical theology. She lives in Minneapolis.

ROBERT GRIMM began his ecumenical career in South Dakota after a two-year World War II stint in the Navy and a three-year seminary career in Rochester, New York, where he was ordained in the Congregational Church. He grew up in the Methodist Church in Evanston, Illinois, and graduated from Denison University in Ohio, where he met his future wife. He says that his sixty years of marriage to Roberta have been the best part of his ecumenical journey as an executive in South Dakota, Erie, Pennsylvania, Syracuse, New York, and Buffalo, New York.

ROBERTA GRIMM is the mother of six children and eighteen grandchildren and a noted liturgical dancer and spiritual leader, especially for women, in her community. She began participating in Church Women United (then the United Council of Church Women) in 1950 and has been active to the present. She has been a local unit and state president in New York and on its national executive council as Northeast coordinator and chair of its celebrations unit. She is the author of "Meditation in Motion" in her specialty of liturgical dance. She says she "is an ecumenical wife." She resides with her spouse, Robert, in Buffalo, New York.

SR. PAUL TERESA HENNESSEE, a Franciscan Sister of the Atonement, has been engaged in ecumenism in local and regional settings and at national and international levels. She is past associate director of the Graymoor Ecumenical and Interreligious Institute and served as interim director of the Faith and Order Commission of the NCCC/USA. Presently she serves on the administrative team of her religious congregation and remains the ecumenical liaison. She is also a member of the WCC Commission on Education and Ecumenical Formation.

THE REV. HORACE H. HUNT served as interim director of the Greater Newark Council of Churches in 1967 and 1968 while serving as pastor of First Baptist Peddie Memorial Church in downtown Newark. In 1969 he resigned as pastor to become the first executive director of the Metropolitan Ecumenical Ministry of Greater Newark. He is a graduate of Denison University and holds two degrees from the Yale Divinity School. He has served pastorates in Ohio, Connecticut, and New Jersey. He spent five years as campus minister at Ohio State University under joint appointment of the Disciples of Christ and the American Baptist Churches. An ordained American Baptist, he also holds ministerial standing in the United Church of Christ. He and his wife, Elva, a founder of Head Start in Newark and a longtime elementary teacher, are now retired and living in Ashville, North Carolina.

DR. KATHLEEN S. HURTY, Ph.D. (University of California—Berkeley), is an educator turned professional ecumenist. She most recently was the general director of the national office of Church Women United. She served for a decade as assistant general secretary and director of the Ecumenical Networks Commission of the NCCC/USA. Prior to that she was a public school principal in Oakland, California, and consultant to the Vesper Society, in San Leandro, California, a Lutheran-based foundation specializing in developing the lay ministry internationally. Hurty has been the recipient of many awards, has written many reports and books, and has served on several boards, such as the Sisters of St. Benedict Ecumenical Monastic Community advisory board. She is a trustee of her alma mater, Bethany College, in Lindsborg, Kansas. A life-long Lutheran, she is married to Lutheran pastor David Hurty. In retirement, they make their home in Oakland, California, and also in Rock Island, Illinois, near one of their sons.

THE REV. DR. ARLEON L. KELLEY, Th.D. (Boston University), is a retired United Methodist minister. In a thirty-five-year ecumenical career, he served the Indiana Council of Churches; the Ohio Council of Churches; in three different positions with the National Council of Churches; in South Asia as co-regional representative (with his spouse) for Church World Service, living in Dhaka, Bangladesh; the New York State Council of Churches; and finally with the Troy Area United Ministries. He has served as the director of this History Project since its beginnings in the mid-1990s. He has published two books, several booklets, more than one hundred research monographs, and numerous articles. He has been the recipient of many awards, including the Fr. Robert F. Kennedy award from the New York State Labor and Religion Coalition for his role as a founding member of New York State's Fiscal Policy Institute and the Bishop's Award for Ecumenical Excellence, given by Bishop Hae Jong Kim. He is married to the Rev. Dr. Donna Meinhard. They live in Elgin, Iowa.

THE REV. DR. ALTON M. MOTTER served in a variety of ecumenical capacities for more than a half century. He was the executive director of the Chicago Sunday Evening Supper Club (a place for Christian young adults to meet with one another and with the great Christian theologians of the time), and his first book was a compilation of the many lectures presented there. In 1954 he served as the press secretary for the Evanston Assembly of the World Council of Churches. He then served in executive positions with the Minnesota Council of Churches, the St. Paul, Minnesota, Council of Churches, and the Williamsport, Pennsylvania, Council of Churches. He has published throughout his career. His most recent book was *Ecumenism 101: A Handbook about the Ecumenical Movement.* Alton was taken from us in July 2003 at age 95, while living in Lewisburg, Pennsylvania. In June 2003 he sent a letter to the team outlining strategies for publicizing this book and asking when we were going to start work on the sequel. We miss Alton and praise God for his life of ecumenical witness.

THE REV. CHARLES W. RAWLINGS held denominational positions in Urban Ministry in the Presbyterian and Episcopal Churches and executive positions with the Greater Cleveland Council of Churches, the New Jersey Council of Churches, and the National Council of Churches. He was lead organizer of the Ecumenical Coalition of the Mahoning Valley.

DR. MARY R. SAWYER, Ph.D., teaches religious studies and African American studies at Iowa State University in Ames. She is the author of *Black Ecumenism: Implementing the Demands of Justice* and *The Church at the Margins: Living Christian Community* and is coeditor of *Peoples Temple and Black Religion in America*. She lives in Ames, Iowa.

THE REV. CHARLES R. WHITE, D.Min., is an honorably retired minister in the Presbyterian Church (USA). He was the pastor of Presbyterian churches in Illinois, Washington state, and Alaska, and of United Methodist churches in California. His work beyond the local church includes service on the staff of the Ecumenical Metropolitan Ministry in Seattle from 1974 to 1978, as executive director of the Buffalo Area Metropolitan Ministries from 1981 to 1992, and as owner and operator of Multifaith Resources, a national resource center for interreligious understanding and cooperation, from 1992 to 2000. He lives in California.

THE REV. HUGH WIRE, a native Californian, has served in many ecumenical capacities, including with the Office of Economic Opportunity program in North Carolina, as a West Coast regional representative for Church World Service, and as executive director of the San Jose Council of Churches. He is an ordained pastor in the Presbyterian Church (USA) and lives with his spouse, Dr. Ann Wire, in Berkeley, California.

THE REV. LAWRENCE E. WITMER served for eighteen years as executive director of the Genesee Ecumenical Ministries and the Greater Rochester (New York) Community of Churches. He is a graduate of Cornell University, the Colgate-Rochester Divinity School (M.Div.), and the University of Chicago Divinity School (M.A. in Social Ethics). He is coauthor of the *Edge of the Ghetto: A Study of Church Involvement in Community Organization.* He is retired and lives with his spouse, Margaret (Peg), in Rochester, New York.

INDEX